CORPORATE CONTROLLER'S HANDBOOK FOR HOSPITALITY

Elisa S. Moncarz, CPA

Nestor de J. Portocarrero, CPA

This publication is designed to provide accurate and authoritative information in regard to the subject matter covered. It is sold with the understanding that the publisher is not engaged in rendering legal, accounting, or other professional services. If legal advice or other professional assistance is required, the services of a competent professional person should be sought.

—From a *Declaration of Principles* jointly adopted by a Committee of the American Bar Association and a Committee of Publishers and Associations

ISBN: 978-0-8080-2386-9

©2010 CCH. All Rights Reserved.
4025 W. Peterson Ave.
Chicago, IL 60646-6085
1 800 248 3248
www.CCHGroup.com

No claim is made to original government works; however, within this Product or Publication, the following are subject to CCH's copyright: (1) the gathering, compilation, and arrangement of such government materials; (2) the magnetic translation and digital conversion of data, if applicable; (3) the historical, statutory and other notes and references; and (4) the commentary and other materials.

Printed in the United States of America

Exhibit 2-4, "Characteristics of Strong Controllers," is from Management Control Systems by Joseph A. Maciarello, Prentice-Hall, Inc., 1984, p. 99, Exhibit 4-9. Adapted with permission.

Exhibit 3-2, "Factors That Determine Shareholder Value," is reprinted with permission from Deloitte Development LLC, © 2004. All rights reserved.

2011 Corporate Controller's Handbook for Hospitality

by Elisa S. Moncarz, CPA, and Nestor de J. Portocarrero, CPA

Highlights

The 2011 *Corporate Controller's Handbook for Hospitality* is a comprehensive reference source designed to provide practical information on major areas of financial management and accounting in a hospitality industry environment. Its goal is to assist sophisticated users, moderately knowledgeable users, and those users who have limited knowledge of financial management but need to become quickly acquainted with specific topics related to accounting and finance in the hospitality industry. The handbook is directed to corporate financial managers, controllers, chief accountants, consultants, small business owners, and others interested in familiarizing themselves with various aspects of hospitality accounting and financial management topics. Applicable to any size company or major segment of the hospitality industry, the handbook covers accounting and finance topics, such as payroll and income tax laws, the Uniform System of Accounts for the Lodging Industry, the Wage and Hour Law, and financial reporting and regulations that impact the industry. It also provides coverage of the many managerial accounting strategies and techniques used to assist managers in their decision making, such as activity-based costing, cost-volume-profit analysis, financial analysis, operations budgeting, turnaround strategies, capital investment analysis, and gross profit and variance analysis.

2011 Edition

The goal of this handbook is to provide practical information on major areas of financial management and accounting in a hospitality industry environment. Several changes have been made in this edition to focus on recent developments and improve relevance as follows:

- Coverage of the latest pronouncements from the Financial Accounting Standards Board (FASB)
- Expanded coverage of the *FASB Accounting Standards Codification ™*, including relevant updates to the standards
- Expanded coverage of measures of performance
- New chapter on turnaround strategies that focuses on turnaround as a significant business strategy for hospitality companies challenged by sustaining their profitability and surviving turbulent times. This chapter examines the financial challenges that hospitality companies have faced in recent times, examines some of the major contributing factors to the declining performance of these companies, and provides selected strategies and turnaround stages for success.
- New chapter on the current status of International Financial Reporting Standards (IFRS). A set of financial statements tentatively proposed by the

International Accounting Standards Board (IASB), based on IFRS reporting is included.

CCH Learning Center

CCH's goal is to provide you with the clearest, most concise, and up-to-date accounting and auditing information to help further your professional development, as well as a convenient method to help you satisfy your continuing professional education requirements. The CCH Learning Center* offers a complete line of self-study courses covering complex and constantly evolving accounting and auditing issues. We are continually adding new courses to the library to help you stay current on all the latest developments. The CCH Learning Center courses are available 24 hours a day, seven days a week. You'll get immediate exam results and certification. To view our complete accounting and auditing course catalog, go to: http://cch.learningcenter.com.

Accounting Research Manager™

Accounting Research Manager is the most comprehensive, up-to-date, and objective online database of financial reporting literature. It includes all authoritative and proposed accounting, auditing, and SEC literature, plus independent, expert-written interpretive guidance.

Our Weekly Summary e-mail newsletter highlights the key developments of the week, giving you the assurance that you have the most current information. It provides links to new FASB, AICPA, SEC, PCAOB, EITF, and IASB authoritative and proposal-stage literature, plus insightful guidance from financial reporting experts.

Our outstanding team of content experts takes pride in updating the system on a daily basis, so you stay as current as possible. You'll learn of newly released literature and deliberations of current financial reporting projects as soon they occur! Plus, you benefit from their easy-to-understand technical translations.

With **Accounting Research Manager**, you maximize the efficiency of your research time while enhancing your results. Learn more about our content, our experts, and how you can request a FREE trial by visiting us at http://www.accountingresearchmanager.com.

12/10

© 2010 CCH. All Rights Reserved.

---

* CCH is registered with the National Association of State Boards of Accountancy (NASBA) as a sponsor of continuing professional education on the National Registry of CPE Sponsors. State boards of accountancy have final authority on the acceptance of individual courses for CPE credit. Complaints regarding registered sponsors may be addressed to the National Registry of CPE Sponsors, 150 Fourth Avenue North, Nashville, TN 37219-2417. Telephone: 615-880-4200.

CCH is registered with the National Association of State Boards of Accountancy as a Quality Assurance Service (QAS) sponsor of continuing professional education. Participating state boards of accountancy have final authority on the acceptance of individual courses for CPE credit. Complaints regarding QAS program sponsors may be addressed to NASBA, 150 Fourth Avenue North, Suite 700, Nashville, TN 37219-2417. Telephone: 615-880-4200.

CONTENTS

Preface vii
Acknowledgments xi
About the Authors xiii

PART I
INTRODUCTION

1. The Scope of Financial Management 1001
2. The Responsibilities of the Controller 2001
3. Corporate Governance 3001
4. Using Computers in Hospitality Financial Management 4001

PART II
FINANCIAL STATEMENT REPORTING

5. The Financial Reporting System 5001
6. Financial Statement Reporting: The Income Statement 6001
7. Financial Statement Reporting: The Balance Sheet 7001
8. Financial Statement Reporting: The Cash Flow Statement 8001
9. Financial Statement Disclosures 9001

PART III
FINANCIAL ANALYSIS

10. Liquidity Analysis 10,001
11. Solvency and Leverage Analysis 11,001
12. Profitability Analysis 12,001
13. Profitability and Investor Analysis 13,001
14. Management Analysis of Operations 14,001
15. Analysis of the Cash Flow Statement 15,001

PART IV
MANAGEMENT ACCOUNTING

16. Maximizing Profit and Minimizing Costs 16,001
17. Different Types of Costs 17,001
18. Cost Allocation 18,001
19. Cost-Volume-Profit Analysis 19,001
20. Taxation 20,001

PART V
INVESTING AND FINANCING DECISIONS

21. Long-Term Financing 21,001
22. Short-Term and Intermediate Financing 22,001
23. Dividend Policy 23,001
24. Capital Investment Analysis 24,001
25. Cost of Capital 25,001

PART VI
RECENT DEVELOPMENTS

26. Turnaround Strategies 26,001
27. International Financial Reporting Standards 27,001

Appendix 1: Present Value Tables 28,001
Appendix 2: Tax Information 29,001
Resources on the Web 30,001
Index 31,001

Preface

Corporate Controller's Handbook for Hospitality provides clear, detailed coverage of accounting and financial management from a hospitality industry perspective. It is designed to serve as a valuable reference tool for making daily operational and financial decisions that create value for hospitality companies. The handbook not only deals with the latest accounting and finance topics, but addresses the impact of recent developments in related areas, such as financing, taxes, turnaround strategies, international financial reporting standards, and computers. It is directed toward corporate financial managers, controllers, chief accountants, consultants, and others involved in the finance and accounting functions of a hospitality company. In addition, others involved in the hospitality industry, such as creditors, investors, and consultants, may also find this information useful.

The handbook covers major aspects of the controller and financial manager's work, including financial reporting activities, capital investment analysis, and managerial analysis and financing. Easy to apply techniques and various practice aids aim to facilitate the decision making process and help financial managers and others perform their jobs more effectively.

Coverage of important issues affecting the industry includes:

- DuPont and leverage analysis for measuring operating and financial performance.
- Cost-volume profit analysis for optimizing operating performance.
- Variance analysis for controlling costs.
- Liquidity, solvency, and profitability analysis.
- Uniform System of Accounts for the Lodging Industry.
- New accounting laws and regulations.
- Wage and Hour Law.
- Capital investment analysis.
- Recent developments in financing assets.
- Forecasting future cash flows.
- Information technology.

Significant questions facing controllers and other financial managers will be answered, such as:

- What is the impact of the Sarbanes-Oxley Act on a public or private firm in the hospitality industry?
- What are some of the most recent developments in computerized technology investments in the hospitality industry?
- How is financial analysis used to optimize performance in the hospitality industry?
- What are the emerging trends in financing a hospitality company?

- How is budgeting used to control operating costs in the hospitality industry?
- How can contribution pricing be used to offset declining sales?
- How does activity-based costing provide better cost determination, a factor to be considered in setting more competitive prices?
- How is management accounting used to maximize revenues and minimize costs in the more competitive hospitality environment of the new millennium?
- How can the cash flow statement be used as an indicator of good financial and investment management?
- What are the early warning signs that a hospitality company is headed to financial distress?
- What are selected turnaround strategies for a hospitality company in financial distress?

The handbook is organized into six parts with 27 chapters, each of which may be examined independently of others.

- Part I (Chapters 1-4) provides an overview of the scope of financial management and the responsibilities of the controller, including the various reports that are prepared in the hospitality industry. The use of computers in hospitality financial management and the role of the Sarbanes-Oxley Act are also discussed.
- Part II (Chapters 5-9) deals with financial reporting in the hospitality industry. It includes in-depth coverage of major hospitality financial statements, including the balance sheet, income statement, and statement of cash flows, as well as financial statement disclosures of hospitality companies.
- Part III (Chapters 10-15) describes and illustrates the usefulness of financial statement analysis to hospitality management. A review of the techniques used by hospitality management to assess a company's financial health and make decisions that enhance the likelihood for survival and success are addressed. It shows how to evaluate a hospitality company's liquidity position, as well as its ability to generate cash flow. It also identifies the factors that drive a company's profitability and its investment potential.
- Part IV (Chapters 16-20) emphasizes managerial accounting concepts and practices for maximizing revenue, as well as planning and controlling costs for hospitality companies. The importance of the budgeting process is illustrated. Consideration is also given to the use of accounting and control information in relation to decision-making. The use of contribution pricing to maximize sales is also discussed.
- Part V (Chapters 21-25) includes five chapters devoted to investing and financing decisions in the hospitality industry. They cover the capital budgeting process in the hospitality industry, as well as long-term, short-term, and intermediate financing decisions. The process used by hospitality

managers to make investment decisions that maximize the company's value is also presented.

- Part VI (Chapters 26 and 27) includes two new chapters on recent developments affecting the hospitality industry. Coverage of the significance of turnaround strategies for hospitality companies in financial distress, as well as an overview of the current status of international accounting standards, is presented.

Acknowledgments

We gratefully acknowledge the assistance and support of those individuals who have contributed to the preparation of this work. First, we wish to acknowledge the role played by thousands of former students in our classes of Accounting and Finance at Florida International University's School of Hospitality and Tourism Management, many of whom currently hold leadership positions in the hospitality industry worldwide. We also want to thank Debra Rhoades, Senior Managing Editor, Sandra Lim, Development Editor, and Holly Whorton, Support Specialist Coordinator.

We also want to express our sincere appreciation to our spouses, Dr. Raul Moncarz and Maria Esperanza de Portocarrero and to our children and grandchildren for their encouragement and understanding and for helping us to keep life in perspective. This book is dedicated to them.

Elisa S. Moncarz, CPA
Nestor de J. Portocarrero, CPA
Florida International University

ABOUT THE AUTHORS

Elisa S. Moncarz is an award-winning author, consultant, speaker, academician, and professional certified public accountant. As a Professor Emeritus in the School of Hospitality and Tourism Management of Florida International University, where she was a Professor of Accounting and Finance for more than three decades, she was the recipient of several awards for outstanding teaching and excellence in research. Professor Moncarz has co-authored seven books and has published numerous articles in leading hospitality academic journals, including the *Cornell Hotel and Restaurant Administration Quarterly*, the *International Journal of Hospitality Management*, the *International Journal of Contemporary Hospitality Management*, and the *FIU Hospitality Review*. Several of her publications have been translated into foreign languages, such as Spanish and Chinese, and adapted to foreign markets, including Canada, Latin America, and Taiwan. She has been ranked among the most prolific researchers in the hospitality field based on studies published in the *Hospitality Research Journal* and the *Journal of Hospitality and Tourism Education*. In 2009, she was the International Council on Hotel, Restaurant and Institutional Education (CHRIE) recipient of the "Article of the Year Award" for a manuscript that she coauthored and published in the *Journal of Hospitality and Tourism Education*. A CPA in New York and Florida, she has extensive financial management and Securities Exchange Commission (SEC) experience with national and international firms in New York and Florida, where she assumed the responsibility for the approval of SEC and audit engagements. She has also served as consultant for many organizations in the United States and abroad and as referee for leading hospitality academic journals, educational institutions, and academic conferences.

Nestor de J. Portocarrero is a Professor of Accounting and Finance in the School of Hospitality and Tourism Management of Florida International University, where he has been a member of the faculty since 1981. He is a certified public accountant and has been involved in the audit of many enterprises. He is a member of the American Institute of Certified Public Accountants. He was a member of the Profit Planning Department of the American Can Company, where he helped develop a formal national budgeting process for the company. He has worked with Panama Airlines in its Miami Office and was the founder of the largest CPA firm in Nicaragua in 1972. He was also involved in the creation of several other business enterprises in Nicaragua.

Professor Portocarrero has co-authored three books and several articles in the hospitality industry. He has received an award for excellence in teaching from the University, two Teaching Incentive Program (TIP) awards from the Florida Board of Regents, and was voted by the Alumni at the 1995 homecoming to receive a plaque recognizing him as the professor who contributed the most to the academic growth of students at the Florida International University School of Hospitality and Tourism Management. He also received an award from the University for Excellence in Service.

PART I

INTRODUCTION

CHAPTER 1
THE SCOPE OF FINANCIAL MANAGEMENT

CONTENTS

Financial Management: Scope and Objectives	1002
Goal of the Company	1002
Importance of Managing for Value Creation	1003
Managing for Value Creation	1003
Making Business Decisions That Create Value	1004
Profit Maximization versus Value Creation	1004
Managerial Actions That Influence Shareholder Value	1005
Separation of Ownership and Control	1005
The Agency Problem	1006
Importance of Cash Flow in Financial Management	1006
The External Environment	1006
Other Stakeholders' Interests	1006
Ethics in Financial Management	1007

The hospitality industry has played a significant role in the service economies of the United States and many other developed nations for years. According to the American Hotel and Lodging Association (AH&LA), the U.S. hotel industry contributes over 100 billion dollars to the nation's economy and employs over 2 million people. Variables, including globalization, competitive and demographic forces, financing challenges and technological advances, have changed the scope of financial management in present-day hospitality companies. Accordingly, financial management responsibility is broadening and becoming more critical to the company's success. In addition to keeping accurate accounting records, preparing financial reports, managing the company's cash position and paying bills, the role of financial management is growing in significance, as the global economy and its financial markets become increasingly interdependent. Factors such as increased company size and complexity, government intervention resulting from corporate scandals, and creativity necessary for raising funds have expanded the scope of financial management. Financial managers require a much broader view of the industry because their influence reaches almost every aspect of the company as well as the external environment. The financial manager is, in essence, the link between the company's operations and financial markets.

FINANCIAL MANAGEMENT: SCOPE AND OBJECTIVES

Financial management is concerned with the acquisition, financing, and management of the hospitality company's resources with the goal of maximizing company value. The main areas requiring sound decision making are

- The investment of resources.
- The financing of these resources.
- The operation of the hospitality company using these resources.

The financial manager works as an integral part of the management team of a modern hospitality corporation. An important aspect of financial management involves the relationship between financial personnel and other departments in the day-to-day management of the hospitality company. On the job, the financial manager must constantly solve business problems using financial tools and techniques.

Financial management can be basic, as in the case of a small, owner-operated hotel or restaurant, or complex, as in the case of a major lodging or restaurant chain. For larger hotels or restaurant organizations the financial management function is distributed between the controller and the treasurer. Although their responsibilities may overlap, the financial area normally consists of both the accounting department, lead by the controller, and the treasury department, headed by the treasurer. Both of these positions report to the chief financial officer (CFO) or vice president of finance. The CFO is the executive in charge of the financial management function; and, in some large hospitality organizations, the CFO may be a member of the board of directors. In addition to overseeing the accounting, treasury, tax, and audit functions, CFOs often are responsible for strategic planning, managing risk from volatile interest rates, and hedging exchange rates risk in foreign currency. Moreover, CFOs must be able to communicate with the investment community concerning the financial performance of the hospitality company.

The controller has responsibility for all accounting-related activities, including the preparation of financial statements and other accounting reports, and taxes and cost control, and is continually becoming more involved with the information technology (IT) function. The treasurer normally is concerned with the acquisition, custody, and expenditure of funds. However, in the case of a small hotel or restaurant company, the treasurer is likely to be the only financial executive. His or her tasks include financial planning; capital investment analysis; raising new capital; and maintaining relationships with banks, stockholders, and the investment community.

GOAL OF THE COMPANY

Efficient financial management requires the existence of a goal, because determination as to whether a financial decision is sound must be made based on a set standard. Although various objectives are possible, it will be assumed in this handbook that the ultimate objective of the hospitality company is to maximize the wealth of its owners as measured by the maximization of the total market value of the company's common stock. With this goal in mind, the job of the financial manager is directed to the creation of wealth for company shareholders.

This goal of value creation makes business common sense. If the financial manager fails to create value for its owners, the company will be unable to attract debt and equity capital and will not be able to survive. Shareholder wealth maximization has another important benefit: It explicitly considers the timing and risk that is expected from stock ownership. As a result, managers must consider the elements of timing and risk when making important financial decisions, such as investing in new hotels or restaurant property and equipment and raising new capital. In this way, financial managers will make decisions that contribute to increased shareholder wealth.

IMPORTANCE OF MANAGING FOR VALUE CREATION

Managing with the goal of raising company value provides the basis for an integrated financial management system that helps the financial manager to evaluate actual business performance and make sound business decisions, as well as to design compensation packages that align the interest of the hospitality company's managers with those of the owners.

Greater value for a company's shareholders does not mean less value for its employees, customers, or suppliers. Successful companies not only have satisfied shareholders but loyal customers, motivated employees, and dependable suppliers. Thus thriving hospitality companies know that dealing successfully with stakeholders is an important element in achieving the ultimate goal of creating value for their owners.

Generally, companies that take care of their customers and employees also deliver value to their shareholders. That is, the ability of a company to create value for its shareholders is related to the way it treats its employees, customers, and community. On the other hand, some hospitality firms that deal successfully with their employees, suppliers, and customers may be unable to translate this outcome into a higher company value. In this case, a revision of the company's current business strategy is required. Otherwise, dissatisfied shareholders may try to force changes or oust the existing management team.

Managing for Value Creation

The financial manager can affect the hospitality company's value by making decisions that influence:

- Projected earnings per share.
- Timing of the earnings stream.
- Risk of these projected earnings.
- Use of debt financing.
- Dividend policy.

Financial managers can maximize shareholder wealth by making investment decisions whose value is greater than the amount of capital invested to finance these investments. Thus financial managers must have the ability to assess the value of potential investments and make the lowest-cost capital acquisitions. However, there are also external factors that can influence a hospitality company's value such as legal constraints.

Making Business Decisions That Create Value

When making operating, financing, or investing decisions the financial manager must consider whether an investment project will create value for the company's owners. If after sound analysis it can be concluded that the decision will result in the creation of value, then management should proceed with the plan; otherwise, the project should be abandoned.

Essentially, financial managers are responsible for deploying external and internal resources and for making decisions to create an economic gain for company owners. This benefit will be reflected in the combination of dividends and share price appreciation received by the owners.

Successful use of resources should result in a net improvement in the economic position of the company's owners. Only if such improvement is achieved has additional shareholder value been created. If the hospitality stock is traded in the public market, its value is determined by the market price of the common stock. If the hospitality company is privately held, its value will be reflected in the price offered by potential buyers of the business.

PROFIT MAXIMIZATION VERSUS VALUE CREATION

Maximizing profits is often considered to be the goal of a hospitality company, but it is narrow in concept when compared to the goal of maximizing the value of the company. The maximization of profits, as reflected through earnings per share growth, is not useful as the central decision-making model for the hospitality company because profit maximization stresses the efficient use of capital resources, but it does not specify the time frame for which profits are to be measured. For example, a financial manager can maximize earnings and earnings per share by reducing food costs by purchasing an inferior quality of meat or poultry. In the short term, these actions might increase profits but in the long term, these actions will lessen customer demand and decrease the company's value.

Another problem associated with profit maximization is that it provides no direct way for financial managers to consider the risk associated with alternative decisions, because profit maximization ignores uncertainty and risk. Projects differ with respect to risk characteristics and to disregard these differences would lead to improper decision making. For instance, a hotel or restaurant can increase earnings per share by increasing the proportion of debt financing used in the company's capital structure; however, the additional use of leverage increases the financial risk. Thus the financial marketplace will recognize the increased risk of financial distress by adjusting the value of the hospitality company.

Accordingly, creation of shareholder value emerges as a critical challenge. Achieving consistency in the choice of accounting alternatives and in making financial decisions is critical to managing a hospitality company's long-term success and shareholder expectations. Therefore, only a well-organized company that takes into account time frame, risk, and time value of money will perform in a way that results in value maximization for hospitality shareholders.

MANAGERIAL ACTIONS THAT INFLUENCE SHAREHOLDER VALUE

Many factors ultimately influence the magnitude, timing, and risk of a company's cash flows and thus the price of its common stock. Creating shareholder value ultimately depends on proper financial management resulting in:

- Identification, evaluation, implementation, and follow-up of investment proposals using sound strategies, financial analysis, and effective management.
- Careful financing of the hospitality company by properly balancing the rewards expected against the risks incurred in using internal and external financing in the capital structure.
- Managing the operations of the hospitality company profitably by making sound decisions and cost-effective use of resources employed.

SEPARATION OF OWNERSHIP AND CONTROL

Managers control company operations of many medium to large hospitality organizations on a day-to day basis, while shareholders own the hospitality company. Clearly, the separation of management and ownership may be an obstacle in the achievement of wealth maximization for the organization. When managers act as agents of owners or stockholders, there is the potential for a conflict of interest between the owners and management interests, which in turn can lead to decision making that will not maximize the company's value but will maximize managerial wealth.

However, enhancing their own personal welfare may lead some managers to be concerned with job security and lead them to limit the amount of risk incurred by the hospitality company. An unfavorable outcome may result in either these managers' dismissal or possible bankruptcy of the company.

The separation of ownership and control has permitted hospitality managers to pursue goals more consistent with their own self-interest, as long as they satisfy owners sufficiently to maintain control of the company. Instead of working toward the goal of value creation, these managers seek acceptable levels of performance while maximizing their own welfare.

There are several ways that managers' actions can negatively affect a company's value, such as by taking on faulty projects, overpaying on a takeover, and incurring excessive debt. These examples are manifestations of the fundamental problem of conflicts of interest between stockholders and managers, where shareholder wealth maximization is likely to take second place to management interests.

The Agency Problem

Hospitality managers are hired to act on the owners' behalf with the objective of maximizing shareholder wealth. To ensure this occurs, owners incur agency costs such as bonding to protect owners from managerial dishonesty, providing stock option plans, and paying a large part of a manager's compensation package in the form of a bonus tied to company performance. Agency costs that result from the separation of ownership and control must be addressed satisfactorily for hospitality companies to prosper.

IMPORTANCE OF CASH FLOW IN FINANCIAL MANAGEMENT

The concept of cash flow is a central consideration in decisions regarding planning, financial analysis, and resource allocation. Cash flow is important because the financial health of the hospitality company depends on its ability to generate sufficient amounts of cash to pay its creditors, employees, suppliers, and owners. Future cash flow is the heart of a hospitality company's true value, which is of interest to both investors and creditors.

Financial managers are concerned primarily with raising funds for use by the hospitality company and investing those funds in assets that can be converted into a stream of cash flow that accrues to the company and its owners. Cash flow generation is closely linked to creating value for the company's owners. For the most part, maximizing shareholder wealth depends on bringing about a positive pattern of cash flow that exceeds investor expectations. When a hospitality business is successfully managed, it will generate cash flow well into the future.

THE EXTERNAL ENVIRONMENT

Although management's actions affect the value of the hospitality company's stock, external factors such as legal constraints; local, domestic, and global economic activity; industry outlook; tax laws; and stock market conditions also influence stock prices. Working within the external environment, financial managers make a set of long-term strategic policy decisions to map the future course of their company.

In addition, a hospitality financial manager should understand how the financial markets function and how a hospitality company raises capital in these markets. The financial markets serve as the arena where market prices are set and investors can exchange their capital.

OTHER STAKEHOLDERS' INTERESTS

Although stockholder wealth maximization should be the primary goal of management, in recent years many firms have expanded this focus to include the interests of other stakeholders. Generally, successful hospitality companies focus on avoiding actions that would prove harmful to other stakeholders. This vision is considered part of the hospitality company's social responsibility and is expected to provide long-term benefits to owners by maintaining positive relationships with employees, creditors, suppliers, and society and minimizing stakeholder turnover, conflicts, and litigation.

ETHICS IN FINANCIAL MANAGEMENT

In recent years, the legality of actions taken by certain businesses has received major media attention. Undoubtedly, business failures involving, for example, Enron, WorldCom, Tyco, Cendant, and Boston Chicken have called into question the effectiveness of the financial reporting and auditing process. These corporate failures and frauds have also called into question the ethics of financial management and its actions as well as the ethics of internal and external auditors. Heightened media exposure has emphasized the importance of sound, ethical management to the proper functioning of the U.S. and global financial markets. Without reliable and accurate financial reporting, hospitality managers would not be able to evaluate the performance of their companies and make appropriate decisions concerning their future growth, and without accurate, dependable financial reporting, creditors and investors could not make sound credit and investment decisions.

Development of meaningful reforms and new ethical standards has been a continuous process due to the widespread publicity surrounding numerous ethical violations and their perpetrators that began with the Enron collapse in late 2001. The financial community's response resulted in the enactment of the Sarbanes-Oxley Act of 2002 by Congress. The goal of the Act is to motivate management at all levels to adhere to both the spirit of the law and the regulations concerned with all aspects of business.

While the recent focus on improved financial reporting and adherence to ethical standards has been positive, hospitality companies must implement policies and procedures whose emphasis remains even after media attention declines. The financial reporting system and related decisions made by financial management will continue to receive close public scrutiny in the foreseeable future. An effective and dependable system serves to ensure the hospitality company's continued success while striving to achieve the company's goal of maximizing shareholder wealth.

CHAPTER 2
THE RESPONSIBILITIES OF THE CONTROLLER

CONTENTS

General Responsibilities of the Controller	2002
Accounting or Record Keeping Function	2002
Significant Factors Affecting the Recording Process	2002
Accrual Entries	2004
Recording and Reporting System Unique to the Hospitality Industry	2005
The Internal Control Function	2009
Internal Audit	2011
The Reporting Function	2011
Financial Accounting and Reporting	2011
Assisting in the Preparation of Other Reports to Outside Stakeholders	2012
Management Accounting and Internal Management Reports	2012
Tax and Insurance Matters	2015
The Controller as Advisor	2015
Accounting Knowledge, Industry Knowledge, and Personal Qualifications	2016
Knowledge of and Currency with Accounting Fundamentals and Pertinent Legal Statutes	2017
Knowledge of the Hospitality Industry	2018
Personal Qualities and Skills	2020
Exhibits	
Exhibit 2-1. Hotel List of Possible Accruals	2005
Exhibit 2-2. Sample Chart of Accounts and Income Statement Compatible with the Uniform System of Accounts for the Lodging Industry	2006
Exhibit 2-3. Requirements for the Controller's Position	2016
Exhibit 2-4. Characteristics of Strong Controllers	2022

A hospitality controller must have knowledge of and involvement in almost every aspect of the industry, thus making the controller's office a crucial hub in the flow of information within the business. The hierarchical structure and relationship of those involved in the financial management of a multiple-entity hospitality company can vary in its complexity. For example, a division controller may report to a division general manager, as well as to a treasurer, who then reports to the vice president of finance or to the chief financial officer (CFO). A division controller may report to a division general manager and to a corporate controller, who reports to the vice president of finance or to the CFO. Usually, a controller of a single hotel is responsible to two managers as well: the operations manager of the hotel or business segment in which the hotel is included and a financial manager at the corporate or division level. Obviously, this places greater demands on a controller, as the division or corporate level financial manager and the local operations manager have different perspectives: the former encompasses the entire organization and the latter focuses on local matters and responsibilities.

GENERAL RESPONSIBILITIES OF THE CONTROLLER

The hospitality controller's responsibilities can be divided into three main categories:

1. *Accounting and recording*—Gathering and recording the financial data of a hospitality company.
2. *Control*—Verifying the integrity of raw data, as well as assuring the accuracy with which the data are recorded and processed in a manner that complies with GAAP.
3. *Reporting*—Exploring new and innovative ways of identifying relationships that might improve management decision making and strategic planning and reporting these to management, as well as assisting the CFO or treasurer in preparing reports to outside stakeholders of the company.

ACCOUNTING OR RECORD KEEPING FUNCTION

Hospitality controllers are responsible for collecting and safeguarding all the financial data of their company, for recording and maintaining accurate records involving assets, liabilities, equity, revenue, and expenses. Within these categories accounts receivable, accounts payable, property and equipment, revenues, and payroll are major accounts. In a restaurant business, payroll and costs of sales are also important, as they can each consume up to 40% of every revenue dollar. Traditionally, the controller has been responsible for recording and presenting all accounting and financial data in an accessible, cost-effective manner for inclusion in reports to internal management and outside stakeholders.

With the increasing implementation by companies of data warehousing, the recording role is gradually being assumed by the information technology (IT) department. Nevertheless, controllers must be aware of the accounting and financial impact of all material changes to the company accounts, and of contracts, such as loans and leases, entered into by the business. In addition, controllers must be knowledgeable about data mining in relation to the warehoused data inherent in property management and business intelligence programs and be able to verify that it is being properly handled in any reports generated by these systems.

Significant Factors Affecting the Recording Process

Every transaction in which a hospitality company participates generates raw financial data. The hospitality controller is responsible for recording or establishing systems that record these data accurately and securely. When recording transactions, a controller must be governed by the basic accounting concepts based on GAAP. The concepts that are most open to subjective interpretation are materiality, realization, matching, consistency, and conservatism.

The Materiality Concept. Although hospitality controllers must comply with basic accounting concepts and GAAP, they should not be obsessed with details. An objective of the controller is not only to organize and manage the controller's department, but also to do so efficiently and cost-effectively. It is important to know when to record items in the most efficient manner. For example, if a central food distribution center carries a large inventory of spices, there should be a spice inventory account, but if each individual restaurant in a chain buys its own spices weekly as they are consumed, it would be an inefficient use of the controller's resources to record weekly purchases of spices in an inventory account rather than record them directly in cost of sales.

The materiality concept can be somewhat elusive, since it states that anything that might significantly affect the opinion of the reader of the financial statements is material. Simple guidelines, such as a rule stating that any amount under 5% of assets is immaterial, are too inflexible. The nature of the account affected by a materiality decision is an important factor. An amount that might be considered immaterial with regard to total assets might be very material with regard to net income, when the recording and presentation format of such an amount can significantly affect the profit or loss, convert a profit into a loss, or vice versa. In addition, when financial statements include the combined amounts of several entities, amounts that might not be material for one particular entity may be offset by amounts in another entity that are significant, resulting in a combined amount that is material but is not visible on the financial statements because of the offsetting nature of the two immaterial errors.

On the other hand, the materiality concept, when properly applied, increases efficiency in the controller's operations because it allows immaterial amounts to be recorded in the most economical manner, even if this method of recording alters, in an insignificant manner, the results presented on the financial statements. Unfortunately, not even the Financial Accounting Standards Board (FASB) has been able to develop a clear definition of the materiality concept.

Item 1 in Appendix 2 provides two links to online discussions of the materiality concept and the inability of the FASB to clearly define it.

The Realization Concept. The hospitality controller must also consider the realization concept when recording revenue. Revenue cannot be recorded merely because cash was received, or it cannot fail to be recorded merely because cash was not received. Although other industries differ, in the hospitality industry only two steps are necessary to require that revenue be recorded:

1. A service must be rendered to, or a product such as food or beverages must be delivered to, a customer, and
2. The exchange value of this service or product must be readily determinable.

Posting room rates in rooms and printing item prices on menus satisfy this second condition. Thus, when a service is rendered, or food or beverages are provided to a customer, a revenue transaction is complete. Recording revenue either before or after the above two conditions are met is a violation of GAAP and can be construed as revenue manipulation. Although in the hospitality industry sales are usually cash sales, including the use of credit cards, corporations or other groups may deal with a hospitality company on a credit basis. Advance deposits paid by customers cannot be recorded as revenue until a service is rendered. Often a portion of a deposit is non-refundable in hotels and is considered revenue because the service rendered is the *reservation* of space in the hotel, not the actual occupancy of a room.

The Matching Concept. The matching concept is the logical complement to the realization concept. It governs a revenue transaction from the point of view of the recipient of the service. It does not allow for the recording of expenses merely because payment has been made, nor is it correct to fail to record an expense solely because payment has not been made. Expenses must be recorded when an asset or a service is consumed regardless of the payment status. The accounting systems of a hospitality company should be designed to avoid over-reporting of revenues and under-reporting of expenses, as defined by basic business concepts and by GAAP. Although these seem to be obvious observations, companies have encountered serious problems as a result of violating these two concepts.

The Consistency Concept. A potential source of trouble to be avoided is the lack of consistency in recording and reporting. Because of the large required investment in tangible property and equipment, depreciation accounts in the hospitality industry are susceptible to tampering by inconsistent depreciation methods. This also applies to the allowance for doubtful accounts and any other accounting procedure based merely on management's judgment. GAAP allows for a certain amount of choice in selecting accounting procedures, but once selected, they may not be altered. The potential for manipulating net income by applying accounting policies inconsistently is obvious.

The Conservatism Concept. The temptation to record expenditures by capitalizing them as opposed to expensing them is ever-present. When there is any doubt, the conservatism concept leads to recording expenditures as expenses, rather than as other possible categories of expenditures, such as debits to assets or to liability reserves, regardless of the negative impact this may have on net income. This concept might apply to management policy concerning the distinction between recording expenditures as maintenance and repairs as opposed to capitalizing them.

Accrual Entries

The recording of accrual entries is an area where a controller must be especially careful to exercise thoroughness. Because these are entries for which no invoice has been received, they can be easily overlooked. To minimize this risk, controllers must be completely conversant with all transactions that affect their particular hospitality business. It is important to establish a procedure with safeguards to ensure proper communication regarding transactions between operating management and the controller's department. Exhibit 2-1, "Hotel List of Possible Accruals," provides a sample list of possible accrual entries that a hospitality company might be required to make.

Exhibit 2-1: Hotel List of Possible Accruals

1. Any outstanding operating expense invoices not posted in accounts payable by the end of the month.
2. Property tax accrual, based on the budget.
3. Mortgage payment accrual (if payment overlaps from month to month).
4. Any prepaid accounts that must be expensed over a period of time (amortization schedules are set up and properly expensed to the correct departments).
5. Payroll accrual.
6. Deposits in transit are accounted for (e.g., cash and credit cards).
7. Deferred revenue.

Recording and Reporting System Unique to the Hospitality Industry

The hospitality industry has developed its own recording and reporting system with regard to the creation of accounts and organization by department. This method of creating and segregating accounts for internal reporting purposes is called the Uniform System of Accounts for the Lodging Industry (USAL) and the Uniform System of Accounts for Restaurants (USAR). These are accounting systems used by management in evaluating the performance of individual managers independent of the overall performance of the company. The USAL has evolved from the original system of hotel accounts devised in 1925, and the USAR was initiated in 1958. A responsibility accounting system must meet the following criteria:

1. It must provide a chart of accounts that allows revenues and expenses to be segregated by department; and
2. It must enable managers to control the revenues and expenses for which they are held responsible. Thus, the following must be true:
    a. The chart of accounts must provide managers with sufficiently detailed information concerning the departments, divisions, or segments for which they are responsible, and
    b. Authority must be assigned along the same lines as responsibility.

The USAL and USAR provide charts of accounts that meet the first criterion. Through the use of departmental schedules, they also provide the detailed information required to effectively control a department, thus meeting item 2a. (Item 2 in Exhibit 2-2 provides an example of the USAL account numbering rationale, a summary income statement, and a department schedule.) With regard to item 2b. above, the hospitality controller should be watchful for situations where management has allocated authority along hierarchical lines different from those according to which responsibility is assigned. This will inevitably result in loss of employee motivation, discontent, and the resulting reduction in employee productivity.

Exhibit 2-2: Sample Chart of Accounts and Income Statement Compatible with the Uniform System of Accounts for the Lodging Industry

A USAL-compatible account number may have several components, as indicated below:

Regional identifier	xxx
Divisional identifier	xxx
Unit identifier	xxx
Responsibility center identifier	xxx
Account identifier	xxx
Sub-account identifier	xxx

Food sales in the revenue department of hotel number 5, which is part of the urban hotels division in the southeastern region of the United States, might have the following account number: 12-03-0005-200-423, and its related cost-of-food-sold account might have number 12-03-0005-200-523, based on the following rationale:

Regional identifier	Divisional identifier	Unit identifier	Responsibility center identifier	Account identifier	Sub-account identifier
12- Southeastern region	03- Urban hotels	0005- Hotel #5	200- Food department	400- Food sales	423- Banquet food sales
12-	03-	0005-	200-	500- Cost of food sales	523- Cost of banquet food sales

Thus it is possible to identify the operating results of various responsibility subcenters.

An income statement based on the numbering system above would have at least two components, a summary income statement and an individual department schedule that provides the necessary detail for managing the food and beverage department. An example of each is presented below.

Summary Income Statement

	Schedule	Net	Cost of sales	Payroll & related	Other	Dept. Income
Operated departments						
Rooms	1	$1,280,000		$200,000	$94,000	$986,000
Food and beverage	2	$570,000	$188,000	227,000	65,000	90,000
Telephone	3	29,000		25,000	9,000	(5,000)
Store rentals	4	51,000				51,000
Total operated departments		$1,930,000	$188,000	$452,000	$168,000	$1,122,000

	Schedule	Net	Cost of sales	Payroll & related	Other	Dept. Income
Undistributed operating expenses						
Administrative and general	5			$130,000	$ 80,000	$ 210,000
Marketing	6			30,000	60,000	90,000
Guest entertainment	7			25,000	70,000	95,000
Property operation maintenance and energy costs	8			27,000	108,000	135,000
Total undistributed operating expenses				$212,000	$318,000	$ 530,000
Totals		$1,930,000	$188,000	$664,000	$486,000	$ 592,000
Management fees	9					93,000
Property taxes, insurance, and rent	10					40,000
Income before interest, depreciation, amortization, and taxes						$ 459,000
Interest	11					25,000
Income before depreciation, amortization, and income taxes						$ 434,000
Depreciation and amortization	12					140,000
Income before income taxes						$ 294,000
Income taxes	13					145,000
Net income						$ 149,000

Exhibit 2-2: Sample Chart of Accounts and Income Statement Compatible with the Uniform System of Accounts for the Lodging Industry (*Continued*)

Food and Beverage Department—Schedule 2

Revenue

Food	$400,000
Beverage	171,000
Total	571,000
Allowances	2,000
Net revenue	569,000
Other income	1,000
Total	570,000

Cost of sales

Cost of food consumed	160,000
Less cost of employees' meals	16,000
Net cost of food sales	144,000
Cost of beverage sales	44,000
Net cost of sales	188,000
Gross profit	382,000

Expenses

Salaries and wages	184,000
Employee benefits	43,000
Total payroll and related expenses	227,000

Other expenses

China, glassware, silver, linen	9,100
Contract cleaning	2,280
Kitchen fuel	5,130
Laundry and dry cleaning	1,710
Licenses	8,800
Music and entertainment	17,700
Operating supplies	18,860
Other operating expenses	1,200
Uniforms	220
Total other expenses	65,000
Total expenses	292,000
Departmental income (loss)	$ 90,000

THE INTERNAL CONTROL FUNCTION

The Committee of Sponsoring Organizations of the Treadway Commission (COSO) defines *internal control* as:

> [A] process, effected by an entity's board of directors, management and other personnel, designed to provide reasonable assurance regarding the achievement of objectives in the following categories:
> - Effectiveness and efficiency of operations.
> - Reliability of financial reporting.
> - Compliance with applicable laws and regulations.

In response to the need for a broader definition of *control*, the Public Company Accounting Oversight Board (PCAOB) introduced the concept of enterprise risk management (ERM) and accepted the definition of *ERM* proposed by COSO. The new definition enumerates the following five processes required to minimize a business's exposure to risk:

1. Establishing a healthy control environment.
2. Assessing areas of risk to a business.
3. Establishing control activities to minimize these risks.
4. Establishing paths for the exchange of information concerning all of the above areas.
5. Monitoring the health of all four of the above factors.

These factors introduce the two new concepts that (1) risk is no longer limited to accounting aberrations risk, but encompasses business risk as well; and (2) everyone in an organization is in some way responsible for the internal control of its assets and procedures. Whether internal control is or is not the explicit responsibility of a particular controller, this broader concept of control adopted by the PCAOB should be taken into consideration by the controller in all of his or her functions relating to the verification and preservation of the integrity of assets and accounting data. Under this definition, the control environment involves ethical values, integrity, and competence. Although these have always been an implied responsibility of the controller within his or her department, this definition makes them explicit and intertwines the internal control responsibilities of all departments.

Because controllers record and evaluate accounting data and translate these data into losses or gains, they are in the best position to be aware of inefficient or particularly efficient procedures and of changes in the value or productive capacity of assets. With this knowledge, the controller is able to reveal a business's progress, failures, and future limitations. The controller has a comprehensive view of all aspects that assist in determining the condition and value of a hospitality business, but most particularly its accounting and financial aspects. Thus, the financial impact of services rendered or food and beverages sold can be determined, and unprofitable endeavors can be eliminated or improved. The controller must catalog, classify, or otherwise deal with all factors that have a financial impact on the business, such as statistics based on stored financial data or relating to properties owned, and the cost of rendering services. Beyond maintaining records of financial investment data, the hospitality controller must also establish safeguards to assure that the accuracy of these records is preserved over time.

In conformity with the definition of *ERM*, the control function can be summarized as follows:

1. It prevents inaccurate or inappropriate recording and reporting of financial data.
2. It establishes systems to detect inaccuracies and deviations from appropriate recording and reporting.
3. It corrects any inaccuracies or deviations discovered by these systems.

These three steps can refer to the verification of compliance with GAAP, government regulations, or procedures designed to attain a company's financial goals. In the hospitality industry, these goals usually involve the verification of compliance with cost and revenue standards (i.e., setting the standards, comparing standards with actual results, and using these comparisons to revise the standards or the service procedures, when necessary, to optimize results).

When viewed from the perspective of the value maximization formula,

$$\text{Market Value} = \text{Price Earnings Ratio} \times \left(\frac{\text{Net income}}{\text{Common shares outstanding}} \right)$$

the controller's efforts are mostly dedicated to maximizing the numerator of this fraction by providing management with the required data and expense analyses necessary for making decisions conducive to minimizing expenses, by:

- Establishing safeguards to ensure that expense control will be maintained,
- Establishing systems that will detect deficiencies in these safeguards, and
- Establishing corrective measures when such deficiencies are detected.

Control over the denominator of this fraction, common shares outstanding, falls within the purview of the CFO or treasurer.

These activities not only involve designing the internal control system; they also evaluate its system's control elements by weighing their cost against the additional security they may provide and, as an ongoing responsibility throughout the year, perform internal audits on a continuous, rotating basis to determine whether the internal controls are functioning effectively. The result of this constant evaluation of internal controls should lead to improvements in the system, either by adding or eliminating security functions, to ensure that the company's assets are safeguarded and that all pertinent transactions are accurately recorded in a way that is cost-effective and facilitates reporting to outside stakeholders according to GAAP. As a part of this responsibility, hospitality controllers must report to the company's audit committee or board of directors. The controllers must also work with external auditors and participate in assuring compliance with all pertinent government regulations, such as the Foreign Corrupt Practices Act of 1977, the Sarbanes-Oxley Act of 2002 (SOX), and SEC regulations, as well as compliance with any requirements stipulated by the board of directors in the minutes of their meetings or in covenants with outsiders. If a company is listed on a stock exchange, there will be additional compliance requirements. These are discussed in Chapter 5, "The Financial Reporting System."

In addition to the control over internal data, when finance-related activities such as employee pension fund investments and stockholder records are outsourced, the controller is responsible for verifying, or assisting the CFO or treasurer in verifying, the accuracy with which the relevant agencies are performing these duties. If any IT functions are outsourced, there are additional audit requirements based on Statement of Auditing Standards (SAS) No. 70, *Service Organizations*.

Internal Audit

In organizations that have separate internal audit and internal control departments, responsibility for the following previously listed items falls within the purview of the control department, which is responsible for supervising the internal control structure:

- Establishing systems that will detect deficiencies in these safeguards, such as automatically reporting data concerning the same transaction from two different independent sources; and
- Establishing corrective measures when such deficiencies are detected.

THE REPORTING FUNCTION

The hospitality controller has a twofold reporting responsibility that involves

1. Assisting the CFO or treasurer in the preparation of external reports (e.g., financial statements) to outside stakeholders in the business, as well as preparing those reports solely to organizations, such as the SEC. The reports might include the historical analysis of growth in a particular division or region.
2. Preparing internal reports to (a) aid management in making decisions and (b) enable management to verify that proper control is being maintained either with regard to only the controllership responsibilities, or to both controllership and internal audit/control responsibilities. These reports might consist of detailed accounts concerning the growth in various sales categories, broken down by type and geographical location, or reports containing bank reconciliations or proofs of cash.

The former reports usually deal with financial matters, which fall within the CFO's or treasurer's area of responsibility; the latter reports more often fall within the realm of management accounting, which is one of the controller's areas of competency.

Financial Accounting and Reporting

Financial accounting involves recording supporting data in preparation for reports to hospitality company stakeholders (e.g., stockholders, creditors, suppliers, employees and their labor unions and retirement benefits funds, and local or federal government agencies). The corporate controller is responsible for gathering the data on which these reports are based and may be called on to assist in their preparation. Because financial reporting may involve litigation or competitive and political risks, it is the CFO or treasurer who is ultimately responsible for the preparation of these reports.

Another function in which financial accounting may be involved is benchmarking. For example, in comparing the company's processes to those of a widely accepted standard, the controller may be requested to contribute data. Further, financial accounting is involved in the long-term planning of a hospitality company. As opposed to merely reporting historical amounts, financial accounting includes such concepts as the market value of assets, the time value of money, cash flows, and off-balance-sheet financing. A list of some possible reports to outside stakeholders, according to their periodicity, that might be prepared by a non-publicly owned hotel in Florida is provided as follows:

- Monthly basis
  — Sales tax (state and county)
  — Beverage surcharge (state)
- Yearly basis
  — Real and personal property tax assessment (county)
  — Capital expenditure survey (government)
  — Information technology purchase survey (government)
  — Tax returns (government)
  — 401k (government testing and evaluations)
  — Keeping current all licenses, franchise names (state)

A publicly owned hospitality company would have to add to this list both financial statements and reports to the SEC.

Similar to providing the sales tax information provided to many state, county, and city governments, hospitality controllers must provide financial information to U.S. agencies, such as the IRS and Departments of Commerce and Labor, as well as to local government agencies.

Assisting in the Preparation of Other Reports to Outside Stakeholders

If a hospitality company is publicly owned, the controller often assists in the preparation of reports required by the SEC and financial statements for presentation to outside stakeholders. The controller must ascertain that the company annual report includes adequate disclosure of all material matters that might significantly affect the opinion of the user of these statements and may be asked to suggest imaginative use of graphs and other illustrations to help clarify the information contained in the report.

Management Accounting and Internal Management Reports

Management accounting involves the organization and presentation of data for internal operating use. Whereas financial management reports are concerned primarily with reporting historical information, management accounting reports are also intended to facilitate future decision making. Accounting reports are designed to assist management in both day-to-day decision making and strategic planning, based on the forward-looking application of historical data. Management accounting provides the information needed for (1) planning the operations of a hospitality company, (2) controlling and evaluating the results, and (3) using this information for making future decisions.

In its white paper titled "Leading Hospitality into the Age of Excellence," the International Hotel and Restaurant Association (IHRA) states:

> In conclusion, the hospitality industry is competing in a challenging marketplace where investors seek maximum returns and minimum risk, putting greater pressure upon executives to invest in products and services that add significant value to the business. Additionally, the risks associated with each investment have to be identified and accurate predictions regarding their impact on the cash flow stream will have to be assessed. Put differently, the need to forecast future earnings streams will be as important as setting up the right accounting and control systems. Foresight will be as essential as hindsight but more difficult to get right, underlining the need for a more complete blending of financial and strategic management.

Areas of controller involvement are being identified ever more clearly not only by regulatory agencies but by the hospitality industry itself, and these responsibilities are broader than had been formerly realized. The controller is no longer solely a provider of historical accounting and financial information, nor solely responsible for minimizing expenditures and expenses. Although this has always been a controller's implied responsibility, stockholders and potential investors are now demanding forward-looking decision making, thus placing more explicit responsibility on the controller. To adequately fulfill this responsibility, the controller must work closely with management to understand its information needs and be conversant with and help shape its future outlook.

A hospitality controller must prepare reports that enable the company to:

- Maximize, not merely increase returns.
- Minimize, not merely decrease risk.
- Identify those services that add significant value as opposed to those that are merely profitable.
- Identify the risks associated with future investments.
- Predict accurately the risks' impact on the cash flow stream.
- Forecast future earnings accurately.

The controller must devise methods of calculating the return on investment (ROI) for the purchase of items such as management software, whose benefits are nebulous and difficult to quantify. A restaurant may be involved in deciding whether to buy handheld, point-of-sale (POS) input devices for its waiters, another difficult-to-quantify decision. Data warehousing programs now provide hotels with additional information concerning their guests to the point where return visits by guests can almost be predicted. This information must be taken into account when preparing budgets and other forward-looking reports. The increased investment in data warehousing facilitates more accurate customer count predictions on a daily, weekly, and monthly basis. The increased accuracy that is facilitated must be assigned a monetary value and must be factored into the financial projections of a restaurant or hotel.

Following is a list of internal management reports that a hospitality controller of a privately owned hotel might be required to present, segregated according to their periodicity:

- Monthly basis
  - Financial statements
  - Cash flow statements
  - Capital expenditures reports
  - Statistics (e.g., information regarding rooms, food and beverages, golf, spa)
  - Explanation and analysis of the financial statements
  - Forecasts
  - Cost/benefit analyses
  - Ratio analyses (e.g., accounts receivable turnover, aging schedule)
  - Purchasing reports (bid reviews, cost increases, buying trends)
- Daily basis
  - Statistics (e.g., regarding rooms, food and beverages, golf, spa)
  - Payroll
  - Night audit discrepancies
  - Revenue forecasts

The internal management reports must be tailored to provide the type of information that will enable a hospitality company to comply with greater investor and stockholder expectations with regard to maximizing, not merely increasing, value. These reports enable a company to establish effective corporate governance.

Accounting can be regarded as a type of shorthand language because voluminous information can be extracted from a two- or three-page set of financial statements or reports. It is the controller's responsibility to present this information to management in a timely, clear, and meaningful manner in appropriate reports that help management to satisfy not only investors' expectations of increasing shareholder value while maximizing risk, but also of making accurate earnings and cash flow projections. As the IHRA expresses in its white paper, "the need to forecast future earnings streams will be as important as setting up the right accounting and control systems."

Hospitality controllers are expected to cooperate in strategic planning with operations management using traditional tools such as preparing budgets using revenue and cost forecasting techniques. Budgets should not only be analyzed and compared to actual results through the preparation of variance analysis and operating ratio reports, but their potential future impact must also be explored. The hospitality controller will be asked to provide cost information for use in setting room rates and menu pricing. Cost analysis reports, including concepts such as cost allocation, cost-volume-profit (CVP) analysis, and analytical techniques (e.g., standard cost analysis and comparative, common size, and operating ratio analyses), should be prepared with forward-looking commentary and suggestions to assist operations management in minimizing these costs. To the extent it contributes to strategic planning, management accounting may also involve present-value and rate-of-return calculations. The impact of inflation on the hospitality company's pricing policies, costs, and profits should be analyzed using indexing techniques. Preparing reports based on responsibility accounting and reports based on management-by-exception by their very nature go beyond merely providing data. Management-by-exception reports highlight those areas where results fall outside of an acceptable range and hence need immediate attention. In addition to these management accounting reports, the controller is responsible for preparing all the financial reports that are required internally as well as reports, such as ratio analyses, that assist operating management in interpreting the standard financial statements, and help in identifying trends based on the voluminous historical data to which the hospitality controller's office has access.

The controller and marketing departments should work closely to develop ways to appraise the elasticity of demand of the goods and services rendered by a hospitality company, develop revenue management techniques, and prepare reports concerning investment decisions. In "Leading the Hospitality Industry into the Age of Excellence" the IHRA states:

> Perhaps the biggest challenge will be the need for a new business model for the marketing function. Having been viewed in the past as a cost necessary to drive revenue, the marketer is becoming a full participant in investment decisions that drive value. This white paper goes on to state: [This evolution] will call for improved estimates of revenues and costs associated with the intangibles of today's hospitality offering, improved analysis of the risks incurred and greater objectivity in evaluating all marketing options.

Tax and Insurance Matters

Hospitality controllers are responsible for presenting reports accompanied by opinions concerning the possible future tax implications of management decisions and for informing management of any potential negative tax consequences of specific management decisions already taken or planned. The controller is responsible for reviewing and reporting on tax opinions given by external tax accountants and consultants and must also review and report on the adequacy of insurance coverage carried by the company. Because the controller's office is at the center of the information flow of a business, the type and number of reports the controller may be asked to provide are wide-ranging in scope and content.

The Controller as Advisor

The controller is the principal advisor to management due to the vast amount of information that circulates through the controller's office. As an advisor, the controller is responsible for assisting management in making informed judgments that may be outside management's area of expertise. In addition, the controller should help management avoid illogical thinking based on unperceived and erroneous assumptions. The controller should be disciplined and, if appropriate, diplomatically prompt management to:

- Understand the logic behind a decision.
- Identify all assumptions and double-check them.
- Collect the data that will support or disprove these assumptions.
- Deliberately consider the situation from multiple frames of reference.
- Take into account the company's employees and their skills.
- Think from both short-term and long-term perspectives.

Thus, the controller not only becomes a provider of information but also helps to assure that the information is used correctly.

ACCOUNTING KNOWLEDGE, INDUSTRY KNOWLEDGE, AND PERSONAL QUALIFICATIONS

A controller must possess (1) a thorough knowledge of accounting fundamentals; (2) knowledge of the hospitality industry and the various segments of the business where the information is employed; and (3) a broad set of personal qualities, abilities, and skills.

Exhibit 2-3, "Requirements for the Controller's Position," presents a recent announcement for employment as a controller in the hospitality industry. It lists the required responsibilities and the desired qualifications for the position.

Exhibit 2-3: Requirements for the Controller's Position

Summary:

Direct the financial accounting, reporting, and control activities of the organization by performing the following duties personally or with the controller's department personnel.

Responsibilities:

1. Assume responsibility for all accounting functions.
2. Lead, mentor, and train accounting staff, as required.
3. Review and evaluate the accounting practices and procedures of the company and assure that they are in compliance with GAAP.
4. Research accounting issues and establish written policies and procedures for applying them within the organization.
5. Assist in establishing internal control procedures and accounting policies to comply with SOX.
6. Ascertain that there is adequate control of all assets, data, and expenses.
7. Organize the controller's department to perform its functions efficiently.
8. Propose and carry out changes to remedy any deficiencies in the above areas.
9. Periodically prepare accurate financial statements for internal financial reporting in a timely manner.

10. Prepare periodic analyses of balance sheets and income statements, and prepare periodic budget variance analyses.
11. Review all external financial reports for accuracy, completeness, and compliance with external regulatory and internal management requirements.
12. Assist in the external audit process to ensure that audit schedules are prepared and reviewed on a timely basis.
13. Prepare any necessary internal management accounting reports to assist in the proper operation of the business.
14. Participate in the strategic planning and decision-making process of the business.

Required knowledge, skills, experience, and education:
1. Possession of a certified public accountant (CPA) certificate and a thorough knowledge of accounting.
2. A thorough understanding of GAAP.
3. Experience in preparing SEC reports.
4. Knowledge concerning the application of section 404 of SOX.
5. Hospitality industry experience.
6. Ability to take the initiative in problem solving and decision making.
7. Ability to maintain commitments.
8. Ability to take responsibility for actions.
9. Possession of adequate interpersonal skills to work with management and staff.

Knowledge of and Currency with Accounting Fundamentals and Pertinent Legal Statutes

The controller must have a mastery of established accounting procedures and conceptual knowledge involved in financial and management accounting, as specified by GAAP, and must stay abreast of the latest developments in GAAP, as developed by authoritative organizations including:

- American Accounting Association (AAA)
- American Institute of Certified Public Accountants (AICPA)
- Committee of Sponsoring Organizations of the Treadway Commission (COSO)
- Emerging Issues Task Force (EITF)
- Financial Accounting Standards Board (FASB)
- Public Company Accounting Oversight Board (PCAOB)
- Securities Exchange Commission (SEC)

The controller must be familiar with the latest accounting procedures (e.g., activity-based costing, asset management). In addition, because of the increased interaction between the marketing and accounting departments, the controller should be familiar with accounting-related marketing procedures, such as yield management, a hospitality industry innovation designed to maximize the sale of expiring inventories, such as rooms in a hotel and seats in a restaurant.

Furthermore, the controller must be familiar with the following laws pertaining to business ethics and accounting:

- SEC Acts of 1933 and 1934
- Racketeer Influenced and Corrupt Organizations Act of 1970 (RICO)
- Foreign Corrupt Practices Act of 1977 (FCPA)
- Sarbanes-Oxley Act of 2002 (SOX)

The controller of an international hospitality corporation must also be familiar with international accounting GAAP as promulgated by organizations such as the International Accounting Standards Board (IASB). This Board and its offshoots have issued the following guidance to the international accounting standards:

- Framework for the Preparation and Presentation of Financial Statements
- International Financial Reporting Standards (IFRS)
- International Accounting Standards (IAS)
- Interpretations by the International Financial Reporting Interpretations Committee (IFRIC)

These standards were completed in 2004. The European Union countries adopted the IFRS in 2005, and other countries, as well as stock markets, are also adopting the standards. Hospitality companies with European subsidiaries or that are subsidiaries of Europe-based companies are affected by this adoption. The FASB has initiated a program called the Norwalk Agreement to work toward convergence of international accounting standards and GAAP. The International Auditing and Assurance Standards Board (IAASB), an independent branch of the International Federation of Accountants (IFAC), is also working to harmonize worldwide accounting and reporting standards.

Examples of differences between GAAP and IFRS are:

- *Revenue recognition.* GAAP is based on many different rules that tend to result in differences in revenue as reported by IFRS.
- *Asset impairment.* The international standards of testing for impairment, as well as the calculation of impairment, are different from the GAAP standards.
- *Property and equipment costs and investment costs.* Unlike GAAP, IFRS allows these costs to be revaluated upward.

Knowledge of the Hospitality Industry

The hospitality controller should be familiar with the unique characteristics of the industry and thoroughly understand its competitive environment. He or she must be familiar with the accounting aspects and problems of the company's individual segments, such as a hotel restaurant, catering department, or casino. The controller must be aware of the company's unique business profile, such as whether it is a resort, an extended stay hotel, or a business-traveler-type company. In the food service industry, a restaurant may be identified as full-service, take-out, family, or luxury. The controller must be aware of how the company intends to realize its business model, the often confidential subtleties that distinguish one business from another. For example, although it may be difficult for an outsider to distinguish between two quick service restaurants, the executives of these two corporations would likely be able to list several identifying characteristics that make their companies unique.

Large amounts of capital are required for the construction of hotels and restaurants, which make the hospitality industry highly capital-intensive. Hospitality inventories such as rooms and seats expire if not sold. The revenue that might have been generated from an empty room in a hotel or an empty seat in a restaurant can never be recovered. In addition, whereas in other industries the inventories of physical products may be considerable, in restaurants and hotels such inventories may be very small. For example, in restaurants fresh food is quickly perishable, and in hotels services are not physical products and expire if not used.

The hospitality controller must understand the importance of controlling food and labor costs. Costs of food and beverages sold can amount to 35% to 40% of every sales dollar. In addition, because it is a service industry, labor costs consume 30% to 40% of every sales dollar. In hospitality businesses that serve food (or food and beverages), combined labor and cost of sales can consume between 65% and 75% of revenue. In addition to their high labor requirements, hospitality companies have to deal with a labor force culled from what has been called the "entitlement" generation. As the IHRA states in its white paper,

> The new worker will expect more freedom and will not tolerate the rigid leadership styles inherited from the era of the manufacturing based economy.

In addition, recruiting and training labor is an increasingly serious challenge for the hospitality industry. An aging workforce, decreasing populations in many developed countries, increasing demand for jobs in less developed countries, and the need to improve service to avoid competing purely on the basis of price are labor concerns facing the hospitality industry.

Because most hospitality companies only generate a net income of 8% to 10% of sales, a slight degree of carelessness in controlling costs of sales and labor can quickly reduce profits sharply or totally eliminate them. Assuming these two expenses total 70% of sales, if they are allowed to go over budget by as little as 5% of 70% (3.5%), this can reduce the hospitality company's net income by 2.5% after taxes (assuming a 40% income tax rate: 60% × 3.5% = 2.5%). This would represent a 25% reduction of net income.

Two other characteristics of the hospitality industry that make it critical for a controller to exercise tight control of cash are that (1) revenue is usually received in the form of cash or cash-equivalent credit card sales and (2) points of sale in a hospitality establishment are often numerous.

Finally, a hospitality controller must be familiar with current developments in the industry through membership in national and state associations. See "Hospitality Management Resources on the Web," for a list and for Web sites of organizations that provide information on current hospitality industry developments, as well as associations of interest to financial managers.

Personal Qualities and Skills

In addition to accounting and industry knowledge, the controller must possess a set of skills that enable him or her to use this knowledge to help the company achieve its goals. A controller must have good analytical abilities to see beyond the numerical data gathered by the controller's department to identify trends and use numerical analysis not only to describe what occurs, but also to present one or more possible causal factors and be able to project into the future the potential consequences of past events. The controller must apply good business judgment when suggesting ways of avoiding or correcting any problems or potential problems identified through this analysis, as well as suggesting future actions to be taken to maximize the value growth of the business.

However, a hospitality controller's extensive knowledge, analytical skills, and good judgment cannot effectively impact the hospitality industry environment without the proper communication and persuasion skills that enable him or her to successfully present ideas, opinions, and points of view. These include the ability to articulate verbally and have the imagination necessary to complement the oral presentation with appropriate graphs and illustrations. Also important is the ability to perform research required to obtain company or industry data that might support or contradict the controller's point of view. Familiarity with one or more of the basic computer programs such as word processors, spreadsheets, databases, and slide show presentation programs is essential in making these presentations.

In addition to having knowledge of the unique characteristics of a company's business model, the controller must be aware of the corporate culture in which he or she works and must have the ability to form good working relationships not only with accounting employees the controller supervises, but also with the non-accounting personnel. There is some historical precedent for an antagonism between operations management personnel and accounting and financial managers. Operations managers, especially those in the area of marketing, tend to view accounting and financial personnel as being unaware of the marketplace and the actual occurrences within a business. An ineffective controller will be viewed as a cost cutter or small spender who does not understand the negative impact of his or her suggestions rather than as an essential team member who helps a hospitality business manage its costs and expenses so that it grows in a coherent, profitable manner. The hospitality controller should be seen as a proponent of incurring those costs that are appropriate to the planned growth of a business.

The task of establishing positive working relationships is made more difficult by the fact that the controller usually is accountable to two superiors in the organization: an operations manager (usually at a lower local level within the organization) and a corporate financial manager. The controller must have the interpersonal skills to be able to resolve conflicts that may arise from these two potentially conflicting points of view. For example, an operations manager may desire funds for an investment that the manager considers essential currently, whereas a corporate financial manager may have longer-range priorities. To work effectively in such an environment, controllers must possess a diplomatic personality that opens the way for them to apply their knowledge and abilities with maximum effect.

In view of the long list of requirements and responsibilities placed on hospitality controllers, they must be motivated and enterprising. Ideally, within the accounting and financial arenas, they should consider themselves entrepreneurs who are constantly thinking of more efficient, less costly ways of gathering and presenting data and devising new ways of benefiting the company by reducing costs, enhancing growth, or otherwise maximizing value. Imagination as well as curiosity and mental agility play a part in this controllership function. Controllers must view their role from various perspectives in order to understand what is required at the local, division, or corporate financial management levels. They should have the self-confidence to admit to and inform themselves concerning anything they do not understand, as well as to inquire about occurrences throughout the company and in its various management levels. Self-confident controllers will take the initiative in presenting information that management was not aware of or was not aware would be useful in a specific decision-making process. Controllers must understand the company's operations to the point of anticipating the need for, and preparing on short notice, any information that management might require for decision making.

Although the controller's department is considered a staff department, as opposed to a line (decision-making) department, a controller must possess leadership qualifications that enable him or her to oppose management decisions, if necessary. In addition, a controller must have the self-confidence to create and implement changes in the organization of the controller's department to increase its efficiency. A controller must be able to motivate and lead his or her department personnel. As an effective leader, the controller must be supportive in order to gain employee confidence, both by being helpful and by representing employee interests within the company. To do this effectively, controllers must have, and be seen to have, the respect of company management.

Last, hospitality controllers must possess integrity. Given the recent developments in the arena of business ethics, it would seem that controllers should possess this personal quality in heroic portions. They should have the integrity and courage to oppose any misleading, unethical, or illegal approach proposed by management, regardless of the personal consequences. This goes beyond simply avoiding the overstatement of revenues and assets or the understatement of expenses and liabilities. It encompasses the clarity with which financial information is presented so that it is highly improbable that it will be misunderstood or misleading. Exhibit 2-4, "Characteristics of Strong Controllers," presents a summary of the personal qualities that a hospitality controller should possess.

Exhibit 2-4: Characteristics of Strong Controllers[1]

Number	Description	Specific Attributes
	Personal Qualities	
1.	Personal energy and motivation	Is a doer Is aware of everything going on Takes the initiative
2.	Personal integrity and professional commitment	Is unbiased source of information Doesn't try to bluff—States: "I don't know but I'll find out." Is the conscience of the division Is not a "Yes" man or woman Is candid
	Technical Competence	
3.	Accounting knowledge	Technical ability is not in question
4.	Analytical skill	Determines not only what happened but also why it happened Is good at arranging and rearranging numbers Is able to spot a trend before it becomes a reality Is able to dig below the numbers
	Business Judgment	
5.	Understands what management needs to run the business effectively	Is a good businessperson Has good business judgment Is familiar with other parts of the company Understands the company's business Anticipates future business problems Recommends action to deal with future business problems Keeps an eye on the whole business Is not always concerned about not spending

Number	Description	Specific Attributes
	Communication Skills	
6.	Ability to judge what is important to management and make recommendations	Does not think only of financial control
Is able to summarize quickly and accurately
Mentally makes the same decisions as the division general manager
Provides management with information even before they realize they need it
Thinks the way the division manager thinks
Quickly grasps information of real concern to management
Is willing to estimate
Does not emphasize accuracy as an end in itself
Is able to judge the degree of accuracy needed
Does not get lost in allocating costs
Speaks the language used by management
Keeps his or her audience in mind
Is able to come to grips with facts and make recommendations
	Interpersonal Skills	
7.	Building relationships and developing influence	Gets along with everyone
Is accepted in all functional areas
Is part of the management team
Is management's trusted counselor
Is flexible in meeting management's demands
Is the general manager's alter ego
Is a sounding board for management when sensitive issues are discussed
Opens up communications
Is respected by management
Is trusted by management and builds trust
8.	Ability to challenge management constructively	Asks the right questions
Thinks about the impact of numbers
Continually challenges management's analysis and plans
Knows when to risk fights and when to give in
Is always asking questions
Does not hesitate to question management's action after it is taken
Does not hesitate to criticize management plans and actions

Number	Description	Specific Attributes
	Managing Dual Accountability	
9.	Recognizes important responsibility to both local and corporate management	Understands corporate expectations
Recognizes responsibility to corporate management
Good judgment is recognized by management
Is able to judge what is important and what is not
Has good rapport with corporate management
Is the eyes, ears, and sense of management

[1] Management Control Systems, by Joseph A. Maciarello, Prentice-Hall, Inc., 1984, p. 99, Exhibit 4-9. Adapted with permission.

CHAPTER 3
CORPORATE GOVERNANCE

CONTENTS

Perspectives on Corporate Governance and Its Importance	3002
The Agency Problem and Various Instruments of Corporate Governance	3002
Impact of the Sarbanes-Oxley Act on Corporate Governance	3004
Traditional Mechanisms of Good Corporate Governance	3004
Corporate Governance and the U.S. Stock Exchanges	3013
A Brief History of Corporate Governance	3016
Defining Corporate Governance, Accounting Accuracy, and Transparency	3018
Accounting Accuracy	3019
Transparency	3020
Complexity of Ethical Decision Making	3020
Corporate Culture, Control Environment, and Principles-Based Accounting	3021
Real and Potential Drawbacks of Corporate Governance	3022
Real Drawback—Out-of-Pocket Cost	3023
Potential Drawback—Inhibited Management	3023
Rewards of Good Corporate Governance	3024
Compliance Mechanisms Used to Meet Strategic Goals and Improve Operating Efficiency	3024
Compliance Mechanisms Used to Establish a Culture of Change	3025
Compliance Increases Market Value	3025
International Concept of Corporate Governance	3028
Improving Corporate Governance	3029
Increasing Transparency through the Corporate Web Site	3036
Exhibits	
Exhibit 3-1. Reports Required by Sections 13(a) and 15(d) of the Securities Exchange Act of 1934	3008
Exhibit 3-2. Factors That Determine Shareholder Value	3027
Exhibit 3-3. Measures for Improving Corporate Governance	3030
Exhibit 3-4. Questions Directed to Management Regarding the Sarbanes-Oxley Act	3032

Because of the greatly increased focus on corporate governance brought about by recent governance abuses, it is important for hospitality industry financial officers to be thoroughly familiar with the implications of the new perspective on corporate governance created by recent legislation. This new perspective requires corporate controllers as well as financial managers to act not only in the interest of stockholders, but also in the interest of other stakeholders.

Some of the abuses that have brought corporate governance to the forefront of the business arena are:

- Misleading reports (e.g., presenting pro-forma data without reconciling to a GAAP measure, or misusing special-purpose entities, also referred to as variable-interest entities).
- Outright managerial fraud.
- Earnings management (e.g., by manipulating accruals).
- Exaggerated compensation.

KPMG International's Economist Intelligence Unit surveyed senior executives worldwide. The survey showed that 29% responded that corporate governance is one of their top ten priorities, 32% responded that it is one of their top three priorities, and 14% indicated it is their top priority. Altogether, 75% of executives considered it to be at least one of their top 10 priorities. It, therefore, behooves the controller, as the principal financial advisor to management, to be familiar with the potential impact resulting from this new focus on corporate governance.

PERSPECTIVES ON CORPORATE GOVERNANCE AND ITS IMPORTANCE

The hospitality controller should be aware that two significantly different definitions of *corporate governance* are generally accepted: (1) the United States and England definition and (2) the broader international definition. The United States and England definition concentrates on the primary responsibility of managers to stockholders and defines *corporate governance* as a process designed to compel managers to act in the interests of, and report accurately to, the stockholders. The internationally accepted definition of *corporate governance* broadens this responsibility to include other stakeholders. In 1999, the Organization for Economic Cooperation and Development (OECD) defined *corporate governance* as:

> [T]he system by which business corporations are directed and controlled. The corporate governance structure specifies the distribution of rights and responsibilities among different participants in the corporation, such as the board, managers, shareholders and other stakeholders, and spells out the rules and procedures for making decisions on corporate affairs. By doing this, it also provides the structure through which the company objectives are set, and the means of attaining those objectives and monitoring performance.

Overall, the goal of good corporate governance is (1) transparency of the company's objectives, governance policies, and structure; (2) honesty on the part of managers and employees; and (3) accurate reporting on the results of operations of the corporation to its stockholders.

THE AGENCY PROBLEM AND VARIOUS INSTRUMENTS OF CORPORATE GOVERNANCE

The need for corporate governance arises out of what is often called "the agency problem," initially discussed in Chapter 1, "The Scope of Financial Management." Proper management should act on behalf of a company's stockholders, but managers sometimes set their own interests above those of the stockholders. For example, a manager might avoid certain investments that increase shareholder value because he or she is risk-averse and more concerned with preserving his or her job. On the other hand, if a manager perceives that any personal risk is low or if the manager sets as a goal immediate corporate growth instead of maximizing long-term value, he or she may involve the company in ventures in which the risks outweigh the potential benefits to shareholders. In addition, upper management may feel deserving of increased remuneration even in years when the company's profits remain flat or decline, or there is a loss. In fact, when profits increase annually, upper management may reward itself with a higher remuneration than is justified by its performance, and its board of directors may acquiesce to the increases because of upper management's influence on the selection of the Board. This conflict of interest between managers' explicit or implicit desire to further their own self-interest at the expense of their responsibility to pursue the interests of stockholders is often called the "agency cost."

Strong corporate governance is intended to defeat the cross-purposes mentioned above and align the interests of management with those of a company's stakeholders. In the past, the following 10 mechanisms have been relied on to promote and even to guarantee good corporate governance:

1. Oversight by the board of directors.
2. Need for increased transparency to reduce increasing cost of capital.
3. Management's potential legal liability and loss of reputation.
4. Executive compensation used as a motivator.
5. Audits by external auditors to verify that reported financial information presents fairly the results of operations and the financial position of the company.
6. Potential of having bad management uncovered, resulting in negative reviews of the company's stock (and thus an increased cost of capital).
7. Oversight by stockholders owning large blocks of stock (e.g., wealthy individuals, pension funds, insurance companies, mutual funds).
8. Oversight by lenders and the repayment discipline imposed on managers who grow their company with borrowed funds.
9. Risk of takeover if a corporation is ineptly managed.
10. Discipline imposed on management by market competition in dynamic markets (e.g., corporations managed by a team that sets its own job preservation ahead of stockholder value maximization may choose a low-risk, slow-growth approach that results in loss of market share to dynamic, risk-taking competitors).

Unfortunately, extreme cases of failure involving these mechanisms, as well as various studies on their effectiveness, have raised doubts about their dependability. The Sarbanes-Oxley Act (SOX) approaches this problem by attempting to increase the efficacy of the first six of the above mechanisms through various measures.

IMPACT OF THE SARBANES-OXLEY ACT ON CORPORATE GOVERNANCE

The Sarbanes-Oxley Act applies to public companies with debt or equity securities registered with the SEC, regardless of whether the companies are based in the United States or internationally. SEC reporting requirements are discussed in Chapter 5, "The Financial Reporting System."

Some of the corporate governance requirements of SOX were already contemplated by the SEC and the Financial Accounting Standards Board (FASB), the latter in their financial accounting and auditing standards (see Chapter 5 for additional information on SOX). For example, the independent auditor's letter states that management is responsible for the content of the financial statements. SOX requires management's response in a written statement by the chief executive officer (CEO) and chief financial officer (CFO) of public companies to indicate, among other things, that they are aware of and assume this responsibility. This pattern of reinforcing and making more explicit corporate governance mechanisms that were already in place typifies the remedies imposed by SOX. Perhaps the most original provision of SOX is the requirement of Section 108 that the SEC study ways to abandon rules-based accounting and switch to principles-based accounting, a concept that is more prevalent in the accounting rules framework established by the International Accounting Standards Board (IASB). In the United States the FASB attempts to establish regulations for every possible transaction rather than establish principles by which to evaluate the method of accounting for each transaction. This approach enables managers to comply with the letter of the law even though they may, under certain circumstances, be violating the spirit of the law.

Traditional Mechanisms of Good Corporate Governance

The traditional mechanisms that assure good corporate governance can be separated into three categories:

1. Governance mechanisms internal to the corporation (Items 1 to 4 above);

2. Governance supervision by gatekeepers of the corporation (Items 5 to 6 above); and

3. External mechanisms such as creditors, stock markets, and large players in these markets (Items 7 to 10 above).

SOX attempts to strengthen the six governance mechanisms included in Items 1 and 2 by:

- Strengthening the credibility and independence of the board of directors.

- Supporting the board's independence by protecting whistleblowers.

- Supporting the board's independence by requiring attorneys to report unresolved issues.

- Increasing the transparency of public corporations by requiring additional disclosures.

- Increasing the accounting responsibility and legal liability of executives.

- Attempting to restore compensation and reputation as mechanisms for corporate governance.
- Strengthening independence of external auditors and increasing their liability.
- Diminishing the potential for security analyst conflict of interest.
- Setting forth minimum standards of professional conduct for attorneys.

Strengthening the Credibility and Independence of the Board of Directors. Section 301 of SOX requires that each member of the audit committee of a public corporation be a member of the board of directors of the issuer and be independent. *Independent* means that no members of the audit committee may receive any consulting, advisory, or other fee from the corporation of which they are directors, except for director fees. It also means they are not affiliated with the corporation or its subsidiaries in any manner other than as directors. It establishes that the audit committee is responsible for the appointment, compensation, and oversight of the work of any public accounting firm employed by the corporation. The audit committee is responsible for establishing procedures for the receipt, retention, and treatment of complaints concerning accounting, internal controls, and auditing. The audit committee shall have the authority, and the corporation must provide funds to enable the committee, to hire independent counsel or consultants, as necessary, to fulfill its duties.

Section 402(a) prohibits public corporations from giving personal loans to executives or directors, with few exceptions. Consumer credit companies may make home improvement and consumer credit loans and issue credit cards to its directors and executive officers if it is done in the ordinary course of business on the same terms and conditions made to the general public.

Supporting the Board's Independence by Protecting Whistle-Blowers. Section 806, dealing with corporate and criminal fraud accountability, requires that employees of companies and accounting firms be extended whistle-blower protection. This prohibits the employer from retaliating against employees who lawfully reveal private employer information to parties in a judicial action where fraud may be involved. Whistle-blowers must also be remunerated by the company for any damages and attorney's fees incurred.

Supporting the Board's Independence by Requiring Attorneys to Report to It Unresolved Issues. Section 307 requires attorneys to report evidence of a material violation of securities law by a company to the chief legal counsel or the CEO and, if there is no appropriate response, to report the evidence to the audit committee of the board of directors or to another committee of the Board comprised solely of directors not employed directly or indirectly by the issuer, or to the board of directors.

Increasing the Transparency of Public Corporations by Requiring Additional Disclosures. The sections of the act discussed below are designed to increase the transparency of public companies, although Section 201 also enhances the independence requirements for external auditors. (See below for further discussion.)

Section 201 requires the audit committee to disclose to investors any non-audit service that is preapproved to be rendered by a company's external auditors. The services that an external auditor is prohibited from providing contemporaneously with an audit are listed in the "Strengthening Independence of External Auditors" section below. However, SOX allows an auditor to render other services that are not on the above-mentioned list, including tax services, as long as they are approved in advance by the audit committee of the client corporation and are disclosed to investors in the periodic reports mandated by Section 13(a) of the Securities Exchange Act of 1934.

Section 401(a) of SOX deals with disclosures in periodic reports and requires the following disclosures.

- Financial reports required to be prepared in accordance with generally accepted accounting procedures (GAAP) will reflect all material correcting adjustments that have been identified by a registered accounting firm.
- Each annual and quarterly financial report shall disclose all material off-balance sheet transactions and other relationships with unconsolidated entities that may have a material current or future effect on the financial condition of the issuer.

These disclosures should be made in the "Management Discussion and Analysis" section of the annual report.

Furthermore, Section 401(b) of the Act mandates that the SEC issue rules that pro-forma financial information must not contain an untrue statement or omit a material fact so that the pro-forma financial information presented is not misleading. In other words, any non-GAAP measure of performance, such as earnings before interest, taxes, depreciation and amortization (EBITDA) must be reconciled to a GAAP financial measure.

Section 401(c) mandates that the SEC study and report to Congress:

- The extent of off-balance-sheet transactions (including assets, liabilities, leases, losses, and the use of special-purpose entities); and
- Whether GAAP are adequate to reflect the full impact of these off-balance-sheet transactions on investors in a transparent fashion.

Section 403 involves disclosures of transactions or changes of ownership percentage in the company's stock by directors, officers, and 10% owners. These transactions must be reported by the end of the second business day following the day on which the transaction was executed rather than the previous 5- to 15-day period, which provided non-related investors insufficient time to react to these insider transactions.

Section 407 requires the SEC to issue rules requiring public corporations to disclose whether at least one member of its audit committee is a financial expert. In defining the term *financial expert*, the SEC is instructed to:

[C]onsider whether a person has, through education and experience as a public accountant or auditor or a principal financial officer, comptroller, or principal accounting officer of an issuer, or from a position involving the performance of similar functions:

- An understanding of generally accepted accounting principles and financial statements;
- Experience in the preparation or auditing of financial statements of generally comparable issuers and the application of such principles in connection with the accounting for estimates, accruals, and reserves;
- Experience with internal accounting controls; and
- An understanding of audit committee functions.

Section 409 requires the disclosure by public corporations of any information on material changes in the financial condition or operations of the company on a rapid and current basis.

Increasing the Accounting Responsibility and Legal Liability of Executives. Section 302 requires that the principal executive officer and the principal financial officer, or persons performing similar functions, certify in each annual or quarterly report filed or submitted under either Section 13(a) or 15(d) of the 1934 Act:

1. The signing officer has reviewed the report.
2. Based on the officer's knowledge, the report does not contain any untrue statement of a material fact or omit to state a material fact necessary to make the statements not misleading.
3. Based on such officer's knowledge, the financial statements and other financial information included in the report fairly present in all material respects the financial condition and results of operations of the issuer as of, and for, the periods presented in the report.
4. The signing officers are responsible for establishing and maintaining internal controls and have designed internal controls to ensure that material information relating to the issuer and its consolidated subsidiaries is made known to the officers by others within those entities, particularly during the period in which the periodic reports are being prepared.
5. The signing officers have evaluated the effectiveness of the issuer's internal controls as of a date within 90 days prior to the report, and have presented in the report their conclusions about the effectiveness of the internal controls based on their evaluation as of that date.
6. The signing officers have disclosed to the issuer's auditors and the audit committee of the board of directors (or persons fulfilling the equivalent function):
    a. All significant deficiencies or material weaknesses in the design or operation of internal controls that could adversely affect the issuer's ability to record, process, summarize, and report financial data have been identified for the issuer's auditors.

b. All fraud must be reported, whether or not material, involving management or other employees who have a significant role in the issuer's internal controls.

7. The signing officers have indicated in the report whether there were significant changes in internal controls or in other factors that could significantly affect internal controls subsequent to the date of their evaluation, including any corrective action with regard to significant deficiencies and material weaknesses. No criminal penalties are specified in Section 302.

Section 906 of SOX specifies penalties for making misstatements in "Each periodic report containing financial statements" required to be presented under Section 13(a) or 15(d) of the 1934 Act. Certifications (per Title IX of SOX) by the CEO and CFO are required in all these reports. A list of these reports is presented in Exhibit 3-1.

Exhibit 3-1: Reports Required by Sections 13(a) and 15(d) of the Securities Exchange Act of 1934

Required by Section 13(a)

13a-1	Annual Reports
13a-2	Annual Reports of Predecessors
13a-3	Reporting by Form 40-F Registrant
13a-10	Transition Reports
13a-11	Current Reports on Form 8-K
13a-13	Quarterly reports on Form 10-Q and Form 10-QSB
13a-14	Certification of Disclosure in Annual and Quarterly Reports
13a-15	Reports on Controls and Procedures
13a-16	Reports of Foreign Private Issuers on Form 6-K

Required by Section 15(d)

15d-1	Annual Reports
15d-2	Special Financial Report
15d-3	Reports for Depository Shares Registered on Form F-6
15d-4	Reporting by Form 40-F Registrant
15d-5	Reporting by Successor Issuers
15d-6	Suspension of Duty to File Reports
15d-10	Transition Reports
15d-11	Current Reports on Form 8K
15d-13	Quarterly Reports on Form 10-Q and Form 10-QSB
15d-14	Certification of Disclosure in Annual and Quarterly Reports
15d-15	Reports on Controls and Procedures
15d-16	Reports of Foreign Private Issuers on Form 6-K
15d-21	Reports for Employee Stock Purchase, Savings, and Similar Plans

Section 906 is somewhat broader than Section 302 in that it includes any report that contains financial statements, whereas Section 302 applies only to each annual or quarterly report filed or submitted.

A violation of Section 906 may be committed knowing that the periodic report accompanying the statement does not comport with all the requirements set forth in this section or it can be committed willfully knowing that the periodic report accompanying the statement does not comport with all the requirements set forth in this section. In the former case, Section 906 specifies that an executive can be fined no more than $1 million and imprisoned for no more than 10 years. In the latter case, the intention to commit fraud is present, and therefore, the Section 906 penalties are greater, with a $5 million maximum fine and up to 20 years' imprisonment. However, hospitality executives who claim ignorance of the existence of any misleading facts have to explain why the internal control system they established and vouched for, as required by Section 404 and explained below, did not inform them of the error or fraud, and therefore made them unknowing accomplices.

In addition, Section 404 requires that each annual report include an assessment of internal controls by company management. This must take the form of a statement containing an internal control report that:

- Affirms the responsibility of management for establishing and maintaining an adequate internal control structure and procedures for financial reporting; and
- Contains an assessment, as of the end of the issuer's fiscal year, of the effectiveness of the issuer's internal control structure and procedures for financial reporting.

Furthermore, each issuer's external auditor shall attest to, and report on, the assessment made by management of the company issuing the report when the external auditor performs the issuer's annual audit; although, per Regulation S-K, the CEO and CFO must certify their company's disclosure of controls and procedures on a quarterly basis.

Section 406 directs the SEC to require each issuer to disclose whether it has adopted a code of ethics for its senior financial officers that is applicable to its principal financial officer and comptroller or principal accounting officer or persons performing similar functions. In addition, the SEC is instructed to require prompt disclosure on Form 8-K and dissemination by the Internet or by other electronic means of any change in or waiver of this code of ethics.

Section 802 makes it a felony to knowingly destroy or create documents to impede, obstruct, or influence any existing or contemplated federal investigation. In addition, the statute of limitations on securities fraud claims is increased to the earlier of five years from the fraud, or two years after the fraud is discovered, instead of three years and one year, respectively.

Title IX of SOX requires that the periodic report containing financial statements filed with the SEC must be certified by the CEO and CFO. The certification must state that the report fully complies with the requirements of section 13(a) or 15(d) of the 1934 Act, and that they fairly present, in all material respects, the operations and financial condition of the issuer. Maximum penalties for willful and knowing violations of these sections are a fine of not more than $500,000 and/or imprisonment of up to five years.

Section 1102 makes it a crime for any person to corruptly alter, destroy, mutilate, or conceal any document with the intent to impair the object's integrity or availability for use in an official proceeding or to otherwise obstruct, influence, or impede any official proceeding, or attempt to do so. Those found committing these acts are liable for a maximum of 20 years in prison and/or a fine.

Attempting to Restore Compensation and Reputation as Mechanisms for Corporate Governance. Section 305 authorizes the SEC to issue an order to prohibit, conditionally or unconditionally, permanently or temporarily, any person who has violated section 10(b) of the 1934 Act from acting as an officer or director of an issuing corporation if the SEC has found that such person's conduct demonstrates unfitness to serve as an officer or director of any such issuer.

Sections 1103 and 1105 extend this authority by modifying section 21C of the 1934 Act to include granting the SEC authority to prohibit a person from serving as an officer or director of a public company if the person's conduct demonstrates unfitness to serve as an officer or director of any such issuer.

Titles VIII, IX, and XI of SOX criminalize willful violations of the provisions of the Act by those to whom the Act applies and increases or clarifies the penalties for such violations.

Section 304 restricts and even requires the forfeiture of bonuses and compensation if an issuer is required to prepare a restatement due to material noncompliance with financial reporting requirements. The CEO and the CFO shall reimburse the issuer for any bonus or other incentive-based or equity-based compensation received during the 12 months following the issuance or filing of the noncompliant document and any profits realized from the sale of securities of the issuer during that period.

Section 1103 authorizes the SEC to freeze the payment of an extraordinary payment to any director, officer, partner, controlling person, agent, or employee of a company during an investigation of possible violations of securities laws.

Furthermore, if any action is brought by the SEC for violation of the securities laws, the SEC is authorized to request, and the federal courts are authorized to grant, any equitable relief that may be appropriate or necessary for the benefit of investors.

Strengthening the Independence of External Auditors and Increasing Their Liability. Section 201 renders it unlawful for a registered public accounting firm to provide any of the following non-audit services to an issuer contemporaneously with the audit:

- Bookkeeping or other services relating to the accounting records or financial statements of the client;
- Financial information systems design and implementation;

- Appraisal or valuations services, fairness opinions, or contribution-in-kind reports;
- Actuarial services;
- Internal audit or outsourcing services;
- Management functions or human resources;
- Legal services and expert services unrelated to the audit; and
- Any other service the Board determines, by regulation, is impermissible.

The Board may, on a case-by-case basis, exempt from these prohibitions any person, issuer, public accounting firm, or transaction, subject to review by the SEC.

SOX allows an accounting firm to engage in any non-audit service, including tax services, that is not listed above only if the activity is pre-approved by the audit committee of the issuer and such pre-approval is disclosed to investors periodically in compliance with section 13(a) of the 1934 Act.

Section 203 requires that the lead audit or coordinating partner and the reviewing partner must rotate off of the audit every five years.

Section 204 requires the external auditor to report to the audit committee:

- All critical accounting policies and practices to be used;
- All alternative treatments of financial information within GAAP that have been discussed with management, ramifications of the use of such alternative disclosures and treatments, and the treatment preferred by the registered public accounting firm.

Section 206 specifies that the CEO, controller, CFO, chief accounting officer, or person in an equivalent position cannot have been employed by the company's audit firm during the one-year period preceding the audit.

Section 303 renders it unlawful for any officer or director of an issuer to take any action to fraudulently influence, coerce, manipulate, or mislead an auditor engaged in the performance of an audit for the purpose of rendering the financial statements materially misleading.

Section 802 increases the liability of auditors by requiring that they retain audit workpapers for a period of five years from the end of the fiscal period in which the audit or review was concluded. The section imposes fines and jail terms of up to 10 years for violations of this part of the section. It also imposes fines and jail terms of up to 20 years on anyone who knowingly alters, destroys, mutilates, conceals, covers up, falsifies, or makes a false entry in any record, document, or tangible object with the intent to impede, obstruct, or influence the investigation or proper administration of any matter within the jurisdiction of any department or agency of the United States or any case filed under Title 11, or in relation to or contemplation of any such matter or case.

Finally, SOX created the Public Company Accounting Oversight Board (PCAOB), which is charged with establishing and supervising quality control and ethics standards applicable to public accounting firms in the preparation and issuance of audit reports on public companies. The PCAOB is also charged with inspecting and reviewing public auditing firms either annually or tri-annually, depending on the number of public companies that they audit.

Diminishing Potential for Security Analyst Conflict of Interest. Section 501 enhances the independence of reporting by securities analysts by requiring registered securities associations or national securities exchanges to enact rules with the following objectives:

- Pre-publication clearance of research reports must be authorized only by legal or compliance staff.
- Securities analysts must be supervised and their remuneration determined only by officials not engaged in investment banking activities.
- Brokers may not retaliate against or threaten a securities analyst employed by them as a result of an adverse or otherwise unfavorable research report.
- Periods should be defined during which brokers or dealers who have participated, or are to participate, in a public offering of securities as underwriters or dealers should not publish or otherwise distribute research reports relating to such securities or to the issuer of such securities.
- Structural and institutional safeguards should be established with registered brokers or dealers to assure that securities analysts are separated by appropriate informational partitions within the firm from the review, pressure, or oversight of those whose involvement in investment banking activities might potentially bias their judgment or supervision.
- Each securities analyst should be required to disclose conflicts of interest that are known or should have been known by the securities analyst or the broker, such as:
  — Debt or equity investments in the issuer.
  — Receipt of any compensation.
  — Whether an issuer, the securities of which are recommended in a research report, currently is, or during the one-year period preceding the date of the report has been, a client of the registered broker or dealer, and if so, state the types of services provided to the issuer.
  — Whether the securities analyst received compensation for a research report based on the revenues of the investment banking division of the broker.
  — Other disclosures of conflicts of interest that are material to investors, research analysts, or the broker or dealer as the Commission, or such association or exchange, determines appropriate.

Setting Forth Minimum Standards of Professional Conduct for Attorneys. SOX mandated the SEC to set forth minimum standards of professional conduct for attorneys appearing and practicing before the Commission in any way in the representation of issuers. This is in addition to the minimum requirements of attorneys' professional conduct previously mentioned.

The most onerous sections would seem to be Sections 302, 404, and 906. As stated in the SurfControl white paper titled "Corporate Governance: The Growing Importance of Data and Network Security," the CEO and CFO must now "sign off on the validity of financials, processing and reporting of which they have no hands-on knowledge, trusting to their employees and technology to back up those certifications." Furthermore, with regard to the internal control network on which these executives must now rely, the Apani Networks white paper titled "The Sarbanes-Oxley Act of 2002 and Its Impact on IT Security," states, "One challenge companies will face in complying with Sarbanes-Oxley is choosing an appropriate methodology and developing a sequence of steps from which to evaluate their internal controls for financial reporting. Since an internal control is not clearly defined in the Act, nor . . . any recommended guidelines for evaluating them, this area is . . . open to interpretation among organizations seeking compliance." Additional guidance is provided by a report of the Committee of Sponsoring Organizations of the Treadway Commission (COSO) titled "Control Objectives for Information and Related Technology (COBIT)" and by Auditing Standard No. 2, *An Audit of Internal Control over Financial Reporting Performed in Conjunction with an Audit of Financial Statements,* of the PCAOB, which establishes the procedures to be used by auditors when they audit management's evaluation of its internal controls.

Another consequence of SOX is that hospitality companies may have to engage two auditing companies, one company to perform an audit and another company to assist in correcting any deficiencies discovered during the audit. Auditors can no longer perform any consulting work for companies that they audit.

Finally, SOX increases the maximum for fines imposed by Section 32(a) of the 1934 Act from $5 million to $20 million for individuals, thereby adding more bite to convictions for securities fraud. Thus SOX underlines compliance risk as another risk that management must consider in addition to business risk. Although this risk always existed, its extent and consequences were tenuous and nebulous. After the passage of SOX, responsibilities are more clearly assigned, and the consequences of failing to carry them out are more significant.

CORPORATE GOVERNANCE AND THE U.S. STOCK EXCHANGES

In compliance with SOX, the New York Stock Exchange has established certain rules. An extract of these rules is presented below. The NASDAQ has a similar set of governance rules, which differ mainly in some of the dollar amounts delimiting independence, where these are applicable.

Extract of Corporate Governance Rules of the New York Stock Exchange

- A listed hospitality firm must have a majority of independent directors.

- Listed hospitality firms must disclose whether directors qualifying as "independent":

- Have no material relationship with the listed company either directly or through a relationship with a company that has a relationship with this company.
- Has not worked for, nor has any immediate family member serving as an executive officer of said company during the previous three years.
- Has not received more than $100,000 in direct compensation from the company other than director fees during the previous three years.
- Has not worked for a former or present internal or external auditor of the company during the previous three years.
- Is not an employee of another company where the executives of this company work as members of that company's compensation committee.
- During the previous three years the director, or immediate family, have not worked for another company that has a business relationship with this company in excess of $1,000,000 or 2% of the other company's consolidated gross revenues.

- The non-management directors of each hospitality company must meet at regularly scheduled executive sessions without management.
- A listed company must have a nominating/corporate governance committee composed entirely of independent directors. The committee must have a written charter that expresses its purpose and responsibilities which are, at minimum, to: (a) identify individuals qualified to become board members; (b) develop and recommend to the board a set of corporate governance principles applicable to the corporation; (c) oversee the evaluation of the board and management; (d) carry out an annual performance evaluation of the committee.
- A listed company must have a compensation committee composed entirely of independent directors, and it must have a written charter that addresses the committee's purpose and responsibilities—which, at minimum, must be to have direct responsibility to review and approve corporate goals and objectives relevant to CEO compensation, evaluate the CEO's performance in light of those goals and objectives, and, either as a committee or together with the other independent directors (as directed by the board), determine and approve the CEO's compensation level, including non-salary compensation, based on this evaluation. The committee must also produce a compensation committee report on executive compensation as required by the SEC to be included in the company's annual proxy statement or annual Form 10-K filed with the SEC, and it must carry out an annual performance evaluation of the compensation committee itself.
- A listed company must have an audit committee of at least three members who satisfy the requirements of the SEC Act of 1934 and the New York Stock Exchange (NYSE) tests for independence. It must have a written charter stating the committee's purpose which, at minimum, must be to:
    - Inform board oversight of the integrity of the company's financial statements;
    - The company's compliance with legal and regulatory requirements;
    - The independent auditor's qualifications and independence;

- The performance of the company's internal audit function and of the independent auditors;
- Prepare an audit committee report as required by the SEC to be included in the company's annual proxy statement;
- Prepare an annual evaluation of itself;
- At least annually obtain and review a report by the independent auditor describing:
    - The firm's internal quality-control procedures;
    - Any material issues raised by the most recent internal quality-control view of the firm or by any inquiry by governmental or professional authorities, within the preceding five years;
    - Any steps taken to deal with such issues.
- Discuss the company's annual audited financial statements and quarterly financial statements with management and the independent auditor, including the company's disclosures under "Management's Discussion and Analysis of Financial Condition and Results of Operations;"
- Discuss the company's annual audited financial statements and quarterly financial statements with management and the independent auditor, including the company's disclosures under "Management's Discussion and Analysis of Financial Condition and Results of Operations;"
- Discuss policies with respect to risk assessment and risk management;
- Meet separately, periodically, with management, with internal auditors (or other personnel responsible for the internal audit function) and with independent auditors;
- Review with the independent auditor any problems or difficulties and management's response;
- Set clear hiring policies for employees or former employees of the independent auditors; and report regularly to the board of directors.

* Each listed company must have an internal audit function. It must maintain an internal audit function to provide management and the audit committee with ongoing assessments of the company's risk management processes and system of internal control.
* Listed companies must adopt and disclose corporate governance guidelines that address the following subjects:
    - Director qualification standards including policies limiting the number of boards on which a director may sit, and director tenure, retirement and succession.
    - Director responsibilities such as attendance at board meetings and advance review of meeting materials.
    - Director access to management and independent advisors.
    - Director compensation. The board should critically evaluate emoluments exceeding what is customary, as well as question substantial charitable contributions to organizations in which a director is affiliated, or provides other indirect forms of compensation to a director.
    - Director orientation and continuing education.

- Management succession.
- Annual performance evaluation of the board. The board should conduct a self-evaluation at least annually to determine whether it and its committees are functioning effectively.

• Listed companies must adopt and disclose a code of business conduct and ethics for directors, officers and employees, and promptly disclose any waivers of the code for directors or executive officers. At a minimum this code should address the following topics:
  - Conflicts of interest.
  - Taking personal advantage of corporate opportunities.
  - Confidentiality.
  - Fair dealing.
  - Protection and proper use of corporate assets.
  - Compliance with laws, rules and regulations (including insider trading laws).
  - Encouraging the reporting of any illegal or unethical behavior.

• Listed foreign private issuers must disclose any significant ways in which their corporate governance practices differ from those followed by domestic companies under NYSE listing standards.

• Listed company CEOs must certify to the NYSE each year that they are not aware of any violation of NYSE corporate governance listing standards by the company.

• Each listed company CEO must promptly notify the NYSE in writing after any executive officer of the listed company becomes aware of any material noncompliance with any applicable provisions of this Section 303A.

• The NYSE may issue a public reprimand letter to any listed company that violates a NYSE listing standard.

Because regulations are by their nature more specific than the broad concepts contained in SOX, the New York Stock Exchange (NYSE) rules may create further compliance problems in areas, for example, involving the extensive responsibilities of the audit committee. It is therefore interesting to note that a comment is attached to the last provision of the NYSE rules, which states that suspending trading in or delisting a company can be harmful to the very shareholders that the NYSE listing standards seek to protect. Therefore, the NYSE must have the ability to apply a lesser sanction to deter companies from violating its corporate governance standards. This is almost an admission that the NYSE feels it will be very difficult for companies to readily meet these standards.

A BRIEF HISTORY OF CORPORATE GOVERNANCE

To better understand the current climate of corporate governance, it is worthwhile briefly to review its history. At the end of the nineteenth century and the beginning of the twentieth century, corporations were by and large governed by dominant founding families. These families zealously watched over management because their own interests were at stake, and they had the power to make immediate management changes. During the trust-busting era of the United

States in the early 1900s, families tended to divest themselves of majority ownership, and gradually corporate management came into its own. This was more befitting the intent of creating the corporate entity, which was intended to be a person, albeit a legal person as opposed to a natural person, independent of its stockholders. During and immediately after World War II, a management technocracy arose that served pretty much as its own self-governance mechanism. The technocrats watched over each other. Generally speaking, the goal of managements at that time was to maximize the market value of their company's shares and thus maximize shareholder value, by maximizing net income. The following equation, previously discussed in Chapter 2, "The Responsibilities of the Controller," demonstrates this relationship.

$$\text{Market Value} = \text{Price Earnings Ratio} \times \frac{\text{Net income}}{\text{Common shares outstanding}}$$

Increased earnings resulted from growth into new markets or from innovation. However, during the late 1960s and early 1970s the easy market penetration had already been experienced, and management began to experiment with maximizing shareholder value through creative financing. This also coincided with the beginning use of stock options to try to align management interests with those of shareholders. In the hospitality industry, creative financing took the form of leasing as a type of off-balance-sheet financing. The builders would own the hotels and restaurants they had built and then would lease them (i.e., for almost the buildings' entire useful lives) back to the hotel and restaurant operators. This minimized the need for borrowing and eliminated the negative impact of loans on the debt-equity ratio of the company. An excessively high debt-equity ratio would have required corporations to dilute earnings by selling more stock. One group of the stakeholders of the companies, the debtholder, objected to this approach as being deceptive, and the Accounting Principles Boards (APB) of the AICPA, which was later replaced by the FASB, agreed with them, thus creating the concept of capital leases.

In the late 1970s and early 1980s, the United States experienced a huge inflationary spike. As a result, the real estate owned by hotels became so valuable that in many cases hotel companies realized they would earn a higher net income by selling the real estate and investing the money to earn interest in a bank or in bonds. They began to divest themselves of their properties and limited themselves to engaging in management contracts. But one hospitality company, Marriott, went even further. Marriott saw the potential of using the depreciation on high building values as a tax shelter. Marriott began to build hotels with the intention of selling them to Real Estate Investment Trusts (REITS), or other investors, and then negotiating contracts to manage these hotels. When anti-tax-shelter legislation was passed and the Federal Reserve Bank ended the inflationary cycle, Marriott was left with many hotels that it could not sell. The recession of 1991 was in sight, so it decided to split the company in two. One company, Marriott International, took most of the profitable hotels and management contracts, while the other company, Host Marriott, was left with the unprofitable, heavily debt-laden hotels. Fortunately, both companies survived due to the stock market bubble years in the late 1990s. In 1988, Shoney's executed a corporate reorganization that included the payment of an approximately $1 billion dividend, some of which was paid out of borrowed money.

The point is that, when companies ran out of the traditional growth techniques that maximized easy market penetration and innovation, they began to manipulate the outstanding common stock. In the bubble years, it was evident that the very governance mechanism that had been intended to align management interests with those of shareholders, the granting of stock options to management, did the opposite. Stock options motivated management to inflate the market value of a company's shares in any way possible and then quickly bail out by selling their stock. Pro-forma earnings were reported almost as being equivalent to net income. Management, with the acquiescence of their board of directors, bought back huge amounts of their company's shares with the objective of increasing the earnings per share, and thus the market value of their own shares, by reducing the outstanding float. Ultimately, management was forced to engage in massive layoffs in an effort to preserve their companies' profitability. However, at the same time the managers were laying off large numbers of employees to preserve their companies' earnings, they were rewarding themselves with large, sometimes huge, increases in remuneration—again, with the acquiescence of their boards. Managers tried to further their own interests at the expense of the employees. These managers often attained their goal of achieving the quarterly earnings growth by sacrificing long-term growth.

DEFINING CORPORATE GOVERNANCE, ACCOUNTING ACCURACY, AND TRANSPARENCY

Taking into account the various ways that managers have dealt with corporate governance, it is important to consider what constitutes strong corporate governance and what is in the best interests of shareholders. Therefore, the following questions should be considered:

- Is it in the best interest of managers to mislead banks and other stakeholders by having them believe the company has less debt than it actually does through the use of off-balance-sheet financing?
- Is it in the shareholders' best interest to fend off a nonexistent but potential takeover by incurring an enormous debt to pay dividends to shareholders or use other measures to avoid being acquired?
- Is it in the shareholders' best interest to meet quarterly earnings growth targets at the expense of long-term growth or by earnings management by manipulating accruals?
- Is it in the shareholders' best interest to increase the value of their shares by buying back company stock even though this is an admission that management cannot increase value by growing earnings?
- Is it in the shareholders' best interest to pay huge management salaries because they are warranted by a disproportionate growth in shareholder value?

- Is it in the shareholders' best interest to avoid losses even at the cost of having to lay off large numbers of employees, some of whom may be critical for the company to resume its growth when market conditions improve?
- Has the focus on meeting quarterly earnings goals been at the expense of implementing the latest information technology because rates of return for this type of investment are difficult to calculate and often produce significant results only over the medium- and long-term?
- Does it increase shareholder value to borrow large amounts of money to pay a huge dividend to stockholders?

The question might also be raised as to whether an increase in shareholder value represents an increase in a corporation's contribution to the economy and to society. In July 2005, Wendy's was pressured by major stockholders to spin off the Tim Hortons chain and franchise all of its hamburger restaurants because it reported a 1% drop in quarterly profits and lowered its earnings outlook for the year. One stockholder retained Blackstone Group LP as financial advisors to explore strategic alternatives for Wendy's. Ultimately, Wendy's announced that it would spin off 18% of its holdings in Tim Hortons and its stock soared. An analyst in Prudential Equity Group stated, "Fundamentals have not been the driver of the investment story here, but rather strategic actions to create shareholder value." Therefore, the exchange of stock ownership did not create any additional value on an absolute scale, and if Wendy's did not become more cost-effective and profitable, the increase in shareholder value created by shareholder expectations would disappear. Nevertheless, if the shareholders had sold their stock in time, they would have been rewarded for an event that did not add any absolute value to society.

SOX does not attempt to deal with the questions above; rather, the Act expects the board of directors, conjointly with management, to handle them on a case-by-case basis. The Act does attempt to assure that the process of answering these questions will be devoid of self-interest on the part of management or the Board, or that it will be transparent to shareholders. In addition, the Act attempts to ensure that those who verify and inform investors concerning how these questions are being answered do so in an objective and non-self-serving manner. SOX also increases the penalties, such as establishing remuneration forfeitures, for those who do not behave in a transparent, non-self-serving manner. A relationship between management performance and compensation is also encouraged through their requirement mandating an independent compensation committee.

Accounting Accuracy

The director of McKinsey's corporate governance practice stated, "The notion that there is one true figure that reveals how companies perform is a myth." In fact, net income depends on the judgment of management when making many adjusting entries, presumably acting under the advice of the controller. Assessing asset lives and the choice of depreciation method can have a very significant impact on the hospitality industry, which is highly invested in real estate and expensive equipment. The value of brands and franchises, the choice of structuring a lease as an operating lease or a capital lease, and company policy toward maintenance and repairs expenses are all areas open to judgment.

Expensing postretirement benefits is another area subject to imprecise calculation. During the late 1990s, the chairman of the SEC stated that the SEC would target public companies that announced restructuring of liability reserves and major write-offs. See Chapter 5, "The Financial Reporting System," for a discussion of SEC reporting requirements.

Materiality is another area that is open to judgment and thus also to earnings management, a euphemism for manipulation. The FASB, in Accounting Concepts Statement No. 2, *Qualitative Characteristics of Accounting Information*, defines *materiality* as "The magnitude of an omission or misstatement of accounting information that, in the light of surrounding circumstances, makes it probable that the judgment of a reasonable person relying on the information would have been changed or influenced by the omission or misstatement." Traditionally, up to a 5% deviation from normalized net income has been considered immaterial. However, in Staff Accounting Bulletin No. 99, *Materiality*, the SEC states that "exclusive reliance on certain quantitative benchmarks to assess materiality . . . is inappropriate." Evaluating a corporation's performance is an exercise in approximation and an area where transparency can be frustrated with impunity.

Transparency

The definition of *transparency* is often subject to individual interpretation. For example, if an auditor encounters a false statement about an immaterial item, is this sufficient to bring into question the transparency of the entire company? Enron disclosed all facts concerning its accounting procedures but in such an obtuse fashion that no one understood what was really occurring. Even if the non-management board members correctly disclose that they are technically independent, they may have hidden loyalties. For instance, board members who were employed by a bank more than three years ago may still be loyal to that bank, therefore leading the company of which they are now directors to incur unnecessary debt or engage in other business with that bank even though conditions are not the most favorable. A study made by Wharton finance professor Geoffrey Tate, Stanford finance professor Ulrike Malmendier, and Burak Guner concluded that "financial experts on corporate boards do not necessarily improve shareholder value" because "often the desire to act in the interests of a bank seems to trump the interests of the company's shareholders."

Complexity of Ethical Decision Making

The inevitable conclusion is that one cannot legislate morality. Corporate governance is based on personal standards. The more specific the legislation designed to defeat a particular problem, the more clearly it delineates how to skirt it. Karl Schulze, a partner in the law firm Schulze, Haynes and Company, states:

> The only difference [between personal and business ethics] is where your responsibilities lie. In business you have to answer to regulatory bodies, your

employer and boss, customers and clients, vendors and shareholders. . . . [I]t's easy to say, "I would not have made those decisions. I would have done the right thing." [But] the right path is not always obvious. You've got to know when it's time to put on the brakes or blow the whistle or take whatever action is appropriate.

CORPORATE CULTURE, CONTROL ENVIRONMENT, AND PRINCIPLES-BASED ACCOUNTING

The KPMG white paper titled "Corporate Governance: The New Strategic Imperative" states that corporate scandals of great magnitude occurred in the United States, a highly legalistic country, which points out the danger of placing too much emphasis on form. Boards of directors and the audit committee need to be given more freedom to determine whether a company's financial statements present its position fairly and in a manner that is clear to all stakeholders. The IASB establishes the principle by which boards of directors and executives should be guided as that of "truth and fairness."

Corporate governance should encompass more than the mere accuracy of a set of numbers, which are to a greater or lesser extent the result of someone's judgment at several stages of the accounting process. Good corporate governance presupposes the existence of proper policies, structures, and procedures or, in other words, a good control environment. Yet, good corporate governance cannot truly exist without a corporate culture that reinforces correct, responsible behavior on the part of all within the corporation. A former managing partner of Bain, the consulting firm, stated "Corporate culture determines how people behave when they are not being watched."

Thus, the CEO, CFO, treasurer, controller, other top executives of the corporation, and the board of directors are all directly responsible for good corporate governance. They must look beyond the rules-based legislation and infuse their companies with a desire to comply with the spirit of the law. This can be done by creating various channels of communication throughout the company, by making sure that everyone is familiar with the company's code of ethics, by making it known that whistle-blowers will be protected, and by truly empowering the audit committee to search for breaches of the company's code of ethics. A good control environment begins *at the top*. If upper management is suspected of being deceitful or self-serving, acceptance of this type of behavior will filter down to other employees. Based on the July 2002 Economist Intelligence Unit survey, discussed previously, the following percentage breakdown indicates what were considered to be the major obstacles to good corporate governance:

- Cultural and managerial hostility to whistle-blowing on dubious practices — 51%
- Increased focus from shareholders and investors on operating cash flow measures rather than earnings per share — 34%
- Lack of financial understanding on the part of senior executives and the board — 30%
- Lack of financial understanding on the part of line managers and middle managers — 27%
- Lack of business understanding on the part of external auditors — 26%
- Lack of business understanding on the part of the board — 23%

- Technology constraints that make it difficult to get a decent integrated picture of the financial accounts quickly — 21%
- Cost of implementing and communicating corporate governance policies throughout the organization — 20%

This study revealed the following opinion of these executives concerning the level of understanding of the business possessed by non-management directors.

- An excellent understanding — 12%
- A good understanding — 44%
- A satisfactory understanding — 28%
- An unsatisfactory or poor understanding — 14%
- Other — 2%

This study appears to support the concept that good internal control structures are not sufficient. Good corporate governance depends on people and their ethics and skills.

In this regard, a very important aspect of SOX was its mandate that the SEC study the possibility of the United States adopting a principles-based accounting system. It recognized what was stated earlier—namely, that rules-based legislation leads to concentration on complying with the letter of the law while losing sight of possible violations of the spirit of the law. However, in his testimony before the U.S. Senate in September of 2003, former SEC chairman William Donaldson stated:

> After considering the issue, our staff found that standards reflecting only a stated principle of accounting ("principle-only standards") would present enforcement difficulties because they would provide little guidance or structure for exercising professional judgment in applying that principle. The staff also found that accounting standards that are too detailed ("rules-based standards") often provide a vehicle for circumventing the intention of the standard.
>
> As a result, the staff indicated that the best approach would be to develop accounting standards that:
>
> - Are based on a conceptual framework;
> - Clearly state the accounting objective of the standard;
> - Provide sufficient detail and structure so the standard may be applied on a consistent basis;
> - Minimize exceptions from the standard; and
> - Avoid the use of percentage tests that allow financial engineers to achieve technical compliance with the standard while evading the intent of the standard.
>
> The staff's recommendation is consistent with the approach currently being developed by the Financial Accounting Standards Board.

REAL AND POTENTIAL DRAWBACKS OF CORPORATE GOVERNANCE

A belief that may hamper a more wholehearted acceptance of the need to improve corporate governance is that a company has engaged in no wrongdoing and consequently the additional costs of corporate governance are not warranted, that improving corporate governance involves unnecessary additional costs and makes the execution of the company's business model more difficult and complex. In fact, there are drawbacks to improving corporate governance, such as the added monetary cost, the impairment of the ability to make decisions quickly, the hesitancy to react to threats immediately, and the impairment of the willingness to take reasonable risks.

Real Drawback—Out-of-Pocket Cost

It has been estimated that the cost of implementing compliance with SOX can be as high as twice the amount that companies were previously spending on their auditing and other compliance activities prior to SOX. The average expenditure for Sarbanes-Oxley compliance, including the required information technology modifications, is estimated to be $2.7 to $3.5 million for companies with revenues of $1 to $5 billion. According to a 2004 survey by the law firm Foley & Lardner LLC in association with KRC Research, the average annual cost of being a public company, for companies with revenues lower than $1 billion, went from $1.25 million prior to the Act up to $2.86 million in 2003. Because of the additional document retention requirements and the permanent monitoring of internal controls required by SOX, one of the major cost elements is the modification of a company's information technology structure to make it more flexible, adaptable, and capable of storing and analyzing considerably greater amounts of data. Corporate emails provide supporting evidence of activity and exchanges that take place prior to engaging in many transactions and must be preserved. External auditor fees have doubled. The higher qualifications for being a director imposed by the Act and the stock exchanges, plus the additional risks and responsibilities involved in being a director, make qualified directors harder to find and more expensive to hire. Julie Daum, head of board services for Spencer Stuart, stated that "The reason fees are going up is the work load is going up—dramatically." She continues, "There's a huge demand for directors and a limited supply." PricewaterhouseCoopers identifies the following compliance-related areas in which companies expect to make long-term improvements:

- Risk identification and assessment processes   67%
- Financial reporting processes   50%
- Internal audit   46%
- Compliance management   46%
- IT security strategy and implementation   44%
- IT oversight and operations   41%
- Risk mitigation processes   33%

Potential Drawback—Inhibited Management

The KPMG white paper, mentioned previously, and other studies conclude that there can be a basic conflict between corporate governance and risk taking (a basic component of innovation and growth) within a corporation. If management perceives that the rewards for successful risk taking do not match the penalties for failure, management will tend to make conservative decisions that may lead not only to slower growth, but to contraction due to loss of market share to more aggressive corporations. Because SOX applies only to public companies, some corporations have chosen to become private companies to avoid what they consider the onerous and management-inhibiting requirements of this Act. Perhaps in the current environment, the hoteliers of the late 1960s and early 1970s would never have engaged in the aggressive off-balance-sheet financing that prompted the FASB to create the capital lease concept. Leaving aside intentionally or accidentally deceiving or dishonest behavior, corporate governance boils down to controlling the risks that come with innovation and growth. The hospitality industry already has a tradition of being conservative and prone to risk avoidance. Managers must not only face the traditional business risks, but these risks now come packaged with another risk: the risk that legitimately taken risks may be misconstrued by a second-guessing (inept and ignorant) board of directors or by stockholders themselves as being a violation of management's agency compact with the stockholders.

To avoid stifling management, the board should concentrate on clearly defining the risks that a company can take and make them consistent with the goals of its stockholders, rather than attempting to micro-manage the corporation and second-guess every management decision. The company should consider whether stockholders want a less indebted, slower growing company that pays out a regular annual dividend or a rapidly growing company that does not pay dividends but instead reinvests all of its earnings and is not afraid to borrow any additional funds it needs to achieve its rapid growth goal. But, more important, the corporation should use this new information-demanding corporate governance to help it define its corporate goals, improve its operating processes, and direct the corporation toward its goals while incorporating a culture that is flexible and capable of adapting to changes in technology and in the marketplace.

REWARDS OF GOOD CORPORATE GOVERNANCE

Good corporate governance should be viewed as a tool for increasing shareholder value. Instead of seeing the new information gathering and storing requirements of SOX as a useless expense to check an internal control system that is working well, management should use this information to effectively apply the resources of the company competitively.

Compliance Mechanisms Used to Meet Strategic Goals and Improve Operating Efficiency

Management should modify the company's information technology infrastructure to monitor its business procedures and performance, which can provide valuable feedback on company operations and any required improvements. The controller should advise management to invest in this area and develop ways to calculate rates of return on information technology enhancements. In addition, it may be worthwhile to expand an information technology system beyond the information gathering and storing requirements of SOX to gather and provide information concerning individual customer profiles and to generate revenue patterns based on these profiles. Research by Ittner et al. (2003) indicates that companies that create and monitor business models have a 2.9% higher return on assets and a 5% higher return on equity.

Compliance Mechanisms Used to Establish a Culture of Change

Companies should extrapolate constant internal control-monitoring requirements into a process for establishing and monitoring a culture of change. They should make Sarbanes-Oxley-related expenditures not merely a goal of complying with regulations and checking on internal control, but also a goal of devising more efficient operational procedures and using the additional monitoring to improve the compliance of the business with their own strategic initiatives. Competition through change is the key to success in the hospitality industry in this new century. A competitive advantage based on a single, fixed approach to costs and to product or service differentiation is being replaced by rapidly advancing technology, which efficiently spreads information to employees and customers. As the CEO and CFO infuse the company with a culture of regulatory compliance and the need for constant changes in internal controls due to growth of the business, they should take advantage of the opportunity to instill employees with the concept of flexibility and constant changes in the business model. This will give employees an image of their company as one that can compete in any market by providing different products or services in many niche markets and geographic locations and in which the employees can contribute to these significant elements of change.

Compliance Increases Market Value

There is some evidence that the transparency fostered by good corporate governance encourages investors to pay a higher multiple for earnings, thereby reducing a corporation's cost of capital. A study of stockholder value executed by Andrew Metrick, Paul A. Gompers, and Joy L. Ishii discovered that the most shareholder-friendly companies (companies that are transparent and do not attempt to interfere with the equities market as a mechanism for enforcing good corporate governance) had average annual returns 8.5% higher than the less shareholder-friendly firms, and 3.5% higher than Standard and Poor's 500 index. McKinsey and Co. conducted the Global Investor Opinion Survey in 2002 in which investors indicated that they were willing to pay a premium ranging from 12% in North America and Western Europe to 30% in Eastern Europe and Africa for companies with good corporate governance. Corporate governance was considered as important as financial indicators in their evaluation of a company. The converse is also true: companies whose corporate governance is shaky are penalized by the stock market. Between May 2004 and August 2005, the market value of Krispy Kreme stock plummeted.

In August 2005, a special committee of the board of directors of Krispy Kreme announced that "The Krispy Kreme story is one of a newly public company experiencing rapid growth that failed to meet its accounting and financial reporting obligations to its shareholders and the public." The emphasis that Krispy Kreme placed on growth versus compliance is an attitude toward corporate governance that SOX has attempted to change. Today's shareholders and investors are much more knowledgeable about their investments, as they demand not only increases in shareholder value, but also transparency of management. A poison pill, such as the one used by Shoney's when it borrowed $1 billion to pay out dividends, is a practice that stockholders no longer tolerate. This type of practice interferes with the functioning of the ninth corporate governance mechanism mentioned previously in the section "The Agency Problem and Various Instruments of Corporate Governance."

Chapter 3: Corporate Governance

Exhibit 3-2: Factors That Determine Shareholder Value[1]

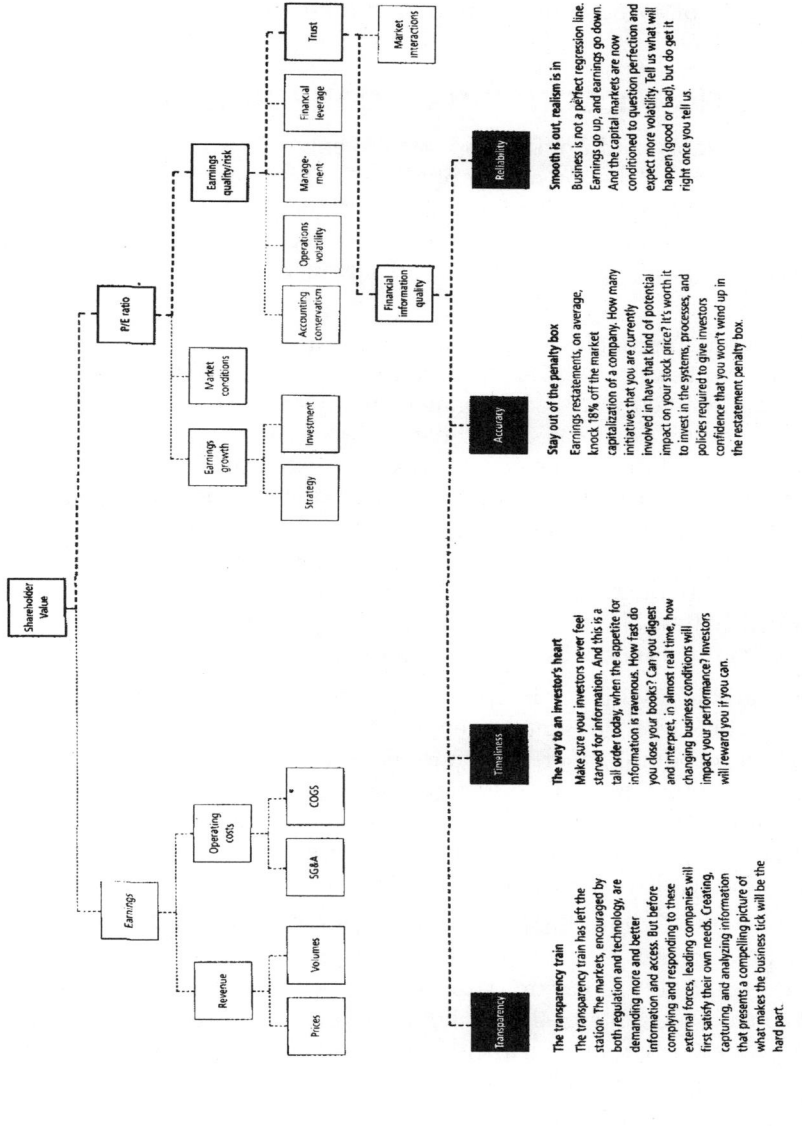

Shareholder Value branches into **Earnings** and **P/E ratio**.

Earnings → Revenue (Prices, Volumes), Operating costs (SG&A, COGS)

P/E ratio → Earnings growth (Investment, Strategy), Market conditions, Earnings quality/risk (Accounting conservatism, Operations volatility, Management, Financial leverage, Trust → Market interactions)

Financial information quality: Transparency, Timeliness, Accuracy, Reliability

Transparency — The transparency train
The transparency train has left the station. The markets, encouraged by both regulation and technology, are demanding more and better information and access. But before complying and responding to these external forces, leading companies will first satisfy their own needs. Creating, capturing, and analyzing information that presents a compelling picture of what makes the business tick will be the hard part.

Timeliness — The way to an investor's heart
Make sure your investors never feel starved for information. And this is a tall order today, when the appetite for information is ravenous. How fast do you close your books? Can you digest and interpret, in almost real time, how changing business conditions will impact your performance? Investors will reward you if you can.

Accuracy — Stay out of the penalty box
Earnings restatements, on average, knock 18% off the market capitalization of a company. How many initiatives that you are currently involved in have that kind of potential impact on your stock price? It's worth it to invest in the systems, processes, and policies required to give investors confidence that you won't wind up in the restatement penalty box.

Reliability
Smooth is out, realism is in. Business is not a perfect regression line. Earnings go up, and earnings go down. And the capital markets are now conditioned to question perfection and expect more volatility. Tell us what will happen (good or bad), but do get it right once you tell us.

[1] Copyright ©2004 Deloitte Development LLC. All rights reserved.

Exhibit 3-2, "Factors That Determine Shareholder Value," provides additional perspective on the influence that good corporate governance can have on shareholder value. Quality and risk are on a par with earnings growth and market conditions in determining a hospitality company's price earnings ratio. As this exhibit indicates, two of the five factors that impact earnings quality and risk are (1) accounting conservatism and (2) quality of financial information (trust), both of which are enhanced by an effective system of corporate governance.

INTERNATIONAL CONCEPT OF CORPORATE GOVERNANCE

The United States' and English approach to engendering good corporate governance is known as the "control approach." This approach aims to strengthen controls by viewing the behavior of those persons or entities involved in the role of corporate governance, the gatekeepers, as needing to be controlled and made to behave ethically while preserving management's focus on maximizing shareholder value.

The more commonly accepted international approach is to establish a system of checks and balances within corporate governance by imposing a more varied set of goals in an effort to reduce management's focus on shareholder value. This approach entitles corporate stakeholders other than shareholders (i.e., employees, creditors, suppliers, the community, and advocates for the natural environment) to have a voice in the activities and governance of a corporation. Thus, the pressure to maximize shareholder value found in the control approach is softened by the existence, for example, of representatives of employees, creditor banks, boards of directors, and much stricter environmental controls than exist in the United States. The goal of running a company for the purpose of long-term job preservation is not considered outlandish in this approach.

The problem with the international approach is that it can make the drawbacks of corporate governance even more onerous. If a company does not properly incorporate governance into its culture by establishing good operating systems, adopting proper strategic goals, and infusing its employees with a culture of change, then distracting management with these additional governance goals will make a corporation unwieldy and unable to quickly adapt to changing competitive circumstances.

Hospitality Extraordinaire, a French firm, is an example of a company that has adapted to and thrives under the international model of governance despite its size of 165,000 rooms in 1,200 properties dispersed in most major cities worldwide. It has state-of-the-art information technology systems, offers a variety of properties (from apartments and time-shares to luxury hotels) and has imbued its employees with the philosophy of being the best. Success with such a varied portfolio of properties and dispersed sites is the new challenge facing United States hospitality companies, where in the past standardization has been the secret of success.

Hotels have also begun forming green associations, such as the "Green" Hotels Association, the Audubon Green Leaf Eco-Rating Program for Hotels, and Green Globe 21. Green Globe has created four environmental standards: (1) the company standard, (2) the community standard, (3) the design and construction standard, and (4) the ecotourism standard. It represents itself as the worldwide benchmarking and certification program, which facilitates sustainable travel and tourism for consumers, companies, and communities. The Marriott Hotel (Calgary), Hotel Sofitel (Chicago), Courtyard Marriott (Toronto), and Colony Hotel (Kennebunkport, Maine) are participants in the Audubon Green Leaf Eco-Rating Program. It is becoming increasingly apparent that implementing environmentally friendly policies and investments can bring savings to a hospitality company. For example, The Holiday Inn at Harbourview, Halifax, saves $65,000 annually with energy-conserving practices and over $30,000 annually for garbage and laundry eco-efficiency practices. A survey of the members of the "Green" Hotels Association conducted by the National Association of Institutional Linen Management found that hotels can save over $6.50 a day per occupied room on laundry by using a simple towel-rack hanger and sheet-changing card being offered by the "Green" Hotels Association. The towel-rack hanger encourages guests to use towels more than once and the sheet-changing card, which is left on a pillow, suggests that guests staying more than one night opt to not have their sheets changed unless necessary. Other companies have discovered that an ecologically friendly workplace can increase employee retention, one of the major cost-cutting challenges in the hospitality industry.

Thus, the international governance standards provide their own advantages. Increasingly, United States hospitality companies are taking into account concepts such as sustainability and environmental consciousness in their corporate governance pacts. As globalization advances, it is only logical to expect that there will be a confluence of the two approaches to corporate governance.

IMPROVING CORPORATE GOVERNANCE

There are ways in which a hospitality company can help to ensure that it has good corporate governance. Some of the following suggestions are internal measures that help to ensure compliance with the regulatory environment; others are designed to help a hospitality company comply with its own strategic goals and enhance its operating efficiencies; yet others are designed to demonstrate to its stakeholders that it takes corporate governance seriously and has implemented the necessary measures to make its governance effective as a guarantor of accuracy and transparency. The checklists in Exhibit 3-3, "Measures for Improving Corporate Governance," and Exhibit 3-4, "Questions Directed to Management Regarding the Sarbanes-Oxley Act," present questions to assist the company in determining its exposure to risk resulting from inadequate or improper corporate governance as revealed by violations of SOX.

Exhibit 3-3: Measures for Improving Corporate Governance

Measures Designed to Improve Compliance with the Regulatory Environment

		Yes	No
1.	Is the company's code of conduct and ethics openly respected by top executives, and is its importance communicated to the rest of the corporation?		
2.	Have the board of directors and management determined the company's mission and corporate strategy and suffused it throughout the organization?		
3.	Are there regular meetings and debate on these matters between management and the Board?		
4.	Has the Board established systems that automatically inform the Board concerning important financial and operating variables, including its employee relations and impact on the community, environment, and other stakeholders; and does the Board address any problem areas?		
5.	Do the advisory committees consist of independent directors only?		
6.	Does the audit committee have adequate powers to ascertain the accuracy of financial reporting?		
7.	Is all important information relating to the company presented to the board of directors, no matter how sensitive or potentially compromising it may be?		
8.	Are nonmanagement directors given responsibility for specific areas of the business and formal training concerning the business, and are visits to business sites programmed?		
9.	Are directors allowed to participate in all meetings of high-level corporate executives with top personnel of any important stakeholders, such as security analysts, employee unions, and institutional investors?		
10.	Are directors allowed to meet with top personnel of any important stakeholders, such as security analysts, employee unions, and institutional investors without any management directors or personnel present at the meetings?		
11.	Does the company tie the remuneration of top officers of the corporation to the performance of the business, and does it avoid the use of stock options as the principal means of remuneration?		
12.	Are nonmanagement Board members encouraged to meet regularly without management board members?		
13.	Does management explain to the board of directors how good judgment has been used in regard to financial statement preparation, including items such as leasing and off-balance-sheet financing?		

	Yes	No

14. Does the company establish and maintain an interchange of ideas between executives and board members regarding current risks to the business, as well as potential future risks? _____ _____
15. Is there a limit regarding the number of other boards that nonmanagement board members may join? _____ _____

Measures Designed to Improve Compliance with a Company's Strategic Goals and Enhance Its Operating Efficiencies

	Yes	No

1. Are processes established to keep top officers and managers more informed concerning the business realities of their company? _____ _____
2. Do top executives make corporate governance a top priority and view it as an instrument for adding value to the company rather than as another burdensome bureaucratic requirement? _____ _____
3. Do the top executives communicate this view down through the company hierarchy? _____ _____
4. Do information technology and other operating systems incorporate feedback not only on regulatory compliance but also concerning compliance with the company's strategic goals and process efficiencies to assist it in achieving goals more effectively and at a lower cost? _____ _____
5. Is the flow of information to top management concerning both regulatory compliance and operational compliance adequate and thorough? _____ _____

Measures Designed to Demonstrate to Stakeholders That Corporate Governance Is Taken Seriously

	Yes	No

1. Does the company have, and does it publish, a code of business conduct and ethics—preferably on a company Web site? _____ _____
2. Does the company include on the company Web site other information, such as how to initiate a proxy vote, how many meetings nonmanagement directors have missed; and, for international companies, is the Web site in the languages of the countries where the company has a major presence? _____ _____
3. Does the company avoid anti-takeover measures, such as staggered elections of the board of directors, poison pills, or dual class recapitalizations? _____ _____
4. Does the company comply with either generally accepted accounting principles or the international accounting standards in recording and presenting financial information and report results according to these rules before reporting any pro-forma data? _____ _____

	Yes	No
5. Does the company discuss financial results with both media and financial analysts present at the same time?	_____	_____
6. Does the company explain to stakeholders clearly, and as accurately as possible, the future prospects of the corporation and the probability of occurrence of each prospective outcome?	_____	_____
7. Does the Board take measures to remedy issues and enhance relationships with all stakeholders?	_____	_____

Exhibit 3-4: Questions Directed to Management Regarding the Sarbanes-Oxley Act

Section 301

	Yes	No
1. Was the public accounting firm that performs independent audits selected and appointed by the audit company?	_____	_____
2. Is each member of the committee also a member of the board of directors?	_____	_____
3. Do the members of the audit committee meet the following independence criteria:		
• They do not receive any consulting advisory or any other fee except as members of the board of directors or one of its committees.	_____	_____
• They are not an "affiliated person" with regard to this company.	_____	_____
4. If they do not meet these conditions, has the SEC granted an exemption?	_____	_____
5. Has the audit committee established procedures for the receipt, retention, and treatment of complaints regarding accounting, internal accounting controls, or auditing matters?	_____	_____
6. Has the audit committee established procedures for the receipt of confidential, anonymous submissions by employees regarding any concerns as to questionable accounting or auditing matters?	_____	_____
7. Does the audit committee have the authority to engage independent counsel and other advisors that it deems necessary to fulfill its responsibilities?	_____	_____
8. Has the audit committee been granted the funds to pay for:		
• Independent audit?	_____	_____
• Independent counsel?	_____	_____
• Independent advisors?	_____	_____

	Yes	No

Section 302

Has the principal executive officer or officers and the principal financial officer or officers, or persons performing similar functions certified in each annual or quarterly report filed or submitted under either Section 13(a) or 15(d) of the Securities Exchange Act of 1934 that:

- The signing officer has reviewed the report; _____ _____
- To the best of the officers' knowledge, the report does not contain any false statement of material fact or does not omit any material necessary to ensure the statements made are not misleading; _____ _____
- The financial statements, and other financial information included in the report represent fairly in all material respects the financial condition and results of operations as of, and for, the periods presented in the report? _____ _____

Have all signing officers:

- Been responsible for establishing and maintaining internal controls? _____ _____
- Designed such internal controls to make certain that material information relating to the company and its consolidated subsidiaries is made known to such officers by those within these entities especially during the period in which the periodic reports are being prepared? _____ _____
- Evaluated the effectiveness and integrity of internal controls as of a date within 90 days prior to the report date? _____ _____
- Included in their report their conclusions about the effectiveness and integrity of internal controls based on their evaluation as of that date? _____ _____

Have the signing officers disclosed to the auditors and the audit committee of the board of directors (or persons fulfilling the equivalent function):

- Any deficiencies and or weaknesses in the design or operation of internal controls which could adversely affect the company's ability to record, process, summarize, and report financial data? _____ _____
- Any evidence of fraud, whether material or not, that involves management or other employees who have a significant role in internal controls? _____ _____

Have signing officers reported whether any significant changes in internal controls or other factors could affect these controls subsequent to the date of their evaluation? _____ _____

	Yes	No

Section 303

Has any officer or director, or any person/s acting under the direction thereof taken any action to fraudulently influence, coerce, manipulate, or mislead an independent public or certified accountant engaged in the performance of an audit of the financial statements? _____ _____

Section 306   Yes   No

Did any director or executive officer of any equity security (other than an exempted security) unlawfully purchase, sell, or otherwise acquire or transfer any equity security directly or indirectly (other than an exempted security) during any blackout period?   _____   _____

Section 401   Yes   No

1. Has each financial report been prepared in accordance with GAAP and does each one reflect all material correcting adjustments that have been identified by a registered accounting firm?   _____   _____
2. Has each annual and quarterly financial report disclosed all material off-balance sheet transactions and other relationships with unconsolidated entities that may have a material current or future effect on the company's financial condition?   _____   _____
3. Does any pro-forma financial information included in a periodic or other report filed with the SEC, or in any public disclosure, or press or other release, contain an untrue statement of a material fact or omit a material fact?   _____   _____

Section 402   Yes   No

Has the company extended any credit or arranged for the extension of any credit to directors or officers of the company? _____   _____

Section 403   Yes   No

Have all executive officers or directors of the company reported to the SEC all transactions they made in the company's stock per the requirements of this section?   _____   _____

Section 404   Yes   No

1. Does each annual report:
   - Contain an internal control report that states that it is the responsibility of management to establish and maintain an adequate internal control structure and procedures for financial reporting?   _____   _____
   - Contain an assessment, as of the end of the fiscal year, of the effectiveness of the internal control structure and procedures for financial reporting? _____   _____
2. Has each auditor reported on the assessment made by management?   _____   _____

Section 406   Yes   No

1. As directed by the SEC, has the company disclosed whether it has adopted a code of ethics for senior financial officers and has it disclosed the contents of that code?   _____   _____
2. Has the company reported to the SEC any changes to this code of ethics, or any waivers granted?   _____   _____

Section 407

Is at least one member of the audit committee a financial expert as defined by this section?

Yes _____ No _____

Section 409

Has the company disclosed information on material changes in the financial condition or operations on a rapid and current basis?

Yes _____ No _____

Section 601

Yes _____ No _____

1. Do all persons representing the company before the SEC possess the requisite qualifications to represent others, conform to the minimum standards for professional conduct set by the SEC, and show integrity; and are they free of any direct violations of securities laws?

2. Have any securities professionals (public accountants, public accounting firms, investment bankers, investment advisors, brokers, dealers, attorneys) working on behalf of the company been found to have aided and abetted a violation of federal securities laws?

3. Has the company remunerated a securities analyst or broker, or dealer in securities in relation to a research report, excluding the exemptions provided in this section? If so, has this been properly disclosed by the securities analyst or broker?

4. Has the company been a client of a broker or related securities analyst within the year preceding the appearance of a research report concerning the company prepared by either the securities analyst or broker? If so, has this been properly disclosed by the securities analyst or broker?

Sections 801 and 1102

Has the company knowingly destroyed, altered, or created documents, or other objects to impede or obstruct or influence any existing or contemplated federal investigation?

Yes _____ No _____

Section 806

Has the company, or any officer, employee, contractor, subcontractor, or agent of the company discharged, demoted, suspended, threatened, harassed, or in any other manner discriminated against an employee because of any lawful act done by the employee to provide information, cause information to be provided, or otherwise assist in an investigation regarding any conduct which the employee reasonably believes constitutes a violation of this act, or of any rule or regulation of the SEC, or any provision of federal law relating to fraud against shareholders?

Yes _____ No _____

	Yes	No
Section 906 Have all financial statements filed with the SEC been certified by the CEO and CFO? (The certification must state that the financial statements and disclosures fully comply with provisions of the Securities Exchange Act of 1934 and that they fairly present, in all material respects, the financial condition and results of operations of the company.)	___	___
Section 1001 Has the CEO signed the federal income tax returns of a corporation?	___	___

INCREASING TRANSPARENCY THROUGH THE CORPORATE WEB SITE

One of the principal venues available to a company for conveying to its stockholders and other stakeholders the extent of its corporate governance policies and its commitment to transparency in its corporate governance is the company's Web site. Some of the topics that may be covered in hospitality Web sites regarding corporate goverenance in general are listed below:

- Board of directors: method of selection, charter, and ethics code
- Board of directors: names, qualifications, independent members, and financial expert
- Nominating and corporate governance committee: members, charter, ethics code, and financial expert
- Compensation committee: members, charter, ethics code, and financial expert
- Audit committee: members, charter, ethics code, and financial expert
- Attendance statistics of board and committee members
- Management succession
- The mechanics of how to initiate a proxy vote
- Whistle-blower procedures—Indicate whom employees can contact to report violations of the code and explain the safeguards protecting them from retaliation. Also indicate whom employees can consult if they are in doubt about the ethical nature of a particular situation, their responsibility in such a situation, or the propriety of an order given them by a superior
- SEC filings and quarterly reports to shareholders
- Major issues confronting the corporation and management measures to resolve them
- Company code of ethics

Some of the topics to be dealt with in the company code of ethics are:

- Outlining who is subject to the code
- Definition of principles-based compliance

- Statement by top executives concerning their own intention to observe the code
- Consequences of violating the code
- Definition and importance of honest, ethical, transparent conduct on and off the job
- Fairness in all dealings
- Nonpermitted outside activities and commitments (executives and board)
- Acceptance of gifts related to company activities or position
- Other personal opportunities resulting from an employee's position in the company
- Political contributions
- Proper use and preservation of company resources
- Definition of other types of conflicts of interest
- Confidentiality regarding sensitive company information
- Compliance with laws and regulations
- Compliance with the company's strategic plan and operating procedures
- Accuracy and integrity in accounting
- Definition of materiality and required full disclosure of all material information
- Integrity in decision making, especially regarding investments and long-term commitments
- Discussion of insider trading, including that of family members, and the significance of information that has not been publicly released

CHAPTER 4
USING COMPUTERS IN HOSPITALITY FINANCIAL MANAGEMENT

CONTENTS

Overview	4002
Computers as Data-Processing Tools	4003
Computer Networks	4003
Computer Application Programs	4004
Use of Information Technology to Maximize ROI	4014
Basic Hospitality Industry Programs	4016
Property Management Systems	4017
Point-of-Sale Systems	4017
Minibar Systems	4018
Call Accounting Systems	4018
Other Property Management Support Systems	4018
Guest-Tracking Software	4018
Restaurant Management Systems	4018
Maximizing Revenues and Minimizing Costs	4020
Programs Designed to Improve Operational Efficiency and Strategic Alignment	4021
Systems That Increase Competitive Advantage	4022
Revenue Management Systems	4022
Risks of Using Application Service Providers	4026
Customer Relationship Management Systems	4026
Supply Chain Management Systems	4027
Data-Warehousing and Data-Mining Systems	4028
Global Distribution Systems	4029
Business Intelligence Programs	4029
Business Performance Management Systems	4030
Other Strategic Planning Computer Systems	4031
Calculating ROI and the Purchasing Process	4035
Calculating ROI for Investments in IT	4035
The IT Asset Purchasing Process	4040
Exhibit	
Exhibit 4-1. Considerations to Be Made Prior to Investing in IT-Related Assets	4036

In the 1960s and 1970s, computers were used solely as electronic data processors (EDP)—machines that could process most of the traditional paperwork of a business in a short time. As computers began to process nontraditional information, EDPs were subsumed into the broader concept of management information systems (MIS). In the 1980s and 1990s, the emergence of the personal computer, with its ability to network easily with other computers; the development of advanced programming capabilities; and the worldwide access provided by the Internet led to the creation of a much broader concept called information technology (IT). As part of this broader concept, the machine that began as a tool to save costs by reducing the need to process large volumes of paper manually became a part of a technology that increasingly determines corporate strategy, especially in the extensive geographic marketplaces serviced by the hospitality industry.

OVERVIEW

Computers are of interest to hospitality controllers for two reasons:

1. They serve in their original function as transaction processors. Computers and the programs that run them serve as an interface between the company reports and financial statements that are created and the data that are manually entered. This interface is vulnerable to corruption through accidental mishandling, ignorance, or intentional tampering. Insofar as a controller is in charge of the internal audit or control function, the computer system is another area in the business process that must be controlled and audited to verify the accuracy with which transactions are recorded and classified. This verification process is presented in two steps:

    a. The verification of the accounting data to determine that there has not been any (1) omission of legitimate data; (2) introduction of false data; (3) double data entry; or (4) corruption of data in the (a) data input stage, (b) the processing stage, or (c) the output stage. If an information technology (IT) department exists, this verification may be performed conjointly with that department.

    b. The verification of compliance with regulatory requirements (most recently the Sarbanes-Oxley Act of 2002), with the company's board of directives, and with loan or other contract covenants.

2. They are used as strategic tools in the hospitality industry. The controller must view them as centers for which a return on investment (ROI) must be calculated. However, the data might not be easy to obtain because some of the benefits that computer systems provide are qualitative and are difficult to express in terms of dollar returns. It is easy to quantify a reduced acquisition cost per guest reservation; however, it is difficult to place a dollar value on a more satisfied guest. This may lead a hospitality company to delay the implementation of the latest advances in IT in favor of investments in other areas that lend themselves to a more precise calculation of ROI.

To determine a hospitality company's IT needs (e.g., data warehousing and supply chain management), computers must be evaluated from at least two perspectives:

1. How beneficial is the current computer system in terms of business process efficiency? Is the system creating operational excellence, maximizing profits, and minimizing expenses?

2. Is the current computer system consistently aligning the company with its strategic long-term goals (e.g., maintaining leadership in the implementation of IT or maintaining the maximum flexibility to adapt to new market conditions)?

The IT and accounting departments must work together closely, as they share the common goal of maximizing profitability for the company. Hospitality controllers must therefore have a good working relationship with the company's chief information officer (CIO). In order to communicate effectively with the CIO, the controller and all company executives can no longer be on the periphery of the IT revolution. To determine whether the company is maximizing its current and potential future revenues and minimizing costs, hospitality controllers need to understand the limitations of IT as well as its potential. Hospitality controllers must ascertain that the company is appropriately positioned on the IT development curve and recognize and recommend the correct time to advance to the next level of IT implementation. To achieve this integration, in some organizations the CIO reports to the CFO or, in some cases, to the controller.

Hospitality controllers must apply their accounting and financial expertise, as well as their interpersonal skills, to assist the CIO and the IT department in answering the following questions:

- What is the actual total cost of a planned investment in IT?
- Is there a less expensive way of achieving the same result by interfacing with legacy systems that are already installed or will this defeat the purpose of the investment?
- How is the ROI measured?
- How can one determine if an investment was successful in achieving the expected ROI and is increasing the profitability of the hospitality company?
- How can one ascertain that the existing or prospective IT systems are in alignment with the strategic objectives of the hospitality company?
- How can a CIO maintain open lines of communication with the financial and operating management of the company in order to respond quickly to developing IT needs and sustain the ability of the hospitality company to respond to rapidly changing market demands that are required to remain competitive?

COMPUTERS AS DATA-PROCESSING TOOLS

Initially, computers were used to simply process data and generate traditional reports faster and more accurately, in contrast to their current additional use as strategic management tools. However, their initial data-processing functions are still valid and useful functions, as discussed below.

Computer Networks

Computer networks are integral to a high-quality IT system. Local area networks (LANs) are the most common type of IT system and are used in small companies, because they cover small geographic areas such as a group of buildings. Virtual local area networks (VLANs) can be created within a LAN, such as the VLAN of a human resources department. VLANs are a group of hosts with a common set of requirements that communicate as if they were attached to a broadcast domain, regardless of their physical location. A VLAN is conceptually and physically separate from the LAN but is encompassed within the overall LAN. On a broader scale are wide-area networks (WANs) that can extend over more than two miles. WANS can be connected wirelessly; by T1 phone lines, which are dedicated lines used by a single entity; or by coaxial cable, the latter being more secure in case of electromagnetic attack. The transactional security of these networks depends on the implementation of safety measures such as secure sockets layers (SSLs) and the use of certificates, such as those issued by VeriSign. Attached to these networks are application servers, file servers, and peripheral servers.

Hospitality companies can also operate a company intranet. An intranet is a series of computers owned by the company that are connected to each other (i.e., a LAN) and use the Internet protocol (language), TCP/IP. The advantage of using TCP/IP is that, as a generally accepted protocol, it allows another intranet, such as that of a supplier, to have access to the hospitality company's intranet to retrieve certain information such as inventory levels. When an outside party is given access to the company intranet it is called an extranet. When communicating with third parties, such as suppliers, it is more efficient to use intranets and extranets, because TCP/IP is a standard language or protocol that is commonly used. LANs and WANs have protocols that may not be compatible with those of third parties.

The most common use of an extranet is to maintain a supply chain connection with a supplier, which enables the supplier to know when its customers will need deliveries of particular items and provides important IT benefits—namely, the use of just-in-time inventory control. Inventory delivered on time means less money invested in inventory and more money available for investing in revenue-generating assets.

Computer Application Programs

A hospitality controller may require the following types of generic programs:
- Spreadsheets
- Databases
- Graphics programs
- Statistical analysis, forecasting, risk calculation
- Accounting
- Tax

Spreadsheets. The most commonly used spreadsheet is Microsoft's *Excel*, although IBM's *Lotus* 1-2-3 and Corel Corporation's *Quattro Pro* spreadsheets provide similar features. Because of its flexibility, a spreadsheet can be used to execute almost any type of accounting or financial project and can even be made to perform simple database functions. But many of these projects or calculations are more easily performed by using programs dedicated to each type of calculation. Dedicated programs are standardized and can be used by different entities within an organization to input data and then consolidate it for the entire organization. A spreadsheet can also be standardized by using its cell-protection function, although this is a more difficult and time-consuming process.

For example, there are dedicated programs for preparing financial statements, for calculating payrolls and depreciation schedules, or for budgeting. These dedicated programs are much easier to use than having to program a spreadsheet to perform all these functions. Below is a partial list of accounting and financial uses for which the Microsoft Excel spreadsheet is particularly well suited:

- Analyzing operating ratios.
- Performing common size analysis (vertical, horizontal, and trend).
- Performing What-if? analysis (e.g., cost-volume-profit analysis, modeling, time value analysis, and tax planning).
- Analyzing lease versus purchase options.
- Analyzing cash flow.
- Examining revenues and expenses.
- Analyzing prepaid expenses.
- Performing accounts receivable and accounts payable analyses.
- Analyzing inventory.
- Calculating economic order quantity for inventory.
- Formatting financial statements in a way different from the standard off-the-shelf accounting program or integrating customized schedules with these financial statements.
- Generating management reports not included in the standard accounting program.
- Converting from cash to accrual basis and vice versa.
- Performing merger and acquisition analysis.
- Analyzing capital investments.
- Using simple or small database functions (simple indexing and pivot tables).
- Performing standards and subsequent variance analysis.
- Evaluating a hotel or restaurant service line.
- Creating comma-delimited data files for exporting to other programs, such as statistical, graphics, or large database programs.
- Importing and creating comma-separated value (CSV) files.
- Using macro-activated workbooks to perform automated tasks.
- Analyzing XML financial data in Excel.
- Combining Microsoft Access (database) and Microsoft Excel to prepare financial charts.

- Importing financial data into Excel from various sources.
- Collaborating on accounting functions by using shared workbooks.
- Using conditional formulas to analyze financial data and highlight financial performance.
- Incorporating balanced scorecards into the budgeting process.
- Determining cost behavior for effective budgeting.
- Comparing two lists of data.
- Using an AutoFilter to analyze sales data.
- Determining the compound annual growth rate.
- Separating fixed and variable costs.
- Creating a scenario analysis for Web site budgeting.
- Communicating budget data to management.
- Creating business plans.
- Performing decision and risk analysis.
- Providing a graphic representation of data.
- Performing regression analysis.
- Analyzing goal-seeking data.

"Resources on the Web" contains Internet sites where further information concerning the major spreadsheets can be obtained.

Tips for using spreadsheets include:

- When formatted spreadsheets containing formulas or functions are used for data input, the cell-protection feature of the spreadsheet should be used to protect all cells to which input is not desired.
- The output of all spreadsheets should be tested immediately after they are created and periodically thereafter.
- When writing a long function or formula into a cell in Excel, it is best to precede it with an apostrophe so that it will be entered as text. This prevents Excel from wrapping the formula into the cell and enables moving or copying the formula without the spreadsheet's cell-referencing feature that changes the cell names used in the formula.

Excel Add-in Programs. There are many available programs that are designed as additions to Excel. These add-in programs provide templates that are already structured to apply many of the Excel features listed above. Two of them that may be of use to hospitality controllers are:

1. *@Risk*—A risk evaluation program whose Web site is http://www.palisade.com/.
2. *EOQ*—A program designed to determine the economic order quantity for inventories may be found by going to http://www.sharewareorder.com and entering "EOQ" in the search window.
3. *Lease vs. Purchase*—A program to assist in making the decision whether to lease or buy an asset. A program for this purpose may be found by

going to http://www.sharewareorder.com and entering "Lease vs. Purchase" in the search window.

"Resources on the Web" at the back of the book contains sites where Excel add-ins may be found.

Databases. A database is a list of grouped data organized in a tabular format. Each characteristic of a member of the group is called an attribute. Thus, if a hotel's front desk creates a database of all guests and records each of their (1) names, (2) room numbers, and (3) their country of origin, each of these three items is an attribute of the members of the data group. A relational database, the standard type of database currently in use, is capable of relating two databases through a common attribute. And if the food and beverage department of the hotel records a guest's room number, whether or not the guests order wine with their meals and the type of wine order, a relational database can be made to relate the guests' countries of origin with their wine preferences by using the attribute that is common to both databases, which is the room number.

This is done by writing a query. Different databases have their own query languages. Standard query language (SQL), as the name states, is the standard. Access, a Microsoft database, has its own query language. A database query is a simple form of what is now called data mining, except that data mining is usually performed by using complex algorithms that extract information from extremely large databases stored in data warehouses. A data warehouse can include the data gathered by all the hotels of a chain. The different parts of this data warehouse can be connected via an intranet (called a storage area network or SAN) and can give hotels access to any information they may require. Information may be used to forecast occupancy, set optimum rates during the year, or mail special rate offers to former guests based on their historic travel pattern.

Commonly used small databases include:

- Microsoft Access
- Wordperfect Suite Database

Higher capacity databases include:

- Centura Software—SQLBase
- Computer Associates—Ingres
- IBM—DB2
- Informix Software—Informix-SQL
- Microsoft—SQL Server
- Oracle—Database 10g
- Sybase—Sybase SQL Server

Studies comparing Oracle's Database with Microsoft's SQL Server can be found by typing: "Oracle database vs. Microsoft SQL" in a search engine such as Google.

Graphics. Creating graphs is an important part of the hospitality financial manager's job, as they assist in analyzing and communicating important information to upper management. Graphs can be used to clarify a concept, emphasize a statement, or present a large volume of information succinctly.

Eight common graph types are:
1. Bar charts
2. Line graphs
3. Pie charts
4. Expansion charts
5. Area charts
6. Statistical charts
7. Scattergrams
8. Bubble charts

Examples of the first seven types of graphs are presented below.

EXAMPLE 1: A bar chart is used primarily to clarify statements such as: "Corporate profits fluctuated during the year, while consumer prices and personal income experienced a steady increase."

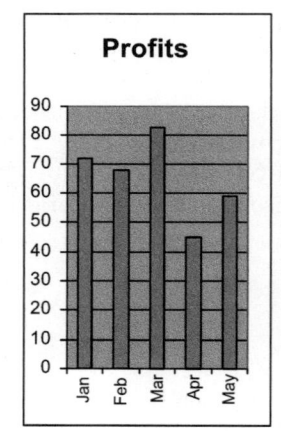

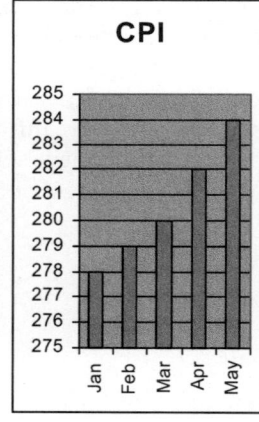

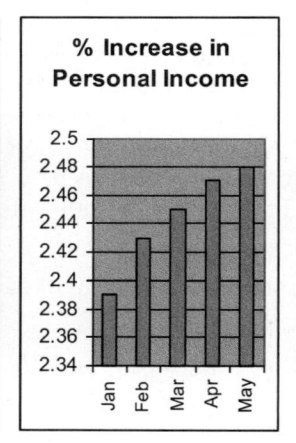

Chapter 4: *Using Computers in Hospitality Financial Management* **4009**

EXAMPLE 2: A line chart is used primarily to clarify statements such as: "Pizza Chain's restaurant sales increased fourfold while sales to franchisees increased ten times."

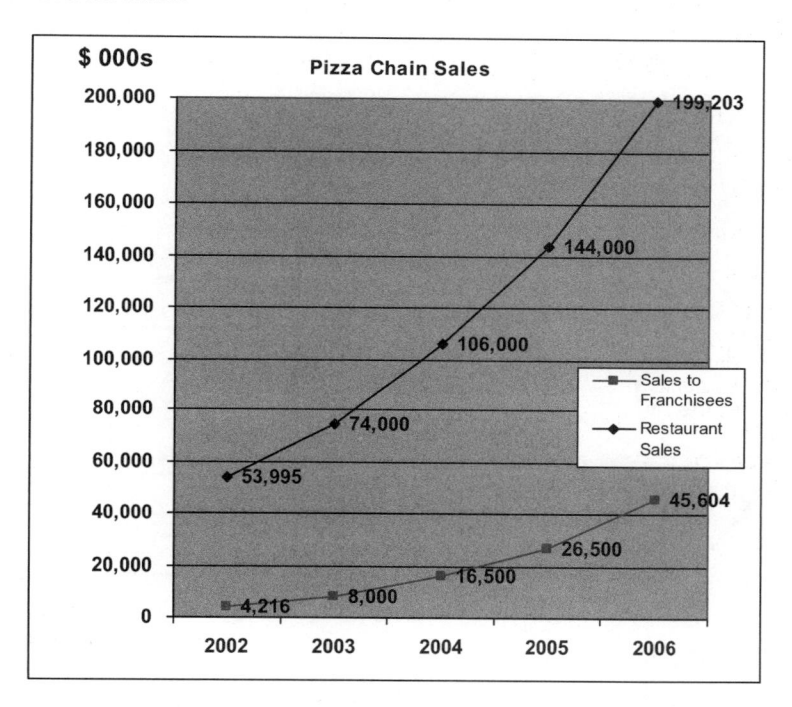

Pizza Chain Sales ($ 000s)

Year	Restaurant Sales	Sales to Franchisees
2002	53,995	4,216
2003	74,000	8,000
2004	106,000	16,500
2005	144,000	26,500
2006	199,203	45,604

EXAMPLE 3: A pie chart is used primarily to clarify statements such as: "Cost of Sales is 35% of sales, payroll is 30% of sales, other expenses are 25% of sales, and net income is 10% of sales."

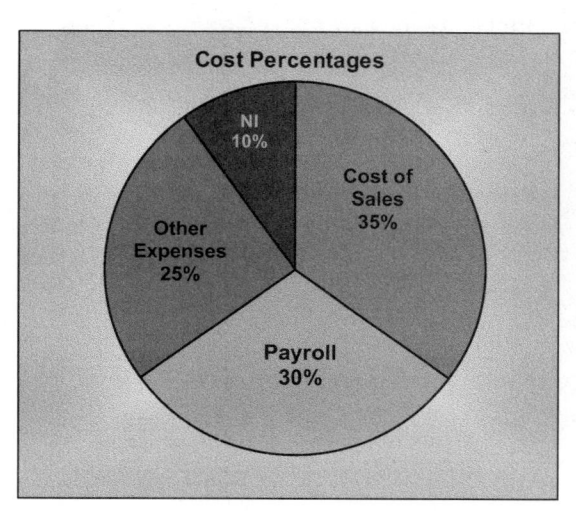

Cost Percentages
- Cost of Sales 35%
- Payroll 30%
- Other Expenses 25%
- NI 10%

EXAMPLE 4: An expansion chart is used primarily to clarify statements such as: "Total assets amount to $1,284,167, of which current assets were $176,168. Current assets consisted of cash, $27,050; certificates of deposit, $17,371; short-term investments, $71,714; accounts receivable, $25,995; inventories, $17,361; and prepaid expenses, $16,677."

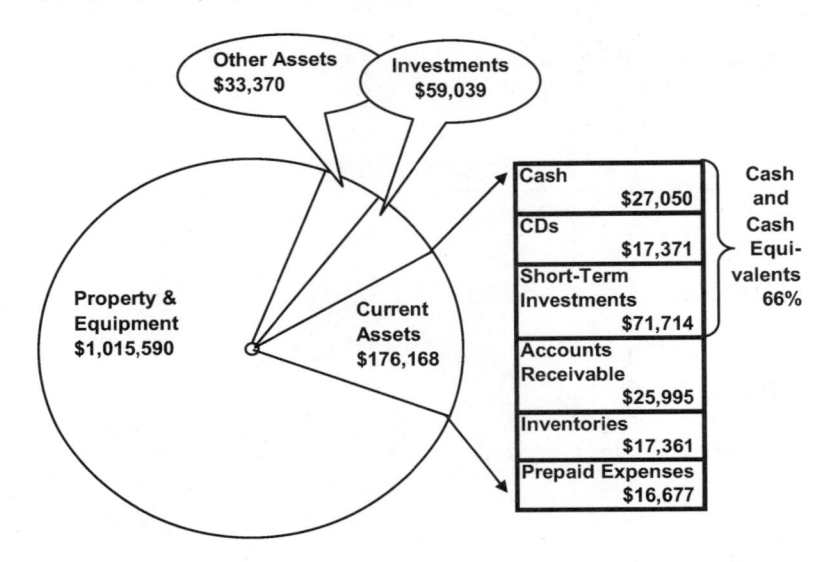

EXAMPLE 5: An area chart is used primarily to clarify statements such as: "In the timeshare segment of the hospitality industry the increase in marketing costs outstripped sales, rising from 35% of sales in 20X0 to 50% of sales in 20X6."

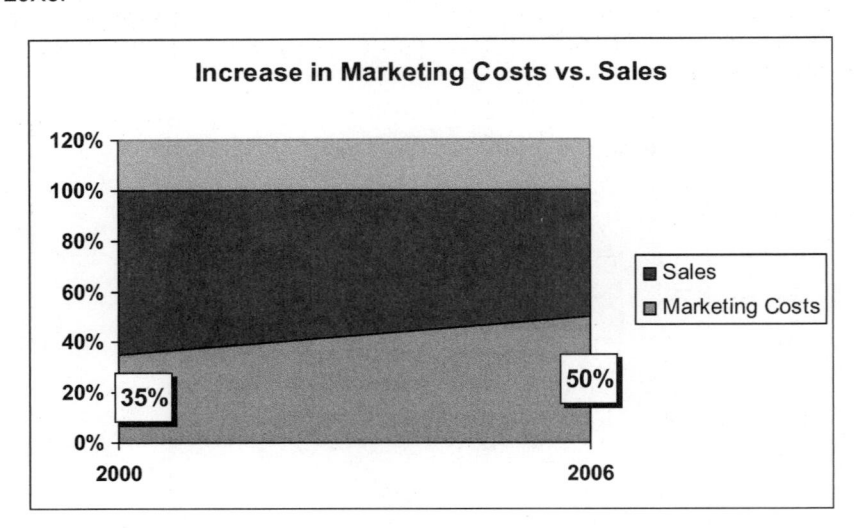

EXAMPLE 6: A statistical chart is primarily used to clarify statements such as:

Three star hotels experienced a 5.13% increase in average daily rate (ADR) between 20X4 and 20X5, which was offset by an occupancy rate decrease of 5.55%, resulting in no change in revenue per available room (RevPAR). Although two star hotels' ADR increased by only 3.42%, the fact that their occupancy rate also increased led to their having the highest percent increase in RevPAR—6.33%. Two star hotels' ADR, RevPAR, and occupancy rates remained flat over this same period.

Hotel Markets by Class

	4 Star	3 Star	2 Star
ADR 2004	146 €	78 €	54 €
ADR 2005	151 €	82 €	54 €
Percent change	3.42%	5.13%	0.00%
RevPAR 2004	79 €	46 €	35 €
RevPAR 2005	84 €	46 €	35 €
Percent change	6.33%	0.00%	0.00%
Occupancy Rate 2004	54.2%	59.5%	65.4%
Occupancy Rate 2005	55.8%	56.2%	65.2%
Percent change	2.95%	−5.55%	−0.31%

ADR = Average daily rate
RevPAR = Revenue per available room
€ = Euro

EXAMPLE 7: A scatter chart is used primarily to clarify statements such as: "The manager of the rooms department did not control variable expenses well during the first half of 20X8. Rooms department expenses did not seem to respond to sales in an approximately linear manner."

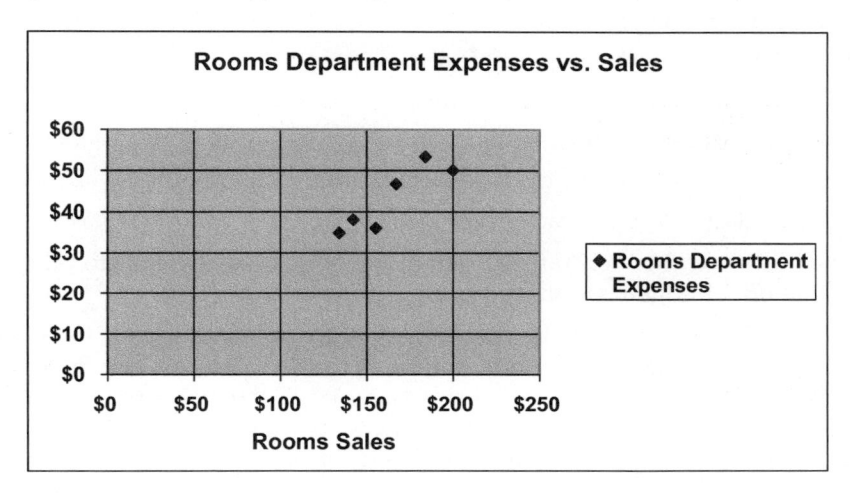

Popular graphics programs for creating these charts include:
- Fireworks, by Macromedia
- Painter, by Corel
- Corel Draw
- Paint Shop Pro, by JASC
- Photoshop, by Adobe
- Excel (basic graphics capability)

Information concerning most of these programs may be found at: http://www.Websitetips.com/graphics/.

Statistical Analysis, Forecasting, and Risk Analysis. Statistical programs are useful for three purposes:
1. Forecasting
2. Statistical analysis
3. Risk analysis

Forecasting is an integral part of budgeting, and therefore, most budgeting programs include a forecasting capacity. In the hospitality industry, forecasting is important because of the seasonal nature of the business. Commonly used forecasting programs include:
- John Galt Forecast Software (johngalt.com)
- Forecast Pro (www.forecastpro.com)
- Roadmap Global Planning Solution (http://www.roadmap-tech.com)
- FRx Forecaster Professional (enter "FRx Forecaster" in a search engine such as google)
- Smart Software (www.smartforecasts.com)
- Forecaster Analytics—Microsoft Business Solutions (www.rossinc.com)
- OutlookSoft (www.outlooksoft.com)
- Brittenford Systems, Inc. (www.brittenfordsystems.com)
- Budget Maestro (www.centage.com)
- Clarity Systems (www.claritysystems.com)
- Quantitative Micro (www.eviews.com)

"Resources on the Web" at the back of the book contains links to other sites or lists that offer budgeting and forecasting software.

Statistical analysis is the process of gathering, analyzing, and interpreting seemingly diverse data in an attempt to discern a pattern that may be of assistance in either describing that data (descriptive statistics) or using relationships discovered in the data for making decisions (inferential statistics). Using statistics to draw a graph, calculate an average, or project past sales and expense trends into the future is a descriptive use of statistics. Inferential statistical analysis is useful, for instance, in extracting information (called *data mining*) from a large database (such as a data warehouse) in a meaningful manner to facilitate making pricing decisions. Inferential analysis is based on extracting a significant sample from all the available data (called *the population*). Some sites with business-related statistical analysis information and access to statistics programs are:

- Electronic Textbook Statsoft (http://www.statsoft.com/textbook/stathome.html)
- Statistical Thinking for Managerial Decisions (http://home.ubalt.edu/ntsbarsh/statdata/Topics.htm)
- Statistical Analysis Pages (http://statpages.org)

Risk analysis is also important in the hospitality industry because of the broad international exposure of many hospitality companies and the uncertain nature of the political and social environment, as well as the currently developing exposure to highly sophisticated competition in most markets. Some of the better known statistical and risk analysis programs include BrainMaker, NeuroShell, Minitab, SPSS, Matlab, CubiCalc, @Risk, RiskCalc, SAS Application System, and FuzzyCalc.

Modelling. Modelling software enables financial managers to simulate the performance of a business, an activity within a business, or an individual asset. This type of program is useful for creating simulations regarding:

- Weighted average cost of capital
- Project finance
- Valuation
- Risk analysis
- Return on investment (ROI) analysis

Examples of this type of product may be found at:

- www.a3solutions.com
- www.modeladvisor.com

Financial Software. Financial software is useful for making calculations such as time value and amortization schedules.

The following financial software programs are available:

- TValue 5 by Time Value Software (www.timevalue.com)
- FinCalc by JDP Sofware
- The Mortgage Office (www.abstmo.com/fc.asp)

A useful (and free) application service provider (ASP) site where many types of simple financial calculations can be performed is www.dinkytown.net.

Accounting and Tax Programs. The following programs may also be required if their functions are not incorporated into the hospitality-specific programs, such as the property management system program and the restaurant management system program.

- General ledger
- Accounts payable

- Accounts receivable
- Fixed assets and depreciation
- Payroll and payroll taxes
- Income taxes
- Budgeting
- Audit

Programs within these categories and related information can be obtained from the Internet.

Suggested accounting software for mid-size hospitality companies are:
- Microsoft Great Plains
- SAP Business One
- Made2Manage
- Sage MAS 90/Sage MAS 200
- Everest Advanced
- Sage Accpac/Sage Pro
- Exact Financials

Suggested accounting software for small hospitality companies are:
- MS Small Business Financials
- Everest Advanced
- QuickBooks Enterprise
- Cougar Mountain
- NetSuite Small Business
- Sage MAS 90 Small Business
- Microsoft Solomon

"Resources on the Web" at the back of the book contains links to these and other business management programs.

Another option is for companies to outsource their payroll tax accounting function to companies dedicated exclusively to this type of service. Companies can transfer their employees to companies that provide this service and then lease them back, thus transferring all payroll tax responsibility to the service companies. Another advantage is that as employees of the leasing companies, the transferred employees may join the leasing companies' health insurance and 401k plans.

USE OF INFORMATION TECHNOLOGY TO MAXIMIZE ROI

Important to the success of the hospitality business is the use of computers in ways that will increase the business's ROI and thus its competitive advantage. Investment in IT is all the more meaningful because advanced IT applications in the hospitality industry are in the early stages of development. Therefore, investment in this area offers a greater competitive advantage to those companies willing to fully exploit IT's potential.

In a world where employees qualified to render such personalized services are becoming increasingly more difficult and expensive to engage, outstanding hospitality companies attempt to counteract the trend toward commoditization of certain types of accommodations, food and beverage services, and products by making guests' experiences unique and personalized by investment in IT. For example, although guests may make reservations at hotels and restaurants over the Internet without making personal contact, a well-designed customer relationship management system remembers a guest's personal preferences and thus individualizes each guest's experience with the company. When properly integrated into all properties in a chain, investments in IT have the potential to increase the ROI of all its hotels or restaurants.

There are at least four ways in which the more advanced IT systems can be used to increase revenues and reduce expenses:

1. Make business processes more efficient and therefore less costly.
2. Better align these processes with the hospitality company's strategic objectives.
3. Facilitate compliance with (a) government regulations, (b) board of director dictates regarding factors such as risk, and (c) contractual covenants such as loan constraints.
4. Expedite and strengthen the internal control processes of the company.

Ways that investment in IT increases business process efficiency and aligns processes more completely with a hospitality company's strategic objectives include:

- Assisting in minimizing expenses by:
  — Permitting the consolidation of worldwide markets and allowing them to be serviced from one geographical location;
  — Reducing the costs of information transferred vertically from the parent corporation to divisions and horizontally among individual divisions, regions, hotels, or restaurants;
  — Increasing the accuracy of inventory planning, which applies to beverage and nonperishable food inventory, perishable food inventory, and expiring unsold rooms and restaurant seats inventory;
  — Making the purchase of food and beverage inventory less time-consuming and therefore less costly;
  — Facilitating central purchasing of food and beverages, thereby allowing for greater volume discounts and better quality control;
  — Enabling better tracking of seasonality and thus better labor and inventory control, an important cost savings in an environment where trained employees are becoming scarcer and more sought after; and
  — Allowing for standardizing processes on a systemwide basis, rather than every property having its own unique processes, thereby saving in training costs while providing guests with a familiar venue.

- Facilitating maximizing short-term revenue by:
  - Reducing costs of booking reservations;
  - Increasing exposure of the hospitality companies via Internet and global distribution systems;
  - Increasing repeat sales by customers accustomed to a particular access system and service pattern and familiarity with their personal tastes;
  - Increasing table turnover;
  - Enabling better tracking of seasonality and thus better planning of promotional efforts directed toward seasonal non-repeat or low-repeat customer preferences;
  - Enabling hotels to sell more of their rooms at bargain rates anonymously without harming their brand name and regular pricing structure either through last-minute bargain sites, such as Expedia.com, or through auction Web sites; and
  - Allowing hospitality companies to access markets where specific types of products are promoted, such as eco-tourism hotels.
- Improving customer service and brand awareness by:
  - Providing customers, guests, and potential customers easier worldwide access to the services offered by hospitality companies;
  - Allowing for the recording and tracking of customer tastes and preferences on a systemwide basis regardless of geographical boundaries; and
  - Enabling better tracking of VIP and high-repeat-visit guests, as well as their preferences, as opposed to non-repeat or low-repeat customers.
- Facilitating the minimizing of costs and maximizing of revenues through better long-term planning by:
  - Enabling the calculation of complex nontraditional ratios such as revenue per available guest (REVPAG) and lifetime value of guest (LVoG);
  - Providing better long-term planning by enabling hotels to calculate revenue per available room (REVPAR) by day of week and by market segment, as well as by distribution channel; and
  - Allowing hotels and restaurants to calculate the profits per market type or per distribution channel.

BASIC HOSPITALITY INDUSTRY PROGRAMS

There are basic systems for managing both individual hotels and restaurants. It is practically inconceivable to run a hotel or restaurant without at least a simple version of these systems. The basic systems presented here are precursors to more sophisticated and complex systems that will be discussed later and which hospitality controllers should investigate for their high ROI potential. Hospitality controllers should bear in mind that sometimes older systems, known as legacy systems, can be interfaced with modern systems as add-ons in a more cost-effective way than buying an entirely new package, although this would generally be true mostly for smaller properties and chains.

Property Management Systems

A property management system is the basic control system of a hotel. It enables guests to make reservations and check in and out. It records all guest transactions in hotel restaurants or any other hotel sales points, and, like a local customer relationship management system, the property management system records all guest activities for strategic marketing purposes. Furthermore, the system assists in the management of rooms by keeping track of the following information:

- Room number
- Type of room and its facilities
- Condition of the room or its facilities (e.g., clean or dirty)
- Guest preferences if a room is occupied
- Guest departure date

Finally, the system tracks other hotel facilities, including their condition and any maintenance requirements. For example, the heating, ventilating, and air-conditioning (HVAC) and the energy management system (EMS) are controlled by the property management system, enabling more efficient temperature control of the property, as well as the closing off of certain areas of the hotel in a slow season.

Fidelio (recently purchased by Micros), Springer-Miller, Visual One Systems, and Epicor offer hotel management programs. Links to these and other programs are provided in "Resources on the Web."

Point-of-Sale Systems

A property management system must include point-of-sale (POS) systems. POS systems record sales and post them to the guest ledger on a real-time basis. Thus, for example, even if a guest signs for breakfast and then immediately checks out, the bill will be instantly added to the guest's ledger by the time the guest checks out. Areas where a POS system is important include restaurants; hotel-owned stores; spa or recreational facilities sales; Internet, computer or printer-use-related charges; and in-room pay-per-view, minisafe, or room services (e.g., shoe shining, laundry, and meals).

POS terminals may be located in specific locations of a restaurant, but some establishments provide waiters with personal data assistants to take orders and transmit them wirelessly to the kitchen. Table computers are also used not only for order-taking, but also to provide detailed dietetic information concerning menu items and as temporary entertainment devices for guests waiting to be served. Leading POS system vendors are listed in "Resources on the Web" at the back of the book. (**Note:** The Micros site listed there contains case studies relating to the implementation of POS systems.)

A more advanced property management system should be able to interface with programs designed to enable managers to enhance the operational efficiency and strategic alignment of the hotel's functions. These systems will be discussed in a later section of this chapter.

Minibar Systems

Hotels with minibars in guest rooms require a minibar system to record sales and manage inventory and should be interfaced with its property management systems, such as CrunchTime! Information Systems' Minibar Manager contains bar-coding features that perform the following functions:

- Integrate seamlessly to room folios.
- Reduce time spent processing minibar transactions.
- Track product use on a room-by-room basis.
- Provide accurate accountability of staff (both time and product).
- Produce customizable reports detailing all minibar transactions.

Call Accounting Systems

The call accounting system keeps track of all guest use of a hotel's private branch exchange (PBX), although voice-over Internet protocol (VoIP) is gradually replacing the PBX system. A VoIP system is entirely computer-driven. These systems must also be interfaced with the property management system.

Other Property Management Support Systems

The introduction of plastic electronic room access keys enables the property management system to track the date and time that cards were used in each room and by whom (e.g., guest, room attendant, or maintenance personnel). The key code can also be easily and centrally changed through the property management system, thus enhancing guest security. In addition, if the hotel caters to groups or conventions, it may need to have a sales and catering system (SCS) interfaced with or incorporated into the property management system to keep track of catering functions and revenues.

Guest-Tracking Software

Guest-tracking software enables hotels to track guests from the moment they make a reservation to the end of their stay at the hotel. These programs have limitations, as they lack the ability to perform extensive analyses of guest patterns and provide information for use in encouraging repeat visits by guests. Customer relationship management programs, discussed later in this chapter, provide these additional services. A strong property management system will have guest-tracking capabilities incorporated into it.

Restaurant Management Systems

Similar to property management systems for hotels, restaurant management systems facilitate the performance of the mundane, day-to-day tasks involved in managing a restaurant. A restaurant's operations can be divided into (a) the front of the house: the dining and bar area; and (b) the back of the house: the kitchen and office area.

There are programs that help to enhance a guest's dining experience even before the guest arrives at the restaurant. The programs help manage guest reservations and then organize the assignment of tables based on guest preferences. Depending on its degree of sophistication, a restaurant management system may permit the accumulation of guest preferences over time, thus enabling the restaurant to remind guests of their previous preferences in order to offer them the same type of service. Using Internet services such as OpenTable to increase reservations is also an option with an appropriate restaurant management system.

Table management systems, which can be incorporated into restaurant management programs, allow the company to enter the location of all tables into the system. When customers are seated, their table identifier is input into the system, as well as the customers' ordering information, which enables the program to know the stage of each customer's meal (e.g., appetizer, entrée, or dessert). Thus, if a large group arrives that requires four tables, the program knows which four adjacent tables are most likely to be available and can give an approximate time for their availability. An example of table management software is ReServe Interactive (www.reserveinteractive.com).

A successful restaurant management system integrates the front of the house with the kitchen by creating a real-time environment that encompasses both the front of the house and kitchen seamlessly through instant communication. Thus, when a waiter takes an order and enters it in a POS terminal, the order becomes instantly visible to kitchen personnel, the manager, the host, and anyone else who might need the information to provide knowledgeable service to a guest. Rather than have individual POS stations, the trend is for waiters to use handheld POS tablets or leave the tablets in the hands of guests for personal use in addition to placing their orders.

A deeper level of integration between the front and back of the house is achievable through the use of programs that assist in menu planning. There are programs to help balance menu offerings dietetically, as well as to rank menu items according to their popularity. In addition, programs help classify menu items from the perspective of their gross profit on a single-item basis or based on the single-item gross profit combined with order volume. EatecNetX, by the Eatec Corporation, is an example of such a program.

To assist with kitchen functions, there are programs that help track inventory items, control inventory costs, and automate the reordering of certain items by interfacing with supply chain management programs.

A restaurant management system keeps track of all financial transactions, such as sales information, cost of sales, payroll, and inventory and supplies purchases. If the system does not have full-fledged accounting functionality, it may be able to interface with an accounting system in order to transfer the above information without double entries. Excel spreadsheets to aid in restaurant cost controls and functions are available at http://www.rrgconsulting.com. Sites to other restaurant management programs are provided in "Resources on the Web" at the back of the book.

Maximizing Revenues and Minimizing Costs

The ways in which property management and restaurant management programs, along with their POS terminals, help increase revenues and decrease costs include:

Sales-maximizing benefits:
- Enable the calculation and storing of sales statistics on a daily and seasonal basis, thus allowing for better planning for maximizing sales.
- Facilitate the analysis of customer or guest preferences with regard to services and/or products sold (calculations are all performed instantly), enabling better planning for maximizing sales.
- Because they are integrated with a property management, restaurant management, or other accounting system, POS systems facilitate the profit analysis of items and services sold, enabling better planning for maximizing profit.
- Decrease waiting time by transmitting information instantly to the kitchen and to every other person who needs the information, thereby maximizing guest satisfaction and return visits.
- Compare the dollar amounts sold by each employee, as well as which items are sold by each employee, enabling better focus of training in order to maximize sales.
- Maximize sales by preparing healthier menus and using this as a promotional tool.
- Interface the restaurant management system with Internet reservations services such as OpenTable.
- When coupled with table management software (TMS), the restaurant management system better utilizes tables by indicating tables that are not yet cleared or guests who have lingered longer than usual. In addition, it alerts employees to the need for a certain table for a proximate reservation arrival.

Cost-minimizing benefits:
- Diminish the probability of error by avoiding having to enter order or purchase information more than once, thereby reducing costs in the kitchen by allowing it to work more efficiently.
- Enable each transaction to be traced to an individual employee so that errors or theft can be minimized and traced through a comparison of cash totals by employee, thereby reducing losses and theft, as well as reducing verification costs.
- Reduce the required training time for employees, thereby reducing training costs.
- Because inventory levels change on a per-order basis, POS systems facilitate the reorder process by keeping track of consumption, thus saving employee time. For nonperishables, the reorder process can be automatic when interfaced with a supply chain management program.

- Analyze par stock levels (i.e., the minimum amount of each item that must be kept in inventory) in relation to volumes consumed, which can be changed quickly from one central location to another if necessary.

- Communicate information regarding out-of-stock items or other matters to the POS terminals instantly, which minimizes customer frustration and repeated order taking.

- Identify an employee who removes an item through inventory control programs, thus minimizing theft. It is estimated that more than 25% of all restaurant failures are due to employee theft.

- Alert the manager to the time delay between order taking and order serving or, in the case of take-out restaurants, order delivery to the counter or drive-by window, which minimizes costs and maximizes customer satisfaction.

PROGRAMS DESIGNED TO IMPROVE OPERATIONAL EFFICIENCY AND STRATEGIC ALIGNMENT

Information technology is shaping the hospitality industry, as hospitality companies are realizing the need to implement the latest IT into their functions to stay competitive. Calculations such as revenue per available guest (REVPAG) and lifetime value of guests (LVoG) cannot be made without the capabilities of data warehousing, data mining, and high-powered computers. The information cannot be applied on a systemwide geographical basis without the Internet and without the assistance of customer relationship management programs. POS computers are becoming increasingly sophisticated, with the introduction of the tablet computer that allows customers to enter their food orders at their tables or in their rooms.

In a pilot program, Intercontinental Hotel Group (IHG) adopted a Tablet PC using Windows XP and 802.11 wireless connectivity to provide menus for their hotel restaurants. The Tablet PC provides images, ingredients, and nutritional breakdown of each item. It has an adjustable font size for those with poor eyesight; it translates into multiple languages; and it keeps a running total for the bill during customer orders. The tablet can suggest menu items that are compatible with particular dietary requirements as well as wines that are compatible with the meal. In addition, menu items can be changed from the central computer to adjust for the time of day and to eliminate items that are sold out. The kitchen can also use the menu tablet to advertise daily specials. Guests can use the tablet to page a server or manager, entertain children, check their flight status, or send a document to a printer in the lobby of the hotel.

This investment not only provides cost savings; it also improves the guests' experience and enhances brand awareness and identification, thereby increasing the likelihood of guests returning. Guest satisfaction can be measured in real time through surveys that the guests can be invited to take on the tablet. It is estimated that this system will pay for itself if it fills one additional room every three nights or if it generates an additional four daily meals. A related case study, and other hospitality-related case studies, can be found at http://www.microsoft.com/industry/hospitality/casestudies.mspx.

Harrah's uses its data warehousing system and customer relationship management program to stratify its services based on the frequency of customer stays and other related factors. For instance, from the vast amount of information that a data warehouse holds and the data mining provided by a customer relationship management program, Harrah's has discovered that only about 5% of its customers generate 25% of its revenues. By identifying these customers, management can devise ways to encourage more frequent visits.

In response to the growing importance of IT in the hospitality industry, the American Hotel and Lodging Association, the Financial and Technology Professionals organization, and hotel companies such as Diplomat Hotels and Bass Hotels & Resorts are developing a set of standards—the Hospitality Information Technology Integration Standards (HITIS)—to enable hospitality industry-oriented programs to easily interface with each other. For instance, a property management system will be able to process signals from any brand of customer relationship management, POS, or other HITIS-compliant system.

SYSTEMS THAT INCREASE COMPETITIVE ADVANTAGE

IT can promote the proper functioning of key business processes and increase the productivity of labor and assets. Because IT is so intimately intertwined with revenue maximization and cost reduction, the major IT programs and systems for achieving these types of objectives are discussed here. Hospitality financial managers should be familiar with these programs and, if appropriate, encourage their companies to consider them as possible investments to enhance competitive advantage and provide more timely and accurate accounting and financial information.

Revenue Management Systems

Revenue management's goal is to maximize revenue. In the lodging industry, it means planning to sell every room in the hotel at its maximum rate to customers who will spend the maximum amount using the other services the hotel has to offer while the hotel spends as little as possible to acquire the customer. The hotel industry uses the REVPAG calculation, which enables revenue management programs to take a much broader approach in examining the amount of money certain categories of guests spend on dining, recreation (e.g., spa, golf, gaming, water sports, and excursions), and meeting and banquet services. The ideal room rate is then set based on a prospective guest category's total spending package and assigning higher-spending guest categories lower room rates. Casinos often grant free stays to guests who gamble in the casino—an extreme example of this rate-setting philosophy.

Revenue management systems use both historical and current data to forecast room occupancy for transients or conventions and set rates accordingly. The systems control allowed length of stay, room availability by category, and overbooking policies. As they accumulate information, the systems become familiar with a particular property's occupancy patterns. Revenue management systems can be connected to property management systems to automatically change room rates based on predicted patterns and changing conditions. Although these systems are automated, revenue is ultimately the responsibility of management. In hospitality companies where these revenue management positions exist, the general manager, the director of sales and marketing, and the revenue manager must work together to ensure the revenue management system is working properly.

Procedures that are currently being incorporated into revenue management programs include:

- Constantly and automatically reviewing changes in demand resulting from automatic occupancy and other sales data from a data bank or warehouse, as well as any data input manually that affects demand, such as special events or competitive changes.
- Forecasting future demand and allocating capacity to the most profitable customers.
- Determining the future mix of market segments and the average length of stay for each segment.
- Determining a guest's total value based on all guest purchases, not just room rates and lengths of stays.
- Calculating price elasticity based on past buying patterns.
- Predicting the impact of price changes on revenue, gross profit, and units sold.
- Providing simulation capacity to study the impact of proposed price changes.
- Providing alerts when certain pre-set parameters, such as forecast occupancy percentages, are violated.
- Providing market basket analysis, which is an indication of which services or products customers tend to buy together.
- Minimizing over-blocking of rooms to meet contractual requirements.

Some of the above procedures go beyond revenue management to yield management, discussed below. Nucleus Research (www.nucleusresearch.com) reports, "Companies using Manugistics revenue and profit optimization models for revenue management reported net revenue increases of 2.5 to 7.5%." Similar increases are claimed by other companies that sell revenue management services. It has been estimated that a company can recover its investment in installing a revenue management system in approximately 9 to 12 months.

Revenue Management Products. Because the major revenue management service providers are all ASPs whose programs reside on their own servers, these systems may require only a small investment in hardware. Most of the investment involves the time company personnel spend in educating the revenue management service provider concerning the characteristics of the hospitality company and tailor the system to these unique specifications, and then train company personnel to use the system. Three major revenue management service providers are listed in "Resources on the Web."

Channel Management. Channel management is a useful supplement to a revenue management system because it allows specific portions of inventory to be allocated to different channels according to their distribution characteristics, taking into account factors such as cost, markup, and type of customer targeted by each channel. The revenue management system can take these factors into account when it automatically establishes room rates for each distribution channel. Various channel markets include:

- Cross-selling among all the hotels or restaurants in a hospitality chain using a central reservation system and a single image inventory.
- Selling through a reservation system of an airline or other external hospitality entity.
- Selling through Internet sites—auction sites or unique market sites.
- Selling through travel agents.

To determine which channels to emphasize in their sales efforts, hospitality companies should consider their decisions from two points of view: (1) how the customer views the channel; and (2) what the channel distribution costs are.

Central Reservation Systems and Single-Image Inventory. Single-image inventory is another useful supplement to a revenue management system. It consists of a centralized inventory of all properties in a system, which enables the property's distribution channels to sell from a single optimized inventory using a central reservation system. This allows a revenue management system to deal with one single inventory, thus simplifying the program's rate-setting process and increasing input into the system of market conditions in different areas. Starwood Hotels uses a central reservation system to allow customers to book business meetings in any of their hotels online through its Web site: www.meetingsinamoment.com.

Yield Management. Revenue management is concerned with obtaining the highest possible rate per room or the highest possible profit per room by maximizing price in a rational manner, based on historical guest occupancy rates and spending patterns. Yield management is more concerned with protecting profit margins rather than only selling rooms. Revenue management might indicate that a 200-room hotel can be filled with lower-paying tourists. However, yield management would examine past history to determine if there is a high probability of selling 80 rooms at a higher rate to business travelers and then block off the sale of these rooms to those travelers, thereby maximizing revenue. For a hotel with a 10% profit margin, it is obvious that a 1% increase in revenue will create a 10% increase in net income.

On the other hand, assuming not all 80 rooms are sold to business travelers, yield management would make available these unsold rooms a few days ahead of occupancy so that they can be sold at auction sites based on the theory that some revenue is better than none.

Thus, yield management programs are activated when revenue management projections are not being met and there is expiring inventory to be sold. When a revenue management system delivers an alert that occupancy percentages are lower than projected, yield management calculates minimum room rates, examines unoccupied rooms, calculates probabilities of occupancy at different prices (perhaps using elasticity-of-demand calculations), and attempts to sell the rooms at a lower cost. Constraints can be established for the yield management system so that it will not sell these rooms in a way that will harm the brand image and formal pricing structure of the company. The two basic conditions under which yield management should be used are:

1. The existence of excess capacity that is not likely to be sold at regular prices.
2. The excess capacity that is sold in a market different from the regular profitable market of the hospitality company so that the lower prices will not harm the formal pricing structure.

For example, a hotel's revenue management system indicates that there will be 200 unoccupied rooms next weekend. The yield management system might then switch these rooms to the "no reservations" market segment and make them available to a cut-rate Internet site or an auction site, such as Priceline.com, at extremely low prices. The yield management approach attempts to sell rooms at the market rate when rooms cannot be sold at full value.

Because they take into account elasticity of demand factors, yield management programs do not always lower rates for last-minute sales. If market conditions change unexpectedly and demand is expected to be inelastic (e.g., demand is high and guests will pay any rate for a room), the yield management program will sense the increased demand through a rapid sales increase and will raise rates. For example, a yield management program would raise the rates of hotel rooms near a local airport that suddenly is closed due to prolonged unfavorable weather conditions.

Yield management systems are mainly beneficial for their ability to increase length of stay and thus smooth out demand by filling in the gaps between peek periods. In their rate-setting process, these systems compare the value of group business, including guest spending in all areas, to the transient guests that might be displaced by a larger group. In addition, they consider demand in "shoulder seasons" (i.e., the seasons immediately before and after peak seasons).

Yield management systems make hotel pricing much more consistent and less arbitrary among the various hotels in a chain. Major companies selling yield management products include the IdeaS product, E-Yield, which is a stand-alone product that forecasts demand by market segment, and Micros' Opus products, which can be integrated with a property management or sales and catering system to automatically retrieve information and change rates and prices in the system accordingly. Yield management programs can be used by hotels with at least 60 rooms to over 5,000 rooms. The major yield management service providers are all ASPs whose programs reside on their own servers. Links to yield management system sites are listed in "Resources on the Web."

Profit per Available Room. More sophisticated revenue management systems allow for the tracking of profit per available room (PROFPAR) in addition to REVPAR. Harrah's Casino, which is considered to have one of the most advanced and sophisticated revenue management systems, uses a Manugistics system to maximize PROFPAR. Although it is sold as part of a revenue management system, maximizing PROFPAR is actually the result of implementing a yield management approach because it takes into account the variable expenses incurred in selling one additional room or meal or rendering other hotel services.

Risks of Using Application Service Providers

Whenever a company uses the Internet or an intranet to obtain information or to transmit confidential guest data to a third party, such as an ASP, the following risks arise:

- The connection with the ASP server can be broken, causing damaging downtime.
- Information can fall into the hands of unscrupulous persons who are willing to use the information for illegal purposes (e.g., selling to the competition, identity theft).
- Information can be lost for other reasons.

Experience has shown that downtime risk has been minimal and not seriously disruptive. To protect against the other risks, companies transmit guest information in a generic manner without including any personal guest information, and they make appropriate backups of all information delivered by the ASP. In addition, some companies buy their own servers and place them with the ASP to be used exclusively for their own data, thus minimizing the risk of contamination with other ASP client data and of data theft because fewer workers will have access to the private server. When possible, a check calculation can be devised to monitor the hospitality company's data before they are transmitted to the ASP and after they are returned by the ASP.

Customer Relationship Management Systems

Most of the latest IT systems must work in conjunction with each other to exploit their full potential. However, the customer relationship management system has the greatest capacity to create competitive advantage. There systems began as simple contact databases used for tracking known sales prospects. In the 1990s, the systems took on additional responsibilities, such as making reservations electronically. Most recently, however, they have evolved into the front ends of huge data gathering and storing data warehouses. The systems make this information available to all interested parties using different levels of security clearance. Thus, guests become part of the hospitality organization and can input appropriate information, such as making online reservations, as well as access any information instantly, such as verifying that reservations are made correctly. In addition, guests can access and make appointments for various hotel services such as spa and fitness facilities. Back office information is also available to guests and employees regarding payments and billing, as well as invoices, letters, reservation requests, and emails. Managers can receive detailed information on each employee and guest interaction, including conversations, to ensure optimal service and guest satisfaction. If a hotel grants a concession to another company to run their parking operations, the hotel will be able to access information related to any damages and claims made by its guests against the parking concessionaire. Supply chain management systems (see below) can be interfaced so that suppliers will know what kind of demand their customer (the hotel) expects and be prepared to meet it.

Most important, the hotel can store guest preferences. For example, in the Miami Mandarin Oriental Hotel, if a dining guest requests no onions, the preference is input into the data warehouse so whenever that guest dines at a Mandarin Oriental Hotel anywhere in the world, that hotel will know the guest does not like onions. Guests can personalize their stay, a fact that reduces the importance of such revenue-draining incentives as price, location, and points programs. Because guest loyalty is greatly enhanced, the cost of implementing such a system should be partially offset by the reduced customer acquisition cost.

The customer relationship management system stores guests' histories with the hotel, thereby enabling a hotel to calculate data, such as incremental revenue per guest (as opposed to per room)—REVPAG and lifetime value of a guest—LVoG. This information enables hotels and restaurants to use their resources more efficiently by concentrating their sales effort on the 30% of guests who bring in 80% of the revenue.

Developers of customer relationship management programs include: Micros Systems, Inc.; Microsoft, Inc. (Business Solutions-CRM division); Siebel Systems, Inc.; SAP Corporation; and Oracle Corporation.

Supply Chain Management Systems

Supply chain management can optimize the timely delivery and quality of food and beverages to guests to minimize inventory cost. Supply chain management begins when food and beverages are supplied and ends when they are delivered to the customers. Other considerations include labor cost versus food cost (e.g., purchasing expensive, portion-packed foods that are sized and trimmed versus preparing foods in a warehouse or restaurant).

Advantages of an efficient supply chain management program include:
- Buying from the lowest-cost provider
- Reducing food theft, waste, and spoilage by reducing over-ordering
- Reducing food over-portioning
- Saving time in placing orders with distributors by using a direct interface with suppliers
- Using perpetual inventories to reduce inventory counting costs and increase inventory accuracy
- Reducing inventory levels by approximately 25% as a result of accurate, timely orders and deliveries

Supply chain management programs can cut food costs by approximately 3% to 4% of sales. Considering that food cost consumes approximately 35% to

40% of every food revenue dollar and that restaurant net incomes hover at around 10% to 15%, a savings equivalent to 1% of sales can amount to a 7% to 10% increase in net income. A well-known provider of supply chain management and other restaurant management systems is eRestaurant Services, Inc.

Data-Warehousing and Data-Mining Systems

A data warehouse is essentially a huge database or repository of very large amounts of information. Data warehouses can store hundreds of bits of information concerning each guest, such as room and food preferences, allergies, and travel patterns. The data is stored in data marts, which group specific categories of information. The information can then be passed on to a global distribution system, which makes it available to third-party programs such as centralized revenue management, yield management, central reservations, or customer relationship management systems.

Data mining involves delving into this mass of data to extract meaningful information, such as the average spending pattern of a guest per stay in a hotel or per visit to a restaurant. These third-party programs are designed to extract or mine all important information from a data warehouse through the use of their own proprietary algorithms, which they sell as revenue management, yield management, central reservation, or other business intelligence-generating services. Data warehouses do not require business intelligence to operate, since reporting tools can generate reports from data warehouses. However, the information mined from a data warehouse can be more useful and pertinent if it is passed through a business intelligence system.

For example, Carlson Hotels Worldwide inquires about which pricing strategy will increase marginal revenues from the top 15% of the millions of guests who have stayed at the company's hundreds of hotels. The huge capacity of a data warehouse can assist the company in obtaining this information, as it must collect data from hundreds of locations worldwide.

Data warehouse servers can be placed in a single location or they may be scattered worldwide and connected through an intranet or storage area network (SAN). Because the information transmitted to and from a data warehouse can often be corrupted and unreliable, it is important to adopt some form of data management strategy. Two companies that sell such services are listed in "Resources on the Web."

RTTs is a company that deals with the security and other issues involved in on-shore and off-shore outsourcing. Its Web site is www.rttsweb.com/outsourcing

Suggested data warehouse server and search engine providers include:

- Terradata, whose fastest double-server system with 750 billion bytes of storage capacity costs $1,100,000, is thought to be the most expensive.
- Microsoft SQL Server
- Oracle, Inc.
- Sybase, Inc.

- WhereScape (www.wherescape.com) is a leading source of enterprise-class data warehouse lifecycle management software for the design, construction, and operation of data warehouses, data marts, business intelligence environments, and decision support systems.

More information on data warehouse servers and data warehouse engine vendors can be found at www.information-management.com and in "Resources on the Web" at the back of the book.

Global Distribution Systems

Global distribution systems, which originally consisted of airline reservation centers, are currently used by hospitality companies to reach repeat and new customers. These systems include the data warehouse; the communications technology, such as WAN, Internet, or intranet; the programs for transmitting data to and extracting data from the data warehouse; the company's reaction to this information (its business strategy); and the employees who interact with this system and whose attributes can either defeat the system or render it a success. The design of the global distribution system determines how costly and how cost-effective it will be. In addition, a hospitality company may opt to sell its global distribution services to another hospitality company. Thus, the global distribution system can be both an internal and an external profit center.

A global distribution system should be used to:

- Build a database of information regarding guests, potential guests, or customers, and market conditions. Besides storing the history of successful sales, it can obtain information from queries made through the system based on their number, type, origin, and desired destination.

- Disseminate information concerning the hospitality company. The more upscale the company, the more detailed the information that will usually be required. High-priced hospitality companies tend to have more varied and unique characteristics, which must be transmitted to potential customers.

- Provide current and valid information concerning rooms and restaurant reservation availability. Preferably this will be through a single image inventory connected to a central reservations system.

Business Intelligence Programs

Most companies collect large amounts of data from their business operations. To keep track of this information, business intelligence programs store, access, and analyze the data in one location. Business intelligence programs usually require data warehousing to store the data, as well as a data mining system. One emerging system, called online applications processing (OLAP), quickly provides reports based on complex analytical queries. OLAP takes a snapshot of a relational database and restructures it into dimensional data against which queries can be run. For complex queries, OLAP can produce an answer in approximately 0.1% of the time for the same query on relational data. An OLAP structure created from the operational data is called an OLAP cube. For example, a set of customers can be grouped by city, by district, or by country. With 50 cities, 8 districts, and 2 countries, there are 3 hierarchical levels with 60 members. These customers can be considered in relation to products. Thus, if there are 250 products with 20 categories, 3 families, and 3 departments, then there are 276 product members. With just these 2 dimensions, there are 16,560 possible aggregations. As the data considered increase, the number of aggregations can quickly total tens of millions or more. These aggregations make up an OLAP cube. Further information on OLAP can be found at www.olapreport.com.

Business intelligence systems magnify the usefulness of the information obtained as a result of data mining by applying to it data rules engines, as well as statistical and other analytical techniques. Business intelligence systems can inform managers in the areas of customer profiling, customer support, market and industry research, market segmentation, product profitability, statistical analysis, competitor analysis, and inventory and distribution analysis. The systems assist hospitality managers in making better decisions by assessing the business environment and providing managers with accurate, relevant, and timely information as needed. A hospitality business should organize and apply its business intelligence system to give the business a sustainable competitive advantage, thus possibly becoming one of its core competencies.

Business intelligence systems gather information from internal business sources, which assist managers in evaluating performance. In addition, these systems gather information from external sources, which may include customer needs; customer decision-making processes; the competition and competitive pressures; conditions in relevant industries; and general economic, technological, and cultural trends.

A business intelligence system can be directed to support one or more organizational goals of the hospitality company, which may be based on a vision statement and may involve maximizing quarterly results on a short-term basis and maximizing shareholder value, market share, and company size on a long-term basis.

The implementation of business intelligence can be extremely expensive, such as the time and labor costs. Prices vary widely between high- and low-end systems, and there are companies that provide this service on an outsourced basis, which enables a hospitality company to use a business intelligence system without having an IT department. Some outsource services allow the application of payments toward the future ownership of the business intelligence system.

Business Performance Management Systems

Business performance management systems analyze not only data, but business procedures such as planning and forecasting. These systems assist companies in implementing the most efficient use of human and material resources for optimum performance. It is integrated software that enables consolidation, planning, forecasting, budgeting, reporting, analysis, and dashboard creation. Key performance indicators such as budget accuracy, customer service levels, and market forecast accuracy can be incorporated into these systems. The indicators may also be used for establishing performance goals for management use.

Other Strategic Planning Computer Systems

There are other systems with more limited goals that might be useful to hospitality companies that cannot afford the implementation of more comprehensive systems.

Business Process Integration Systems. Business process integration or business process management refers to a set of activities that companies can perform to optimize individual or selected business processes, as opposed to the comprehensive process of analyzing and integrating all data that is offered by business process management systems. These activities are usually implemented through specific software tools; thus the term *business process integration* is often used synonymously to refer to the software tools themselves. These software programs allow for the direct implementation of business processes without having to develop in-house software. In addition, the programs report on the effectiveness of the business processes, thereby enabling management to analyze performance and make any necessary changes. Using these new programs, the modified processes can easily be made operational.

Business process integration includes or is included in other performance evaluation paradigms, such as Total Quality Management, Six Sigma, Performance Management, and Balanced Scorecard. While business process reengineering deals with piecemeal changes to the company, business process management incorporates the process of change through analysis seamlessly into the company by facilitating the monitoring and reengineering of the processes themselves. Some business process integration allows for the simulation of processes in order to test them before they are implemented.

The business process management system category of software is developed to allow a business process to be defined in computer language so that it can be executed by the computer. The computer either uses services in connected applications to perform business operations (e.g., calculating a repayment plan for a loan) or sends messages to employees requesting them to perform certain tasks that cannot be well automated. In order to work effectively, the system often requires that the underlying software be constructed according to the principles of a service-oriented architecture, making the system a difficult feature to integrate into existing legacy systems.

A business process management system enables process monitoring by tracking individual processes and providing statistics on the performance of one or more processes. For example, the system will track the status of a reservation, the stage of a guest's stay at a hotel, or the payment status of that guest so problems can be identified and corrected. In addition, this information can be used to work with suppliers and better serve customers. Although such functions may be currently performed by other applications, the use of a business process management system is expected to ease the development of such monitoring and reporting. Business process management is regarded as the crucial backbone of enterprise content management.

Enterprise Application Integration. Enterprise application integration is the use of software and architectural principles to integrate enterprise-wide computer applications. Widely used since 2004, enterprise application integration is used not only to share data between applications but to share business processes. It is viewed as being necessary for the efficient exploitation of business applications such as customer relationship management and supply chain management. Newer enterprise application integration technologies involve using Web services to integrate service-oriented architecture.

Enterprise application integration prevents computer systems from working in their own "silos," thereby potentially decreasing the value of individual systems. Integration must be carried out with a formal enterprise application integration strategy to prevent excessive point-to-point connections in an organization, resulting in a difficult-to-maintain system often referred to as "spaghetti." The number of connections needed to have adequately integrated point-to-point connections is $[n(n-1)]/2$. To integrate five applications on a point-to-point basis, $(5\times4)/2=10$ point-to-point connections are required. Each enterprise application is connected to a bus. This facilitates evolution, makes it highly scalable, and makes investment in such a system unlikely to become a "sunk" cost. Calculating ROI for such a system is easier now that the benefits of customer relationship management and supply chain management programs are more readily identifiable and quantifiable.

An Internet reference site for enterprise application integration is eai.ittoolbox.com.

Enterprise Resource Planning. Enterprise resource planning systems integrate data from the different departments of a hospitality company, such as accounting and marketing information, and permit all appropriate employees access to this information. These systems can be incorporated into a business process management system; however, they are specially tailored to provide information to middle- and upper-level executives to assist them in making strategic decisions. Recently, factors that can influence management decisions, such as the economy, are being incorporated into enterprise resource planning systems. They are being programmed to automatically access sites where such information is available and use artificial intelligence to weigh its impact, based on historical data, before presenting recommendations to management.

The benefits that can be derived from an enterprise resource planning system include:

- Organization-wide access of appropriate personnel to all information pertinent to their job functions, resulting in better decision-making potential. The system allows management to consolidate all pertinent information for consideration when making decisions. Recent developments may result in the system actually making recommendations.
- Lower recordkeeping and accounting costs by avoiding duplication of entries.
- Less equipment investment by avoiding duplication of equipment.
- Facilitation of customer interaction with the hospitality company.

- More individual treatment of customers (customers' likes and dislikes can be entered into the system and made known to all personnel who may come in contact with them).

All of the above lead to lower costs, greater sales volume (market share) due to higher customer satisfaction and greater dollar sales due to less need for discounting. In other words, they lead to higher profits. A seller of enterprise resource planning systems can be found at www.exact.com.

Decision Support Software. Decision support software (DSS) systems provide a front-end interface with the systems that gather and store data. DSS systems can be programmed to provide data in a format desired by management so that it is transformed into understandable information. The function of DSS is to support operations, financial management, and strategic decision making. Increasingly, this type of program is being incorporated into property and restaurant management systems and other programs designed to aid in hospitality management. Various types of DSS and its functions are listed as follows:

- *Passive DSS*—Presents the desired information in the desired format.
- *Active DSS*—Goes one step further by using the data to present management with specific suggested decisions.
- *Cooperative DSS*—Allows a hospitality executive to modify any decision suggestions by interacting with the DSS.
- *Data-Driven DSS*—Uses both stored and external historical data pertinent to the hospitality company.
- *Document-Driven DSS*—Uses stored information to fill in various predefined documents.
- *Model-Driven DSS*—Uses stored financial, statistical, or simulation models.
- *Knowledge-Driven DSS*—Provides information based on stored facts and rules.
- *Web-Based DSS*—Uses a Web browser, such as Internet Explorer, that accesses the Internet or a corporate intranet.
- *Simulation-Based DSS*—Helps managers make decisions through simulation analysis.
- *Communication-Driven DSS*—Allows more than one person to access and discuss the same data. Examples of this type of DSS are Microsoft's "Net-Meeting" and "Groove."

Executive Information Systems. An executive information system is a specific form of DSS that presents in a more graphical format the information required by management to make decisions. In the hospitality industry lower-level managers, such as department managers, generally use numerical information, such as number of occupied rooms, rooms being cleaned, and table turnover. Mid-level managers, such as the hotel manager, use both numerical and graphical information. While specific numbers are important, they also need to have a quickly analyzed and absorbed overview of a property's operations, which is best presented graphically. Upper-level managers, those at corporate headquarters, and divisional or regional managers rely on graphical information to the greatest extent because it provides an overall picture of the strategic position of the company and its operational status in the marketplace, financially, and compliance-wise. These managers do not have time to review the vast numerical, financial, and accounting data generated by a hospitality company and so must rely on graphical information to call their attention to those areas that require it. Executive information systems are usually used in conjunction with a data warehouse, which enables managers to penetrate several levels of detail if warranted.

Asset Management Systems. Asset management systems are used to obtain the maximum benefit from a hospitality company's physical assets through maintenance and repair and maximum utilization. These systems can assist in properly maintaining accounting records concerning the assets of the company (recording the purchase, depreciation, or sale of these assets) or capitalizing a company's IT assets through an asset register that indicates the location and value of IT assets (an asset register describes the IT infrastructure). It can also include a configuration management system that indicates how the IT assets work together.

An asset management system enables a hospitality company to analyze how well or poorly it is using its IT assets, where it needs additional investment, and where it may have over-invested, resulting in under-utilized IT assets. The annual cost of supporting and maintaining a corporate desktop computer is approximately $8,000. A good asset management system can save approximately 10% of this cost by aligning its IT structure with its strategic objectives more clearly. Thus, a good asset management system should be part of a hospitality company's financial strategic plan.

An asset management system has features that:
- Track all physical IT assets.
- Monitor the maintenance and repair history of IT assets.
- Track assets without performing a visual physical inventory.
- Record the use of individual computers.
- Monitor available disk space and its location.
- Monitor available memory and its location.
- Monitor licensing use and compliance with license terms.
- Monitor the use of leased assets and compliance with lease terms.
- Track operating systems in use.
- Track various applications programs in use.
- Perform analysis of idle capacity, projected demand growth for IT capacity, and cost when combined with a business integration program.
- Incorporate the current market value of systems owned into any cost-benefit analysis.

If integrated with a configuration management system, any bottlenecks that are slowing down the entire IT infrastructure can be detected, and the cost benefit of remedying these situations can be easily calculated. Further information concerning IT systems can be obtained at www.cio.com or www.bitpipe.com.

CALCULATING ROI AND THE PURCHASING PROCESS

Computers are becoming the backbone of the hospitality industry business. They must be considered an investment that will increase revenue and decrease expenses, and an attempt must be made to measure the return provided by these additional revenues and savings. This is not always easy to do because, as mentioned earlier, it is difficult to measure certain benefits, such as the impact on revenue of increased customer satisfaction.

Calculating ROI for Investments in IT

The approach to calculating ROI for IT investments should include estimating the value received in one or more of the areas listed below. Consideration should also be given to the potential cost of not making the investment (e.g., costs such as risks of business interruption, obsolescence, and competition).

1. *Cost savings*. Will it save labor or energy?
2. *Revenue augmentation*. Will it increase revenue directly by introducing a new chargeable service, or will it better align a business process with the company's strategic goals and thereby indirectly increase sales?
3. *Productivity*. Will it enhance productivity by allowing the company to render existing services better or faster, thereby improving its image or brand, although these services will not increase revenue directly? Will it increase the speed of an existing process, enabling greater output at the same cost?
4. *Business impact*. Will it augment the benefits of business management systems, such as central reservation management, or does it prepare the business to better withstand disruptions in its IT infrastructure? Will it create or increase a barrier to entry for the competition?
5. *Security*. Does it increase security of business data or guest information during storage and transmission?

Because of the elusive and tenuous nature of some of the benefits obtained from investment in IT, it is sometimes difficult to put a dollar value on these benefits for purposes of calculating a quantifiable return.

To attempt to overcome this problem, the questions in Exhibit 4-1, "Considerations to Be Made Prior to Investing in IT-Related Assets," should be answered, and the measuring process should be broken down into the basic components involved in the particular business process being considered. The result should be:

- A list of the alternatives. (Note that not making the investment is an alternative.) After taking into account the following considerations, rank them from highest to lowest ROI.

- A list of tangible revenue increases and cost savings for each alternative (to which a dollar value can be assigned), including an evaluation of the probability of achieving these revenue increases or cost savings.
- A list of the intangible business improvement benefits of each alternative, including an evaluation of the probability of achieving these results.
- A list of the investment costs and annual operating costs related to each alternative.

Exhibit 4-1: Considerations to Be Made Prior to Investing in IT-Related Assets

1. **Have the following costs of the investment been taken into account?**
    a. Purchase costs
    b. Financing costs
    c. Transportation costs
    d. Site modification costs
    e. Installation costs
    f. Transition downtime costs or loss of revenue
    g. Time spent by company personnel in educating the service provider concerning the unique characteristics of their hospitality company
    h. Training costs
    i. Consulting costs
    j. Cost of interfacing with existing legacy or nonlegacy systems
    k. Costs of converting any existing data

2. **Have the following potential tax savings related to this investment been considered?**
    a. Are all deductible expenses included in the ROI calculations?
    b. Have all tax credits and tax deductions been included in the ROI calculations?
    c. Have other tax considerations, such as local and sales taxes, been considered?
    d. If dealing with multinational companies, in what country should the investment be made to obtain the greatest tax benefits?
    e. Should this asset be leased or purchased?
    f. If the asset is leased, is it better to structure the lease terms as an operating lease or capital lease?

3. **Has the process affected by this investment been reduced to its minimum component to facilitate the calculation of ROI?**

    For example, assume that consideration is being given to purchasing a remote order-taking terminal for waiters. A study should be made to determine how much time they devote per table. Assume the study reveals that they devote 30 minutes to a table, including taking an order, serving food, water, and other items, and then cleaning up the table.

4. **What is the cost per minimum service component?**

   The study further reveals that waiters spend 10 minutes on average taking an order without the remote terminal, and 2 minutes explaining the use of the remote terminal on average to all guests, both first-time and repeat guests (most of whom will not need an explanation).

5. **What is the saving per minimum service component?**

   Assume further that a waiter is assigned to five tables. Using the remote terminal will result in an approximate time saving of 8 minutes times 5 tables, or 40 minutes. Thus the waiter would be able to wait on an additional table as a result of this investment. The waiter cost per table would be reduced from 20% of the waiter's wages to 16-2/3% of his or her wages (100%/6 tables).

6. **What is the additional revenue per minimum service component?**

   Is this investment going to be used merely to reduce waiter labor cost or is it going to reduce a labor bottleneck? In the latter case the implication is that there is sufficient demand so that in addition to the cost savings, additional revenue will be generated from serving an additional customer. This should be factored in based on statistical forecasting of the probability of obtaining the additional customer.

7. **What is the total return that will be created for the business as a whole?**

   By applying this calculation to the entire organization, the total return, both in savings and additional revenue, can be calculated and related to the cost of the investment. To aid in the calculation, a grid of the entire organization can be visualized. This grid might indicate the departments that will be affected by the acquisition, whether an existing IT system is in place, whether the existing system will be replaced, or whether only a new interface will be required. A simplified example of such a grid is presented here:

Exhibit 4-1 Considerations to Be Made Prior to Investing in IT-Related Assets

	Existing System in Place	First-Time Installation Required	Change required: Change Existing System	Only New Interface Required	Area of Conceptual Impact	Detailed Specifications
Rooms:						
Front office						
Concierge	Yes	Yes			Strategic alignment of operational process	New terminal required
Housekeeping						
Reservations						
Engineering						
Food department						
Beverage department						
Gift shops						
Human resources						
Finance:						
Accounting						
Internal control						

	Existing System in Place	Change required:			Area of Conceptual Impact	Detailed Specifications
		First-Time Installation Required	Change Existing System	Only New Interface Required		
Regulatory and contractual compliance						
Information technology and management decision support:						
Data processing						
Data warehousing and data mining	Yes			Yes	Operational process	Capture guest reception preferences
Customer relations management	Yes		Yes		Strategic alignment	Modify program to output guest preferences

Note: A similar spreadsheet can be developed on a property-by-property basis, listing the possible IT improvements in the vertical column and the properties horizontally.

8. **What intangible value will be created for the customer and consequently for the business?**

   In addition to the immediate increase in customer count that may be generated as a result of pent-up demand, this investment may bring another benefit to the business: the enhancement of its image or brand identity. This should be taken into account as a long-term benefit superimposed on, and added to, the short-term benefits of the investment.

The ROI calculation should be made on a time-adjusted cash flow basis, as well as on the accrual basis in order to offset, with a potentially high initial cash flow, the negative impact that initial accrual losses may have when evaluating the investment. "Resources on the Web" contains a link to a site, and a list of topics covered, where further information on investment in IT is available.

The IT Asset Purchasing Process

The purchasing process for IT-related assets requires several steps, each of which must be thoroughly analyzed and developed. The steps are as follows:

1. A set of requirement specifications must first be developed. These specifications will later be incorporated in a request for proposal (RFP). The specifications should be developed as follows:

   a. In sufficient detail to avoid confusion in the bids and should include:

      (1) Technical requirements

      (2) Delivery time frame

      (3) Request for costs in relation to the delivery time frame

   b. With consensus among all the affected departments of the organization. This is of the utmost importance because an unrepresented department will tend to sabotage any choice.

   c. With the approval of the CEO and CFO.

   A poorly developed specification set wastes the time not only of bidding suppliers, but also of the purchaser in terms of time spent dealing with suppliers prior to the realization that the bids do not supply the company's real needs in addition to the time spent to reconstruct a corrected set of requirement specifications. It is better to construct a proposal correctly the first time than to deconstruct and reconstruct a poorly written set of specifications. The possibility of hiring a consultant to assist in the preparation of the specifications should be considered.

   The specifications should be based on a conceptual set of requirements. This concept should be the result of answering the question "What do I want this system to do for my organization?" When a satisfactory answer to this question has been obtained, it must be translated into the physical components required to produce the desired results.

   In developing the specifications, the possibility of using or interfacing with legacy systems already in place should be considered.

2. Once the requirement specifications have been developed, an RFP should be created so that various purchase options may be compared. The RFP should contain the requirement specifications in sufficient detail to enable vendors to submit bids for software, hardware, IT services, or a combination of these items.

3. Create a list of all possible vendors of such systems.

4. Research the vendors, their capabilities, and their past service records. If possible, create a hypothetical scenario with which each vendor can demonstrate its system. Research the latest developments in the field and read financial analysts' reports on the company. In addition to giving an updated picture of the industry segment as a whole and of the individual vendors being considered, these reports often include the names of comparable competitors that the company might have missed. From this research a short list of vendors can be developed.

5. After sending the RFPs and receiving the proposals, study them in depth. The company should follow up on any additional references provided, verify information, and, if possible, request a demonstration or other evidence that the service provider has the integrity and ability to follow through on its proposal prior to making a final choice. The upkeep cost of all systems should be a major factor in the decision.

PART II

FINANCIAL STATEMENT REPORTING

CHAPTER 5
THE FINANCIAL REPORTING SYSTEM

CONTENTS

The Financial Reporting System	5001
General Principles and Measurement Rules	5002
The Financial Accounting Standards Board	5002
The Securities Exchange Commission	5004
The Securities Act of 1933	5004
The Securities Act of 1934	5004
Annual Reports to Hospitality Shareholders	5005
Hospitality Financial Statements	5006
Notes to the Hospitality Financial Statements	5006
Management Discussion of Financial Condition and Results of Operations	5007
Auditor's Report	5007
The Uniform System of Accounts	5007
Internal Reports	5008
Prospective Financial Statements	5008

Hospitality companies issue financial statements and other accounting reports to communicate to internal and external users the operating performance and financial health of the business. The financial manager is fully accountable for the form and content of the financial statements. In the case of publicly held companies, section 302 of the Sarbanes-Oxley Act of 2002 (SOX) contains provisions requiring chief executive officers (CEOs) and chief financial officers (CFOs) to certify that to the best of their knowledge the financial statements are accurate.

The financial manager has the ultimate responsibility for choosing accounting methods, gathering accounting data, and preparing the company's financial statements. Collectively, the financial statements and footnotes are intended to provide relevant, reliable, and timely information essential for making investment and credit decisions. The most important sources of information for managerial decision making are found in the financial statements and other internal accounting reports.

THE FINANCIAL REPORTING SYSTEM

The primary goal in financial reporting is the preparation of financial statements that present in a clear and straightforward manner the profitability and financial position of the hospitality company. The financial statements and other data generated by the financial reporting system can help management, creditors, investors, and others to assess the performance of the hospitality entity and its future direction.

The most common form in which financial and operating information is available is the set of financial statements issued under guidelines of the FASB. In the United States, the SEC governs these guidelines in the case of companies whose securities are publicly traded. As an agency of the federal government, the SEC has the ultimate legal authority to set accounting principles. Although the SEC has delegated most of its responsibility to the FASB, in recent years the SEC has enacted its own requirements as part of SOX. The financial statements are prepared according to GAAP. They usually contain balance sheets as of a given date, income statements for given periods, and cash flow statements for the same periods. A special statement highlighting changes in stockholders' equity on the balance sheet is usually provided as well.

General Principles and Measurement Rules

Generally accepted accounting principles determine the valuation and measurement methods used in financial statement reporting. The financial statements recognize events and transactions meeting certain criteria. Under accrual accounting, for instance, revenues are recognized when services are rendered by the hospitality company (e.g., sale of rooms), and expenses are reported as services are used rather than when cash is collected or paid by the hotel or restaurant. Accrual accounting is based on the matching concept, which states that expenses incurred by the hospitality company must be matched against the revenues they help to generate.

Financial statements are prepared using a monetary unit of measurement, (e.g., the U.S. dollar). Assets are normally reported at historical cost unless there is evidence that cost cannot be recovered. In those cases, relying on conservatism, hospitality companies must provide for possible losses by reporting assets at their lowest possible value on the balance sheet.

Financial reporting also relies on the going-concern assumption, which states that, unless there is evidence to the contrary, the hospitality company will continue operations for an indefinite period of time. Based on this assumption, the hotel building is depreciated over its estimated useful life rather than at its disposal value.

In evaluating whether financial reports of hospitality entities are reliable and relevant, they must adhere to two additional conventions: materiality and consistency. Materiality is an accounting convention that states that only significant information should be considered in financial reporting. Consistency requires that similar events should be subject to the same accounting treatment by the hospitality company from period to period.

The Financial Accounting Standards Board

The FASB is an independent body with seven full-time members. The Board sets accounting standards for all hospitality companies issuing audited financial statements. Such standards are essential to the efficient functioning of the economy because investors, creditors, and others rely heavily on credible, reliable, and comparable financial information.

Chapter 5: The Financial Reporting System 5003

Because the SEC recognizes FASB statements as authoritative, there is only one body of GAAP applicable to the United States. There are a few instances in which private companies are exempted from certain FASB requirements. A case in point is the disclosure of earnings per share on the income statement.

Before issuing a new pronouncement, the FASB often works with a task force composed of public accountants, university professors, business executives, regulators, and financial analysts. After public comments are received and hearings held, the FASB staff prepares an exposure draft for public comment.

Until 1973, GAAP were heavily influenced by the Accounting Principles Board (APB), which was part of the AICPA. Since 1973, the FASB has been the designated organization in the private sector for establishing standards of financial accounting and reporting. All opinions, research studies, and statements enacted by the APB and the FASB were considered to have authoritative support unless they were superseded by a subsequent FASB pronouncement. The FASB is constantly responding to new accounting problems as they arise by amending and expanding the body of GAAP.

On July 1, 2009, the FASB released the authoritative version of the FASB Accounting Standards Codification™ (ASC) as the single source of authoritative nongovernmental GAAP. FASB ASC is a major restructuring of accounting and reporting standards designed to simplify user access to all authoritative GAAP by providing the authoritative literature in a topically organized structure. Accordingly, the ASC became the single source of authoritative GAAP, superseding existing FASB, AICPA, Emerging Issues Task Force, and related literature. All other accounting literature not included in the Codification is nonauthoritative. The Codification became effective for interim and annual periods ending after September 15, 2009.

It is important to note that the Codification does not change GAAP. Instead, it introduces a new structure—one that is organized into a user-friendly online research system. It reorganizes the thousands of U.S. GAAP pronouncements into approximately 90 topics and displays all topics using a consistent structure. The codification content is arranged within (a) Topics, (b) Subtopics, (c) Sections, and (d) Subsections. The FASB developed a hybrid classification system for the Codification where XXX = Topic, YY = Subtopic, ZZ = Section and PP = Paragraph.

Topics represent a collection of related guidance and correlate to standards issued by the International Accounting Standards Board (IASB). They reside in four main areas: Presentation, Financial Statement Accounts, Broad Transactions, and Industries (e.g., Airlines, Real Estate); below the topic level are subtopics sections and subsections. Subtopics represent subsets of a Topic and are generally distinguished by type and by scope. Sections represent the nature of the content in a Subtopic such as measurement and disclosure. Sections are further broken down into Subsections, Paragraphs and Subparagraphs. For example,

- Topics-FASB ASC 805 to access Business Combinations
- Subtopics-FASB ASC 805-10 to access the Overall Subtopic
- Sections- FASB ASC 805-10-15 to access the Scope Section

- Paragraph-FASB ASC 805-10-15-2 to access paragraph 2 of Section 805-10-15

Effective July 1, 2009, changes to the FASB Accounting Standards Codification™ are communicated through an Accounting Standards Update. Updates are now published for all authoritative U.S. GAAP promulgated by the FASB, as well as for amendments to the SEC content in the FASB Codification and for editorial changes.

The Securities Exchange Commission

The SEC was established to protect investors by providing them with full and fair disclosure of financial information needed to make investment decisions. The major responsibility of the SEC is to ensure enforcement of the Securities Act of 1933 and the Securities Act of 1934. As previously mentioned, SOX has also strengthened the SEC's disclosure rules.

In addition to annual reports submitted to its shareholders, the SEC requires a publicly held hospitality company to file annually a 10-K report, which is a more detailed document used by regulators, institutional investors, and analysts to make decisions concerning publicly held hospitality companies.

The accounting rules of the SEC are enumerated in articles 3A through 12 of Regulation S-X, Financial Reporting Releases (FRRs), Accounting and Audit Enforcement Releases (AAERs), and Industry Guides.

To enhance the value of the Codification for public companies, relevant portions of authorative content issued by the SEC, and selected staff interpretations and administrative guidance have been included for reference in the FASB Accounting Standards Codification™ (e.g., Regulation S-X, Financial Reporting Releases, Interpretive Releases (IR) and SEC Staff Observer Comments). Nonetheless, the Codification does not include content related to matters outside the basic financial statements, such as Management's Discussion and Analysis.

The Securities Act of 1933

The Securities Act of 1933 was intended to protect investors from deceptive activity following the 1929 stock market crash. It requires a hospitality company to file a registration statement with the SEC before offering securities to the public. The SEC has exempted small offerings, securities of government units, private securities, and certain other securities from the provisions of the Act. The registration statement, which is provided in a prospectus to potential investors, includes financial statements and a number of disclosures about the registrant and the securities being offered. Its main goal is to prevent misrepresentation and other misleading activity in the sale of securities by hospitality (and other) companies.

The Securities Act of 1934

The Securities Act of 1934 was designed to regulate the subsequent trading of securities in secondary markets. It also requires disclosure of information concerning securities, and prohibits fraudulent practices and establishes regulations of market participants. The Act extended disclosure requirements to all hospitality companies whose securities are publicly traded on stock exchanges or over the counter. As noted earlier, publicly held hospitality companies are required to file periodic reports with the SEC. The annual Form 10-K and the quarterly Form 10-Q are the most common types of reports required by the 1934 Act. The information included in these reports is generally available to the general public.

10-K Report. The Form 10-K is an annual report that publicly held companies must file annually with the SEC. It is due three months following the end of the hospitality company's fiscal year. SEC Regulation S-X governs the form and content of the financial statements included in Form 10-K, which are audited. This form contains more detailed information than other financial statements distributed by hospitality companies to their shareholders. For example, Form 10-K must include information on the market for the holders of common stock and related securities, including high and low stock prices and frequency and amount of dividends. In addition, the form must include disclosure of foreign and domestic components of pre-tax income if it is deemed material to the hospitality reporting entity.

10-Q Report. The SEC requires that publicly held hospitality companies file a quarterly report (Form 10-Q) 45 days following the end of the quarter. This quarterly report, which is not required for the last quarter of the year, includes far less information than the annual reports filed with the SEC on Form 10-K. Form 10-Q comprises unaudited financial statements and a management discussion and analysis section. Although it is not as reliable and complete as the 10-K report, Form 10-Q contains the most recent information about the hospitality company's financial and operating performance.

ANNUAL REPORTS TO HOSPITALITY SHAREHOLDERS

In addition to complying with SEC reporting requirements, every publicly traded hospitality company must issue an annual report to its shareholders. Two types of information are given in the annual report: first, there is a section often presented as a letter from the president and/or chairman of the board of the company that contains a statement about the company's results from the previous year and about prospects for the future. The annual report also provides a financial statement section where the balance sheet, income statement, statement of shareholders' equity, and statement of cash flow are presented along with appropriate footnotes.

In addition, hospitality companies provide quarterly reports to their shareholders. These reports are unaudited and less comprehensive than annual reports; however, the quarterly reports include the most recent information available about the company.

In the recent past, a number of large hospitality companies have turned their annual reports into flashy management platforms in which glossy pictures of restaurants and hotels are shown in order to present their companies in the best possible light. Although the financial section is still the sole responsibility of the

CFO, the director of public relations is in charge of producing this type of annual report.

Hospitality Financial Statements

Financial statements and their accompanying notes contain a wealth of useful information regarding the company's financial position, the success of its operations, the policies and strategies of management, and insight into its future performance. Financial statements report the hospitality company's position at a specific time, as well as the results of its operations over a past period of time. The real value of financial statements is that they can be used to predict the company's future earnings and dividends, which is useful information for the investor. From a management standpoint the analysis is useful for anticipating future conditions and planning actions that will influence the future course of events.

A corporate annual report consists of three basic financial statements:

1. The balance sheet shows the financial position of the hospitality company at a point in time. It represents a snapshot of the assets the company owns, such as hotel buildings, and all the claims against those assets in the form of liabilities (e.g., mortgages payable) and shareholders' equity (e.g., common stock).

2. The income statement presents the results of operation for a specific period of time. It includes revenues (e.g., room sales), expenses (e.g., cost of food sold), gains or losses, and the resulting net income or net loss.

3. The statement of cash flows provides information about cash inflows and outflows from operating (e.g., collection of accounts receivables), financing (e.g., issuance of common stock or debt), and investing activities (e.g., purchase of restaurant chain) during the accounting period.

In addition, annual reports include a statement of stockholders' equity. This statement reconciles the beginning and ending balances of all accounts that appear in the stockholders' equity section of the hospitality company's balance sheet.

Notes to the Hospitality Financial Statements

Immediately following the financial statements is the "Notes to the Financial Statements" section. Also referred to as footnotes, the notes are governed by the basic accounting principle of full disclosure. This principle requires the disclosure of all facts that might influence the decision-making process of a financial statement user. The notes are, in fact, an integral part of the hospitality financial statements and must be read to acquire a full understanding of the information included in the financial statements. Additional coverage of financial statement disclosures is provided in Chapter 9, "Financial Statement Disclosures."

Management Discussion of Financial Condition and Results of Operations

The SEC requires that a hospitality company include in its annual report a section about favorable and unfavorable trends in the areas of liquidity, capital resources, and results of operations. This "Management Discussion and Analysis" section also provides information about future events and trends that might affect future business operations of the hospitality company.

Auditor's Report

Management has full responsibility for the preparation and integrity of the hospitality financial statements, including the footnotes. The accounting firm or independent auditor is charged with examining the company's financial statements and rendering an opinion as to whether the statements fairly present the hospitality company's financial results. The auditor's letter report attests to the fairness of the presentation of the financial statements and is included in the hospitality company's annual report to its shareholders.

THE UNIFORM SYSTEM OF ACCOUNTS

In preparing financial statements for internal purposes, most hospitality organizations use a uniform system of accounts appropriate for their particular segment of the industry. These uniform systems of accounts, which have been developed for lodging properties, clubs, and restaurants, are available from the American Hotel and Lodging Association, the National Restaurant Association, and the Club Management Association of America. The Hotel Association of New York City developed the original Uniform System of Accounts for the Lodging Industry (USAL) in 1925. The USAL (previously known as the Uniform System of Accounts for Hotels) was adopted by the American Hotel and Lodging Association and has been updated on several occasions to keep it current. The USAL is widely used throughout the lodging industry and has served as the basis for formulating other uniform systems in various segments of the hospitality industry. The system was designed for classifying and presenting financial information so that uniformity prevails to facilitate comparability among lodging properties.

An additional feature of the appropriate uniform system is the ability of interest groups and associations to compile industrywide statistics and results, information that can be collected on a regional, national, or international basis from similar organizations within the industry. This makes possible the development of industry averages, which can then be used to compare a hotel's or restaurant's information with the performance of the industry overall. By analyzing these systems of accounts and determining where variances exist and then examining the causes, managers of individual hospitality properties can decide what type of corrective action is required, if any.

The uniform systems of accounts are also excellent tools that give high priority to management's need for information on which to base operating judgments. These systems are fairly flexible and are easily adapted to the needs of individual properties. However, it is important to recognize that the USAL as well as other uniform systems of accounts widely used in the hospitality industry are not mandatory.

INTERNAL REPORTS

In addition to SEC reporting, the controller is responsible for communicating useful and accurate information to senior-level management, the board of directors, divisional managers, employees, and interested third parties. It is essential that reports be issued in a timely manner and that these reports are understood by a diverse audience. The needs of management vary from one hospitality organization to another. Management reports should be sufficiently simple to understand to enable the reader to center his or her attention on problems or issues that may or could arise. Consistency and uniformity in report format and issuance can only enhance the organization's operational effectiveness and efficiency. The data presented in reports issued to management, employees, and third parties should be based on facts that may be corroborated by underlying financial and accounting data.

The accounting department collects all data needed to perform its reporting and record keeping function. In some large hotels or resorts there might be other collection points for data, such as the front desk, food and beverage outlets, and other revenue-producing departments. These secondary collection points eventually transfer most of their data to the accounting department.

Reports based on this data should be tailored to the needs of the specific management level for which they are prepared. At the department level, the information is specific in providing information that will enable the department head to immediately isolate deficiencies in the company's operations. At higher operating levels, the information tends to be broader and more general in nature, in keeping with the broader upper management perspective. This information is usually condensed in the process of preparing financial statements, budgets, operating statistics, and other internal reports, discussed in Chapter 2, "The Responsibilities of the Controller."

PROSPECTIVE FINANCIAL STATEMENTS

Prospective financial statements consist of financial forecasts and projections that present the hospitality entity's expected financial position and results of operations and cash flows based on assumptions about anticipated conditions and the course of action that is expected.

A financial forecast may be provided as a single monetary amount based on the best estimate or as a reasonable range, which should be chosen carefully so it does not result in deceptive reporting. These projections are prospective in that they present the hospitality company's financial position, results of operations, and cash flows based on assumptions about conditions that are expected to be present and the strategies that are expected to be followed, given one or more hypothetical (i.e., what-if) postulations.

CHAPTER 6
FINANCIAL STATEMENT REPORTING: THE INCOME STATEMENT

CONTENTS

The Income Statement: Objectives and Scope 6002
Income Statement Formats 6002
Income Statement Components 6003
  Revenue 6003
  Franchise Fee Revenue 6004
  Expenses 6004
  Income Taxes 6005
  Gains and Losses 6005
Basic Structure of a Hospitality Income Statement 6005
The Uniform System of Accounts 6006
The Summary Operating Statement 6007
  Section I—Operated Departments 6008
  Section II—Undistributed Operating Expenses 6012
  Section III—Fixed Charges 6014
Special Income Statement Items 6014
  Extraordinary Items 6014
  Discontinued Operations 6015
  Cumulative Effect of a Change in Accounting Principle 6016
  Restructuring Charges 6016
Earnings per Share 6017
  Basic Earnings per Share 6017
  Diluted Earnings per Share 6018
Comprehensive Income 6020

Exhibits

Exhibit 6-1. Example of a Single-Step Income Statement 6002
Exhibit 6-2. Basic Structure of the Summary Operating Statement 6007
Exhibit 6-3. USAL Summary Operating Statement 6008
Exhibit 6-4. Example Inn Food Department Sub-Schedule 2-1 6010
Exhibit 6-5. Statement of Income and Comprehensive Income 6020

The statement of income, also called the statement of earnings or the statement of operations, reflects the results of operations of the hospitality company for a particular period of time (a month, a quarter, or a year). It indicates whether management has achieved its primary objective of securing an acceptable level of earnings for the owners of the hospitality organization, which is done by reporting the revenues earned from the sale of goods or services, the expenses associated with earning revenues, and the resulting net income or net loss for the period reported.

THE INCOME STATEMENT: OBJECTIVES AND SCOPE

The information concerning profit-oriented activities is of utmost importance to all parties interested in the hospitality company, but the information that is required is different for internal and external purposes. Internally, hospitality management requires a report of the determination of income or loss by department or segment of the business in addition to the performance of the company as a whole. Certainly, the income statement represents a tool for measuring operating as well as management performance. External users, on the other hand, do not require the same amount of detail concerning revenues and expenses, and thus the required income statement is not as elaborate as the statement prepared for internal purposes. For example, the operations of a hotel might include room rentals, food and beverage sales, and telecommunications, thus making it highly departmentalized. As a result, the manager of a lodging business must be apprised of the performance of all major revenue-producing departments or activities in order to conduct an effective operational analysis as the basis for making sound decisions. Through the development of the Uniform System of Accounts for the Lodging Industry (USAL), as well as for other segments of the hospitality industry, this specific need for information is effectively addressed.

INCOME STATEMENT FORMATS

There are two general formats for income statements: (1) single-step and (2) multistep. The single-step format is as follows: (1) all revenues and gains are totaled; (2) total expenses and costs are deducted from total revenues to arrive at the income before income taxes; and (3) income taxes are deducted in determining the amount of net income for the period. Conversely, the multistep income statement arrives at net income in various steps and provides more detailed information about operations (see below). Exhibit 6-1, "Example of a Single-Step Income Statement," is normally used for external reporting purposes.

Exhibit 6-1: Example of a Single-Step Income Statement

MADISON TRAVEL AGENCY
Income Statement
For the year ended December 31, 20X8

Revenues		
Commissions		$50,000
Other income		3,000
		53,000
Expenses		
Salaries and wages	$6,000	
Supplies	1,000	
Administrative and general	5,000	

Marketing	3,000	
Interest	1,000	
Depreciation	2,000	
Other expenses	1,000	
		19,000
Income before income taxes		34,000
Income taxes		11,000
Net income		$23,000

INCOME STATEMENT COMPONENTS

The basic components of an income statement are revenues, expenses, gains, and losses. These elements can be combined in various ways to obtain several measures of enterprise performance. While the resulting net income (or net loss) is the final measure of operating performance, several intermediate components can be utilized to evaluate operating results. Intermediate components in a hotel income statement include items such as operating departmental income and earnings before interest, taxes, depreciation, and amortization (EBITDA). Operating income in the hospitality industry might also include gross profit (or gross margin).

Revenue

Revenue has been defined as the inflow of cash or other properties in exchange for goods and services. A more formal definition of *revenue* is incorporated in the FASB Statement of Financial Accounting Concepts No. 6 (SFAC 6), *Elements of Financial Statements*. SFAC 6 states that revenue is an inflow or other enhancement of assets of an entity or settlements of its liabilities (or a combination of both) from delivering or producing goods, rendering services, or other activities that constitute the entity's ongoing major or central operations. Revenue results in an increase in equity attributable to the normal operations of the hospitality organization.

Generally, revenue encompasses all income-producing activities of the company resulting from sales of products, services, or commissions. A typical hospitality company earns revenue by offering various services to the public, such as accommodation services: a country club offers its members the use of its pool, tennis courts, and other facilities; a restaurant offers its customers a dining experience. Other sources of revenue include interest income, franchise fees, management fees, and dividend income.

Recognition of revenue is an area of major concern to the hospitality industry inasmuch as early recognition of revenue not only has a major effect on the determination of net income; it also produces a corresponding increase in equity. In accordance with the realization concept of accounting, revenue is to be recognized at the time it is earned, which generally occurs when goods are sold or services are rendered. Revenue is to be measured by the cash received plus the fair market value of any other asset received.

Franchise Fee Revenue

Special revenue recognition guidelines apply to the recognition of franchise fee revenue based on ASC 952, *Franchisors* (FAS-45), *Accounting for Franchise Fee Revenue*. According to ASC 952 (FAS-45), the franchisor should recognize franchise fee revenue from the initial sale of the franchise only when all significant services and obligations have been substantially performed or satisfied by the franchisor. Based on this pronouncement, substantial performance is deemed to have occurred when the initial services have been rendered and there is nothing material to be done by the franchisor. Unless special circumstances are present, the earliest time that substantial performance can occur is at the franchisee's start of operations.

If it is probable that the franchisor will ultimately repurchase the franchise, payment of the initial fee is not recognized as revenue. Instead, the payment is deferred and treated as a reduction of the repurchase price. Related expenses are also deferred and matched against revenue in the year in which revenue is recognized. According to ASC 952, *Franchisors* (ASC 952-50-2), initial franchise fees should be segregrated from other franchise fee revenue, if material. In the event that initial franchise fee revenue will decline in the future because sales predictability reaches a saturation point, disclosure should be made. In the event that it is not apparent, disclosure of the contribution to net income of initial franchise fee revenue is required.

Franchise fees (or royalties) paid by the franchisee on a continuing basis are recognized when earned, while related costs are expensed. In cases where the price charged for the continuing services to the franchisee is lower than the price charged to third parties, part of the initial fee has to be deferred and recognized as an adjustment of the revenue from the sale of services at bargain prices.

If the franchisor sells equipment (e.g., kitchen appliances) or other property to the franchisee at a profit, a receivable and a payable are recorded but no revenue or expense recognition is given. Conversely, in the case of a repossessed franchise, refunded amounts to the franchisee reduce current revenue. If there is no refund, the franchisor records additional revenue for the consideration retained that was not previously recorded.

Expenses

Expenses are goods or services consumed in the regular operations of a business by virtue of the process of earning revenues. In SFAC 6, the word *expenses* is defined as outflows or decreased assets, or incurred liabilities (or a combination of both) as a result of delivering or producing goods, rendering services, or carrying out other activities that constitute the entity's ongoing major or central operations.

As previously noted, the proper matching of expenses against revenues during each accounting period is a crucial objective in the preparation of an income statement. For instance, salary and wage expenses are recorded in the period of employment, regardless of when the wages or salaries are paid. If hotel employees are paid on Friday and the end of the accounting period falls on Wednesday, two-fifths of that week's wage expense is reported in the income statement of the following period.

Income Taxes

Income tax, which is the last expense reported on a corporate income statement, reflects the portion of the corporate earnings paid or due to be paid to the government in compliance with the rules and regulations of the IRS and any other government agencies responsible for the collection of income taxes. Since federal and state income tax laws have been designed with objectives that are different from GAAP, it is not unusual that the financial statement treatment of certain transactions will differ from their tax treatment. A typical example is the difference between book depreciation and tax depreciation.

In these cases, there is a need to account for the effects of timing differences between accounting and book income (on the financial statements) and taxable income (on the tax return). This results in deferred income tax, which simply represents the accumulated value of postponed taxes—that is, the total amount of taxes the hospitality company defers by using tax treatments resulting in lower taxable income than the book income (income before income taxes) shown on the income statement. In addition, there is a need to segregate on the income statement the amount of income taxes currently payable (current income tax) and the amount deferred (deferred income tax), if applicable.

Gains and Losses

Gains is defined in SFAC 6 as increases in equity (net assets) from peripheral or incidental transactions of an entity and from all other transactions and events and circumstances affecting the entity during a particular period except for those increases that result from revenue or investments by owners. Losses are decreases in equity (net assets) from peripheral or incidental transactions of an entity and from all other transactions and other events and circumstances affecting the entity during a particular period except for those that result from expenses or distributions to owners. In other words, gains and losses are increases (or decreases) in equity resulting from transactions not related to the entity's main operations. They are considered secondary activities. Examples include losses related to assessments of fines to a restaurant or damages assessed by courts.

BASIC STRUCTURE OF A HOSPITALITY INCOME STATEMENT

While commercial companies rely on gross profit from sales as a basic measure of profitability, hospitality companies emphasize the determination of departmental income in the evaluation of operating performance. The basic structure of a hospitality company income statement is summarized as follows:

Departmental revenue	$xx
Less: Departmental expenses	xx

Departmental income	xx
Less: Indirect expenses	xx
Income before income taxes	xx
Less: Income taxes	xx
Net income	$xx

This format places emphasis on the determination of departmental income from which indirect expenses are deducted to arrive at income before income taxes. The term *indirect expenses* implies that these are expenses not directly related to specific revenue-producing activities or departments of the hospitality entity. Indirect expenses include both operating and nonoperating items.

Another unique feature of hospitality industry income statements is the great significance of labor costs to the industry. While the cost of sales is normally the major expense for manufacturing and merchandising companies, payroll costs represent the principal expense category for hospitality companies as a result of the labor-intensive nature of the industry. In fact, for many hospitality companies, payroll costs are well over one-third of total revenue.

Moreover, fixed expenses (e.g., depreciation and interest) are very important in the evaluation of a hospitality company's operating results, as they denote the capital-intensive nature of the industry. These fixed costs do not vary in direct proportion with changes in sales and are treated as indirect expenses in the formal income statement.

All of these operating characteristics of hospitality industry companies have been taken into account in the development of the USAL, an all-inclusive (multistep) income statement format that embraces nearly all the major sources of hospitality service revenues.

THE UNIFORM SYSTEM OF ACCOUNTS

The Hotel Association of New York City developed the Uniform System of Accounts for the Lodging Industry in 1925, thereby creating a common language in the reporting of financial statements within the industry. The USAL (previously known as the Uniform System of Accounts for Hotels) was approved by the American Hotel and Lodging Association and has been updated on several occasions. The latest revision (the tenth edition), published in 2006, includes a number of changes needed for the financial statements to conform to new pronouncements of the FASB and to recent industry practices.

The USAL has served as the foundation in the formulation of other uniform systems in the hospitality service industries, including the Uniform System of Accounts for Restaurants, supported by the National Restaurant Association, and the Uniform System of Accounts for Clubs, sponsored by the Club Managers Association of America. Through the development of a uniform presentation of financial statements, the following objectives are achieved:

- Facilitation of comparisons between financial statements of hospitality companies.

- Efficient flow of managerial information is achieved by showing the operating results of each major revenue-producing unit or department.
- A convenient and effective accounting system is provided, which can be used by any operation within the applicable segment of the hospitality industry, including a standardized format of organizing, classifying, and preparing financial statements.
- Simplification of the development of regional, national, and global industry statistics in the hospitality industry.

The USAL provides a convenient and efficient method of presenting the results of operations of specific segments of the industry. Although it has become the generally accepted manual for reporting lodging industry operating results, it is not mandatory. Supporting departmental schedules are prepared for all revenue and expenses included in the summary operating statement, thereby providing detailed information to lodging managers.

THE SUMMARY OPERATING STATEMENT

The summary operating statement (previously known as the long-form income statement or summary income statement) is used by internal management and is not in accordance with GAAP in all respects. It summarizes the results of operations of the hotel in greater detail than is contained in the traditional short-form (single-step) income statement prepared for external purposes. The summary operating statement or USAL is also designed to facilitate the comparison of results between different lodging companies and to enable comparison to a standard consisting of combined data for multiple properties. The arrangement of revenue and expense items reported in this multiple-step format makes possible the effective measurement of all major revenue-producing activities of the lodging operation.

The USAL income statement is divided into three major sections: (1) operated departments, (2) undistributed operating expenses, and (3) selected fixed charges. The basic structure of the summary operating statement is shown in Exhibit 6-2.

Exhibit 6-2: Basic Structure of the Summary Operating Statement

Section I

Operated departments	
Revenue	$xx
Less: Departmental expenses	xx
Total departmental income	xx

Section II

Less: Undistributed operating expenses	xx
Gross operating profit	xx
Less: Management fees	xx
Income before fixed charges	xx

Section III

Less: Fixed charges*	xx
Net operating income	xx
Less: Replacement reserves	xx
Adjusted net operating income**	$xx

* Only rent, property, and other taxes, and insurance are included.
** Adjusted net operating income excludes deductions for depreciation, interest, or income taxes. Hence, the summary operating statement does not link to net income as reported on the income statement prepared for external reporting purposes.

Section I—Operated Departments

The main objective of Section I is to set aside all revenue and expenses applicable to each revenue-producing activity of the hotel to determine the department income (or loss). This also serves as a basis for evaluating department performance. While major revenue-producing departments (or activities) of the operation are shown on a separate line on the statement, minor revenue-producing departments and other miscellaneous sources of department revenue are combined into one heading.

The tenth revised edition of the USAL includes four revenue categories: (1) rooms, (2) food and beverage, (3) other operated departments, and (4) rentals and other income. Exhibit 6-3 presents a sample summary operating statement of a sample hotel based on the most recent revised edition of the USAL. Note the format is referred to as a summary operating statement, because most of the lines have a supporting schedule (e.g., rooms and food and beverage).

Exhibit 6-3: USAL Summary Operating Statement

Example Hotel
Summary Operating Statement
for the Year Ended December 31, 20X8
In Thousands of Dollars

Revenue	
Rooms	$1,700
Food and beverage	900
Other operated departments	50
Rentals and other income	5
Total revenue	2,655
Departmental expenses	
Rooms	700
Food and beverage	670
Other operated departments	45
Total departmental expenses	1,415
Total departmental income	1,240

Undistributed operating expenses	
Administrative and general	204
Sales and marketing	106
Property operation and maintenance	70
Utilities	90
Total undistributed operating expenses	470
Gross operating profit	770
Fixed charges	
Rent	60
Property and other taxes	80
Insurance	60
Total fixed charges	200
Net operating income	570

Rooms. Room revenue is generally a major source of income for a lodging operation; thus, it is listed first on the summary operating statement. A supporting schedule contains additional information concerning the composition of the rooms department heading, which is summarized on the formal statement.

Room revenue is classified into transient, group, contract, and other, depending on whether the guest has established residency in the hotel for an extended period. Contract room revenue is derived from a contract with a third party for a consistent block of rooms for an extended period of over 30 days, whereas other room revenue includes no-shows, late or early departure fees, and item rentals such as rollaway beds and cribs. The net revenue of the rooms department consists of total room revenues less allowances given in the form of adjustments for rebates and overcharges.

The expenses directly attributable to the rooms department are broken down in the room's department schedule into two categories: (1) payroll and related expenses and (2) other expenses. Cost of sales does not apply to the rooms department, because room rentals involve only services, not goods.

Because the rooms department is mainly concerned with a service activity, payroll and related expenses representing the cost of staffing the rooms department of the hotel is a major expense category. Not only are salaries and wages included here, but also payroll taxes and employee benefits applicable to employees of the rooms department, such as the front office manager, desk clerks, maids, housekeepers, doorpersons, and bell persons and porters.

Other expenses reported in the rooms' department schedule relate primarily to the materials used in making up the rooms (laundry and cleaning supplies, and linens and guest supplies), contract services, commissions, telecommunications, complimentary services and gifts, and training.

Food and Beverage. As a result of the close ties between the food and beverage departments, which are generally under the responsibility of a food and beverage director, one combined heading for food and beverage operations is included on the summary operating statement.

Food and beverage departments can be presented as a single department with a combined schedule or as separate departments with food and beverage sub-schedules that are combined into a single schedule. Exhibit 6-4, "Example Inn Food Department Sub-Schedule 2-1," provides the necessary information with respect to revenue and expense categories of the food department. The calculation of food department income entails the deduction of three expense categories (cost of food sales, payroll and related expenses, and other expenses) from net food revenue.

Food revenue includes sale of food and non-alcoholic beverages. The revenue may be classified by the type of operation from which it is generated, such as restaurant, coffee shop, banquets, and room service. A major cost in the food department is cost of food purchased, representing the raw materials used in the preparation of meals served to guests. Cost of food sales does not include the cost of food used in preparation of meals provided for employees during the workday even if employees are charged for food consumed.

Exhibit 6-4: Example Inn Food Department Sub-Schedule 2-1

Total revenue	$603
Less: Allowances	3
Net revenue	600
Cost of food sales	150
Gross profit	450
Expenses:	
Salaries and wages	180
Employee benefits	20
Total payroll and related expenses	200
Other expenses:	
China, glassware, silver, and linen	25
Laundry and dry cleaning	3
Operating supplies	20
Training	12
Licenses and permits	12
Other	18
Total other expenses	100
Total expenses	300
Department income (loss)	$150

Another significant expense category in the food department is payroll and its related expenses—that is, the cost of staffing the food operation (e.g., salaries and wages, payroll taxes, and employee benefits provided to cooks, chefs, dishwashers, servers, and cashiers). In addition, the cost includes any expense associated with contract labor.

Other operating expenses applicable to the food operation are the cost of items used in serving the guests (e.g., china, glassware, flatware, and linen) and the cost of utility items (e.g., cleaning supplies, paper supplies, kitchen fuel, and guest supplies).

Beverage revenue includes the revenue generated from the sale of alcoholic beverages and other drinks. Sales may be classified by the type of operation from which revenue is generated, such as restaurant, lounge, or mini-bar. In addition, beverage revenue includes revenue generated from cover charges to customers for entrance to special events where beverages are sold.

The cost of beverages sold includes the cost of wine, liquor, beer, mineral water, syrups, and other items that are used in the preparation of mixed drinks. Payroll and related expenses include cost of staffing the beverage operation (e.g., salaries and wages, payroll taxes, and employee benefits provided to beverage purchasers, stewards, and bartenders). Other operating expenses applicable to the beverage operation are china, glassware, silver and linen, contract services, licenses, permits, uniforms, and other expenses directly attributable to the beverage operation.

Other Operating Departments. The telecommunications department (previously known as the telephone department) includes revenue derived from the use of telecommunication facilities by guests, including local and long-distance calls, facsimile services, Internet services, and other telecommunication services. Revenue should not include telecommunication services used by management or other departments of the hotel.

Telecommunication expenses include cost of sales, payroll and related expenses, and other expenses. The cost of sales, also known as cost of calls, includes the total amount billed by the telecommunication companies for long-distance and local calls through the switchboard. Payroll and related expenses include salaries and wages, payroll taxes, and benefits of the telecommunications manager, telephone operators, supervisors, and technicians. Other expenses include contract services, cost of employee uniforms, and cost of printing service manuals and telecommunication vouchers.

In addition to telecommunications, there are several other departments operated by the hotel, as opposed to similar services operated by others under rental or concession arrangements. Examples include health club, guest laundry, golf course, tennis, newsstand, swimming pool, garage and parking, and gift and apparel shop departments. The hotel must include a sub-schedule for each operated department and a consolidated schedule for all minor operated departments. The format of the other operated department sub-schedules follows the same base outline as the department schedules for the rooms and food and beverage departments.

Other operated departments receive the same treatment as the major departments. The department income or loss is determined by deducting the appropriate department expenses (cost of sales, payroll and related expenses, and other expenses) from the department net revenue.

Rentals and Other Income. Rentals and other income include all revenue-producing activities of the company not listed as part of a specific operated department. Examples include store and office rental income, interest income, vending machine income, and dividend income. Since rentals and other income are part of the "department" section of the summary operating statement, they are taken into consideration in the calculation of total department income or loss, but because these revenue sources do not constitute an actual operated department, any related expenses are generally treated as a direct reduction from the revenue generated.

Major sources of revenue reported as rentals and other income include revenue generated from the rental of space within the property, commissions received for services, such as automobile rentals, cash discounts for early payment to vendors, and interest earned on cash investments. It is important to recognize that some of the items listed under rentals and other income might not clearly fit the description of operating income. A typical example is interest income, normally included after operating income. Hence, in certain situations where contractual agreements state that interest income should not be included in operating income, it is reported separately as a line item below gross operating profit.

Department Income or Loss. The department income (or loss) is determined by deducting from total department net revenue the sum of department expenses. It reflects the total income generated by all revenue-producing departments and activities of the operation. The overall profitability of the operation will depend on whether the total contribution of the operated departments covers all other operating costs as well as the fixed expenses of the organization.

Section II—Undistributed Operating Expenses

The undistributed operating expenses are considered the overhead expenses of a hotel—that is, they are incurred for the benefit of the overall organization and hence are not allocated to any specific department, because it is not possible or practical to do so. The undistributed operating expenses include four groups of expenses: (1) administrative and general, (2) sales and marketing, (3) property operation and maintenance, and (4) utilities.

Administrative and General Expenses. Administrative and general expenses include costs of a general nature that relate to all departments. That is, they benefit the entire operation and are broken down into two headings on department schedules: (1) Payroll and Related Expenses and (2) Other Expenses.

Salaries and wages, payroll taxes, and employee benefits associated with the employment of the general manager, accounting office personnel, and other administrative employees are part of administrative and general payroll and related expenses inasmuch as these expenses provide a general benefit to all units. Likewise, a department schedule includes detailed information concerning the composition of other expenses, such as professional fees, payroll processing, transportation, security, printing, stationery and postage, and dues and subscriptions.

Sales and Marketing. Sales and marketing encompass all costs incurred by the organization with the prime objective of obtaining and retaining customers. Included here are the salaries, wages, and other payroll-related expenses associated with employees—namely, sales managers, advertising managers and staff, research analysts, and public relations managers and staff who work toward the marketing effort.

Marketing expenses are broken down by the different activities of the marketing functions (i.e., sales, advertising, merchandising, public relations, and other selling and promotional expenses). In addition to payroll costs, other marketing expenses are aimed at the creation of customers' perception of hotel services. They include travel and entertainment, printing, radio and television fees, and trade show expenses.

Property Operations and Maintenance. Property operation and maintenance costs are a separate line item. The costs include operation of the heating, refrigeration, air conditioning, and other mechanical systems in the hotel.

Similar to other undistributed operating costs, the costs of property operations and maintenance are broken down into payroll costs and other costs. Payroll and other expenses refer to personnel, such as the chief engineer and assistants, plumbers, electricians, and elevator mechanics. Other expenses include the costs of materials used in repairing buildings, furniture, fixtures and equipment, painting and decorating supplies, as well as licenses and permits and equipment rental.

Utilities. Utilities include the costs of electricity, gas, oil, and steam purchased from outside producers, as well as water, sewer, and taxes assessed by utility companies. If reimbursements for these costs are received from separate entities, such as managed condominiums or timeshare units, they are deducted from the total utility costs.

Gross Operating Profit. Gross operating profit (previously known as income before fixed charges or house profit) represents the amount of income after deducting the total undistributed operating expenses from total operated department income. The remaining expenses, not yet recognized, are mainly capital costs, which are not directly related to operating performance.

Gross operating profit is regarded as the best measure of overall managerial efficiency, because all revenue and expenses that are under the responsibility and control of operating management are considered in its calculation. Because gross operating profit is considered to be a good indicator of managerial performance and operating success, bonuses given to the general manager are often based on the amount of gross operating profit.

Section III—Fixed Charges

The final section of the USAL summary operating statement includes selected fixed charges such as rent, property taxes and other taxes, and insurance. These are the capital costs of the hospitality organization. As previously noted, the USAL summary operating statement does not link to the net income reported on the company's income statement prepared for external parties, because it does not include the deduction of interest, depreciation, amortization, or income taxes. Because fixed expenses are a function of investment and financing decisions and thus are beyond the control of operating management, they are considered nonoperating, noncontrollable costs.

Theoretically, many of the indirect costs (undistributed operating expenses and fixed expenses) could be allocated to operated departments. Marketing expenses can be allocated on the basis of department revenues, and utility costs can be apportioned on the basis of space occupied or based on meter readings. Other base of apportioning indirect costs to operated departments might be total department payroll, number of persons employed in each department, and total department earnings.

In previous editions of the USAL, general insurance (i.e., premiums relating to liability, fidelity, and theft coverage) was included under undistributed operating expenses based on the premise that it was under the control of operating management. However, currently, especially in the case of managed operations, the owner controls general insurance costs; therefore, they are now included under fixed charges.

SPECIAL INCOME STATEMENT ITEMS

In addition to reporting revenue earned and expenses incurred during the accounting period, the income statement might include special items, such as gains and losses from discontinued operations, extraordinary gains and losses, restructuring charges, and the cumulative effect of changes in accounting principles.

Extraordinary Items

Extraordinary items are events and transactions that are distinguished by their unusual nature and by the infrequency of their occurrence, which means the transaction is not expected to take place in the foreseeable future, taking into account the corporate environment. Materiality is considered by evaluating the items separately, not collectively. However, if they arise from a single event, they should be combined.

If material, the extraordinary item (net of the corresponding income tax effect) is deducted from income before extraordinary items on the income statement. In addition, appropriate disclosure of specific details concerning extraordinary items is required in a note to the financial statements.

Examples of extraordinary items include fire loss and other casualty losses (e.g., losses from natural disasters such as earthquakes) that cause property damage to hospitality companies. Other examples of extraordinary gains or losses include gain on life insurance proceeds, gain on troubled debt restructuring, and losses on expropriation of property by the government of a foreign country.

Discontinued Operations

Gains and losses from the disposal of a segment of a hospitality business should be reported separately from the operating results of the continued operations on the statement of income. The results of the discontinued operations of a segment of a hospitality business that has been sold, abandoned, or otherwise disposed of (but is still operating), together with the gain or loss on the sale, are shown on the income statement under discontinued operations.

The expression "a segment of a business" refers to a portion of a company that represents a major line of business or class of customer. For instance, when a hospitality chain sells the restaurant division while continuing to operate the hotel division, operating results of the restaurants disposed of, together with the gain or loss on the sale, are reported as a discontinued operation on the statement of income.

Once management develops or adopts a formal plan for the sale or disposal of a business segment, the operating results of the segment are segregated within the income statement. The company is required to accrue any estimated loss from operations during the phaseout period and any estimated loss on sale or disposal. However, any gain on disposal of expected operating losses during the phaseout period can only be reported when realized.

The income or loss of a component of a company that either has been disposed of or is held for sale is reported in discontinued operations only if both of the following criteria are satisfied:

1. The company will not have any material continual involvement in the operations of the component subsequent to the disposal transaction.
2. The cash flows and operations of the component have been (or will be) eliminated from the continued operations of the company because of the disposal transactions.

ASC 360, *Impairment or Disposal of Long-Lived Assets* (ASC 360-10-05-4) (FAS-144, *Accounting for the Impairment or Disposal of Long-Lived Assets*, requires specific disclosures for discontinued operations. They are:

- A description of the facts and circumstances leading to the expected disposal, the expected manner and timing of that disposal, and, if not separately presented on the face of the statement, the carrying amount(s) of the major classes of assets and liabilities included as part of a disposal group.
- In the year in which a component or division of a hospitality company is disposed of or is considered for disposition or sale, the income statement for the current and previous years must separately disclose the income or loss of the division, including any gain or loss recognized in discontinued operations.

- The results of discontinued operations net of tax effect are reported as a separate component of income before extraordinary items and the cumulative effect of a change in an accounting principle.
- The profit (or loss) of a component of a company that either has been disposed of or is held for sale is reported in discontinued operations if the company will not have any material continual involvement in the operations subsequent to the disposal and the cash flows and operations of the component have been (or will be) eliminated from the continual operations of the company because of the disposal transaction.

Cumulative Effect of a Change in Accounting Principle

When a hospitality company changes from one acceptable accounting policy to another, such as changes in depreciation or inventory valuation methods, it needs to report the effect of the accounting change in the period of change. Although changes in accounting policy may be voluntary, other changes are mandated by FASB or SEC pronouncements.

Any cumulative impact on prior period earnings is reported net of tax after extraordinary items and discontinued operations on the income statement. In some cases, prior period results are restated. In those instances, the portion of the cumulative impact applicable to periods preceding those for which an income statement is presented is shown as an adjustment to the beginning balance of retained earnings.

Financial statement users need to know what cumulative effect the accounting change would have had on net income of prior years in order to facilitate comparisons between accounting periods. Accordingly, hospitality companies are required to provide footnote disclosure of the impact of the change on current period operations (and on each period, if restated) and their justification for the change. Additional information on accounting change disclosures is included in Chapter 9, "Financial Statement Disclosures."

Restructuring Charges

SEC Staff Accounting Bulletin No. 67, *Income Statement Presentation of Restructuring Charges*, requires restructuring charges to be expensed and presented as a separate component in computing income from operations. For example, expense and liability should be accrued for employee termination benefits in a restructuring. In addition, disclosure should be made of the group and number of workers laid off.

An exit plan requires the recognition of a liability for the restructuring charges incurred if there is no future benefit to continuing operations. Exit costs incurred are presented as a separate item as part of income from continuing operations. The expense for the estimated costs should be made on the commitment date of the exit plan. Expected gains from assets to be sold in connection with the exit plan should be recorded in the year realized. These gains are not allowed to offset the accrued liability for exit costs.

Disclosures associated with an exit plan include the terms of the exit plan, a description and the amount of exit costs incurred, activities to be exited from and method of disposition, expected completion date, and liability adjustments. For example, with regard to employee terminations, disclosure of the group and number of workers laid off should be made.

EARNINGS PER SHARE

GAAP requires the disclosure of earnings per share in the income statement. ASC 260, *Earnings per Share* (FAS-128, *Earnings per Share*), covers the computation, reporting, and disclosures associated with earnings per share.

Based on ASC 260 (FAS-128), there are two components of earnings per share: (1) basic earnings per share and (2) fully diluted earnings per share. Basic earnings per share consider only the actual number of outstanding common shares during the period (and those contingently issuable in certain cases). Diluted earnings per share include the effect of common shares actually outstanding and the effect of convertible securities, stock options, stock warrants, and their equivalents. Diluted earnings per share should not assume the conversion, exercise, or contingent issuance of securities having an antidilutive effect (increasing earnings per share or decreasing losses per share) because it violates conservatism.

Basic Earnings per Share

Basic earnings per share are simply the net income of the hospitality company (less preferred dividends, if applicable) divided by the weighted average number of common shares outstanding. Common stock equivalents are no longer included in the calculation of earnings per share. When a prior period adjustment occurs that causes a restatement of previous years' earnings, basic earnings per share should also be restated. Examples 1 and 2 present the calculation of basic earnings per share for two hospitality companies.

EXAMPLE 1: The following data are presented for A Hospitality Company:

Net income	$120,000
Preferred stock, $10 par, 5% cumulative, 40,000 shares issued and outstanding	400,000
Common stock, $1 par, 100,000 shares issued and outstanding	100,000

The preferred stock cash dividend is $20,000 (5% × $400,000)

Basic EPS = $1.00, as follows:

Net income ($120,000) less preferred dividends ($20,000) = $100,000

$100,000 ÷ 100,000 shares outstanding = $1.00

EXAMPLE 2: Delectable Restaurant had the following shares outstanding on January 1, 20X9:

5% Cumulative preferred stock, $100 par value	4,000 shares
Common stock, $3 par value	300,000 shares

During the year, the following transactions took place:
- On April 1, 20X9, the company issued 100,000 shares of common stock.
- On September 1, 20X9, the company declared and issued a 10% stock dividend.
- For the year ended December 31, 20X9, the net income was $1,000,000.

Basic earnings per share for 20X9 equal $2.38 ($980,000 ÷ 412,500 shares) computed below:

Earnings available to common stockholders:

Net income	$1,000,000
Less: Preferred dividend (4,000 shares × $5)	20,000
Earnings available to common stockholders	$ 980,000

Weighted-average number of outstanding common shares is determined as follows:

1/1/20X9 to 3/31/20X9 (300,000 × 3/12 × 110%)	82,500
4/1/20X9 to 8/31/20X9 (400,000 × 5/12 × 110%)	183,333
9/1/20X9 to 12/31/20X9 (440,000 × 4/12)	146,667
Weighted-average outstanding common shares	412,500

When shares are issued as a result of a stock dividend or stock split, the computation of weighted-average common shares outstanding mandates retroactive adjustments as if the shares were outstanding at the beginning of the year.

Diluted Earnings per Share

Hospitality companies report diluted earnings per share when they have stock options, convertible securities, and other instruments that are convertible into shares of common stock that could potentially reduce the common shareholders' proportionate share of earnings if the instruments were presented on the income statement.

Pursuant to ASC 260 (FAS-128), the calculation of diluted earnings per share assumes that convertible securities will be converted, and options and warrants are exercised. This requires adding back any interest (net of taxes) on convertible bonds, or dividends on convertible preferred stock, that the company subtracted in computing net income available to the hospitality common shareholders. The denominator of diluted earnings per share equals the weighted-average outstanding common shares for the period plus the assumed issue of common shares arising from convertible securities plus the assumed shares issued because of the exercise of stock options or stock warrants, or their equivalent.

According to Accounting Standards Update (ASU) No. 2009-08, *Earnings per Share—Amendments to ASC 260 Section 260-10-S99*, if convertible preferred stock is converted into other securities issued by the hospitality company pursuant to an inducement offer, the excess of (1) the fair value of all securities and other consideration transferred in the transaction over (2) the fair value of the securities issuable pursuant to the original conversion terms should be deducted from net income in arriving at net income available to common shareholders in the calculation of diluted earnings per share.

EXAMPLE 3: Based on the same information provided in Example 2 on basic earnings per share and the additional data below:

Potentially diluted securities outstanding include 5% convertible bonds (each $1,000 bond is convertible into 20 shares of common stock) having a face value of $1,000,000. There are options to buy 10,000 shares of common stock at $10 per share. The average market price for common shares is $25 per share for 20X9. The tax rate is 30%. The company is expected to repurchase 4,000 shares of its common stock at $10 per share.

Diluted earnings per share for 20X9 are $2.31 ($1,015,000 ÷ 438,500 shares) as computed below.

Income for diluted earnings per share:

Earnings available to common stockholders		$ 980,000
Interest expense on convertible bonds ($1,000,000 × 5%)	$50,000	
Less: Tax savings ($50,000 × 30%)	(15,000)	
Interest expense (net of tax)		35,000
Income for diluted earnings per share		$1,015,000
Shares outstanding for diluted earnings per share:		
Weighted-average outstanding common shares		412,500
Assumed issued common shares for convertible bonds (1,000 bonds × 20 shares)		20,000
Assumed issued common shares from exercise of option	10,000	
Less: Assumed repurchase of treasury shares (10,000 × $10 = $100,000 ÷ $25)	4,000	6,000
Shares outstanding for diluted earnings per share		$ 438,500

If convertible bonds are included in the denominator of earnings per share, they are considered equivalent to common shares. Thus, interest expense (net of tax) is added back in the numerator. A stock conversion occurring during the year or between year-end and the audit report date may have materially affected earnings per share if it had taken place at the beginning of the year. Thus, supplementary footnote disclosure should be made reflecting on an as-if basis what the effects of these conversions would have had on earnings per share if they were made at the start of the accounting period.

Basic earnings per share and diluted earnings per share (if required) must be disclosed on the face of the income statement. Reconciliation is required of the numerators and denominators for basic and diluted earnings per share. Disclosure of earnings per share should include information on the capital structure, explanation of the computation of earnings per share, identification of common stock equivalents, assumptions made, and number of shares converted. Rights and privileges of the securities should also be disclosed. Disclosure includes dividend and participation rights, call prices, conversion ratios, and sinking fund requirements.

When comparative financial statements are presented, there is a retroactive adjustment for stock splits and stock dividends. Assume in 20X9 a 10% stock dividend occurs. The weighted-average shares used for previous years' computations have to be increased by 10% to make earnings per share data comparable. When a prior-period adjustment occurs that causes a restatement of previous years' earnings, earnings per share should also be restated.

COMPREHENSIVE INCOME

According to ASC 220, *Comprehensive Income* (FAS-130, *Reporting Comprehensive Income*), hospitality companies must report total comprehensive income either on the face of the income statement, in the statement of shareholders' equity, or in a separate financial statement.

Comprehensive income represents the change in equity of a business enterprise during a period from transactions and other events resulting from nonowner sources. It includes all changes in equity except those resulting from owners' investments and distribution to owners.

According to ASC 220 (FAS-130), comprehensive income has two components: (1) net income and (2) other comprehensive income. No changes were made on items included under net income. Other comprehensive income includes foreign currency translation adjustments and unrealized gains and losses on investments in debt and equity securities. A restatement of previous years' financial statements is needed when presented for comparative purposes.

The requirement to report comprehensive income in a financial statement can be satisfied in one of three ways:

1. *The one-statement approach*—Uses a single income statement to report net income and comprehensive income.
2. *The two-statement approach*—Reconciles net income to comprehensive income in a separate Statement of Comprehensive Income.
3. *The statement of changes in equity approach*—Reports comprehensive income within the statement of changes in shareholders' equity.

Exhibit 6-5 presents an example of comprehensive income within the income statement.

Exhibit 6-5: Statement of Income and Comprehensive Income

Net income		$100,000
Other comprehensive income:		
Foreign currency loss	($10,000)	
Unrealized gain on available-for-sale securities	20,000	
Minimum pension liability adjustment	10,000	
Total other comprehensive income		20,000
Total comprehensive income		$120,000

CHAPTER 7
FINANCIAL STATEMENT REPORTING: THE BALANCE SHEET

CONTENTS

The Balance Sheet: Scope and Objectives	7001
The Classified Balance Sheet	7002
Assets	7003
Current Assets	7003
Property and Equipment	7005
Other Assets	7008
Liabilities	7010
Current Liabilities	7010
Long-Term Liabilities	7011
Other Liabilities	7013
Accounting for Compensating Absences	7013
Contingencies	7014
Owners' Equity	7014
Shareholders' Equity	7014
Exhibits	
Exhibit 7-1. Sample Balance Sheet	7002
Exhibit 7-2. Stockholders' Equity for Brinker, Fiscal Year 2004	7015
Exhibit 7-3. Outback Steakhouse Consolidated Statement of Stockholders' Equity	7020

The balance sheet, also called the statement of financial condition or statement of financial position, presents a snapshot of the resources of a hospitality company (the assets) and the claims on those resources (its liabilities and shareholders' equity) at a specific point in time. The balance sheet depicts the assets controlled by the hospitality entity and how those assets are financed with the funds provided by creditors (liabilities), with the capital provided by owners (equity), or with both.

THE BALANCE SHEET: SCOPE AND OBJECTIVES

The balance sheet is a reflection of the fundamental accounting equation:

$$\text{Assets} = \text{Liabilities} + \text{Owners' Equity}$$

The balance sheet is a very important financial report because it provides valuable information about a hospitality company's liquidity—its ability to pay short-term obligations as they become due. It is used to determine both the financial strength and financial risk. In general, the greater the amount of debt relative to equity, the higher the financial risk. The balance sheet also provides information concerning profits that have been retained in the hospitality entity as a way to finance its expansion or to reduce external financing from creditors.

THE CLASSIFIED BALANCE SHEET

In achieving the balance sheet's major objective of providing useful and reliable information concerning the financial position of the company, the assets and liabilities are classified in account categories. However, it is important to recognize that financial officers have a fair degree of discretion in the way they report assets and liabilities. The amount of detail shown depends on the company's size and complexity and on the type of business organization used.

Some lodging and restaurant operators prefer their balance sheet simplified as much as possible because it makes it easier to read. Yet others prefer a more detailed balance sheet in order to use the information internally for decision making. As a rule, balance sheets prepared for external purposes are more concise than internally generated balance sheets. A detailed review of the individual balance sheet categories follows. A sample balance sheet for ERM Hotels is presented in Exhibit 7-1.

Exhibit 7-1: Sample Balance Sheet

ERM Hotels
Balance Sheet
(In Thousands)

	As of December 31, 20X9	As of December 31, 20X8
ASSETS		
Current assets		
Cash and cash equivalents	$ 8,810	$ 6,143
Trade and other receivables, net	9,140	7,400
Inventories	4,544	4,257
Prepaid expenses	3,423	1,198
Total current assets	25,917	18,998
Property and equipment at cost less accumulated depreciation and amortization	286,450	198,340
Other assets	34,340	28,420
	$346,707	$245,758
LIABILITIES AND SHAREHOLDERS' EQUITY		
Current liabilities		
Current portion of long-term debt	$ 7,235	$ 5,340
Accounts payable	7,340	4,420
Accrued liabilities	8,456	4,768
Customer deposits	3,978	2,498
Total current liabilities	27,009	17,026

	As of December 31,	
	20X9	20X8
Long-term debt, net	123,191	81,473
Shareholders' equity		
Common stock, $.01 par value; 200,000,000 shares authorized; 190,000,000 and 180,000,000 shares issued	1,900	1,800
Additional paid-in capital	108,023	76,339
Retained earnings	87,818	70,354
Treasury stock (45,000 shares at cost)	(1,234)	(1,234)
Total shareholders' equity	196,507	147,259
	$346,707	$245,758

ASSETS

According to FASB Statement of Financial Concepts No. 6 (SFAC 6), *Elements of Financial Statements*, paragraph 25, assets are probable future economic benefits obtained or controlled by an entity as a result of past transactions or events. They are listed on the balance sheet in order of liquidity—that is, how quickly they are expected to be converted into cash. Assets may be tangible, such as food inventory, land, and buildings, or may be intangible, such as trademarks and goodwill. Assets are divided into categories such as current assets, property and equipment, and other assets.

Current Assets

Liquidity, or a resource nearest to cash, determines the sequence of current assets reported on the balance sheet. Current assets typically include cash, marketable securities, accounts receivable, notes receivable, food and beverage inventories, housekeeping supplies inventories, and prepaid expenses. The definition of *current assets* excludes restricted cash, investments for purposes of control, long-term receivables, the cash surrender value of life insurance, and long-term prepayments.

Cash and Cash Equivalents. Cash is the ultimate measure of liquidity. It includes negotiable checks and unrestricted balances in checking accounts as well as cash on hand. In addition, it includes investments with maturities of up to three months at the time of purchase. Cash that is restricted for the payment of bonds or for other long-term purposes should be included under noncurrent assets. Based on the most recent edition of the Uniform System of Accounts for the Lodging Industry (USAL), cash is classified on the balance sheet in the following categories: house banks, demand deposits, and temporary cash investments.

Short-Term Investments. Short-term investments, also called marketable securities, are highly liquid investments that are intended to be converted into cash or cash equivalents within a year from the balance sheet date. Under FASB Statement No. 115 (FAS-115), *Accounting for Certain Investments in Debt and Equity Securities* (ASC 320, *Investments-Debt and Equity Securities*), the valuation of marketable securities on the balance sheet depends on the intent of the investor. Held-to-maturity securities apply to those debt securities that the company intends to hold to maturity. These securities are reported at amortized cost. Similarly, trading securities are debt and equity securities that are held for resale in the short term and should be reported at fair value with the unrealized gain or loss included in comprehensive income. The basis of valuation of these short-term investments should be disclosed in the notes to the financial statements.

Receivables. Accounts receivable represent the customer balances outstanding on credit sales. They are reported on the balance sheet at their net realizable value, which represents the actual amount of the account less an allowance for doubtful accounts. These accounts are carried in the hospitality industry's guest and city ledgers. Accounts that are not expected to be collected within one year should be included under other assets. If material, any accounts due from owners, officers, employees, and affiliated companies should be disclosed separately.

Pursuant to the conservatism concept of accounting, assets should be recorded at their lowest possible value. Thus, financial personnel must estimate the amount of accounts receivable they expected to be uncollectible, as experience shows that not all receivables can be collected in full. Accounts that become uncollectible are written off against the allowance account, which is adjusted at the end of each period.

Notes receivable include notes that are expected to be collected within a year from the balance sheet date. If material, notes receivable from owners, officers, employees, and affiliated companies should be reported separately. Notes that are not expected to be collected within one year from the balance sheet date should be reported under other assets. If payable in installments, the current maturities of noncurrent receivables will include amounts that are expected to be collected within one year.

FASB Statement No. 114 (FAS-114), *Accounting by Creditors for Impairment of a Loan* (ASC 310, *Receivables*), stipulates that if it is probable that some of the principal or interest on a note is uncollectible, the loan is deemed "impaired." A loss on an impaired loan is recorded immediately by debiting bad debt expense and crediting a valuation allowance.

Inventories. In the hospitality industry inventories are generally insignificant in relation to a company's total assets. They consist of merchandise held for sale (e.g., food and beverages) and items used in the production of revenues, such as housekeeping and office supplies. Inventories also should include the cost of reserve stocks of china, glassware, linen, and uniforms. Based on the conservatism concept of accounting, inventories are reported at the lower of cost or market value applied on a total, category, or individual basis. The basis of valuing inventory should be disclosed in the notes to the financial statements and, if individual categories are significant, they should be separately disclosed.

Prepaid Expenses. Prepaid expenses represent the portion of expenditures paid in advance of the use of a service or goods. It represents amounts that have been paid but have not been fully incurred. Additional benefits will be realized after the balance sheet date. Examples of prepaid expenses include insurance, taxes, promotion costs, advertising, licenses, rent, and early payments on long-term contracts.

Other Current Assets. Other current assets include items not shown previously that are reasonably expected to be converted into cash or consumed by the business within one year from the balance sheet date. For instance, for financial and income tax purposes, deferred income taxes current represents the tax effects of temporary differences between the bases of current assets and current liabilities. If the allowance for doubtful accounts, for instance, is not deductible for tax purposes, it will result in a current deferred tax asset.

Property and Equipment

Property and equipment include the productive, long-lived assets that a hospitality company uses in operations to produce revenue. They include land, buildings, and improvements, kitchen equipment, and construction in progress. Due to the capital-intensive nature of the hospitality industry, most companies have substantial investments in property and equipment.

The balance sheet reports property and equipment at historical cost and then subtracts the accumulated depreciation recognized on these assets since acquisition. Historical cost includes the purchase price, freight costs, taxes, installation costs, and other expenditures necessary to acquire an asset and prepare it for its intended use. Land improvements (e.g., hotel parking lots, sidewalks) are capitalized and depreciated over their estimated useful life. Conversely, ordinary repairs, such as painting a restaurant, are expensed because they provide a current benefit to the company.

Determining costs to capitalize (capital expenditures) and costs to expense (revenue expenditures) is very important because of the impact on earnings and earnings per share. For example, if $5,000 of maintenance costs incurred during the year is improperly capitalized to a building account, the assets will be overstated, while the $5,000 will be incorrectly spread across 40 years of estimated useful life instead of being expensed in the current year. This will result in an understatement of expenses and an overstatement of earnings and earnings per share.

Hospitality companies may purchase two or more assets as a group or in a basket for a single amount. For example, a lodging business may pay one price for both land and a building. The company must identify the cost of each asset and then allocate the total cost to the assets according to their relative fair market values. If a hotel building is demolished to create space for a new hotel, the costs of demolishing the old hotel are charged to the land account.

Except for land, property and equipment decline in service potential over their useful lives. The allocation of an asset's net cost (after reduction of estimated salvage value) over its estimated useful life is referred to as depreciation.

There are several methods used by hospitality companies for depreciation, including the straight line, declining balance, and sum-of-year's digit method. Many hospitality companies use the declining-balance method for tax purposes and the straight-line method on the income statement. The use of different methods of depreciation for tax and financial statement purposes requires recording the timing difference as deferred income taxes.

The financial manager must consider several issues when recording depreciation. Estimating the useful life of each asset poses a major challenge to some hospitality companies, which might require changes based on experience and new information. For example, the Walt Disney Company revised depreciation for the amended useful lives of its theme-park property and equipment. The following note to the financial statements of Walt Disney, included in its annual report, explained the accounting change:

> The company extended the estimated useful lives of certain theme park assets based upon engineering studies. The effect of this change was to decrease depreciation by approximately $8 million (an increase in net income of approximately $4.2 million ...).

When a company's assets are acquired during the period rather than at the beginning of the period, most companies use the half-year convention to record depreciation. That is, they use one half of a year's depreciation on all assets acquired or sold during the year. For example, a company purchases a piece of kitchen equipment for $20,000 on June 7, 20X5, with an estimated useful life of 10 years and an estimated residual value of $2,000. Using the half-year convention, depreciation is calculated as follows:

Year	Straight Line	200% Declining Balance	Sum of the Years' Digits
20X5	$1,800* × 1/2 = $900	$20,000 × 20% = 4,000 × 1/2 = $2,000	$18,000 × 10/55 = 3273 × 1/2 = $1,637
20X6	$1,800*	$18,000 × 20% = $3,600	$18,000 × 9/55 = 2945 × 1/2 = $1,473

* Straight-line depreciation 20,000 − 2000 = 18,000 × 10% = 1,800.

When property and equipment cease to serve their purposes, the company will dispose of the asset by either selling or exchanging it. If the asset cannot be sold or exchanged, it will be discarded. Regardless of the method used to remove the asset, the hospitality company must record the disposal by reducing (crediting) the asset account and removing the accumulated depreciation from the books (e.g., debiting accumulated depreciation). The difference between the sale proceeds and the eliminated account balances is either a gain or a loss. If assets are scrapped before being fully depreciated, the company records a loss equal to the asset's net book value. For example, X Hospitality Company had equipment costing $6,000 and accumulated depreciation of $5,000. Management decides to remove the equipment, thus generating a loss of $1,000 recorded in the following manner:

Accumulated depreciation—kitchen equipment		$ 5,000
Loss on disposal of kitchen equipment		1,000
Kitchen equipment		$ 6,000
To dispose of kitchen equipment.		

Hospitality companies often exchange their old property and equipment for newer, more efficient models. For instance, Domino's Pizza may exchange a seven-year-old delivery truck for a newer model. To record the exchange, the restaurant must remove the balances of the old delivery truck and its accumulated depreciation while adding the new delivery truck, as follows:

Transportation equipment (new delivery truck)	$ 25,000	
Accumulated depreciation (old delivery truck)	18,000	
Transportation equipment (old delivery truck)		20,000
Cash		$ 23,000

To record the exchange of an old delivery truck for a new one by paying $23,000.

Leasehold and Leasehold Improvements. It is not unusual in the hospitality industry to have buildings constructed on leased land or substantial improvements made to rented premises. These leasehold improvements are reported under property and equipment and are amortized over the life of the improvement or the remaining period of the lease, whichever is shorter.

Construction in Progress. Construction in progress represents costs incurred for hotel and restaurant projects under construction. These costs are included in property and equipment during the construction process and then transferred to the appropriate building account on completion of the project. Accordingly, these costs are not depreciated until they are placed in service.

Operating Equipment. Operating equipment includes china, glass, silver, linen, and uniforms. Based on previous editions of the USAL, hospitality companies have used different methods in accounting for the approximate value of china, glass, silver, linen, and uniforms. While some operations considered these items as part of their inventory, others capitalized the base stock of china, glass, silver, linen, and uniforms and then expensed the cost of items subsequently purchased and placed in service. However, a major change in the treatment of operating equipment has been included in the tenth revised edition of the USAL. Operating equipment, with a period of consumption of more than one year, is currently recorded under Other Assets, whereas operating equipment that is determined to have a period of consumption of one year or less is recorded under Current Assets. Operating equipment is then expensed ratably to the appropriate department expense account over its estimated useful life.

Properties under Capital Leases. From the lessee's perspective, leases take two forms: (1) operating leases or (2) capital leases. Capital leases transfer to the lessee the risks and benefits that are incident to ownership. In order to be treated as a capital lease, a lease contract must be noncancelable and meet at least one of the following criteria:

1. Ownership is transferred to the lessee at the end of the lease term.

2. Transfer of ownership at the end of the lease term is likely because the lessor has a bargain purchase option (e.g., the right to purchase the leased property at a specified future date for a price substantially lower than the fair value of the property at that time).
3. The lease extends for at least 75% of the property's estimated useful life.
4. The present value of the minimum rental payments equals or exceeds 90% of the fair value of the property at the inception of the lease.

If a lease meets one of the above criteria, it is a capital lease; otherwise, the lease is an operating lease. Property and equipment leased under a capital lease are included under "property and equipment" and shown net of accumulated amortization. The initial journal entry to record a capital lease would increase (debit) the property under a capital lease and credit a long-term liability (an obligation under a capital lease) for the present value of the minimum rental payments over the life of the lease.

Other Assets

Other assets include resources with a long-term future value not used in operations to produce revenues. Examples include long-term investments, long-term receivables, cash surrender value of life insurance, deferred charges, and intangible assets.

Investments. Long-term investments, usually stocks and bonds of other companies, are often held to maintain a business relationship or to exercise control. Investments may include special funds set aside for payment of specific obligations such as bonds or pensions.

Debt securities are classified as either held-to-maturity or available-for-sale securities. Debt securities classified as held to maturity are those that the hospitality company intends to hold to maturity. They are carried at amortized cost and thus the amortization of any bond premium or discount is recorded in the investment account. Conversely, debt securities classified as available for sale are carried at fair value.

Equity securities reported under investments are to be carried at cost except in cases where the company can exert significant influence over the investee. For example, when a hospitality company owns between 20% and 50% of the common stock of another corporation, it is presumed that the company has significant influence over the financial and operating activities of the investee. As a result, the common stock investment will be accounted for using the equity method, under which the cost is adjusted for the proportionate share of the rise or fall in the accumulated profits of the subsidiary (investee). In addition, dividends declared by the subsidiary reduce the investment account, because they are considered a return on the investment. For example, a parent company owns 30% of a subsidiary purchased at a cost of $500,000. When the subsidiary company earns $200,000, the parent company increases the investment account by $60,000 (30% of $200,000). When the investee declares a dividend of $30,000, the parent company decreases the investment account by $9,000 (30% of $30,000).

Cash Surrender Value of Life Insurance. Cash surrender value of life insurance represents the amount by which insurance premiums may exceed the actual insurance cost and is refundable on cancellation or surrender of the policy. In other words, it represents a future value in the form of the amount that an insurance company will pay the insured (i.e., the hospitality company) if a life insurance policy is canceled. Changes in the amount of the cash surrender value should be accounted for as an adjustment to insurance expense.

Intangible Assets. Intangible assets have a long-term future value to the company but no physical substance. The hospitality entity exercises a right, including a legal right, to assist the company in generating future revenues. Patents, copyrights, goodwill, trademarks, and franchises exemplify intangible assets. Amortization of intangible assets is on a straight-line basis, and usually a contra account is not used. Instead, the intangible asset decreases as amortization is recorded in each period. Accounting Principles Board Opinion No. 17 (APB 17), *Intangible Assets*, FASB Statement No. 141 (FAS-141), *Business Combinations*, and FASB Statement No. 142 (FAS-142), *Goodwill and Other Intangible Assets* (ASC 350, *Intangibles—Goodwill and Other*) cover the accounting for intangible assets.

In December 2007, the FASB issued Statement of Financial Accounting Standards No. 141 (Revised 2007) (FAS-141R), *Business Combinations* (ASC 805, *Business Combinations*), which replaces FAS-141, *Business Combinations*. Under FAS-141R (ASC 805), an acquiring entity will be required to recognize the assets acquired, the liabilities assumed, and any noncontrolling interest in the acquiree, measured at their fair values as of the acquisition date.

A trademark is a distinctive name or symbol under which a right is granted indefinitely, as long as the owner uses it in connection with the product or service and files the paperwork.

A franchise is the legal right to operate under a particular corporate name (e.g., McDonald's, Holiday Inn) at a specific time and location. This right is normally stated in an agreement that defines the geographical area as well as the terms of the franchise relationship. The cost of obtaining the franchise is shown on the balance sheet, net of amortization over the duration of the franchise.

A patent represents the exclusive right granted to an inventor for a period of 20 years and is valued at acquisition cost and amortized over its legal or useful life, whichever is shorter.

Goodwill represents the excess of the purchase price over the fair value of the net assets acquired in the purchase of a business. It may result from talented personnel, strategic location, or outstanding management. Prior to the enactment of FAS-141, goodwill was amortized (written off) over a period not to exceed 40 years. Pursuant to FAS-141R (ASC 805), goodwill is recorded in a business combination using the purchase method when the purchase price exceeds the fair market value of the acquired net assets. Therefore, assets of the acquired company are stated at fair value using appraised values provided by an independent appraiser. If the purchase price is less than the fair market value of the net assets acquired, negative goodwill is created. According to FAS-141R (ASC 805), negative goodwill is proportionately allocated as a reduction of the acquired assets, with some exceptions (e.g., deferred tax charges or deferred pension assets).

FAS-142 (ASC 350) involves the subsequent accounting treatment of intangible assets and goodwill. Purchased goodwill is no longer amortized, but it is subject to annual impairment reviews. Generally, a long-term asset is viewed as impaired if the sum of the asset's estimated future cash flows is less than its carrying value. If the hospitality company meets this test, it will write down the asset to its estimated fair market value.

In the case of goodwill, the test of impairment involves estimating the fair value of the entire acquired business unit and comparing that value to its book value at that time. If the fair value is less than the book value, goodwill may be impaired. The amount of impairment is then measured by comparing the implied fair value of goodwill to the book value of the entity's goodwill. The implied fair value of goodwill is the difference between the estimated fair value of specific assets in the business unit and the fair value of the business unit as a whole. Once the impairment loss for goodwill is recorded, the adjusted book value becomes the intangible new cost basis. Goodwill is not revalued upward even if the implied fair value increases in the future.

Footnote disclosures for goodwill and other intangible assets include the amortization period and expected amortization expense for the next five years, the amount of any significant residual value, the method of determining fair value, the total amount of impairment losses, and the information related to the changes in the carrying value of goodwill both in total and by reporting unit.

Deferred Expenses. Deferred expenses (sometimes referred to as deferred charges) are long-term prepayments that are to be written off (or amortized) over future years. Examples include the discount or prepaid interest on a mortgage and preopening expenses.

LIABILITIES

Liabilities represent the hospitality company's obligations to make payments of cash or services within a reasonable future time for benefits or services received. SFAC 6, paragraph 36, defines *liabilities* as probable future sacrifices of economic benefits arising from present obligations of a particular entity to transfer assets or provide services to other entities in the future as a result of past transactions or events. Most liabilities are usually classified as either current or long-term, and are monetary items that require payments of a fixed amount of cash.

Current Liabilities

Current liabilities are those liabilities that must be satisfied in one year from the balance sheet date. They include accounts and notes payable, accrued expenses, the current portion of long-term debt, and unearned revenue. In addition, current deferred income taxes are reported under current liabilities when the tax effects of temporary differences result in a net current liability. For instance, revenue recognized in the income statement before it becomes taxable will result in current deferred income taxes because the revenue will be taxable in a future accounting period.

Accounts Payable. Accounts payable are short-term obligations that arise from credit extended by suppliers for the purchase of food inventory, supplies, or other goods and services. Amounts due to concessionaires for guest charges collected by the property may be included with accounts payable or shown separately, according to the most recent version of the USAL.

Notes Payable. Notes payable are short-term obligations in the form of promissory notes mainly to financial institutions. A short-term note may be given to secure an extension of time in which to pay an account payable or may arise when a company borrows money from a bank. Normally, the bank will collect interest when the note is repaid.

Current Portion of Long-Term Debt. When a company has mortgages or other forms of long-term debt outstanding, the portion of the principal that is due to be repaid during the upcoming year is classified as a current liability. Since it represents an amount owed within one year from the balance sheet date, it is deducted from the total long-term debt and shown as a current liability on the balance sheet.

Accrued Expenses. Accrued expenses represent expenses incurred but not due to be paid as of the balance sheet date. Examples include salaries and wages, interest, management fees, rent, and payroll taxes.

Unearned Revenue. Unearned revenue represents revenue collected or billed in advance of the performance of a service. Thus, the hospitality entity is indicating that a future service is owed to the customer and those services are forthcoming. For example, customer deposits received by a hotel or restaurant on room or banquet reservations represent unearned revenue, because these amounts are not recognized as revenue until the customer receives the service. In the same way, the unearned portion of transportation revenue received by a cruise or airline company is included under unearned revenue or is listed separately as an advance deposit under current liabilities.

Long-Term Liabilities

Long-term liabilities are those amounts due beyond one year from the balance sheet date. Examples include mortgages payable (net of current portion), bonds payable, and notes payable due after one year from the balance sheet date.

Bonds Payable. A bond payable is a form of interest-bearing note payable issued by hospitality companies in denominations of $1,000. It may be issued at face value, above face value (at a premium) or below face value (at a discount). A bond is issued at face value when the stated interest rate is the same as the market interest rate. If HR Corporation issues 200 five-year 10% bonds dated January 1, 20X9, at 100 (100% of face value), the entry to record the issuance is:

Jan 1	Cash	200,000	
	Bonds payable		200,000

To record issuance of bonds at face value.

When bonds are sold at a discount or premium, the stated rate is either higher or lower than the market interest rate. For instance, when a hospitality company issues 10% bonds at a time when other bonds of similar risk are paying 12%, the company will issue the bonds at a discount (below face value) because investors will not be willing to buy the bonds at 10%. To record the issuance of 200 five-year 10% bonds at 98, the entry will be:

Jan 1	Cash	196,000	
	Discount on bonds payable	4,000	
	Bonds payable		200,000

To record issuance of bonds at a discount.

Similarly, when bonds are issued at a premium (above face value), the entry will result in a credit to premium on bonds payable. Premium on bonds payable is added to bonds payable on the balance sheet, whereas the discount on bonds payable is deducted from bonds payable on the balance sheet.

Over the term (life) of the bond, entries are required for bond interest. During this time, the premium or discount on the bonds is amortized (written off) over the life of the bond. The sale of bonds above face value causes the total cost of borrowing to be less than the bond interest paid because the borrower is not required to pay the bond premium at the maturity date of the bond. Thus, the premium is considered to be a reduction in the cost of borrowing. Conversely, the discount on bonds is considered an additional cost of borrowing that is recorded as bond interest expense over the life of the bonds.

There are two methods of amortizing bond discount or bond premium: (1) the straight-line method and (2) the effective interest method. The straight-line method results in a constant dollar amount of amortization but a different effective rate each period. The effective interest method (the preferred method) results in a constant rate of interest but different dollar amounts each period.

Bonds may be redeemed before maturity. This decision is made by the financial officer in order to reduce interest cost while removing debt from the balance sheet. When bonds are retired before maturity, it is necessary to eliminate the carrying value of the bonds at the redemption date and recognize the gain or loss on redemption. The carrying value of the bonds is the face value of the bonds less unamortized bond discount or plus unamortized bond premium on the redemption date. For example, RT Hospitality retires at 103 bonds sold at a premium. If the carrying value of the bonds at the redemption date is $100,500, the entry to record the redemption at the end of the fourth interest period is:

Jan 1	Bonds payable	100,000	
	Premium on bonds payable	500	
	Loss on bond redemption	2,500	
	Cash		103,000

To record redemption of bonds at 103.

Note that the loss of $2,500 is the difference between the cash paid: $103,000, and the carrying value of the bonds: $100,500.

Other Liabilities

Some items do not meet the criteria for being classified as current or long-term liabilities on the balance sheet. These items usually represent long-term obligations of the hospitality company arising from the operation of the business and are presented as a separate line item immediately after long-term liabilities. Examples include deferred income taxes, minority interest, and pension obligations.

Deferred Income Taxes. As previously noted, using different accounting methods for tax and financial reporting purposes causes deferred income taxes. The most significant timing difference to a hospitality company is associated with using an accelerated method of depreciation for tax purposes (e.g., double-declining balance), while using straight-line depreciation on the income statement. This causes tax expense on the income statement to be higher than taxes actually payable. The difference is deferred income tax.

Pursuant to FASB Statement No. 109 (FAS-109), *Accounting for Income Taxes* (ASC 740, *Income Taxes*), the liability method must be used to account for deferred income taxes. The deferred tax liability (or asset) is measured at the tax rate under current law that will exist when the temporary difference reverses. In addition, the deferred tax liability (or asset) must be adjusted for changes in tax laws or tax rates. Accordingly, tax expense will be equal to taxes payable plus the tax effects of all timing differences.

A hospitality company is required to report a breakdown of its deferred income taxes into a current and noncurrent amount, depending on the classification of the asset or liability responsible for the temporary difference. The net current amount could result in a current asset or liability being reported, whereas the net noncurrent amount could result in a noncurrent asset or a noncurrent liability being reported. For instance, a deferred tax liability resulting from the excess of tax depreciation over income statement depreciation would be reported as a noncurrent liability or as a separate line item.

Accounting for Compensating Absences

Based on FASB Statement No. 43 (FAS-43), *Accounting for Compensated Absences* (ASC 710, *Compensation—General*), the hospitality entity has to record a liability for employee compensation for future absences. To record the accrual, it is necessary that employee rights have vested and employee services have already been performed. In addition, the amount of estimated liability must be able to be reasonably determined. Compensated absences include sick leave (only in cases when the company allows employees to take accumulated sick leave days), holiday, and vacation time.

Contingencies

Contingencies are events with uncertain outcomes and are recognized by rules established by FASB Statement No. 5 (FAS-5), *Accounting for Contingencies* (ASC 450, *Contingencies*). To record a liability, the loss must be probable, and the amount must be reasonably estimated. If the hospitality company can determine a reasonable estimate of the expected loss and if it is probable the loss will occur, then the company should accrue for the loss by increasing (debiting) a loss account and crediting a liability, if material. Examples of probable loss contingencies include expropriation of property by a foreign government and casualties (e.g., fire or hurricane losses).

In cases where the above conditions are not met (e.g., the loss is more than remote and less than likely), the hospitality company should disclose the basic facts regarding the contingency in the notes to its financial statements. For example, in the case of lawsuits or environmental hazards, the company cannot predict the outcome; nonetheless, information about the contingency must be disclosed in the notes to the financial statements. The disclosure will include the nature of the contingency and the estimate of possible loss. In cases where an estimate of the loss is not possible, a disclosure of this fact is made. In cases of remote contingencies (with a very minimal chance of occurring), disclosure is usually not made. However, some remote contingencies are normally disclosed (e.g., loan guarantees).

OWNERS' EQUITY

The owners' equity represents the owners' claims on the hospitality company. It is presented in different ways for sole proprietorships, partnerships, and corporations, depending on the type of legal organization. In the case of an unincorporated business, one or more capital accounts represent the equity section of the balance sheet.

SHAREHOLDERS' EQUITY

The ownership interests in a corporation are represented in the final section of the balance sheet as shareholders' or stockholders' equity. It is a residual interest or claim to the assets of the company. That is, the owners have a claim on all assets not required to meet the claims of creditors. Hence, the valuation of assets and liabilities in the balance sheet determines the valuation of total shareholders' equity. Common stock and additional paid-in capital are part of paid-in capital, which is the amount contributed by original investors through public offerings and other sources.

The stockholders' equity section of the balance sheet may include the following accounts:

- Preferred stock
- Common stock
- Additional paid-in capital
- Retained earnings

- Treasury stock
- Comprehensive income

Exhibit 7-2, "Stockholders' Equity for Brinker, Fiscal Year 2004," presents an example of shareholder's equity reported in the Brinkers International Inc. 2004 annual report.

Exhibit 7-2: Stockholders' Equity for Brinker, Fiscal Year 2004 (In Thousands)

	2004	2003
Shareholders' Equity:		
Common stock 250,000,000 authorized shares; $.10 par value: 117,499,541 shares issued and 90,647,745 shares outstanding at June 30, 2004, and 117,499,541 shares issued and 97,854,952 shares outstanding at June 25, 2003	$ 11,750	$ 11,750
Additional paid-in capital	357,444	344,486
Accumulated other comprehensive income	737	609
Retained earnings	1,277,298	1,123,337
	1,647,229	1,480,182
Less:		
Treasury stock, at cost (20,851,796 shares at June 30, 2004 and 19,644,589 shares at June 25, 2003)	(619,806)	(337,946)
Unearned compensation	(1,350)	(1,986)
Total shareholders' equity	$1,026,073	$1,140,250

Preferred Stock. Where a second class of stock exists, it is normally referred to as preferred stock.

Preferred shareholders have preferential rights over other classes of stock. They receive a fixed dividend prior to common shareholders, share in liquidation prior to common shareholders, and may have preemptive and voting rights over common shareholders. Preferred stock may also be fully participating, cumulative, and convertible into common stock.

Financial statement disclosures of preferred stock include shares authorized, issued, and outstanding, as well as liquidation preferences, call prices, and cumulative dividends in arrears.

In the case of fully participating preferred stock, preferred shareholders are entitled to receive a dividend that is higher than the preferred dividend rate. For instance, a 12% fully participating preferred stock is entitled to a 12% preference rate plus a proportionate share of the excess dividend based on the total par value of the common and preferred stock.

Regarding cumulative preferred stock, dividends not paid in a specific year are accumulated so that dividends in future years must be paid before dividends on common stock and noncumulative preferred dividends are paid.

In cases where preferred stock is converted into common stock, the preferred stock and paid-in capital accounts are eliminated, while the common stock and paid-in capital accounts are created (credited). If a deficit results, the retained earnings account would be debited.

Common Stock. Common stock represents ownership that has voting and liquidation rights. In the event of liquidation, the liquidation rights of common stockholders give them claims to company assets after all creditors' and preferred stockholders' rights have been fulfilled.

The total amount contributed by shareholders is the same for both par value stock and no-par stock. In some states, no-par stock can be issued, whereas in other states a stated value must be assigned to each share, and this stated value per share has the same legal status as par value per share. If common stock is retired, an entry debiting common stock and crediting cash is recorded. In cases where the common stock is retired for less than par value, additional paid-in capital is also credited, whereas in cases where the common stock is retired for more than par value, additional paid-in capital is debited for the original premium, and the retained earnings are debited for the excess over the original premium. Retained earnings cannot be credited when retiring common stock.

As shown in Exhibit 7-2, Brinker issued 117,499,541 shares at the end of fiscal 2004, of which 90,647,745 shares were outstanding. Brinker has a policy of buying back its own shares, which are recorded as treasury stock, thus reducing the number of shares outstanding.

Additional Paid-in Capital. The additional paid-in capital or contributed capital in excess of par represents the excess paid by shareholders over the par value of the issued shares. For example, if a hospitality company sold 3,000 shares of $1 par value stock for $5 per share, the common stock account would be $3,000 and additional paid-in capital would total $2,000.

Reference to the additional paid-in capital for Brinker reveals that the company's common stock was issued at a price substantially higher than its par value of $.10 per share. The additional paid-in capital account is not affected by fluctuation in stock prices resulting from stock trading subsequent to its original issue.

Retained Earnings. The retained earnings account is the sum of the total amount earned by the hospitality company since its inception net of distribution of these earnings (i.e., dividends) in the form of cash or stock. Since retained earnings represent the link between the income statement and the balance sheet, details as to the transactions affecting retained earnings from the beginning to the end of the period are shown on a separate statement of retained earnings.

Retained earnings can be set aside for specific uses, in which case the amount is not available for the payment of dividends. The entry to record an appropriation of retained earnings will debit retained earnings while crediting appropriated retained earnings. Examples include appropriations for company expansion, debt retirement, sinking funds, and other general contingencies. Once the contingency actually takes place, the aforementioned entry is reversed.

When retained earnings are negative, the accumulated losses and dividends exceed the accumulated profits, which is termed a *deficit*. Quasi-reorganization provides a fresh start for a financially troubled company with a deficit instead of retained earnings. It is implemented to avoid bankruptcy by revaluing the assets and eliminating the deficit or by reducing paid-in capital.

Dividends represent a distribution of profits paid to the company's stockholders out of retained earnings. Once the board of directors of the corporation declares the dividend on the declaration date, it becomes a liability of the company. A journal entry is recorded on the declaration date debiting dividends (or retained earnings) and crediting dividends payable.

In order to qualify to receive dividends, shareholders must be registered as owners of the stock on the record date. They will receive the dividend in the form of cash or stock on the payment date, at which time the company will debit dividends payable and credit cash (or common stock).

Stock dividends are issued in the form of common stock. If the stock dividend is less than 25% of the outstanding shares on the declaration date, retained earnings are debited in the amount of the market price of the shares. If the stock dividend is more than 20% to 25% of the outstanding shares, retained earnings are debited for the par value of the shares issued.

Treasury Stock. Treasury stock represents issued shares that have been repurchased by the hospitality company rather than retired. They are reported as a reduction in total stockholders' equity. Hospitality companies often repurchase shares of their own stock for (1) employee stock option and retirement plans, (2) to defend against a potential takeover, (3) as an investment use of excess cash holdings, and (4) to increase earnings per share by reducing the number of shares outstanding.

There are two methods available to account for treasury stock: (1) the par value method and (2) the cost method. The par value method records the treasury stock at par or stated value. This method removes the paid-in capital in excess of par (or stated value) from the original issue. Thus, the treasury stock is reported as a reduction from paid-in capital. The cost method records treasury stock at the price paid to acquire the stock. Most hospitality companies record treasury stock at cost.

If the repurchased shares are not retired, they are shown as an offsetting account in the shareholders' equity section of the balance sheet when the cost method is used. Brinker held 20,851,796 shares of treasury stock on June 30, 2004. The cost of the shares is shown as a reduction of shareholders' equity.

Comprehensive Income. Comprehensive income represents the change in total shareholders' equity from all sources other than transactions involving owners. Since the enactment of FASB Statement No. 130 (FAS-130), *Reporting*

Comprehensive Income (ASC 220, *Comprehensive Income*), companies must report comprehensive income or loss for the period. There are two types of comprehensive income: (1) net income and (2) other comprehensive income. As noted in Chapter 6, "Financial Statement Reporting: The Income Statement," other comprehensive income can be reported in a separate equity account on the balance sheet generally referred to as accumulated other comprehensive income (expense). This account includes:

- Foreign currency translation adjustments resulting from converting financial statements from a foreign currency to U.S. dollars.

- Unrealized gains or losses in the market value of investments on available-for-sale marketable securities. Debt and equity securities classified as available-for-sale securities are carried at fair value. Unrealized holding gains and losses are included in a separate category within stockholders' equity until realized. This accounting treatment applies only to securities available for sale. Trading securities are reported at their fair value on the balance sheet, and unrealized gains and losses are included in income of the current period.

- Changes in the excess of additional pension liability over unrecognized prior service cost. Accounting standards require a reduction in stockholders' equity for a minimum pension liability under a defined benefit plan.

- Certain gains and losses on derivative financial instruments. Derivative instruments are financial instruments or other contracts where rights or obligations meet the criteria of assets or liabilities. The gain or loss from some derivative instruments is reported in current earnings. For other derivative instruments, the gain or loss is reported as a component of other comprehensive income.

FAS-130 (ASC 220) provides considerable flexibility in reporting comprehensive income. Exhibit 7-3, "Outback Steakhouse Consolidated Statement of Stockholders' Equity," provides an example of comprehensive income reported in a separate equity account on the balance sheet.

The details of stockholders' equity are considered important enough to warrant their own statement, which provides details of activities in all accounts in the stockholders' equity section. The consolidated statement of stockholders' equity, presented in Exhibit 7-3, consists of columns that summarize the specific changes that occurred between the beginning and ending balance sheet amounts in each of the equity accounts. In a separate column of this statement, the company presents the comprehensive income, which represents the results of the current period's income (loss), as well as other non-owner changes in equity for the period, which do not appear on the income statement.

Employee Stock Purchase Plans. Under a qualified employee stock purchase plan, a hospitality entity may offer stock to employees at a discount of up to 15% for a period of five years. The employee can purchase no more than $25,000 of stock in any year. This is considered a noncompensatory plan as long as the discount is not material.

Stock Options. Stock options are perks given to employees that allow them to buy shares of their company's stock in the future at a set price. If the stock rises before the options are exercised, the employee can buy the stock at the predetermined lower price and then sell it at the higher price. Stock options have become an increasingly important form of remuneration in the recent past. Most large hospitality companies offer options to at least some of their employees. There have been ongoing debates about whether the fair value of employee stock options should be expensed on the income statement. Expense recognition of stock options can have significant effects on net income and earnings per share.

Prior to the enactment of FASB Statement No. 123R (FAS-123R), *Share-Based Payment* (ASC 718, *Compensation—Stock Compensation*), a hospitality company's cost of issuing stock options only had to be disclosed in a footnote to its financial statement, not deducted from the income statement. However, FAS-123R (ASC 718) currently requires publicly held companies to measure the cost of employee services received in exchange for an award of equity instruments based on the grant date fair value of the award. That cost will be recognized over the period during which an employee is required to provide service in exchange for the award; that is, the requisite service period (normally the vesting period). No compensation cost is recognized for equity instruments for which employees do not render the requisite service.

Exhibit 7-3: Outback Steakhouse Consolidated Statement of Stockholders' Equity (*Source:* Outback 2003 Annual Report)

Outback Steakhouse, Inc. and Affiliates
CONSOLIDATED STATEMENT OF STOCKHOLDERS' EQUITY
(In Thousands)

	Common Stock Shares	Common Stock Amount	Additional Paid-In Capital	Retained Earnings	Accumulated Other Comprehensive Loss	Treasury Stock	Total
Balance, December 31, 2000	76,632	$785	$216,056	$570,746	$—	$(46,119)	$741,468
Issuance of common stock	40	1	272	—	—	—	273
Purchase of treasury stock	(1,210)	—	—	—	—	(31,250)	(31,250)
Reissuance of treasury stock	1,451	—	—	(9,346)	—	35,365	26,019
Stock option income tax benefit	—	—	5,835	—	—	—	5,835
Stock option compensation expense	—	—	1,004	—	—	—	1,004
Net income	—	—	—	124,738	—	—	124,738
Balance, December 31, 2001	76,913	786	223,167	686,138	—	(42,004)	868,087
Issuance of common stock	196	2	6,998	—	—	—	7,000
Purchase of treasury stock	(2,691)	—	—	—	—	(81,650)	(81,650)
Reissuance of treasury stock	1,462	—	—	(6,767)	—	36,706	29,939
Dividends ($0.12 per share)	—	—	—	(9,101)	—	—	(9,101)
Stock option income tax benefit	—	—	8,580	—	—	—	8,580
Stock option compensation expense	—	—	1,338	—	—	—	1,338
Net income	—	—	—	150,090	—	—	150,090
Balance, December 31, 2002	75,880	788	240,083	820,360	—	(86,948)	974,283
Purchase of treasury stock	(3,784)	—	—	—	—	(143,191)	(143,191)
Reissuance of treasury stock	2,183	—	—	(19,133)	—	68,331	49,198
Dividends ($0.49 per share)	—	—	—	(36,917)	—	—	(36,917)

Outback Steakhouse, Inc. and Affiliates
CONSOLIDATED STATEMENT OF STOCKHOLDERS' EQUITY
(In Thousands)

	Common Stock Shares	Common Stock Amount	Additional Paid-In Capital	Retained Earnings	Accumulated Other Comprehensive Loss	Treasury Stock	Total
Stock option income tax benefit	—	—	13,189	—	—	—	13,189
Stock option compensation expense	—	—	1,580	—	—	—	1,580
Net income	—	—	—	170,206	—	—	170,206
Foreign currency translation adjustment	—	—	—	—	(2,078)	—	(2,078)
Balance, December 31, 2003	74,279	$788	$254,852	$934,516	$(2,078)	$(161,808)	$1,026,270

In the case of nonpublic entities, FAS-123R (ASC 718) requires the company to measure the cost of employee services received in exchange for an award of equity instruments based on the grant date fair value of those instruments, except in certain circumstances. In cases where it is not possible to reasonably estimate the fair value of equity share options and similar instruments because it is not feasible to approximate the expected volatility of the entity's share price, a nonpublic hospitality entity is required to measure its awards of equity share options based on a value calculated using the historical volatility of the appropriate lodging or restaurant industry sector index instead of the expected volatility of its share price.

As a result of the enactment of FAS-123R (ASC 718), hospitality companies are required to record the stock option as compensation expense on the income statement. The notes to financial statements of both public and nonpublic entities will also disclose information to assist users of financial information to understand the nature of share-based payment transactions and the effects of those transactions on the financial statements. The new pronouncement became effective for fiscal periods beginning after June 15, 2005. For private companies and small business issuers, the standard applies for fiscal years beginning after December 15, 2005.

Stock Splits. A stock split involves the issuance of additional shares to stockholders according to their percentage ownership. It results in the reduction of the par value per share and the increase in the number of shares outstanding. If a company had 2,000 shares of common stock outstanding, a 2-for-1 stock split would result in 4,000 shares outstanding. However, the par or stated value of the stock is changed in proportion to the stock split and no change is made to common stock, or retained earnings, or to any other equity accounts. The purpose of the stock split is to increase the marketability of the stock by lowering the market value per share.

CHAPTER 8
FINANCIAL STATEMENT REPORTING: THE CASH FLOW STATEMENT

CONTENTS

The Cash Flow Statement: Objectives and Scope	8001
Preparation of the Cash Flow Statement	8002
Cash Flow Statement Components	8003
Cash Flow from Investing Activities	8004
Cash Flow from Financing Activities	8004
Cash Flow from Operating Activities	8004
Direct Versus Indirect Approach	8005
Schedule of Noncash Financing and Investing Activities	8008
Cash and Cash Equivalents	8008
Management of Cash Flows	8009

Exhibits

Exhibit 8-1.	Format of the Statement of Cash Flows	8002
Exhibit 8-2.	Major Operating, Investing, and Financing Cash Inflows and Outflows	8003
Exhibit 8-3.	Indirect Method of Computing Cash Provided by Operations	8006
Exhibit 8-4.	Adjustments to Net Income—Indirect Approach	8006
Exhibit 8-5.	Format of Cash Flow Statement—Indirect Approach	8007
Exhibit 8-6.	Hilton Hotels Cash Flow Statements	8009

The statement of cash flows presents the movement of cash in and out of the company during a specific period of time, which is the same period that is used for the income statement. FASB Statement No. 95 (FAS-95), *Statement of Cash Flows* (ASC 230, *Statement of Cash Flows*), requires that all hospitality companies issue a cash flow statement and provides guidelines regarding its format. On the statement, cash flows are segregated by operating, investing, and financing activities.

THE CASH FLOW STATEMENT: OBJECTIVES AND SCOPE

The objective of the statement of cash flows is to furnish useful information regarding a company's cash receipts and cash payments for the period. This information is not directly available from either the income statement or the balance sheet. FAS-95 (ASC 230) requires a reconciliation of net income and net cash flow from operations, as well as the disclosure of certain information applicable to noncash investing and financing transactions.

Some hospitality companies may report high earnings but still not be able to pay obligations to employees, creditors, or suppliers. The statement of cash flows provides detailed information about the cash inflows and outflows of the company to help detect these types of weaknesses. Thus, this information offers insights into a company's management of its cash flows and the underlying quality of its earnings.

The main goal of the hospitality company is to maximize the owners' value. To accomplish this objective in the case of corporate entities, operating profits are paid to owners as dividends. However, the ability of the hospitality company to pay dividends is a function of the cash flow that is available for that purpose. The statement of cash flows demonstrates the ability of the company to finance expansion, pay dividends and, most important, repay obligations.

PREPARATION OF THE CASH FLOW STATEMENT

The statement of cash flows explains the change in cash and cash equivalents for the period. It is prepared by calculating the changes in all the balance sheet accounts, including cash, then listing the changes in all the accounts except cash as inflows or outflows, and categorizing the flows by operating activities, financing, or investing activities. The inflows minus the outflows balance to and explain the change in cash during the period.

Exhibit 8-1, "Format of the Statement of Cash Flows," presents the general format of the statement of cash flows and provides examples of the categories often found in hospitality published statements. As shown, each type of transaction listed in the statement of cash flows reflects an increase in cash (inflow) or a decrease in cash (outflow).

Exhibit 8-1: Format of the Statement of Cash Flows

	Increase	(Decrease)
Cash flow from operating activities:		
Cash received from customers		$xx
Cash paid for salaries and wages		(xx)
Cash paid to suppliers		(xx)
Cash paid for income taxes		(xx)
Cash paid for interest		(xx)
Cash flow from operating activities:		$xx
Cash flow from investing activities:		
Cash paid for the purchase of property and equipment	$(xx)	
Cash received from sales of investments	xx	
Cash received from sale of property and equipment	xx	
Net cash flow (used) by investing activities		(xx)
Cash flow from financing activities:		
Cash received from the sale of common stock	$ xx	
Cash paid for dividends	(xx)	
Net cash provided (used) by financing activities		xx

	Increase	(Decrease)
Cash flow from operating activities:		
Net increase (decrease) in cash		$xx

FAS-95 (ASC 230) requires the reconciliation of operating cash flows to the net income reported on the income statement based on accrual accounting. Accordingly, when using the above direct format to report cash flow from operating activities, a separate schedule is prepared showing the reconciliation of operating cash flow to net income.

CASH FLOW STATEMENT COMPONENTS

The statement of cash flows classifies cash receipts and cash payments of a hospitality business into three principal activities: (1) investing, (2) financing, and (3) operating. Each group of activities can result in inflows and outflows of cash, and the statement of cash flows includes a listing of all cash flows classified under the three groups of activities. Exhibit 8-2, "Major Operating, Investing, and Financing Cash Inflows and Outflows," summarizes the classifications of cash flows under financing, investing, and operating activities.

Exhibit 8-2: Major Operating, Investing, and Financing Cash Inflows and Outflows

ACTIVITIES

Operating Activities

Cash Inflow
- Sale of rooms
- Collection of accounts receivables
- Advance collection of sales

Cash Outflow
- Payment of salaries
- Payment of taxes
- Payments to vendors

Investing Activities

Cash Inflow
- Sale of property and equipment
- Sale of investments
- Collection of loans

Cash Outflow
- Increase in property and equipment
- Granting loans to others
- Purchase of investments

Financing Activities

Cash Inflow
- Issuance of preferred and common stock
- Issuance of short-term debt
- Issuance of long-term debt

Cash Outflow
- Repayment of debt
- Payment of dividends
- Purchase of treasury stock

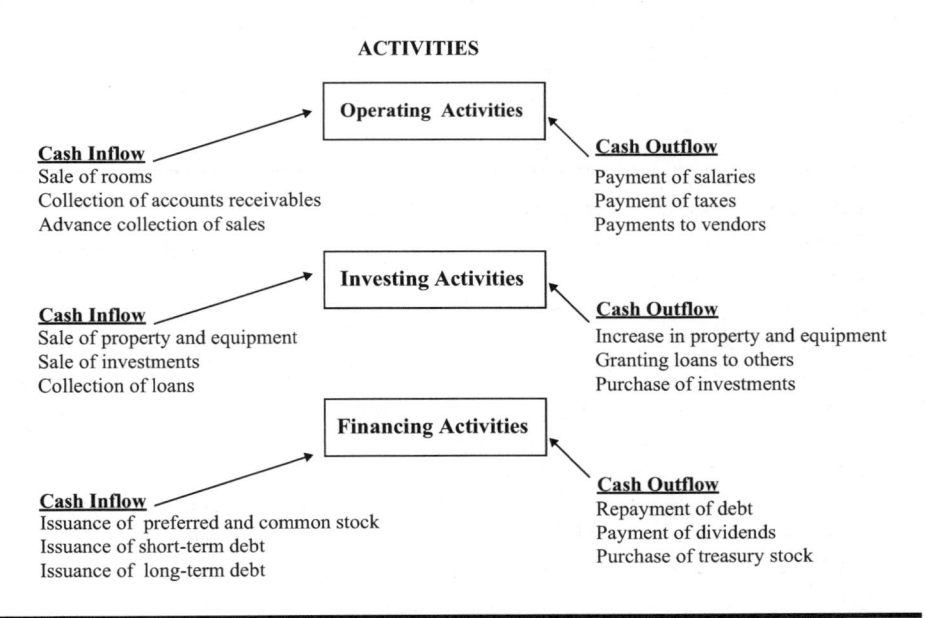

Because operating activities are their only internal source of cash, hospitality companies that are able to satisfy most of their cash needs from operating cash are generally considered to be in stronger financial health and better credit risks.

If a cash receipt or cash payment applies to more than one classification (i.e., investing, financing, or operating), sorting is made as to the activity that is the main source of that cash flow. For instance, the purchase and sale of equipment to be used by the hospitality company is typically reported as an investing activity.

Cash Flow from Investing Activities

Investing activities involves the cash flow effect of transactions related to the hospitality company's long-term assets, including property and equipment, and investments. Examples include cash paid for the construction or purchase of hotel or restaurant properties, acquisitions of other companies, and purchase of debt and equity securities of other entities.

Cash inflows from investing activities comprise receipts from sales of equity or debt securities of other companies, amounts received from the sale of hotel or restaurant properties, and collections or sales of loans made by the hospitality entity. Cash outflows for investing activities include payments to buy equity or debt securities of other companies; payments to purchase property and equipment, such as kitchen equipment or lodging properties; and disbursements for loans made by the company. For growth hospitality companies, the cash from investing activities will normally be a net outflow, although this depends on the company's growth strategy.

Note that gains or losses of long-term assets are included as investing activities along with any related assets. These gains or losses are not included in net cash flow from operating items. Thus, they are reported as an adjustment to net income in obtaining cash flow from operations.

Cash Flow from Financing Activities

Financing activities incorporate the long-term inflow of capital to the hospitality company in the form of cash from investors. These include both the equity investments of stockholders and the loans from bondholders and other creditors—that is, transactions involving changes in long-term liabilities and stockholders' equity items.

Financing activities include the issuance and repayment of debt, such as mortgages and notes payable, as well as issuances and repurchases of stock and payment of dividends. Cash inflows from financing activities are composed of cash received from the sale of the hospitality company's common or preferred stock and cash obtained from the issuance of mortgages or bonds. Cash outflows for financing activities include repayment of debt obligations, repurchase of stock, dividend payments, and other payments to long-term creditors. Note that stock dividends, stock splits, and appropriations of retained earnings are not included under financing activities because they are noncash transactions. Gains or losses from the early extinguishment of debt are part of the cash flow related to the repayment of the amount borrowed as a financing activity.

Cash Flow from Operating Activities

Cash flow from operating activities includes cash outflows from the sale of rooms, food and beverages, and other hospitality services, and from expenses associated with the generation of those sales.

Cash flow derived from operating activities typically applies to the cash effects of transactions entering into the calculation of net income. Cash inflows from operating activities include:

- Cash sales or collections on receivables arising from the initial sale of food or beverages;
- Rendering of services or unearned revenue received, such as customer deposits;
- Cash receipts from returns on loans, debt securities (e.g., interest income), or equity securities (e.g., dividend income) of other entities;
- Cash received from licensees and lessees;
- Receipt of a litigation settlement; and
- Reimbursement under an insurance policy.

Cash outflows for operating activities include:

- Cash paid for raw material or merchandise for resale;
- Principal payments on accounts payable arising from the initial purchase of goods;
- Payments to suppliers of operating expense items (e.g., office supplies, advertising, and insurance);
- Salaries and wages;
- Payments to government agencies (e.g., taxes);
- Interest expense;
- Lawsuit payments;
- Charitable contributions; and
- Cash refunds to customers.

DIRECT VERSUS INDIRECT APPROACH

The two approaches to presenting cash flow from operations are the direct method and the indirect method. FAS-95 (ASC 230) allows the use of either method, as both methods produce identical results of cash received from operations. Yet, there is essentially one difference in statement presentation between the direct and indirect method, which relates solely to the operating section. Under the direct method, the hospitality company reports cash received from revenue-producing activities and then subtracts its cash payments for expenses. With this method, the reconciliation of net income to cash flow from operations is presented in a separate schedule. An example of the direct method format is shown in Exhibit 8-1.

Under the indirect method, gross cash receipts and gross cash payments from operating activities are not shown. Instead, the company reports net cash flow from operating activities indirectly by adjusting net income through its reconciliation to net cash flow from operating activities. This is shown in the operating section within the body of the statement of cash flows or in a separate schedule. If presented in a separate schedule, the net cash flow from operating activities is presented as a single line item.

8006 Part II: Financial Statement Reporting

Although the direct method is preferred, most hospitality companies use the indirect method because it is simpler to prepare. Exhibit 8-3, "Indirect Method of Computing Cash Provided by Operations," presents an example of the reconciliation process of net income to cash flow from operating activities.

Exhibit 8-3: Indirect Method of Computing Cash Provided by Operations

	Add (+) or deduct (−) to adjust net income
Net income	$xxx
Adjustments required converting net income to cash basis:	
Depreciation, amortization expense, and loss on sale of noncurrent assets	+
Amortization of deferred revenue, amortization of bond premium, and gain on sale of noncurrent assets	−
Add (deduct) changes in current asset accounts affecting: revenue or expenses[a]	
Increase in the account	−
Decrease in the account	+
Add (deduct) changes in current liability accounts affecting revenue or expenses[b]:	
Increase in the account	+
Decrease in the account	−
Add (deduct) changes in the deferred income taxes account:	
Increase in the account	+
Decrease in the account	−
Cash provided by operations	$xxx

[a] Examples: Accounts receivable, inventory and prepaid expenses.
[b] Examples: Accounts payable, accrued expenses and unearned revenue.

Exhibit 8-4, "Adjustments to Net Income—Indirect Approach," provides an analysis of major transactions in which reconciliation of net income to net cash is required when using the indirect approach.

Exhibit 8-4: Adjustments to Net Income—Indirect Approach

Adjustments to Net Income	Explanation	Adjustment
Depreciation and amortization	Reduces net income but has no effect on cash	Add back depreciation or amortization
Increase in receivables	Increases net income but has no effect on cash	Deduct increase in receivables from net income
Decrease in receivables	Increases cash but has no effect on net income	Add decrease in receivables to net income

Adjustments to Net Income	Explanation	Adjustment
Increase in inventory	Decreases cash but has no effect on net income	Deduct increase in inventory from net income
Decrease in inventory	Reduces net income but not cash	Add decrease in inventory to net income
Increase in payables and other current liabilities	Expenses exceed related payments to creditors	Add increase in current liabilities to net income
Decrease in payables and other current liabilities	Cash payments to creditors exceed related expenses	Deduct decrease in current liabilities from net income
Increase in deferred taxes	Income tax expense exceeds amount payable to the government	Add increase in the deferred income tax account to net income
Decrease in deferred taxes	Amount currently payable to the government exceeds income tax expense	Deduct decrease in deferred income tax from net income
Gain on sale of assets	Cash effect shown on the investing section	Deduct gain from net income
Loss on sale of assets	Cash effect shown on the investing section	Add loss to net income

Exhibit 8-5, "Format of Cash Flow Statement—Indirect Approach," presents the complete cash flow statement format required when using the indirect approach in presenting the operating section of the cash flow statement.

Exhibit 8-5: Format of Cash Flow Statement—Indirect Approach

Cash flow from operations:
  Net income:
  Add:
    Depreciation and amortization
    Losses on sales of noncurrent assets and liabilities
    Increases in current (operating) liabilities
    Decreases in current (operating) assets other than cash
  Deduct:
    Gains on sales of noncurrent assets and liabilities
    Increases in current (operating) assets other than cash
    Decreases in current (operating) liabilities
Cash flow from investing:
  Add:
    Proceeds from sale of or decrease in noncurrent assets and nonoperating current assets
    Proceeds from dispositions of other companies
  Deduct:
    Purchase of or increase in noncurrent assets and nonoperating assets
    Acquisitions of other companies

Cash flow from financing:
   Add:
      Issuance of short-term or long-term debt
      Issuance of common or preferred stock
   Deduct:
      Repayment of debt
      Payment of dividends
      Stock repurchases

SCHEDULE OF NONCASH FINANCING AND INVESTING ACTIVITIES

Generally accepted accounting principles (GAAP) requires the disclosure of transactions involving significant noncash financing and investing activities as supplemental information on the statement of cash flows. Separate disclosure shall be made of investing and financing activities impacting assets or liabilities that do not affect cash flow. Examples of noncash activities of an investing and financing nature are conversions of bonds and preferred stock into common stock, purchase of property and equipment by the incurrence of a mortgage payable, capital leases, and nonmonetary exchange of assets. These disclosures may be footnoted or shown in a separate schedule within the statement of cash flows as follows:

EXAMPLE 1:

Noncash investing and financing activities:	
Purchase of land by the issuance of common stock	$300,000
Conversion of bonds payable to common stock	100,000
	$400,000

CASH AND CASH EQUIVALENTS

On the statement of cash flows the term *cash* includes both cash and highly liquid short-term marketable securities, also called *cash equivalents*. A cash equivalent is a short-term, very liquid investment satisfying the following criteria: (1) it is easily convertible into cash; and (2) it is very near the maturity date so there is hardly any chance of change in market value due to interest rate changes. Typically, this last condition is applicable solely to investments having original maturities of three months or less.

Examples of cash equivalents are commercial paper, money market funds, and Treasury bills. Disclosure should be made of the company's policy for determining items that represent cash equivalents. A change in policy is accounted for as a change in accounting principle requiring the restatement of previous years' financial statements for comparative purposes, if material.

In the case of foreign currency cash flows, the exchange rate at the time of the cash flow should be used in reporting the currency equivalent of foreign currency cash flows. The effect of changes in the exchange rate on cash balances

MANAGEMENT OF CASH FLOWS

held in foreign currencies should be reported as a separate element of the reconciliation of the change in cash and cash equivalents for the period.

Although a company may be profitable, it will not be successful without a consistently healthy cash flow. When planned expenditures necessitate more cash than that which planned activities are likely to produce, financial managers must develop a plan for confronting the shortfall. They may decide to obtain debt or equity financing or dispose of some property or business segment. Alternatively, they may decide to reduce planned activities by modifying operational plans, such as by postponing expansion plans; or they may decide to revise planned payments to financing sources, such as reducing or eliminating dividend payments. Whatever is decided, the goal should be to balance, over the short- and long-term, the cash available while maximizing the use of resources.

The cash flow statement provides insights into the effectiveness with which a hospitality company manages its cash flows, as well as evidence of the underlying quality of its earnings flows. Management of cash flows is an important activity in a hospitality business. If a hotel or restaurant's operating cash flows are insufficient to meet operating cash outflow demands, the company may be forced to engage in additional borrowing or to issue stock or sell long-term assets to meet cash needs. The analysis of the statement of cash flows is presented in Chapter 15, "Analysis of the Cash Flow Statement." Exhibit 8-6 presents the Hilton Hotels' statements of cash flows for 2002, 2003, and 2004, taken from the company's 2004 annual report.

Exhibit 8-6: Hilton Hotels Cash Flow Statements

Hilton Hotels Corporation and Subsidiaries
Consolidated Statements of Cash Flow
(in millions)

	Year Ended December 31,		
	2002	2003	2004
Operating Activities			
Net income	$198	$164	$238
Adjustments to reconcile net income to net cash provided by operating activities:			
Depreciation and amortization	348	334	330
Amortization of loan costs	9	13	9
Net loss on asset dispositions and other	14	6	5
Loss of non-operating affiliates	—	—	6
Impairment loss and related costs	21	22	5
Change in working capital components:			
Inventories	13	(34)	45
Accounts receivable	12	37	(24)
Other current assets	55	2	(9)

	Year Ended December 31,		
	2002	2003	2004
Accounts payable and accrued expenses	26	(26)	59
Restricted cash	(15)	(39)	(90)
Change in deferred income taxes	(39)	(48)	27
Change in other liabilities	(22)	35	49
Unconsolidated affiliates' distributions in excess of earnings	19	17	20
Change in timeshare notes receivable	(36)	(73)	(105)
Other	21	(30)	(17)
Net cash provided by operating activities	624	380	548
Investing Activities			
Capital expenditures	(245)	(202)	(178)
Additional investments	(32)	(25)	(72)
Proceeds from asset dispositions	174	279	80
Payments received on notes and other	21	8	38
Acquisitions, net of cash acquired	(71)	—	—
Net cash (used in) provided by investing activities	(153)	60	(132)
Financing Activities			
Change in revolving loans	(550)	(510)	(160)
Long-term borrowings	373	562	—
Reduction of long-term debt	(278)	(513)	(14)
Issuance of common stock	18	40	131
Repurchase of common stock	—	—	(48)
Cash dividends	(30)	(30)	(31)
Net cash used in financing activities	(467)	(451)	(122)
Increase (Decrease) in Cash and Equivalents	4	(11)	294
Cash Equivalents at Beginning of Year	16	20	9
Cash and Equivalents at End of Year	$ 20	$ 9	$303

CHAPTER 9
FINANCIAL STATEMENT DISCLOSURES

CONTENTS

Notes to the Financial Statements	9002
Summary of Significant Accounting Policies	9002
Accounting Changes	9003
Changes in Accounting Principles	9003
Changes in Accounting Estimates	9004
Changes in Reporting Entity	9005
Prior-Period Adjustments	9006
Commitments	9007
Long-Term Debt	9007
Pension Plans and Other Postretirement Benefit Plans	9007
Contingencies	9008
Environment Reporting and Disclosures	9009
Disclosures for Derivatives	9009
Stock Options	9010
Income Tax Disclosures	9010
Segment Reporting	9011
Subsequent Events	9012

One of the basic principles of financial reporting requires that financial statements disclose all facts that might influence the judgment of an informed reader. If the hospitality entity uses accounting methods or techniques that represent a departure from official FASB pronouncements (codified in ASC), disclosure of such departure should be made, along with the justification for this position. Additional disclosures covered by the Sarbanes Oxley Act of 2002 (SOX) are discussed in Chapter 3, "Corporate Governance."

Because of the complexity of many hospitality companies and the increased expectations of the public, which have been exacerbated with the recent corporate scandals and the passage of SOX, full disclosure has become one of the most difficult concepts for the financial manager to enforce. In the recent past, lawsuits have charged some hospitality companies and its auditors with failure to make proper disclosures. Since financial managers have the ultimate responsibility for reporting requirements and selecting accounting policies, it is important that they become familiar with the general rules that govern the appropriate disclosures on the financial statements and its footnotes.

NOTES TO THE FINANCIAL STATEMENTS

Several methods of disclosure exist, such as parenthetical explanations, supporting schedules, cross-references, and footnotes. In most instances the required disclosure is included in a note to the financial statements, often called footnotes, in order to explain the situation accurately. Details of stock option and pension plans, long-term leases, provisions of long-term debt and other commitments, for instance, are usually disclosed in the notes to the financial statements.

Notes to the financial statements are considered an integral part of the statements. They are ruled by accounting principles requiring the full disclosure of the facts needed by statement users to reach informed conclusions and thus to make the financial statements not misleading. These footnotes expand and clarify the information contained on the balance sheet, income statement, cash flow statement, and statement of shareholder's equity. Accordingly, a review of the footnotes to the financial statements is essential for a complete and accurate interpretation of the hospitality company's financial and operating performance.

SUMMARY OF SIGNIFICANT ACCOUNTING POLICIES

The accounting policies of a hospitality entity are the specific accounting principles and methods selected by the financial manager. Accounting policies used should be those that are most appropriate in the circumstances to fairly present the financial position and results of operations for the period.

A description of the accounting policies followed by management is normally included on the first footnote to the financial statements known as "summary of significant accounting policies." The information provided by this footnote assists users of hospitality industry financial statements in assessing the credibility and quality of earnings so that users becoming familiar with the company's choices in the selection of conservative accounting principles in conformity with GAAP. Moreover, it enables hospitality companies to make comparisons with competitors.

The following list includes some of the major disclosures found in the summary of significant accounting policies:

1. Basis of presentation of financial statements.
2. Method of determining inventory cost and basis for stating inventories.
3. Method of calculating depreciation.
4. Practices and accounting methods unique to the segment of the hospitality industry in which the company operates.
5. Unusual application of GAAP.
6. Basis for accounting for revenue recognition and related costs (e.g., franchise fee revenue, and unearned revenue).
7. Basis for allocating asset costs to current and future periods (e.g., deferred charges, goodwill).
8. Basis for calculating earnings per share.

The application of GAAP requires the use of managerial judgment where alternative acceptable principles are available and where varying methods of applying a principle to a given set of facts exist. Disclosure of these principles and methods is vital to the full presentation of financial position and operations so that meaningful economic decisions can be made.

Only annual reports are normally required to disclose the summary of significant accounting policies. Quarterly unaudited statements, for instance, do not disclose accounting policies unless there has been a policy change since the previous reporting period and the statements are not intended for internal use.

ACCOUNTING CHANGES

Based on the ever-changing industry environment, hospitality companies may have to change accounting methods to meet conditions they may be facing. ASC 250, *Accounting Changes and Error Corrections* (FAS-154, *Accounting Changes and Error Corrections*), supersedes Accounting Principles Opinion No. 20 (APB 20), *Accounting Changes*, and became effective for fiscal years ending after December 15, 2006. Its goal is to provide uniformity in disclosing accounting changes by presenting a clear explanation of the nature and justification of the changes in accounting principles and their effect on earnings and earnings per share.

ASC 250 (FAS-154) presents three classifications of accounting changes: (1) a change in accounting principles, (2) a change in accounting estimates, and (3) a change in reporting entity. Consistent with APB 20, ASC 250 (FAS-154) takes the position that corrections of errors are not accounting changes.

Changes in Accounting Principles

When a hospitality company changes from one generally accepted accounting principle to another, it is considered a reportable change in accounting principle. An example is a change in inventory method from last in, first out (LIFO) to first in, first out (FIFO).

Under ASC 250 (FAS-154), all changes in accounting principles must be retrospectively applied to previous period financial statements, unless such application is impracticable or the FASB mandates another approach. As a result, hospitality companies no longer report the impact of the change in the current period financial statements, nor do they report the cumulative effect adjustments to current income, as previously required by APB 20. Instead, the company reports any necessary change as an adjustment to the opening balance of retained earnings for the earliest period presented.

ASC 250 (FAS-154) requires that the nature and justification for the change in accounting principle be disclosed in a footnote, as well as the impact on earnings and earnings per share. In addition, this disclosure should include the reasons why the new principle is preferable. Proper justification may take the form of a new FASB pronouncement, new AICPA recommended practice, a change in circumstances, and a change to conform more readily to industry practices. A company must justify a change in an accounting principle other than one resulting from the issuance of a new standard by the FASB. Hospitality companies also should describe the prior-period information they retrospectively adjusted and present the effect of the change on income from continuing operations and net income and related per share amounts for the current period and any prior periods retrospectively adjusted. In addition, the company should disclose the cumulative effect of the change on retained earnings as of the earliest period.

Changes in Accounting Estimates

A change in an accounting estimate is caused by new conditions or events that require management to revise prior estimates, such as a change in salvage value or useful life of kitchen equipment.

ASC 250 (FAS-154) includes new rules for changes in depreciation and amortization for property and equipment. These events are treated as a change in accounting estimates affected by a change in accounting principles. Accordingly, the hospitality company will no longer show the cumulative effect of the change on its income statement in the period of change and no restatement of prior periods. Instead, the company allocates any remaining depreciation or amortization over the remaining life of the asset in question using the newly adopted approach, as shown in Example 1.

EXAMPLE 1: In 20X9, RYT Hospitality changed from the double declining balance method of depreciation to the straight-line method for its $500,000 equipment. Acquired in January 1, 20X6, the equipment had a $20,000 salvage value and an estimated life of eight years. The company policy is to take a full year of depreciation in the year of acquisition and none in the year of disposal.

Pursuant to ASC 250 (FAS-154), the change in accounting estimate is as follows:

Net book value as of 12/31/X8 (500,000 less 289,062.50)	$210,937.50
Less salvage value	20,000.00
Remaining depreciation	190,937.50
Remaining life (original life 8 years – 3 years already used) divided by 5	
Revised annual depreciation	$ 38,187.50

Consistent with APB 20, a change in an accounting estimate must be accounted for in the current period if it affects only that period, or in the period of change and future periods if it affects more than one period. If a change in estimate is associated with a change in accounting principle and the effects cannot be differentiated, it is accounted for as a change in estimate. For instance, a capitalized expenditure may be expensed because future benefits may be doubtful. In this case, the change will be considered a change in accounting estimate.

Footnote disclosure is required in the period of change for the effect on income before extraordinary items, net income, and earnings per share. However, these disclosures are not required for estimate changes in the ordinary course of business when deemed not material, such as when revising estimates of uncollectible accounts.

Example 2 presents a recorded change in an accounting estimate as follows:

EXAMPLE 2: Hotel furniture was purchased on January 1, 20X6, for $80,000, having an original estimated life of 10 years, with a salvage value of $8,000. On January 1, 2X10, the estimated life was revised to 8 remaining years, with a new salvage value of $7,500. The journal entry on December 31, 2X10, to record depreciation expense is:

Depreciation	$5,463	
Accumulated depreciation		5,463

The calculation of the depreciation expense recorded above is:

Book value on January 1, 2X10:
Original cost	$80,000
Less: Accumulated depreciation	28,800
Book value	$51,200

$$\frac{80,000 - \$8,000}{10 \text{ years}} = 7,200 \times 4 = 21,800$$

Depreciation for 2X10:
Book value on January 1, 2X10	$51,200
Less: New salvage value	7,500
Depreciable cost	$43,700

$$\frac{\text{Depreciable cost}}{\text{New life}} = \frac{\$43,700}{8 \text{ years}} = \$5,463$$

Footnote disclosure is required in the year 2X10 for the impact of the revised number of years of estimated useful life on earnings and earnings per share.

Changes in Reporting Entity

A change in reporting entity, such as business combinations between two hotels, is accounted for by restating prior years' financial statements as if both companies had been previously combined. ASC 250 (FAS-154) does not change the way hospitality companies are required to account for changes in reporting entities; these changes continue to be applied retrospectively. Companies should restate financial statements of all prior periods presented.

Restatement due to a change in reporting entity is necessary to facilitate comparability between financial statements and past summaries. The accounting treatment for the change is to restate all prior periods of the change and to disclose the nature and reason for the change only in the year of change, as well as the effect on income before extraordinary items, net income, and earnings per share for all periods presented. The restatement process does not have to include more than the past five years.

Examples of changes in reporting entity include:
- Presentation of consolidated statements instead of individual company statements.
- Change in subsidiaries included in consolidated or combined statements.

PRIOR-PERIOD ADJUSTMENTS

ASC 250 (FAS-154) does not change the way a hospitality company accounts for and reports error corrections. Companies should report the correction of errors in previously issued financial statements as prior-period adjustments, with a restatement of prior-period financial statements. The carrying value of the assets and liabilities should be adjusted for the cumulative effect of the error for periods before the earliest period presented.

When a single year is presented, prior-period adjustments adjust the beginning balance of retained earnings. The presentation follows:

Retained Earnings—1/1 Unadjusted
Prior-Period Adjustments (net of tax)
Retained Earnings—1/1 Adjusted
Add: Net Income
Less: Dividends
Retained Earnings—12/31

Errors may be due to numerical mistakes, misapplication of accounting principles, or misuse of facts existing when the financial statements were prepared. Moreover, a change in principle from one that is not in accordance with GAAP to one that is in accordance with GAAP is considered a correction of an error. Disclosure should include the nature of the error and its effect on earnings and earnings per share.

Since a correction of an error affects previous years, this retroactive adjustment must be disclosed when comparative financial statements are presented. The retroactive adjustment is disclosed by showing the effects of the adjustment on previous years' earnings and component items of net income (see Example 3).

EXAMPLE 3: A restaurant purchased 20 dishwashers on January 1, 20X8, for $100,000, with a $1,000 salvage value and a five-year estimated useful life. By mistake, repairs expense was charged. The error was discovered on December 31, 20X9, before closing the books. The correcting entry follows:

Depreciation expense	19,800	
Kitchen equipment	100,000	
Accumulated depreciation		39,600
Retained earnings		80,200

Accumulated depreciation of $39,600 is calculated below:

$$\frac{\$100{,}000 - 1{,}000}{5 \text{ years}} = 19{,}800 \text{ per year for 2 years} = \$39{,}600$$

The credit to retained earnings reflects the difference between the incorrect $100,000 repairs expense amount instead of recording depreciation expense of $19,800 in 20X8. Accordingly, the statement of retained earnings for the year 20X9 will disclose the prior-year adjustment (net of tax effect) as a reduction of the beginning balance of retained earnings.

COMMITMENTS

Commitments are contractual obligations of the hospitality entity. The major commitments disclosed by a hospitality company are related to construction contracts, leasing, and long-term debt. Leasing commitment disclosures contain the general description of the leasing arrangement, including minimum annual rentals and restrictions imposed by the lease agreement. For capital leases, the imputed interest is also disclosed.

Long-Term Debt

Due to the highly leveraged nature of the hospitality industry, the long-term debt commitment is normally a very long footnote containing information related to the different types of debt, including their maturities, interest rates, and restrictions pursuant to the terms of long-term debt agreements.

For each type of outstanding debt instrument, the hospitality company discloses the nature of the issue, interest rates, assets given as collateral for the debt, maturity dates and amounts, as well as restrictive debt covenants associated with maintaining specific amounts of working capital and financial ratios, payment of dividends, and other limitations imposed by the terms of the loan agreement.

Pension Plans and Other Postretirement Benefit Plans

When applicable, it is necessary to disclose the nature of the hospitality company's pension plan, describing employee groups covered, funding policies, and provisions for the current period pension cost.

ASC 715, *Compensation—Retirement Benefits* (FAS-87, *Employers' Accounting for Pensions*), governs accounting and disclosure for two types of pension plans: (1) defined contribution plan and (2) defined benefit plan. In a defined contribution plan, the actual contributions by the hospitality company are specified instead of the benefits to be paid. Conversely, in a defined benefit plan, the determinable pension benefit (considering factors such as age, salary, and service years) to be received by participants upon retirement is given.

Pursuant to ASC 715 (FAS-87), footnote disclosure for pension plans includes:

- A description of the pension plan, including employee groups that are covered, type of benefits provided, funding policy, benefit formula, and retirement age.

- Components of pension expense (e.g., service cost, prior service cost, interest on projected benefit obligation).
- Assumptions used for interest rates, mortality rates, and employee turnover.
- Present value of vested and nonvested benefits.
- Weighted-average assumed discount rate in measuring the projected benefit obligation.

In addition to these disclosures, ASC 715, *Compensation—Retirement Benefits* (FAS-132, *Employers' Disclosures about Pensions and Other Postretirement Benefits*), requires additional disclosures about the management and allocation of plan assets for defined-benefit pension plans. These expanded requirements provide additional information about pension plan assets, obligations, benefit payments, contributions, and net benefit cost. They include:

- The percentage of fair value of total plan assets for each major category of plan assets such as equity securities, debt securities, real estate, and other assets.
- A narrative description of investment policies and strategies, which should be specific for the entity, and include the important policies followed by the entity with regard to the plan asset investment.
- A description of the basis used to determine the overall expected long-term rate of return on assets.
- The amount of accumulated benefit obligation for all defined benefit plans.
- The benefits to be paid in each of the next five fiscal years and the aggregate of the expected benefits for the next five fiscal years thereafter.
- The funded status of the pension plan and both the employer and participant contribution.
- The estimate of contributions to be paid to the plan during the next fiscal year in addition to the employer and participant contribution.
- The weighted-average assumptions for the discount rate or rate of compensation increase if the plan is related to pay and expected rate of return on plan assets.

CONTINGENCIES

Contingencies refer to existing conditions whose ultimate effect is uncertain, and their resolution depends on specific future events. Examples of contingencies include pending lawsuits, tax examinations, and cosigning of a note by another party. The disclosures might provide an estimate of the possible loss (if applicable) or state that a reasonable estimate cannot be determined. In addition, the nature of the contingency will be disclosed.

ASC 450, *Contingencies* (FAS-5, *Accounting for Contingencies*), states that contingent gains should not be reported until they are realized. Footnote disclosure of a contingency that might result in a gain is desirable as long as it includes no misleading implications concerning the likelihood of its realization. In the case of contingency losses, ASC 450 (FAS-5) requires that such losses should be reported in the period's financial statements if it is probable that an asset has been impaired or a liability has been incurred and the amount of the loss can be reasonably estimated. In the absence of those conditions, disclosure should be made when there is a reasonable possibility that a loss may be incurred. The footnote will disclose the nature of the contingency and an estimate of the amount of the loss, or range of loss, or a statement that such an estimate cannot be made.

A remote contingency (i.e., remote possibility of loss) need not be disclosed in the financial statements except in cases of guarantees of indebtedness, standby letters of credit, or agreements to repurchase properties. An example would be loss contingencies having the characteristic of a guarantee with the right to proceed against an outside party. If R Hotels borrows money on a note that is cosigned by K Hotels, the latter would disclose the possible obligation because this remote contingency involves a guarantee and a right to proceed against an outside party.

ENVIRONMENT REPORTING AND DISCLOSURES

Hospitality companies are faced with federal and local compliance requirements regarding environmental issues, which provide specifications with which companies must comply. The costs of compliance could significantly increase a company's expected cost of projects and processes. Failure to follow environmental laws could result in substantial costs and risks, including civil and criminal prosecution and fines. The hospitality company must monitor compliance with environmental laws in order to prevent the payment of fees and penalties.

The Environmental Protection Agency (EPA), for instance, imposes federal laws regulating pollution, solid waste disposal, water supply, and ocean dumping. These regulations have heavily affected the cruise industry. EPA regulations require adherence to specific pollution-detection measures, such as leak testing, and installation of corrosion protection and leak-detection systems applicable to underground storage tanks.

An effective compliance program is essential in minimizing environmental risks. The financial manager must ascertain that appropriate accounting, reporting, and disclosures for environmental issues are being practiced by the hospitality company.

DISCLOSURES FOR DERIVATIVES

ASC 815, *Derivatives and Hedging* (FAS-133, *Accounting for Derivative Instruments and Hedging Activities*), defines *derivative* as a financial instrument or contract having an underlying price based on an asset or liability that contains a required or allowable net settlement and no net investment or a smaller initial net investment than would be anticipated for a contract with similar terms linked to changing market conditions. Examples of derivatives are interest rate swaps, dual-currency bonds, variable-coupon redeemable notes, floating rate notes, and zero coupon bonds.

Based on ASC 815 (FAS-133) and some additional SEC requirements, certain disclosures are associated with reporting for derivatives, including financial instruments and commodities (e.g., futures, forwards, options, and swaps). These disclosures include:

- The types and nature of derivative instruments to be accounted for.
- The accounting method used for derivatives, such as the fair value, accrual, and deferral method. Disclosure should be made where gains and losses associated with derivatives are reported.
- The risks associated with the derivatives.
- Identification of derivatives used for trading as opposed to nontrading purposes.

STOCK OPTIONS

ASC 718, *Compensation—Stock Compensation* (FAS-123R, *Share-Based Payment*), requires public and nonpublic companies to recognize stock-based compensation as an expense on the income statement. The notes to the financial statements of both public and nonpublic entities will also disclose information to assist readers in understanding the effects of stock options, as well as stock-based compensation plans. The following disclosures are generally included for stock options:

- Weighted-average grant date fair value of options and other equity instruments granted during the year.
- Description of the method and assumptions used to estimate the fair value of options. A method that has been widely used is the Black-Scholes model. This model calculates the present value of the stock option at the grant date based on specific information about the terms of the option and assumptions about future stock price performance.
- Major changes in the terms of stock-based compensation plans.
- Amendments to outstanding stock option awards.

INCOME TAX DISCLOSURES

ASC 740, *Income Taxes* (FAS-109, *Accounting for Income Taxes*), requires that a deferred tax liability or asset be measured at the tax rate under the current law that will exist when the temporary difference reverses. As previously noted, deferred taxes are the result of temporary differences in the recognition of revenues and expenses in the calculation of taxable income relative to reported income. The tax liability method must be used to account for deferred income taxes. Under this method, tax expense equals taxes payable plus the tax effects of all temporary differences. Temporary differences arise because certain revenue or expense items (e.g., accelerated depreciation) are includable on the tax return either before or after being recognized on the income statement.

Deferred taxes are classified as current and noncurrent on the balance sheet, corresponding to the classifications of related assets and liabilities underlying the temporary difference. A deferred tax asset or liability that is not related to an asset or liability for financial reporting purposes is classified according to anticipated reversal or benefit (e.g., loss carryforwards). Accordingly, the deferred tax account can conceivably appear on the balance sheet as a current asset, current liability, long-term asset, or long-term liability.

The income tax footnote included the following disclosures based on GAAP and SEC requirements:

- Significant year-to-year changes in deferred tax accounts.
- Reference to the types of timing differences.
- Reconciliation between the amount of reported income tax expense and the amount expected.
- Estimated dollar amount of the underlying causes for the difference between the effective and statutory tax rates.
- Increases or decreases to the tax provision caused by tax rates in foreign countries that differ from U.S. tax rates.
- Operating loss carryforwards not recognized in the loss period along with expiration dates.
- Any other unused deductions or credits together with their expiration dates.

Accounting Standards Update (ASU) No. 2009-06, *Income Taxes (Topic 740)—Implementation Guidance on Accounting for Uncertainty in Income Taxes and Disclosure Amendments for Nonpublic Entities,* eliminates some disclosures for nonpublic entities (i.e., tabular reconciliation of the amounts of unrecognized tax benefits at the beginning and end of the year, total amount of unrecognized tax benefits). Users of private company financial statements have indicated that these disclosures do not provide useful information for decision-making. These amendments became effective for interim and annual periods ending after September 15, 2009.

SEGMENT REPORTING

ASC 280, *Segment Reporting* (FAS-131, *Disclosures about Segments of an Enterprise and Related Information*), requires the assets and operations of publicly held hospitality companies to be apportioned into reportable business segments. Determination of the company's industry segments is primarily left to the judgment of the financial manager guided by standard classifications systems, the nature of the products and services that are provided, the geographic marketing area, and the types of customers.

According to ASC 280 (FAS-131), a segment is considered to be reportable if any one of the following three criteria is met:

1. Segment revenue is 10% or more of combined revenue, including intersegment revenue.
2. Segment operating profit or loss is 10% or more of the greater of the combined profit of all segments with a profit, or the combined loss of all segments with a loss.
3. Segment assets exceed 10% or more of the combined assets of all segments.

The segment information that is disclosed includes revenue, operating earnings and losses, identifiable assets, depreciation expense, capital expenditures, and other material information. It should be disclosed for each material reporting segment or industry in which the hospitality company operates. Hilton Hotels Corporation provides an example of segment information disclosures on note 15 of its 2004 annual report, as described in Example 4.

> **EXAMPLE 4:** Hilton identifies three reportable segments based on similar products or services: (1) hotel ownership, (2) managing and franchising, and (3) timeshare. Its hotel ownership segment derives revenue primarily from owned, majority-owned, and leased hotel properties. The managing and franchising segment provides services, including hotel management and licensing of Hilton's brands to franchisees, and generates revenue from fees charged to hotel owners. The timeshare segment consists of multi-unit timeshare resorts and derives revenue from the sale and financing of timeshare intervals and operating timeshare resorts.

SUBSEQUENT EVENTS

Disclosure of events that occurred subsequent to the balance sheet is required by GAAP to prevent the financial statements from being misleading. Examples of subsequent events are the purchase of new companies, mergers or business combinations; fire losses, hurricane losses or other casualties; settlement of litigation; and the issuance of bonds or capital stock.

An entity, including a public company, expected to widely distribute its financial statements to shareholders and other financial statement users, has been required to evaluate subsequent events through the date that the financial statements are issued, according to ASC 855, *Subsequent Events* (FAS-165, *Subsequent Events*). All other entities were to evaluate subsequent events through the date that the financial statements were available to be issued. Financial statements are considered available to be issued when they are complete in a form and format that complies with GAAP and have all the approvals (e.g., from management, the board of directors or significant shareholders) necessary for issuance. ASC 855 (FAS-165) applies to interim and annual periods ending after June 15, 2009.

ASC 855 (FAS-165) introduced the concept of statements being *available to be issued*. It requires (1) disclosure of the date through which an entity has evaluated subsequent events and (2) the basis of the date, meaning whether the date represents the date the financial statements were issued or were available to be issued. This disclosure informs users of the financial statements that an entity has not evaluated subsequent events after that date in the set of financial statements being presented.

Accounting Standards Update (ASU) No. 2010-09, *Subsequent Events (Topic 855)—Amendments to Certain Recognition and Disclosure Requirements,* issued in February 2010, removes the requirement for an SEC filer to disclose a date in both issued and revised financial statements. If the financial statements have been revised, a hospitality entity that is not an SEC filer should disclose both the date that the financial statements were issued or available to be issued and the date that the revised financial statements were issued or available to be issued. An SEC filer is an entity that is required to file or furnish its financial statements with the SEC based on Section 12(i) of the Securities Exchange Act of 1934, as amended; this change alleviates potential conflicts between ASC Subtopic 855-10 and the SEC's requirements. It is effective for interim or annual periods ending after June 15, 2010.

PART III

FINANCIAL ANALYSIS

CHAPTER 10
LIQUIDITY ANALYSIS

CONTENTS

Overview	10,001
Managing Working Capital	10,002
Current Ratio	10,002
Owners versus Creditors	10,004
Quick Ratio	10,004
Accounts Receivable Analysis	10,005
Accounts Receivable Turnover	10,005
Average Collection Period	10,006
Accounts Receivable Percentage	10,006
Cash Ratio	10,007
Composition of Current Assets and Current Liabilities	10,007
Cash	10,007
Short-Term Investments	10,008
Receivables	10,008
Inventories	10,008
Current Liabilities	10,009
Other Liquidity Considerations	10,009
Sources of Industry Averages	10,010

Liquidity refers to a company's ability to meet current obligations as they become due. A company's short-term debt-paying ability is of utmost importance to creditors, investors, employees, and other financial statement users, because it provides insights into the company's capability to remain solvent during periods of economic or financial instability. A company that reports high earnings on its income statement may still be forced out of business because of its inability to meet short-term obligations. It is liquidity, not profitability, that determines a company's short-term debt-paying ability.

OVERVIEW

The resources (i.e., cash and assets) of a hospitality company are judged based on their availability or convertibility to cash (i.e., liquidity) in a reasonable period of time. Liquidity ratios are used to determine whether a company has a sufficient amount of cash or assets that can be quickly converted to cash. They also assist management in determining a company's position for obtaining short-term credit. When using these ratios, it is assumed that current assets are the principal source for paying current liabilities.

When analyzing a company's short-term debt-paying ability, the main focus is on the relationship between current assets and current liabilities. Several measures are used to determine a hospitality company's short-term debt-paying ability, such as working capital, current ratio, quick ratio, and cash ratio. In addition, the evaluation of the liquidity of accounts receivable is determined by the accounts receivable turnover, the accounts receivable percentage, and the average collection period. Inventory ratios may also be used to determine if there is an over-investment in inventories.

MANAGING WORKING CAPITAL

Working capital is an indication of liquidity and is calculated by deducting current liabilities from current assets:

$$\text{Working capital} = \text{Current assets} - \text{Current liabilities}$$

The key to strong liquidity is the proper management of working capital. If a hospitality company's working capital requirement is not controlled and properly financed, liquidity problems arise. In order to achieve effective management of a company's working capital, the two major components of working capital, accounts receivable and inventory, must be kept at their minimum levels relative to sales. This allows the hospitality company to set aside any cash it would have needed to finance a larger amount of receivables and inventories.

In addition, a hospitality company can minimize future liquidity problems by using long-term debt financing at a higher proportion to its normal working capital requirements. This protects the company during seasonal business trends, as well as during unforeseen economic and natural events, where receivables may fluctuate substantially from period to period. The use of this strategy will also provide a margin a safety to meet unforeseen cash needs that would have to be financed by an increase in short-term borrowings.

Internal auditors can also minimize a company's present and future liquidity problems through their assessment of the company's ability to meet its short-term debt obligations. For example, an audit may uncover management fraud, where low amounts of working capital encouraged management to manipulate financial statements to mislead investors and creditors. In fact, the AICPA lists inadequate working capital as one of several red flags alerting external auditors to possible fraud in the workplace.

CURRENT RATIO

The current ratio measures the relationship between current assets and current liabilities. This ratio reflects whether the assets expected to be converted into cash within one year are greater than the liabilities that are expected to be paid during that period. The current ratio is calculated for X Hotel as follows:

$$\text{Current Assets} = \frac{\text{Current assets}}{\text{Current liabilities}} = \frac{\$200{,}000}{\$160{,}000} = 1.25 \text{ to } 1$$

This indicates that X Hotel has $1.25 of current assets for every dollar of current liabilities.

A current ratio of 1 to 1 is generally considered to be reasonable in the hospitality industry. In contrast to merchandising or manufacturing companies, hospitality company inventories seldom exceed one-half percent of total assets. Instead, the major asset sold is the guest rooms or airplane seats, which are reported as property and equipment on the balance sheet. The larger the current ratio, the greater the likelihood that the company will meet its short-term debt obligations. A comparison of the hospitality company's current ratio with prior periods and industry averages will help determine whether its ratio is high or low. Possible reasons for high or low ratios can be found in the underlying current assets (i.e., cash, accounts receivables, inventories) or current liabilities.

The current ratio is considered a rough measure of the hospitality company's short-term debt-paying ability, since it ignores the revolving cycle of receivables, inventory, and other current accounts. The implication is that all current assets will be converted into cash to pay current obligations in the event of insolvency. Clearly, this is not possible in the hospitality industry because, in most instances, inventories consist of perishable foods, beverages, and housekeeping supplies of immaterial value in the event of the company's demise.

Creditors generally prefer a relatively high current ratio because it provides some assurance that the hospitality company will meet its payments of interest and principal when due. Possible actions to increase the current ratio include:

- Issuing preferred or common stock.
- Paying current debts with cash if current ratio is higher than 1 to 1.
- Postponing the declaration of dividends.
- Obtaining long-term loans.
- Selling long-term investments.

The above actions vary in terms of timing regarding implementation. In some instances, the improvement in the current ratio may misrepresent the company's liquidity position. An example of a practice known as window dressing follows:

EXAMPLE 1: On December 31, 20X6, VTY Restaurant has $300,000 in current assets and $260,000 in current liabilities. Thus, its current ratio is 1.15 to 1. If the company needs to maintain a current ratio of $1.20 to 1 based on the terms of a loan agreement, it might decide to pay off $60,000 of accounts payable from cash (and short-term investments) on December 31, 20X6. Accordingly, the current ratio temporarily improves, as follows:

$$\frac{\text{Current assets}}{\text{Current liabilities}} = \frac{300{,}000 - 60{,}000}{260{,}000 - 60{,}000} = \frac{240{,}000}{200{,}000} = 1.20 \text{ to } 1$$

It is evident that the current ratio of VTY has improved as a result of the early payment to creditors on the last day of the accounting period. However, this is considered an artificial enhancement to the company's liquidity position.

Therefore, once the company's current ratio increases, it appears to be more capable of paying its short-term debt obligations. Because this ratio does not take into account the composition of current assets, an assessment of a more specific measure of liquidity is needed (i.e., quick ratio).

Owners versus Creditors

Owners of hospitality companies prefer a relatively low current ratio, because they are mainly concerned with maximizing the value of the company. They perceive investments in current assets as less productive than investments in property and equipment and other long-term assets.

Creditors prefer a relatively high current ratio, because it provides assurance that they will receive timely payments. Thus, loan agreements may incorporate certain minimum dollar amounts of working capital or minimum current ratio requirements to ensure the company maintains sufficient liquidity to meet its loan repayment schedule. Violation of these debt covenants could result in the lender demanding immediate payment of the loan.

Conversely, an extremely high current ratio may indicate poor management if it is the result of an excessive amount of available cash or a very high investment in receivables or inventories. Idle cash should be invested to produce adequate returns to the hospitality company and its owners. High receivables might also arise because of liberal credit policies or inadequate follow-up of slow collections from customers.

Managers concerned with satisfying both owners and creditors while simultaneously maintaining adequate working capital and liquidity may be encouraged to manipulate the financial statements. These managers may sometimes artificially enhance a company's liquidity position as a way to exercise discretion over the accounts in the current section of the balance sheet. Thus, manipulation of financial statements by management has reduced the credibility of the statements, which, in the long term may hinder the company's ability to raise debt and equity capital.

QUICK RATIO

The quick ratio, sometimes called the acid-test ratio, serves as a supplement to the current ratio in assessing liquidity. It measures how quickly and easily a company's assets can be converted to cash in relation to its current liabilities. Accordingly, the quick ratio provides a more rigorous measure of liquidity than the current ratio. Quick assets include cash, temporary investments (or marketable securities), and net receivables.

The quick ratio of X Hotel is computed as follows:

$$\text{Quick ratio} = \frac{\text{Cash, marketable securities and receivables}}{\text{Current liabilities}}$$

$$= \frac{150{,}000}{160{,}000} = .94 \text{ to } 1$$

The quick ratio of X Hotel indicates that it has 94 cents of liquid assets for each dollar of current liabilities. The difference between the current ratio and the quick ratio depends on the inventory amounts (and prepaid expenses) relative to current assets. In some hospitality establishments, the difference between the current ratio and the quick ratio will be small, while in others it will be fairly high. In the case of X Hotel, there is a fairly small difference between the current ratio and the quick ratio, because the inventory amounts are small in proportion to total current assets and a very rapid turnover.

The perspective of owners, creditors, and management toward the quick ratio is similar to the perspectives they hold about the current ratio. Accordingly, owners of hospitality companies prefer a fairly low quick ratio; creditors prefer a high quick ratio; and management is once more caught in the middle.

ACCOUNTS RECEIVABLE ANALYSIS

To further assess a hospitality company's liquidity position, it is important to appraise the quality of the accounts receivables included in the calculation of both current and quick ratios. In some cases, there might be high-risk receivables that require further evaluation, such as receivables due from customers experiencing financial difficulties. The receivable ratios commonly used in the hospitality industry include the accounts receivable turnover, the average collection period, and the accounts receivable percentage.

Accounts Receivable Turnover

The accounts receivable turnover ratio measures the speed of the conversion of accounts receivables into cash—that is, the number of times, on average, that accounts receivables are collected during the year. The accounts receivable turnover is determined by dividing the total revenue (or net sales) by the average accounts receivable. Although only credit sales should be used in the calculation of the accounts receivable turnover ratio, it is common to use total sales, because the amount of credit sales may not be available. However, the calculations should be consistent from period to period. The formula used for the accounts receivable turnover follows:

$$\text{Accounts receivable turnover} = \frac{\text{Net sales or total revenue}}{\text{Average accounts receivable}}$$

Average accounts receivables for the period is the beginning accounts receivable balance plus the ending accounts receivable balance divided by two. However, in the case of seasonal hotel operations, monthly or quarterly sales figures are used to calculate the average receivables, because sales fluctuate during the year. A higher accounts receivable turnover is normally desirable because it indicates faster collections; yet an excessively high accounts receivable turnover may indicate a credit policy that is too strict and thus hinders potential sales growth. Accordingly, hospitality companies must consider maximizing revenue as well as the risks inherent in selling to less creditworthy customers.

Owners prefer a high accounts receivable turnover, because this reflects lower investment in nonproductive assets. In addition, a high accounts receivable turnover indicates that accounts receivable are being collected in a timely manner. Yet, increasing receivable turnover may put downward pressure on the company's sales by eliminating slow-paying customers. Accordingly, it is important for management to properly balance the desire to maximize sales with the potential collectibility problems in selling to less creditworthy customers.

The faster the receivables turn over, the more credibility the current and quick ratios have in liquidity analysis. Although the accounts receivable turnover measures the overall promptness of collections, it fails to address the collectibility of individual accounts. This matter is resolved by preparing an aging schedule of outstanding accounts receivable. This schedule lists all of the uncollected guest accounts based on the month in which the original charge occurred and the length of time each account has been outstanding.

Average Collection Period

A variation of the accounts receivable turnover is the average collection period, also referred to as the number of day's sales uncollected. This ratio expresses the number of days that an average accounts receivable remains uncollected beyond its sales day. It is calculated by dividing the accounts receivable turnover by 365 (the number of days in a year), as follows:

$$\text{Average collection period} = \frac{365}{\text{Accounts receivable turnover}}$$

A significant increase in the number of day's sales uncollected might be a reflection that customer's balances will be uncollectible. Further, accounts receivables outstanding in excess of the normal due date and relative to industry averages suggest a higher likelihood of uncollectibility. To determine the collection period for customer balances, it is important to compare a company's ratios with industry standards, which have ranged from 15 to 30 days in the case of the lodging industry. The collection period may be considerably lower in certain segments of the hospitality industry, with a high proportion of cash sales or credit card sales that provide daily collections. These factors tend to increase the turnover ratio and decrease the collection period.

Accounts Receivable Percentage

The accounts receivable percent expresses the percent of sales that is in the form of uncollected accounts receivable and thus has not been converted into cash. The average accounts receivable at the beginning and end of the period is used in the calculation: it is simply the reciprocal of the accounts receivable turnover. The calculation of the accounts receivable percent follows:

$$\text{Accounts receivable percentage} = \frac{\text{Average accounts receivable}}{\text{Total revenue or net sales}}$$

The financial manager should appraise the trends in bad debts to accounts receivables and to sales. An unwarranted decrease in bad debts may indicate that the hospitality company is manipulating its financial statements and thus lowers the quality of earnings. This may occur when a company reports a decline in bad debts expense while showing an increasing trend in sales to less creditworthy customers. In this case, sales and accounts receivables are overstated and thus the reported earnings are distorted.

CASH RATIO

The cash ratio, a very conservative approach in the assessment of a hospitality company's liquidity position, is used only when the company is experiencing major liquidity problems. The calculation of the cash ratio follows:

$$\text{Cash ratio} = \frac{\text{Cash + Cash equivalents + marketable securities}}{\text{Current liabilities}}$$

The cash ratio indicates the immediate liquidity of the hospitality company by considering only cash and short-term investments for payment of current obligations. It measures the company's ability to pay short-term debt obligations with cash, cash equivalents, and short-term investments. A cash ratio that is extremely low suggests that the company will have immediate difficulties in meeting its short-term debt obligations. Conversely, a very high cash ratio may suggest that the company is not fully utilizing its cash.

COMPOSITION OF CURRENT ASSETS AND CURRENT LIABILITIES

Current assets include the most liquid assets of a hospitality company. They are cash, assets to be realized in cash within one year from the balance sheet date, and assets that will conserve the use of cash within a year from the balance sheet date. The five categories of current assets listed in order of liquidity are (1) cash, (2) short-term investments, (3) receivables, (4) inventories, and (5) prepayments.

Current liabilities are obligations of the hospitality company that are expected to be met using current assets or creating other current liabilities. As a result, current liabilities correlate to current assets. Typical items include accounts payable, notes payable, accrued expenses, customers' deposits, and current portion of long-term debt.

Cash

Cash is the ultimate measure of liquidity. The cash account on the balance sheet will typically be referred to as cash or cash equivalents. This cash classification includes currency, cashier's checks, and unrestricted funds on deposit with a bank.

The relative size of the cash account on the balance sheet varies among hospitality companies. Although a hospitality company should not maintain an excessive cash balance, some companies retain relatively large amounts of money as part of their plan for strategic growth, such as acquiring hotels, restaurants, or cruises, while other companies retain large amounts of cash to run their operations (i.e., casinos).

To be classified as a current asset and thus affect the liquidity position of the hospitality company, cash must be free from restrictions. If cash is restricted for specific short-term liabilities, it may be classified as a current asset, although the restriction must be disclosed in a footnote. When assessing a company's liquidity, cash restricted for short-term debt (as well as long-term debt) should be eliminated along with the related amount of short-term debt. Cash should be available for payment of short-term obligations to be considered as part of the appraisal of a hospitality company's liquidity position.

Short-Term Investments

Hospitality companies with excess cash typically invest in interest-bearing marketable securities or short-term investments until the cash is needed for operations, expansion, or other purposes. These short-term investments only include investments in equity or debt securities of other companies with the intention of disposing of the stock when cash is needed. Often considered cash equivalents, these short-term investments represent highly liquid current assets, which are included in calculating both current and quick ratios.

Receivables

A common characteristic of receivables is that the hospitality company expects to receive cash within one year from the balance sheet date. To determine the likelihood of accounts receivable collections within the expected time frame, it is important to conduct an independent evaluation of the liquidity position of the receivables.

In the hospitality industry, accounts receivables are from the sale of rooms, food, or beverages on account. They neither bear interest nor involve claims against specific resources of the customers. Notes receivables from franchisees, affiliates, and officers are interest-bearing and may have repayment periods extending beyond a year. At times, an accounts receivable may be converted into an interest-bearing note receivable.

Based on generally accepted accounting principles, an allowance for doubtful accounts is deducted from accounts or notes receivable on the balance sheet, which provides for estimated uncollectible accounts. In addition, the impairment of receivables may result from other factors, such as sales allowances or discounts earned. The hospitality company normally considers all of the reasons that might result in the impairment of receivables in recording the allowance for doubtful accounts.

Inventories

Although inventories normally represent a very significant portion of the assets of most manufacturing and merchandising companies, in the hospitality industry they generally represent an immaterial portion of the company's assets. They include food and beverages available for sale as well as supplies consumed by the company in the generation of revenues. Accordingly, for many hospitality companies, inventory is not emphasized in the evaluation of a company's liquidity. However, there might be some exceptions for hospitality companies that manufacture a product (e.g., coffee) or maintain a very large inventory of alcoholic beverages due to the nature of their operations. In those cases, there will be a large difference between the current and quick ratios and strict monitoring of changes in business activity and inventory costs is required.

Current Liabilities

Current liabilities represent obligations expected to be met with current assets. These include accounts payable, accrued expenses, short-term debt, current portion of long-term debt, income taxes payable, and unearned revenue.

In some segments of the industry, unearned revenue may represent a significant portion of current liabilities on the balance sheet and thus will have a negative impact on the company's overall liquidity. For example, airline and cruise reservations are routinely paid several months before they are used. These prepayments are not earned until used by the customers and thus are reported under current liabilities. Similarly, hotel customer deposits or coupons sold by restaurants before they can be exchanged for meals are reported as unearned revenue on the balance sheet.

OTHER LIQUIDITY CONSIDERATIONS

A hospitality company may have superior or inferior liquidity than indicated on the financial statements. Examples of situations in which the hospitality company is deemed to be more liquid than indicated by ratio analysis include:

- *Unused bank credit lines.* Credit lines would have a positive impact on liquidity because the hospitality company would have immediate access to cash when needed. These credit lines are disclosed in footnotes.
- *Long-term assets that can be converted into cash quickly.* These assets represent investments that can be sold when cash is needed.
- *Ability to issue debt or stock.* This helps to relieve a severe liquidity problem in a reasonable amount of time.

Examples of situations that result in less liquidity than indicated by ratio analysis include:

- *Discounted notes.* When a hospitality company discounts a note receivable, it is selling the note to a bank with recourse. Accordingly, notes discounted in which the other party has recourse against the hospitality company result in a contingent liability to the hospitality company. Discounted notes are disclosed on notes to the financial statements.
- *Lawsuits.* If the hospitality company is being sued for a material amount, this contingency may have a negative impact on the company's overall liquidity position. Material lawsuits are disclosed in footnotes.
- *Loan guarantees.* If the hospitality company has guaranteed a bank loan for another company, there might be a negative impact on the company's liquidity position. Loan guarantees are disclosed in the notes to the financial statements.

SOURCES OF INDUSTRY AVERAGES

There are a number of financial services and library sources that provide industry averages for several segments of the hospitality industry. They include:

- *Robert Morris Associates Annual Statement Studies.* Published annually by Robert Morris Associates, the association of lending and credit risk professionals, this publication provides common size balance sheets, income statements, and several ratios, as well as five-year comparisons of historical data that presents companies in various segments of the hospitality industry.
- *Standard and Poor's Industry Surveys.* Each report contains a five-year summary on several companies within the lodging and restaurant groups.
- *Almanac of Business and Industrial Financial Ratios.* Published by CCH, provides comparative benchmarch data for 199 industry groups based on more than five million IRS corporate tax returns. Data is categorized by asset size within an industry group, and includes income and expenses, balance sheets, and key business ratios. Expense detail includes cost of sales, salaries and wages, officer compensation, taxes, interest, amortization and depreciation, advertising, employee benefits, and other expenses as a percentage of sales.
- *Industry Norms and Key Business Ratios.* Published by Dun & Bradstreet, this publication includes annual data consisting of condensed balance sheets; income statements in dollars and common size; and several liquidity, solvency, and profitability ratios. Dun and Bradstreet includes both current and quick ratios in rating the creditworthiness of large U.S. companies in many industries, including hospitality.
- *Hotel Operating Statistics (HOST) Study.* Compiled annually by Smith Travel Research, the study provides lodging operating statistics used by investors, lenders, and owners in evaluating operating performance and financial projections.
- *Trends in the Hotel Industry.* Published annually by PKF Consulting, the report provides operating statistics on the U.S. lodging industry.

Business periodicals and financial services provide current hospitality industry averages online. They include marketguide.com and finance.yahoo.com. Moreover, business and industry periodicals such as *Business Week, Forbes, Fortune, Nation's Restaurant News,* and the *Wall Street Journal* provide summary data on a few financial ratios on a regular basis.

Several factors must be taken into consideration when using industry averages or in comparing a hospitality company's and competitor's ratios. For example, companies with different financial policies might be included in the same industry average, or some industry averages may not be representative of hospitality industry performance. Moreover, the use of different accounting methods or different year-ends may affect the data analysis. Accordingly, it is imperative not to expect complete reliance on industry averages, as the financial manager must use judgment when formulating an evaluation of the financial condition of a company.

Although comparisons with lodging or restaurant industry averages do not always reveal financial strengths or weaknesses, they are useful in identifying hospitality companies that are not operating at optimum capacity. Where a significant deviation occurs, it is important to determine the reasons. In some cases, it may be established that the industry itself is overly liquid, and the hospitality company is basically sound. On the other hand, the hospitality establishment may be too liquid relative to the industry, with the implication that it is not using its resources effectively and thus may be forgoing added profitability.

CHAPTER 11
SOLVENCY AND LEVERAGE ANALYSIS

CONTENTS

Overview	11,001
Balance Sheet Approach	11,002
Solvency Ratio	11,002
Debt Ratio	11,003
Minority Interest	11,003
Deferred Taxes	11,004
Reserves	11,004
Debt to Equity Ratio	11,004
Asset to Equity Ratio	11,005
Long-Term Debt to Capitalization	11,005
Income Statement Approach	11,006
Interest Coverage	11,006
Fixed Charges Coverage	11,006
Special Items That Impact Long-Term Debt-Paying Ability	11,007
Capital Leases	11,007
Contingencies	11,008
Joint Ventures	11,009
Impact of Historical Cost Accounting	11,009

Solvency refers to the ability of a hospitality company to meet its long-term debt obligations when they become due, including principal and interest on long-term borrowings. A major aspect of evaluating a hospitality company's financial condition (or solvency) is to determine the proportion of equity and debt financing in the company's capital structure. Long-term creditors (e.g., banks, insurance companies, bondholders) are especially interested in whether a company has adequate resources on its balance sheet to satisfy long-term debt obligations when they mature. Solvency also depends on the earning power of the company, because a hotel or restaurant company may not be able to pay its interest or the principal debt repayments unless it is profitable.

OVERVIEW

Financial leverage describes the impact of debt financing on the returns of a company to its owners. If the income generated by investment in assets is greater than the cost of debt, the owners of the hospitality company will benefit from the use of positive leverage. Since assets are primarily financed by lenders and owners, the risk of insolvency is dependent on the amounts of cash supplied by each. Hospitality companies that are highly leveraged are considered more risky and less solvent than those that use moderate or low leverage to finance their business.

Solvency and leverage ratios are important to creditors, because they indicate a company's earning capacity in terms of supporting interest and other fixed charges, and show whether there are sufficient assets to meet debt obligations. The greater the predictability of returns, the larger the amount of acceptable debt, as it is less likely the company will be faced with conditions that prevent it from fulfilling its debt obligations.

A hospitality company's long-term debt-paying ability can be determined through two approaches: (1) analysis of the income statement and (2) analysis of the balance sheet. It is important to recognize that stability in earnings and cash flow from operations enhances the confidence in the hospitality company's ability to meet long-term debt obligations and interest.

Successful use of leverage enhances returns for owners of hospitality companies because the returns earned on these funds are higher than the cost of debt (i.e., interest costs). Interest and principal obligations must still be met even when earnings do not exceed or fall short of the interest cost. This fixed payment commitment increases the break-even point and risk of the hospitality company.

BALANCE SHEET APPROACH

The amount of debt in relation to the size of the hospitality company reveals the amount of leverage used by the company to finance its asset investment. If a high proportion of funds have been provided by lenders, they obviously take on the risks involving repayment. The company's ability to carry debt, as indicated by the balance sheet, can be evaluated by considering the solvency ratio, debt ratio, debt to equity ratio, and asset to equity ratio.

Solvency Ratio

The solvency ratio measures the relationship of the hospitality company's total assets to its total liabilities. It provides an estimate of the company's ability to pay debts on liquidation. The calculation of the solvency ratio for X Hotel follows:

$$\text{Solvency ratio} = \frac{\text{Total assets}}{\text{Total liabilities}} = \frac{\$1,085,000}{\$770,000} = 1.41 \text{ to } 1$$

The calculation above shows that X Hotel has $1.41 of book assets for every dollar of liabilities. The higher the solvency ratio, the greater the likelihood of obtaining debt financing, since it serves as a reflection that there will be an adequate amount of book assets available to cover obligations in the event of liquidation. However, because most assets are reported on the balance sheet using historical cost, the data do not represent the assets' true economic or liquidating values. In addition, the solvency ratio does not provide any evidence regarding earnings fluctuations that might affect current interest and principal payments.

A high solvency ratio represents the amount of debt that the hospitality company is including in its capital structure. If the solvency ratio is relatively high, it indicates that the company is using low leverage in financing its asset investment in comparison to what might be considered acceptable in any specific segment of the hospitality industry. If the solvency ratio is relatively low, the hospitality company is using a high proportion of debt in financing its assets in relation to what might be considered reasonable in the segment of the industry in which it operates.

Debt Ratio

The debt ratio, also called debt to asset ratio, indicates the company's long-term debt paying ability by expressing the percentage of assets that were financed through the use of debt financing. It helps determine how well creditors are protected in the event of insolvency. The debt ratio is calculated for X Hotel as follows:

$$\text{Debt ratio} = \frac{\text{Total liabilities}}{\text{Total assets}} = \frac{\$770{,}000}{\$1{,}085{,}000} = 71\%$$

The above calculation indicates that 71% of the hotel's assets are currently financed with borrowings. Total liabilities might include current liabilities (some may not be interest-bearing), long-term debt, deferred tax liabilities, minority shareholders' interest, pension obligations, other post-retirement obligations, reserves, and other noncurrent liabilities.

The higher the debt ratio, the greater the expected risk to the lender. The risk is exacerbated in the presence of cash deficiencies. Because creditors are not well protected, the company will not be in a good position to issue additional debt. Conversely, the lower the debt ratio, the stronger the hotel or restaurant's financial position.

The debt ratio should be compared with competitors and with industry averages, which indicate that companies with stable earnings can take on more debt than companies with cyclical earnings. However, this comparison can be misleading if one of the companies has a significant hidden value, such as substantial real property carried at original cost.

As the debt ratio increases, the returns to the owners of the hospitality company will increase, as long as the return on the company's assets is higher than the interest costs on the borrowed funds. However, because financial risks associated with the hospitality company will also increase in the presence of higher leverage, debt agreements will often include precise limits of debt levels that the company cannot exceed.

Minority Interest

Some hospitality companies exclude the minority shareholder's interest when calculating debt ratios because this amount does not represent an obligation to pay funds to outsiders. Instead, minority interest results when a firm has consolidated another company of which it owns less than 100%. Nonetheless, other hospitality companies include the minority interest when calculating debt ratios, because the funds were provided by outsiders and are part of the total funds used by the hospitality company. This latter approach is considered more conservative.

Deferred Taxes

Some hospitality companies exclude deferred tax liabilities and assets when calculating the debt ratio because of the uncertainty of whether the deferred tax liability or asset will be paid or received. However, this is inconsistent with GAAP, which recognize deferred taxes as specified in ASC 740 (FAS-109). The statement clearly stipulates that deferred taxes should not be recorded unless they are likely to be paid or received.

Reserves

Reserve accounts may be used by hospitality companies for the repayment of funds in the future. They are charged to an expense on the income statement and a corresponding increase in a reserve account on the balance sheet. Since reserve accounts do not represent distinct commitments to meet future fund obligations, some hospitality companies do not include them in the calculation and analysis of the debt ratio; however, this is not the conservative position.

Debt to Equity Ratio

The debt to equity ratio is another calculation that determines the amount of leverage used by a hospitality company based on creditor financing relative to owner (shareholder) financing. The calculation of the debt to equity ratio for X Hotel follows:

$$\text{Debt to equity ratio} = \frac{\text{Total liabilities}}{\text{Total equity}} = \frac{\$770,000}{\$315,000} = 2.4 \text{ to } 1$$

X Hotel's, creditors have provided $2.40 in debt financing for every dollar of the owner's investment. Creditors view the debt to equity ratio as an indicator of the risk involved in extending credit to the company, and the cost of debt (interest expenses) will be closely related to this risk factor, as will all the terms and conditions of the loan. The ratio is also considered a quick indicator of future borrowing capacity.

When making credit decisions, creditors prefer moderate debt to equity ratios, because lower leverage provides additional security against losses in the event of liquidation. In general, it is difficult for a highly leveraged hospitality company to locate sources of borrowed funds at even the highest interest rates.

Many companies in the lodging or airline segments of the hospitality industry (and, in some instances, in the restaurant industry) have industry averages for the debt to equity ratio of 2 to 1, a reflection of the high proportion of debt financing in relation to equity financing in their capital structure. The capital-intensive nature of the hospitality industry induces these companies to rely on long-term debt instruments to finance the large investments that are required.

Asset to Equity Ratio

The asset to equity ratio is another calculation used to determine a hospitality company's leverage. It measures the proportion of assets that are financed by owners of the hospitality company. If the ratio of assets to equity is 100%, the hospitality company would be totally financed by its owners. A company with a high asset to equity ratio finances a large proportion of its assets with debt or is considered to be highly leveraged. The calculation of the asset to equity ratio for X Hotel follows:

$$\text{Assets to equity} = \frac{\text{Assets}}{\text{Equity}} = \frac{\$1,085,000}{\$315,000} = 3.4 \text{ to } 1$$

The asset to equity ratio of X Hotel indicates that the company has used high leverage in financing its assets, as the company has $3.40 of assets for every dollar financed by its owners. Thus, the hotel's creditors have invested $2.40 in debt financing for every dollar of the owner's investment.

Because of the expanding use of management contracts, joint ventures, and leasing and other financing and expansion strategies in the hospitality industry, leverage ratios must be carefully evaluated before conclusions can be drawn. In some cases, the amount of asset investment required to be financed is relatively low compared to that required by lodging companies that are very capital-intensive.

Long-Term Debt to Capitalization

A more refined version of the debt proportion analysis involves using the long-term debt to total capitalization ratio. This ratio provides a long-term perspective in relation to the company's capitalization, which is defined as the sum of long-term claims against the hospitality business, both debt and owner's equity but does not include short-term liabilities. The calculation of the long-term debt to capitalization follows:

$$\text{Long-term debt to total capital} = \frac{\text{Long-term debt}}{\text{Long-term debt} + \text{equity}}$$

Bondholders and bankers typically prefer low debt to capitalization ratios, which provide greater security for their loans. Since equity holders' returns might be enhanced with the use of positive leverage, some shareholders may prefer higher leverage. Many loan agreements of both publicly held and private hospitality companies contain covenants regulating the company's allowed maximum debt exposure expressed in terms of long-term debt to total capital. Overall, management is responsible for ensuring the company maintains a strong financial position to meet its long-term debt obligations while following leveraged strategies that result in the magnification of returns to the company's owners.

INCOME STATEMENT APPROACH

In evaluating a company's long-term debt-paying ability and the risk involved with the use of leverage, a hospitality company must examine its past earning ability to meet its interest payments and to cover significant fixed charges. Two ratios commonly used are the times interest earned ratio and the fixed asset coverage ratio.

Interest Coverage

The times interest earned ratio, a measure of interest coverage, expresses the extent to which earnings cover interest costs associated with debt financing. It indicates the ability of the company to generate earnings to pay its interest expense. The interest coverage of X Hotel is calculated as follows:

$$\text{Times interest earned} = \frac{\text{Earnings before interest and taxes (EBIT)}}{\text{Interest expense + Capitalized interest}}$$

$$= \frac{\$10{,}000}{\$5{,}000} = 2 \text{ times}$$

Times interest earned reflects the hospitality company's ability to pay annual interest on debt from its earnings. This ratio indicates the margin of safety or the times earnings can decline and still meet interest obligations. It is important to recognize that interest coverage represents a company's ability to survive during periods of economic and financial instability. An interest coverage ratio of less than 1 suggests that the hospitality company's earnings are not sufficient to meet its interest commitments.

Since the typical income statement format does not provide disclosure of EBIT, this amount must be determined by adding net income to interest and income taxes. The interest capitalized represents the interest paid during the construction period of a new hotel or restaurant, which results in interest being added to property and equipment on the balance sheet instead of expensing it on the income statement. The capitalized interest should be included in the denominator of the times interest earned ratio because it is part of the interest payment.

The averages for interest coverage in the hospitality industry have fluctuated between 2 and 5 times. The higher the interest coverage, the greater the likelihood of obtaining additional debt financing, because it represents a margin of safety for creditors. Negative interest coverage is an indication that the hospitality company incurred an operating loss and could not generate profits from operations to meet interest payments.

Fixed Charges Coverage

In the recent past, many hospitality companies have supplemented debt with leasing as a way of acquiring property and equipment. For example, restaurants often lease their kitchen equipment, thus engaging in long-term lease contracts that require periodic fixed rent payments. Because they do not meet the conditions required by GAAP for capitalization, these leases are called operating leases and are also referred to as off-balance-sheet financing. The leases carry the same long-term commitment implications as that of interest. To measure a hospitality company's ability to cover these lease payments, as well as the interest expense, the fixed charge coverage is utilized.

This coverage relates the earnings before interest, rent, and taxes to the total interest expense plus all lease costs. It is similar to the times interest earned ratio but is more inclusive in that it takes into account fixed lease payment commitments. The formula for fixed charge coverage relates the earnings before interest, taxes, and lease expenses to the total interest and lease costs as follows:

$$\text{Fixed charge coverage ratio} = \frac{\text{EBIT + Lease expenses}}{\text{Interest + Lease expenses}}$$

The fixed charge coverage ratio is a broader assessment of earning capability than the times interest earned ratio because it includes the fixed payments associated with leasing. Lease payments are added back in the numerator because they are deducted as an operating expense to calculate operating income. Lease payments are similar in nature to interest expense in that they both represent fixed obligations that must be met on an annual basis. The fixed charge coverage is important to hospitality companies that make extensive use of operating and capital lease financing.

SPECIAL ITEMS THAT IMPACT LONG-TERM DEBT-PAYING ABILITY

There are a number of special items that need to be considered in evaluating a hospitality company's long-term debt-paying ability. They include:

- Long-term capital leasing.
- Contingencies.
- Impact of historical cost accounting.

Capital Leases

Leases are considered a form of long-term financing. They can be considered operating leases, which are off-balance-sheet financing because they only impact the income statement, or capital leases, which also impact the balance sheet. When a lease contract includes any one of the following four conditions, ASC 840, *Lease* (FAS-13, *Accounting for Leases*), requires that it be capitalized:

1. Ownership passes automatically from the lessor to the lessee at the end of the lease term.
2. The lease contract includes a bargain purchase option at the end of the lease term.
3. The life of the lease covers 75% or more of the expected useful life of the leased asset.
4. The present value of the minimum future lease payments is 90% or more of the cash value of the leased asset at the time the lease is signed.

The decision to capitalize a lease involves other considerations, such as whether certain attributes of ownership are transferred to the lessee. These may include the payment of property taxes or the obligation to maintain and repair the property. These attributes tend to convert the lessor-lessee relationship into a seller-buyer relationship.

Capital leases are reported on the balance sheet as part of property and equipment. The amount that is reported is the present value of the minimum future lease payments. An offsetting long-term liability amount is reported as long-term capital lease obligations. Accordingly, capital leases are considered in the calculation, and evaluation of leverage ratios and the corresponding implied interest expense are included with interest expense when calculating the times interest earned ratio.

Operating leases are reported as rent or lease expense on the income statement, usually accompanied by explanatory footnotes indicating the length of the lease contract and any contingent rent liability. Because of their long-term financial impact, the fixed nature of minimum lease payments and the potential impact of contingent lease payments, operating leases should also be considered when evaluating the hospitality company's debt structure. Operating lease payments directly compete with interest and principal payments for the funds a hospitality company might have available for acquiring resources such as assets or operating leases.

In general, approximately two-thirds of the total long-term operating lease payment commitments are usually allocated to principal, the remainder being implied interest. Therefore, operating leases can be quickly added to a GAAP balance sheet to allow for the recalculation of the asset-liability relationship, presenting a more conservative supplemental view of the company's long-term debt-paying ability.

As of this writing, a joint FASB/IASB exposure draft on lease accounting being proposed, will replace ASC 840 (FAS-13) in the United States and IAS 17 in countries using international financial reporting standards. Essentially, it will eliminate the distinction between operating and capital leases and require that all leases be reported on the balance sheet. The proposal does this by eliminating the so-called 90% rule currently effective.

Contingencies

As defined by ASC 450, *Contingencies* (FAS-5, *Accounting for Contingencies*), a *contingency* is an existing condition, situation, or set of circumstances involving uncertainty as to possible gain or loss to an enterprise that will ultimately be resolved when one or more future events occurs or fails to occur. Accordingly, a contingent liability is a potential liability that may become an actual liability contingent on the occurrence of an uncertain event. The most common contingent liabilities in the hospitality industry are:

- Joint ventures.
- Lawsuits.
- Tax examinations.

- Discounted notes.
- Acting as guarantor for another's debts.

ASC 450 (FAS-5) does not require or allow contingent liabilities to be included in the financial statements unless they are likely to become actual liabilities. If the likelihood increases, the liabilities must be included on the balance sheet as specified by GAAP. However, these liabilities should be taken into consideration even prior to becoming probable or actual liabilities when evaluating the solvency position of a hospitality company.

Joint Ventures

Joint ventures have been widely used as a form of financing growth in the hospitality industry. A *joint venture* is an association of two or more companies established for a special purpose (e.g., the development and operation of a hotel property). Many times the hospitality company entering into a joint venture makes commitments in the form of guarantees on bank loans for the joint venture or a long-term contract to purchase supplies for the joint venture. In those cases, there might be significant potential contingent liabilities or commitments that are not reported on the balance sheet. These commitments or contingencies must also be considered in the evaluation of a company's long-term debt-paying ability. For additional information on the reporting of contingencies on the financial statements, refer to Chapter 9, "Financial Statement Disclosures."

Impact of Historical Cost Accounting

The use of historical cost accounting based on GAAP creates the need for further analysis in the evaluation of a hospitality company's ability to meet its long-term payment commitments. Assets are shown at their historical cost, except when they are impaired, in which case their value is reduced. However, assets are usually not marked up to market value. Thus, when evaluating a hospitality company's solvency from the perspective of the balance sheet, GAAP statements conceal the difference between an asset's original purchase cost (historical cost) and its current market value, which in the case of real property is usually higher and can be significant. Looked at from a balance sheet perspective, this hidden value may cause the solvency of a company to be understated.

On the liability side of the balance sheet, although the market value of debt can change because of movement in interest rates in the open market, such changes usually lead to less dramatic differences between book and market values than those that exist in the asset or equity sections of the balance sheet.

Because the equity section of the balance sheet responds to changes in the market value of both assets and liabilities, it is the section most likely to present differences when comparing GAAP net book value to the same net equity value after conforming assets and liabilities to their current market value. Consequently, the book value of the equity accounts is likely to be very different from the market value of a company's stock.

Because the typical hospitality company is heavily invested in real property, hotels more so than restaurants, whose market value tends to increase consistently, there tends to be a greater than usual disparity between a hospitality company's market value and its total book value in owner's equity, with the equity being understated because asset value cannot be marked up to market value. This leads to debt-equity ratios that make debt appear disproportionately large. To overcome this, many financial analysts replace the book value of equity with the total market value of common stock, computed as the number of shares outstanding times the market price per share.

CHAPTER 12
PROFITABILITY ANALYSIS

CONTENTS

Measures of Profitability	12,001
Fixed Asset Turnover	12,002
Return on Equity	12,002
Return on Assets	12,003
Net Return on Assets	12,004
Profit Margin	12,005
Asset Turnover	12,005
Operating Efficiency Ratio	12,006
DuPont and Leverage Analysis	12,006
Drivers of Return on Equity	12,007
Measures of Profitability by Managerial Area of Responsibility	12,008
Common Size Analysis	12,008
Vertical Analysis	12,009
Horizontal Analysis	12,009
Sustainable Sales Growth	12,009
Exhibits	
Exhibit 12-1. Drivers of Return on Equity	12,008
Exhibit 12-2. CED Sustainable Growth Rate Relative to Growth in Sales	12,010

Profitability is the ability of the hospitality company to generate earnings. Analysis of profitability is of vital concern to owners of the hospitality company, as they invest in the company with the objective of deriving income from profit distributions (dividends) and from increases in the price of common stock. Profitability analysis is also important to creditors because the ability of the hospitality company to pay interest and principal is a reflection of its ability to generate earnings. At the same time, management relies on profitability analysis as a means to appraise the company's performance.

MEASURES OF PROFITABILITY

Profitability ratios measure management's overall effectiveness, as indicated by returns on sales (profit margin and operating efficiency ratio), returns on assets (return on assets and net return on assets), and return on equity. Profitability ratios determine whether a hospitality company's earnings are reasonable, considering the amount of capital invested.

Profitability ratios are among the most closely scrutinized ratios. Many hospitality companies link employee bonuses to profitability ratios, and stock market prices react sharply to unforeseen changes in these ratios.

Commonly used measures of profitability analysis in the hospitality industry include profit margin, return on equity, return on assets, net return on assets, asset turnover, and operating profit percentage or operating income margin.

Fixed Asset Turnover

The fixed asset turnover, also referred to as the sales to fixed assets ratio, measures a hospitality company's ability to make productive use of its property and equipment to generate revenues. This ratio can be helpful in evaluating the use of assets to generate sales revenue in comparison to other companies in the industry. A high turnover suggests that the property is being used effectively in generating sales. Conversely, a low fixed asset turnover suggests that the hospitality entity is not making effective use of its property and equipment to generate sales. The fixed asset turnover is calculated as follows:

$$\text{Fixed asset turnover} = \frac{\text{Net revenue or net sales}}{\text{Average property and equipment}}$$

Factors that affect fixed asset turnover include the age of the property, the depreciation method used, and the location. Because the fixed asset turnover ignores the market value of property and equipment, it could unfairly penalize newer hotels that were built at higher costs. On the other hand, hotel companies that own very old properties will have a relatively high fixed asset turnover, because the hotels were built at lower costs and a major portion of those costs have been depreciated.

The fixed asset turnover in most segments of the hospitality industry (e.g., lodging, cruise lines) is relatively low in comparison to other industries as a result of the large investment required to operate those segments and the fact that there is no way of raising output at times of maximum demand.

Many hotels or restaurants with properties under construction may exclude these fixed assets in the calculation of the fixed asset turnover, because the properties under construction do not contribute to current sales and thus will result in the understatement of the sales to fixed assets ratio.

Return on Equity

The return on equity (ROE) or return on stockholders' equity ratio presents the overall effectiveness of the hospitality company in managing its total investment in assets and in generating a return to shareholders. It is useful in evaluating managerial performance in achieving profits for the owners of the company. In developing an acceptable ROE requirement for a business plan, management must first prepare sales forecasts for several years, which, in turn, are used to prepare a capital budgeting plan.

The formula for this ratio depends on the capitalization of the company, which might consist of both common stock and preferred stock. If only common stock has been issued, the equation is:

$$\text{Return on equity} = \frac{\text{Net income}}{\text{Average shareholders' equity}}$$

When preferred stock is outstanding, a variation of ROE is the return on common shareholders' equity. It is calculated by dividing net income less preferred dividends by average common stockholders' equity. From the viewpoint of the common shareholder, any time preferred stock or debt can be issued at a cost lower than the cost of investing those funds, the return on common equity is enhanced.

In evaluating the change in ROE, it is important to consider decisions and events that might impact stockholders' returns in the future. For example, the exercise of stock options will reduce or dilute the existing shareholders' control of the company, as well as their claims against the company's earnings, thereby having the potential of negatively impacting ROE. Similarly, the inclusion of restrictive covenants on bank loan agreements places a restriction on retained earnings. Moreover, when a hospitality company repurchases stock, there is a reduction in shareholders' equity due to the decrease in the number of shares outstanding. Accordingly, stock repurchases will lead to an increase in ROE (other things being equal).

ROE is important because it is a measure of the efficiency with which management employs shareholder's capital. But ROE can conceal a number of potential problems. Companies can resort to financial strategies to artificially maintain a strong ROE and hide deteriorating performance in business fundamentals. Growing use of financial leverage and stock buybacks can help to maintain a company's ROE even though operational profitability is eroding. Mounting competitive pressure combined with very low interest rates, characteristic of recent times, creates a potent incentive to engage in these strategies to keep investors content.

Excessive use of leverage is a significant impediment for a hospitality company when market demand for its brands decline, as many companies discovered during the recent economic downturn. In reality, it results in increased risk for a company during troubled times. If underlying profitability continues to deteriorate, more stock buybacks or increasing leverage will be necessary to maintain ROE, further increasing the hospitality entity's exposure to unanticipated downturns or financial market crises. Yet, the alternative of allowing ROE to decline will have an instant negative affect on stock performance.

The aforementioned concerns with ROE reflect the need to pay less attention to ROE and increase focus on other measures of profitability (e.g., return on assets (ROA)) to analyze long-term profitability trends across hospitality companies. ROA avoids the potential distortions created by financial strategies such as those mentioned above.

Return on Assets

The return on assets (ROA) expresses the earning power of the investment capital employed in the hospitality business independent of the pattern of financing this asset investment. It is used by owners and financial managers in determining the return on the company's investment in assets and to assist in financing decisions. Because ROA seeks to determine the earning power of the company's assets, its calculation ignores debt financing by using EBIT, as follows:

$$\text{Return on assets} = \frac{\text{Earnings before interest and taxes}}{\text{Average assets}}$$

Essentially, ROA is a measure of the true productivity of the hospitality company's assets, without considering leverage or tax factors. As a result, the interest cost of borrowed funds is omitted because it is a variable that is determined by the amount of debt financing used by the company. In this way, the resulting ROA ratio provides a gauge by which the earning potential of assets can be compared with the interest rate on the debt capital used in financing those assets. In order for leverage to be positive, the ROA must be higher than the interest rate on the borrowed funds. The financial manager can use this comparison as a first step in making leverage decisions regarding the expansion of the company's assets.

Hospitality companies can increase their ROA by increasing the profit yield on each dollar of sale by raising the operating profit margin or improving asset utilization in the generation of sales. The first approach will result in an increase in operating income that is higher than the rise in sales (e.g., by enhancing food or beverage cost controls). In the second approach, improving asset utilization entails increasing sales more than assets. One way to accomplish this is by disposing of unprofitable hotels or restaurants.

Using ROA as a key performance indicator places immediate emphasis on management's ability to utilize the assets required to operate the business. Accordingly, ROA may foster a better view of fundamentals of the hospitality business. As economic pressures rise, management must focus on the assets they are distinctively capable of managing in order to maximize the company's value.

Net Return on Assets

The net return on total assets (net ROA) indicates the amount of net earnings relative to the level of investment in assets. Therefore, this ratio measures a hospitality company's ability to utilize its assets to generate earnings. It relates the after-tax income to stockholders and lenders on the total investment that they have in the hospitality company. The net ROA is used by large conglomerates to assess the performance of their subsidiary corporations operating in the hospitality industry. It is affected by the extent of leverage that the hospitality company is using, and thus interest expense and income taxes are deducted in the calculation of net income. The formula follows:

$$\text{Net return on assets} = \frac{\text{Net income}}{\text{Average assets}}$$

Profit Margin

The profit margin, also known as net profit margin or return on sales, provides a measure of net income dollars generated by each dollar of sales. It represents the hospitality firm's ability to translate sales dollars into earnings and serves as an expression of the overall cost and price effectiveness of the hospitality operation. Although it is desirable that the net profit margin be high, competitive forces within an industry, economic conditions, use of high leverage, and high fixed costs may have a negative impact on profit margin. The calculation of the net profit margin follows:

$$\text{Net profit margin} = \frac{\text{Net income}}{\text{Net sales}}$$

The profit margin is considered a measure of the extent of protection of the hospitality company against future losses that can occur because of increasing costs or declining sales. For example, a profit margin of 2% demonstrates that if restaurant sales decrease by 2% or expenses increase by 2%, the company may need to report losses on the income statement.

A variation of the profit margin is the gross profit margin, which measures the percentage of each sales dollar after deducting the cost of goods used to generate those sales. This ratio is more widely used in the retail and manufacturing industries than in the hospitality industry.

The profit margin ratio of hospitality companies depends largely on two factors: (1) operating costs and (2) pricing policies. The profit margin may decline, for example, because management has reduced room rates in anticipation of raising the total sales volume or because costs are increasing while selling prices remain constant.

Asset Turnover

Asset turnover measures the utilization of the hospitality company's assets and its ability to generate sales through the use of its asset investment. It is used to appraise the hospitality company's ability to use its asset base efficiently in the generation of sales revenue. The calculation of asset turnover follows:

$$\text{Asset turnover} = \frac{\text{Total revenue or net sales}}{\text{Average assets}}$$

A low asset turnover ratio may result from an excessive asset investment in relation to the sales that are being derived from the utilization of those assets. If that is the case, the hospitality entity may consider the consolidation of its present operation by selling some properties and investing funds in high yielding investments or using them to expand into more profitable segments of the hospitality industry or other industries.

It is also important to recognize that hotels, cruise lines, and restaurants will have a very low asset turnover during periods of aggressive expansion because of increasing assets at a higher pace than sales revenue.

Operating Efficiency Ratio

The operating efficiency ratio, also known as operating income ratio, is a measure of operating performance. It is considered a superior gauge of operating performance than the profit margin ratio because it only considers expenses that are under the control of operating management. It is determined by dividing income before fixed charges by total revenue. Income before fixed charges is also referred to as income after undistributed operating expenses (or income before occupancy expenses in the restaurant industry). Fixed charges are not under the control of operating management because they are based on decisions of owners or boards of directors and thus are beyond the control of active management. The calculation of the operating efficiency ratio for lodging companies follows:

$$\text{Operating efficiency ratio} = \frac{\text{Income before fixed charges}}{\text{Total revenue}}$$

A variation of the operating efficiency ratio for restaurants and other segments of the hospitality industry is the operating income margin. This ratio indicates the profitability of sales before deducting nonoperating revenues and expenses. These items are not directly associated with the generation of sales and are not under the control of operating management. The operation income margin is calculated as follows:

$$\text{Operating income margin} = \frac{\text{Operating income}}{\text{Total revenue}}$$

DUPONT AND LEVERAGE ANALYSIS

E.I. DuPont de Nemours and Company developed the DuPont and Leverage system. This internal management tool is an excellent way to evaluate managerial performance and future investment opportunities and to rate managerial effectiveness at different levels. DuPont and Leverage analysis separates the net ROA into its component parts, profit margin and asset turnover, as follows:

$$\text{Profit margin} \times \text{Asset turnover} = \text{Net return on assets}$$

$$\frac{\text{Net income}}{\text{Net sales}} \times \frac{\text{Net sales}}{\text{Assets}} = \frac{\text{Net income}}{\text{Assets}}$$

The DuPont equation reveals the way in which a hospitality company's earning power can be enhanced by a combination of strategies undertaken by its operating or asset management. For example, a restaurant can improve its earning power by either increasing its profit margin by raising sales more than expenses (e.g., offering a larger hot dog at a higher price) or by increasing its asset turnover by reducing assets more than sales (e.g., reducing inventories).

Separating the net ROA into profit margin and asset turnover allows for identifying the causes of the change in the net ROA. Example 1 presents the DuPont Analysis for XYZ Hotel for 20X6 and 20X5. It indicates that XYZ Hotel's ROA improved because of an increase in the profit margin. That is, a good control of expenses by the company's operating management was able to offset the slowdown in asset turnover caused by assets growing at a faster pace than sales.

EXAMPLE 1: The Dupont analysis for XYZ hotel is as follows:

	Profit margin	×	Asset turnover	=	Net return on assets
20X6	6%	×	.60 times	=	3.6%
20X5	5%	×	.70 times	=	3.5%

By multiplying net ROA by the ratio of assets to equity, it is possible to conduct a more in-depth analysis of ROE and determine how the use of positive leverage can enhance the return to common shareholders. The product of these two ratios equals the return on equity. This extension of the DuPont equation is used to determine the impact of leverage on ROE, since the asset to equity ratio is another way to express the extent of leverage that a hospitality company is including in its capital structure. The expanded equation follows:

Net return on assets × Leverage = Return on equity

$$\frac{\text{Net income}}{\text{Average assets}} \times \frac{\text{Average assets}}{\text{Average shareholders' equity}} = \frac{\text{Net income}}{\text{Average shareholders' equity}}$$

Drivers of Return on Equity

Exhibit 12-1 depicts the main drivers of ROE. As previously noted, the DuPont system allows the hospitality company to break down its ROE into a return on sales component (profit margin), the efficiency of the company in utilizing its assets to generate revenue (asset turnover), and the financial leverage component (asset to equity ratio). This enables management, as well as financial analysts, to study the impact of each of these factors in the overall return on common shareholders' equity.

Exhibit 12-1: Drivers of Return on Equity

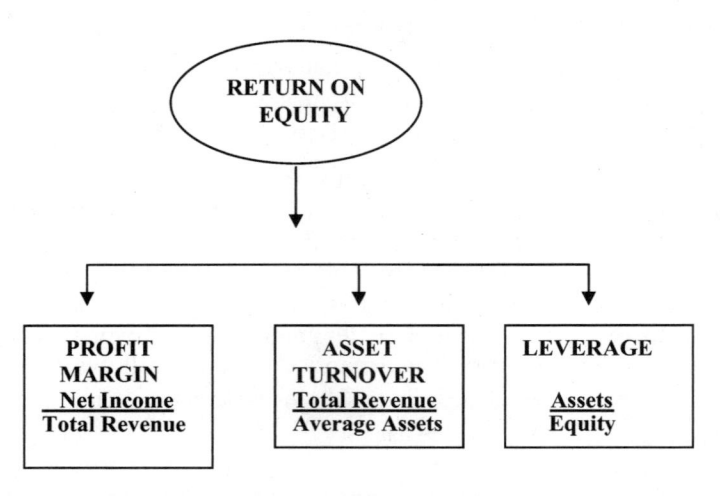

```
                    RETURN ON
                     EQUITY
                        |
        ┌───────────────┼───────────────┐
        ▼               ▼               ▼
     PROFIT          ASSET           LEVERAGE
     MARGIN         TURNOVER
    Net Income    Total Revenue       Assets
   Total Revenue  Average Assets      Equity
```

MEASURES OF PROFITABILITY BY MANAGERIAL AREA OF RESPONSIBILITY

The measure of profitability that is used depends on the hospitality manager's area of responsibility. For example, a director of sales will focus on profit margin, as this ratio reflects a return on sales. Conversely, the manager of a hospitality operating unit, with responsibilities for that unit's assets, would choose ROA (or net ROA). At the same time, the chief executive officer (CEO) is mainly concerned with the overall return to the shareholders who invested capital in the hospitality company. Accordingly, the CEO would pay attention to ROE. Likewise, the operating efficiency ratio is of utmost concern to the general manager, as it is usually used to evaluate the ability of management to operate profitably and serves as a basis to pay bonuses to the general manager.

In chain operations, hotel managers may be evaluated based on the ROA of their individual units. As a result, hotel managers may hesitate to replace inefficient equipment because the replacement may lower income and ROA through the increased asset base and depreciation.

COMMON SIZE ANALYSIS

Common size analysis is a technique that enables management to determine the structure and composition of the hospitality company's financial statements. The analysis can either be horizontal (across years) or vertical (within a year). Common size analysis expresses all numbers in a financial statement in percentage form, thereby revealing significant trends and identifying areas of wide deviation in need of further attention. There are two types of common size analysis: horizontal analysis and vertical analysis.

Vertical Analysis

Vertical common size analysis can be used to make valuable comparisons of operating performance between a hospitality company and industry performance. As reflected in industry studies, it expresses all the numbers in financial statements as a percent of a common base figure. In the case of the income statement, the base figure is net sales. In so doing, it shows the relationship between expenses and income items and revenue, as provided in the following example:

EXAMPLE 2: The vertical common size income statement of XER Hotels for the year ended December 31, 20X8, is as follows:

Net sales	$120,000	100%
Cost of sales	35,000	29%
Gross profit	85,000	71%
Operating expenses	60,000	50%
Net income	$ 25,000	21%

Vertical analysis is helpful in disclosing the internal structure of the hospitality business and identifies potential strengths and problem areas. For example, a comparison of the percents of the cost of sales section of the income statements can be an indication of the effectiveness of controlling these costs and of the potential impact of the mix of food and beverage sales.

Horizontal Analysis

Horizontal analysis expresses all the numbers on a financial statement as a percent of a common base year. All items in the first year (base year) are stated at 100%, and in the following years each item is expressed as a percent of the same item in the base year. By focusing on the horizontal common size analysis, it is possible to examine the relative change in individual revenue, expense, and net income amounts. Horizontal analysis is very useful in establishing trends and preparing financial projections.

SUSTAINABLE SALES GROWTH

Sustainable sales growth is the maximum expansion in sales that the hospitality company can achieve without having to raise external funds. It relies on the ROE model and is the guiding criteria used by management in planning capital expenditures.

Sustainable growth is essentially the rate of growth the hospitality company can support without changing its dividend policy and the factors affecting the ROE ratio. A hospitality company cannot grow faster than its sustainable growth rate for an unlimited amount of time using internal financing only. If actual growth were to exceed the sustainable growth rate, management would need to find additional resources to support the company because operations could not provide sufficient funds.

Part III: Financial Analysis

In addition, the calculation assumes that the company does not issue any new common stock. To calculate the sustainable growth rate, the following formula is used:

$$\text{Sustainable growth rate} = \text{Retention rate} \times \text{Return on equity}$$

$$\text{Where: Retention rate} = \frac{\text{Retained earnings}}{\text{Net income}} \text{ and ROE} = \frac{\text{Net income}}{\text{Equity}}$$

The main factors that determine a company's ability to grow without raising additional equity capital include its operating policy, its dividend policy in terms of retaining earnings for future expansion, the effective tax rate, and its current use of financial leverage. If these factors continue unchanged, a hospitality company will not be able to expand its sales faster than the calculated sustainable growth rate unless it issues new equity capital. Exhibit 12-2 presents the sustainable growth rate of CED Hospitality Company compared to its actual growth in sales for the two years (20X7 and 20X8).

Exhibit 12-2: CED Sustainable Growth Rate Relative to Growth in Sales

Year	Retention rate $\frac{\text{Retained earnings}}{\text{Net income}}$	Return on equity (ROE) $\frac{\text{Net income}}{\text{Equity}}$	Self-sustainable growth rate Retention rate × ROE	Sales growth
20X8	0.50	20%	.50 × 20% = 10%	15%
20X7	0.60	18%	.60 × 18% = 10.8%	8%

In 20X8, the company expanded at a faster pace than its sustainable growth rate. Since this growth rate is unsustainable, CED Hospitality Company had to revise its financing policies in order to fund the gap in the sustainable growth rate and its growth in sales. Generally, companies with sales that exceed their sustainable growth rate will ultimately experience a cash deficit and problems obtaining funding.

Conversely, in 20X7, CED sales grew less than the company's sustainable growth rate. A company that is unable to increase sales as quickly as its sustainable growth rate will experience investing difficulties and have a cash surplus. A hospitality company confronted with these circumstances must determine the most efficient use of its cash surplus in order to create value for its business. If the company is not capable of devising value-creating strategies for investing its money, it may have to consider returning the excess cash to owners through a special dividend payment or by repurchasing shares of the company's stock.

13,001

CHAPTER 13
PROFITABILITY AND INVESTOR ANALYSIS

CONTENTS

Profitability for Investors' Analysis	13,001
Measures of Profitability for Investors	13,002
Earnings per Share	13,002
Price Earnings Ratio	13,004
Dividend Payout Ratio	13,006
Dividend Yield	13,006
Book Value per Share	13,008
Market Value and Market to Book Value	13,008
Beta Analysis	13,009
Exhibits	
Exhibit 13-1. Caesars Entertainment Basic and Diluted EPS Disclosure	13,003

The financial manager must be aware of the various factors affecting investment decisions. One of the major factors investors take into account when choosing equity investments is the relationship between return and risk, for which investors have different degrees of tolerance. Even with identical attitudes toward risk, investors might choose different investments because of constraints associated with liquidity, tax status, and regulatory restrictions.

The financial manager should acquire an understanding of the main objectives of equity investors of publicly held hospitality companies, because they provide vital risk capital to these companies. The analysis of risk from the investor's perspective, also referred to as stock valuation analysis, is of special concern to investors of publicly held companies. Stock valuation analysis provides an appraisal of the hospitality company in terms of its investment potential and is used by investors to determine if they should buy, hold, or sell its stock.

PROFITABILITY FOR INVESTORS' ANALYSIS

Of all users of financial statements, investors and potential investors have the need for the most extensive amount of information. In deciding to provide equity investment, these investors must take into account the relationship between risk and returns while considering all facets of liquidity, profitability, financial condition, and capital structure. Every equity investor, and potential investor in a hospitality company, may expect one or more of the following three principal types of returns on their investment:

1. Cash dividends

2. Stock appreciation

3. Special distributions such as rights and warrants

Hospitality companies tend to follow a precise growth pattern. Young companies initially tend to grow by attracting venture capital investors. During middle age, their established success enables them to complement equity capital with large amounts of debt capital to further finance their rapid growth. Their goal is to capture the maximum amount of market share before competitors enter the market. Accordingly, these companies retain most of their earnings and invest them in future growth. As they mature, their market penetration allows for less rapid growth and less demand for capital. At this stage, the hospitality companies tend to switch to a dividend-paying strategy.

MEASURES OF PROFITABILITY FOR INVESTORS

Earnings per Share

Earnings per share (EPS) is the most commonly published investment statistic used by the financial press as the primary measure of a hospitality company's performance. It is the amount of income earned on a share of common stock during the period. EPS applies only to investors of publicly held hospitality companies; nonpublic companies, because of cost-benefit considerations, are not required to report EPS. As noted in Chapter 6, "Financial Statement Reporting: The Income Statement," GAAP requires that publicly held hospitality companies report EPS on the face of the income statement and are also required to disclose separately the specific EPS associated with:

- Income from continuing operations (after tax),
- Disposal of business segments,
- Extraordinary items, and
- Changes in accounting principles.

Basic Earnings per Share. Basic EPS is calculated by dividing net income by the weighted-average common shares outstanding, as follows:

$$\text{Earnings per share} = \frac{\text{Net income}}{\text{Weighted-average number of common shares outstanding}} = \frac{200{,}000}{1{,}000{,}000} = .02$$

If the hospitality company has preferred stock outstanding, the dividends paid and accumulated on the stock are deducted from net income in the calculation of EPS. Because earnings pertain to a full period, they should be related to the common shares outstanding during that time. Thus, the denominator of the equation is the weighted-average number of common shares outstanding. Chapter 6, "Financial Statement Reporting: The Income Statement," presents an example of the calculation of the weighted-average number of shares outstanding.

Diluted Earnings per Share. In addition to disclosing basic EPS, GAAP requires the disclosure of diluted EPS for hospitality companies that have the potential for significant dilution. Many hotel or restaurant companies, for instance, have issued and presently have outstanding options to purchase their common stock or preferred stock or bonds that can be converted to common stock in the future. When and if these options and conversion privileges are exercised, the number of common shares outstanding will increase. This in turn will dilute the ownership interests of the existing common shareholders. The calculation of diluted EPS reflects these possibilities by effectively increasing the number of common shares outstanding, thus diluting a corporation's net income among a larger number of shares. The extent of potential dilution of EPS can be information that is useful to existing or prospective stockholders, who are concerned with maintaining the value of their investments.

In evaluating profitability for investors, diluted EPS is perceived as an accounting creation used to consider the complex capital structure of companies that have securities outstanding, which can be converted into common stock. EPS depends on net income and the number of shares outstanding (plus a certain amount of dilution potential), and fluctuations in EPS can be caused by one or both factors. Exhibit 13-1 shows the presentation of basic and diluted EPS included in Caesars Entertainment's 2004 Annual Report as follows:

Exhibit 13-1: Caesars Entertainment Basic and Diluted EPS Disclosure

	Years ended December 31		
	2004	2003	2002
Basic earnings (loss) per share:			
Income from continuing operations before cumulative effect of accounting change	$0.60	$0.23	$ 0.55
Income (loss) from discontinued operations, net of taxes	0.36	(0.08)	(0.04)
Cumulative effect of accounting change	—	—	(3.25)
Net income (loss)	$0.96	$0.15	$(2.74)
Diluted earnings (loss) per share:			
Income from continuing operations before cumulative effect of accounting change	$0.58	$0.23	$ 0.55
Income (loss) from discontinued operations	0.36	(0.08)	(0.04)
Cumulative effect of accounting change	—	—	(3.22)
Net income (loss)	$0.94	$0.15	$(2.71)

Chapter 6, "Financial Statement Reporting: The Income Statement," provides examples of basic and diluted EPS calculations.

Earnings per Share and Analysts' Forecasts. Historical EPS can be stated as either basic or diluted; both statistics are available from the income statement. EPS becomes important when looking at future growth rates, when making comparisons to stock price and other measures, and when forecasting future EPS.

Changes in EPS must be carefully evaluated. An increase in EPS, for instance, might be attributed to the company's purchase of its own stock (treasury stock), which reduces the number of shares outstanding. Conversely, EPS might increase as a hospitality company reinvests earnings in its operations because of the resulting rising profits without any change in the number of shares outstanding.

Annual reports are not issued until approximately 90 days after the end of the fiscal year, but EPS are announced a few days after the end of each period. Accordingly, quarterly EPS are used by present and prospective investors in making investment decisions. Particularly important is the actual quarterly EPS compared to analysts' expectations or forecasts. If actual EPS have increased from the amount reported in the previous quarter but fall short of analysts' forecasts, the price of the stock will usually fall.

Price Earnings Ratio

The price earnings ratio (P/E) is one of the most widely used measures of performance among analysts and investors of publicly held hospitality companies. This measure involves the market price of a company's common stock. In essence, the P/E reflects how much the investing public is willing to pay for the hospitality company's prospective earnings. This ratio is the simple calculation of current stock price divided by EPS and is best interpreted as the stock price premium for current (and future) EPS. It expresses the multiple that the stock market places on a hospitality company's current earnings. Basically, the P/E ratio reflects an investor's expectations about the hospitality company's future performance. If two publicly held restaurant companies, for instance, had annual earnings of $1.00 per share, and Company A shares sold for $20 per share and Company B shares sold for $30 per share, investors placed a different value on the same $1 earnings. The reason for this $10 divergence lies in the collective expectations of investors about the ability of Company B to achieve faster growth in earnings and cash flow than Company A.

A hospitality company's P/E ratio depends on several factors, including its performance history, quality of earnings, future earnings prospects, and risks associated with those earnings. A high P/E ratio is usually associated with a high growth hospitality company that is expected to generate substantial and rapid increases in EPS for the foreseeable future, while a low P/E usually is associated with hospitality companies whose future earnings growth is expected to be low, erratic, or slow, thus resulting in a substantial drop in stock price. Conversely, if a hospitality company has a year of poor earnings performance but is expected to recover in the near future, the P/E ratio may be high.

The P/E numerator is market price per share, which changes throughout the trading day and has a new closing price daily. The P/E ratio fluctuates as stock prices change. The denominator is the basic EPS for the latest fiscal year. If diluted EPS differs significantly from basic EPS, both calculations should be made. The P/E ratio of a hypothetical hospitality company XRT would be determined as follows:

	20X7	20X6	20X5
Market price per share	35	30	34
Earnings per share	2.2	2	2

$$\text{Price earnings ratio} = \frac{\text{Market price per share}}{\text{Earnings per share}} = \frac{35}{2.2} = 16 \quad \frac{30}{2} = 15 \quad \frac{34}{2} = 17$$

In this case investors in XRT Hospitality are willing to pay between 15 and 17 times what the company earned during the year. The P/E ratio is higher in 20X7 than in 20X6 but is below the 20X5 level, which could be the result of developments in the economy or the market in general, or due to investors reacting to changes in earnings performance. Another factor could be risks associated with prospective earnings or a potential for the reduction of dividend payments. A decline in the hospitality company's P/E ratio not explainable by the general decline in stock market valuations is cause for concern. Management should compare its P/E ratio with those of competing hospitality companies to determine its ranking in the marketplace.

Financial managers generally prefer a hospitality company's P/E ratio to be high, as this allows the company to raise a given amount of equity capital by selling a lesser amount of shares, thus creating less dilution of earnings. Conversely, many investors prefer to buy stocks whose P/E is below the current market average for the industry because their market valuation does not depend so much on fulfilling extraordinary growth expectations. Companies with strong growth prospects normally have a high P/E ratio. However, paying such high valuations for a company's stock entails taking the risk that the expected earnings underlying the high P/E ratio might not materialize. In general, a high price to earnings ratio implies greater investment risk, but such high P/E ratios are normally only granted to companies with a lower degree of financial leverage. High leverage is normally associated with a low P/E because leverage increases the volatility in the company's future earnings, and thus its financial risk.

Most hospitality company P/E ratios range between 10 and 30 times earnings. On July 3, 2008, for instance, McDonald's P/E was 27.1 times, whereas Marriott International's was 15.2 times. However, some hospitality companies (e.g., Hilton Corporation in 1996) have traded over 50 times (or more) of their current earnings. These exceptionally high P/E ratios have been attributed to the market valuing exceptional growth opportunities, such as the development of a new concept or entrance into a new market such as China.

Nonetheless, most investors pay careful attention to a hospitality company's P/E ratio in the belief, usually well founded, that among low P/E stocks they are more likely to find bargains than among high P/E stocks. Investors prefer to acquire a claim on a dollar of earnings as cheaply as possible, as is the case when a company's P/E ratio is low. For example, if a company's P/E ratio is 10, the investor will pay $10 per share for every dollar of current earnings, whereas if the P/E ratio is 20, the hospitality investor will pay twice as much for a claim on the same one dollar of the current earnings.

Dividend Payout Ratio

The dividend payout ratio, which is determined by dividing cash dividends per share by EPS, measures the proportion of earnings paid out to shareholders in the form of cash during a given period. It is calculated for XRT Company as follows:

	20X7	20X6	20X5
Dividends per share	.37	.40	.40
Earnings per share	2.2	2	2

$$\text{Dividend payout ratio} = \frac{\text{Dividends per share}}{\text{Earnings per share}} = \frac{.37}{2.2} = 17\% \quad \frac{.40}{2} = 20\% \quad \frac{.40}{2} = 20\%$$

There are no set standards for the dividend payout ratio in the hospitality industry; yet, the relationship between dividends per share and EPS significantly portrays the style of the company's top management and board of directors, who ultimately must authorize any dividends. High-growth hospitality companies tend to pay out relatively low proportions of earnings because they prefer to reinvest earnings to support profitable growth. Stable- or moderate-growth companies tend to pay a larger than average percentage of their earnings to shareholders. Other factors may also affect the dividend policy of the hospitality company, including tax law revisions, anticipated changes in economic performance, and interest rates.

In the above calculation of dividend payout, it is evident that XRT Company reduced its dividend in 20X7. To explain the reduction, management might have stated that this decline in dividends per share was the result of adopting a new policy to reduce dividend payments in order to have additional internal funds available for more rapid expansion. However, it is rather unusual for companies to reduce dividend payments in the presence of an increase in EPS. In many cases such a decision can lead to a negative signal regarding future earnings outlook.

Because most boards of directors are inclined to pay fairly stable dividends per share, and adjust them only slowly, the payout ratio of a company may vary widely in the short run in response to changes in earnings performance. However, over a period of several years, the dividend payout ratio can often be used to indicate the propensity of directors to reinvest funds in the business instead of paying out earnings to hospitality shareholders.

Dividend Yield

Dividend yield is a measure of the return on the owner's investments in a company's stock provided by the current dividend payment. As stated earlier young, growing hospitality companies pay little or no cash dividends. Conversely, matured hospitality companies that have limited growth prospects and consequently have less debt service obligations are more likely to pay out a higher portion of earnings in dividends. At the same time, boards of directors try to smooth out seasonal variations in earnings, so typical in the hospitality industry, by maintaining a dividend payment proportional to the long-run prospects of the hospitality company. In general, hospitality companies have historically paid low dividends in comparison to other industries and thus may not attract investors who need current income. These investors are likely to focus on stocks that pay high dividends, with earnings growth a lesser concern. The calculation of the XRT Company's dividend yield relates the current market price of the company to the annual dividend payment as follows:

$$\text{Dividend yield} = \frac{\text{Dividends per share}}{\text{Market price per share}} = \frac{.37}{35} = 10\% \quad \frac{.40}{30} = 13\% \quad \frac{.40}{34} = 12\%$$

(20X7, 20X6, 20X5)

In this case XRT's dividend yield ranged from 10%-13% during the period 20X5–20X7, which is considered to be a very high dividend yield for a hospitality company. One might not expect a negative response from the company's investors as a result of the dividend reduction in 20X7; however, investors become uneasy during times of change or market price fluctuations.

Equity investors in hospitality companies also expect the growth in future dividends that results from wise investment of the profits retained by the company. Usually, companies with higher dividend yields are expected to have lower growth in future dividends as they find additional sources to increase returns to their owners. Thus, there is a trade-off between current dividends and future dividend growth. As stated earlier, many successful hospitality companies invest their earnings for expansion purposes rather than distributing them as dividends. In those cases, the dividend yield will be extremely low or even zero.

Many hotels and restaurants have never paid a dividend and publicly state that they do not have any plans to do so in the foreseeable future. Successful hospitality companies make such statements because they are reinvesting most of their earnings in profitable opportunities such as opening more hotels, more restaurants, or otherwise growing their companies rather than returning earnings directly to the stockholders. As long as these companies provide an above average capital appreciation in the future that is greater than the one expected by the level of risk associated with the stock, investors will be willing to finance these companies.

Dividend Yield and Interest Rates. Hospitality financial managers should be aware of how investors view the interplay between dividend yield and interest rates. Because they are constantly looking for maximum current returns, when interest rates exceed dividend yields there is a tendency to transfer funds from stocks to bonds or other interest-paying investments.

It is interesting to note that that some investors also transfer their funds out of stocks when interest rates increase. They foresee that interest rate increases, by making borrowed funds more expensive, will negatively affect the financial leverage that growth-seeking companies normally use. Therefore, increasing interest rates tend to lessen growth of market value.

Tax Impact on Dividends. Another reason some investors want hospitality companies to reinvest their earnings rather than pay them out as dividends is that reinvested earnings are taxed only once. If a corporation pays out part of its earnings as dividends, the stockholder must pay taxes on these dividends in addition to the tax already paid by the corporation. Thus, when these investors reinvest any dividends received after paying taxes on them, they will have less money to reinvest than if the hospitality corporation had kept the earnings and reinvested them itself.

Book Value per Share

The book value of a hospitality company is equal to total stockholders' equity (also called net assets) less the par value of preferred shares. It reflects the amount that common shareholders would receive if the company's liabilities are paid and all of its assets sold at their balance sheet value. Book value is calculated on a per-share basis by dividing net assets less the par value of preferred shares by the number of common shares outstanding, as follows:

$$\text{Book value per share} = \frac{\text{Total shareholders' equity} - \text{Preferred stock}}{\text{Number of common shares outstanding}}$$

If book value per share is a true reflection of the economic value of the hospitality company, then book value should be the same as market value. However, in most cases, the market value of a hospitality company is greater than its book value. This is due to at least three factors:

1. Market value is a function of perceived or real earnings potential.
2. Book value results from the depreciation of real estate properties.
3. Market value is affected by inflation.

Higher market premiums indicate that investors have greater confidence in the future performance of a hospitality company (its shares will sell at a price higher than book value). When market value is below book value, investors perceive the hospitality company as lacking earnings growth potential.

Inflation and the fact that buildings and other tangible property, in which hospitality companies invest heavily due to their capital-intensive nature, are depreciated also tends to increase the difference between book value and market value. While the book value of these assets is being reduced by the hospitality company through depreciation, inflation causes their market value to increase due to the decrease in value of current dollars.

MARKET VALUE AND MARKET TO BOOK VALUE

The *market value* of a hospitality company (also called market capitalization or market cap) is calculated by multiplying the stock price by the number of shares outstanding. Stock market value changes can be caused by several factors, including:

1. The daily changes in investor sentiment, which affects individual stocks. (These may be caused by real changes within a company or by perceived, but unfounded, changes.)

2. Long-term changes in investor sentiment (usually due to macro-economic factors), which cause values in the entire market or in an entire market segment to increase or decrease.
3. The buyback of a hospitality company's own shares (usually held as treasury stock).

Large market declines can reduce the market cap of big companies by billions of dollars. This not only affects current shareholder value; it also makes it more costly, in terms of dilution and loss of control, for such companies to raise additional equity capital.

The market-to-book-value ratio is calculated by dividing the market price of a share of a hospitality company's common stock by its book value minus the par value of any preferred shares (i.e., its common shareholders' equity per share).

At times investors consider the stock of a hospitality company with a low market-to-book value to be a safer investment because they perceive the book value as a base supporting the market value. Investors view book value as the level below which market price will not fall because the company always has the option to liquidate or sell its assets for their book values. This is especially true in the case of hospitality companies that have high investments in well-located properties. A low market-to-book value is seen by some investors as providing a margin of safety, and some analysts will reject high market-to-book-value hospitality companies in their stock selection process.

BETA ANALYSIS

Finance theory suggests that *Beta* is a measure of nondiversifiable risk, as opposed to portfolio risk, which changes according to the mix of investments held in a portfolio. Beta represents the hospitality company's sensitivity to market performance and also reflects the market risk of investing in any individual hospitality company. For example, the expected return of a hospitality company with a beta of 1 is equal to the market's return on any given day. If beta is greater than 1, the change in a company's stock price is expected to be greater than the change in the general market—either up or down. The converse is true if the beta of a hospitality company's stock is less than 1.

Hospitality companies that are considered higher risks tend to have lower P/E ratios and lower market-to-book ratios, and many investors use a high P/E as an initial filter when selecting stocks for investment.

CHAPTER 14
MANAGEMENT ANALYSIS OF OPERATIONS

CONTENTS

Analyzing Operations Using Standard Operating Ratios	14,003
Commonly Used Hotel Operating Ratios	14,004
Commonly Used Restaurant Operating Ratios	14,013
Beverage Operations	14,018
Less Commonly Used Operating Ratios	14,021
Basis for Evaluating Operating Ratios	14,022
Cyclical Comparisons	14,023
Comparative Analysis	14,023
Common Size Analysis—Including a Sample Analysis	14,025
Vertical Analysis	14,025
Horizontal Analysis	14,026
Trend Analysis (Percent Change)	14,028
Indexing Analysis	14,030
Indexing Analysis and Operating Ratio Analysis Example	14,032
Indexing Analysis of Twin Restaurants	14,032
Operating Ratio Analysis of Twin Restaurants	14,033

Exhibits

Exhibit 14-1. Rooms in Hotel	14,006
Exhibit 14-2. Room Occupancy Statistics and Operating Ratios for Leisure Hotel	14,007
Exhibit 14-3. Ratios to Measure the Number of Rooms Being Used for Various Purposes	14,008
Exhibit 14-4. Ratios to Evaluate the Number of Rooms Occupied by More than One Guest	14,009
Exhibit 14-5. Ratio to Measure the Average Length of a Guest's Stay	14,010
Exhibit 14-6. Ratios to Evaluate Room Rates Charged	14,010
Exhibit 14-7. Major Hotel Cost Ratios	14,012
Exhibit 14-8. Determination of Cost of Food Consumed	14,014
Exhibit 14-9. Most Commonly Used Food Operating Ratios	14,016
Exhibit 14-10. Food Sales per Cover by Meal Period	14,018
Exhibit 14-11. Food Sales per Cover by Hypothetical Dining Area or Category	14,018
Exhibit 14-12. Determination of Cost of Beverages Consumed	14,019
Exhibit 14-13. Most Commonly Used Beverage Operating Ratios	14,020
Exhibit 14-14. Rule-of-Thumb Relationship Between Food and Beverage Inventory Days	14,021
Exhibit 14-15. Step One of the Comparative Analysis of Twin Restaurants	14,024
Exhibit 14-16. Step Two of the Comparative Analysis of Twin Restaurants—Segment Statements	14,024

Exhibit 14-17.	Vertical Analysis of Twin Restaurants' Income Statements	14,025
Exhibit 14-18.	Vertical Analysis of Twin Restaurants' Segment Statements	14,025
Exhibit 14-19.	Horizontal Analysis of Twin Restaurants' Income Statements	14,027
Exhibit 14-20.	Horizontal Analysis of Twin Restaurants' Segment Statements	14,027
Exhibit 14-21.	Trend Analysis of Twin Restaurants' Income Statements	14,028
Exhibit 14-22.	Trend Analysis of Twin Restaurants' Segment Statements	14,029
Exhibit 14-23.	Calculation of Indexed Sales	14,031
Exhibit 14-24.	Indexing Analysis of Twin Restaurants	14,032
Exhibit 14-25.	Operating Ratio Analysis of Twin Restaurants	14,033

The analysis of operations in the hospitality industry can be approached from five perspectives:

1. Operating ratio analysis
2. Comparative analysis
3. Common size analysis
4. Indexing
5. Fundamental analysis

Operating ratio analysis relates to units of input of a hospitality company (e.g., sales, cost of sales, payroll) to units of output (e.g., covers sold, rooms sold). Comparative analysis is based on the comparison of total dollar amounts of revenues and expenses to each other over a sequence of periods, as well as a comparison of segment expense accounts to their related segment revenue. Common size analysis relates individual revenue sources and expenses to total revenue, base year amounts, or the immediate preceding period's amount. Indexing translates revenues and expenses into constant dollar amounts, thus enabling management to remove the impact of inflation. These types of analyses allow management to identify areas that require attention either because they are poorly managed and require remedial action or because they are managed exceptionally well and could be emulated by other departments, hotels, restaurants, divisions, regions, or segments of the hospitality entity. These types of analysis are best performed in spreadsheet programs.

A study of the numerical relationships involved in operating ratio, comparative, and common size analysis may highlight the need to review the business model from a fundamental, qualitative perspective. The fundamental approach to management's analysis of operations requires that management study the various aspects of the business model itself. This may include an analysis of strategic objectives, a conceptual analysis of sales components and cost elements to determine their degree of alignment with these strategic objectives, and an evaluation of the operational excellence of the business processes themselves.

ANALYZING OPERATIONS USING STANDARD OPERATING RATIOS

For purposes of analysis, ratios have the following advantages compared to the use of absolute numerical amounts. Ratios:

- Facilitate the detection of small changes that might portend larger, more significant changes in the near future and thus allow for taking corrective action sooner.
- Allow for comparison of entities of different sizes by eliminating the bias of size.
- Allow for comparison of entities at different stages of their growth. (The management of two hotels of different sizes can be compared on the basis of percent occupancy to avoid the bias in number of rooms occupied favoring the larger hotel.)

Operating ratios compare units of input to units of output, or they can compare units of input and output to each other. Units of input are those resources that are used to generate revenues and expenses. Units of output are items sold or services performed, measured either financially or on a unit basis. By relating revenues and expenses to units of input and output, or by relating units of input and output to each other (e.g., employees per restaurant, per kitchen, per rooms department, per hotel), certain trends stand out. Occupancy percents are an example of operating ratios that relate units of output (e.g., various categories of occupied rooms) to units of input (i.e., available rooms). Revenue per occupied room is an example of one unit of output being compared to another unit of output.

Units of input include:
- Available rooms
- Tables
- Seats
- Square feet
- Number of employees (various categories)
- Waiters
- Payroll dollars
- Food cost
- Phone line rental cost
- Hotel or restaurant departments
- Entire hotels or restaurants
- Hours worked or hours open

Units of output include:
- Various categories of occupied rooms
- Double-occupied rooms
- Room revenue

- Restaurant revenue
- Covers served
- Checks
- Guests/customers
- Conventions or other types of groups
- Catered events

Units of input and output can be measured by activity or department or for an entire entity, region, division, or organization as a whole.

In the hospitality industry, there are two major cost categories that consume up to 75% of every revenue dollar—cost of food sold (30–40% of sales), cost of beverages sold (20–26% of sales), and payroll (30–40% of sales). Furthermore, there are two types of inventory: (1) expiring and (2) physical. Expiring inventory consists of rooms in a hotel and seats in a restaurant. The revenue from unoccupied rooms or seats cannot be recovered. Inventory management in the hospitality industry involves not only (1) minimizing the cost of food and beverages sold, but also (2) maximizing hotel and restaurant occupancy rates. It is not surprising, therefore, that most of the operations control ratios in the hospitality industry are designed to help management evaluate how well it is achieving these two objectives, as well as achieving effective control of payroll and payroll-related expenses. Because of their predominance in the income statement of a hospitality company, overspending by merely 2% in food, beverage, and payroll costs can lead to a 10% decrease in net income. A 2% excess in these categories, which consume 70% of revenue, represents 1.4% of sales. Assuming a net income of 10% and an income tax rate of 30%, this 1.4% translates into a 10% reduction of net income (70%×1.4% = 1%, which is 10% of an assumed 10% net income).

Commonly Used Hotel Operating Ratios

A hotel's room revenue depends on two sets of factors: (1) those that are under the control of management and owners and (2) those beyond their control. The following factors are controllable by management:

1. Size of the hotel (room count)
2. Class of the hotel (luxury, economy, gaming)
3. Location of the hotel (optimal versus marginal location, central versus peripheral location, or resort location)
4. Occupancy percent (percent of rooms occupied)
5. Number of days hotel is open (seasonal hotels often close during off-season)
6. Adequate or inadequate capital to weather difficult periods
7. Credit granting and collection policies
8. Maintenance of physical plant
9. Timeliness of hotel concept and design
10. Quality of management

11. Training and quality of nonmanagement personnel
12. Marketing and publicity

Factors that are beyond management and ownership control are:
1. Overbuilding and pressure from competitors
2. The state of the economy

Most of these factors determine the rates the hotel can charge. Average room rates tend to increase as occupancy percent increases. In addition, the higher the class of the hotel and the more optimal the hotel's location, the higher the room rates the hotel can charge.

Room revenue consists of the following four components:

$$\text{Average room rate} \times \text{Number of available rooms} \times \text{Occupancy percent} \times \text{Days open} = \text{Annual rooms revenue}$$

The above formula can be summarized and broken down into two relationships as follows:

$$\text{Average room rate} \times \text{Total rooms sold} = \text{Annual rooms revenue}$$

This simplified equation indicates two ways to increase revenues in a hotel: (1) by increasing the room rate or (2) by increasing the occupancy percent (selling more rooms). In this regard, it should be noted that every percentage increase in a room rate is applied entirely to an increase in net income because no additional expenses are incurred when room rates are increased. However, increasing revenue by selling more rooms does involve an increase in variable expenses, and therefore not all the revenue increase will be applied to an increase in net income. Thus, it is better to increase revenue by increasing room rates; yet, this may result in a decrease in occupancy percent. Yield management programs are designed to reconcile these two potentially conflicting revenue drivers to maximize revenues.

Hotel operating ratios are designed to pinpoint the percent of available rooms that are being used for revenue or nonrevenue-generating purposes, as well as to identify costs per room and costs in relation to sales. The major concern of a hotel is to maximize its paid occupancy. This is made especially urgent by the fact that room inventory expires. In other words, the revenue from an unsold room cannot be recovered.

The broadest category is simply "rooms in hotel." This category includes the total number of rooms in a hotel and can be divided into subcategories, as shown in Exhibit 14-1.

The impact of these new definitions in the exhibit above is to increase the occupancy percents for "paid rooms occupied" and "rooms available for sale," consequently decreasing the average rates for these two occupancy categories.

Exhibit 14-1: Rooms in Hotel

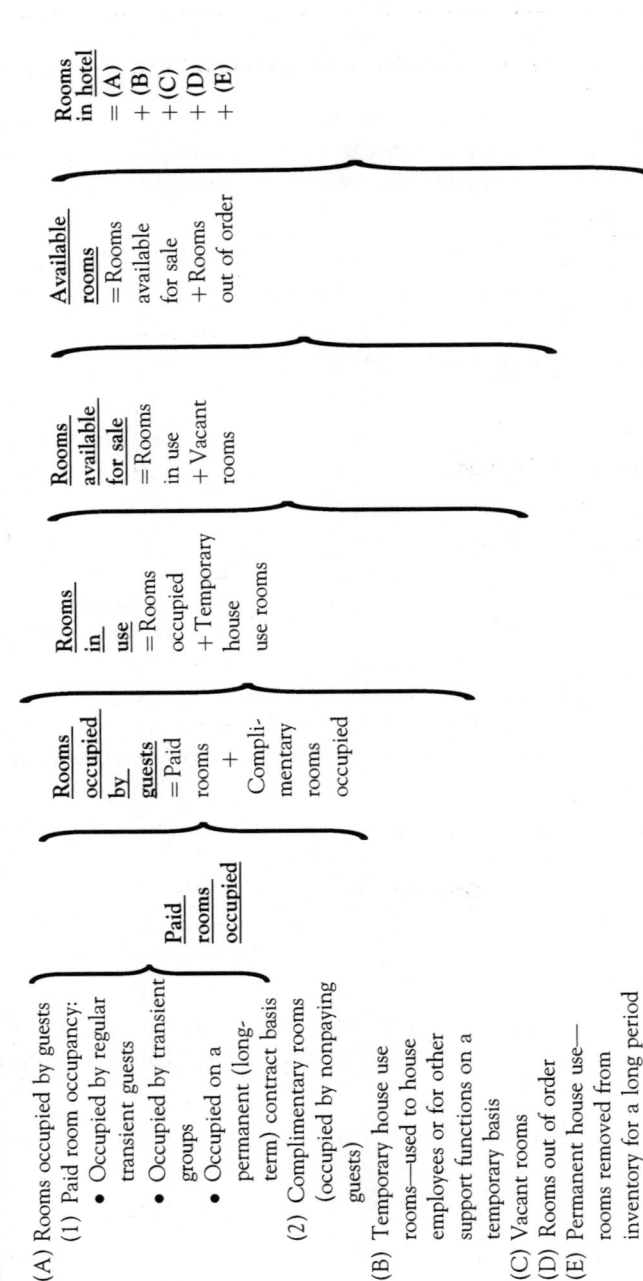

(A) Rooms occupied by guests
  (1) Paid room occupancy:
    • Occupied by regular transient guests
    • Occupied by transient groups
    • Occupied on a permanent (long-term) contract basis
  (2) Complimentary rooms (occupied by nonpaying guests)

(B) Temporary house use rooms—used to house employees or for other support functions on a temporary basis

(C) Vacant rooms

(D) Rooms out of order

(E) Permanent house use—rooms removed from inventory for a long period of time

Paid rooms occupied

Rooms occupied by guests = Paid rooms + Complimentary rooms occupied

Rooms in use = Rooms occupied + Temporary house use rooms

Rooms available for sale = Rooms in use + Vacant rooms

Available rooms = Rooms available for sale + Rooms out of order

Rooms in hotel = (A) + (B) + (C) + (D) + (E)

Note:

1. In the new (10th edition) of the Uniform System of Accounts for the Lodging Industry (USAL), a room is not considered "out of order" unless it has been out of order for at least six months due to events beyond the control of management (e.g., due to floods, hurricanes) or if an entire department in the rooms division has been closed for at least 30 days.

2. In the 10th edition, a complimentary room cannot be a room that is based on a contract with a guest, such as when guests are given additional nights free as a result of a specified length paid occupancy. It must be a room that is provided free purely for marketing purposes.

Chapter 14: *Management Analysis of Operations* **14,007**

An example of the calculation of the various room categories and their corresponding ratios for Leisure Hotel is presented in Exhibit 14-2.

Exhibit 14-2: Room Occupancy Statistics and Operating Ratios for Leisure Hotel

	Rooms Occupancy Statistics	Operating Ratios
Number of Rooms in Hotel	267	100.0%
Less: Permanent House Use	4	1.5%
= Available Rooms	263	98.5%
Number of Paid Rooms Occupied:		
Transient: Regular	86	32.7%
Transient: Group	90	34.2%
Permanent—Long-Term Contracts	10	3.8%
= Total Paid Rooms Occupied	186	70.7%
+ Number of Complimentary Rooms	7	2.7%
= Rooms Occupied by Guests	193	73.4%
+ Temporary House Use Rooms	0	0.0%
= Rooms in Use	193	73.4%
+ Number of Rooms Vacant	62	23.6%
= Rooms Available for Sale	255	97.0%
+ Rooms Out of Order	8	3.0%
= Available Rooms	263	100.0%

Occupancy Percents:	
Rooms in Use %	73.4%
Transient: Regular %	32.7%
Transient: Group %	34.2%
Permanent %	3.8%
Paid Occupancy %	70.7%
Complimentary Rooms %	2.7%
Guest Occupancy %	73.4%
Temporary House Use %	0.0%
Total Occupancy %	73.4%
Rooms Out of Order %	3.0%
Percent of Available Rooms Not Available for Sale	5.7%

Part III: Financial Analysis

Average Daily Rate:

(Revenue per room type/No. rooms per room type)	
Transient: Regular	$135.00
Transient: Group	$ 92.00
Permanent (Contract Guests)	$ 60.00

Number of Guests:

Transient: Regular	203
Transient: Group	115
Permanent	26
Paid Guests	344
Complimentary Guests	13
Paid Guests per Paid Rooms Occupied	1.85

In Exhibit 14-2, the occupancy percents most commonly used in the industry are presented separately. These enable a hotel manager to quickly determine what percent of available rooms are occupied by paying guests, temporarily set aside for the hotel's use, occupied by guests on a nonpaying basis, or out of order. The total of these last three percents indicates the percent of available rooms that are not generating revenue and are not available for sale.

Evaluating Rooms Revenue. The ratios traditionally used to measure the productive use of rooms, directly and indirectly, evaluate (1) the number of rooms in use, (2) the number of rooms occupied by two or more guests, and (3) the average length of a guest's stay. Ratios to measure these parameters are listed in Exhibits 14-3, 14-4, and 14-5.

Exhibit 14-3: Ratios to Measure the Number of Rooms Being Used for Various Purposes

$$\text{Regular transient} = \frac{\text{Rooms occupied by regular guests}}{\text{Available rooms}}$$

$$\text{Group transient} = \frac{\text{Rooms occupied by groups}}{\text{Available rooms}}$$

$$\text{Contract guests} = \frac{\text{Rooms occupied by contract guests}}{\text{Available rooms}}$$

$$\text{Paid occupancy} = \frac{\text{Paid rooms occupied}}{\text{Available rooms}}$$

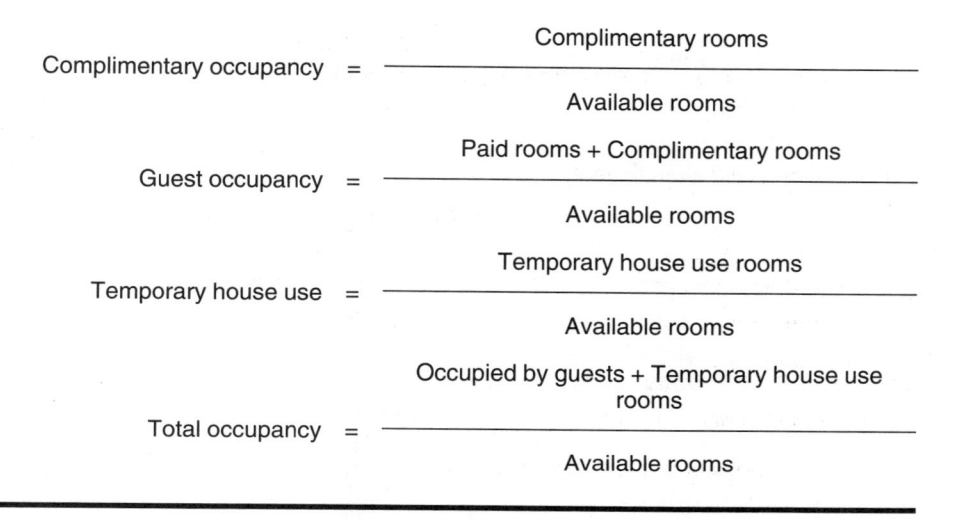

$$\text{Complimentary occupancy} = \frac{\text{Complimentary rooms}}{\text{Available rooms}}$$

$$\text{Guest occupancy} = \frac{\text{Paid rooms} + \text{Complimentary rooms}}{\text{Available rooms}}$$

$$\text{Temporary house use} = \frac{\text{Temporary house use rooms}}{\text{Available rooms}}$$

$$\text{Total occupancy} = \frac{\text{Occupied by guests} + \text{Temporary house use rooms}}{\text{Available rooms}}$$

The key ratios that should be maximized are "paid occupancy" and its three components: (1) regular transient, (2) group transient, and (3) contract guest rooms.

The first two of the four ratios in Exhibit 14-4, guests per occupied room and multiple occupancy percentage, are ratios that can be viewed from two perspectives. If there are 100 rooms and 100 guests, it is better to have one guest per room than to have 50 rooms occupied by two guests each (single-occupancy rates are higher per guest than double-occupancy rates). However, if all rooms are occupied, it is better to have them occupied by more than one paying guest. In this case, double occupancy is better than single occupancy because the average room rate will be higher. It is important to interpret the following ratios accordingly. The third ratio below, average rate per guest, tends to decrease as the number of double-occupied rooms increases. If the single-occupied room rate is $100 and the double-occupied room rate is $140, then two people in separate rooms will generate $200 of revenue, whereas in a double-occupied room they will generate only $140 of revenue. The average rate per guest will be $100 in the first instance versus $70 in the latter instance. Although the average guest rate decreases with double occupancy, revenue per occupied room (REVPOR) will increase as more rooms are double-occupied.

Exhibit 14-4: Ratios to Evaluate the Number of Rooms Occupied by More than One Guest

$$\text{Guests per occupied room} = \frac{\text{Total guests}}{\text{Paid rooms occupied}}$$

$$\text{Multiple occupancy percent*} = \frac{\text{Rooms occupied by two or more guests}}{\text{Paid rooms occupied}} \times 100$$

14,010 Part III: *Financial Analysis*

$$\text{Average guest rate} = \frac{\text{Rooms sales}}{\text{Number of guests}}$$

$$\text{Revenue per occupied room (REVPOR)} = \frac{\text{Rooms sales}}{\text{Paid rooms occupied}}$$

* Also referred to as "Double occupancy percent."

The number of guests per room is important for two reasons. First, if the number of guests per room increases at the same time that occupancy percentages decrease, it may indicate that guests, especially in the business travel category, are sharing rooms to save on hotel expenses. Second, spending on hotel services will likely increase as the number of guests increase. Even if there is no additional charge for a third guest in a room, that guest is likely to increase the hotel's revenue in other ways.

Another important statistic is the average length of time that a guest stays at the hotel. Exhibit 14-5 presents this ratio as follows:

Exhibit 14-5: Ratio to Measure the Average Length of a Guest's Stay

$$\text{Average length of guest's stay} = \frac{\text{Total guests during period}}{\text{Arrivals during the period}}$$

This ratio should be watched carefully because it helps the marketing department refine its approach. If the length of guest stay falls below the norm, then the marketing department may want to include incentives, such as reduced rates for longer stays, in its marketing plan.

Because dollar sales are a factor for both rooms sold and the room rate, it is important for hospitality managers to evaluate room rates in addition to occupancy rates. The ratios in Exhibit 14-6 enable a hotel manager to do this.

Exhibit 14-6: Ratios to Evaluate Room Rates Charged

Average regular transient daily rate

$$= \frac{\text{Regular transient guest revenue less regular allowances}}{\text{Paid rooms occupied by transient regular guests}}$$

Average group transient daily rate

$$= \frac{\text{Group transient guest revenue less group allowances}}{\text{Paid rooms occupied by transient group guests}}$$

Average permanent (long-term contract) daily rate

$$= \frac{\text{Permanent guest revenue less permanent allowances}}{\text{Paid rooms occupied by contract (long-term) guests}}$$

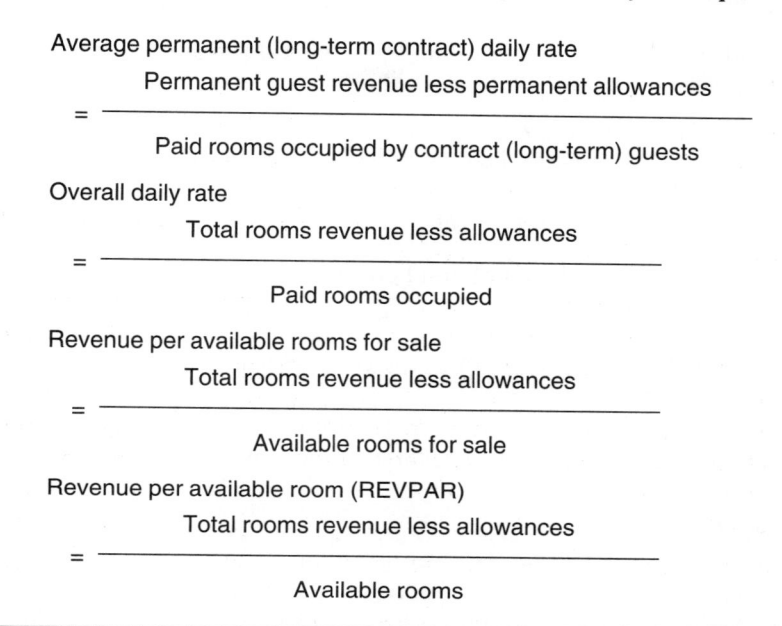

Overall daily rate

$$= \frac{\text{Total rooms revenue less allowances}}{\text{Paid rooms occupied}}$$

Revenue per available rooms for sale

$$= \frac{\text{Total rooms revenue less allowances}}{\text{Available rooms for sale}}$$

Revenue per available room (REVPAR)

$$= \frac{\text{Total rooms revenue less allowances}}{\text{Available rooms}}$$

The "overall daily rate" measures the average rate charged for all occupied rooms, whether they are transient regular, group, or contract rates. The revenue per "available room for sale" dilutes the overall daily rate by including the "complimentary rooms" and the "temporary house use" rooms plus the number of "vacant rooms" in its calculation. The revenue per available room dilutes the overall daily rate by including all of the above nonpaying categories plus "rooms out of order." Thus, the dilutive impact on individual rooms revenue produced by having vacant rooms, complimentary rooms, rooms used by management temporarily, and rooms out of order can be measured progressively by these ratios.

The calculation of revenue per available rooms (REVPAR) excludes only those rooms removed from inventory for a long period of time. REVPAR is the most important ratio for evaluating room management because it penalizes management performance for:

- Complimentary rooms
- Temporary house use rooms
- Unsold rooms
- Rooms out of order

REVPAR is a popular evaluation tool because it encourages managers to keep the above nonpaying room categories to a minimum.

Evaluating Food and Banquet Revenue in a Hotel. As mentioned earlier, even when there is no additional room charge for a third guest per room, it is in the hotel's interests to maximize guest count because this increases the use of other services the hotel may provide, such as the spa or restaurant. The following ratios can be used to measure spending by guests at a hotel's food and beverage

14,012 *Part III: Financial Analysis*

sales points, as well as to determine the dependency each restaurant or bar has on guest spending.

Percent of guests dining in the hotel

$$= \frac{\text{Covers sold in the hotel's restaurants to guests}}{\text{Number of guests in the hotel}}$$

Percent of restaurant patrons that are not hotel guests

$$= \frac{\text{Covers sold in the hotel's restaurants to non-guests}}{\text{Total covers sold in the restaurant}}$$

The latter ratio indicates how dependent each service point is on the hotel guest count. When calculated by meal period (breakfast, lunch, and dinner) this can be determined for each period.

As discussed in Chapter 4, "Using Computers in Hospitality Financial Management," through the use of tablet computers, guests who eat at their hotel can provide valuable information concerning their point of origin, destination, and personal preferences. This information can be stored in a data warehouse, made available to appropriate personnel anywhere within the hotel chain, and be used to guide guests to other hotels within the chain and market to them more effectively at any of these other hotels.

Because of higher markups, the cost of food sold at banquets is usually about 10% lower than that of the restaurants (20%–30% vs. 30%–40%). This ratio is shown below:

$$\text{Banquet sales to total sales} = \frac{\text{Banquet sales}}{\text{Total food sales}}$$

The ratio of banquet food sales to total food sales indicates how much of an influence increasing banquet sales versus restaurant sales may have on the cost of food sold, as reflected in a decrease of the cost-of-food-sold percent.

Evaluating Expenses. Controlling costs is another important factor in the profit equation. The following ratios are used to evaluate room department costs from a broad perspective. Exhibit 14-7 lists the major cost ratios calculated by hotels. The most significant ratios are cost per available room and individual expenses or total cost as a percentage of room sales. Many hotel managers place a great deal of emphasis on cost per available room and make decisions concerning the incurrence of additional costs based on their impact on cost per available room.

Exhibit 14-7: Major Hotel Cost Ratios

$$\text{Individual expenses per room sales} = \frac{\text{Individual expense amounts}}{\text{Room sales}}$$

$$\text{Individual expenses per total sales} = \frac{\text{Individual expense amounts}}{\text{Total sales}}$$

$$\text{Cost per available room} = \frac{\text{Total rooms department cost}}{\text{Total rooms minus permanent house use rooms}}$$

$$\text{Cost per occupied room} = \frac{\text{Total rooms department cost}}{\text{Rooms occupied by guests}}$$

$$\text{Labor cost percentage} = \frac{\text{Payroll and related expenses}}{\text{Total revenue}}$$

$$\text{Revenue per front desk employee} = \frac{\text{Total revenue}}{\text{Total number of front desk employees}}$$

$$\text{Revenue per rooms department employee} = \frac{\text{Total revenue}}{\text{Total number of rooms department employees}}$$

Revenue per front desk employee is calculated because these are among the highest paid nonmanagement employees in a hotel. Payroll expense, by far the largest operating expense in a hotel, constitutes more than 50% of all operating expenses (all expenses excluding fixed charges). Payroll expense constitutes 50% of all the expenses by which the hotel's general manager is evaluated. All revenues and expenses, including the lesser nonpayroll expenses, can be further evaluated and controlled by comparison with:

- The previous month
- The same month in the previous year (to eliminate the impact of seasonality)
- An average of a number of previous months (to determine if a trend exists)
- Budgeted amounts

These figures can also be evaluated and controlled by the use of common size analysis, which will be discussed later in this chapter.

Commonly Used Restaurant Operating Ratios

In addition to the sales ratios, the major expenses in a restaurant are (1) cost of sales and (2) salaries and wages expense. These two expenses consume up to 70% of every revenue dollar in a restaurant. In addition to the traditional calculation of cost of sales, restaurants will calculate the prime cost, which is the cost of food sold plus the payroll cost.

Restaurant Sales. Restaurant sales are the result of several drivers that can be similarly related to hotel sales. The full revenue equation and its compressed version are presented below:

$$\text{Average check} \times \text{Number of available seats} \times \text{Seat turnover} \times \text{Days open} = \text{Annual revenue}$$

$$\text{Average check} \times \text{Total checks} = \text{Annual revenue}$$

In addition, menu price increases directly increase net income, whereas sales increases resulting from selling more seats involve additional expenses and result in a net income increase equivalent to the additional revenue minus all incremental expenses. These incremental expenses are usually the cost of food sold, but may also involve increases in wages if additional kitchen staff and table attendants to service the additional sales are required. Menu engineering and analysis techniques are used to attempt to maximize net income, as opposed to maximizing revenue alone. Menu engineering and analysis is discussed in Chapter 16, "Maximizing Profit and Minimizing Costs in the Hospitality Industry."

Accounting for Food Consumed. Because food is such an important cost, restaurants must maintain control over the cost-of-food-sold expense. Food cost includes light beverages but usually excludes alcoholic drinks. Depending on whether a periodic or perpetual inventory system is used, a restaurant will calculate the ending inventory or the cost of sales first. Under the periodic inventory system, there is no control over issues; therefore, consumption is determined by the cost-of-sales equation based on a physical count at the end of a period. A periodic inventory is used when the value of the inventory is small and fast access is necessary, such as in a kitchen pantry or the daily use of a fast-food restaurant.

Under a perpetual inventory system, there is a storeroom keeper who records purchases and issues (withdrawals of food or beverages). Under this system, the issues are recorded first, along with any inventory shortages, to reconcile with the ending inventory value maintained by the accounting department. Because of this higher degree of control, high-value inventories should be maintained under a perpetual inventory system. The calculations under both systems are presented in Exhibit 14-8.

Exhibit 14-8: Determination of Cost of Food Consumed

Determination of Cost of Food Consumed When a Periodic Inventory Is Used	
Beginning food inventory	$ 10,000
Plus:	
Purchases	100,000
Transportation costs	1,000
Food available for sale	111,000

Determination of Cost of Food Consumed When a Periodic Inventory Is Used

Minus:
Ending inventory (per physical count)		(13,000)
Cost of food consumed		98,000

Determination of Cost of Food Consumed When a Perpetual Inventory Is Used

Beginning food inventory		$ 10,000
Plus:		
Purchases		100,000
Transportation costs		1,000
Food available for sale		111,000
Minus:		
Per issues requisitions	$(97,500)	
Shortage	(500)	
Cost of food consumed		(98,000)
Ending inventory (per accounting records—		
purchases less issues requisitions less shortage)		$ 13,000

The shortage under a perpetual inventory is determined by a gradual count of inventory: comparing the count with the amount on each item's perpetual inventory card. No end-of-period physical inventory is required to determine the cost of food consumed, as is the case with a periodic inventory. This gradual count allows a business to count individual items several times during the period, during store-room or other department employees' idle time, rather than have to pay overtime at the end of the period to count all items at once. The end-of-period count is not only more expensive but disruptive. A perpetual inventory system also reduces theft and errors because someone is responsible for the integrity of the inventory; and, for every item that is removed from inventory, there must be an authorized issues requisition.

Under a perpetual inventory, food cost is determined by totaling the issues requisitions and adding shortages. The shortage is an extremely important number: if it exceeds 2%, then it should be investigated. In quick service restaurants, a .5% shortage is significant. The shortage may be caused by theft or by improper recordkeeping in the storeroom.

Food consumed can be broken down into the following categories.
- Cost of food sold
- Cost of food per manager's checks
- Cost of employee meals
- Cost of food transferred to the bar

Because no bill or check is issued to identify what is consumed in employee meals, the cost of these is estimated based on an approximation differentiating breakfast, lunch, and dinner costs to improve accuracy of the estimates.

Food Operating Ratios. The most commonly used food operating ratios are listed in Exhibit 14-9.

Exhibit 14-9: Most Commonly Used Food Operating Ratios

$$\text{Prime cost per cover} = \frac{\text{Cost of food sold plus kitchen labor}}{\text{Number of covers* sold}}$$

$$\text{Food cost percentage} = \frac{\text{Cost of food sold}}{\text{Food sales}}$$

$$\text{Average food sales per cover} = \frac{\text{Food sales}}{\text{Number of covers sold}}$$

$$\text{Food inventory turnover} = \frac{\text{Cost of food sold}}{\text{Average food inventory over the period}}$$

$$\text{Average number of days food is held in inventory} = \frac{365 \text{ days}}{\text{Food inventory turnover}}$$

$$\text{Number of days food on hand} = \frac{\text{Cost of food sold}}{\text{Ending-inventory food}} \times 365 \text{ days}$$

* **Note**: A cover is a table setting for one person. A top refers to the number of covers that can be set at a table. Thus, a table with four tops can be set with four or less covers.

Prime cost per cover and food cost percent are key ratios in the control of a restaurant's predominant expenses—cost of food sold and labor. The food cost percent and the average food inventory ratio are the most important ratios.

Factors that affect food cost percent include:

- Category of restaurant (lower-priced quick service menus are based on smaller gross profit margins, whereas higher-priced, full service, restaurant menus are likely to have a lower cost of food sold percent)
- Menu mix (proportion between high markup and low markup items)
- Seasonal factors
- Purchasing procedure (bulk purchases and existence of a purchasing department tend to lower costs in large operations)
- Use of economic order quantity (EOQ) calculations
- Cost of storage facilities
- Efficiency of receiving procedures (clerical efficiency and efficiency in the physical movement of food when received)

- Promotional pricing from suppliers
- Price spikes due to natural disasters either locally (resulting in excessively costly transportation) or in the food source locations (resulting in scarcity)
- Waste (excess trimmings or trimmings not used in other menu items)
- Over-portioning
- Spoilage due to inadequate employee training
- Poor physical control over the inventory resulting in theft or excessive spoilage
- Unrecorded inventory transfers to other departments

The food inventory turnover ratio and the "average number of days food held in inventory" ratio help to determine how well a restaurant is minimizing investment in inventory, which is a factor in minimizing investment in working capital. Food inventory turnover indicates how frequently the inventory is sold on average throughout the period. The "average number of days food held in inventory" indicates the number of days, on average, that food has stayed in the storeroom. The "number of days food on hand" indicates the number of days more or less the existing inventory will last. This is an approximate measure because some items might run out, necessitating additional purchases to complete menu items.

Average food inventory can be calculated by adding beginning and ending amounts and dividing by 2, or, for annual averages, by adding monthly amounts and dividing by 12. Monthly food inventory turnover ratios can vary from 1.5 to 3 times, and annual turnover ratios should be within the range of 18 to 36 times. Like all ratios, they can also be calculated on a seasonal basis.

The factors affecting inventory turnover are:

- Spoiled inventory not removed from the account
- Missing inventory still being carried in the account
- Disproportionate amounts of inventory in relation to required menu ingredients
- Wrong type of inventory with regard to local area demand
- Too much of each inventory item
- Frequency and amount of purchases
- Use of EOQ calculations
- Location of restaurant in relation to storage, or in relation to suppliers, may require larger purchases due to inaccessibility
- Inventory storing and processing procedures (portion-pack inventory versus bulk, day's inventory processed in advance)
- Future sales forecasts (projected increases or decreases in sales)
- Disasters

The goal of inventory management is to carry as little inventory as possible without running out, thus minimizing investment in inventory and lowering the carrying costs of inventory: costs of storage, spoilage, and obsolescence (due to changing customer tastes). The more often inventory is sold, the less inventory must be held on hand. Therefore, management should attempt to maximize inventory turnover.

The food sales per cover ratios help to determine how well a restaurant is maximizing food sales. Food sales per cover can be calculated per meal period, as indicated in Exhibit 14-10.

Exhibit 14-10: Food Sales per Cover by Meal Period

$$\text{Average breakfast food sales per cover} = \frac{\text{Breakfast food sales}}{\text{Number of breakfast covers sold}}$$

$$\text{Average lunch food sales per cover} = \frac{\text{Lunch food sales}}{\text{Number of lunch covers sold}}$$

$$\text{Average dinner food sales per cover} = \frac{\text{Dinner food sales}}{\text{Number of dinner covers sold}}$$

This ratio can also be calculated per dining area or per category. Some ratios are based on a breakdown of dining category, as presented in Exhibit 14-11.

Exhibit 14-11: Food Sales per Cover by Hypothetical Dining Area or Category

$$\text{Average food sales per cover: Buffet} = \frac{\text{Food sales}}{\text{Number of covers sold in buffet area}}$$

$$\text{Average food sales per cover: Table service} = \frac{\text{Food sales}}{\text{Number of covers sold in table service area}}$$

$$\text{Average food sales per cover: Groups} = \frac{\text{Food sales}}{\text{Number of covers sold to groups}}$$

Beverage Operations

The major expenses with regard to beverage sales are also cost of sales, and salaries and wages expense. These two expenses consume up to 60% of every revenue dollar in a bar. Because the markup in a bar tends to be higher, the cost of beverages sold tends to be lower in relation to sales. Control of theft in the bar is particularly difficult to achieve. Diluted drinks allow a bartender to divert beverages from paying customers while maintaining the cost-of-beverages-sold ratio within bounds. This is one of the methods that bartenders frequently use to divert beverages for their own benefit. Because of an often hectic pace behind the bar, it is difficult to supervise bartenders effectively.

Accounting for Beverages Consumed. The beverages account usually includes alcoholic beverages as opposed to nonalcoholic drinks, which are considered part of food cost. Accounting for beverages consumed also includes accounting for food sold or given away at the bar. Exhibit 14-12 demonstrates the corresponding calculations under both a periodic and perpetual inventory system.

Exhibit 14-12: Determination of Cost of Beverages Consumed

Determination of Cost of Beverages Consumed in a Periodic Inventory System

Beginning beverage inventory		5,000
Plus:		
Purchases		1,000
Transportation costs		100
Food cost from cost of food consumed		200
Beverages available for sale		6,300
Minus:		
Ending inventory (per physical count)		(4,800)
Cost of beverages consumed		1,500

Determination of Cost of Beverages Consumed When There Is a Perpetual Inventory System

Beginning beverage inventory		5,000
Plus:		
Beverage purchases		1,000
Transportation costs		100
Food purchases		200
Beverages available for sale		6,300
Minus:		
Per beverage issues requisitions	(1,250)	
Per food issues requisitions	(160)	
Shortage	(90)	
Cost of food consumed		(1,500)
Ending inventory (per accounting records—purchases less issues requisitions less shortage)		4,800

As mentioned previously, the shortage under a perpetual inventory is determined by a gradual count of inventory, comparing the count with the amount on each item's perpetual inventory card. No end-of-period physical inventory is required to determine the cost of beverages consumed, as with periodic inventory. This gradual count allows a business to count individual items several times during the period, during store-room or other department employees' idle time, rather than have to pay overtime at the end of the period to count all items at once. The end-of-period count is not only more expensive but disruptive. A perpetual inventory system also reduces theft and errors because someone is responsible for the integrity of the inventory; and, for every item that is removed from inventory, there must be an authorized issues requisition.

Under a perpetual inventory, beverage cost is determined by totaling the issues requisitions and adding shortages.

Beverage Operating Ratios. The most commonly used beverage operating ratios are listed in Exhibit 14-13. The factors that affect food cost percent and food operating ratios apply to the respective beverage cost percent and beverage operating ratios (see above). The one significant difference between food and beverage operating ratios is that the cost of beverages sold tends to be lower in relation to sales because a higher markup is required for beverages to compensate for what is usually a lower beverage turnover. Beverages have a lower turnover because of the required investment in a variety of beverages. In addition, due to the fact that beverages are usually not perishable, volume discounts are often accepted by the hospitality company. Exhibit 14-14 presents a very approximate rule-of-thumb relationship between the food and beverage inventory days.

Food Sales versus Beverage Sales. Because of their higher markup and because they require no kitchen labor, beverage sales tend to generate most of the profit in a combined food and beverage operation. Although they usually generate only about 25% to 35% of sales, the profits these sales generate is usually about two and one half times their sales percentage. A restaurant whose beverage sales are 25% of total sales will obtain approximately 62% of its profits from beverage sales. Thus a change in the sales mix between food and beverages can be a powerful profit stimulator, even though combined sales may remain the same. The cost of food and labor in a restaurant can be as high as 70% of sales, whereas the cost of beverages and beverage labor usually tops out at 40% to 45%.

Standard Ratios. A major cost control tool in both hotels and restaurants, but especially in restaurants, involves controlling costs through the use of standard ratios. (See Chapter 16, "Maximizing Profit and Minimizing Costs in the Hospitality Industry.")

Exhibit 14-13: Most Commonly Used Beverage Operating Ratios

$$\text{Beverage cost percent} = \frac{\text{Cost of beverages sold}}{\text{Beverage sales}}$$

$$\text{Average beverage sales per cover} = \frac{\text{Beverage sales}}{\text{Number of covers sold}}$$

$$\text{Beverage inventory turnover} = \frac{\text{Cost of beverages sold}}{\text{Average beverage inventory over the period}}$$

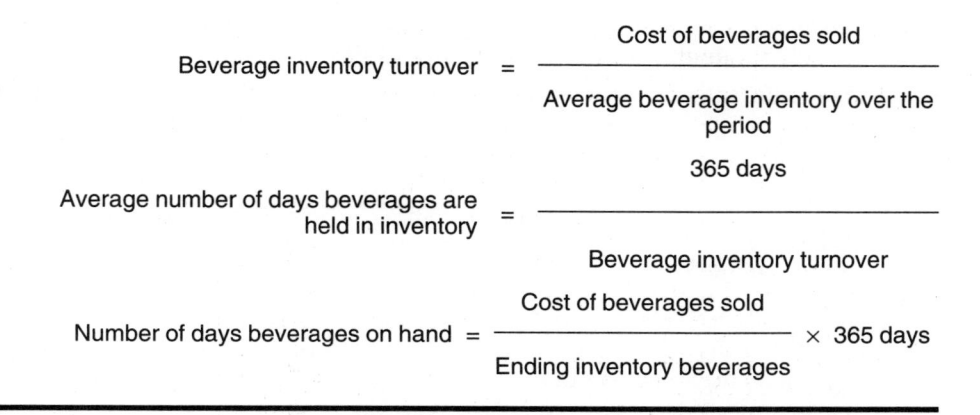

$$\text{Average number of days beverages are held in inventory} = \frac{365 \text{ days}}{\text{Beverage inventory turnover}}$$

$$\text{Number of days beverages on hand} = \frac{\text{Cost of beverages sold}}{\text{Ending inventory beverages}} \times 365 \text{ days}$$

Exhibit 14-14: Rule-of-Thumb Relationship Between Food and Beverage Inventory Days

	Food Only	Beverages Only	Combined Food and Beverages	
			2/3 Food 12 Days	1/3 Beverages 20 Days
Average number of days inventory held =	18 Days	60 Days	32 Days	

Less Commonly Used Operating Ratios

Analyses based on the most commonly used hotel and restaurant operating ratios were presented earlier in this chapter. Because of the innumerable combinations of these other units of input and output, they cannot all be analyzed individually. Thus it is the financial manager's responsibility, based on the hospitality industry segment, to select the appropriate operating ratios for his or her organization from the following list and further refine them based on the perceived information needs.

Other examples of restaurant operating ratios include:

- *Food and/or beverage sales per total square feet*—Restaurant, banquet hall, group lunch space
- *Food and/or beverage sales per square feet*—Seating area, restaurant, banquet hall, group lunch space
- *Food and/or beverage sales per square feet*—Nonseating area, restaurant, banquet hall, group lunch space
- *Food sales*—Per restaurant, per seat, per catering event (banquet hall or other location)
- *Beverage sales*—Per restaurant, per seat, per catering event (banquet hall or other location)

- *Combined food and beverage sales*—Per seat, per restaurant, per catering event (banquet hall or other location)
- Beverage sales as a percent of food sales
- *Average number of employees*—Per kitchen, per back of the house, per front of the house
- *Sales*—Per all employees, per waiter, per kitchen employee
- *Salaries*—Per salary-earning employee, per seat, per restaurant, per catering event
- *Wages*—Per wage-earning employee, per seat, per restaurant, per catering event
- Salaried employee pay in relation to wage-earning employee pay
- Employee benefits in relation to total labor cost

Other examples of hotel operating ratios include:
- Room service sales per occupied room
- *Sales*—Per employee, per front desk employee, per manager, per hotel, per square foot in rooms department, per total square feet
- *Salaries*—Per salary-earning employee, per room, per room category, per department
- *Wages*—Per wage-earning employee, per room, per room category, per department
- Salaried employee pay in relation to wage-earning employee pay
- Employee benefits in relation to total labor cost
- Restaurant ratios can be used to analyze restaurants in hotels
- Rental revenue per square feet of rented area

Ratios that can be extracted from the above list, as well as from the units of input and output listed earlier include:
- Meals per hours open
- Meals per employee hour
- Kitchen labor cost or total labor cost per meal
- Kitchen labor cost or total labor cost per hour
- Revenue per square foot
- Net income or operating income per square foot
- Change in number of employees

Basis for Evaluating Operating Ratios

Operating ratios may be evaluated by comparing them to:
- The same ratio on a daily, weekly, monthly, or quarterly basis
- Industry averages when available
- Averages developed by the organization or chain for different types of restaurants or hotels within the chain
- Budgeted amounts

Variances or differences can be screened according to their amount, thus instituting management by exception. Those variances below a certain threshold can be overlooked, while the remaining variances are analyzed in depth.

Industry averages are available for purchase from sources such as:

- The National Restaurant Association
- Host Report, published by Smith Travel Research
- Consulting firms such as Pannell, Kerr, Forster

Cyclical Comparisons

Because most segments in the hospitality industry are subject to seasonal variations, it is important for a hospitality operation to compare ratios not only on an annual basis, but also on a seasonal basis. Vacation destinations in warm weather areas, such as south Florida, tend to have a high peak winter season and a more moderate peak season in summer, between its shoulder seasons (the seasons next to peak seasons). However, spas are often a destination themselves, and their clientele tend to be composed mostly of retirees, resulting in an even occupancy rate throughout the year. Other hotels, such as downtown business hotels, airport hotels, and highway hotels experience weekly fluctuations.

COMPARATIVE ANALYSIS

Comparative and common size analyses are crucial procedures for analyzing the health of a hospitality company's operations. Any consistent and significant changes in revenues and expenses will show up in these types of analysis over time. Furthermore, a given hospitality company's revenues and expenses can be compared to industry averages using these techniques. Such comparisons help identify discrepancies in performance that may be small at present but warn of future trouble.

The first step in comparative analysis is to align the revenues and expenses in adjacent vertical columns. This facilitates detecting any obvious changes that, due to their large magnitude, do not require a ratio analysis to detect. The purpose of comparative analysis is to note any easily detectable discrepancies in the dollar amounts of the listed data without formally calculating any ratios. Once detected, these large variations or irregularities can serve as the basis for a more thorough investigation through the use of common size and indexing analysis (to be discussed later) and can also be studied using operating ratio analysis. The simplified income statements in Exhibit 14-15, along with the customer count, are analyzed using comparative, common size, operating ratio and indexing analysis techniques. These income statements are for a restaurant company, Twin, which owns two separate restaurants, Twin-1 and Twin-2. A comparative analysis of these income statements reveals that although sales have been increasing from year 1 to year 4, gross profit and net income decreased between years 2 and 3. Further investigation through the use of common size, operating ratio, and indexing analysis reveals the cause.

Exhibit 14-15: Step One of the Comparative Analysis of Twin Restaurants
Simplified Consolidated Income Statements
Twin Restaurants

	Year 1	Year 2	Year 3	Year 4
Sales	$15,000	$16,425	$17,175	$20,000
Cost of sales	4,500	4,950	6,150	7,200
Gross profit	10,500	11,475	11,025	12,800
Salaries and wages	3,000	3,250	3,300	3,475
Other expenses	4,000	4,300	4,400	4,600
Rent	2,000	2,100	2,200	2,300
Net income	$ 1,500	$ 1,825	$ 1,125	$ 2,425
Customers served	2,000	2,500	3,000	3,000

But before proceeding to these analyses, a second step in comparative analysis should be performed. Twin Restaurants consists of two restaurants. For the sake of simplicity, it is assumed that only the cost of sales expense can be identified separately for each restaurant. This comparative analysis step involves relating the restaurants' expenses to their corresponding revenue, as indicated in Exhibit 14-16.

Exhibit 14-16: Step Two of the Comparative Analysis of Twin Restaurants—Segment Statements

Segment Statements
Twin-1

	Year 1	Year 2	Year 3	Year 4
Sales	6,000	6,675	7,500	9,836
Cost of sales	3,000	3,150	3,750	4,582
Gross profit	3,000	3,525	3,750	5,254

Segment Statements
Twin-2

	Year 1	Year 2	Year 3	Year 4
Sales	9,000	9,750	9,675	10,164
Cost of sales	1,500	1,800	2,400	2,618
Gross profit	7,500	7,950	7,275	7,546

A review of these departmental statements indicates that it is the decrease in Twin-2's gross profit that is responsible for the anomalous decrease in the combined net income of Twin Restaurants in year 3 despite growing sales. Its gross profit decreased by $675 from $7,950 to $7,275, while Twin-1's gross profit increased by only $225.

COMMON SIZE ANALYSIS—INCLUDING A SAMPLE ANALYSIS

Similar to ratio analysis, common size analysis enables management to detect small changes in revenues and expenses, changes that might not be detected when reviewing the absolute dollar amounts in the revenue and expense accounts. Early detection of unwarranted decreases in revenue accounts and increases in expense accounts enable management to take preventive remedial action, if required, before a serious problem develops.

There are three types of common size analysis: (1) vertical analysis, (2) horizontal analysis, and (3) trend analysis. A sample set of income statements for the hypothetical Twin Restaurants is used to demonstrate the usefulness of these types of analyses.

Vertical Analysis

Vertical analysis reveals the significance or importance of each individual revenue and expense account with relation to total revenues. The appropriate percentages are calculated by dividing each source of revenue (if there is more than one revenue source) or expense by total revenues, as shown in Exhibits 14-17 and 14-18 for Twin Restaurants and its individual restaurants, Twin-1 and Twin-2.

Exhibit 14-17: Vertical Analysis of Twin Restaurants' Income Statements

Vertical Analysis
Twin Restaurants

	Year 1		Year 2		Year 3		Year 4	
Sales	$15,000	100%	$16,425	100%	$17,175	100%	$20,000	100%
Cost of sales	4,500	30%	4,950	30%	6,150	36%	7,200	36%
Gross profit	10,500	70%	11,475	70%	11,025	64%	12,800	64%
Salaries and wages	3,000	20%	3,250	20%	3,300	19%	3,475	17%
Other expenses	4,000	27%	4,300	26%	4,400	26%	4,600	23%
Rent	2,000	13%	2,100	13%	2,200	13%	2,300	12%
Net income	$1,500	10%	$1,825	11%	$1,125	7%	$2,425	12%

This vertical analysis indicates that in year 3 the combined cost of sales expense jumped upward from 30% to 36%, a 6% increase that accounts for the decrease in net income in year 3 despite the fact that sales were higher in year 3 than in year 2.

Exhibit 14-18: Vertical Analysis of Twin Restaurants' Segment Statements

Vertical Analysis of Segment Sales

	Year 1		Year 2		Year 3		Year 4	
Sales Twin-1	6,000	40%	6,675	41%	7,500	44%	9,836	49%
Sales Twin-2	9,000	60%	9,750	59%	9,675	56%	10,164	51%

Part III: Financial Analysis

Vertical Analysis of Segment Sales

	Year 1	Year 2	Year 3	Year 4
Total sales	15,000 100%	16,425 100%	17,175 100%	20,000 100%

Vertical Analysis of Segment Statements
Twin-1

	Year 1	Year 2	Year 3	Year 4
Sales	6,000 100%	6,675 100%	7,500 100%	9,836 100%
Cost of sales	3,000 50%	3,150 47%	3,750 50%	4,582 47%
Gross profit	3,000 50%	3,525 53%	3,750 50%	5,254 53%

Vertical Analysis of Segment Statements
Twin-2

	Year 1	Year 2	Year 3	Year 4
Sales	9,000 100%	9,750 100%	9,675 100%	10,164 100%
Cost of sales	1,500 17%	1,800 18%	2,400 25%	2,618 26%
Gross profit	7,500 83%	7,950 82%	7,275 75%	7,546 74%

A review of the segment vertical analysis indicates that sales of Twin-1 have been increasing from 40% to 49% of total sales, while sales of Twin-2 have been decreasing from 60% to 51% of total sales. When this data is compared with the segment income statements for Twin-1 and Twin-2, it appears that Twin-1, with the lower gross profit, is the restaurant whose sales have been growing most rapidly.

This raises the question of whether the company is erroneously emphasizing the growth of Twin-1, with apparent mismanagement, or whether the market for Twin-2 style restaurants is decreasing and the company is trying to replace its sales with the sales of Twin-1 restaurant. The fact that the company is gradually increasing the gross profit of Twin-1, perhaps in the hope that it will eventually equal that of Twin-2's gross profit before it began its decline, seems to reinforce the latter assumption.

Other expenses decreased to 23% from 26% in year 4, probably due to a fixed expense component in them. The reduction in labor cost percent from 20% in years 1 and 2 to 17% in year 4 is probably due both to the existence of fixed salaries and perhaps to a more efficient use of personnel allowed by the Twin-1 restaurant's concept.

Horizontal Analysis

Horizontal analysis reveals the amount of increase or decrease in individual revenue and expense accounts as compared to a base period. The period used may be any length of time, such as weekly, monthly, quarterly, or annually. The base period is usually the oldest period, although this does not have to be the case. Any period within the analysis range can be designated to be the base period, as is explained later. A horizontal analysis is performed by dividing each period's individual revenue and expense accounts by its corresponding base period amount. Twin Restaurants' horizontal analysis is presented in Exhibit 14-19.

Exhibit 14-19: Horizontal Analysis of Twin Restaurants' Income Statements

Horizontal Analysis
Twin Restaurants
Base Year

	Year 1	Year 2	Year 3	Year 4
Sales	$15,000 100%	$16,425 110%	$17,175 115%	$20,000 133%
Cost of sales	4,500 100%	4,950 110%	6,150 137%	7,200 160%
Gross profit	10,500 100%	11,475 109%	11,025 105%	12,800 122%
Salaries and wages	3,000 100%	3,250 108%	3,300 110%	3,475 116%
Other expenses	4,000 100%	4,300 108%	4,400 110%	4,600 115%
Rent	2,000 100%	2,100 105%	2,200 110%	2,300 115%
Net income	$ 1,500 100%	$ 1,825 122%	$ 1,125 75%	$ 2,425 162%

This analysis demonstrates that in year 3, the year that net income unexpectedly decreased, cost of sales expense increased 37% from its base year, while sales had only increased by 15%, causing net income to decrease to 75% of the base year amount. The difference in amount of growth between sales and cost of sales became even greater in year 4, going from 22% (137% to 115%) to 27% (160% to 133%). However, the vertical analysis in Exhibit 14-18 indicates that as a percent of sales, the cost of sales remained the same at 36%. All other expenses increased by a lesser amount than sales, thus indicating evidence of a fixed expense component, as well as improved management in the area of salaries and wages. These facts allowed net income in year 4 to become the highest of the four years as sales increased by 18% (133% to 115%) between years 3 and 4.

An examination of the horizontal analysis of the individual segment income statements in Exhibit 14-20 reveals that Twin-2 is having difficulty controlling its cost of sales, which grew 60% from the base year, while its sales grew only 8% from the base year. This explains the source of the increase in Twin Restaurants' combined cost of sales percentage from 30% to 36% identified in the vertical analysis.

Exhibit 14-20: Horizontal Analysis of Twin Restaurants' Segment Statements

Horizontal Analysis of Segment Sales

	Year 1	Year 2	Year 3	Year 4
Sales Twin-1	6,000 100%	6,675 111%	7,500 125%	9,836 164%
Sales Twin-2	9,000 100%	9,750 108%	9,675 108%	10,164 113%
Total sales	15,000 100%	16,425 110%	17,175 115%	20,000 133%

Part III: Financial Analysis

Horizontal Analysis of Segment Statements
Twin-1

	Year 1	Year 2	Year 3	Year 4
Sales	6,000 100%	6,675 111%	7,500 125%	9,836 164%
Cost of sales	3,000 100%	3,150 105%	3,750 125%	4,582 153%
Gross profit	3,000 100%	3,525 118%	3,750 125%	5,254 175%

Horizontal Analysis of Segment Statements
Twin-2

	Year 1	Year 2	Year 3	Year 4
Sales	9,000 100%	9,750 108%	9,675 108%	10,164 113%
Cost of sales	1,500 100%	1,800 120%	2,400 160%	2,618 175%
Gross profit	7,500 100%	7,950 106%	7,275 97%	7,546 101%

The horizontal analysis also reveals that in year 2, Twin-2's cost of sales grew faster (20%) than its sales (8%). Although this disproportion between sales and cost of sales is not easily detected by examining the dollar amounts, it does stand out very clearly in a horizontal analysis. Thus, this analysis indicates the possibility of greater problems occurring in the future, which in this case did materialize, and provides management with sufficient time to take corrective measures before the problems escalate.

Trend Analysis (Percent Change)

Trend analysis indicates the speed with which individual revenue and expense accounts are growing. It is calculated by dividing the change between the most recent two years by the earlier year's amount. This is a standard mathematical percent change calculation.

Exhibit 14-21: Trend Analysis of Twin Restaurants' Income Statements
Trend Analysis
Twin Restaurants

	Year 1	Year 2	Year 3	Year 4
Sales	$15,000	$16,425 10%	$17,175 5%	$20,000 16%
Cost of sales	4,500	4,950 10%	6,150 24%	7,200 17%
Gross profit	10,500	11,475 9%	11,025 −4%	12,800 16%
Salaries and wages	3,000	3,250 8%	3,300 2%	3,475 5%
Other expenses	4,000	4,300 8%	4,400 2%	4,600 5%
Rent	2,000	2,100 5%	2,200 5%	2,300 5%
Net income	$ 1,500	$ 1,825 22%	$ 1,125 −38%	$ 2,425 116%

The trend analysis in Exhibit 14-21 reveals what is already known about the company; that is, in year 3 cost of sales expense grew much faster than sales, creating a 38% decrease in net income. In addition, it is evident that all the other expenses grew at a slower pace than sales, probably due to a fixed-element component in expenses that causes their growth rate to lag behind sales and behind cost of sales, which, as a variable expense, normally grows at the same rate as sales.

Another point that stands out in this analysis is that in year 4, cost of sales continued to grow faster than sales (17% versus 16%), which indicates that the problem of controlling cost of sales may not be resolved. It is also evident that after decreasing their growth rate from 8% to 2% between years 2 and 3, salaries and wages and other expenses increased their growth rate to 5% in year 4, which requires further investigation.

Exhibit 14-22: Trend Analysis of Twin Restaurants' Segment Statements

Trend Analysis of Segment Sales

	Year 1	Year 2		Year 3		Year 4	
Sales Twin-1	6,000	6,675	11%	7,500	12%	9,836	31%
Sales Twin-2	9,000	9,750	8%	9,675	−1%	10,164	5%
Total sales	15,000	16,425	10%	17,175	5%	20,000	16%

Trend Analysis of Segment Income Statements
Twin-1

	Year 1	Year 2		Year 3		Year 4	
Sales	6,000	6,675	11%	7,500	12%	9,836	31%
Cost of sales	3,000	3,150	5%	3,750	19%	4,582	22%
Gross profit	3,000	3,525	18%	3,750	6%	5,254	40%

Trend Analysis of Segment Income Statements
Twin-2

	Year 1	Year 2		Year 3		Year 4	
Sales	9,000	9,750	8%	9,675	−1%	10,164	5%
Cost of sales	1,500	1,800	20%	2,400	33%	2,618	9%
Gross profit	7,500	7,950	6%	7,275	−8%	7,546	4%

A trend analysis of the segment statements, as shown in Exhibit 14-22, indicates that cost of sales expense increased more rapidly than sales even in Twin-1 (19% versus 12%). Furthermore, the year 4 growth rate of cost of sales in

Twin-1 is much higher than in Twin-2 (22% versus 9%). Fortunately, the sales of Twin-1 are also increasing at a much faster pace (31% versus 5%), thus signifying its fastest gross profit growth rate of the four years. However, with a gross profit growth rate of 4% in year 4, Twin-2 does not appear to have recovered the 6% gross profit growth rate that it enjoyed between years 1 and 2.

INDEXING ANALYSIS

Inflation deflates the value of a standard monetary unit. It arises when governments increase the money supply faster than a country's output of goods and services. There are more dollars than goods and services to buy, therefore the monetary price of these goods and services is bid up so that it costs more dollars in any given period to buy exactly the same basket of goods as a lesser amount of dollars would have purchased in an earlier period. There is another alleged cause of inflation, price-push as opposed to the demand-pull inflation described above, but the net result is the same. Generally, governments try to create a certain small amount of inflation in the belief that this stimulates the economy. Yet, when inflation exceeds 1% or 2% per year, it can move the distribution of goods and services away from those who have relatively fixed incomes to those whose incomes will rise with the inflation rate even when this rate is high, reducing the purchasing power of the general population and, consequently, economic growth.

Thus, in the hospitality industry, like-kind room rates, menu prices, and salaries and wages tend to increase from year to year due to this inflationary pressure. When there is 2% annual inflation, for instance, a hotel that has $1,000,000 in room sales in one year might generate sales of $1,020,000 the following year while selling exactly the same number of rooms. The increase in revenue would be due to the increase in room rates produced by the inflationary push. Thus, the sales increase presumably would be totally offset by a similar inflation-generated increase in costs. An increase in dollar sales may not be the result of generating a greater real sales volume—that is, selling additional rooms or covers, but rather the result of selling the same number of rooms at a higher price. Although revenue may be increasing, the revenue-generating activities of a hospitality company may not actually be increasing. As mentioned above, an inflation-induced increase in sales is less beneficial than a price increase in a noninflationary environment because, in an inflationary environment costs also increase. To eliminate the impact of inflation on the sales of a hospitality company, the sales must be indexed to the inflation rate. This implies converting previous years' sales into current dollars in order to determine whether there was real growth in activity, not solely in prices. Of course, costs also should be indexed to evaluate the impact that inflation has on them.

It is possible that a company may be growing its sales by increasing the number of rooms sold without increasing its room rate, at least over a short period of time. If a hospitality company is efficiently run and is aggressively controlling its costs, it may be able to offset increases in the cost of its inputs with increases in efficiency. Or it may be willing to accept a lower overall profit to avoid raising rates or prices in order to gain market share. Or both situations may apply.

Indexing can be performed using the consumer price index (CPI) or the producer price index (PPI). Usually the CPI is used to measure real purchasing capacity, whereas the PPI is used as a revenue deflator to translate the cost of certain products, such as food, into constant dollars. In the hospitality industry, the CPI is used to calculate the growth in sales in terms of constant purchasing-power dollars of consumers. The PPI should be used to eliminate inflationary cost increases in expenses. Indexing is performed by dividing the CPI of a previous year into the current year's CPI and multiplying the previous year's sales by the resulting factor. Exhibit 14-23 demonstrates the calculation of indexed sales based on the data presented in the exhibit.

Exhibit 14-23: Calculation of Indexed Sales

Data:

Year	1	2	3
Sales	$100,000	$102,000	$103,000
CPI	234	238	242

Calculation:

Year				Current dollar sales		Indexed sales
1	Current CPI / Year 1 CPI	$\frac{242}{234}$	×	$100,000	=	$103,419
2	Current CPI / Year 2 CPI	$\frac{242}{238}$	×	$102,000	=	$103,714
3	Current CPI / Year 3 CPI	$\frac{242}{242}$	×	$103,000	=	$103,000

Although apparently, in current year dollars, the sales of this entity grew consistently from year 1 to year 3, if the increase due to inflation is removed from these sales, it is evident that sales grew from year 1 to year 2, but decreased from year 2 to year 3. The assumption above is that the increase or additional revenue-generating activities were not worth $2,000 between years 1 and 2 and were not worth $1,000 between years 2 and 3 but, rather, that only $295 worth of new revenue-generating activities occurred between years 1 and 2 and there was actually a decrease in revenue-generating activities of $714 between years 2 and 3. However, this may not be the case, as the growth in current dollar sales may be due to the sale of more rooms or food, but at the original year 1 prices. Although this is not likely, it may be true, at least over a short time period, for some hospitality companies operating in low-price (economy) market segments. (**Note:** The CPI and PPI are calculated and published monthly by the Bureau of Labor Statistics.)

INDEXING ANALYSIS AND OPERATING RATIO ANALYSIS EXAMPLE

Because of the variety of combinations of all units of input and output, it is not feasible to present an example that includes all possible operating ratios and their interpretation. The following analysis of Twin Restaurants includes only a sample of the types of operating ratios mentioned earlier in this section.

Indexing Analysis of Twin Restaurants

After applying indexing analysis to the Twin Restaurants, as presented in Exhibit 14-24, it is evident that the sales of Twin Restaurants have not been increasing in terms of constant dollars, whereas the cost of sales has been increasing in terms of constant dollars. This explains in part the increase in cost of sales experienced by the company. In terms of constant dollars, in year 3 the company's sales actually decreased from $20,979 to $18,531. Although sales rose to their previous level in year 4, the increase was not enough to compensate for the consistent increase in cost of sales experienced by the company over the four-year period. In other words, it was not transferring the increase in food costs to its customers.

Exhibit 14-24: Indexing Analysis of Twin Restaurants

Indexing Analysis of Sales and Cost-of-Sales
Twin Restaurants

	Year 1	Year 2	Year 3	Year 4
Sales	$15,000	$16,425	$17,175	$20,000
Cost of sales	$ 4,500	$ 4,950	$ 6,150	$ 7,200
CPI	300	321	380	410

Year	Indexing of Sales		Current dollar sales		Indexed sales
1	$\dfrac{\text{Current CPI}}{\text{Year 1 CPI}}$	$\dfrac{410}{300}$ ×	15,000	=	$20,500
2	$\dfrac{\text{Current CPI}}{\text{Year 1 CPI}}$	$\dfrac{410}{321}$ ×	16,425	=	$20,979
3	$\dfrac{\text{Current CPI}}{\text{Year 1 CPI}}$	$\dfrac{410}{380}$ ×	17,175	=	$18,531
4	$\dfrac{\text{Current CPI}}{\text{Year 1 CPI}}$	$\dfrac{410}{410}$ ×	20,000	=	$20,000

Year	Indexing of Cost-of-Sales		Current dollar cost-of-sales		Indexed cost-of-sales
1	$\dfrac{\text{Current CPI}}{\text{Year 1 CPI}}$	$\dfrac{410}{300}$ ×	4,500	=	$6,150
2	$\dfrac{\text{Current CPI}}{\text{Year 1 CPI}}$	$\dfrac{410}{321}$ ×	4,950	=	$6,322

3	Current CPI / Year 1 CPI	410/380	×	6,150	=	$6,636
4	Current CPI / Year 1 CPI	410/410	×	7,200	=	$7,200

Operating Ratio Analysis of Twin Restaurants

Only two operating ratios are calculated in Exhibit 14-25, average cover price and average cover cost, to indicate how such ratios can be used to understand the underlying factors affecting a hospitality company. Average cover relates sales (a revenue source) to covers (a unit of output) by dividing sales by covers and cost of sales by covers.

Exhibit 14-25: Operating Ratio Analysis of Twin Restaurants

Operating Ratio Analysis of Sales and Cost of Sales
Twin Restaurants

	Year 1	Year 2	Year 3	Year 4
Sales	$15,000	$16,425	$17,175	$20,000
Cost of sales	$ 4,500	$ 4,950	$ 6,150	$ 7,200
Customers served	2,000	2,500	3,000	3,000
Average cover price	$ 7.50	$ 6.57	$ 5.73	$ 6.67
Average cover cost	$ 2.25	$ 1.98	$ 2.05	$ 2.40

Change in average cover price from year 1 to year 4 = −11.1%
Change in average cover cost from year 1 to year 4 = 6.7%

This analysis confirms the conclusion reached with regard to Twin Restaurants based on the indexing analysis, namely that it is not passing on to its customers the increase in costs that it is experiencing due to inflation. Operating ratio analysis reveals that the average non-indexed cover price decreased by 11.1% over the four-year period, while the average non-indexed cover cost increased by 6.7% over this same period, enhancing the cost-price squeeze identified through indexing analysis.

The previous ratio analyses have all assumed that neither the menu items nor their recipes were changed. A change in either the menu items or in their preparation costs will change the cost-of-sales percentage in a way that is unrelated to inflation. The use of better, more expensive, ingredients would cause a cost-of-sales percent increase that is not produced by inflation.

Operating ratio analysis can be performed in greater detail by calculating the average cover price and cost for each of the two restaurants, Twin-1 and Twin-2, individually, to determine which restaurant is most responsible for this cost-price squeeze. In addition, an operating ratio analysis of other expenses can be performed.

CHAPTER 15
ANALYSIS OF THE CASH FLOW STATEMENT

CONTENTS

Components of the Cash Flow Statement	**15,002**
Supplementary Cash Flow Information	**15,002**
Supplementary Disclosure of Noncash Investing and Financing Activities	**15,003**
Change in Cash	**15,003**
Analyzing Operating Activities	**15,005**
Adjustments of the Income Statement Due to Noncash or Nonoperating Transactions	**15,006**
Indicator of Working Capital Management Efficiency	**15,006**
Warning Signs in the Operating Activities Section	**15,007**
Analyzing Investing Activities	**15,007**
Indicator of Company Growth	**15,008**
Ability to Finance Growth Internally	**15,008**
Quality of Growth	**15,009**
Analyzing Financing Activities	**15,009**
Financing Investments	**15,010**
Financial Restructurings	**15,010**
Analyzing the Cash Flow Statement as a Whole	**15,015**
Summary of Restructurings Encompassing Entire Statement	**15,015**
The Cash Flow Statement and the Business Life Cycle	**15,017**
Other Cash Flow Ratios	**15,018**
Free Cash Flow	**15,018**
Commonly Used Cash Flow to Debt Ratios	**15,019**
Importance of the Cash Flow Statement	**15,020**
Increasing Importance of the Cash Flow Statement and EBITDA	**15,020**
Cash Flow Ratios Reveal More Than Accrual Ratios	**15,022**
Constant Evaluation of the Uses of Cash and Sources of Financing	**15,024**
Typical Cash Flow Questions	**15,024**
Shortcomings of the Cash Flow Statement	**15,026**
The Best Approach to the Cash Flow Statement and What It Does Not Reveal	**15,026**
Potentially Misleading Operating Cash Flow Reporting	**15,029**
Exhibits	
Exhibit 15-1. Cash Flow Statement of ABC Restaurant	**15,003**
Exhibit 15-2. Operating Activities Section of ABC Restaurant	**15,005**
Exhibit 15-3. Examples of Simple Restructurings in Five Financing Activity Transaction Categories	**15,011**
Exhibit 15-4. Possible Cash Flow Statement Profiles	**15,015**

Exhibit 15-5. Cash Flow Patterns at Different Stages of a Business's Development	**15,018**
Exhibit 15-6. Commonly Used Cash Flow to Debt Ratios	**15,019**
Exhibit 15-7. Cash Flow Ratios Reveal More Than Accrual Ratios	**15,023**
Exhibit 15-8. Example of Two Direct-Method Operating Cash Flow Sections That Are Consistent with a Single Indirect-Method Presentation	**15,027**

The format of the cash flow statement and the alternative presentation option for the operating activities section of the cash flow statement were discussed in Chapter 8, "Financial Statement Reporting: The Cash Flow Statement." This chapter explains how to extract and interpret the information contained in the cash flow statement, the only one of the four statements required by GAAP that reports the nonoperating activities of a hospitality company. In addition to its uniqueness from this perspective, the cash flow statement has acquired greater importance in light of the accounting scandals uncovered in the early twenty-first century because cash flow is less subject to management manipulation and is easier to verify than accrual net income. The analysis of this statement is presented here on a section-by-section basis, from the perspective of the statement as a whole and from the point of view of the life cycle of a hospitality business, product, or service. Ratio analysis of the cash flow statement is also explained.

COMPONENTS OF THE CASH FLOW STATEMENT

The cash flow statement contains three sections: (1) Operating Activities, (2) Investing Activities, and (3) Financing Activities. Together, the data included in both the income statement and the cash flow statement, when added to the account balances of the balance sheet for the beginning of a period, generate an accurate and complete balance sheet for the end of the period.

When the indirect method of preparing the operating activities section of the cash flow statement is used, two other sections must be added to the three sections that constitute the body of the statement: (1) Supplementary Cash Flow Information and (2) Supplementary Disclosure of Noncash Investing and Financing Activities. When the direct method is used, the first of the supplementary sections is omitted because the information is contained in the operating activities section in the body of the statement.

Supplementary Cash Flow Information

In addition to the cash basis transactions reported in the body of the indirect method cash flow statement, FASB Statement No. 95 (FAS-95), *Statement of Cash Flows* (ASC 230, *Statement of Cash Flows*), requires that (1) cash amounts be paid for interest, net of any capitalized interest, and (2) income taxes be presented separately below the cash flow statement. Capitalized interest paid is included in the investing activities section of the cash flow statement as construction in progress.

Chapter 15: Analysis of the Cash Flow Statement

Supplementary Disclosure of Noncash Investing and Financing Activities

Finally, any noncash investing and financing activities must be listed, and their dollar amounts must be shown below the cash flow statement as well. When the indirect method is used, these noncash transactions are listed after interest and income taxes paid.

CHANGE IN CASH

The first step in analyzing the cash flow statement is to determine the change in cash from one period to the next. This is shown in the last three lines of the body of the statement. The cash flow statement of ABC Restaurant, which will be used in this analysis, is presented in Exhibit 15-1.

Exhibit 15-1: Cash Flow Statement of ABC Restaurant

(Indirect Method)
Statement of Cash Flows
ABC Restaurant
for (period) ended xx/xx/xxxx

Cash flows (used in) provided by operating activities		
Net income		$34,612
Reconciliation of net income to cash provided by operations:		
Depreciation and amortization	$12,000	
Provision for doubtful accounts	700	
Deferred income taxes	5,000	
Gain on sale of property and equipment or investments	(2,000)	
Change in operating assets and liabilities:		
Decrease (increase) in accounts receivable	12,000	
Decrease (increase) in other receivables	(1,200)	
Decrease (increase) in inventory	(9,000)	
Decrease (increase) in prepaid expenses	1,000	
Increase (decrease) in current payables	(5,000)	
Increase (decrease) in accrued expenses	4,000	
Increase (decrease) in interest payable	1,500	
Increase (decrease) in taxes payable	16,000	35,000
Cash (used in) provided by operating activities		69,612
Cash flows (used in) provided by investing activities		

15,004 Part III: Financial Analysis

Purchase of hotels	(60,000)	
Payments for leasehold improvements	(13,000)	
Initial payment on equipment purchase	(19,000)	
Net cash (used in) provided by investing activities		(92,000)
Cash flows (used in) provided by financing activities		
Net borrowings on line-of-credit	4,000	
Loan from First Bank	30,000	
Repayment of loan	(3,000)	
Sale of common stock	3,000	
Purchase of treasury stock	(18,000)	
Dividends paid	(4,000)	
Net cash (used in) provided by financing activities		12,000
Increase (decrease) in cash and cash equivalents		(10,388)
Cash and cash equivalents at beginning of period		12,000
Cash and cash equivalents at end of period		1,612

(for indirect method only):

Supplemental disclosures of cash flow information

Cash paid during the year for:

Interest (net of amount capitalized)	1,900
Income taxes	1,500

(for both direct and indirect methods):

Supplemental schedule of non-cash investing and financing activities:

The company issued 10,000 additional shares of common stock to extinguish $100,000 of long-term debt.

The company purchased equipment in exchange for a $40,000 note payable in three years.

The last three lines of the body of this statement reveal that the company had $12,000 at the beginning of the period, used $10,388 during the period, and had $1,612 at the end of the period. The fact that it ended the period with less cash than it started with may not necessarily be negative, because it is not possible to arrive at any valid conclusion concerning this reduction in cash until the individual components of this statement have been analyzed and the questions raised by this cash flow statement have been answered. Generally, it is better to have as little cash as possible in the bank because investing cash in a bank account is not very profitable.

ANALYZING OPERATING ACTIVITIES

The operating activities section of the cash flow statement is the only section that FAS-95 (ASC 230) allows to be prepared in two different ways: by the direct method and by the indirect method. This analysis is based on the indirect method because it is the most commonly used method. However, in another section of this chapter a comparison with the direct method will be presented. The discussion of the analysis of the operating activities section will use the data presented in Exhibit 15-2.

Exhibit 15-2: Operating Activities Section of ABC Restaurant

(Indirect Method)
Statement of Cash Flows
ABC Restaurant
for (period) ended xx/xx/xxxx

Cash flows (used in) provided by operating activities		
Net income		$34,612
Reconciliation of net income to cash provided by operations:		
Depreciation and amortization	$12,000	
Provision for doubtful accounts	700	
Deferred income taxes	5,000	
Gain on sale of property and equipment or investments	(2,000)	
Changes in operating assets and liabilities:		
Decrease (increase) in accounts receivable	12,000	
Decrease (increase) in other receivables	(1,200)	
Decrease (increase) in inventory	(9,000)	
Decrease (increase) in prepaid expenses	1,000	
Increase (decrease) in current payables	(5,000)	
Increase (decrease) in accrued expenses	4,000	
Increase (decrease) in interest payable	1,500	
Increase (decrease) in taxes payable	16,000	35,000
Cash (used in) provided by operating activities		$69,612

Adjustments of the Income Statement Due to Noncash or Nonoperating Transactions

The first step in analyzing the operating activities section is to determine that depreciation expense is reasonable in relation to the property and equipment accounts on the balance sheet. Under-reporting depreciation is a way of artificially augmenting net income. Because the hospitality industry is so capital-intensive, the depreciation expense should be approximately equal to net income, except for those companies that manage but do not own hotels, and those companies that use operating leases to obtain the use of their facilities.

The hospitality financial manager should determine whether there are any large nonoperating category gains deducted from net income, such as the sale of a segment of a restaurant chain or the sale of a large hotel. Such events tend to be nonrepeating and consequently lower the quality of the reported earnings of the hospitality company. In addition, they may indicate the downsizing of the company. Large losses on sales of property and equipment are also suspect because they may indicate that the asset was either purchased for too high a price (future market erosion was not detected or utopian earnings projections were made) or mismanaged, resulting in a drop in its market value.

Indicator of Working Capital Management Efficiency

The subsection titled "changes in operating assets and liabilities" excludes non-operations-related accounts such as short-term notes payable and the current portion of long-term debt. These are analyzed in the investing activities section of the cash flow statement.

The remaining accounts are usually accounts directly related to operations, such as those listed in Exhibit 15-2, whose creation involves increases or decreases to an income statement account. The changes in these accounts indicate whether investment in working capital is being minimized. When the accounts generate cash, this indicates that investment in working capital is decreasing, which is a favorable development.

Decrease (increase) in accounts receivable	12,000	
Decrease (increase) in other receivables	(1,200)	
Decrease (increase) in inventory	(9,000)	
Decrease (increase) in prepaid expenses	1,000	$19,300
Increase (decrease) in current payables	(5,000)	
Increase (decrease) in accrued expenses	4,000	
Increase (decrease) in interest payable	1,500	
Increase (decrease) in taxes payable	16,000	

The changes in these accounts total a positive $19,300, indicating that there was a net reduction in working capital and a consequent release of $19,300 into the cash flow stream of ABC Restaurant. This cash is available to be used in one of the following four productive ways:

1. To purchase revenue-generating assets (increases revenue), or cost-reducing assets (decrease expenses)

2. To repay interest-bearing debt (reduces expenses)
3. To purchase treasury stock (increases earnings per share)
4. To purchase dividends (increases market valuation of shares)

An outflow of cash from these accounts indicates the hospitality company is redirecting its funds to customers and suppliers instead of placing them in potentially lucrative investments. Increases in accounts payable and decreases in accounts receivable decrease investment in working capital by reducing the amount of money held by customers and increasing the amount of suppliers' funds held by the hospitality company. Thus, this section of the cash flow statement serves as a control panel to monitor the efficient management of each individual working capital account.

Warning Signs in the Operating Activities Section

The major accounts in this section of the cash flow statement are accounts receivable and accounts payable. Because they are intimately related to sales and expenses, it is important to take into account any large increases when evaluating net income. A large increase in net income that is accompanied by an equally large increase in accounts receivable is highly suspect for obvious reasons. Although it was previously stated that management should try to maximize accounts payable in order to work with suppliers' funds, an unusually large increase in accounts payable is also suspect, as it may indicate an inability to pay for needed services or supplies, especially if it is accompanied by an unusually large increase in expenses or a severe decrease in ending cash. However, hospitality managers should determine whether the cash decrease was caused by useful investing or financing activities before labeling the decrease as detrimental. Even when not accompanied by an unusually large increase in expenses, working with negative working capital or having current liabilities that are larger than current assets involves greater risk and demands a more agile management style, such as maintaining customer satisfaction while simultaneously meeting debt obligations.

Generally, any increase in operating cash generated by net income and less working capital should not remain in a bank account; it should be used in one of the four productive ways indicated earlier. The first involves using cash for investments.

ANALYZING INVESTING ACTIVITIES

The investing activities section of the cash flow statement is used to record two types of nonoperating transactions: (1) the purchase of noncurrent assets and (2) the sale of noncurrent assets. This section, in conjunction with any noncash investing transactions listed in the supplementary disclosures of the noncash investing and financing activities section, indicates whether a company is growing or contracting, and whether it is growing by investing in assets that add significant value to the company. The accounts in the investing activities section of ABC Restaurant's cash flow statement are:

Cash flows (used in) provided by investing activities	
Purchase of hotels	(60,000)
Payments for leasehold improvements	(13,000)
Initial payment on equipment purchase	(19,000)
Net cash (used in) provided by investing activities	(92,000)

Indicator of Company Growth

The investing activities section of the cash flow statement indicates that the company is growing because its (1) investing activities are using cash, not providing cash, and (2) the cash used is greater than 1.5 to 2 times the amount of depreciation, which in Example 15-2 is $12,000. New investment should be greater than depreciation to compensate for inflationary increases involved in the recent purchases of assets, as opposed to purchases many years ago.

If a hospitality company is selling more assets than it is acquiring, the net cash (used in) provided by investing activities will be positive. Although it would seem that a positive cash flow is generally desirable, in this section of the cash flow statement it is unfavorable because it may indicate that the hospitality company is contracting or that management cannot devise or perceive any worthwhile investments. However, this would not be the case if the company were selling bonds, shares of other companies, or making other investments that do not generate revenue in the main course of business. These types of investments do not generate high rates of return, and the fact that a hospitality company has a positive net cash flow in the investing activities section of its cash flow statement because it is eliminating this type of investment can be considered a favorable reduction in the assets (size) of the company.

Ability to Finance Growth Internally

The investing activities section also helps to determine whether the company can finance its growth internally. The two internal sources of cash are (1) cash provided by operating activities and (2) cash and cash equivalents on hand at the beginning of the period. When the total of these two sources is greater than the amount spent investing in new assets, then the company has the ability to finance its growth internally. When making this comparison, any noncash investments revealed in the supplementary disclosure of the noncash investing and financing activities section should be added to the net cash used in investing activities. In this example, ABC Restaurant purchased $40,000 of equipment in exchange for long-term notes payable. Therefore, it invested $92,000 plus $40,000 in its growth, totaling $132,000. Its operating activities provided $69,612 and the restaurant had $12,000 of cash and cash equivalents at the beginning of the period, totaling $81,612. Thus, the company lacked $50,388 in order to finance its growth internally and had to borrow to be able to finance its investments in noncurrent assets. Of this amount, $40,000 was financed by a purchase loan that does not appear in the body of the cash flow statement, thus leaving the company short $10,388. This $10,388 amount was financed by reducing its beginning cash balance from $12,000 to $1,612.

Another way to measure a hospitality company's ability to finance its growth with internal funds is to relate the cash flow from operating activities to the cash flow used in investing activities, as in the following equation:

$$\text{Cash flow from operations to cash flow used in investing} = \frac{\text{Operating cash flow}}{\text{Cash used in investing activities}}$$

This ratio indicates the percent of cash used for investing activities that is generated internally by the hospitality company on a continuing basis. Another ratio that can be used to measure the ability to replenish its assets internally results from relating operating cash flow to the total pre-depreciated cost of noncurrent assets.

$$\text{Operating cash flow to noncurrent assets} = \frac{\text{Operating cash flow}}{\text{Noncurrent assets} + \text{accumulated depreciation}}$$

Although it appears to be favorable for a company to finance its growth internally, as such funds are interest-free and do not require the issue of income-diluting new shares, the reliability of cash from operating activities depends on the quality of the funds, as explained above and discussed later in this chapter. It is, therefore, necessary to remove any nonrecurring or suspect sources of cash to arrive at a truly reliable operating cash flow that can be used to finance sustainable growth.

Quality of Growth

The investing activities section of the cash flow statement also should reveal the type of assets in which a company is investing. This is a determining factor in the quality and sustainability of its growth. Investing in revenue-generating assets represents the highest quality of growth and portends future growth in operating cash flows. Investing in cost-reducing assets is a close second, but lacks the expansive aspect. Sometimes a hospitality company may be required to invest in improvements necessary to comply with government regulations or laws. This type of investment does not add value to the company because it is non-revenue-generating. A company may also invest in stocks or bonds of other companies on a long-term basis; however, this too is not a high-quality investment. Although it does generate some revenue for the hospitality company in the form of interest or dividends, unless there is an ulterior strategic motive for investing in other companies—a motive that will ultimately increase the company's own revenue-generating capacity—such investments are indicative of a lack of perceived investment opportunities within the hospitality company's own industry segment.

ANALYZING FINANCING ACTIVITIES

The financing activities section is used to record five types of nonoperating transactions:

Part III: Financial Analysis

1. Borrowings
2. Repayments of borrowings
3. Sale of stock
4. Purchase of a company's own stock (treasury stock)
5. Payment of dividends

The discussion in this section is based on the following data of ABC Restaurant:

Cash flows (used in) provided by financing activities		
Net borrowings on line of credit	$ 4,000	
Loan from First Bank	30,000	
Repayment of loan	(3,000)	
Sale of common stock	3,000	
Purchase of treasury stock	(18,000)	
Dividends paid	(4,000)	
Net cash (used in) provided by financing activities		$12,000

Financing Investments

The financing activities section of the cash flow statement reveals (1) the sources of funds a hospitality company is using to finance its growth in those instances when it cannot finance its growth internally and (2) the types of financial restructuring a company is executing. Any activity in this section that remains after removing the source of cash used to finance the difference between operating cash flow and investments is a financial restructuring not required to fund the growth of the hospitality company.

Financial Restructurings

ABC Restaurant determined that it could not finance $50,388 of its growth internally. After deducting the $40,000 worth of bonds not included in the body of the cash flow statement, the company was unable to finance $10,388 of its growth internally. The only remaining source for this amount is the $30,000 loan listed in its financing activities. After removing this transaction from the financing activities section, this section of the statement would appear as follows:

Cash flows (used in) provided by financing activities		
Net borrowings on line of credit	$ 4,000	
Proceeds from the $30,000 loan from first bank after deducting the $10,388	19,612	
Repayment of loan	(3,000)	
Sale of common stock	3,000	
Purchase of treasury stock	(18,000)	
Dividends paid	(4,000)	
Net cash (used in) provided by financing activities		$(2,388)

The $1,612 amount is ABC's remaining cash in the bank. It is questionable as to why ABC engaged in so many financial transactions merely to end up with $1,612 in the bank. Moreover, it could have simply borrowed a modest sum, such as $5,612 (to pay the $4,000 dividend and have $1,612 left in the bank), without engaging in other financing-related activities. One reason is that, after engaging in so many transactions, it is impossible to predict the amount of cash left at the end of a period. In the case of ABC, however, there appears to be a pattern to the remaining financial transactions. If all equity transactions are combined with each other, as well as all remaining debt transactions, it appears that the company is restructuring its finances by going out of equity (buying back a net amount of $15,000 of its own stock), and going into debt (by borrowing $20,612—net of the $10,388 used to finance the purchase of property and equipment).

Simple Financial Restructurings. Financial restructurings may be simple or complex. Simple financial restructurings involve a transaction in a single activity. Exhibit 15-3 presents examples of how a financing activities section would appear when simple restructurings occur in each of the five categories of transactions normally recorded in the financing activities section of the cash flow statement.

Exhibit 15-3: Examples of Simple Restructurings in Five Financing Activity Transaction Categories

Cash flows (used in) provided by financing activities		
Borrowings	$ 10,000	
Net cash (used in) provided by financing activities		10,000
Cash flows (used in) provided by financing activities		
Repayment of borrowings	(10,000)	
Net cash (used in) provided by financing activities		(10,000)
Cash flows (used in) provided by financing activities		
Sale of stock	10,000	
Net cash (used in) provided by financing activities		10,000
Cash flows (used in) provided by financing activities		
Purchase of treasury stock	(10,000)	
Net cash (used in) provided by financing activities		(10,000)
Cash flows (used in) provided by financing activities		
Dividends paid	(10,000)	

Net cash (used in) provided by financing activities	$ (10,000)

Complex Restructurings. Simple financial restructurings rarely occur; however, visualizing them helps to understand complex restructurings. To analyze complex restructurings, it is best to combine all financing activities into their five categories and then analyze the composition of each individual category. This provides a framework for analyzing the individual components of this section. The reduced financing activities section of ABC Restaurant would appear as follows:

Cash flows (used in) provided by financing activities	
Borrowings	$ 19,612
Repayment of loan	(3,000)
Sale of common stock	3,000
Purchase of treasury stock	(18,000)
Dividends paid	(4,000)
Net cash (used in) provided by financing activities	$(2,388)

Note that in the above example, net borrowings on the line of credit and proceeds from the sale of bonds were combined because they both fall into the "borrowings" category.

Debt to Debt. A company moves from debt to debt when it obtains and repays loans during the same period. In this case, the company is repaying $3,000 and borrowing $19,612, of which the $3,000 of that amount was used to make the repayment. Therefore, the new net borrowing amount is $16,612.

By identifying debt to debt restructurings, the financial manager can determine the cause, which may be due to:

1. A short-term cash requirement (cash borrowed and repaid within the same accounting period)
2. A desire to refinance a loan at a lower interest rate or otherwise better terms
3. An inability to repay a loan that has matured

The first two reasons for a debt to debt transaction do not necessarily have negative connotations. However, the last reason indicates a possible liquidity or solvency problem.

By looking at the individual transactions in the borrowing and repayment transaction categories, the nature of each transaction can be determined. Because the amount of debt to debt transactions is small and involves a line of credit, it is probably due to a short-term cash need.

Debt to Equity or Equity to Debt. Two other types of major restructurings that can occur are debt to equity and equity to debt. To analyze these, it is best to net sales of stock against purchases of stock, and borrowings against repayment of loans. After these reductions, ABC Restaurant's cash flow statement would appear as follows:

Cash flows (used in) provided by financing activities

Net increase in borrowings	$ 16,612
Net purchases of stock	(15,000)
Dividends paid	(4,000)
Net cash (used in) provided by financing activities	$(2,388)

It is evident that this company is moving from equity to debt in the amount of $15,000. It is increasing debt by a net amount of $1,612 and paying dividends amounting to $4,000. Two reasons for this might be:

1. There is a recession, and the market value of the company's stock has decreased plus the recession has resulted in lower interest rates, making borrowing attractive.

2. The company is engaged in some merger, acquisition, or divestiture transaction that requires it to restructure its finances in this manner.

If further investigation reveals that one of the above is occurring, then this restructuring is probably beneficial. But if neither of these is occurring, then it may reveal mismanagement of company finances due to lack of foresight or inability to evaluate future prospects. For example, if the economy were at its peak, then interest rates and the market value of stocks would likely be at a high point. It would be a mistake to borrow and repurchase treasury stock under such conditions. In fact, under these conditions hospitality companies should give serious consideration to selling stock and using the cash to repay loans.

Treasury Stock. In the prior analysis it was recommended that treasury stock purchases be netted against sales of stock, which was germane for that analytical procedure. However, independent of the above analysis, the purchase of treasury stock requires a valid reason such as the following:

1. To have stock on hand to sell to holders of stock options without diluting earnings per share (EPS);

2. The determination that it is the best investment the company can make at the time;

3. To fend off a hostile takeover by giving another company majority control.

However, none of these reasons can ever be assumed to be beneficial without an in-depth investigation.

Although options may exist as a result of mergers, divestitures, or other major financial events, they are usually issued to compensate or motivate management. In this case, the purchase and sale of treasury stock to holders of options raises the question of whether the company is excessively using stock options as compensation.

If the company is buying treasury stock to increase EPS, this raises the following questions:

- Has the company reached market saturation to the extent that it cannot do a better job of increasing EPS by investing in revenue-generating assets?
- Can management detect or devise any cost-reducing investments?
- Is the cost of equity capital greater than the cost of debt?
- Is the company taking advantage of a temporary drop in the market value of its stock?

Finally, if the company is trying to ward off a hostile takeover by buying its own shares to give another company majority control, the question arises as to why the company is in this position. The hostile company may be interested in the company because:

- It is well managed and the hostile company wants to add it to its portfolio of successful companies.
- It is poorly managed from an operating standpoint, and the hostile company believes it can do a better job of increasing earnings.
- It is suffering from poor financial management and has excessive amounts of cash or unleveraged assets that the hostile company desires to put to profitable use.

Dividends. Although the dividends category in the cash flow statement only includes dividends that were actually paid in cash, ultimately all dividends are paid. Shareholders are compensated for investing in corporations by receiving dividends and by the increase in market value of their shares, an increase they can realize by selling their shares. Therefore, some hospitality companies that have a history of paying dividends, and whose shares are owned by safety-conscious, income-seeking investors, are under pressure to pay their dividends consistently.

However, if a hospitality company is unable to pay its dividends from earnings, the financing activities section of the cash flow statement will indicate that it is borrowing or selling stock to raise the cash it needs for dividend payments. For example, ABC Restaurant borrowed $1,612 to help pay its $4,000 in dividends with excess cash remaining at the end of the period.

Having to borrow or sell stock in any given year to maintain a dividend payment is not necessarily an indicator of a poor financial condition. A company may be temporarily illiquid because it is using its operating cash to take advantage of good investment opportunities. This seems to be the case for ABC Restaurant because it is generating a significant amount of cash from its operations, the cash flow is good quality, and it is using its cash to make investments in revenue-generating assets. However, it is unhealthy for a company to borrow or sell stock over a period of years in order to maintain its dividend payment because it is not generating enough cash from operations.

ANALYZING THE CASH FLOW STATEMENT AS A WHOLE

After examining the cash flow statement in detail, it is also important to view it as a whole, which can reveal additional information about the financial health of a company. The following charts and discussions present this perspective on the cash flow statement as a whole.

Summary of Restructurings Encompassing Entire Statement

The chart presented in Exhibit 15-4 summarizes the possible profiles of the three sections of the cash flow statement, excluding noncash transactions that are listed in the supplementary schedule after the body of the cash flow statement. Noncash transactions can be added separately to the appropriate sections, such as the investing activities and financing activities sections in the case of property and equipment purchased on credit or by issuing stock.

Exhibit 15-4: Possible Cash Flow Statement Profiles

	Operating Activities	Investing Activities	Financing Activities	Interpretation	Analysis—Potential Problems
1	Positive	Positive	Positive	Company is accumulating cash.	Company is very liquid and may be losing its revenue-generating capacity because it may be selling its productive assets.
2	Positive	Positive	(Negative)	Company is obtaining cash from operations and the sale of property and equipment and using it to repay debt or buy treasury stock.	Company is very liquid and may be losing its revenue-generating capacity because it may be selling its productive assets. It may also have problems with creditors if they are requiring immediate repayment of loans.
3	Positive	(Negative)	(Negative)	Company is obtaining cash from operations and using it to: (1) buy property and equipment, (2) repay debt, (3) or buy treasury stock.	Company is obtaining cash from its operating activities and is using it to: (1) increase revenues, (2) reduce interest expense, or (3) increase earnings per share by decreasing outstanding common stock.

Part III: Financial Analysis

	Operating Activities	Investing Activities	Financing Activities	Interpretation	Analysis—Potential Problems
4	Positive	(Negative)	Positive	Company is using cash from operations, from borrowings, or sale of stock to invest in assets.	Company is growing if it is buying more than 1-1/2 to 2 times the productive assets it is depreciating. It is financing this growth with operating cash flow and financing activities. This is a potentially favorable situation.
5	(Negative)	Positive	(Negative)	Company needs to sell property and equipment to: (1) cover its operating cash outflow, (2) pay its debts, (3) buy treasury stock, or (4) pay dividends.	Its liquidity seems to be threatened and it may be losing its revenue-generating capacity if it is selling productive assets to raise cash to pay off loans.
6	(Negative)	Positive	Positive	Company is losing cash in its operations and is making up for it by: (1) selling assets, (2) borrowing, or (3) selling stock.	Its liquidity seems to be threatened, and it may be losing its revenue-generating capacity if it is selling productive assets and borrowing or selling stock to raise cash and increase liquidity.
7	(Negative)	(Negative)	Positive	Company is losing cash through its operations and purchasing property and equipment and is financing these outflows by selling stock.	Its liquidity seems to be threatened but it is growing if it is buying more than 1-1/2 to 2 times the productive assets it is depreciating.

	Operating Activities	Investing Activities	Financing Activities	Interpretation	Analysis—Potential Problems
8	(Negative)	(Negative)	(Negative)	Company is drawing on cash that it had in the bank to: (1) finance operations, (2) buy property and equipment, (3) repay debts, (4) buy treasury stock, or (5) pay dividends.	It is growing if it is buying more than 1-1/2 to 2 times the productive assets that it is depreciating. But its liquidity is threatened. It is losing cash in all three types of activity. The only possible source of cash it may have is the cash it had in its bank account. The question is: Will this cash last long enough to allow the assets it is purchasing to start generating positive cash flow?

* Usually a company needs to buy 1-1/2 to 2 times as much property and equipment as it is depreciating to be considered a growing company. Depreciation expense is based on old assets purchased and recorded in dollars that were worth more than current dollars. It costs more in current dollars to replace these assets.

THE CASH FLOW STATEMENT AND THE BUSINESS LIFE CYCLE

Another perspective on the cash flow statement is based on a company's stage of development. Companies tend to present typical patterns at each stage of development. The diagram in Exhibit 15-5 is a simplified version of these patterns. The exhibit highlights the cash flows of the different sections of this statement over the life cycle of a company. Initially, a hospitality company obtains cash from external financing activities such as the sale of stock or borrowing. Gradually, the company's earnings begin to generate cash flow although it continues to supplement this operating cash flow with external financing (borrowing or selling stock) to purchase new assets and replace old assets. Near the end of their life cycle companies have a larger positive cash flow from operating activities, which they use to replace worn out assets, repay debt, buy treasury stock, or distribute profits as dividends.

Exhibit 15-5: Cash Flow Patterns at Different Stages of a Business's Development

	Operating Activities	Investing Activities	Financing Activities
Stage 1	Cash outflow ←	Cash outflow ↙	→ Cash inflow
Stage 2	Cash inflow ↘	Cash outflow ↖	↙ Cash inflow
Stage 3	Cash inflow ↘	Cash outflow ↖	→ Cash outflow

	Stage 1	Stage 2	Stage 3
Operating activities	(70,000)	250,000	600,000
Investing activities	(550,000)	(440,000)	(140,000)
Financing activities	620,000	190,000	(460,000)
Net cash flow	0	0	0

The above cash flow patterns also tend to apply to new services, hotels, and restaurants, as well as entire businesses.

OTHER CASH FLOW RATIOS

As with the balance sheet and income statement, the use of ratios is crucial to the analysis of the cash flow statement. The significance of most of the amounts in the financial statements depends on their relationship to other key amounts. The only conclusions the hospitality manager can safely arrive at when looking at balance sheet and income statement dollar amounts relate to their size and the size of the company. To determine whether individual account balances or changes in these balances are reasonable, it is necessary to relate them to certain other pertinent accounts on the income statement, balance sheet, or cash flow statement.

Free Cash Flow

Free cash flow is a term in search of a definition. The differences in the various definitions hinge on the meaning of the word *free*. The most common definition of *free cash flow* is:

Cash from Operating activities less:	$100,000
Cash used in capital expenditures	(70,000)
Cash used to pay dividends	(20,000)
Free cash flow	$ 10,000

However, assuming the company needs to spend only $40,000 to maintain its operating assets in their current condition, *free cash flow* may be defined as follows:

Cash from Operating activities less:	$100,000
Cash used in capital expenditures to maintain operating assets without growth	(40,000)
Cash used to pay dividends	(20,000)
Free cash flow	$ 40,000

This calculation is based on the assumption that the $30,000 the hospitality company used to increase its capital assets is actually a discretionary expenditure, and the $30,000 spent was available to (1) pay interest-bearing debts, (2) buy treasury stock, or (3) pay dividends. In fact, $40,000 of cash flow was available for such discretionary spending, not solely the $10,000 identified by the first calculation.

However, another term is *total free cash* (TFC). This definition applies to off-balance-sheet financing, such as operating leases and rentals, under the assumption that they are financing activity outflows. The calculation of TFC would be made as follows:

Net income

plus : accrued and capitalized interest

plus : depreciation and amortization

plus : operating lease and rental expense

less: capital expenditures

less: declared dividends

equals: total free cash

The importance of calculating free cash flow lies in its use as a predictor of future earnings growth. Companies with large amounts of cash that exceed their requirements are logically more capable of investing for future growth. Consistent with this use of the ratio, one-time events that produce inordinately large operating cash inflows or outflows are usually excluded from cash from operating activities as they are nonrecurring and hence not likely to contribute to, or detract from, future operating cash flows.

Commonly Used Cash Flow to Debt Ratios

Two other commonly used cash flow ratios are (1) the current cash debt coverage ratio and (2) the cash debt coverage ratio, which are shown in Exhibit 15-6.

Exhibit 15-6: Commonly Used Cash Flow to Debt Ratios

$$\text{Current Cash Debt Coverage Ratio} = \frac{\text{Cash Provided by Operations}}{\text{Average Current Liabilities}}$$

$$\text{Cash Debt Coverage Ratio} = \frac{\text{Cash Provided by Operations}}{\text{Average Total Liabilities}}$$

The former equation is used as a measure of short-term liquidity, and the latter as a measure of long-term solvency. A more conservative version of the above ratios excludes dividends from cash provided by operations. When this version is used, the numerator of both ratios would be cash provided by operations minus cash dividends.

IMPORTANCE OF THE CASH FLOW STATEMENT

Income statement and cash flow statement ratios are more significant than balance sheet ratios because they deal with operating and nonoperating results produced over extended periods of time. Balance sheet amounts exist only as of the balance sheet date, thereby allowing them to be more easily manipulated by short-term accounting transfers in or out of key accounts.

Increasing Importance of the Cash Flow Statement and EBITDA

Analysts are increasingly wary of the income statement as a basis for evaluating the performance of a business. Because net income is affected by numerous adjustments related to depreciation, amortization, allowance for doubtful accounts, company policies regarding the capitalization of expenditures versus expensing them, consolidation of special-purpose entities or variable interest entities, and other adjustments, net income is more easily subject to manipulation than the cash flow statement. However, the cash flow statement is tied to a company's bank accounts, can be more easily verified, and is more dangerous to alter. It is interesting to note that paragraph 33 of FAS 95 (ASC 230-10-45-45.3) states:

> Financial statements shall not report an amount of cash flow per share. Neither cash flow nor any component of it is an alternative to net income as an indicator of an enterprise's performance, as reporting per share amounts might imply.

The above excerpt indicates the FASB may be attempting to minimize the growing importance assigned to cash basis accounting versus adjustment-ridden accrual basis accounting. However, this does not impede a hospitality financial manager from calculating this interesting ratio for internal company use.

For this reason, amounts such as earnings before interest, income taxes, and depreciation and amortization (EBITDA) are gradually acquiring as much, if not more, importance than net income and operating cash flow. The problem that some analysts find with operating cash flow is that it is also subject to some degree of manipulation. Net income can be manipulated by intentional or unintentional errors in management judgment when making legitimate accounting adjustments. Operating cash flow can be manipulated by short-term changes in the operating assets and liabilities accounts. Temporary transfers, as of the date that ratios are calculated, in or out of accounts receivable, inventories, accounts payable, and accruals accounts can significantly change a hospitality company's operating cash flow, but, because these transfers need to be reversed, the apparent operating cash flow is not in fact the real operating cash flow. EBITDA avoids this type of manipulation by using operating cash flows before it is modified by changes in the operating assets and liabilities of the company.

Another way to detect manipulation of the working capital accounts related to operations is to calculate the following ratios and compare them to each other:

$$\text{Profit margin} = \frac{\text{Net income}}{\text{Sales}}$$

$$\text{EBITDA margin} = \frac{\text{EBITDA}}{\text{Sales}}$$

$$\text{Operating cash flow margin} = \frac{\text{Operating cash flow}}{\text{Sales}}$$

These ratios indicate the amount of cash flow per dollar of sales and facilitate a comparison with a company's profit margin. In addition, if the EBITDA margin is significantly lower than the operating cash flow margin, it may indicate short-term manipulation of working capital account balances to increase period-end operating cash flow.

There is no single indicator of a hospitality company's operating and financial health; yet, an analysis of the cash flow statement ties together income statement and balance sheet accounts much more than does an analysis of any other financial statements. Even prior to a ratio analysis, cash flow statement analysis forces the reader to interpret results of operations, cash from operations, beginning and ending cash balances, changes in investments (cash in the body of the statement and noncash in a supplementary schedule), sources of external financing, and dividend payments, as well as interest and income taxes paid. These encompass most of the critical areas of a hospitality business. The only major items omitted are cost of food and beverage expense, labor expense, and an accurate appraisal of the size of a company, which only occurs if the more popular indirect method of preparing the operating activities section is used.

The cash flow statement is more difficult to interpret than the income statement or balance sheet and requires the reader to have a more thorough understanding of the business, as well as an understanding of the interplay of all four financial statements required by GAAP. This additional knowledge makes the statement more useful and important to those reviewing it.

Free Funds Cash Ratio. An important ratio that helps to analyze a company's ability to service its debt is the free funds cash ratio (FFCR). This ratio is shown below:

$$\text{FFCR} = \frac{\text{EBITDA}}{\text{Interest expense} + (\text{Annual Principal Payment}/[1 - \text{Income tax rate}])}$$

Because EBITDA is a pre-tax amount and the annual principal payment (APP) must be made in after-tax income, this amount must be converted into a pre-tax amount by dividing the APP by "1—income tax rate." This step is not applied to interest expenses because interest is tax deductible and is paid from pre-tax income.

Cash Flow Ratios Reveal More Than Accrual Ratios

Exhibit 15-7 presents a comparative analysis of two hypothetical hospitality companies, ABC Company and DEF Company, using two balance sheet ratios as opposed to two cash flow ratios. The balance sheet ratios, the current ratio and the quick ratio, indicate that ABC Company is stronger than DEF Company. ABC's current ratio and quick ratio are higher than those for DEF Company as follows:

Exhibit 15-7: Cash Flow Ratios Reveal More Than Accrual Ratios

Balance Sheets

ABC

Cash + accounts receivable:	10,000	Operating liabilities:	9,000
Other operating assets:	4,000	Interest-bearing debt:	270,000
Operating Assets:	14,000		
All other assets:	285,000	Equity:	20,000
	299,000		299,000

DEF

Cash + accounts receivable:	80,000	Operating liabilities:	100,000
Other operating assets:	35,000	Interest-bearing debt:	800,000
Operating Assets:	115,000		
All other assets:	885,000	Equity:	100,000
	1,000,000		1,000,000

	ABC		DEF
Sales	120,000	Sales	1,300,000
Expenses	(130,000)	Expenses	(600,000)
EBITDA	(10,000)	EBITDA	700,000
Depreciation + amortization	(30,000)	Depreciation + amortization	(160,000)
Interest expense	(18,900)	Interest expense	(72,000)
Earnings before income taxes	(58,900)	Earnings before income taxes	468,000
Income tax expense 40%	23,560	Income tax expense 40%	(187,200)
Net income	(35,340)	Net income	280,800

Net income	(35,340)	Net income	280,800
Depreciation + amortization	30,000	Depreciation + amortization	160,000
Decrease in operating assets	6,000	Decrease in operating assets	(34,000)
Increase in operating liabilities	5,000	Increase in operating liabilities	(10,000)
Operating cash flow	5,660	Operating cash flow	396,800

Annual Principal payment	30,000	Annual Principal payment	80,000
Interest paid	11,000	Interest paid	70,000
Income taxes paid	2,000	Income taxes paid	185,000

Cur Ratio	1.56	Cur Ratio	1.15
Quick Ratio	1.11	Quick Ratio	0.80
Current Cash Flow Ratio	0.63	Current Cash Flow Ratio	3.97
FFCR	(0.24)	FFCR	4.67

ABC		DEF	
Current Ratio	1.56	Current Ratio	1.15
Quick Ratio	1.11	Quick Ratio	0.80

Nevertheless, ABC's negative current cash flow ratio and its negative free funds cash ratio (FFCR) (see Exhibit 15-7) both indicate that ABC is in financial trouble.

On the other hand, DEF is financially sound despite the fact that its balance sheet ratios indicate that it is not as healthy as ABC. Their respective current cash flow ratios, less than 1 for ABC and 3.97 for DEF, and their respective FFCRs, (0.24) for ABC and 4.67 for DEF, reveal ABC's true lack of financial health.

In fact, cash flow ratios do not have to be negative to indicate the existence of a problem. A negative ratio indicates that cash flow is negative; that is, expenditures are greater than cash receipts. Nevertheless, any cash flow ratio that is less than "1" indicates an inability to meet the specific cash requirement measured by that ratio.

Constant Evaluation of the Uses of Cash and Sources of Financing

Financial managers of successful hospitality companies are constantly faced with the choice of whether to use their company's excess cash to buy revenue-generating assets, buy cost-reducing assets, pay interest-bearing debt, buy treasury stock, or pay dividends. In addition, they face the decision of how to finance future asset purchases, whether with debt or by issuing stock. The cash flow statement presents the changes in all these accounts in one statement.

In fact, in recessions or in periods of slow economic growth, when interest rates fall and stock market values decline, it is almost an indication of derelict management if a hospitality company that is near market saturation does not borrow to buy treasury stock. The opposite transition, from debt to equity, should be observed at the peaks of economic cycles, when interest rates and stock market valuations are high. It is sometimes difficult to exceed the cash return a hospitality company can obtain by buying treasury stock in a down cycle and selling it in an up cycle. Although the profit realized on such transactions cannot be reported on the income statement but must instead be credited to an additional paid-in capital account, the EPS increase generated by the purchase of treasury stock is normally reflected in the market value of stockholders' shares.

The above transaction is not appropriate for companies that have not achieved significant market penetration. Such companies should use all of their cash to expand during down cycles in the hope that, by the time the economy recovers, their expansion process will enable them to increase profits significantly as a result of their larger market presence. Buying and selling treasury stock generates a one-time net cash inflow, whereas well thought-out investments in revenue-generating assets provide a recurring profit accompanied by growth.

Typical Cash Flow Questions

Although the cash flow statement does not provide complete answers to many questions, it points readers in a direction that may enable them to obtain appropriate answers. Questions that this statement helps to answer, based on historic data, include:

1. Why does the hospitality company have a shortage of cash although sales are increasing rapidly?

Note: It is common for new businesses or ventures to consume cash in their operating activities operations because of their investment in inventory. They must also grant extended credit terms to gain market share and sell at lower prices to obtain competitive advantage. Thus, profits are small, inventory and supplier payments are large, and collections from credit customers are slow. This places a new business in the position of having a small amount of cash that only becomes greater if it continues to outgrow it.

2. Why did net cash increase despite the fact that a net loss is reported on the income statement?

Note: It is possible that noncash expenses, such as depreciation, amortization, and deferred income taxes, are greater than the accrual basis loss, thus resulting in a cash inflow despite the accrual basis losses on the income statement.

3. Is the hospitality company managing its operating assets and liabilities efficiently?

Note: It is favorable to negotiate extended credit terms with suppliers, collect accounts receivable as quickly as possible, and maintain low inventories. This enables a company to work with negative working capital. Although riskier, negative working capital provides capital for investment in revenue-generating assets. The cash flow statement enables a hospitality manager to determine whether the changes in the operating assets and liabilities section of the cash flow statement indicate an increasing or decreasing investment in working capital.

4. Is the hospitality company buying assets that add value to the business or is it buying low-return assets such as stocks and bonds?
5. How did the hospitality company pay for the purchase of assets?
6. Was there a large fluctuation in debt repayments?
7. How much stock did the hospitality company issue or how much treasury stock did it buy?
8. Was there a large fluctuation in dividend payments?
9. Does the hospitality company have enough operating cash flow to increase dividend payments?
10. Is the hospitality company allowing too much cash to accumulate in its bank accounts?
11. What was the cash gain or loss from currency transactions?

When making decisions, the above questions lead to others that the hospitality manager may want to consider as follows:

1. Did the company finance its asset purchases using the optimum cash sources in terms of interest expense versus earnings dilution?
2. How should the hospitality company finance future asset purchases?
3. How will the hospitality company be able to repay its debts?

4. Is the use of external sources of financing coherent with the economic cycle?
5. Is the hospitality company hedging its foreign currency transactions properly?
6. Will the company be able to maintain its dividend payments?
7. Is rapid growth forcing the hospitality company to incur too much debt and hence risk?
8. How should the company use the excess cash in its bank accounts?
9. In case of a catastrophe, does the hospitality company have an alternate emergency source of cash?
10. Should the company finance its additional cash needs during peak season by borrowing, or should it invest excess cash during the slow season in certificates of deposit, treasury bills, or other cash equivalents that can easily be converted to cash in the peak season?

SHORTCOMINGS OF THE CASH FLOW STATEMENT

The cash flow statement is not easy to interpret. More than for the other required financial statements, the reader must understand the source of the information presented on the statement in order to interpret its significance. Furthermore, though the cash flow statement points the reader to those areas where further investigation is required, the reader must be alert to any of the warning signs that may appear, as mentioned in this section.

The Best Approach to the Cash Flow Statement and What It Does Not Reveal

Cash flow statements should be viewed on a comparative basis over several periods. This is especially true in the operating activities section. There are gray areas in GAAP that may allow companies to classify expenditures as investments that should be classified as expenses. The financial manager should watch for sudden increases or decreases in accounts receivable or accounts payable, or sudden sharp increases or decreases in inventory. These may indicate that sales, cost of sales, or other expenses are being manipulated. The hospitality financial manager should also be alert to one-time events that distort the operating cash flow in a particular year. For instance, for tax purposes companies can deduct the noncash cost when their employees exercise stock options. This results in a decrease in income taxes paid, which might not repeat in subsequent periods. As mentioned earlier, regarding the use of external financing to maintain dividend payments, if the hospitality company is not using its operating cash to increase investments, this may indicate a persistent lack of liquidity and be a precursor to future profitability issues.

Furthermore, the cash flow statement does not present a company's entire financial profile. Therefore, it is important to review balance sheet and income statement data in conjunction with the cash flow statement. A $10,000 increase in accounts receivable is much more significant for a company that has $50,000 of accounts receivable than for a company that has $300,000 in accounts receivable. This is true of all the account changes shown in a cash flow statement.

The indirect method of preparing the operating activities section of the cash flow statement is ambiguous because it does not reveal a company's total cash inflows and outflows. It is possible to match many different income statements and their related direct-method operating cash flows with a single operating activities section prepared using the indirect method. Exhibit 15-8 presents an indirect-method operating activities section that is consistent with two different hypothetical operating activities sections prepared using the direct method. Although GAAP requires the supplementary presentation of an indirect-method operating activities section when the direct-method format is used in the body of the statement, it does not require a supplementary direct-method presentation when the indirect method is used in the body of the cash flow statement.

Exhibit 15-8: Example of Two Direct-Method Operating Cash Flow Sections That Are Consistent with a Single Indirect-Method Presentation

Hypothetical Example A

Operating Activities Section of Cash Flow Statement

(Direct Method)

Cash receipts		
Sales	913,000	
Increase in accounts receivable	(13,000)	900,000
Cash payments		
Cost of food sold	(344,000)	
Decrease in food inventory	2,000	
Cash paid to other suppliers	(138,000)	
Increase in accounts payable	16,000	
Cash paid to employees	(233,000)	
Interest paid (net of capitalized interest)	(24,000)	
Income taxes paid	(64,000)	(785,000)
Cash (used in) provided by operating activities		$115,000

Hypothetical Example B

Operating Activities Section of Cash Flow Statement

(Direct Method)

Cash receipts		
Sales	1,700,000	
Increase in accounts receivable	(13,000)	1,687,000
Cash payments		
Cost of food sold	(651,000)	
Decrease in food inventory	2,000	
Cash paid to other suppliers	(321,000)	

15,028   Part III: Financial Analysis

Increase in accounts payable	16,000	
Cash paid to employees	(530,000)	
Interest paid (net of capitalized interest)	(24,000)	
Income taxes paid	(64,000)	(1,572,000)
Cash (used in) provided by operating activities		$115,000

Operating Activities Section of Cash Flow Statement
(Indirect Method)

Net income		$100,000
Depreciation		10,000
Changes in operating assets and liabilities		
Increase in accounts receivable	($13,000)	
Decrease in food inventory	2,000	
Increase in accounts payable	16,000	5,000
Cash (used in) provided by operating activities		$115,000

The cash flow statement brings to management's attention the four important decision points in any business. These are the decisions that determine the degree to which stockholder value is maximized (reflected in a stock's market value) as shown in the following equations:

Market value per share (MV) = Price earnings ratio (PE)
× Earnings per share (EPS)

$$\text{EPS} = \frac{\text{Net Income}}{\text{Common shares outstanding}}$$

EPS can be maximized by the following activities, as reflected in the indicated sections of the cash flow statement:

Investing activities section

1. *Investing in assets that will either increase revenue or reduce expenses*—This increases net income by either increasing revenue or reducing expenses, or both.

Financing activities section

2. *Paying back interest-bearing debts*—This reduces interest expense and increases net income.

3. *Buying treasury stock*—This reduces the denominator of the EPS fraction and increasing EPS.

4. *Increasing the dividend payout*—Increasing the dividend payout makes a stock more attractive to investors who desire immediate income as opposed to rapid growth over the long-term. In this case, a higher dividend payout will cause the P/E of a stock to rise, thus increasing its MV per the first equation above.

The best use of a company's free cash flow depends on the proper evaluation of all the factors that affect the above equations. The evaluation of these factors should take into account whether they will impact the company favorably over the short-term, the long-term, or ideally over both the short- and long-terms. Using some free cash to buy treasury stock at a current low price and sell it at a higher price in one or two years may not delay a company's growth plans because other non-financial factors may inhibit it from investing the funds temporarily invested in treasury stock during that period. This is an example of a strategy that would benefit the company over both the short- and long-term.

Potentially Misleading Operating Cash Flow Reporting

The cash flow statement is subject to several misleading reporting practices. One of the reasons why analysts emphasize a hospitality company's cash from operation is its recurring nature. However, certain accounting and reporting practices that are not entirely in violation of GAAP can compromise its recurring nature by introducing some nonrecurring items into operating cash flow:

- Cash overdrafts should be reported in the financing activities section when they are the result of financing arrangements with banks. Yet GAAP requires them to be reported as current liabilities. As such, an increase in the overdraft can become an operating source of cash, as opposed to a financing source.
- Because of their seasonal nature, in the slow season hospitality companies may invest their excess cash by purchasing short-term marketable securities. If these are classified as trading securities, the cash inflows or outflows from the sale or purchase of these securities may increase operating cash flows on a one-time or infrequently recurring basis.
- Company policy with regard to capitalizing versus expensing certain asset-related expenditures can also artificially increase operating cash flow by increasing net income when they are capitalized and later increasing cash flow through their amortization.
- Selling accounts receivable or securitizing them can also increase operating cash flows on a nonrecurring basis. Postponing the payment of accounts payable, either in violation of credit terms or by negotiation with suppliers, also introduces a one-time surge in operating cash flow.
- The tax benefits derived from large nonoperating gains or losses can also distort operating cash flow on a one-time basis, as can tax benefits to the company when stock options are exercised. Another one-time tax benefit is produced when tax laws allow the amortization of goodwill from certain acquisitions.
- Cash generated by discontinued operations is also correctly included in operating cash flow, yet they are nonrecurring.

Operating cash flow must, therefore, be closely examined in order to determine what portion of it is truly recurring in nature and can thus be counted on as a source of cash to repay long-term financing commitments, make progress payments on large-asset construction projects, or make large purchases using installment payments.

PART IV

MANAGEMENT ACCOUNTING

CHAPTER 16
MAXIMIZING PROFIT AND MINIMIZING COSTS

CONTENTS

Maximizing Restaurant Contribution Margin	16,002
Restaurant Design	16,004
Menu Design	16,005
Menu Pricing	16,005
Base Selling Price	16,012
Menu Sales Mix Analysis	16,012
Elasticity of Demand	16,015
Ratio Analysis	16,018
Procurement	16,019
Determining Optimum Order Size	16,021
Receiving	16,026
Storage	16,027
Consumption	16,030
Maximizing Beverage Revenue	16,033
Beverage Pricing	16,034
Waiters' Suggestion	16,034
Cost/Margin Analysis	16,035
Minimizing Beverage Costs	16,039
Purchasing	16,039
Storage	16,039
Consumption	16,040
Possible Methods of Theft at the Bar	16,045
Minimizing Labor Costs in Restaurants and Hotels	16,046
Staffing Guide	16,046
Standard Ratios and Variance Analysis	16,048
Minimizing Other Costs in Restaurants and Hotels	16,049
Standard Per-Unit Ratios	16,049
Operating Ratios, Common Size Analysis, and Variance Analysis	16,049
Other Factors That May Affect Profits	16,055
Exhibits	
Exhibit 16-1. Mediocre Food and Labor Cost Control—Effect on Net Income	16,003
Exhibit 16-2. Comparison of Mark-Up Price Calculation Methods to Arrive at a $10.00 Sales Price	16,009
Exhibit 16-3. Menu Mix Analysis	16,013
Exhibit 16-4. Hypothetical Situations for Elastic, Inelastic, and Negatively Elastic Demand	16,017
Exhibit 16-5. Calculation of Number of Items to Order—Par Stock Method	16,021
Exhibit 16-6. Calculation of Number of Items to Order—Levinson Method	16,022

Exhibit 16-7. EOQ Calculation	16,023
Exhibit 16-8. Perpetual Inventory Card	16,028
Exhibit 16-9. Flow Chart for a Perpetual Inventory System	16,029
Exhibit 16-10. Two Actual Cost/Standard Cost and Actual Price/Standard Price Scenarios	16,031
Exhibit 16-11. Cost Percents Disguise Collusion	16,032
Exhibit 16-12. Cost/Margin Analysis for Hypothetical Beer Sales	16,036
Exhibit 16-13. Popularity Indicators	16,037
Exhibit 16-14. Per-Unit Price-Cost-Profit Analysis	16,037
Exhibit 16-15. Total Sales-Cost-Contribution Margin Analysis	16,038
Exhibit 16-16. Daily Cost Percentage Calculation Sheet	16,042
Exhibit 16-17. Cost per Ounce and Recipe-Costing Sheets	16,044
Exhibit 16-18. Flow Chart for Preparing and Using a Staffing Guide	16,047
Exhibit 16-19. Calculation of Labor Variances	16,048
Exhibit 16-20. Hypothetical Hotel Income Statements and Averages	16,050
Exhibit 16-21. Vertical and Operating Ratio Analysis	16,052
Exhibit 16-22. Ratio-Analysis-by-Exception Reports	16,054
Exhibit 16-23. Seasonal Cycle of Room Rates	16,054
Exhibit 16-24. Percent Sales per Room Category	16,055

MAXIMIZING RESTAURANT CONTRIBUTION MARGIN

A restaurant's greatest expenses are costs of sales and payroll. Together, these two expenses consume 60% to 70% of every sales dollar. These are called the *prime cost*, although often the prime cost is defined as cost of sales and kitchen labor only and excludes all nonkitchen payrolls. All other expenses combined consume between 20% and 30% of revenue. Thus, with restaurant profits that usually range from 6% to 10%, the impact of even a slight loss of control over these expenses has a significant impact on a restaurant's net income. The following income statements demonstrate the impact of a 5% and 10% increase in cost of food sold and payroll expense on a restaurant with an original net income of approximately 8% (median between 6% and 10% net incomes). A 5% increase in these expenses causes a 29% decrease in net income, whereas a 10% increase in cost of food sold and payroll expenses results in a 58% decrease in net income.

Exhibit 16-1: Mediocre Food and Labor Cost Control—Effect on Net Income

	(A) Company with good cost controls	(B) Reduction in net income due to 5% excess in cost of food sold and payroll	Company with mediocre cost controls	(C) Reduction in net income due to 10% excess in cost of food sold and payroll	Company with poor cost controls
Inter-column relationships			(A) + (B)		(A) + (C)
Sales	$102.00		$102.00		$102.00
Cost of food sold	35.00	(1)1.75	36.75	(2)3.50	38.50
Labor costs	35.00	1.75	36.75	3.50	38.50
Other costs	20.00		20.00		20.00
Earnings before income tax	12.00	3.50	8.50	7.00	5.00
Income tax (33%)	3.96	1.16	2.80	2.31	1.65
Net income	8.04	2.34	5.70	4.69	3.35
Percentage reduction in net income		(3)29%		(4)58%	

(1) $1.75 = 5% × $35.00
(2) $3.50 = 10% × $35.00
(3) 29% = $2.34 / $8.04
(4) 58% = $4.69 / $8.04

Control of food costs begins with the planning and design of the restaurant structure, continues with menu design and menu engineering, and applies to every stage of the food acquisition and service processes from purchasing, receiving, and paying to presenting the food to the customer. As noted earlier, individual expense control deficiencies need not be very large to merit management attention. Restaurants are particularly vulnerable to improper cost controls because of the many stages involved in the process of acquiring food and serving it to customers. These stages can be identified as:

- Purchasing
- Receiving
- Storing
- Consuming
- Paying

At every one of these stages restaurants are vulnerable to cost excesses due to dishonesty or ineptitude on the part of employees, and/or improper handling of food. It is easy to imagine how excess costs equal to 1% of sales, or even more, can be incurred in each of these stages. Should that occur, it would represent a reduction of about 35% of net income on an after-tax basis. See Exhibit 16-1, "Mediocre Food and Labor Cost Control—Effect on Net Income."

In addition, there is the problem of cost-increasing inefficiencies due to poor restaurant design, and the problem of maximizing revenue by optimizing menu pricing, and optimizing menu design and engineering. The subtleties of profit maximization and the many stages at which food cost control can be deficient renders success in the restaurant business difficult to achieve. In fact, 90% of all new restaurants fail within the first five years of their existence.

Because there are so many potential expense leakage points, inadequate control of one process may be accompanied by small control deficiencies in other processes. These small expense excesses, if tolerated, or small cost-reduction opportunities, if dismissed, can quickly result either in failure or in severely curtailed profits. The various control stages in the food preparation and service process are:

- Restaurant design
- Menu design, pricing, and sales mix analysis
- Purchasing
- Receiving
- Paying
- Storing
- Issuing
- Consuming and delivering to customers
- Employee meals

Restaurant Design

A restaurant's layout and design affects profits in two ways:

1. It facilitates revenue maximization in the front of the house, and
2. It provides appropriate food storage and facilitates efficient food preparation and service.

It is beyond the scope of this book to discuss restaurant design, but it is important for the hospitality financial manager to understand that facilities design is a significant underlying factor that can affect a restaurant's ability to maximize revenues and minimize costs. An inefficiently laid out kitchen or an insecure or inadequate food storage facility leads to higher storage and processing costs through excess food waste during processing, or pilferage and spoilage during storage. In addition, an inappropriate concept, incompatible ambience, or inadequate maintenance will limit the restaurant's ability to maximize profits. The appearance of the front of the house usually carries over to the back of the house in the mind of a customer. Thus, when comparing two restaurants with similar menus, the one with the ambience that is more compatible with its menu will be able to charge customers higher prices. Analyzing the impact of the facilities design on pricing potential (value analysis or value engineering) is similar to a manufacturer designing a product by taking into consideration both its sales potential and the simplification of the manufacturing process. Although a great menu can bring success, profit will not be maximized if the facility's design and maintenance are incompatible with the menu's content.

Menu Design

Menu content and design provide an opportunity to minimize costs in several ways. In addition to promising high-quality food, menu presentation (i.e., appealing pictures and descriptions and properly positioned high-margin items) and an appropriate menu selection from the perspective of preparation costs helps maximize profits.

The menu's content should be designed with the following objectives in mind:

- Cost of individual ingredients
- Cross-utilization of ingredients
- Portion size
- Complexity (extensiveness and variety) of menu items

Costs of ingredients should be minimized when developing recipes in a manner consistent with the desired customers' perception of the restaurant's food quality. Costs can also be minimized by using the same ingredients in various menu items. This reduces costs in later stages of the food production process, such as in the purchasing, receiving, payment, storage, and issuing stages. Food costs can obviously be minimized by serving smaller rather than larger portions. Customers may be leaving food on their plates because the portion sizes are too large, especially in a weight-conscious environment. For example, a menu centered on a single theme helps minimize the variety of ingredients, reduces preparation time, more easily promotes cross-utilization of ingredients, and facilitates the standardization of many facets of the food production process.

Menu Pricing

Pricing methodologies are obviously an important part of cost control because food cost percentage is a factor of both food cost and price. An improperly priced menu may make it impossible to meet food cost percentage targets.

Setting the price of a menu item is an art, not a science. Therefore, not only quantitative but qualitative factors, such as demand for a particular item and competitor pricing, should be taken into account when setting menu prices. If demand for a menu item is inelastic, sales will be maximized by maximizing price. If demand is elastic, then the price the competition is charging for a similar item becomes an important factor. Qualitative factors often limit how well quantitative goals such as desired check averages, food cost percentage targets, and gross profit or contribution margin targets can be achieved. Because of the infinite potential combinations of qualitative factors, the decision to override quantitative factors can only be based on experience. The most commonly used price-setting methodologies are:

- Subjective methods (various listed below)
- Objective methods
  - Markup on food costs
  - Markup on food costs plus (pre-prep) payroll
  - Markup on food costs plus all kitchen labor payroll
  - Markup on food costs plus the entire restaurant labor payroll
  - Contribution margin pricing method
  - Pricing per customer
  - Price-by-the-ounce method

Subjective Methods. The oldest pricing method is subjective or intuitive. However, in the hands of experienced restaurateurs, this method is not as haphazard as it may seem. An experienced price setter intuitively takes into account one or more of the following factors when setting menu prices: (1) competitors' prices; (2) value of a menu item as perceived by a typical customer (based on price, portion size, atmosphere, service quality); (3) different menu items with different markups (e.g., hamburgers versus soda and fries).

Consideration of these factors has led to the following subjective pricing methods:

- *Loss leader pricing*—Pricing some items so cheaply that they produce little or no profit in the hope that they will attract customers who will then be motivated to buy other, more profitable items. Discount pricing for different groups or at unusual hours is another application of this approach.
- *Reasonable price method*—The price is based on what one expects is a reasonable price to pay. Unfortunately, this method is sometimes approached solely from the price setter's perspective without some objective testing of what customers consider reasonable.
- *Highest price method*—The price is based on what one expects is the maximum price a customer is willing to pay. This is subject to the same shortcoming mentioned above.
- *Targeting competitors' prices*—Under this method a study of competitors' menus leads to the setting of prices that are lower than the competition.
- *Target pricing*—Target pricing is based on using a market analysis to determine the maximum price that customers will pay for an item and then making a cost study to determine whether that item can be produced at a price that will contribute to maintaining a restaurant's gross profit or its contribution margin.
- *Trial and error method*—This is the catch-all method. Any mistakes made using the other intuitive methods are then corrected by trial and error price changes until a suitable price is reached.

- *Average check target pricing*—Average check target pricing attempts to make it impossible for a customer to spend less than a specific amount. This takes into account the probability of customers ordering side dishes, desserts, or drinks in addition to the entrée. A certain percentage of customers will only order entrées, thus the price of entrées must be high enough to achieve the average check based on the historical percentage of patrons who only order entrées.

Selection of Pricing Method—Sales Volume Considerations. The number of covers sold plays a significant role in the choice of pricing method. When labor costs are excluded from the cost of menu items, they are treated as fixed costs. It is possible that the number of covers sold, combined with a price that does not take labor costs into account, will be insufficient to generate a marginal profit large enough to cover the excluded labor costs. When it is questionable whether a targeted sales volume will be attained, the more all-inclusive methods should be used to minimize this risk.

Objective Methods. The seven objective pricing methods to be discussed are (1) markup on food cost, (2) markup on prime cost in which only direct labor (pre-prep) payroll is included, (3) markup on prime cost in which all kitchen labor payroll is included, (4) markup on prime cost in which all restaurant payroll is included, (5) contribution margin pricing, (6) pricing per customer, and (7) pricing by the ounce. There is also a variation of the markup on food cost that is called the Texas Restaurant Association (TRA) method—a variation of all the prime cost methods that involves calculating payroll costs on a per-item basis rather than using the overall budget percent for each of the three payroll categories used (i.e., direct kitchen labor, all kitchen labor, and all payroll).

The Four Mark-Up Methods and the TRA Method. The procedure for applying the above pricing methods is presented in Exhibit 16-2, "Comparison of Markup Price Calculation Methods." The markup methods involve calculating the standard cost per menu item (the costed-out recipe). These methods also require the use of various cost percentages, presumably based on budget estimates. The TRA method requires a net income percentage. All non-food cost percentages plus the desired profit percentage are added. This amount is then subtracted from 100%. The resulting percent (in decimal format) is then divided into the menu item food cost dollar amount. A variation of the prime cost methods requires the calculation of the applicable labor costs per menu item based on a labor cost study as well as an estimate of the number of each menu item that will be sold. These amounts should all be available because they are the basis for preparing the budget from which the required cost and net income percentages are obtained. The individual restaurateur should select the easiest format to follow.

Contribution Margin Pricing. The contribution margin method is based on achieving a targeted contribution margin per cover. It is similar to the TRA method with the difference that the TRA method adds all expenses and treats them as if they were variable, whereas the contribution margin method attempts to distinguish between variable and fixed expenses. It then allocates the fixed expenses to all menu items and treats all variable expenses, including variable labor, in the per-item way that variable expenses should be treated. Under this method, the cost per menu item includes only those expenses that are truly variable. It is possible to include the variable element of semi-variable (or mixed) expenses here along with the 100% variable cost of food sold. The variable cost of an average cover must be calculated followed by the fixed expenses plus desired net income per cover as follows:

$$\frac{\text{Fixed expenses} + \text{Desired net income}}{\text{Number of covers expected to sell}} = \text{Contribution margin per cover}$$

The standard cost per average cover is then added to the desired contribution margin per cover to arrive at the selling price as follows:

Standard menu item cost + Desired contribution margin per cover = Price

Exhibit 16-2: Comparison of Mark-Up Price Calculation Methods to Arrive at a $10.00 Sales Price

For clarity, these pricing examples are based on the following income statement and on the assumption that this restaurant sells 100,000 units of one single menu item and has no separate beverage department.

		Relevant percentage for mark-up on food cost	Relevant percentage for mark-up on prime cost (direct labor only)	Relevant percentage for mark-up on prime cost (kitchen labor only)	Relevant percentage for mark-up on prime cost (all payroll)	Relevant percentage for TRA (ratio) method
Budgeted number of customers: 100,000						
Budgeted sales	$1,000,000					
Budgeted food cost	$400,000	250.00%				12.50%
Budgeted pre-prep kitchen payroll (direct labor)	$125,000		190.48%			7.50%
Budgeted post-prep kitchen payroll	$75,000			166.67%		10.00%
Budgeted nonkitchen payroll	$100,000				142.86%	
Budgeted other nonfood costs (excluding beverage costs)	$200,000					20.00%
						10.00%
Budgeted net income	$100,000					Total 60.00%

The above are mark-up percentages chosen by management based on including progressively more costs in the per-menu-item total cost. As included costs increase, the mark-up required to achieve the desired total dollar sales decreases.

100% − 60% = 40%

Relevant mark-up percentages (divisor percentage in case of TRA)		250%	190.48%	166.67%	142.86%	
Multiplied by		×	×	×	×	
Calculated cost per menu item*		$4.00	$5.25	$6.00	$7.00	$4.00 ÷ .40
Gives sales price per item		$10.00	$10.00	$10.00	$10.00	$10.00

* For example: $400,000 ÷ 100,000 covers = $4.00; ($400,000 + $125,000) ÷ 100,000 covers = $5.25; etc.

Chapter 16: Maximizing Profit and Minimizing Costs   **16,009**

Texas Restaurant Association (TRA) method: In the TRA method all nonfood costs plus a desired profit percent are added. This total percent is then subtracted from 100% to obtain the percent (in decimal format) by which per-item food costs will be divided to obtain per unit price.
Advantage of the TRA method: The advantage of the TRA method is that all nonfood costs can be automatically tied into the price calculation using a computer program such as Excel. Thus, if the desired net income, nonfood costs, or any other cost category changes, the impact on prices will be automatically observable.

Note: A problem with this method is the difficulty in differentiating between variable and fixed expenses. Truly variable expenses must not only change as sales change but change in the same proportion to increasing or decreasing sales. The fixed salary of kitchen employees is not a variable expense, but the wages of hourly employees are usually considered to be a variable expense. Theoretically, to be perfectly variable, wages should be paid on a per-menu-item basis, not on an hourly basis. Thus, when two portions of any single menu item are sold, the labor cost attached to those two items should double. There are methods discussed in this manual that allow for the calculation of an estimated variable element in expenses that would otherwise have to be considered totally fixed or totally variable, thus reducing the degree of error inherent in these price calculations.

Pricing per Customer. Because it is impossible to develop a standard cost for each item in a salad or food bar, an average-cost approach must be used. Both a standard-cost approach and an average-cost approach involve calculating all the costs associated with the bar, including food, setup, and cleaning expenses. This total cost can be divided by the expected number of customers and an average cost can thus be determined. The cost can be calculated over a period of days or weeks to obtain a valid average, and it can be frequently recalculated to maintain a current average food cost. This cost can then be used to determine the sales price per person by using any of the pricing methods explained previously.

Price by the Ounce. The pricing-by-the-ounce method is used when food is sold by weight. The point of this method is to calculate an approximately accurate cost per ounce when the products that are being sold vary in cost, weight, and customer preference. The steps required in this process are:

1. Make a list of all items to be sold.
2. Calculate the standard cost (costed recipe) per ounce for each item based on yield, not on pre-cooked weight.
3. Reorganize the list so that the most expensive items per ounce are listed first to help make consumption estimates.
4. Estimate the yield pounds of each item that will be consumed per week.
5. Divide this amount by the estimated number of customers expected during the week to obtain the average weight per cover.
6. Calculate the total cost of all food estimated to be consumed during the week.
7. Divide this by the total weight of all items estimated to be sold during the week to obtain a weighted-average cost per ounce sold.
8. Multiply the average cost per ounce by the average ounces expected to be sold per cover to obtain an average cost per average cover.
9. Use any of the markup pricing methods previously described to arrive at a price based on this cost.

An alternative method of pricing by the ounce would change steps 8 and 9 as follows:

8. Estimate the desired average cover price. This amount can be obtained from the budget.
 9. Divide this by the average weight per cover (in ounces) obtained in step 5 to determine what price per ounce must be charged to attain the desired average cover price.

Base Selling Price

The prices determined by using objective pricing methods should often be considered merely as starting points for the pricing process. After an objective price has been determined, it should be reviewed from the perspective of the various subjective pricing viewpoints to determine whether the base price should be modified. Factors affecting demand elasticity should be considered, as well as whether a product's uniqueness warrants an increase above the base price or a decrease based on the competition with the reduced profit compensated for by another product.

Menu Sales Mix Analysis

After optimizing the menu items' price-cost relationship, the menu mix should be analyzed. Menu mix analysis involves choosing the mix of menu items that will maximize profit from food sales. The two major menu mix analysis methods are (1) cost/margin analysis and (2) menu engineering.

Cost/Margin Analysis. In the cost/margin analysis method all menu items are grouped into the following four categories based on food cost percent and total contribution margin (CM), as opposed to per-unit CM:

1. Problems—High food cost percent—Low CM
2. Sleepers—Low food cost percent—Low CM
3. Standards—High food cost percent—High CM
4. Primes—Low food cost percent—High CM

The grouping of menu items into each of these categories depends on their relationship to an (1) average food cost percent for the entire menu or equivalent menu items and (2) an average CM for the entire menu or equivalent menu items. A comparison of this method with the menu-engineering method of menu analysis is provided in Exhibit 16-3, "Menu Mix Analysis."

Menu Engineering Analysis. An alternative basis for menu item analysis is menu engineering. In this method, all menu items are grouped into the following four categories based on units sold and per-unit contribution margin (PCM):

1. Dogs—Low volume—Low per-unit contribution margin
2. Plow horses—High volume—Low PCM
3. Puzzles—Low volume—High PCM
4. Stars—High volume—High PCM

The grouping of menu items into each of these categories depends on their relationship to an (1) average sales volume for all menu items or equivalent

Chapter 16: Maximizing Profit and Minimizing Costs 16,013

menu items and (2) an average contribution margin per item for all menu items or equivalent menu items. A comparison of this method with the menu-engineering method of menu analysis is provided in Exhibit 16-3 below.

Exhibit 16-3: Menu Mix Analysis

Part A—Individual Menu Item Data to Be Used in the Illustration of Both Menu Analysis Methods

		Price	Cost	Unit CM	Volume	Total CM	Total Food Cost	Total Sales	Food Cost %
1	Chicken	$5.00	1.50	$3.50	100	$350.00	$150.00	$500.00	30.0%
2	Fish	6.00	2.00	4.00	70	280.00	140.00	420.00	33.3%
3	Paella	10.00	3.00	7.00	85	595.00	255.00	850.00	30.0%
4	Steak	12.00	5.00	7.00	35	245.00	175.00	420.00	41.7%
5	Lobster	16.00	5.00	11.00	25	275.00	125.00	400.00	31.3%
6	Stew	5.00	2.00	3.00	90	270.00	180.00	450.00	40.0%
7	Shrimp	11.00	5.00	6.00	80	480.00	400.00	880.00	45.5%
8	Soup	3.00	1.00	2.00	60	120.00	60.00	180.00	33.3%
9	Hot dog	2.00	0.25	1.75	30	52.50	7.50	60.00	12.5%
10	Hamburger	4.00	1.00	3.00	40	120.00	40.00	160.00	25.0%
	Totals	$74.00	$25.75	$48.25	615	$2,787.50	$1,532.50	$4,320.00	

Cost/Margin Menu Analysis

↑ Food Cost %

Problems High Food Cost % + Low CM			Standards High Food Cost % + High CM			Average Food Cost %
Steak	41.7%	245.00	Shrimp	45.5%	480.00	
Stew	40.0%	270.00				35.5%

35.5%

Sleepers Low Food Cost % + Low CM			Primes Low Food Cost % + High CM			Average CM per item
Fish	33.3%	280.00	Chicken	30.0%	350.00	
Lobster	31.3%	275.00	Paella	30.0%	595.00	$279
Soup	33.3%	120.00				
Hot dog	12.5%	52.50				
Hamburger	25.0%	120.00				

$279

$ CM →

Part IV: Management Accounting

Menu Engineering Menu Analysis

	Plow horse High Vol. + Low CM			Star High Vol. + High CM			Average Volume
	Chicken	100	$3.50	Paella	85	$7.00	
	Fish	70	4.00	Shrimp	80	6.00	61.5 Items
	Stew	90	3.00				
	Dog Low Vol. + Low CM			Puzzle Low Vol. + High CM			Average per unit,
	Soup	60	2.00	Steak	35	7.00	per item CM
	Hot dog	30	1.75	Lobster	25	11.00	
	Hamburger	40	3.00				$4.53

Volume ↑ 61.5

Per-unit per-item $ CM → $4.5

Part B—Comparison of Cost/Margin and Menu-Engineering Methods Results

Comparison of Menu Engineering and Cost/Margin Methods by Total Contribution Margin

		Eliminate		Include Both		Include Only	
		Dogs	Sleepers	Stars and Puzzles	Primes and Standards	Stars	Primes
		Menu Engineering CM	Cost/ Margin Analysis CM	Menu Engineering CM	Cost/ Margin Analysis CM	Menu Engineering CM	Cost/ Margin Analysis CM
1	Chicken	$350	$350		$350		$350
2	Fish	280					
3	Paella	595	595	$595	595	$595	595
4	Steak	245	245	245			
5	Lobster	275		275			
6	Stew	270	270				
7	Shrimp	480	480	480	480	480	
8	Soup						
9	Hot dog						
10	Hamburger						
	Total Contribution Margin	$2,495	$1,940	$1,595	$1,425	$1,075	$945

Chapter 16: Maximizing Profit and Minimizing Costs

Comparison of Menu Engineering and Cost/Margin Methods by Food Cost Percentage

		Eliminate		Include Both		Include Only	
		Dogs	Sleepers	Stars and Puzzles	Primes and Standards	Stars	Primes
		Menu Engineering Food cost	Cost/ Margin Analysis Food Cost	Menu Engineering Food cost	Cost/ Margin Analysis Food Cost	Menu Engineering Food cost	Cost/ Margin Analysis Food Cost
1	Chicken	$150	$150		$150		$150
2	Fish	140					
3	Paella	255	255	255	255	255	255
4	Steak	175	175	175			
5	Lobster	125		125			
6	Stew	180	180				
7	Shrimp	400	400	400	400	400	
8	Soup						
9	Hot dog						
10	Hamburger						
	Total Food Cost	$1,425	$1,160	$955	$805	$655	$405
	Total Sales	$3,920	$3,100	$2,550	$2,230	$1,730	$1,350
	Food Cost %	36.4%	37.4%	37.5%	36.1%	37.9%	30.0%

The above comparison of the two methods reveals that the menu with the lowest cost percentage does not always generate the highest total dollar contribution margin. The menu-engineering method selects items with a higher cost percent for its two top categories. But because it also takes volume into account, these items generate a higher total dollar contribution margin, sounding a warning against selecting menu items based only on a low cost percent.

Elasticity of Demand

Management must always consider the impact of price, not only on volume, but also on gross profit, or if the variable element of semi-variable costs are being tracked, on contribution margin. A lower price will increase units sold, but it also decreases per-unit gross profit and contribution margin.

Elasticity of demand measures the reaction of units sold (volume) to changes in unit price and is calculated as follows:

$$\% \text{ Change in volume} = \frac{\text{Change in volume}}{1/2 \text{ (Original volume + New volume)}} = x\%$$

$$\frac{}{} = z\%$$

$$\% \text{ Change in price} = \frac{\text{Change in price}}{1/2 \text{ (Original price + New price)}} = y\%$$

Percent change is calculated differently for elasticity of demand because the demand curve is a hyperbola. The divisor is not the original value; rather, it is the average of the original value and the new value.

Exhibit 16-4 presents the following hypothetical situations for elastic, inelastic, and negatively elastic demand:

Elastic demand:
1. A lower per-unit price results in an increase in units sold, an increase in total dollar sales, but a decrease in gross profit.
2. A lower per-unit price results in an increase in units sold, an increase in total dollar sales, and an increase in gross profit.
3. A higher per-unit price results in a decrease in units sold, a decrease in total dollar sales, and a decrease in gross profit.

Note: When demand is elastic, the dollar sales will always increase when unit price is reduced, but the gross profit or contribution margin will not always increase. This is because a price reduction reduces the per-unit gross profit or per-unit contribution margin and the increase in covers sold generated by the lower price, although always sufficient to increase total dollar sales, may not be sufficient to compensate for the lower per-unit gross profit or per-unit contribution margin.

Inelastic demand:
4. A lower per-unit price results in an increase in units sold but a decrease in total dollar sales and a decrease in gross profit.
5. A higher per-unit price results in a decrease in units sold but an increase in total dollar sales and an increase in gross profit.

Negatively elastic demand:
6. A higher per-unit price results in an increase in units sold, an increase in total dollar sales, and an increase in gross profit.
7. A lower per-unit price results in a decrease in units sold, a decrease in total dollar sales, and a decrease in gross profit.

Exhibit 16-4: Hypothetical Situations for Elastic, Inelastic, and Negatively Elastic Demand

	Before price reduction	Elastic Demand			Inelastic Demand			Negatively Elastic Demand	
		1. Decrease price / Increase units sold / Increase dollar sales / Decrease gross profit	2. Decrease price / Increase units sold / Increase dollar sales / Increase gross profit	3. Increase price / Decrease units sold / Decrease dollar sales / Decrease gross profit	4. Decrease price / Increase units sold / Decrease dollar sales / Decrease gross profit	5. Increase price / Decrease units sold / Increase dollar sales / Increase gross profit	6. Decrease price / Decrease units sold / Decrease dollar sales / Decrease gross profit	7. Increase price / Increase units sold / Increase dollar sales / Increase gross profit
Sales	$500,000	$505,875	$522,500	$446,250	$484,500	$509,250	$451,250	$559,125
Cost of sales	$200,000	$213,000	$220,000	$170,000	$204,000	$194,000	$190,000	$213,000
Gross profit	$300,000	$292,875	$302,500	$276,250	$280,500	$315,250	$261,250	$346,125
Unit price	$5.00	$4.75	$4.75	$5.25	$4.75	$5.25	$4.75	$5.25
Unit cost	$2.00	$2.00	$2.00	$2.00	$2.00	$2.00	$2.00	$2.00
Units sold	100,000	106,500	110,000	85,000	102,000	97,000	95,000	106,500

In the above exhibit, for income statement 2, dollar sales have increased after the price reduction from $5.00 to $4.75, units sold have increased to 106,500, and total dollar sales have increased to $505,875, but the gross profit has decreased from $300,000 to $292,875.

Quick Determination Method. From the above exhibit it is evident that one can arrive at a quick determination method of distinguishing between elastic and inelastic demand. Demand is elastic if the unit price and the total dollar sales (not the units sold) move in opposite directions (if price decreases, dollar sales increase, and if price increases, dollar sales decrease). However, total dollar sales increases will not always result in an increase in gross profit under elastic demand conditions, as demonstrated in income statement 1 of the above exhibit. Under the quick determination method, inelastic demand is detected when the unit price and total dollar sales change in the same direction (e.g., if the unit price increases, total dollar sales increase). When inelastic market conditions exist for a product or service, increases in sales will always generate an increase in total dollar gross profit because increasing the unit price also increases its per-unit gross profit.

Snob Demand. Negatively elastic demand might also be called "snob elasticity" because when the price of a product or service is increased there is more demand for the product or service, and, contrary to what occurs under both elastic and inelastic market conditions, the number of units sold increases. High-end restaurants, hotels, and resorts should be aware that a high price may sometimes attract wealthy customers, who believe they are buying the best. In these circumstances, competing with another luxury hospitality establishment by lowering prices, rather than on the basis of amenities and service, may have a negative result.

Ratio Analysis

Operating ratios can be used to identify trends in sales as a complement to standard ratio analysis. Early identification of a negative trend provides the opportunity for timely corrective action. Food-related operating ratios include:

For stand-alone restaurants and in hotels

$$\text{Average cover} = \frac{\text{Food sales}}{\text{Number of customers}}$$

$$\text{Sales per seat} = \frac{\text{Food sales}}{\text{Number of seats}}$$

For restaurants in hotels

$$\text{Food sales to room sales ratio} = \frac{\text{Food sales}}{\text{Room sales}}$$

Chapter 16: Maximizing Profit and Minimizing Costs

$$\text{Food sales per occupied room} = \frac{\text{Food sales}}{\text{Occupied rooms}}$$

Other food-related ratios are included in Chapter 14, "Management Analysis of Operations."

Procurement

The next step in the process of profit maximization involves minimizing food costs in the purchasing stage. From this perspective, a purchasing department or the individual responsible for purchasing should possess the following knowledge and skills:

- Know the lowest-cost suppliers in ranking order.
- Know the suppliers who deliver requested product quality most reliably.
- Know the suppliers who deliver on time.
- Be able to determine the best trade-off among the above qualities when one supplier does not offer all of them.
- Be sufficiently familiar with the food industry to have a general awareness of cost trends.
- Be familiar with kitchen terminology and processes, such as recipe costing, and know the difference between terms such as "as purchased," "edible portion," the product remaining after removing trimmings and before cooking; and "as served" (AS), the weight of the food that is actually served to the customer after cooking. These terms can play an important role in the purchasing process, especially when using the Levinson method (explained below) for determining order quantities.
- Know the number and type of products on hand.
- Know the amount of available storage space and the cost per square foot and cubic foot of space.
- Know the amounts of cash available for purchasing currently and at different periods in the future.
- Be familiar with historical and forecast customer counts and product popularity index on a seasonal basis, if applicable.
- Have the ability to establish a close yet licit relationship with suppliers and elicit favorable treatment from them in terms of price, quality, or delivery times.
- Have the ability to relate well to, and maintain close cooperative contact with, the receiving department.
- Possess an honest and ethical character.

All of the above are important cost-minimizing tools. Ranking suppliers according to cost, optimum quality, and timeliness of deliveries saves costs in several ways. Purchasing products from a low-cost supplier minimizes purchase price; and buying from the optimum-quality provider enables a restaurant to maximize its resale value and also maximizes food freshness, taste, and yields. Knowledge of food industry cost trends enables a buyer to purchase products in advance when costs are expected to rise. In order to do this, the purchaser must know (1) the quantity of product currently available, (2) the amount of available storage space, (3) the amount of available cash to make unusually large purchases, and (4) the projected demand for these products. This same type of analytical process is required when determining whether to accept one-time promotional-price-quantity purchase offers from suppliers.

The purchaser should also know the restaurant's cash availability to be able to appraise the feasibility of benefiting from cash discounts on cash on delivery (C.O.D.) purchases. If sufficiently large quantities are involved, the purchaser should be able to make an evaluation comparing carrying charges as calculated for determining the economic order quantity (EOQ) with the opportunity cost of not making the purchase. When warranted by the value of the purchases, EOQ calculations should also be made to determine the minimum and maximum quantities to have on hand per item (minimum and maximum par stock), as well as the optimum order size. Excessive amounts in inventory make it more susceptible to pilferage and theft and increase the potential for spoilage.

Knowledge of costing techniques used in the kitchen enables the purchaser to communicate readily with kitchen staff and serve as a knowledgeable reviewer of purchase requisitions received. The purchasing department should be familiar with the shelf life of perishable items as opposed to nonperishable items (such as canned goods), also called "value-added" products. The purchaser should know that "as purchased" means the restaurant is paying for all the wasted trimmings that have to be removed to arrive at the edible portion.

Running out of a product is a sales-limiting event that can be avoided by properly gauging inventory requires many of the above listed skills and knowledge. Purchasing too much inventory without a justifiable decrease in purchase cost can lead to unwarranted excessive investment in inventory and its related interest expense, increased storage costs, and loss of capacity to invest in revenue-generating property and equipment. Every dollar invested in working capital is one less dollar that is available to invest in property and equipment that is expected to generate a rate of return (ROR) before fixed charges of 40% or more.

In addition to serving as a repository for these types of information and skills, a purchasing department for multi-restaurant hospitality companies, when a commissary exists, can take advantage of price points by buying in volume for all of its restaurants that use common ingredients. Additional negotiating power provided by volume purchases is usually significant when used judiciously. Small restaurant companies should consider the possibility of joining with other restaurants to form cooperative buying pools to increase their negotiating power.

Honesty is important in all aspects of a business but it is of special importance in the purchasing stage because of the unique temptations to which purchasing department personnel may be exposed (e.g., kickbacks or gifts from suppliers). In addition, the purchaser must be aware that suppliers may attempt to circumvent a purchaser by selling directly to the chef or other kitchen personnel who may have accepted some kind of incentive from the supplier. However, a close but licit personal relationship with suppliers will often enable a purchasing agent to obtain better price, payment, or delivery terms from suppliers, all of which translate into greater profits for the restaurant.

The purchasing agent must know whether suppliers are living up to their commitments. Because the receiving department evaluates the quality of food received, as well as the timeliness of deliveries, it is important for the purchasing agent or department to maintain close ties with the receiving department.

The purchasing department, in conjunction with restaurant management and the chef, must decide when and what food to buy in a semi-processed (value-added) state. Value-added foods, such as portion-packed foods, cost more but, because they are partially processed, save costs in the kitchen and in storage because (1) less labor cost is involved in the final preparation of the food; (2) the trimmings have already been removed so only the edible portion is being purchased; (3) less storage space is required because of reduced size and because no equipment is needed for the initial processing; and (4) no investment in initial processing equipment (e.g., grinders) is required. Portion-packed foods also assure that each customer will receive the same size and quality every time. However, if the restaurant can process trimmings into saleable products, perhaps buying nonprocessed foods is most cost-effective. Food processed entirely in-house is fresher, tends to retain its taste better, and may be one of the restaurant's competitive factors.

Determining Optimum Order Size

Two ways to determine the optimum order size are (1) the par stock method and (2) the Levinson method. The par stock method is used when ordering discrete, fungible products. The Levinson method is best applied to bulk orders of products that are to be divided and portioned in the restaurant.

Par Stock Method. The par stock method of determining order size involves four steps: (1) determining the expected customer count, (2) calculating the popularity index of the menu items for which the product is an ingredient, (3) calculating the amount needed, and (4) calculating the quantity to order. This is presented in Exhibit 16-5 below.

Exhibit 16-5: Calculation of Number of Items to Order—Par Stock Method

Assumptions:
1. Last period there were 4,000 customers.
2. This period a 3% increase in customer count is expected.
3. Last period 2,400 customers ordered steak.
4. Number of steaks on hand is 1,000.

Step 1—Calculate expected number of customers.

Last period customer count:		1+ Expected 3% increase:		Expected customer count:
4,000	×	1.03	=	4,120

Part IV: Management Accounting

Step 2—Calculate popularity index of steak.

		Popularity index
Number of customers who ordered steak:	2,400	= 60%
Last period customer count:	4,000	

Step 3—Calculate number of steaks needed.

Popularity index:	×	Expected customer count:	=	Number of steaks needed:
60%		4,120		2,472

Step 4—Calculate number of items to order.

Par stock:	+	Number of steaks needed after order arrives:	−	Estimated number of steaks on hand:	=	Number of steaks to order:
500		2,472		1,000		1,972

Levinson Method. The Levinson method would be used if instead of buying discrete portion-controlled steaks or any other food item totally unprocessed and in bulk form, the restaurant bought the entire cut of beef from which the steaks are to be portioned. Exhibit 16-6 shows how this seven-step method is applied.

Exhibit 16-6: Calculation of Number of Items to Order—Levinson Method

Assumptions:

1. Last period there were 4,000 customers.
2. This period a 3% increase in customer count is expected.
3. Last period 2,400 customers ordered steak.
4. Number of steaks on hand is 1,000.
5. Pounds per individual steak = .5 pounds per serving.

Step 1—Calculate expected number of customers.

Last period customer count:	×	1+ Expected 3% increase:	=	Expected customer count:
4,000		1.03		4,120

Step 2—Calculate popularity index of steak.

		Popularity index
Number of customers who ordered steak:	2,400	= 60%
Last period customer count:	4,000	

Step 3—Calculate number of steaks needed.

Popularity index:	×	Expected customer count:	=	Number of steaks needed:
60%		4,120		2,472

Step 4—Calculate number of items to order.

Par stock		Number of steaks needed after order arrives		Estimated number of steaks on hand		Number of steaks to order
500	+	2,472	−	1,000	=	1,972

Step 5—Calculate the portion factor.
(number of servings per raw pound)

Raw pounds:		Amount per serving:		Portion factor (PF):
1	÷	0.5	=	2

Step 6—Calculate edible product (EP) portion divider (PD)

PF		Ingredient's edible yield percentage		PD
2	×	75.0%	=	1.5

Step 7—Determine Order Size in Pounds.

Number of steaks to order:		PD:		Pounds to order:
1,972	÷	1.5	=	1,315

Economic Order Quantity. It is important for a food commissary, a buying cooperative, or a large restaurant to have an optimum quantity of inventory on hand. Thus, determining an optimum quantity focuses on having sufficient products at all times, which is important for maximizing sales. However, from a cost viewpoint, the optimum inventory amount is that quantity that minimizes the trade-off between carrying expenses and ordering costs.

As mentioned previously, when considering a larger than usual purchase motivated by a one-time promotional discount, the carrying costs should be compared to the lost opportunity cost of not making the purchase. In a normal EOQ calculation, however, carrying costs are not compared to the lost opportunity cost; rather, they are compared to the normal costs of making repetitive orders. A sample normal EOQ calculation is shown in Exhibit 16-7.

Exhibit 16-7: EOQ Calculation

Assumptions:
1. 10,000 pounds of steak are consumed annually.
2. Cost per pound is $3.00.
3. Storage cost per pound is $0.50.
4. Interest rate paid on borrowed funds is 8%.
5. Traditionally, pilferage and spoilage of inventories amounts to 1% of their cost.
6. Clerical cost of placing an order is $5.00 per order.
7. The supplier ordering charge per order is $3.00.

The EOQ equation is:

$$\sqrt{\frac{2 \times \text{Ordering cost per order} \times \text{Annual item consumption}}{\text{Annual carrying costs per item}}} = \text{EOQ in units}$$

Ordering costs per order, per item:

Clerical costs	=	$5.00
Supplier ordering charge per order	=	$3.00
Total costs per order	=	$8.00

Carrying costs per year, per item:

Storage

Storage cost per pound		$0.10	
Pounds consumed annually	×	10,000	
			= $1,000

Pilferage and spoilage

Pounds consumed annually		10,000	
Cost per pound	×	$3.00	
Total cost of item purchased annually		$30,000	
Pilferage and spoilage percent	×	1.00%	
Total pilferage and spoilage cost			= $300

Interest expense

Total cost of item purchased annually		$30,000	
Interest rate on borrowed funds	×	8.00%	
Total annual interest expense			= $2,400
Total annual carrying charges			$3,700

$$\sqrt{\frac{2 \times \$8.00 \times 10,000}{\$3,700}} = 7 \text{ Units}$$

Clerical costs might include:

Salary of purchasing clerk

Cost of stationery related to purchase order

Cost of dedicated phone line for purchasing clerk

Salary of receiving clerk

Cost of stationery related to receiving

Cost of accounting department time spent processing each order

---

The EOQ calculation is usually only warranted for those items that are purchased in large quantities and have a high value and for frequently ordered items that can be effectively stored. Based on the EOQ calculation, each product's minimum par can be established more cost-effectively.

Ideal Inventory Quantity and Supply Chain Information Technology. The ideal inventory amount from a cost viewpoint is zero. The ideal supplier would deliver food only as needed and grant extended credit terms. The restaurant would take this inventory, cook it immediately, sell it for cash, and use the money to operate the business or invest in more revenue-generating or cost-reducing property and equipment before paying the supplier.

This is an unrealistic scenario, yet an approximation of it can be achieved by using supply chain information technology systems, which allow suppliers to have computer access to a restaurant's or a commissary's inventory modules. Suppliers of choice for each item can view, on a current basis, the restaurant's inventory items as they approach par minimums and can schedule deliveries to meet the restaurant's needs several times per day, daily, weekly, or monthly, as appropriate. Therefore, the restaurant can establish very low minimum par amounts because it can rely on its suppliers for just-in-time (JIT) delivery. JIT delivery is an efficient inventory system created by the Japanese that is widely used in all types of businesses that carry inventory. Essentially, the restaurant's inventory management is outsourced to its suppliers.

Various Approaches to Purchasing. There are various approaches to purchasing. Restaurants of different sizes and types are able to minimize costs by using different purchasing approaches. These approaches are listed here, along with suggestions for their application:

No-bid	This method selects a prime supplier for each menu item and buys from that supplier consistently. It is best suited for small restaurants where the time spent seeking the lowest prices would detract from the owner/operator's time better spent performing other tasks. It is, therefore, more efficient for such restaurants to maximize contribution margin by maximizing sales rather than by minimizing food costs.
Standing order	This method is a variation of the no-bid method. Rather than prepare individual orders for every purchase, a standing (repetitive) order is placed with prime suppliers.
Single supplier	For this method, a restaurant attempts to buy as many different food items as possible from one single supplier. The goal is to simplify the purchasing process while building up volume with the supplier to strengthen the restaurant's price-negotiating stance.
Cash and carry shopping	This method involves buying from individual farmers, farmers' markets, or food warehouses and is a waste of time. The quality of products may be superior, as well as fresher than those products purchased otherwise.

Stockless purchasing	In this case, inventory costs are reduced because the supplier stores the purchased inventory for the restaurant. Some restaurants may simply not have the storage space available, nor the environmental conditions required for storing food.
Contract buying	In this method, a written list of specifications is prepared, a purveyor bid sheet specifying quantities and length of time of the contract. This is sent to a group of pre-qualified suppliers, who then send their bid specifying cost, the quantities they can supply, as well as the length of time for which they are willing to contract.
Competitive bidding	The restaurant prepares a purveyor bid sheet and sends it to a pre-qualified list of suppliers who bid on it.

Purchase Requisition and Purchase Order. Another two stages of the purchasing process where costs can get out of control involve purchase requisitions and purchase orders. It is important to minimize the purchase of nonsellable inventory by authorizing the purchasing agent or department to buy only those items that are requested by the consuming departments through purchase requisitions. This also preempts purchases that might be solicited by suppliers from purchasing agents whom they have compromised with gifts.

The purchase order is important because it is a formal record of all the conditions specified by the restaurant when making a purchase. This record will later be used by the receiving department and accounting department to verify that all supplier commitments have been met. Therefore, in addition to buyer and seller identification, a purchase order should contain at least the following specifications. They should:

- Be dated to determine length of delivery delay.
- Be pre-numbered to impede their use for illicit purposes.
- Be given a required delivery date.
- Specify:
    — Quantity
    — Quality
    — Unit price
    — Number of units ordered
    — Total price
    — Sales tax, if applicable
    — Shipping charge, if applicable

Receiving

A purchase order allows the receiving department to verify that a delivery has in fact been ordered, and that it is of the same quality and quantity that was ordered. This is a crucial step in the purchase-to-consumption cycle, and the person in charge of receiving should be thoroughly trustworthy, in addition to being well supervised. Because food cost is such a large component (30% to 40% of sales), slight differences in weight over the long term can easily add up to a 1%

increase in cost of sales and the resulting reduction of net income. If net income is 10% of sales, an increase in cost of sales equivalent to 1% of sales constitutes a 6.6% after-tax reduction in net income for a company in the 34% income tax bracket.

Storage

The storage time is another period of vulnerability where losses of 1% or more can enter the purchase-to-consumption cycle. Inventory losses can result not only from theft, but also from spoilage due to poor storage conditions. Certain foods may be sensitive to temperature and humidity and should be stored appropriately. Of the two major inventory control methods, the periodic and the perpetual, the perpetual method of inventory control offers far more security.

Periodic Inventory Control. Periodic inventory control involves giving trusted personnel free access to the storeroom. However, if free access to inventory is given to more than one person, excess inventory consumption cannot be traced back to any one individual. Of course, there are circumstances in which the complexity of perpetual inventory controls is inappropriate, such as in a simple kitchen pantry or a quick-serve restaurant. Because consumption can only be determined by a physical count when using the periodic inventory system, it is important to maintain small inventories and frequently survey the physical count so that consumption can be tracked over short periods of time before losses can increase. Ultimately, protection against pilferage or waste that might occur under these circumstances must be provided by verification processes implemented in the consumption stage, which is discussed below.

Perpetual Inventory Control. Under perpetual inventory control, a storeroom keeper is responsible for the physical integrity of the inventory. All issues from the storeroom must be based on issues requisitions from the using departments. Thus, when a physical count is made, the total inventory plus the issues requisitions must equal the cost of the beginning inventory plus purchases. Daily receiving reports and issues reports are sent to the accounting department which enable the department to maintain a correct balance in the inventory account at all times. Under this system inventory is tracked from the time it enters the restaurant to when it is consumed. Perpetual inventory cards are maintained, often by both the storeroom keeper and the accounting department. These cards enable inventory counts to be made on a continuous basis, rather than only when financial statements are prepared. Exhibit 16-8 demonstrates a sample perpetual inventory card. Because there is a check figure for each inventory item, a few items can be counted on a daily or weekly basis and compared to their respective perpetual inventory cards. This not only provides greater control; it also reduces labor costs because items can be counted when employees are less busy. Another advantage of a perpetual inventory is that, because of the continuous monitoring of inventory quantities, par minimums can be established and used as re-order points, and EOQs can be established and used. Exhibit 16-9 contains a sample flow chart for a perpetual inventory system.

Exhibit 16-8: Perpetual Inventory Card

Description:				Minimum Quantity									
				Order Quantity									
				Par Stock									
	Purchases			Issues			Balance			Issued to:		
Date	Quantity	Unit cost	Total cost	Quantity	Unit cost	Total cost	Units	Total value	Issuer	Department	Recipient

Chapter 16: Maximizing Profit and Minimizing Costs   16,029

Exhibit 16-9: Flow Chart for a Perpetual Inventory System

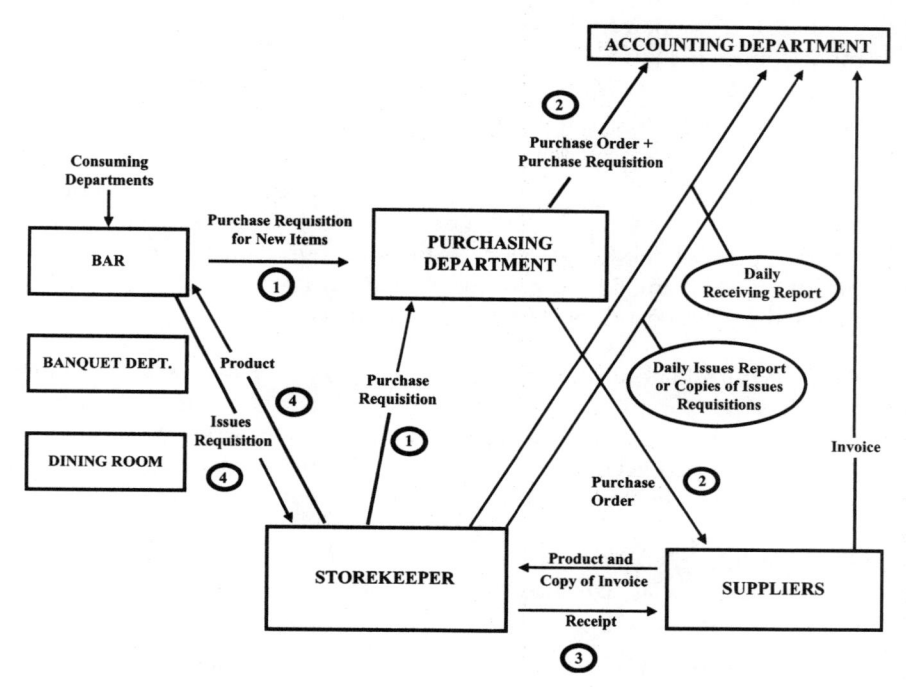

```
                                        ACCOUNTING DEPARTMENT
                                          ↑         ↑         ↑
                                         ②                    
                                   Purchase Order +
                                   Purchase Requisition
  Consuming
  Departments
      ↓         Purchase Requisition
                 for New Items        PURCHASING
    BAR    ─────────────────────▶    DEPARTMENT         Daily
                     ①                                  Receiving Report
              ↑
  BANQUET DEPT.     Product                      Daily Issues Report
                               Purchase           or Copies of Issues
                 ④            Requisition             Requisitions
              Issues
              Requisition           ①                            Invoice
  DINING ROOM    ④                              Purchase    ②
                 ↓                              Order
                                 Product and
              STOREKEEPER  ◀──  Copy of Invoice     SUPPLIERS
                           ──▶    Receipt
                                    ③
```

ADDITIONAL INFORMATION:

(A) Purchase Requisitions

   (1) Originate with the department where they will be consumed when a new product is involved,

                                    OR

   (2) Originate with the storekeeper when restocking a previously ordered product.

(B) The following forms represent a minimum needed to preserve the integrity of the inventory by leaving a paper trail each time an inventory item is transferred. Also shown is the flow of each form between departments.

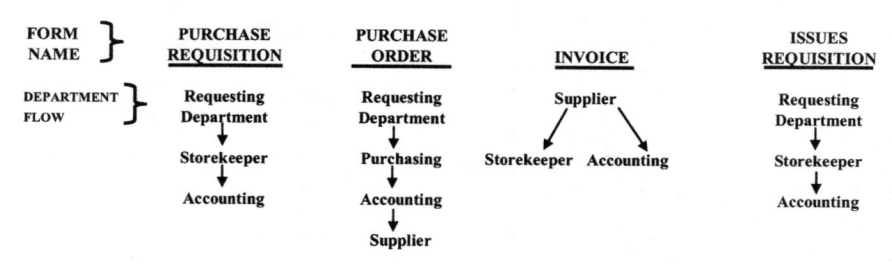

FORM NAME	PURCHASE REQUISITION	PURCHASE ORDER	INVOICE	ISSUES REQUISITION
DEPARTMENT FLOW	Requesting Department ↓ Storekeeper ↓ Accounting	Requesting Department ↓ Purchasing ↓ Accounting ↓ Supplier	Supplier ↙ ↘ Storekeeper Accounting	Requesting Department ↓ Storekeeper ↓ Accounting

Consumption

In the consumption stage of the restaurant operating cycle, losses may occur for many reasons. It is one of the most vulnerable stages of a restaurant operation. The most common losses are improper trimming of food, improper cooking, improper storage in the kitchen area, and pilferage. Two control measures that can be applied at this stage are portion control and standard ratios.

Portion Control. Controlling the size of served portions is an important cost control tool, especially with the more expensive menu items, such as meat and fish. Portion-packed foods are more expensive but, unless there is an expert trimmer in a restaurant, or the restaurant is able to prepare dishes based on the trimmings, the extra cost of portion-packed foods is cost-effective.

Portion control should not be limited only to expensive items. The margins in quick-serve restaurants and other hospitality businesses are so slim that even items as inexpensive as mashed potatoes should be portion-controlled. When U.S. Airways stopped giving out free pretzels, its executives stated that it would save the airline about $1 million per year. In the days when martinis were still served free on flights, the reduction from two olives to one olive per martini saved the airline $300,000 per year. This applies to beverages as well. For instance, in bars, special-size shot glasses should be mandatory.

Standard Ratios and Variance Analysis. Standard ratios are also used to control consumption. Comparing actual cost and price averages to standard costs and prices enables management to identify excessive costs and undercharging. Four ratios that can be used for this purpose are:

$$\text{Standard Cost Percent} = \frac{\text{Standard Cost}}{\text{Standard Price}}$$

$$\text{Actual Cost Percent} = \frac{\text{Actual Cost}}{\text{Actual Price}}$$

$$\text{Actual/Standard Cost Percent} = \frac{\text{Actual Cost}}{\text{Standard Cost}}$$

$$\text{Actual/Standard Price Percent} = \frac{\text{Actual Price}}{\text{Standard Price}}$$

The standard cost is the ideal cost that is obtained by calculating the desired cost of one or several recipes. The actual cost is what it costs to serve the related menu. Based on per-item sales statistics, the standard cost as well as the actual cost can be calculated by computers, and many restaurant management programs perform these calculations. The standard price is based on menu prices.

Chapter 16: Maximizing Profit and Minimizing Costs   16,031

Exhibit 16-10 presents two possible actual cost/standard cost and actual price/standard price scenarios. A discussion follows regarding their possible implications. The calculations are based on the following income statements:

Exhibit 16-10: Two Actual Cost/Standard Cost and Actual Price/Standard Price Scenarios

	October Actual	November Actual	October Standard
Sales	53,950	52,000	54,000
Cost of Sales	21,500	18,900	20,300
Gross Profit	32,450	33,100	33,700
Covers Sold	12,600	11,950	12,600
Per unit prices	$4.28	$4.35	$4.29
Per unit costs	$1.71	$1.58	$1.61

October

$$\text{Standard Cost Percent} = \frac{\$1.61}{\$4.29} = 37.59\%$$

$$\text{Actual Cost Percent} = \frac{\$1.71}{\$4.28} = 39.85\%$$

$$\text{Actual/Standard Cost Percent} = \frac{\$1.71}{\$1.61} = 105.91\%$$

$$\text{Actual/Standard Price Percent} = \frac{\$4.28}{\$4.29} = 99.91\%$$

November

$$\text{Standard Cost Percent} = \frac{\$1.61}{\$4.29} = 37.59\%$$

$$\text{Actual Cost Percent} = \frac{\$1.58}{\$4.35} = 36.46\%$$

$$\text{Actual/Standard Cost Percent} = \frac{\$1.58}{\$1.61} = 98.36\%$$

$$\text{Actual/Standard Price Percent} = \frac{\$4.35}{\$4.29} = 101.41\%$$

Undercollection and Excessive Costs. In the above exhibit, in October, the actual cost percent exceeds the standard cost percent, indicating that the restaurant either is undercollecting or overconsuming, given the number of covers it is selling and their standard cost. A review of the Actual/Standard Cost ratio and the Actual/Standard Price ratio reveals that both over-consumption and undercollection are occurring. The actual average cost is 5.91% greater than the ideal or standard cost, and the actual average price is .09% less than the ideal or standard price. A list of possible causes follows:

Part IV: Management Accounting

Ratio Calculation Result	Possible Causes
Standard cost higher than actual cost	Use of outdated standard costs Use of outdated recipes Over-portioning Spoilage Excessive trimming Theft Unrecorded employee meals Unrecorded transfers to other restaurants within a hotel Temporary supplier price increases Waiter offers customers menu items without charging them with the hope of obtaining a higher tip
Actual price lower than standard price	Use of outdated standard prices Waiter theft Waiter error Cashier theft Cashier error

Overcharging and Underportioning. It is also possible to overcharge customers due to a waiter error or too small a portion. In Exhibit 16-10, the November column reflects this situation. The actual cost is 1.64% less than standard (100.00% − 98.36%), and the actual price is 1.41% higher than standard (101.41% − 100.00%). Although this is temporarily favorable to the restaurant because it results in greater cash receipts and lower expenditures, over the long term it will hurt the image of the restaurant and lower revenues. Overcharged customers tend not to return, and underportioning lowers perceived value received, which also results in nonrepeat customers.

Collusion. Collusion may also be present among employees in the front and back of the house with employees in the accounting department. That type of broad based collusion can result in an Actual Cost Percent that is equal to, or very close to, the Standard Cost Percent, as shown in Exhibit 16-11.

Exhibit 16-11: Cost Percents Disguise Collusion

	October Actual	October Standard
Sales	53,950	54,000
Cost of sales	21,500	20,300
Gross profit	32,450	33,700
Covers sold	12,600	12,600
Per unit prices	$ 4.37	$ 4.29
Per unit costs	$ 1.64	$ 1.61
Cost percent	37.59%	37.59%

In this case, the errors in the Actual/Standard Cost ratio and in the Actual/Standard Price ratio will tend to closely offset each other, as shown below:

$$\text{Standard Cost Percent} = \frac{\$1.61}{\$4.29} = 37.59\%$$

$$\text{Actual Cost Percent} = \frac{\$1.64}{\$4.37} = 37.59\%$$

$$\text{Actual/Standard Cost Percent} = \frac{\$1.64}{\$1.61} = 102.00\%$$

$$\text{Actual/Standard Price Percent} = \frac{\$4.37}{\$4.29} = 102.00\%$$

Although computers will detect this type of collusion if they calculate the Actual/Standard Cost Percent and the Actual/Standard Price Percent, if these calculations are done manually, there might be a tendency to stop after calculating the Actual Cost Percent because it is within the accepted parameters of the Standard Cost Percent. If this occurs, the collusion will go undetected. If collusion occurs in the front of the house, the Actual/Standard Price Percent will be less than 100% and will be compensated for by underportioning. If the theft is in the back of the house, the Actual/Standard Cost Percent will be greater than 100% and will be compensated for by overcharging customers and leaving the money in the cash register.

Possible Error When Using Total Sales and Total Costs. When calculating these ratios manually, per-unit amounts should be used. If standard total sales and standard total cost of sales for months with different numbers of covers sold are compared, a volume variance will be introduced into the calculation and will distort the results.

Built-in Margin of Error. The acceptable margin of error in actual costs and prices varies for different classes of restaurants. Quick-service restaurants rely on high-volume, low markup items. They can tolerate only very small deviations from standard, somewhere in the area of 0.5% (.5 of 1%). Full-service restaurants, because of their higher markups, can tolerate higher margins of error. In any case, the margin of error can be built into the standard cost and price, in which case any deviation from standards will be unacceptable. In this case, actual price and cost will fluctuate undetected within the tolerable limits. Otherwise, standards can be calculated exactly and the deviations from standards will always be visible.

MAXIMIZING BEVERAGE REVENUE

Beverages include liquor, beer, and wine. Included with liquor are liqueurs, beer (both draft and bottled), and wine (both bottle and by-the-glass sales). Other ingredients associated with beverage costs are onions, olives, juice, dairy items, sugar, and sometimes appetizers. Beverages do not include items such as juice, tea, coffee, or soda served with food.

Beverage Pricing

Food markups oscillate around 250% (corresponding to a 60% gross margin); beverage markups are about 450% (corresponding to a 78% gross margin). Usually liquor and mixed drinks have the lowest cost percentage, in the area of 15% to 20%, and the highest gross margin, 80% to 85%. Liquors sold straight have lower markups than those sold as mixed drinks because of the added labor cost of mixing the drink. Ordinary wines and beers are more likely to be consumed with food. Because of their higher turnover, they have lower markups than liquor. The beer cost percentage is in the 25% to 30% range, and wine cost percentages are approximately 30% to 35%. A restaurant should have some fine name wines, which have the highest markups, and some low-end wines that cost no more than two times the average entrée price.

Bars usually have two brands of liquor: (1) a *call brand* and (2) a *house brand*, also called a *well brand* or a *pouring brand*. The call brand is used when customers specify a specific brand for their straight or mixed drinks. The house brand is less expensive than a call brand and is used when customers do not specify a brand. A computerized point-of-sale system that is pre-programmed with all of the possible drink combinations is essential for maintaining accurate price and cost records.

Creating unique and imaginative mixed drinks allows for higher markups. The opposite approach is to create mixed drinks that can be sold at a modest price but that generate high margins because they cost less to prepare.

The ambience in which beverages are sold affects pricing policy. Thus, exotic locations, luxurious environments, or venues providing entertainment allow for higher markups. Other factors to consider when determining beverage pricing are:

- *Overhead costs*. Factors such as whether the location is a high-rent (such as airports) or low-rent area, liquor license costs, or liability risk due to dram shop laws should be taken into account when setting prices.
- *Type of customers*. A monopolistic location where little or no competition exists allows for higher markups. This is also true of locations where customers are transient, nonrepeat customers. Repeat customers tend to be more cost-conscious, with customers in low-income areas being the most cost-conscious.

Waiters' Suggestion

Waiters can often influence a customer's beverage choice. Care should be taken, especially where dram laws exist, to avoid encouraging excessive drinking. A better approach is to suggest that customers switch from a low-margin drink or brand to one with a higher margin. In dram law states an employee-training program is essential to limit liability and the cost of settling any lawsuits that may arise as a result of an act committed by a customer after leaving the establishment.

Cost/Margin Analysis

Cost/margin analysis can also be used to maximize beverage sales. Assume that Exhibit 16-12 presents the cost percent and total contribution margin, the two components needed to prepare a cost/margin analysis, per brand of a hypothetical restaurant or bar that sells beer.

Exhibit 16-12: Cost/Margin Analysis for Hypothetical Beer Sales

	Number of Units of Each Brand Sold	Per Unit Price	Per Unit Cost	Per-Unit Contribution Margin (CM)	Per-Brand Total Actual Sales	Per-Brand Total Actual Cost	Per-Brand Total Actual CM	Cost % per Brand	
Corona	50	$4.00	$0.90	$3.10	$200.00	$45.00	$155.00	22.50%	Prime
Miller	20	$3.25	$0.65	$2.60	$65.00	$13.00	$52.00	20.00%	Sleeper
Heinecken	12	$3.50	$0.95	$2.55	$42.00	$11.40	$30.60	27.14%	Problem
Budweiser	80	$2.75	$0.70	$2.05	$220.00	$56.00	$164.00	25.45%	Standard
Totals	162			$10.30	$527.00	$125.40	$401.60	95.10%	
Averages	40.5			$2.58	$131.75	$31.35	$100.40	23.77%	

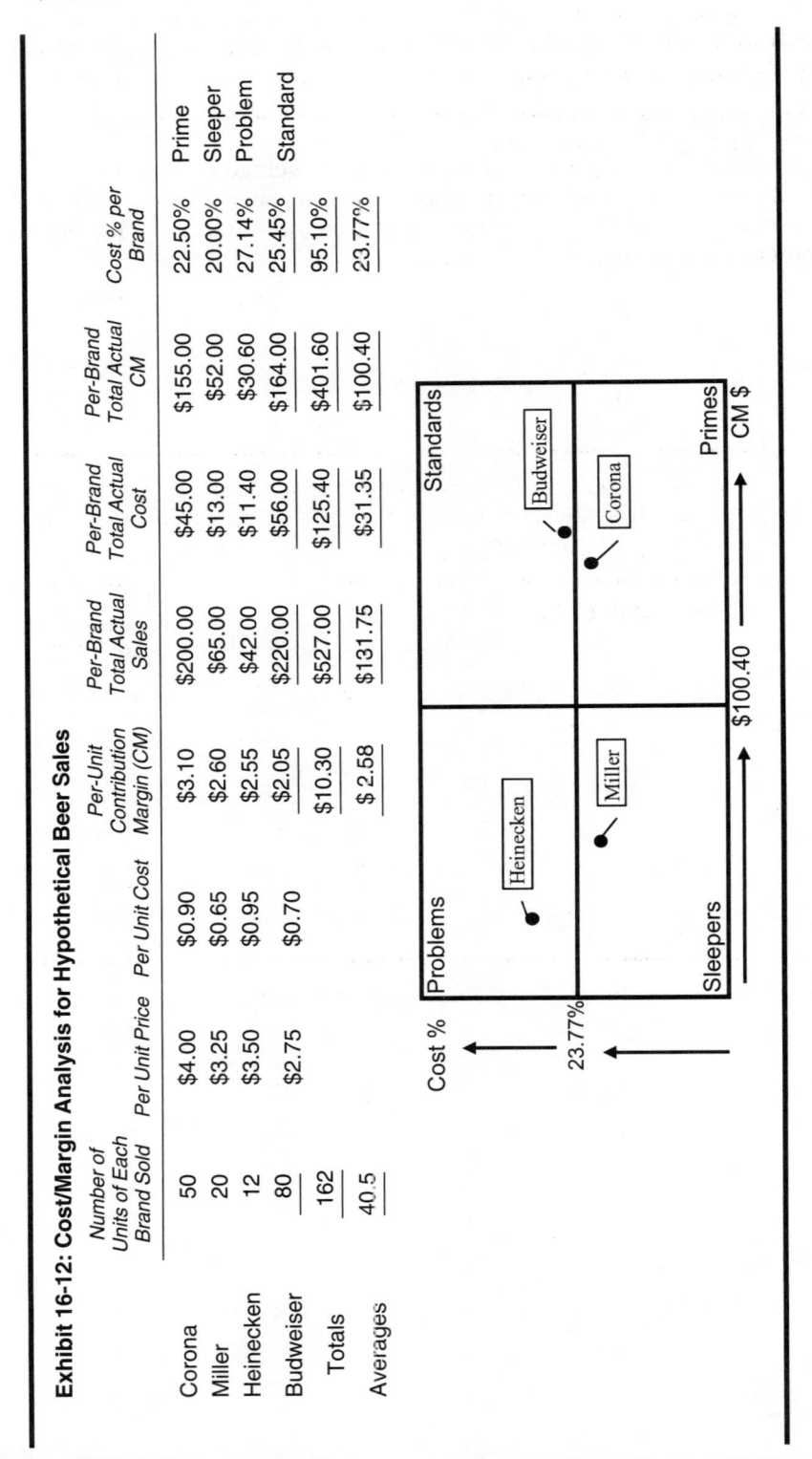

This simplified example illustrates the four types of sales categories and also indicates that Budweiser is close to being a prime instead of a standard. Other methods of analyzing sales are presented in Exhibits 16-13, 16-14, and 16-15.

Exhibit 16-13: Popularity Indicators

	Number of Units of Each Brand Sold	Average Units Sold	Units Sold More or Less Than Average	Percent of Total Units Sold
Corona	50	40.5	9.5	30.86%
Miller	20	40.5	−20.5	12.35%
Heinecken	12	40.5	−28.5	7.41%
Budweiser	80	40.5	39.5	49.38%
	162			100.00%

The popularity indicators show that Budweiser is by far the most popular beer. Thus, the decision to increase its price slightly may bring it into the prime category without affecting its popularity.

Exhibit 16-14: Per-Unit Price-Cost-Profit Analysis

	Per-Unit Price	Per-Unit Cost	Per-Unit Contribution Margin (CM)
Corona	$ 4.00	$0.90	3.10
Miller	$ 3.25	$0.65	2.60
Heinecken	$ 3.50	$0.95	2.55
Budweiser	$ 2.75	$0.70	2.05
Totals	$13.50	$3.20	10.30
Averages	$ 3.38	$0.80	$2.58

A per-unit analysis indicates that in fact Budweiser is the beer with the lowest contribution margin and supports a decision to attempt to increase its price.

Exhibit 16-15: Total Sales-Cost-Contribution Margin Analysis

	Number of Units of Each Brand Sold	Per Brand Total Actual Sales	Per Brand Total Actual Cost	Per Brand Total Actual CM	Percentage of Total Units Sold per Brand	Brand Sales Percentage to Total Sales	Brand Cost Percentage to Total Cost	Brand CM Percentage to Total CM
Corona	50	$200.00	$45.00	$155.00	30.86%	37.95%	35.89%	38.60%
Miller	20	$65.00	$13.00	$52.00	12.35%	12.33%	10.37%	12.95%
Heinecken	12	$42.00	$11.40	$30.60	7.41%	7.97%	9.09%	7.62%
Budweiser	80	$220.00	$56.00	$164.00	49.38%	41.75%	44.66%	40.84%
	162	$527.00	$125.40	$401.60	100.00%	100.00%	100.00%	100.00%

An analysis of the percentage rankings of units sold per brand to similar rankings for total dollar sales, total cost, and total contribution margin per brand might indicate that the Corona brand constitutes only 30.86% of units sold, yet it generates almost as much total contribution margin as the most popular beer, Budweiser. Perhaps demand for Corona beer is sufficiently inelastic that its price can be raised slightly as well without causing an equal percentage decrease in units sold.

The answer to these types of questions lies in experimenting with the prices of these beers. But preparing analyses such as those presented here enable a manager to better quantify and evaluate the possible results of future pricing experiments.

MINIMIZING BEVERAGE COSTS

Beverage costs are controlled in the same manner as food costs and also require exercising control over an extended process that includes purchasing, storage, and consumption.

Purchasing

Beverage purchasing involves setting goals, which should achieve the appropriate quality of beverages purchased at the minimum cost and that are sufficient to maintain the minimum quantity per stock desired for each beverage. The appropriate quality depends on the type of establishment, customer, and location. Minimizing purchase costs varies from state to state, as some states are control states while others are license states. In control states, the state is the only seller, and the price is the same for all buyers. Nevertheless, states may offer promotional prices that can provide an opportunity to lower costs but will require large quantity purchases if the lower price is to have a significant impact on cost of sales. Sometimes only one distributor will carry a brand, thereby eliminating the opportunity for competitive shopping. In such cases, discounts will usually depend on the quantity purchased. Thus, volume purchasing seems to be the best way to reduce beverage purchase costs. Given this situation, the EOQ calculation, explained before, is particularly appropriate. This calculation also determines the optimum minimum quantity (par stock) to have in inventory, taking into account promotional price, ordering cost, storage cost, and other carrying costs, such as interest cost of funds invested in inventory. To use the EOQ calculation, it is necessary to establish a perpetual inventory system, so that daily balances can be monitored. A perpetual inventory card for each item such as the one presented in Exhibit 16-8 facilitates the daily control of balances as well as helping to establish an audit trail for the items issued, the trend in unit costs, and the total value of each item on hand.

Storage

There are two types of inventory control methods for beverages: periodic and perpetual. Because of beverages' high value, it is much more important to make an inventory count of a bar than a food pantry, both of which are maintained under periodic inventory control because of the need for fast access. In addition to accessibility, it is necessary to consider the susceptibility to theft and content spoilage in the storage facility. Because of the higher value of beverages, it is important to establish some type of perpetual control or, if a complete perpetual system is too expensive, to establish individual responsibility by limiting access to one person. It might also be advisable to install some type of surveillance system, both in the storeroom and the bar. Computerized locks to establish entry and exit times also help to ensure the integrity of inventory. It is important to organize the storage areas efficiently to minimize employee access times and misplaced inventory due to storing items in illogical places where they cannot easily be found. It is also important to create a proper storage environment for certain beverages, especially wine, which should be kept at a specific temperature and in a horizontal or inclined position.

One way to maintain a constant inventory at the bar is to require the return of an empty bottle for every new bottle that is issued. It should be kept in mind that minimizing investment in inventory and working capital plays an important role in maximizing profits by making more funds available for investment in revenue-generating or cost-reducing property and equipment. One way to detect bloated inventories is to calculate the turnover rate:

$$\text{Turnover rate} = \frac{\text{Cost of sales for a beverage}}{\text{Average inventory cost}}$$

The average turnover rate for liquor is approximately 1.5 times; and for beer the rate is 2 times. If the turnover rate is higher, the bar may be running out, and if it is lower, there is probably too much investment in inventory. Because of their great variety and price and category differences as well as differences in stocking policies, there is no accepted average inventory turnover for wines.

Maintaining continuous control over beverages from their purchase to their issue is an essential ingredient for success. Exhibit 16-9 contains a sample flow chart for a perpetual inventory system that helps achieve this type of control.

Consumption

Control over beverage sales is more important than control over food sales. Similar to food costs, there are two ways to control beverage costs at the consumption or sales stage: (1) standard ratios and (2) portion control.

Cost Percentage. Calculating the actual monthly, weekly, or daily cost percentage and comparing it to other similar periods is the most basic way to control bar costs after the fact. These calculations can be made by counting empty bottles returned or taking a physical inventory. However, a calculation of the daily cost percentage based on empty bottles returned, which may include bottles that were not consumed the previous day, render it unlikely that a true daily cost for the previous day is obtained. To calculate the cost percentage, an example of a daily cost percentage calculation sheet is shown in Exhibit 16-16.

When calculating cost ratios, transfers from the food department (e.g., appetizers, dairy products, juices) and beverages transferred to the food department should be taken into account, as should drinks given in promotions, or complimentary drinks authorized by management. The expense for transporting beverages to the establishment should be included in their cost. In control states, where alcoholic beverages, if not picked up by the purchaser, must be delivered by bonded agents, this cost can be significant.

Additional columns showing (1) previous 7 days, (2) previous 30 days, (3) week-to-date, or (4) month-to-date amounts might also be added. Furthermore, these calculations can be made for all three types of beverages together to obtain an average cost, or they can be made for liquor, beer, and wine separately, which is the preferable method because it allows for more specific cost control.

Exhibit 16-16: Daily Cost Percentage Calculation Sheet

Date	Beginning Inventory	Issues (+)	Ending Inventory (−)	Transfers In (+)	Transfers Out (−)	Daily Total Cost	Daily Sales	Daily Cost %
2 Mar	$4,000	$2,000	$2,800	$200	$100	$3,300	$8,000	41.25%
3 Mar	$5,000	$1,500	$3,800	$150	$75	$2,775	$7,000	39.64%
4 Mar	$3,500	$800	$900	$100	$110	$3,390	$8,500	39.88%

Transfers in:
Appetizers purchased or from the kitchen
Dairy products purchased or from the kitchen
Other mix ingredients
Inventory count overages

Transfers out:
Beverages transferred to the kitchen
Promotional drinks
Management complimentary drinks
Inventory count shortages

Chapter 16: Maximizing Profit and Minimizing Costs 16,043

Standard Ratios. The problem with comparing cost percentages to historical percentages is that problems that existed in the past may continue to exist without being detected. A more effective cost-control method is to calculate standard (ideal) cost ratios to compare to actual results. Standard costs for beverages may be determined on a per-bottle basis. A liter-sized bottle contains approximately 34 ounces. Therefore, if the bottle costs $17, the standard cost per ounce is $0.50. Multiplying the number of bottles issued by their cost, plus the cost per ounce of partially used bottles, provides the standard cost for a particular brand of beverage. The total standard cost is obtained by totaling the results for all brands.

The calculation of a standard sales value per bottle is more complicated because not every ounce of a specific brand and type of liquor is sold at the same price. An ounce of whiskey sold straight is sold for a different price than when mixed into a cocktail. This difference can be accounted for by calculating a mix differential per cocktail, or calculating an average sale price per bottle based on average sales of straight drinks and mixed drinks monitored during a test period, or using computerized machinery that not only dispenses but also automatically calculates actual and standard costs and prices. Under the former method a record of the specific number of each type of drink sold must be maintained. The standard sales value of a bottle of blended whiskey, assuming all ounces are sold straight, can easily be calculated as follows:

Liquor Brand	Ounces per Liter Bottle	Standard Price per Ounce Sold Straight	Total Standard Sales Value Assuming All Straight Sales
Blended whiskey	34 Ounces	$2.00	$68.00

If sales records indicate that seven Old Fashioned cocktails were sold, that the standard recipe specifies two ounces of whiskey per cocktail, and an ounce of blended whiskey in an Old Fashioned is sold for $3.00 per ounce, then the standard sales value for this bottle would be calculated as follows:

Liquor Brand	Ounces per Liter Bottle	Standard Price per Ounce Sold Straight	Total Standard Sales Value Adjusted for Mixed Sales
Blended whiskey	20 ounces	$2.00	$40.00
	14 ounces	$3.00	$42.00
Total Standard Sales Adjusted for Mixed Sales			$82.00

This calculation can be made using a sales differential of $1.00 per ounce sold in an Old Fashioned as follows:

Liquor Brand: Blended Whiskey	Ounces per Liter Bottle	Standard Price per Ounce Sold Straight	Total Standard Sales Value Assuming All Straight Sales
Sold straight	34 ounces	$2.00	$68.00
		Sales differential for Old Fashioned	Plus or minus all sales differentials
Sold in Old Fashioned cocktails	14 ounces	$1.00	$14.00
Total Standard Sales Adjusted for Mixed Sales			$82.00

Under the average sales mix method, a test period would be studied. Assume that during the test period it was found that 20 ounces per bottle of blended whiskey were sold straight and 14 ounces per bottle were sold in Old Fashioneds. The average standard price per bottle of blended whiskey would then be set at $82.00 per bottle, and the standard sales price per ounce for blended whiskey would be set at $2.4118 per ounce (= $82.00 ÷ 34 ounces). Standard sales per bottle would be calculated as follows:

Liquor Brand	Ounces per Liter Bottle	Standard Price Per Ounce Sold	Total Standard Sales Value Assuming Standard Sales Mix
Blended whiskey	34 ounces	$2.4118	$68.00

One or more of the above calculations are performed by restaurant management computer point-of-sale programs, but at least some of the data (usually the actual consumption) must be manually entered into the computer.

The most advanced cost-control method involves acquiring dispensing machines that not only dispense the exact amount of each ingredient for all the cocktails they are programmed to prepare, but also adjust inventory and calculate standard cost and standard total sales.

Portion Controls. Calculating standard ratios is an after-the-fact control. Portion control is a proactive form of cost control that begins with establishing recipes for each drink and creating a recipe manual. There is more than one way to prepare most mixed drinks, with one recipe using more of the expensive ingredient (the liquor), as opposed to the less expensive other ingredients. A bar can reduce costs by using a recipe that uses smaller quantities of the more expensive ingredients. In those bars where there are many return customers, a bartender might be given the option of using two or three recipes for a certain mixed drink to personalize the customer relationships.

Recipes should be costed by calculating the cost per ounce of the ingredients and then multiplying by the amount of each ingredient used in the recipe. Exhibit 16-17 includes sheets where cost per ounce is calculated and used in a recipe-costing sheet. Only liter-size bottles are shown because it is less expensive per ounce to buy in liter quantities than to buy .750 liter bottles, and 1.75 liter bottles are too heavy for pouring. The last four columns can be used to calculate a new recipe cost when the costs of ingredients changes.

Exhibit 16-17: Cost per Ounce and Recipe-Costing Sheets

Per Ounce Costing Sheet

	ml.	Ounces	Cost per Bottle	Cost per Ounce
Dewar's Scotch White Label	1000	33.8	$24.99	$0.7393
Bombay Gin	1000	33.8	$24.99	$0.7393
Jack Daniel's Whiskey	1000	33.8	$25.99	$0.7689

Recipe Costing Sheet—Mint Julep

Ingredient	Amount	Cost per Ounce	Total Cost	Cost per Ounce	Total Cost	Cost per Ounce	Total Cost
Jack Daniels Whiskey	3 oz.	$0.7689	$2.3067				
Powdered sugar	1 tspn.		.0300				
Dash of bitters			.0400				
Sprig of mint			.0500				
Total Cost			$2.4267				

Recipe control should be accompanied by appropriately sized or measured shot glasses, jiggers, or bottle top pourers. The size of the glass into which drinks are poured should be predetermined as well because this often regulates the quantity of secondary ingredients used in a drink. Also available are automatic liquor dispensers that prepare mixed drinks, record the sale electronically (through a link to the cash register), and reduce inventories. Although these machines offer the best control over cost of beverage sales, they are not universally appealing because of their high cost, inflexibility in drink preparation, and reduced personal contact between the bartender and the customer. Deciding on the most suitable portion control method depends on whether a manager is more intent on maximizing sales (and perhaps accepting a lower profit margin) by providing faster service to customers and giving them more control over their mixed drinks, or whether the manager is more intent on minimizing costs (and perhaps accepting the reduced sales that the cost-cutting process might entail).

Possible Methods of Theft at the Bar

Despite all efforts to preclude it, beverage-related theft is common. Some of the most common methods of theft are:

- *Selling from a phantom bottle.* The bartender brings his own bottle of liquor, sells from this bottle, and keeps the proceeds.
- *Overpouring.* The bartender favors high-tipping customers with larger than standard size pours.
- *Stealing bottles of liquor.* The bartender hides bottles of liquor in a location where they can be retrieved later without being noticed.
- *Serving diluted drinks.* Less than standard amounts of liquor are poured into mixed drinks and the underpoured liquor is later sold to a customer with the bartender keeping the proceeds. This can be done even with a computerized dispenser system by using the dispensed amount to prepare two mixed drinks.
- *Undercharging friends or high-tipping customers.* A drink can be undercharged or a more expensive brand used instead of a house brand with the hope of receiving a larger tip.
- *Underringing sales.* A more expensive drink is charged to the customer but is rung up as a less expensive one, and the bartender keeps the difference;

or the quality of liquor is reduced after customers have had several drinks in the hope they will not notice the difference.
- *Leaving the cash drawer open.* This allows sales to be made without being rung up.
- *Overcharging customers.* One customer is charged for a drink he or she did not consume, allowing the bartender to later sell that drink and keep the proceeds.
- *Ringing up food sales as liquor sales.* Fraudulently increasing liquor sales, disguises the higher cost of liquor consumption that results from stolen liquor.

MINIMIZING LABOR COSTS IN RESTAURANTS AND HOTELS

Labor cost is the other major restaurant cost category in restaurants and the major cost category in hotels. Because it can fluctuate between 30% and 40% of revenue, it must be controlled very tightly. A meager 2.5% of a 40% labor cost is 1% of sales, and 1% of sales is 10% of a 10% profit margin. The factors for controlling labor costs in restaurants and hotels are similar and include the key elements of knowledge, training, planning, implementation, and measurement of results.

Minimizing labor cost begins with a complete knowledge of employee job requirements. In addition, the hospitality manager must consider the basis for performing a particular job in a particular way. These job requirements should then be inserted into a budget forecast, from which a daily staffing guide should be produced. After the fact, actual labor hours consumed and actual hourly rates paid should be compared with the budgeted or standard hours and rates, and variances should be calculated. Knowledge of this process prepares managers to discuss important employment issues, such as wage increases and hours worked, based on concrete facts rather than on emotions.

Staffing Guide

Preparing a staffing guide is a powerful way to control labor costs proactively. When properly prepared and applied, a staffing guide obliges management to take the following steps that are essential to effective labor cost control:
- Analyze a job position to determine if it is necessary.
- Calculate the time that it takes for an employee to perform all the tasks required in that position.
- Prepare a complete and highly detailed job description for the position.
- Train the employee for the position with the same degree of detail that the job description contains.
- Prepare sales volume forecasts.
- Prepare the staffing guide.
- Calculate standard ratio variances for labor cost.

Exhibit 16-18 demonstrates how the various steps listed above should be integrated into the process of preparing the staffing guide.

Exhibit 16-18: Flow Chart for Preparing and Using a Staffing Guide

Job Analysis

At this stage, questions such as the following should be asked and answered:
1) Why is this job being done?
2) By this employee?
3) At this location?
4) At this time?

Personnel Capacity Analysis

This analysis answers the question: What can an employee reasonably be expected to do in one hour or one day?
To answer the question, two steps must be performed:
1) Divide the task into discrete units or motion equivalents.
2) Observe employees (perhaps use time and motion studies) to determine how many motion equivalents a typical employee can perform in a day.

Budget Volume Forecast

Based on budget projections, an estimate should be made to determine the number of times that each task (as defined in the job description) will be performed daily.

Job Description

A job description must be determined by combining the job analysis and the personnel capacity estimates as follows:
1) Define each task minutely in terms of motion equivalents required and their proper sequence.
2) Determine how many times per hour or per day an employee can perform each task.

Staffing Guide

These steps generate the information required to produce a staffing guide. This information is:
1) A list and definition of the tasks that need to be performed.
2) The number of times per day that an employee can perform them.
3) The number of times the budget indicates that these tasks will need to be performed.

This information enables management to plan how many employees will be needed and when they will be needed.

Variance Analysis

A variance analysis can then be performed to determine the areas that need improvement.

Budgeted hours and payroll dollars per the staffing guide	Actual hours worked and payroll dollars spent
• Budgeted revenue • Budgeted labor cost dollars • Budgeted hours worked • Budgeted hourly rate	• Actual revenue • Actual labor cost dollars • Actual hours worked • Actual hourly wage

---

As shown in Exhibit 16-18, to prepare a staffing guide and use it effectively, management must become intimately familiar with a job position and how it fits into the organization as a whole. Not only does a staffing guide promote the efficient use of employee time; it also provides a constructive framework within which to discuss the employee's work.

The advantages of preparing a staffing guide are:

- Unnecessary positions will not be created (job analysis)

- Performing job tasks excessively slowly due to slacking will be reduced (personnel capacity analysis—perhaps time-and-motion studies)

- Performing job tasks excessively slowly due to an inefficient job process will be reduced (detailed job description, employee job manual, proper training)
- The proper number of employees will be hired (budget volume forecast)
- Knowledge of how many employees are on the job (staffing guide)
- The results obtained will be analyzed (variance analysis)

Training. Detailed training of employees is an essential part of the staffing guide preparation process. Without sufficiently detailed training, much of the benefit of the process will be lost. For example, it is not sufficient to train employees to prepare a certain type of menu item or to clean a room. They must also be taught the most efficient manner to perform these tasks, which may require creating a specific step-by-step instruction manual.

Standard Ratios and Variance Analysis

The consumption of labor hours should also be monitored by performing standard ratio calculations. In the case of labor, the two factors to control are the (1) labor rate and (2) labor hours. Thus, the two ratios to be calculated are the (1) labor rate variance and (2) labor efficiency variance, calculated as follows:

$$\text{Labor rate ratio} = \frac{\text{Actual hourly rate}}{\text{Standard hourly rate}}$$

$$\text{Labor efficiency ratio} = \frac{\text{Actual hours worked}}{\text{Standard hours worked}}$$

Exhibit 16-19 demonstrates the calculation of these variances based on a hypothetical scenario.

Exhibit 16-19: Calculation of Labor Variances

	Actual Labor Expense	Standard Labor Expense
Total dollar amounts	$105,000	$100,000
Hours worked	10,200	10,000
Hourly rate	$ 10.29	$10.00

$$\text{Labor rate ratio} = \frac{\$\ 10.29}{\$\ 10.00} = 103\%$$

$$\text{Labor efficiency ratio} = \frac{10,200}{10,000} = 102\%$$

The standards should be verified to ascertain that the correct standards are being used. The labor rate ratio indicates that there was probably some overtime paid, or one or more employees with higher salaries were used to perform tasks that had been designated for employees earning less per hour than was actually paid. The labor efficiency ratio indicates that one or more employees worked more hours than planned or that more employees were needed than had been expected. These cost excesses are very often due to the high turnover that plagues the hospitality industry, which results in a high proportion of employees who are near the bottom of their learning curve. Identifying these deviations from designated goals by such measures as standard ratio analysis serves to motivate management to work to reduce them.

MINIMIZING OTHER COSTS IN RESTAURANTS AND HOTELS

Evaluating and minimizing other expenses involves a similar approach for both restaurants and hotels. Standard ratio calculations and the analysis of operating ratios through the use of comparative, common size, operating ratio, and indexing analysis are the best tools for this purpose.

Standard Per-Unit Ratios

Standard ratio analysis can be used for any expense as long as the expense can be compared to some unit of output. Units of output can be covers sold, seats, rooms occupied, or available rooms. An expense, such as a cleaning expense, can be calculated on the basis of standard covers sold or rooms sold. For example, if it is estimated that 1,000 rooms will be sold and the expense for cleaning common (nonroom) areas is estimated to be $3,000, then the standard cleaning expense per occupied room is $3.00. If the actual cleaning expense is $3,500 and only 950 rooms are sold, then cost of cleaning the common areas per occupied room is $3.68. In this example, a predetermined standard was the basis for comparison to actual results.

Operating Ratios, Common Size Analysis, and Variance Analysis

Another way to identify excessive costs in hospitality industry companies is to compare them to previous periods' results or industry averages using operating ratios such as those suggested below, as well as those discussed in Chapter 14, "Management Analysis of Operations." The advantage of using operating ratios is that they enable management to detect small changes in results, changes that despite their small size might forecast future problems of a serious magnitude. This is based on the premise that the hospitality industry tends to depend on volume sales, so that small cost excesses calculated on a per room, per cover, or per seat basis, when multiplied by the large numbers of rooms, covers, or seats sold, can lead to impaired performance or, in a highly competitive market, to failure. An analysis of the hypothetical hotel income statements and hypothetical industry averages presented in Exhibit 16-20 demonstrates the use of some of these ratios.

Exhibit 16-20: Hypothetical Hotel Income Statements and Averages

	Hotel A Medium Size Low Room Rate	Hotel B Small Size High Room Rate	Industry or Segment Average Large Size Medium Room Rate
Available rooms	370	210	400
Occupied rooms	185	180	320
Occupancy percentage	50.0%	85.7%	80.0%
Revenue			
Rooms	$6,617,450	$8,738,100	$13,432,000
Food	2,701,000	2,299,500	4,438,400
Beverages	894,706	854,100	1,752,000
Telephone	405,150	197,100	467,200
Other operated departments	506,438	262,800	1,985,600
Rentals/other income	219,456	131,400	817,600
Total	$11,344,200	$12,483,000	$22,892,800
Departmental Expenses			
Rooms	2,565,950	2,299,500	4,438,400
Food & beverages	2,363,375	2,628,000	4,788,800
Telephone	324,120	177,390	292,000
Other operated departments	411,903	98,550	1,635,200
Total	$5,665,348	$5,203,440	$11,154,400
Departmental Income	$5,678,853	$7,279,560	$11,738,400
Undistributed Operating Expenses			
Administrative & general	1,620,600	1,576,800	2,102,400
Management fees	270,100	438,000	350,400
Marketing	1,215,450	1,752,000	1,635,200
Property Operation & Maintenance	945,350	700,800	1,284,800
Energy	945,350	1,051,200	1,051,200
Other	0	0	147,168
Total	$4,996,850	$5,518,800	$6,571,168
Income before fixed charges	$682,003	$1,760,760	$5,167,232

A vertical analysis identifies the significance of individual expense categories in relation to revenues. An operating ratio analysis is also performed to relate units of input (available rooms) and units of output (occupied rooms) to revenues and expenses. These are presented in Exhibit 16-21 below.

To identify the ratios that are significantly different from the industry or segment averages, analysis-by-exception reports, such as those shown in Exhibit 16-22, can be prepared.

In the above report, focus should be directed to those areas where revenue is lower than the industry or segment average and those areas where expenses are higher than the industry or segment average. In the case of revenues, it is evident that the food and beverage revenues of Hotel B are lower than the average, and the telephone revenue of Hotel A is lower than the average. Departmental and undistributed operating expenses are all higher than the industry average for both hotels except for room expenses in Hotel B, which are lower than average. This is to be expected based on the sizes of the hotels. Being smaller than average, both hotels probably have a higher proportion of fixed expenses, such as managerial salaries, to sales. Rooms revenue in proportion to total revenue in Hotel B is higher than average (70% vs. 58%), probably because of its higher average room rate. This also results in a lower room expense percentage per room than average (26.3% vs. 33.0%). But it is important to perform a more in-depth operating ratio analysis of room rates by studying their annual pattern at different points in the season, as illustrated in Exhibit 16-23.

Part IV: Management Accounting

Exhibit 16-21: Vertical and Operating Ratio Analysis

	Hotel A Low Room Rate			Hotel B High Room Rate			Segment or Industry Average		
	Per Available Room	Per Occupied Room	%	Per Available Room	Per Occupied Room	%	Per Available Room	Per Occupied Room	%
Available Rooms	370			210			400		
Occupied Rooms	185			180			320		
Occupancy Percentage	50%			86%			80%		
Revenues									
Rooms	$18,130	$ 98.00	58.3%	$23,940	$133.00	70.0%	$36,800	$115.00	58.7%
Food	7,400	40.00	23.8%	6,300	35.00	18.4%	12,160	38.00	19.4%
Beverages	2,451	13.25	7.9%	2,340	13.00	6.8%	4,800	15.00	7.7%
Telephone	1,110	6.00	3.6%	540	3.00	1.6%	1,280	4.00	2.0%
Other Operated Dept.	1,388	7.50	4.5%	720	4.00	2.1%	5,440	17.00	8.7%
Rentals/Other Income	601	3.25	1.9%	360	2.00	1.1%	2,240	7.00	3.6%
Total	$31,080	$168.00	100.0%	$34,200	$190.00	100.0%	$62,720	$196.00	100.0%
Departmental Expenses									
Rooms	7,030	$38.00	38.8%**	6,300	$ 35.00	26.3%**	12,160	$ 38.00	33.0%**
Food & Beverages	6,475	35.00	65.7%**	7,200	40.00	83.3%**	13,120	41.00	77.4%**
Telephone	888	4.80	80.0%**	486	2.70	90.0%**	800	2.50	62.5%**
Other Operated Dept.	1,129	6.10	81.3%**	270	1.50	37.5%**	4,480	14.00	82.4%**
Total	$15,522	$83.90	49.9%*	$14,256	$ 79.20	41.7%*	$30,560	$ 95.50	48.7%*

Chapter 16: Maximizing Profit and Minimizing Costs

	Per Available Room	Per Occupied Room	%	Per Available Room	Per Occupied Room	%	Per Available Room	Per Occupied Room	%
Departmental Income	$15,559	84.10	50.1%*	$19,944	110.80	58.3%*	$32,160	100.50	51.3%*
Undistributed Operating Expenses									
Admin. & General	4,440	$24.00	14.3%	4,320	$24.00	12.6%	5,760	$18.00	9.2%
Management Fees	740	4.00	2.4%	1,200	6.67	3.5%	960	3.00	1.5%
Marketing	3,330	18.00	10.7%	4,800	26.67	14.0%	4,480	14.00	7.1%
Property Operations & Maintenance	2,590	14.00	8.3%	1,920	10.67	5.6%	3,520	11.00	5.6%
Energy	2,590	14.00	8.3%	2,880	16.00	8.4%	2,880	9.00	4.6%
Other	0	0.00	0.0%	0	0.00	0.0%	403	1.26	0.6%
Total	$13,690	$74.00	44.0%	$15,120	$84.00	44.2%	$18,003	$56.26	28.7%
Income Before Fixed Charges	$1,869	$10.10	6.0%	$4,824	$26.80	14.1%	$14,157	$44.24	22.6%

* Percent of Total Departmental Expense and Total Departmental Income to Total Revenues
** Percent of Individual Departmental Revenue

Exhibit 16-22: Ratio-Analysis-by-Exception Reports

Report indicating which revenue and expense relationships are higher or lower than the industry or segment average

	Hotel A Lower	Hotel A Higher	Hotel B Lower	Hotel B Higher	Industry or segment average
Revenue Analysis					
Rooms revenue to total revenue				70.0%	58.7%
Food revenue to total revenue		23.8%	18.4%		19.4%
Beverage revenue to total revenue			6.8%		7.7%
Telephone revenue to total revenue	1.8%			3.1%	2.0%
Departmental Expense Analysis					
Rooms Expenses to Room Sales		43.9%	26.3%		33.0%
Food and beverage expenses to food and beverage sales		65.7%		89.6%	77.4%
Telephone expenses to telephone sales		80.0%		90.0%	62.5%
Undistributed Expenses Analysis					
Administrative & general to total revenues		14.3%		12.6%	9.2%
Management fees to total revenues		2.4%		3.5%	1.5%
Marketing to total revenues	6.7%			14.0%	7.1%
Property operation and maintenance to total revenues		8.3%			5.6%
Energy to total revenues		8.3%		8.4%	4.6%

Exhibit 16-23: Seasonal Cycle of Room Rates

Percent of rooms sold at various rates during seasonal cycle

	Hotel A Rates from	Hotel A To		Hotel B Rates from	Hotel B To	
Peak season	150	200	25.0%	175	325	30.0%
	100	149	30.0%	125	174	60.0%
	75	99	45.0%	100	124	10.0%
			100.0%			100.0%
Shoulder season	120	140	20.0%	160	225	25.0%
	100	119	30.0%	75	124	45.0%
	90	99	50.0%	50	74	30.0%
			100.0%			100.0%
Off season	100	125	25.0%	125	150	30.0%
	90	99	35.0%	100	124	25.0%

Percent of rooms sold at various rates during seasonal cycle

	Hotel A			Hotel B		
	Rates from	To		Rates from	To	
	75	89	40.0%	75	99	45.0%
			100.0%			100.0%

The exhibit above indicates that Hotel B sells a higher percent of rooms at the high end of its room rate range than Hotel A. This is likely due to Hotel B's higher marketing expense per room ($26.67) than both Hotel A and the average. But it may also be due to greater liberty given to the front desk clerks to grant small room rate discounts to keep potential guests from losing interest. Another factor to consider is the percent of the different categories of rooms that are sold, as analyzed in Exhibit 16-24.

Exhibit 16-24: Percent Sales per Room Category

	Hotel A			Hotel B		
	Available	% Available Rooms	% of Total Rooms Sold	Available	% Available Rooms	% of Total Rooms Sold
Luxury Suites	111	30.0%	20.0%	63	30.0%	35.0%
Standard Suites	111	30.0%	25.0%	69	33.0%	30.0%
Standard rooms	148	40.0%	55.0%	78	37.0%	35.0%
	370	100.0%	100.0%	210	100.0%	100.0%

The analysis of sales per room category reveals that Hotel A is under-utilizing its higher room categories. Although 30% of its rooms are luxury suites, only 20% of annual sales are generated by these suites.

On the positive side, it is evident that Hotel B has a higher average room rate than the industry or segment average ($133 vs. $115) which resulted in its having a lower room-expense-to-room-sales ratio (26.3% vs. 33.0%) than the average.

Other Factors That May Affect Profits

Several factors affect the profits of a hospitality company negatively and may result in failure. These are:

- *Natural disasters.*
- *Economic recession.*
- *Competition.* Competitors are better managed or they overbuild.
- *Inadequate sales or excessive expenses.* Basically these are due to incompetent management. The four basic management skills are (1) working capital management, (2) financial management, (3) investment management, and (4) operating management. Operating management is responsible for maximizing revenues and minimizing expenses, but its performance is limited or enhanced by a hospitality company's working capital manage-

ment, financial management, and investment management, as indicated below. Some factors that affect the maximization of sales are:

1. *Management*—Is management able to develop or identify new sources of sales?
2. *Product or service concept in relation to the target market.*
3. *Promotional activities.*
4. *Pricing strategy.*
5. *Personnel training*—Promotion attracts customers to the restaurant or hotel the first time. Good service likely will bring them back.
6. *Plant design and maintenance*—A well-designed and maintained restaurant or hotel increases the number of repeat customers. (Investment management)
7. *Investment in current assets*—Is there sufficient inventory and are the company's credit and collection policies on par with those of the competition or are they too strict? (working capital management)
8. *Efficient asset composition*—Does the company maximize non-interest-bearing current liabilities so that it can use the excess of current liabilities over current assets to purchase revenue-generating assets? (working capital and financial management)
9. *Debt financing*—Resistance to using borrowed funds to expand limits a company's ability to buy new revenue-generating assets. (financial management)

Several of the above factors can also be responsible for inhibiting a company's ability to minimize expenses, such as, for example, a poorly designed facility that hampers the efficiency of employees. Additionally, a poorly designed system of operational cost controls and a dysfunctional system of internal controls to verify the efficiency of operational controls lead to excessive costs.

This chapter is devoted to the review of operating management. Nevertheless, financial managers should consider the other aspects of management when evaluating their company's operating performance.

CHAPTER 17
DIFFERENT TYPES OF COSTS

CONTENTS

Management Accounting and Cost Accounting	17,001
Variable, Mixed, and Fixed Costs	17,002
Variable Expenses	17,003
Mixed Expenses and Contribution Margin	17,004
Fixed Expenses	17,005
Separating Mixed Expenses into Their Variable and Fixed Elements	17,007
Relevant Range	17,008
Contribution Pricing	17,010
Conditions Required to Use Contribution Pricing	17,013
Direct Costs versus Indirect Costs	17,014
Expanded Income Statement	17,017
Service/Product Costs versus Period Costs	17,017
Joint Costs and the Yield Ratio	17,018
Relevant Costs, Incremental Costs, and Sunk Costs	17,018
Controllable versus Noncontrollable Costs	17,019
Standard Costs	17,020
Opportunity Cost	17,020
Exhibits	
Exhibit 17-1. Summary Long-Form Income Statement for Hotel Charles	17,015
Exhibit 17-2. Expanded Income Statement	17,017

It is important to be able to identify different types of expenses because they each interact in unique ways under specific circumstances and reveal different aspects of a hospitality company's actual or hypothetical performance. Some expenses may be used to make management decisions regarding the future direction of a hospitality company, while others may be used to evaluate managers' individual performance in addition to management decision making. In order to advise operating managers of a hospitality company correctly or evaluate management performance, it is essential that financial managers understand how different expenses behave in specific scenarios—for example, to determine what alternative investment to make, how to better structure a hospitality company to maximize future profit growth, whether to close a division, whether managers are making correct decisions, or whether employees are working efficiently.

MANAGEMENT ACCOUNTING AND COST ACCOUNTING

Management accounting involves gathering, organizing, and reporting costs or expenses internally in a compact, logical format, usually requiring cost allocation, to enable managers to make future decisions and plans that will maximize the value of a business to its stakeholders. Management accounting also involves evaluating the efficacy with which these decisions and plans are executed, as well as their ultimate impact on the value of the business to its stakeholders.

While management accounting and cost accounting aim to maximize shareholder value, cost accounting is limited to determining the cost of goods and services rendered. Management accounting, on the other hand, includes the broader objectives of determining how well costs are being controlled. In addition, financial accounting is concerned primarily with providing historical information to outside stakeholders, while cost accounting is concerned mainly with providing internal information necessary for making decisions about the future sale of goods and services.

In the hospitality industry, *goods* are usually food and beverages (i.e., alcoholic drinks only), and services may represent transportation to a desired destination or lodging at that destination. Fresh food is perishable because of its short shelf life; and rooms, seats, and cabins are perishable because they cannot be stored. If not sold, their potential revenue is permanently lost. For this reason, yield management and revenue management, which involve lowering rates, sometimes drastically, to capture at least some of the revenue that might otherwise be permanently lost, are an essential part of the hospitality industry. To use these tools properly, accurate knowledge of the relevant costs of the goods and services provided is critical. The required large fixed investment in property and equipment (hotels, restaurants and their equipment, airplanes and cruise ships) and the high cost of rendering personal services require a constant high level of expenditures, even when the customer count is low. A more than 90% failure rate during the first five years of a hospitality industry business is not usually because of a bad concept, but rather because of insufficient initial funding resulting from underestimating costs and failure to identify, properly classify, and control the costs of the ongoing business. When dealing with costs, the following list of questions must be addressed. The first two questions, involving cost identification and classification, are covered in this chapter. The subsequent questions, relating to the broader managerial accounting function, are covered in later chapters:

- What type of cost is it?
- Is it a service/product (direct) cost or a period (indirect) cost?
- If it is a period cost, will it be allocated or remain an indirect cost?
- If it will be allocated, will traditional allocation methods or activity-based costing be used? (See Chapter 18, "Cost Allocation.")
- How will this cost be evaluated and controlled? (See Chapter 16, "Maximizing Profit and Minimizing Costs")
- Which manager's performance will the cost be used to evaluate and what type of variance analysis will be used? (See Chapter 16, "Maximizing Profit and Minimizing Costs")

VARIABLE, MIXED, AND FIXED COSTS

Variable and mixed expenses vary in response to dollar sales or unit sales. However, variable expenses vary both in the same direction and in the same proportion as sales. Mixed expenses vary in the same direction, but not in the same proportion as sales. Fixed expenses are not usually fixed, though they remain stable over longer periods of time than variable and mixed expenses. Fixed expenses tend to change in response to stimuli other than sales, such as inflation, interest rates, and changes in the structure of a business. Usually cost of food or beverages sold is a 100% variable expense. Although when there is a large increase in volume, suppliers may reduce their per-unit cost, causing a reduction in an otherwise constant variable expense percent. Property insurance, property taxes, depreciation, and interest are usually considered to be 100% fixed expenses. In the hospitality industry, most other expenses are mixed.

Variable Expenses

Variable expenses preserve their percentage relationship to sales. They increase and decrease in dollar amounts as sales change. Example 1 presents variable expenses for a hypothetical food establishment.

EXAMPLE 1: Variable expenses for the Hamburger Shoppe are as follows:

	Hamburger Shoppe				
Hamburgers sold	1	200	300	400	
Unit price	$5.00	$ 5.00	$ 5.00	$ 5.00	
Unit cost	$2.00	$ 2.00	$ 2.00	$ 2.00	
Sales	$5.00	$1,000.00	$1,500.00	$2,000.00	Variable Expense %
Variable expenses:					
Cost of food sold	$2.00	$400.00	$600.00	$ 800.00	40.0%
Gross margin	$3.00	$600.00	$900.00	$1,200.00	

Changes in Variable Expense Percent. On a per unit basis, variable expenses do not change, but if either the unit price or the unit total variable cost changes, or they both change in dissimilar proportions to each other, then the variable expense percent will also change.

Step-Like Behavior of Some Variable Expenses. Variable expenses sometimes increase in a step-like pattern. Fixed expenses also increase in a step-like manner, but their relevant range is usually one year or longer. The relevant range is the range over which both variable and fixed expenses can be expected to behave predictably. However, variable expenses respond to changes in sales, whereas fixed expenses do not. The following graph shows room attendants' wages as a step-like variable expense. The graph is based on the assumption that one room attendant can clean five rooms per day.

EXAMPLE 2:

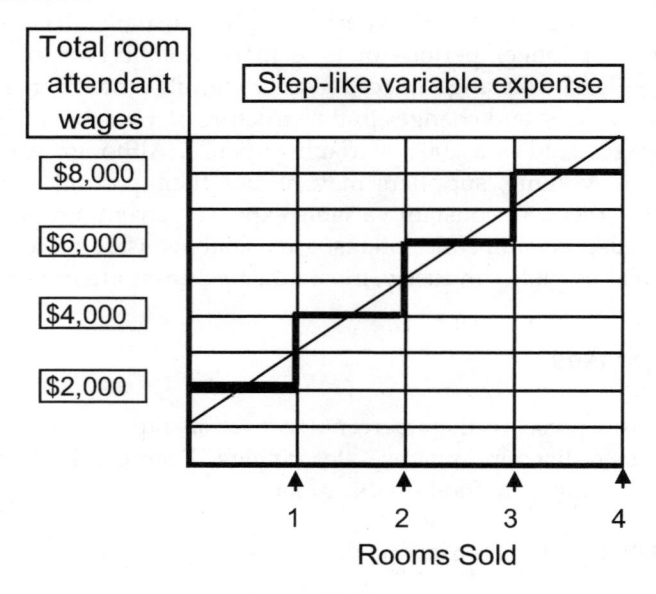

```
Total room
attendant      Step-like variable expense
wages

$8,000

$6,000

$4,000

$2,000

              1    2    3    4
                Rooms Sold
```

Mixed Expenses and Contribution Margin

Because they behave partially like variable expenses (they change in the same direction as sales) and partially like fixed expenses (they are more stable than variable expenses and do not change in the same proportion as sales), mixed expenses can be separated into a variable and fixed element. (See Chapter 19, "Cost-Volume-Profit Analysis.") Total variable expenses consist of:

1. Those expenses that are intrinsically 100% variable
2. The variable element of mixed expenses

EXAMPLE 3: Hamburger Shoppe pays a fixed rent of $100 plus a contingent rent equal to 2% of sales. Rent expense is a mixed expense with a fixed element and a variable element that always maintains its same percent relationship to sales. The income statement shows (1) the 100% variable cost of sales expense; (2) the variable element of the mixed expense (rent); and (3) the contribution margin—that is, revenues minus all variable expenses:

Hamburger Shoppe

Hamburgers sold	1	200	300	400	
					Variable Expense %
Unit price	$5.00	$ 5.00	$ 5.00	$ 5.00	
Unit cost	$2.00	$ 2.00	$ 2.00	$ 2.00	
Sales	$5.00	$1,000.00	$1,500.00	$2,000.00	

Chapter 17: Different Types of Costs 17,005

Hamburger Shoppe

Variable expenses:						
(a) Cost of food sold	$2.00	$ 400.00	$ 600.00	$ 800.00	40.0%	**100% Variable**
Gross margin	$3.00	$ 600.00	$ 900.00	$1,200.00		
(b) Contingent rent	$0.10	$ 20.00	$ 30.00	$ 40.00	2.0%	**Variable element**
Total variable expenses	$2.10	$ 420.00	$ 630.00	$ 840.00	42.0%	
Contribution margin	$2.90	$ 580.00	$ 870.00	$1,160.00		

Fixed Expenses

Total variable expenses can consist of expenses that are 100% variable, plus the variable element of mixed expenses. Total fixed expenses can consist of expenses that are 100% fixed, plus the fixed element of a mixed expense.

EXAMPLE 4: If the previously specified fixed rent amount of $100 is added to the above income statement and it is assumed that its depreciation expense (a 100% fixed expense) is $200, then the income statements can be completed as follows:

Hamburger Shoppe

Hamburgers sold	1	200	300	400		
Unit price	$ 5.00	$ 5.00	$ 5.00	$ 5.00		Variable Expense %
Unit cost	$ 2.00	$ 2.00	$ 2.00	$ 2.00		
Sales	$ 5.00	$1,000.00	$1,500.00	$2,000.00		
Variable expenses:						
(a) Cost of food sold	$ 2.00	$ 400.00	$ 600.00	$ 800.00	40.0%	**100% Variable**
Gross margin	$ 3.00	$ 600.00	$ 900.00	$1,200.00		
(b) Contingent rent	$ 0.10	$ 20.00	$ 30.00	$ 40.00	2.0%	**Variable element**
Total variable expenses	$ 2.10	$ 420.00	$ 630.00	$ 840.00	42.0%	
Contribution margin	$ 2.90	$ 580.00	$ 870.00	$1,160.00		

Hamburger Shoppe

Fixed expenses:					
(c) Fixed rent payment	$100.00	$100.00	$100.00	$100.00	**Fixed element**
(d) Depreciation expense	$200.00	$200.00	$200.00	$200.00	**100% Fixed**
Total fixed expenses	$300.00	$300.00	$300.00	$300.00	
Net income	($297.10)	$280.00	$570.00	$860.00	

Note: Variable expenses per unit do not change automatically as sales change; however, fixed expenses per unit do. For example, an increase in sales causes per unit fixed expenses to decrease. In Example 3, the fixed expenses per unit when 200 units are sold is $1.50 per unit (= $300/200 units), but they decrease to $0.75 per unit (= $300/400 units) when 400 units are sold. This is called the *operating leverage,* which is discussed in Chapter 19, "Cost-Volume-Profit Analysis." The following graphs serve to clarify this point.

Chapter 17: Different Types of Costs   **17,007**

Total variable expense	Total variable expenses increase as sales increase.
	Variable expense ratio is constant.

$2,000
$1,500
$1,000
$500

Variable expenses = 50% of sales

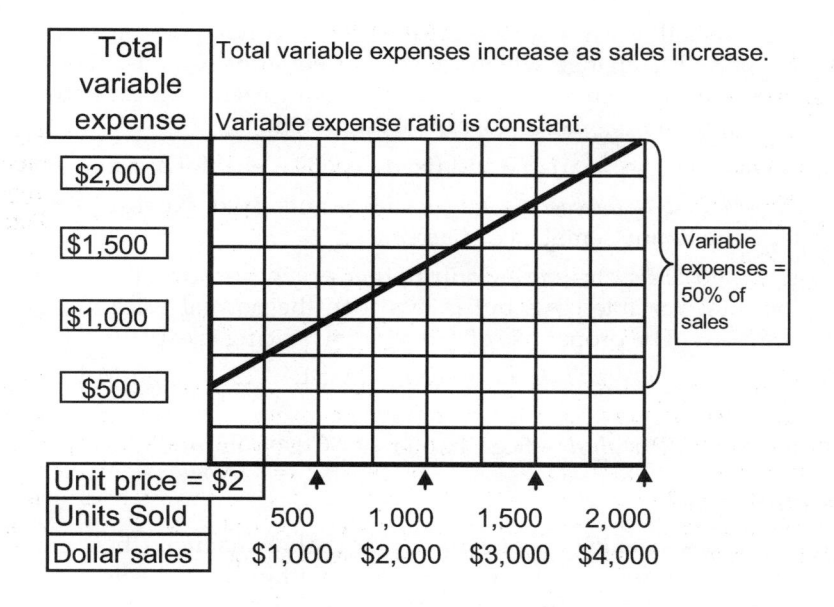

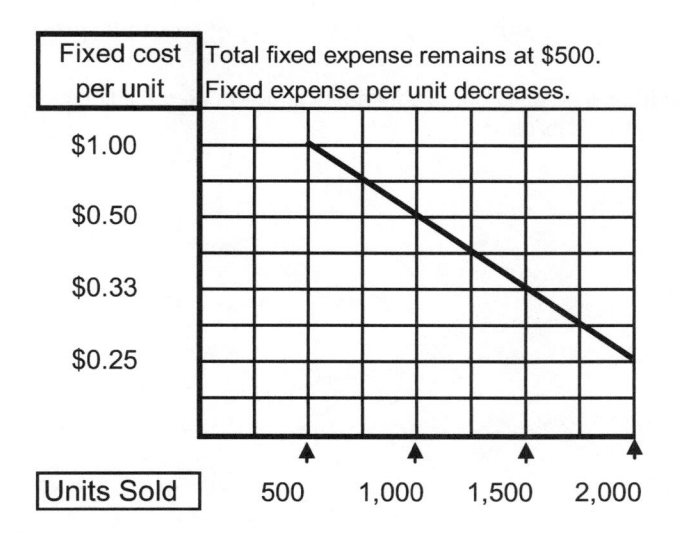

Unit price = $2				
Units Sold	500	1,000	1,500	2,000
Dollar sales	$1,000	$2,000	$3,000	$4,000

Fixed cost per unit	Total fixed expense remains at $500.
	Fixed expense per unit decreases.

$1.00
$0.50
$0.33
$0.25

Units Sold	500	1,000	1,500	2,000

Separating Mixed Expenses into Their Variable and Fixed Elements

In Chapter 19, "Cost-Volume-Profit Analysis," the process of separating mixed expenses into their variable and fixed element is explained. Mixed expenses should be separated into their variable and fixed elements because mixed expenses cannot be projected with any degree of accuracy due to the fact that they have different proportions of fixed and variable elements. This causes some mixed expenses to be more responsive to changes in sales, while others will be less responsive. Variable expenses can be projected because they maintain a fixed percent relationship to sales, provided the unit price and unit total variable cost do not change disproportionately. Fixed expenses can be projected because they remain fixed, usually over a period of one year, or undergo a one-time change during this period, a change which can be closely approximated. For example, property taxes usually change in the same month each year and the change, based on previous annual increases, can be estimated.

The ability to project variable and fixed expenses enables a manager to:

1. *Prepare budget forecasts*—Only variable and fixed expenses can be projected with any semblance of accuracy.
2. *Use contribution pricing*—Contribution pricing is any price that exceeds the total variable costs but is less than the normal price charged by a company. The proper use of contribution pricing is explained below.
3. *Prepare break-even graphs*—See Chapter 19, "Cost-Volume-Profit Analysis."
4. *Perform CVP analysis*—See Chapter 19, "Cost-Volume-Profit Analysis."

Relevant Range

Variable expenses usually behave in a predictable manner (they maintain a constant percentage relationship to sales) only within limited sales parameters. Fixed expenses also remain fixed only over a specific period of time or a specific range of sales called *relevant ranges*. The following example presents a variable food cost expense.

EXAMPLE 5: A dairy offers volume-incentive price reductions, which affects the cost of milk, as follows:

Chapter 17: Different Types of Costs   17,009

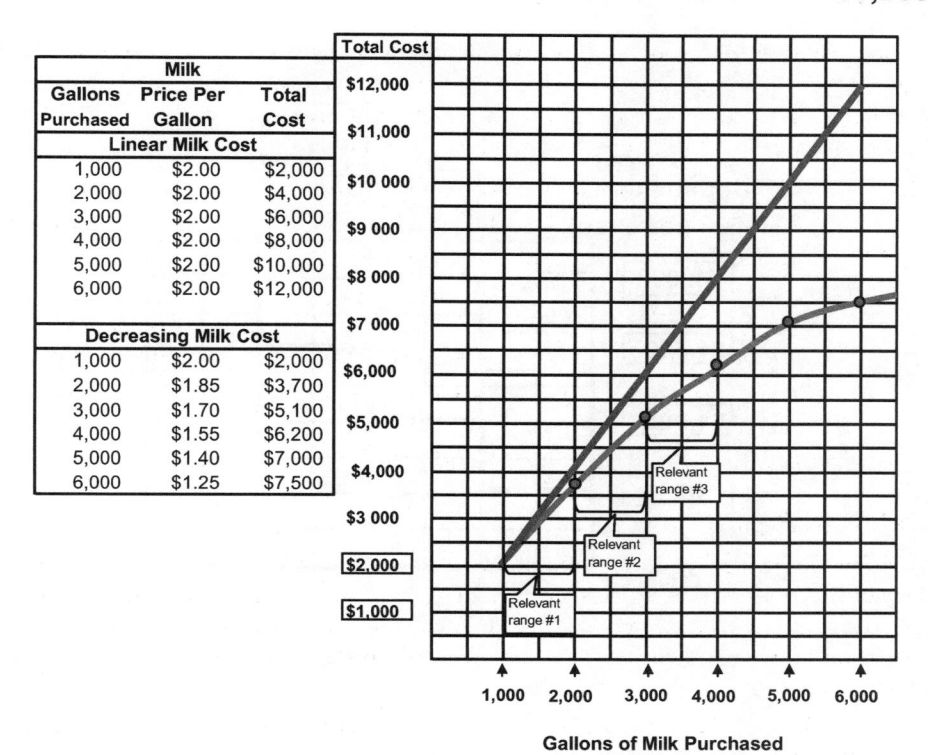

Gallons Purchased	Milk Price Per Gallon	Total Cost
Linear Milk Cost		
1,000	$2.00	$2,000
2,000	$2.00	$4,000
3,000	$2.00	$6,000
4,000	$2.00	$8,000
5,000	$2.00	$10,000
6,000	$2.00	$12,000
Decreasing Milk Cost		
1,000	$2.00	$2,000
2,000	$1.85	$3,700
3,000	$1.70	$5,100
4,000	$1.55	$6,200
5,000	$1.40	$7,000
6,000	$1.25	$7,500

When the cost of a variable expense is nonlinear, its percentage relationship to sales is constant only over the relevant ranges between volume price break points. In Example 5, the relevant ranges would be, for example, between 1,000 and 2,000 gallons or 2,000 and 3,000 gallons.

EXAMPLE 6: Assuming the milk is resold for $6.00 per gallon, the variable expense percent would eventually decrease from 33.3% to 20.8% as sales increase from a lower to a higher price point volume:

Gallons purchased	1,000	2,000	3,000	4,000	5,000	6,000
Unit cost	$ 2.00	$ 1.85	$ 1.70	$ 1.55	$ 1.40	$ 1.25
Total cost	$2,000	$3,700	$5,100	$6,200	$7,000	$7,500
Milk sales	$6,000	$12,000	$18,000	$24,000	$30,000	$36,000
Cost of sales	$2,000	$ 3,700	$ 5,100	$ 6,200	$ 7,000	$ 7,500
Variable expense %	33.3%	30.8%	28.3%	25.8%	23.3%	20.8%

Fixed expenses also have relevant ranges, sometimes delimited chronologically, other times delimited by sales volume. An example of a time-delimited relevant range for a fixed expense is property taxes, which tend to increase annually. An example of a sales-delimited fixed expense would be the depreciation on a specialized oven capable of cooking $10,000 worth of a product per day. The relevant range for the depreciation on that oven would be from zero sales to $10,000 sales of that product per day. Example 7 presents this concept graphically.

EXAMPLE 7:

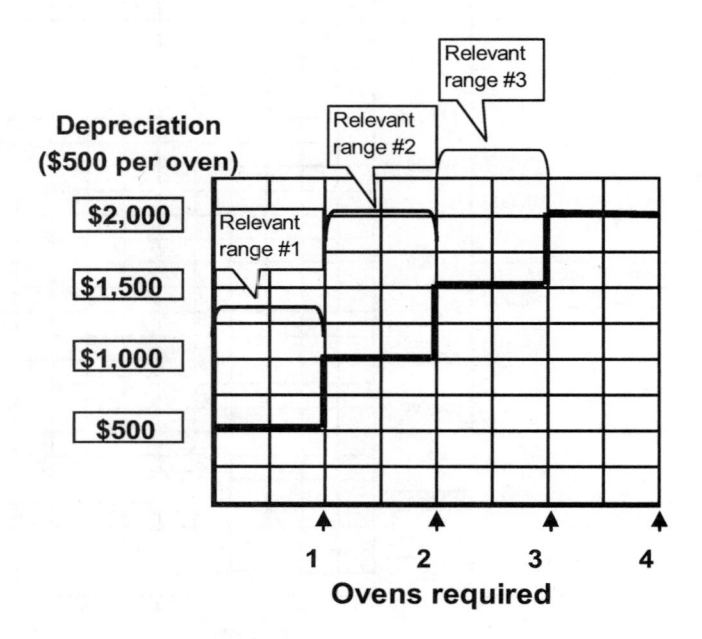

```
Depreciation                         Relevant
($500 per oven)                      range #3
                        Relevant
                        range #2
  $2,000   Relevant
           range #1
  $1,500

  $1,000

   $500


              1       2       3       4
                 Ovens required
```

CONTRIBUTION PRICING

A company prices products or services based on one of the following strategies:

1. Full price based on what an individual or small group of people are willing to pay under normal sales options.

2. Price that covers variable expenses and fixed expenses at a sales level at which the full price strategy has achieved its maximum total sales potential.

3. Price that covers variable expenses and contributes some profit, regardless of whether this profit is sufficient to cover all fixed costs.

Both of the latter two pricing strategies can be called "contribution pricing strategies," because they are not intended solely to generate a profit but merely to cover fixed expenses once the intended sales level is reached. For example, assume that a company has found that its optimum price for maximizing sales is $20 per unit sold, at which price it sells 15,000 units. If it charges more than $20 per unit, the number of units sold will decrease by a higher percent than the increase in unit price, resulting in a lower total net income. Assuming its fixed expenses are $245,000, the company can calculate the necessary charge per unit that will cover its fixed and variable expenses at the 15,000 unit sales level. That price would be $16.33 (=245,000/15,000).

Chapter 17: Different Types of Costs 17,011

			Maximum full price sales level	Variable plus fixed costs at this sales level		
Sales	100,000	200,000	300,000			
Variable Expenses	45,000	90,000	135,000	135,000		
Contribution margin	55,000	110,000	165,000		Total costs at 15,000 unit << sales.	
Fixed expenses	110,000	110,000	110,000	110,000		
				245,000		
Net income	(55,000)	0	55,000			
Units sold	5,000	10,000	25,000	15,000	Unit price required to cover total costs without generating a profit at 15,000 << unit sales.	
Full unit price	$20.00	$20.00	$20.00	$16.33		

If the company were to charge this $16.33 price on all of its sales, it would only break even at 15,000 units sold and generate a $36,667 loss at 10,000 units sold, as demonstrated below:

Income Statements Assuming All Sales Are Made at the Price of $16.33

Sales	81,667	163,333	245,000
Variable expenses	36,750	90,000	135,000
Contribution margin	44,917	73,333	110,000
Fixed expenses	110,000	110,000	110,000
Net income	(65,083)	(36,667)	(0)
Units sold	5,000	10,000	15,000
Price to cover total costs at 15,000 unit sales	$16.33	$16.33	$16.33

The company has already determined that its maximum profit is generated by selling 15,000 units at $20 each. Therefore, lowering the price in its principal market would not be a good decision. However, it should consider selling any additional units above the 15,000 full price units at some price lower than $20 in a market other than its principal full-price market. This new lower price is called a "contribution price." If the company was able to sell 5,000 additional units at this new lower price without affecting its sale of 15,000 units at their full $20 price, its net income would increase by the $44,917 amount, as indicated below:

Sales	81,667 = 5,000 units × $16.33
Variable expenses	36,750
Contribution margin	44,917
Fixed expenses	
Net income	44,917

17,012 Part IV: Management Accounting

Units sold	5,000
Price to cover total costs at $300,000 sales	$16.33

Any price higher than the company's variable expenses would increase its net income, provided that it did not affect its full-price market where it sells 15,000 units at $20 per unit. The company's variable expenses are $9.00 per unit as calculated below:

$$\text{Variable expenses per unit} = \frac{\$135,000}{15,000} = \$9.00$$

If it sells the additional 5,000 units at $9.10, its net income would increase by $500, as calculated below:

Sales	45,500 = 5,000 units × $9.10
Variable expenses	45,000 = 5,000 units × $9.00
Contribution margin	500
Fixed expenses	
Net income	500
Units sold	5,000
Price to cover total costs at $300,000 sales	$9.10

Contribution-priced sales can radically change a restaurant's profits. In the following example, assuming that based on its hypothetical elasticity of demand, the number of tops the restaurant can sell peak at an average price of $18.00 per top. At this price, the profit is barely $194. If the restaurant charges more than $18.00, the percent of the number of seats sold diminishes more than the percent increase in price and its profit will decrease.

Income statement with only full-price sales

Cover sold at full price	3,500	3,000	2,500	2,000	1,500	1,100	950	
Full price	$5.00	$7.00	$9.00	$11.50	$14.00	$18.00	$20.00	
Variable expense per unit	$4	$4	$4	$4	$4	$4	$4	
Full price sales	17,500	21,000	22,500	23,000	21,000	19,800	19,000	
Variable expenses	14,000	12,000	10,000	8,000	6,000	4,400	3,800	
Contribution margin	3,500	9,000	12,500	15,000	15,000	15,400	15,200	
Fixed expenses	15,000	15,000	15,000	15,000	15,000	15,000	15,000	
Net income	(11,500)	(6,000)	(2,500)	0	0	400	200	

If the restaurant engages in contribution pricing by selling its extra tops at a contribution price of $7.00, a price that covers its variable costs and only some of its fixed costs, it can realize a greater profit, as shown in the following income statement:

Income statement with full-price and contribution priced sales

Cover sold at full price	3,500	3,000	2,500	2,000	1,500	1,100	950
Full price	$5.00	$7.00	$9.00	$11.50	$14.00	$18.00	$20.00
Variable expense per unit	$4	$4	$4	$4	$4	$4	$4
Full price sales	17,500	21,000	22,500	23,000	21,000	19,800	19,000
Variable expenses	14,000	12,000	10,000	8,000	6,000	4,400	3,800
Contribution margin	3,500	9,000	12,500	15,000	15,000	15,400	15,200
Fixed expenses	15,000	15,000	15,000	15,000	15,000	15,000	15,000
Net income	(11,500)	(6,000)	(2,500)	0	0	400	200
Covers sold at contribution price of					500	1,000	2,000
Contribution price					$7.00	$7.00	$7.00
Variable expense per unit					$4.00	$4.00	$4.00
Contribution margin per unit on contribution priced sales					$3.00	$3.00	$3.00
Contribution margin per unit times units sold at contribution price					$1,500.00	$3,000.00	$6,000.00
Tops available for sale	3,500	3,500	3,500	3,500	3,500	3,500	3,500
Total covers sold	3,500	3,000	2,500	2,000	2,000	2,100	2,950
Total profit (Full price sales + Contribution priced sales)	(11,500)	(6,000)	(2,500)	0	1,500	3,400	6,200

Conditions Required to Use Contribution Pricing

The following two conditions must exist before a company can engage in contribution pricing:

1. It must have excess unused capacity at the time the contribution-priced customers are rendered a service.
2. It must be selling at the lower-than-full-price rate to a different market than its full-price market.

If the company does not have excess capacity, it will be replacing full-price-paying customers with contribution-price customers, thus lowering its net income. If it is not selling to a different market, the company may lose its full-price-paying customers because other customers are receiving the same service at a lower price. Examples of differentiated markets are:

- *The volume market.* If a customer buys a large number of rooms or covers, he or she is given a lower price. This approach should only be used if a company has excess capacity on a year-round basis.

- *The no-reservations market.* If the hospitality company selects a specific time to render a service, it can schedule the service when it has excess capacity. A highly booked company can also use this approach.
- *Sales to large corporations.*
- *Sales to the government.*

The list of differentiated markets is large. Some hotel companies have more than a hundred different room rates for the same room, designed for sales in different markets.

DIRECT COSTS VERSUS INDIRECT COSTS

Direct costs are costs that can be specifically identified with a particular activity, department, or segment of a business. In a hotel with both a rooms department and a restaurant, waiters' wages can be specifically and exclusively identified with the restaurant and are, therefore, direct expenses of the food department. Furthermore, direct expenses are expenses that will cease to exist if their related activity, department, or segment is eliminated. Thus, if the hotel's restaurant is closed, the waiters' wages would be eliminated.

An indirect cost cannot be specifically, clearly, or exclusively identified with any particular activity, department, or segment of a business. Therefore, its continuance does not depend on any single activity, department, or business segment. Fixed rent payments would be an example of this kind of expense for the hotel mentioned above. If a single amount is paid to rent the entire building in which both the hotel and restaurant are housed, then the exact dollar amount of rent that applies to the rooms department of the hotel, as opposed to the amount that applies to the restaurant, cannot be determined. Furthermore, if the restaurant or hotel is closed, then the rent on the entire building will still be due and payable.

Any specific expense can be both direct and indirect, depending on the context within which it is viewed. This is best observed in the summary long-form income statement shown in Exhibit 17-1. It is constructed in a format similar to that recommended in the ninth edition of the Uniform Chart of Accounts for the Lodging Industry (USAL). Although the current tenth edition does not include this format, the summary long-form income statement is useful because it assists in conceptualizing multi-segment businesses. A similar income statement could be constructed for a restaurant business or any hospitality business with several restaurants or segments. The expenses listed in each line of this income statement are direct expenses of their respective departments. These direct expenses are presented in greater detail in the department schedules whose identifying number appears in the correspondingly titled column. Thus, the expenses listed in the row titled "Administrative and general" are direct expenses of that department. This department renders support services to the other departments of the hotel; however, its expenses are considered indirect with regard to the other departments of the hotel because most of the administrative and general expenses cannot be specifically identified with any other particular department. Thus, they are both direct and indirect expenses, depending on whether they are viewed within the context of the administrative and general department or in relation to other departments of the hotel. When viewing the hotel as a whole, the administrative and general expenses become direct expenses again. This is due to the fact that they can be specifically identified with the hotel. If the hotel closes, these expenses would be eliminated.

Exhibit 17-1: Summary Long-Form Income Statement for Hotel Charles

Hotel Charles
Summary Long-Form Income Statement for the year ended December 31, 20XX

	Schedules	Net Revenues	Cost of Sales	Payroll Expense	Other Expenses	Income (Loss)
Operated Departments						
Rooms	1	$1,023,768		$176,042	$75,664	$772,062
Food	2	598,472	209,465	155,716	64,892	168,399
Telecommunications	3	74,399	50,317	13,169	7,144	3,769
Other Income and Store Rentals	4					27,471
Total Operated Departments		$1,696,639	$259,782	$344,927	$147,700	$971,701
Undistributed Operating Expenses						
Administrative and General	7			46,528	27,751	74,279
Data Processing	8			21,739	10,835	32,574
Human Resources	9			21,942	39,771	61,713
Transportation	10			14,007	6,993	21,000
Marketing	11			34,115	30,682	64,797
Property Operation and Maintenance	12			29,537	49,312	78,849
Energy Costs	13			24,663	80,349	105,012
Total Undistributed Operating Expenses				$192,531	$245,693	$438,224
Income Before Fixed Charges		1,696,639	259,782	537,458	393,393	533,477

	Schedules	Net Revenues	Cost of Sales	Payroll Expense	Other Expenses	Income (Loss)
Rent, Property Taxes, and Insurance	14					86,450
Interest Expense	14					40,301
Depreciation and Amortization	14					97,845
Income Before Income Taxes						308,881
Income Tax	15					120,464
Net Income						$188,417

An important controllership function is that of facilitating the identification of, or identifying, direct costs that may not be easily recognized. A controller should not be a mere provider of historical accounting information; he or she should be a part of the decision-making process by imaginatively and proactively seeking and identifying direct costs that may be mixed with indirect costs that go undetected. Failure to identify all direct costs is conducive to making erroneous decisions. Two instances of hidden direct costs are presented in Example 8.

EXAMPLE 8:

Instance 1

Assume there is a hotel with rooms, food, beverage, and telecommunications departments. A controller might suggest that the electricity consumed by the individual departments be determined through the use of sub-metering, although the USAL income statement groups all utility expenses together and presents them as indirect expenses.

Instance 2

Assume there is a corporation with three restaurants and that there are six employees in the human resources department with the following distribution of responsibilities: two are involved in hiring for all three restaurants, two are responsible for certain types of training, and two are responsible for other miscellaneous duties related to each restaurant. If consideration were given to closing one of the restaurants, the full financial benefits of closing it would not become apparent unless the human resources department responsibilities were restructured so that two employees were made responsible for all the human resources functions for each of the three restaurants. This restructuring would convert what was previously an indirect cost for all three restaurants to a direct cost of each one individually, permitting the elimination of two salaries in the human resources department if one restaurant is closed. The human resources department manager might not be motivated to take the trouble to reorganize the department, but the controller can point out the potential savings involved.

EXPANDED INCOME STATEMENT

The expanded income statement shown in Exhibit 17-2 is based on the assumption that all variable expenses are direct expenses because they change in direct proportion to sales. This expanded income statement demonstrates the relationship between direct, indirect, variable, and fixed expenses. For example, it highlights the fact that decisions regarding the elimination of segments should be made at the segment income level. It also helps to highlight the role of the different types of costs included on this income statement when making incremental pricing and investing decisions.

Exhibit 17-2: Expanded Income Statement

Standard Income Statement
Combined
Restaurants A and B
Sales $500,000
Expenses $450,000
Net Income $ 50,000

Expanded Income Statement

	Restaurants		
	A	B	Total
Sales	$200,000	$300,000	$500,000
Cost of Sales (100% variable)	50,000	100,000	150,000
Gross Profit	150,000	200,000	350,000
Other 100% Variable Expenses	5,000	10,000	15,000
Variable element of direct mixed expenses	20,000	15,000	35,000
Contribution Margin	125,000	175,000	300,000
Fixed Expenses			
Direct Fixed Expenses			
Fixed element of direct mixed expenses	20,000	30,000	50,000
100% fixed direct expenses	10,000	15,000	25,000
Department (Segment) Income	$115,000	$160,000	$225,000
Indirect Fixed Expenses			
Variable element of indirect mixed expenses			15,000
Fixed element of indirect mixed expenses			85,000
100% fixed indirect expenses			75,000
Net Income			$ 50,000

SERVICE/PRODUCT COSTS VERSUS PERIOD COSTS

Another frequently used method of classifying costs is to identify them as direct costs with regard to a particular product (food or beverages) or a particular service (sale of rooms, sale of telecommunications services, sale of parking and garage services). If an expense cannot be specifically identified with either products or services, then the expense is an indirect expense with regard to that product or service and is considered to be a period cost, a cost incurred due to the passage of time. In the hospitality industry, all costs are period costs except for the cost of food and beverage sales; the cost of any other hospitality-related merchandise sale; and the cost of laundry, linen, and guest supplies in a hotel. Although these expenses are few, cost of food and beverage sales consumes between 20% and 40% of every sales dollar. In take-out restaurants, the cost of food sold includes:

- Paper, plastic bags, or other take-out containers
- Napkins, cups, and disposable utensils

The expense category, "Laundry, linen and guest supplies," usually consumes only approximately 2.5% to 3% of every room's revenue dollar. Because the hospitality industry is a service industry, labor, along with cost of sales, is the other major expense category in this industry. Labor can consume up to 20% (hotels) or 50% (restaurants) of every revenue dollar. As opposed to the manufacturing industry, in which direct labor is added to the cost of products sold, labor in the hospitality industry is considered a period cost. Regardless of food and beverage sales, it is necessary to have a certain number of kitchen personnel and waiters on staff, thus salaries and wages are considered period costs.

JOINT COSTS AND THE YIELD RATIO

Joint costs help to generate revenue from more than one source. In the Charles Hotel income statement in Exhibit 17-1, all the costs below the Total Operated Departments' income are joint costs because they offer services to more than one revenue-generating department. Joint costs can also exist on a smaller scale. The cost of trimming meat is a joint cost, a portion of which can be considered the cost of the meat and the remainder of which can be considered the cost of the fat and the trimmings.

When purchasing meat, poultry, or fish from different suppliers, it can be determined that after removing all the unusable parts (the fat and the trimmings), the ratio, by weight, of usable parts to those that must be discarded or sold by the pound as waste by-products will differ for each supplier. This ratio is called the butchering yield factor. It is obviously advantageous to purchase from those suppliers whose product has the highest butchering yield factor. A further loss of weight occurs during the cooking process. The weight of the food left after trimming and cooking can be divided by the original weight invoiced and paid for to derive the overall yield factor, which can be expressed as a percent or a decimal figure. This yield factor can be used in the following formula to determine the pounds of meat, poultry, or fish that must be purchased for a given number of portions:

$$\text{Pounds to purchase} = \frac{\text{Lbs. per portion} \times \text{Portions desired}}{\text{Yield factor (as a decimal)}}$$

In the hospitality industry the revenue received from any by-products, such as fat and trimmings, that are sold is usually deducted from the cost of the principal product—in this case, the meat, poultry, or fish.

RELEVANT COSTS, INCREMENTAL COSTS, AND SUNK COSTS

A relevant cost is a cost that matters when making a future decision. In the decision concerning which of two elevators to buy, if one company charges for a two-year warranty and the other does not, the cost of the warranty is a relevant cost. If all companies charge the same amount for the warranty, then the cost of the warranty is not a relevant cost in deciding which elevator to buy. However, if the elevator takes visitors to an observation platform and there is a charge for this, then the cost of the warranty is a relevant cost insofar as the calculation of the return on investment for this activity is concerned.

An incremental cost is also a relevant cost. Incremental costs are the additional costs that must be incurred to generate additional revenue. For example, a hotel is at 80% occupancy and wishes to increase its occupancy by 10% (to 90%) to generate additional daily income of $3,000. Assume that the hotel would have to spend $1,000 more on publicity, utilities, and room attendant wages. In this case, depreciation expense, property taxes, property insurance, and interest expense would not increase. The incremental expenses—that is, publicity, utilities, and wages, would be relevant to the decision; and depreciation expense, property taxes, property insurance, and interest expense would not. But assume the hotel wanted to increase occupancy by 20% to increase daily income by $6,000, and management believes additional rooms would be required to achieve this goal. If it involves an increase of $3,500 in depreciation expense, property taxes, property insurance, and interest expense, then the increase in depreciation expense, property taxes, property insurance, and interest expense would also be relevant because the $3,500 additional amount incurred would be a necessary incremental cost of generating the additional $6,000 revenue.

A *sunk cost* is a past cost and should not be taken into account in making future decisions. For instance, the purchase last year of an elaborate computer system is a sunk cost. If a breakthrough in computer technology is made in the current year that allows for a much faster computer system that is not compatible with an existing computer system but provides more competitive information, the current year's capital budgeting decisions should not be impacted by last year's computer purchase. If rate-of-return calculations show that investing in a new computer system again this year will bring the highest return, then the decision should be made on its own merits, without regard for any previous purchases of computer systems. Under the above-described conditions, such previous purchases are sunk costs and are not relevant to the current decision.

CONTROLLABLE VERSUS NONCONTROLLABLE COSTS

Costs can be defined as controllable or noncontrollable only within the context of a particular management level. All expenses are controllable at some level of the management hierarchy, if only by closing a particular business entity. The fixed charges of hotels and restaurants are not usually controllable by the managers of these business entities. They are controlled by the owners or, in the case of multientity enterprises, by the regional or divisional manager. In the Hotel Charles shown in Exhibit 17-1, the expenses in each department's row should be controlled by the manager of the respective department. Usually controllable expenses are also direct expenses. It is difficult to imagine an expense that cannot be identified specifically with a department being controlled by the manager of that department. That does not mean that all noncontrollable expenses are indirect expenses. The fixed charges of hotels and restaurants may not be controlled by their general managers, but they are direct expenses of each of these entities because they will be eliminated if the entity is disposed of. Controllable expenses are used to evaluate managerial performance.

STANDARD COSTS

Standard costs are used to evaluate management performance. Standard cost analysis is usually performed in association with the analysis of standard revenue.

Standard costs are ideal costs calculated by management to be used as target costs. By comparing actual costs to standard costs, the degree of management success in achieving ideal costs is evaluated. This comparison is made through the analysis of variances between actual and standard costs. Standard costs can be calculated for food and beverages sold, for services sold, or for the cost of supporting services, such as those provided by the undistributed operating departments shown on the Hotel Charles income statement in Exhibit 17-1. (See Chapter 16, "Maximizing Profit and Minimizing Costs," for a further discussion)

OPPORTUNITY COST

An opportunity cost is not a cost in the sense that it entails an additional consumption of assets or services, the usual measure of an expense. An opportunity cost entails forgoing income from one type of activity in order to use the funds invested in this activity elsewhere. For example, if a restaurant has $100,000 invested in a certificate of deposit that earns 5% interest and it needs to use this money to construct an extension to the restaurant, it must give up this income as part of the cost of building the extension. Assuming the extension increases the restaurant's annual earnings by $25,000, the true increase in earnings is $25,000 less the $5,000 annual interest income previously received from the certificate of deposit. In this sense, the $5,000 of lost interest is a cost of constructing the restaurant extension—the cost of a forgone opportunity.

CHAPTER 18
COST ALLOCATION

CONTENTS

Factors Involved in Cost Allocation	18,002
Allocation of Undistributed Operating Expenses—Cost Objects, Cost Pools, and Direct and Indirect Expenses	18,002
Choosing an Allocation Basis	18,005
Traditional Cost Allocation—USAL Direct Method	18,006
Traditional Cost Allocation—USAL Step Method	18,009
Traditional Cost Allocation—USAL Formula Method	18,011
Activity-Based Costing and Activity-Based Management Examples	18,012
Allocated Costs as Motivators	18,012
Activity-Based Allocation to Measure Productivity	18,013
Activity-Based Allocation to Minimize Unnecessary Use of Services	18,015
Activity-Based Management	18,015
Misinterpreting Post-Allocation Income	18,016

Exhibits

Exhibit 18-1.	Sample Restaurant Income	18,003
Exhibit 18-2.	Sample House Laundry Schedule	18,004
Exhibit 18-3.	List of Possible Allocation Bases	18,005
Exhibit 18-4.	Sample USAL Direct Method Calculations	18,007
Exhibit 18-5.	Resulting Allocated Income Statements	18,008
Exhibit 18-6.	Flowchart of Allocated Costs	18,009
Exhibit 18-7.	Sample USAL Step Method Calculations	18,010
Exhibit 18-8.	Resulting Allocated Income Statements	18,010
Exhibit 18-9.	Flowchart of Allocated Costs	18,011
Exhibit 18-10.	Flowchart of USAL Formula Method	18,012
Exhibit 18-11.	Broad-Brush Traditional Allocation Method	18,013
Exhibit 18-12.	ABC Allocation Method	18,013
Exhibit 18-13.	Post-Allocation Income Statement Based on ABC Allocation	18,015
Exhibit 18-14.	Post-Allocation Income Calculation	18,016

As discussed in Chapter 17, "Different Types of Costs," direct expenses can be specifically identified with a particular activity, department, or segment of a business. For example, the cost of food and beverages sold and the cost of operating supplies can be specifically identified with their respective individual departments and do not need to be allocated to those departments. Indirect expenses cannot be specifically identified with individual entities or activities, and therefore can only be associated with the entities or activities to which they are indirectly related by assigning them, or allocating them, based on some more or less arbitrary basis. Because of this indirect relationship and the arbitrariness of their allocation, segment income statements that include allocated expenses have limited and specific uses.

FACTORS INVOLVED IN COST ALLOCATION

The operating results reported on the basis of allocated expenses can be misleading because (1) they are approximate, (2) they can be easily considered incremental or differential costs in situations in which they are not, and (3) they can lead department managers to give precedence to short-term profit maximization over long-term profit maximization. Despite these drawbacks, there are five reasons why allocating expenses may be advantageous. These are: (1) to evaluate efficient use of resources, such as space; (2) to motivate managers of individual departments; (3) to minimize unnecessary use of the services provided by support departments and thus minimize charges against using departments' income; (4) to motivate support departments to render more efficiently services for which other departments are being charged; and (5) to serve as guidelines in establishing prices of individual services or products on a full-cost basis. This chapter discusses some allocation methods and their advantages and disadvantages.

Cost allocation involves three steps:

1. Identifying a service, product, or entity to which costs need to be allocated (called the *cost object*). These can be profit centers or other cost centers.
2. Identifying the costs that are related to a particular cost object (called the *cost pool*).
3. Selecting a basis for associating or allocating the appropriate amounts of these cost pools with their cost object (called *cost drivers*).

As an examination of the income statement of the Charles Hotel reveals (see Exhibit 17-1 in Chapter 17), the Uniform System of Accounts for the Lodging Industry (USAL) summary income statement does not incorporate cost allocation. Although not evident from a review of this statement, the only expense that is allocated is that of the house laundry. The undistributed operating expenses are reported on the statement as indirect expenses with regard to the other departments despite the fact that they render services to the profit-generating operated departments (profit centers), listed at the top of the income statement, and to the other undistributed operating expense departments (cost centers). Laundry expenses can be allocated because the amount of service rendered to each department is easily identifiable. Other undistributed operating expenses cannot be accurately or fairly allocated, although as was pointed out in the previous chapter with regard to sub-metering electricity expense, a controller should be aware that this limitation does not always apply.

ALLOCATION OF UNDISTRIBUTED OPERATING EXPENSES— COST OBJECTS, COST POOLS, AND DIRECT AND INDIRECT EXPENSES

The potential to allocate expenses only exists when an expense can be related to more than one product, service, activity, or entity. In the case of the summary income statement of the Charles Hotel, every department, both the profit-generating operated departments (profit centers) and the undistributed operating expense departments (cost centers), are potential cost objects. The potential cost pools are the departments that render services to the profit-generating departments. These are the undistributed operating expense departments and the fixed charges of the hotel.

Restaurants differ from hotels in that they do not specifically identify payroll and related expenses, nor do they identify direct operating expenses, with individual revenue-generating activities (such as the food and beverage departments). Only sales and cost of sales are usually reported segmentally on their income statement. Restaurant employees often work in both the food and beverage service areas so that it is usually impossible to identify and associate their individual salaries with only one type of revenue-generating activity. Exhibit 18-1 presents sample restaurant income for Brushfire Grill Restaurant.

Exhibit 18-1: Sample Restaurant Income

Brushfire Grill Restaurant

Sales:	
Food	$2,000,567
Beverages	720,204
Catering	185,389
Total sales	2,906,160
Cost of sales:	
Food	800,227
Beverages	180,051
Catering	46,347
Total cost of sales	1,026,625
Gross margin	1,879,535
Operating expenses:	
Salaries and wages	697,478
Employee benefits	112,497
Direct operating expenses	104,300
Music and entertainment	26,551
Marketing	97,000
Utility services	56,284
Administrative and general expenses	112,736
Repairs and maintenance	41,288
Occupancy costs	120,332
Depreciation	67,393
Other income	(4,421)
Total operating expenses:	1,431,438
Operating income	448,097
Interest	18,522
Income before income taxes	429,575

18,004 Part IV: Management Accounting

Income taxes	171,830
Net income	$ 257,745

There is one cost pool in the USAL for which certain expenses do not appear among the undistributed operating expenses on the summary income statement—that is, the house laundry. Its expenses are regularly allocated to other departments of a hotel because a reliable link can be established between the benefits received by its client departments and the cost of operating the laundry. A somewhat refined cost driver exists for laundry department expenses—namely, pounds of laundry processed. Thus, laundry expenses can be allocated much more precisely than the undistributed operating departments' expenses, almost to the extent that the process is not an allocation at all, but rather a specific identification of the laundry costs incurred by each department, which would make them direct expenses. However, they are direct only to the extent that they meet the essential test of a direct expense. To be direct, an expense must be so closely associated with a department that if the department closes, the related expense will cease to exist. If one of the departments serviced by the laundry disappears, the laundry's expenses may be reduced, but they will not all cease to exist. Those expenses that can be reduced were truly direct expenses of the closed department. There are certain basic expenses of the laundry department, such as the manager's salary, that cannot be eliminated if one or two other departments are closed. This prevents all laundry department expenses from being unallocated direct expenses. Exhibit 18-2 shows a sample house laundry schedule similar to the one prescribed by the USAL.

Exhibit 18-2: Sample House Laundry Schedule

House Laundry Schedule

Payroll and Related Expenses:

Salaries and wages	$66,473
Employee benefits	12,481
Total Payroll and Related Expenses	53,992

Other expenses:

Cleaning supplies	783
Contract services	6,795
Laundry supplies	5,799
Printing and stationery	400
Telecommunications	200
Training	1,348
Uniforms	579
Total Other Expenses	15,904
Total Expenses	69,896

Credits received:

Cost of guest and outside laundry		(19,635)
Concessionaires' laundry		(6,892)
Total Credits		(26,527)
Cost of House Laundry		43,369

Charged to Operated Departments:

Rooms	Schedule _____	20,298
Food	Schedule _____	12,958
Beverage	Schedule _____	5,327
Golf course	Schedule _____	1,311
Other operated departments	Schedule _____	3,475
Total Charged to Operated Departments		$ 43,369

CHOOSING AN ALLOCATION BASIS

Although cost allocations are never accurate or even fair, there are certain concepts that can be considered when determining an allocation basis to minimize the unfairness of the allocation. These are:

- Benefits received by assignee product, service, activity, department, or division.

- Degree to which the assignee product, service, activity, department, or division causes the indirect costs to increase.

For example, marketing department costs can be allocated to each profit-generating department based on their sales. Sales can then serve as the basis for measuring the benefit derived by each department from the marketing activities of the hotel. Administrative and general expenses, on the other hand, can be allocated based on the number of employees of each department. The assumption here is that the expenses of this service department increase or decrease in some general relation to the number of employees in each department.

Exhibit 18-3 presents a list of possible allocation bases that comply with the above two criteria for use with traditional allocation procedures.

Exhibit 18-3: List of Possible Allocation Bases

Some Allocated Undistributed Operating Expenses	Potential Allocation Bases
Telecommunications	Number of telephones
Payroll taxes and employee benefits	1. Number of employees in department 2. Total payroll cost
Administrative and general	1. Number of employees in department 2. Total payroll cost

Some Allocated Undistributed Operating Expenses	Potential Allocation Bases
Information systems Marketing	Number of employees in department 1. Dollar sales 2. Unit sales
Guest entertainment	1. Dollar sales 2. Unit sales
Energy costs Property operation and maintenance	Cubic feet of area occupied 1. Number of repairs plus maintenance activity 2. Square feet
Human resources Transportation	Number of employees in department Number of employees in department
Some Allocated Fixed Costs	**Potential Allocation Bases**
Rent	1. Percent applicable to revenue sources 2. Square feet of area occupied (fixed rent)
Real estate taxes Insurance—building and contents	Square feet of area occupied 1. Square feet of area occupied 2. Square feet plus investment in furniture and fixtures
Interest Depreciation—building	Same Square feet of area occupied
Depreciation—capital leases	1. Department use of leased equipment 2. Square feet of area occupied

Note: Furniture and equipment can be depreciated according to cost records.

Because allocated (indirect) expenses do not cease to exist when a business, division, department, or activity is terminated, they will have to be covered by the remaining businesses, divisions, departments, or activities.

The traditional allocation approach is a broad brush approach in which the cost of entire departments is allocated as one single whole. The USAL proposes three methods of allocating indirect expenses (undistributed operating departments and fixed charges) using the traditional approach. These are the direct method, the step method, and the formula method.

TRADITIONAL COST ALLOCATION—USAL DIRECT METHOD

In the direct method all indirect expenses, fixed charges, and undistributed operating expenses are allocated directly to the profit-generating departments in a single step. An example of this allocation method using overly simplified hotel management statistics to facilitate the calculations is shown in Exhibit 18-4. Income taxes are not allocated, thus the post-allocation department income total equals the income before income taxes.

Exhibit 18-4: Sample USAL Direct Method Calculations

Hotel Small
Summary Long-Form Income Statement
for the year ended December 31, 20XX

	Net Revenues	Cost of Sales	Payroll Expense	Other Expenses	Income (Loss)
Operated departments					
Rooms	$1,023,768		$176,042	$75,664	$772,062
Telecommunications	74,399	$30,411	23,726	7,144	13,118
Total operated departments	1,098,167	30,411	199,768	82,808	785,180
Undistributed operating expenses					
Administrative and general			66,528	17,734	84,262
Energy			34,467	58,456	92,923
Total undistributed operating expenses			100,995	76,190	177,185
Income before fixed charges	$1,098,167	$30,411	$300,763	$158,998	607,995
Property taxes					47,753
Depreciation and amortization					73,947
Income before income taxes					486,295
Income tax					189,655
Net income					$296,640

Expense	Allocation Basis	Department Specifications	
		Square Feet	Employees
Rooms		18,000	8
Telecommunications		400	1
Administrative and general	Number of employees	1,200	2
Energy	Department Floor area	2,000	1
Property taxes	Department Floor area		
Depreciation	Department Floor area		

Direct Method Allocation

Cost Pool		Cost Object	Allocation Basis		Allocated Amounts	
Undistributed operating expenses			Employees	%	Rooms	Telecom.
Administrative and general		Rooms	8	89%	$74,900	
		Telecommuni-cations	1	11%		$74,900
Total	$84,262				$9,362	9,362
		Totals	9	100%		
		Square Feet				
Energy	$92,923		18,000	98%	91,065	91,065
			400	2%		1,858	1,858
Total	$177,185		18,400	100%	$165,964	$11,221	$177,185
Fixed charges						
Property taxes	47,753	Rooms		98%	119,054		$119,054
Depreciation	73,947	Telecommunications		2%		2,646	2,646
Total	$121,700	Totals		100%	$119,054	$2,646	$121,700

In Exhibit 18-5, the resulting allocated income statements are presented in a format similar to that recommended by the USAL for presenting adjusted departmental income.

Exhibit 18-5: Resulting Allocated Income Statements

Hotel Small—Direct Method
Schedule of Post-Allocation Departmental Profit or Loss

	Rooms	Telecom-munications
Net revenue	$1,023,768	$74,399
Expenses	251,706	61,281
Reported departmental income	$772,062	$13,118
Less: Traceable undistributed expenses		
Traceable departmental income	772,062	13,118
Less: Allocated undistributed expenses	165,964	11,221
Less: Allocated fixed charges	119,054	2,646
Post-Allocation departmental income	$487,044	($749)

This statement includes a line for "traceable undistributed expenses," such as electricity expense when sub-metering is used. The combined post-allocation departmental income equals the income before taxes—$486,295.

A flowchart of the allocated costs is shown in Exhibit 18-6.

Exhibit 18-6: Flowchart of Allocated Costs

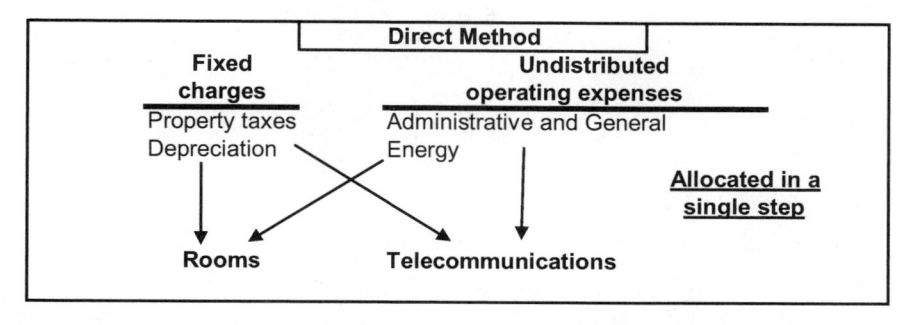

```
┌─────────────────────────────────────────────────────────────┐
│                    Direct Method                            │
│        Fixed                  Undistributed                 │
│       charges               operating expenses              │
│    Property taxes        Administrative and General         │
│     Depreciation              Energy                        │
│           ╲          ╱            │          Allocated in a │
│            ╲        ╱             │           single step   │
│             ╲      ╱              │                         │
│              ╳                    ▼                         │
│            ╱   ╲                                            │
│           ▼     ▼                                           │
│         Rooms    Telecommunications                         │
└─────────────────────────────────────────────────────────────┘
```

TRADITIONAL COST ALLOCATION—USAL STEP METHOD

In the step method, all fixed charges are allocated first to both profit centers and undistributed operating expense service departments. A decision must then be made regarding the sequence of allocation of service departments that render services to other service departments. Usually, the administrative and general department is considered to render services to all other departments, so it is allocated first to both profit centers and service centers based on the selected allocation basis. Then the department that renders services to most of the remaining service departments is allocated, step after step, until all the service department expenses, including the allocations received for fixed charges and from other service departments, are allocated to the profit centers. The calculation process is shown in Exhibit 18-7.

18,010   Part IV: Management Accounting

Exhibit 18-7: Sample USAL Step Method Calculations

Step Method Allocation

Cost Pool	Cost Object	Allocation Basis Square Feet	%	Allocated Amount	Original Amount	New Total Amount
Step #1						
Allocate fixed charges						
Property taxes 47,753	Rooms	18,000	83%	$101,417	$251,706	$353,123
Depreciation 73,947	Telecommunications	400	2%	2,254	61,281	63,535
Total $121,700	Administrative and General	1,200	6%	6,761	84,262	91,023
	Energy	2,000	9%	11,269	92,923	104,192
	Totals	21,600	100%	$121,700	$490,172	$611,872
Step #2						
Allocate administrative and general expenses	Employees					
Administrative and General 91,023	Rooms	8	80%	$72,818	$353,123	$425,941
	Telecommunications	1	10%	9,102	63,535	72,637
	Energy	1	10%	9,102	104,192	113,294
	Totals	10	100%	$91,023	$520,849	$611,872
Step #3						
Allocate energy expenses	Square feet					
Energy 113,294	Rooms	18,000	98%	$110,831	$425,941	$536,772
	Telecommunications	400	2%	2,463	72,637	75,100
	Totals	18,400	100%	$113,294	$498,578	$611,872

In Exhibit 18-8, the resulting allocated income statements are presented in a format similar to that recommended by the USAL for presenting adjusted departmental income.

Exhibit 18-8: Resulting Allocated Income Statements

Hotel Small—Step Method
Schedule of Post-Allocation Departmental Profit or Loss

	Rooms	Telecom- munications
Net revenue	$1,023,768	$74,399
Expenses	251,706	61,281
Reported department income	$772,062	$13,118
Less: Traceable undistributed expenses		
Traceable department income	772,062	13,118

	Rooms	Telecom-munications
Less: Allocated undistributed expenses and fixed charges	285,066	13,819
Post-Allocation departmental income	$ 486,996	($ 701)

Again, the combined post-allocation department incomes equal the income before income taxes—$486,295. A flowchart of the allocated costs is shown in Exhibit 18-9.

Exhibit 18-9: Flowchart of Allocated Costs

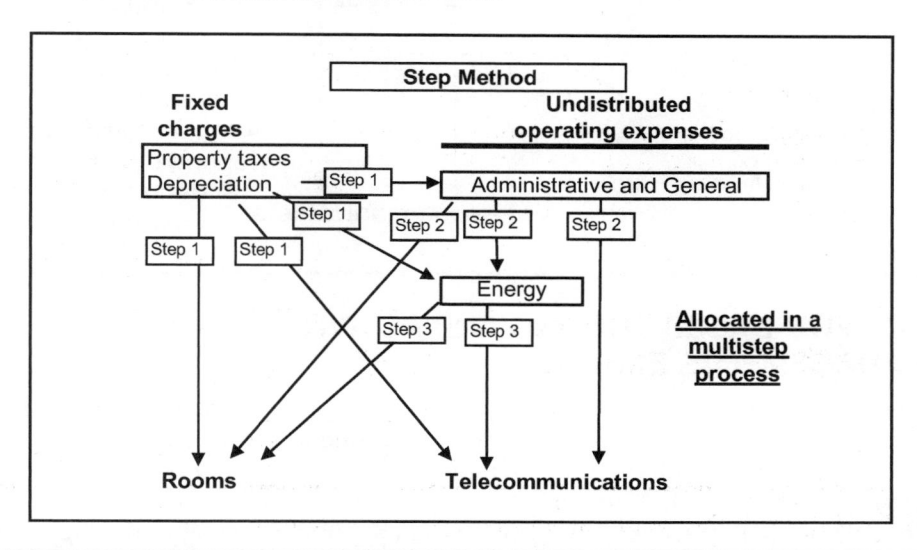

[Flowchart showing Step Method: Fixed charges (Property taxes, Depreciation) and Undistributed operating expenses (Administrative and General, Energy) allocated in a multistep process to Rooms and Telecommunications]

TRADITIONAL COST ALLOCATION—USAL FORMULA METHOD

The formula method is very similar to the step method. Fixed charges are first allocated to all profit and service departments. Then the service departments' costs are allocated to other service departments in a fashion similar to that used in the step method. The difference is that in the formula method, service departments that have received a charge from a service department can then reciprocate by allocating a different charge to the same service department from which it received a charge. This is a complicated method that requires the use of computers. As can be seen by comparing the allocation results using the direct method and the step method, the difference between these methods is not usually significant. A flowchart demonstrating this method with the Small Hotel accounts, which has been used in prior exhibits, appears in Exhibit 18-10. In this example, there are only two departments whose expenses need to reciprocate: the administrative and general department and the energy department.

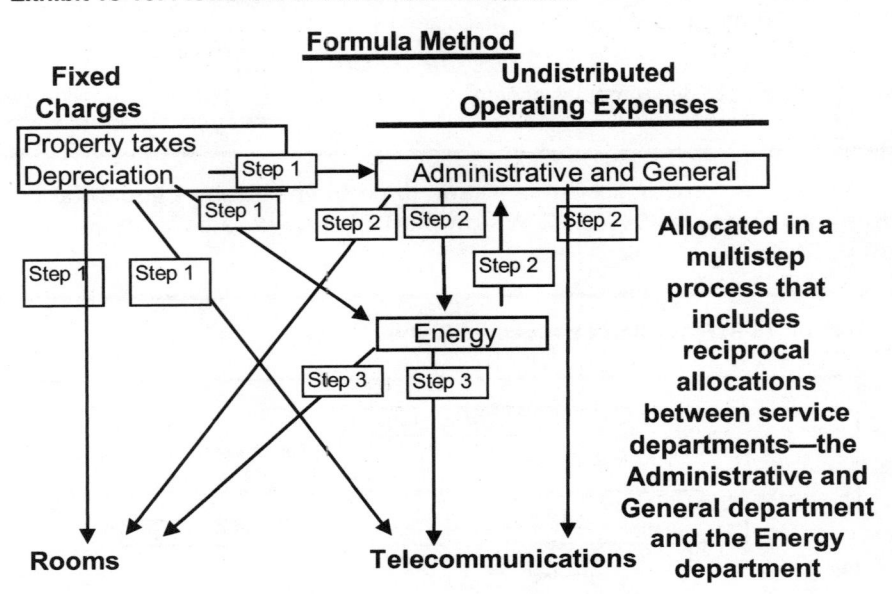

Exhibit 18-10: Flowchart of USAL Formula Method

Formula Method

Fixed Charges: Property taxes, Depreciation

Undistributed Operating Expenses: Administrative and General, Energy

Flows: Step 1, Step 2, Step 3 → Rooms, Telecommunications

Allocated in a multistep process that includes reciprocal allocations between service departments—the Administrative and General department and the Energy department

ACTIVITY-BASED COSTING AND ACTIVITY-BASED MANAGEMENTS EXAMPLES

The activity-based costing (ABC) approach uses a more refined approach by allocating activities, or processes, within departments rather than allocating the costs of an entire department. This allows for the selection of more specific cost drivers. Although this approach provides the benefit of more accurate cost determination, it is also more expensive than the traditional allocation approach. Furthermore, it has the same drawback as traditional methods of allocating indirect costs—namely, that it can mislead management into making buy, sell, or close decisions based on allocated costs that are irrelevant to the decision.

Allocated Costs as Motivators

Whether traditional or ABC allocation methods are used, the process of allocation can serve to motivate managers to maximize revenue or minimize expenses. In Exhibit 18-11, using a broad-brush allocation based on total labor dollars, it appears that the coffee shop is not covering its fair share of the entire organization's indirect expenses. It is generating a post-allocation loss of $2,500.

Exhibit 18-11: Broad-Brush Traditional Allocation Method

	Sales	Cost of Sales	Labor	Other Direct	Departmental Income	Allocated Expenses Undistributed	Allocated Expenses Fixed	Post-Allocation Income
Restaurant	$420,000	$130,000	$160,000	$40,000	$90,000	$37,500	$10,000	$42,500
Coffee Shop	200,000	60,000	100,000	25,000	15,000	$12,500	$5,000	($2,500)
Totals	$620,000	$190,000	$260,000	$65,000	$105,000	$50,000	$15,000	$40,000

Undistributed Operating Expenses
    Administrative and general $50,000   50,000
                 Operating income $55,000

Fixed Charges
    Depreciation $15,000   15,000
        Earnings before income taxes $40,000
    Income taxes   16,000
                Net income $24,000

	Square Feet
Restaurant 1	16,000
Restaurant 2	8,000
Total	24,000

This statement might serve as a stimulus to the person in charge of the coffee shop to increase revenue or improve control of expenses. However, a more refined, activity-based allocation might indicate that the coffee shop is outperforming the restaurant on a per-square-foot basis, as indicated below.

Activity-Based Allocation to Measure Productivity

If an ABC allocation method is used, the administrative and general expenses would not be allocated to the operating departments based on "total labor cost" per operating department. Instead, the labor cost would be allocated to processes within the administrative and general department. These process costs would then be allocated to the operating departments based on more specific cost drivers than "total labor cost." Exhibit 18-12 demonstrates how this might be done.

Exhibit 18-12: ABC Allocation Method

Cost of Processes within the Administrative and General Department

Hiring	16,000
Out-Processing	8,000
Training	15,000
Payroll	6,000
Advising	5,000
Total General and Administrative Expenses	50,000

Cost Drivers Based on Arbitrary Assumptions Regarding Process Usage per Entity

Process	Cost Driver	Restaurant No.	%	Coffee Shop No.	%
Hiring	Employees hired	8	89%	1	11%
Out-Processing	Employees laid off	7	88%	1	13%
Training	Employees hired	8	89%	1	11%
Payroll	Total employees	12	92%	1	8%
Advising	Employees requesting advice	3	100%	0	0%

Dollar Amount Allocated per Entity for Each Process Based on Cost Drivers

	Process Cost	Restaurant %	Restaurant Allocation	Coffee Shop Allocation
Hiring	$16,000	89%	$14,222	$1,778
Out-Processing	8,000	88%	7,000	1,000
Training	15,000	89%	13,333	1,667
Payroll	6,000	92%	5,538	462
Advising	5,000	100%	5,000	0
Total General and Administrative Expenses:	$50,000		$45,094	$4,906

The above, more refined ABC allocation method allocates only $4,906 to the coffee shop based on its actual usage of general and administrative department services, instead of the $12,500 allocated under a traditional broad-brush method that uses the total dollar payroll of the restaurant and coffee shop as the allocation basis. The post-allocation income statement for both entities would appear as shown in Exhibit 18-13.

Exhibit 18-13: Post-Allocation Income Statement Based on ABC Allocation

	Sales	Cost of Sales	Labor	Other Direct	Departmental Income	Allocated Expenses Undistributed	Fixed	Post-Allocation Income
Restaurant	$420,000	$130,000	$160,000	$40,000	$ 90,000	$45,094	$12,500	$32,406
Coffee Shop	200,000	60,000	100,000	25,000	15,000	$ 4,906	$ 2,500	$ 7,594
Totals	$620,000	$190,000	$260,000	$65,000	$105,000	$50,000	$15,000	$40,000

Undistributed Operating Expenses
    Administrative and general $50,000   50,000
        Operating income $ 55,000

Fixed Charges
    Depreciation $30,000   15,000
        Earnings before income taxes $ 40,000
    Income taxes   16,000
        Net income $ 24,000

	Square Feet
Restaurant 1	20,000
Restaurant 2	4,000
Total	24,000

Based on this more refined allocation method it would seem that on a per-square-foot basis, the coffee shop is actually generating a higher post-allocation income per square foot $1.90 (= $7,594 ÷ 4,000 sq. ft.) than the restaurant's $1.60 (= $32,406 ÷ 20,000 sq. ft.) per square foot. Under the traditional allocation method, the coffee shop appears to be generating a $2,500 post-allocation loss.

Activity-Based Allocation to Minimize Unnecessary Use of Services

This ABC method of allocation would stimulate department managers to reduce employee turnover because their departments would be rewarded with a higher post-allocation income. In the hospitality industry, a high turnover industry, these savings can be particularly significant.

Activity-Based Management

Activity-based management is the use of this more refined identification of processes (cost pools) within departments to enable department managers to focus on these processes and make more meaningful and measurable efforts to reduce their cost. In the example above, the processes that constitute the activities of the general and administrative department are now clearly identified. This enables management to focus on minimizing the costs of (1) hiring, (2) out-processing, (3) training, (4) payroll, and (5) advising by addressing them as discrete activities within the department and measuring the cost savings that do or do not result from any remedial actions taken.

MISINTERPRETING POST-ALLOCATION INCOME

Calculating post-allocation income has certain uses, but it is also prone to misinterpretation that can lead to erroneous decision making. The problem arises when allocated costs, whether allocated by the traditional methods or by the ABC method, are confused with direct costs or with incremental costs. For example, in Exhibit 18-14, Restaurant 2 has a negative post-allocation income before income taxes. What management decisions should be taken based on this income statement?

- Should Restaurant 2 be closed immediately?
- Should it be left open while a search for a better concept is conducted?
- Should the manager be replaced?

Exhibit 18-14: Post-Allocation Income Calculation

	Restaurant 1	Restaurant 2	Restaurant 3
Sales	$400,000	$200,000	$300,000
Cost of sales	120,000	80,000	99,000
Gross margin	280,000	120,000	201,000
Variable element of mixed expenses	120,000	70,000	90,000
Contribution margin	$160,000	$ 50,000	$111,000
Direct fixed expenses			
Equipment depreciation	4,000	2,000	3,000
Insurance	2,000	1,000	1,500
Other direct fixed expenses	50,000	30,000	45,000
Pre-allocation income	$104,000	$ 17,000	$ 61,500
Indirect fixed expenses			
Other indirect fixed expenses	10,000	20,000	15,000
Building depreciation	16,000	8,000	12,000
Building insurance	6,000	3,000	4,500
Real estate taxes	4,000	2,000	3,000
Total indirect fixed expenses	$ 36,000	$ 33,000	$ 34,500
Post-allocation income before income taxes	68,000	(16,000)	27,000

(Restaurant Trio spans Restaurants 1, 2, and 3.)

In fact, if Restaurant 2 is closed, the business will lose $17,000 of pre-allocation income. It will not remove a ($16,000) loss from the combined income statement because the indirect fixed expenses will remain and have to be absorbed by Restaurants 1 and 3. Thus, it is best to take one of the other two possible courses of action. This conclusion should be arrived at regardless of whether a broad-brush traditional allocation method was used or a refined ABC method was employed to allocate the indirect expenses. The method of allocation does not change the character of an expense.

In the example of the restaurant and coffee shop presented above, it would be an erroneous conclusion to believe that the $12,500 allocated to the coffee shop using traditional allocation or the $4,906 allocated to the coffee shop using ABC would be eliminated if the coffee shop were closed. Some expenses of the general and administrative department might be eliminated. In that case these would be considered direct expenses of the coffee shop, and a separate income statement based on direct versus indirect expenses should be prepared for the purpose of making such a decision. Such an income statement would also be required for making buy or sell decisions.

CHAPTER 19
COST-VOLUME-PROFIT ANALYSIS

CONTENTS

Four Basic Components of an Income Statement	19,002
Purpose of CVP Analysis	19,003
Examples of CVP Analysis—Single Product or Service	19,004
Top-Down Questions	19,004
Pro Forma Contribution Format Income Statements	19,005
Bottom-Up Questions	19,005
More Bottom-Up Questions	19,007
Example of CVP Analysis—Multiple Products or Services	19,009
Fixed Versus Variable Expenses—Risk versus Rapid Growth	19,011
CVP Graphical Analysis and the Income Statement Equation	19,012
Break-Even Graphs	19,012
Leverage	19,013
Operating Leverage	19,014
Financial Leverage	19,014
Total Leverage	19,015
Factors Affecting Leverage and Favorability of Leverage	19,016
Indifference Earnings before Income Taxes and Margin of Safety	19,018
Indifference EBT	19,018
Margin of Safety	19,019
Concepts Underlying CVP Analysis	19,020
Separation of Mixed Costs into Variable and Fixed Elements	19,021
Graph Method	19,021
Min-Max Method	19,023
Regression Method	19,024
Bottom-Up Pricing	19,025
Bottom-Up Pricing for Hotels (Hubbart Formula)	19,027
Exhibits	
Exhibit 19-1 Four Basic Components of an Income Statement	19,002
Exhibit 19-2. Various Income Statement Component Relationships	19,003
Exhibit 19-3. Pro-Forma Top-Down Income Statements Based on Data from Examples 1-3	19,005

To effectively utilize the flexibility that cost-volume-profit (CVP) analysis provides, it is important to understand that all income statements can be reduced to the four components listed below. By modifying one or more of these components a financial manager can project, hypothetically, the possible future impact on the operating results of a hospitality company. One way of expressing the function of CVP analysis is to state that it enables financial managers to obtain answers to "What if?"-type questions. For example, what would be the net income of this company if its variable per unit cost increases by 2% and its unit

19,002 *Part IV: Management Accounting*

sales volume increases by 0.50%, or what will be the new net income if variable expenses per unit are decreased by 2% and fixed costs increase by 3%?

FOUR BASIC COMPONENTS OF AN INCOME STATEMENT

An income statement contains four basic components:

1. Unit price (UP)
2. Unit variable expenses (VE)
3. Total fixed costs (FC)
4. Number of units sold (US)

Exhibit 19-1 presents their relationship.

Exhibit 19-1: Four Basic Components of an Income Statement

	Dollars	Percent	Per Unit	
Sales	$200,000	100.00%	$20.00	(1)
Variable expenses	110,000	55.00%	$11.00	(2)
Contribution margin	90,000	45.00%	$9.00	
Fixed expenses	75,000			(3)
Earnings before taxes (EBT)	15,000			
Income tax expense (40%)	6,000			
Net income	9,000			
Units sold (covers, menu items, rooms, seats, cabins)	10,000			(4)

Variable expenses change in the same direction and in the same proportion as sales. Fixed expenses are not completely fixed, although they do not change in response to changes in sales and usually remain fixed for the length of an accounting period—one year. Mixed expenses contain both a variable element and a fixed element and change in the same direction but not in the same proportion as sales. Although the variable element does change in response to sales, these expenses do not change in the same proportion as sales because the fixed element does not change in response to sales. For example, electricity expense is a mixed expense. It requires a certain amount of electricity to illuminate, cool, or heat a hospitality establishment. This expense must be incurred regardless of whether sales are generated. When customers enter an establishment, electricity consumption increases, and the variable element of electricity expenses begins to increase in approximate proportion to the number of customers. In Exhibit 19-1, mixed costs have been eliminated from the income statement because they cannot be predicted. Due to the predictive function of CVP analysis, mixed costs must be separated into their variable and fixed elements before CVP analysis can be performed. The process of separating mixed costs into their variable and fixed elements is covered later in this chapter.

Based on a review of Exhibit 19-1, it is evident that the following relationships among the various components of an income statement, as shown in Exhibit 19-2, can be derived.

Exhibit 19-2: Various Income Statement Component Relationships

Contribution margin (CM) = Sales – Variable expenses	$200,000 – $110,000 = $90,000
Contribution margin (CM) = Net income/ (1 – Tax rate) + Fixed costs (FC)	$9,000/(0.60) + $75,000 = $90,000
Unit CM = Unit price – Unit variable expenses (VE)	$9.00 = $20.00 – $11.00
Variable expenses percent = Unit VE/Unit price (UP)	55% = $11.00/$20.00
Variable expenses percent = Total variable expenses/Sales	55% = $110,000/$200,000
CM percent = Total dollar CM/Sales	45% = $90,000/$200,000
CM percent = Unit CM/Unit price	45% = $9.00/$20.00
CM percent = (Unit price – Unit variable expenses)/Unit price	45% = ($20.00 – $11.00)/$ 20.00
CM percent = 100% – Variable expense %	45% = 100% – 55%

Contribution margin is the amount of money left after paying all variable expenses required to generate sales. It is the money available to cover fixed costs and generate net income. Another way of viewing this is to consider the variable expense percent to be the incremental cost of generating an additional $1.00 of sales. In the above example, it costs the company $0.55 (55% of every dollar) to generate an additional $1.00 of sales.

PURPOSE OF CVP ANALYSIS

CVP analysis enables an accountant to evaluate the consequences of changing one or more of the above four basic income statement components and answer what-if type questions. These questions can be asked top-down or bottom-up. Top-down questions are based on specific assumptions concerning sales or fixed expenses in the quest for the resulting net income. Bottom-up questions begin with a desired net income assumption, and/or possible change in fixed expenses, and/or change in variable expenses in the quest for the required sales amount.

Sample questions include:

Top-Down Questions

- What would be the net income if units sold change by a given amount?
- What would be the net income if unit price changes by a given amount?
- What would be the net income if unit variable cost changes by a given amount?
- What would be the net income if fixed expenses change by a given amount?

Part IV: Management Accounting

Bottom-Up Questions
- What sales are required to generate a given net income, with no change in unit price, unit variable cost, or fixed expenses?
- What sales are required to generate a given net income if there is a given change in unit price, unit variable cost, or fixed expenses?
- What sales are required to break even?

Answers to these questions enable an accountant to make better decisions by evaluating the possible consequences of future courses of action.

EXAMPLES OF CVP ANALYSIS—SINGLE PRODUCT OR SERVICE

Top-Down Questions

Top-down questions are best answered by constructing a contribution format pro-forma income statement based on the new assumptions. Following are three examples of top-down "what-if" questions. The calculations are presented first and then incorporated into pro-forma income statment formats in Exhibit 19-3.

EXAMPLE 1: What would be the net income of the above firm if units sold increased by 10%?

New sales would be 110% × 10,000 units × $20.00 =	$220,000
New CM would be 45% of new sales =	$99,000
(New CM – Original CM) =	$99,000 – $90,000 = $9,000
Change in CM × (1 – Tax rate)	$9,000 × (1 – 0.40)
= Increase in NI	= $5,400

EXAMPLE 2: What would be the net income of the above firm if its unit price increased by 10% and its fixed expenses increased by 20%?

New sales would be 110% × $20.00 × 10,000 (US) =	$220,000
New CM % = (New UP – VE per unit)/New UP =	($22.00 – $11.00)/ $22.00 = 50%
New CM (50% of $220,000 new sales) =	$110,000
Increase in CM = New CM – Original CM =	$110,000 – $90,000 = $20,000
Less increase in FC (20% × $75,000) =	($15,000)
Increase in EBT	$ 5,000
Increase in EBT × (1 – Tax rate) = $5,000 × (1 – 0.40) =	$ 3,000

EXAMPLE 3: What would be the net income of the above firm if the covers sold remained the same, but its variable expenses per unit increased by $1.00 and its fixed expenses decreased by 10%?

New CM % = ($20.00 – $12.00)/ $20.00 =	40%
New CM = Sales × New CM % = $200,000 × 40% =	$80,000
Less: New FC (90% × $75,000) =	67,500
New EBT	$12,500
New EBT × (1 – Tax rate) = ($12,500 × 0.60) =	$ 7,500

Pro Forma Contribution Format Income Statements

Based on the above three sets of assumptions, the pro-forma contribution income statements are presented in Exhibit 19-3. Because these are top-down questions, the income statements are constructed beginning with the calculation of sales. On the other hand, bottom-up pro forma statements begin with the calculation of net income and work up toward sales, which are discussed below.

Bottom-Up Questions

Bottom-up questions are solved more easily using the following CVP equation, sometimes called the *break-even formula*. However, they can also be solved using the pro forma income statement approach based on the fact that CM/CM% = Sales. Because net income, income taxes, and fixed expenses are specified in bottom-up questions and because they equal CM, the sales can easily be calculated by dividing the desired new CM by the original or a modified CM%.

The CVP equation (break-even formula) is presented below.

$$\text{Sales (Unit price} \times \text{Units sold)} = \frac{\text{CM } (= \text{Fixed Costs} + \text{Net Income (NI)} / [1 - \text{Tax rate}])}{\text{CM\% } (= 100\% - \text{VE\%})}$$

This formula can be restructured as follows:

$$\text{Sales (Unit price} \times \text{Units sold)} = \frac{\text{VE* } (= \text{Total Cost} - \text{Fixed Costs})}{\text{VE\%}}$$

* VE = Variable expenses

If the answer is desired in terms of units sold, then the formula can be restructured as follows:

$$\text{Units sold} = \frac{\text{CM}}{\text{CM per unit}}$$

Example 4 below demonstrates a bottom-up solution when the answer is desired in terms of dollar sales.

Exhibit 19-3: Pro-Forma Top-Down Income Statements Based on Data from Examples 1–3

Example 1

	10,000 units sold @ $20.00	Changes	11,000 units sold × $20.00
Sales	$200,000	110% × 10,000 × $20.00	$220,000
Variable Expenses	110,000	55% × Sales	121,000
Contribution margin	90,000	45% × Sales	99,000
Fixed expenses	75,000	$75,000 × 120%	75,000

Example 1

	10,000 units sold @ $20.00	Changes	11,000 units sold × $20.00
EBT	15,000		24,000
Income Tax (40%)	6,000		9,600
Net income	$ 9,000		$ 14,400

Example 2

	10,000 units sold × $20.00	Changes	10,000 units sold × $22.00
Sales	$200,000	110% × $20.00 × 10,000	$220,000
Variable Expenses	110,000	55% × Sales	110,000
Contribution margin	90,000	45% × Sales	110,000
Fixed expenses	75,000	$75,000 × 120%	90,000
EBT	15,000		20,000
Income Tax (40%)	6,000		8,000
Net income	$ 9,000		$ 12,000

Example 3

	VE per unit = $11.00	Changes	VE per unit = $12.00
Sales	$200,000	$20.00 × 10,000	$200,000
Variable Expenses	110,000	60% × Sales	120,000
Contribution margin	90,000	40% × Sales	80,000
Fixed expenses	75,000	$75,000 × 90%	67,500
EBT	15,000		12,500
Income Tax (40%)	6,000		5,000
Net income	$ 9,000		$ 7,500

EXAMPLE 4: Solution in Dollar Sales

Based on Example 1 in Exhibit 19-3, what sales are required to generate a 15% increase in net income, assuming fixed costs are $75,000, the CM% is 45%, and the income tax rate is 40%?

Desired new net income = 115% × $9,000 (see Exhibit 19-2) = $10,350

Desired net income translated into earnings before taxes (EBT)

$$= \$ 10,350/(1 - 0.40) = \$17,250$$

$$\text{Sales (Unit price} \times \text{Units sold)} = \frac{FC + \text{New NI}(1 - \text{Tax rate})/250}{45\% \, (= 0.45) \, \text{CM \%}}$$

Required sales would be $205,000.

Example 5 demonstrates a bottom-up solution when the answer is desired in terms of number of units sold.

EXAMPLE 5: Solution in Units Sold Instead of Dollars

To obtain the required sales in units instead of dollars, CM per unit is substituted for CM% in the equation shown in Example 4. Assume the CU per unit is $9.00.

$$\text{Dollar sales} = \frac{FC + \text{New NI} \times (1 - \text{Tax rate})}{\$9.00 \, \text{CM per unit}} = \frac{\$75,000 + \$17,250}{\$9.00} = 10,250 \text{ Units}$$

The company would be required to sell 10,250 units to achieve its net income goal under the specified assumptions.

More Bottom-Up Questions

A company may desire to know how many covers it must sell to increase its current net income by 10%, based on the following three options:

1. Decrease unit price by 2%   (Example 6)
2. Increase advertising expenses by 3% of sales   (Example 7)
3. Increase advertising expenses by a fixed $4,000 amount   (Example 8)

It may desire to know how many dollars it must have or how many units it must sell to break even, that is, to have a net income of zero.

4. Dollar sales required to break even   (Example 9)
5. Unit sales required to break even   (Example 9)

It may desire to know how much it must sell to break even on a cash basis, that is, neither increasing cash nor decreasing cash.

6. Dollar sales required to break even on a cash basis   (Example 10)

These examples are all based on the continued assumption that the income tax rate is 40%.

EXAMPLE 6: Decrease Unit Price by 2% of the Original Price

The fixed expenses remain the same and the desired net income is 10% greater than the current $9,000 NI, resulting in a $9,900 new net income. To generate this new net income, an EBT of $16,500 ($9,900/[1 − 0.40]) is required. Because of the 2% decrease in unit price, a new CM per unit must be calculated, and it must be in units because the desired answer is in units.

The new CM per unit is calculated as follows:

$$98\% \times \$20.00 \text{ Unit price} = \text{New unit price} = \$19.60.$$

New unit price less per unit CM of $11.00 = new CM per unit of 8.60.

Applying these amounts to the CVP equation below, the answer is that approximately 893 more units (10,893 − 10,000 original units) must be sold to increase the current net income by 10% if the unit price is decreased by 2%.

$$\text{Unit Sales required} = 10{,}893 \text{ (rounded)} = \frac{FC + \text{New NI}/(1 - \text{Tax rate})}{\$20.000 - \$11.60 = \$8.40 \text{ New CM/unit}} = \frac{\$75{,}000 + \$16{,}500}{\$8.40}$$

EXAMPLE 7: Increase Advertising Expenses by 3% of Sales

The fixed expenses remain the same at $75,000, and the desired net income is 10% greater than the current $9,000 net income, resulting in a $9,900 new net income. Because of the 3% increase in variable expenses, a new CM per unit must be calculated, and it must be in units because the desired answer is in units.

The new CM per unit is 3% × $20.00 Unit price = $0.60 = increase in CM per unit (New CM per unit is $11.60).

Applying these amounts to the CVP equation below, the answer is that 640 more units (10,640 − 10,000) must be sold to increase the current net income by 10% if advertising expenses are increased by 3% of sales.

$$\text{Unit Sales required} = 10{,}640 \text{ (rounded)} = \frac{FC + \text{New NI}/(1 - \text{Tax rate})}{\$19.60 - \$11.00 = \$8.60 \text{ New CM/unit}} = \frac{\$75{,}000 + \$16{,}500}{\$8.60}$$

EXAMPLE 8: Increase Advertising Expenses by a Fixed $4,000 Amount

The fixed expenses increase by $4,000 to $79,000, and the desired net income is 10% greater than the current $15,000 net income, resulting in a $16,500 new net income. The contribution margin percent will not change, but the CM per unit will be used in the CVP equation because the desired answer is in units.

Applying these amounts to the CVP equation below, the answer is that 611 more units (10,000 − 10,611) must be sold to increase the current net income by 10% if advertising expenses are increased by 3% of sales.

$$\text{Unit sales required} = 10{,}611 \text{ (rounded)} = \frac{FC + \text{New NI}/(1 - \text{Tax rate})}{\$9.00 \text{ Original CM/unit}} = \frac{\$79{,}000 + \$16{,}500}{\$9.00}$$

EXAMPLE 9: Break-Even Sales

Determination of break-even sales is simply a bottom-up question in which the desired net income is zero. This is the sales level at which fixed expenses are exactly equal to contribution margin and are determined for our sample company as follows:

Chapter 19: Cost-Volume-Profit Analysis 19,009

$$\text{Break-Even Sales} = \$166{,}667 = \frac{\text{FC} + \text{Zero NI}}{\text{CM\%}} = \frac{\$75{,}000 + 0}{45\% \,(= 0.45)}$$

In hotels and restaurants, the break-even sales are usually determined in terms of occupied rooms or covers sold. In such cases, the desired answer will be in units sold instead of dollars sold, and would be calculated as follows:

$$\text{Break-Even Sales in Units} = 8{,}333 \text{ units} = \frac{\text{FC} + \text{Zero NI}}{\text{CM per unit}} = \frac{\$75{,}000 + 0}{\$9.00}$$

EXAMPLE 10: Break-Even Point Based on Cash

To obtain the break-even sales required to preserve the current cash flow (net income + noncash expenses) the following equation is appropriate, assuming that depreciation is $25,000 and that there is no amortization expense:

$$\text{Cash Break-Even Sales} = \$111{,}111 = \frac{\text{FC} - \text{Noncash expenses}}{\text{CM\%}} = \frac{\$75{,}000 - \$25{,}000}{45\% \,(= 0.45)}$$

EXAMPLE OF CVP ANALYSIS—MULTIPLE PRODUCTS OR SERVICES

When more than one product is sold, the calculation of CM percent is affected by changes in the relative sales percentages of each product. Thus, to determine the break-even sales, a weighted-average CM per unit or CM percent must be calculated by weighting each product or service contribution margin according to the percentage of total sales that the product or service generates, as illustrated in Examples 11 and 12.

EXAMPLE 11: What are the break-even sales for the following restaurant?

	Hamburgers	Fries	Drink	Total
Units sold	5,000	3,000	4,000	
Unit price	$3.00	$0.75	$1.25	
Unit cost of food sold	$1.00	$0.15	$0.10	
Other variable expenses per unit	$0.20	$0.13	$0.05	
Sales percent	67.4%	10.1%	22.5%	100.0%
Dollar sales	100.0% 15,000	2,250	5,000	22,250

19,010 Part IV: Management Accounting

	Hamburgers		Fries		Drink		Total
Cost of food sold	33.3%	5,000	26.7%	600	16.0%	800	6,400
Gross margin (GM)	66.7%	10,000	73.3%	1,650	84.0%	4,200	15,850
Other variable expenses	6.7%	1,000	17.8%	400	4.0%	200	1,600
Contribution margin	60.0%	9,000	55.6%	1,250	80.0%	4,000	14,250
Fixed expenses							10,000
Net income							4,250

First the weighted average contribution margin must be calculated by multiplying each product's sales percent by its CM ratio, as follows:

	Hamburgers	Fries	Drink	
Weighted-average CM Ratio =	(67.4% × 60.0%) +	(10.1% × 55.6%) +	(22.5% × 80.0%)	= 64%

Then the CVP formula may be applied as follows:

$$\text{Break-even sales} = \$15{,}625 = \frac{10{,}000 + 0}{64\% (0.64)}$$

EXAMPLE 12: Suppose that this restaurant's manager believes that most customers pay attention to the price of the hamburger and tend to disregard the price of the fries and drink, and he arrived at the following estimated unit sales amounts for the new prices indicated below. What would the restaurant's new net income be?

	Hamburgers		Fries		Drink		Total
Units sold	6,000		2,800		3,900		
Unit price	$2.75		$1.00		$1.40		
Unit cost of food sold	$1.00		$0.15		$0.10		
Other variable expenses per unit	$0.20		$0.13		$0.05		
Sales percent		66.6%		11.3%		22.1%	100.0%
Dollar sales	100.0%	16,500	100.0%	2,800	100.0%	5,460	24,760
Cost of food sold	36.4%	6,000	21.4%	600	14.7%	800	7,400
Gross margin (GM)	63.6%	10,500	78.6%	2,200	85.3%	4,660	17,360
Other variable expenses	7.3%	1,200	13.0%	364	3.6%	195	1,759
Contribution margin	56.4%	9,300	65.6%	1,836	81.8%	4,465	15,601

	Hamburgers	Fries	Drink	Total
Fixed expenses				10,000
Net income				5,601

The new weighted average contribution margin would be:

	Hamburgers	Fries	Drink	
New weighted average CM Ratio	= (66.6% × 56.4%)	+ (11.3% × 65.6%)	+ (22.5% × 80.0%)	= 63.1%

Although net income has increased, the CM ratio has decreased because the CM% on the major sales generator, hamburgers, has decreased from 60.0% to 56.4%.

This will result in a slightly higher break-even sales amount, which increases the risk involved as a result of the new pricing structure.

$$\text{New break-even sales} = \$15,848 = \frac{10,000 + 0}{63.1\%(0.631)}$$

FIXED VERSUS VARIABLE EXPENSES—RISK VERSUS RAPID GROWTH

Fixed expenses do not increase in response to increases in sales, thus their impact on every additional sales dollar diminishes as sales increase. Therefore, profits increase more rapidly in a company that has replaced variable expenses with fixed expenses. Conversely, if sales decrease, the impact of fixed expenses on every dollar of sales becomes greater. Because fixed expenses do not decrease in response to decreases in sales, the break-even sales amount is higher for the company, thereby increasing risk. The following simple example demonstrates this concept.

EXAMPLE 13: Suppose there are two restaurants selling hot dogs at $2.00 each. One restaurant, called "High Labor," hires additional employees to cook hot dogs as sales increase. The other restaurant, called "High Automation," bought a continuous feed oven that can cook up to 5,000 hot dogs with only one person inserting the hot dogs and another removing them at the other end.

Their hypothetical income statements appear below:

	High Automation (Low variable expense ratio)			High Labor (High variable expense ratio)		
Sales	$4,286	$5,000	$10,000	$3,750	$5,000	$10,000
Variable expenses	1,286	1,500	3,000	2,250	3,000	6,000
Fixed expenses	3,000	3,000	3,000	1,500	1,500	1,500
Net income	$ 0	$ 500	$ 4,000	$ 0	$ 500	$ 2,500
Fixed Expense/Sales	$ 0.70	$ 0.60	$ 0.30	$ 0.40	$ 0.30	$ 0.15

Both restaurants start out at $5,000 sales, at which sales level they both have total expenses of $4,500. Restaurant "High Automation" has a lower percentage of total expenses that are variable expenses ($1,500 variable and $3,000 fixed), whereas restaurant "High Labor" has a higher percentage of total expenses that are variable ($3,000 variable and $1,500 fixed). High Automation's profits will therefore increase faster than High Labor's. However, if sales decrease, High Labor's sales can decrease more (to $3,750) than High Automation's sales ($4,286) before it begins to generate a loss.

For high automation, profits are greater at $10,000 sales than they are for high labor ($4,000 vs. $2,500). But the break-even sales point of $4,286 is also higher for high automation than for high labor ($3,750).

Note: In a growth environment, to maximize profit growth potential, it is a good idea to endeavor to transform variable expenses into fixed expenses.

CVP GRAPHICAL ANALYSIS AND THE INCOME STATEMENT EQUATION

Top-down and bottom-up CVP questions can also be answered approximately through the use of break-even graphical analysis. However, only the results of changing unit sales or dollar sales can be viewed on a specific graph, thereby limiting the flexibility of this method. Assumptions concerning the other three basic income statement components: (1) unit price, (2) unit variable costs, and (3) fixed expenses cannot be changed without drawing a new graph. Despite this limitation, the following seven types of questions can be answered directly from any specific break-even graph.

These questions are divided into the two groups: top-down and bottom-up.

Top-Down

1. What is the profit or loss at a given sales level?
2. What are the total expenses at a given sales level?
3. What are the variable expenses at a given sales level?

Bottom-Up

4. What are the break-even sales in dollars or units?
5. At what sales level is any specified profit or loss achieved?
6. At what sales level is any specified total expense amount attained?
7. At what sales level is any specified variable expense amount attained?

In addition to permitting a quick and approximate answer to the above questions, break-even graphs also facilitate a comparison of the speed with which the future earnings of two or more companies or activities will grow, as sales increase, as well as their break-even points.

Break-Even Graphs

Dollar amounts are plotted on the Y (diagonal) axis and units sold are plotted on the X (horizontal) axis. The income statements for high automation and high labor are plotted on the correspondingly named graphs as follows:

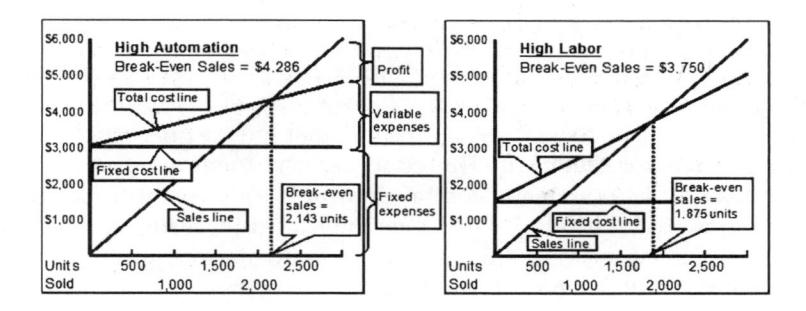

Notice that the vertical distance between the sales line and the total cost line is exactly the same for both companies at sales of 2,500 units. This is confirmed by a review of their income statements above. At 2,500 unit sales, the dollar sales are $5,000 (unit price is $2.00), and at $5,000 sales, both companies earn a $500 profit. However, though the vertical distance between the total cost and the sales lines at 2,500 units sold is the same for both High Labor and High Automation, the angle between the sales and total cost line is greater for High Automation, indicating that as sales increase, the profits of High Automation will grow more rapidly than those of High Labor.

LEVERAGE

Leverage, when applied to lifting a weight, implies exerting a relatively small amount of downward pressure to enable one to lift a large weight. In accounting there are two kinds of leverage: (1) operating leverage and (2) financial leverage. In both situations the concept of leverage implies using a relatively small increase in fixed expenses, which remain constant, to obtain a larger increase in total contribution margin.

Operating leverage involves transforming variable expenses into fixed expenses. This enables a hospitality company's profit to increase more rapidly when sales increase because variable expenses increase in proportion to sales, whereas fixed expenses remain relatively constant, usually for the period of a year. The reduction in variable expenses enables the company's contribution margin to grow more rapidly as sales increase.

Financial leverage involves a similar principle. Revenue-generating or cost-reducing assets are purchased at a fixed cost—the interest expense on the money borrowed to invest in these assets. Yet, these assests increase sales, and, if the investment is a wise investment, increase contribution margins as sales increase, while the interest incurred on the money used to buy these assets remains constant or fixed.

The same principle is at work in both situations—contribution margin is increased as a result of increasing fixed expenses. Under operating leverage, the increase in contribution margin arises from a decrease in variable expenses (which are converted into fixed expenses). Under financial leverage, the increase in contribution margin arises from an increase in sales or a reduction in expenses, which result from adding a fixed expense, interest.

Operating Leverage

What can be observed in the previous example is the effect of operating leverage. Leverage increases when the variable expense ratio decreases because, as sales increase, having higher fixed expenses results in a higher proportion of expenses that decrease on a per unit basis. This continuous reduction of fixed expenses on a per unit basis as sales increase, combined with lower variable expenses, causes profits of the more highly leveraged company to grow faster as sales increase. The formula for calculating the ratio of growth in operating earnings EBIT (earnings before interest and income taxes) to sales growth can be calculated in one of the following two ways:

Operating Leverage

Percent Change Calculation Method

$$\frac{\text{Percent change in EBT}}{\text{Percent change in sales}} = \frac{(\text{New EBIT} - \text{Original EBIT})/\text{Original EBIT}}{(\text{New sales} - \text{Original sales})/(\text{Original sales})}$$

Unit Values Calculation Method

$$\frac{\text{Percent change in EBT}}{\text{Percent change in sales}} = \frac{(\text{Unit price} - \text{unit variable cost}) \times \text{units sold}}{([\text{Unit price} - \text{unit variable cost}]) \times \text{units sold} - \text{Fixed costs}}$$

For a hotel with an average room rate of $100 per room, a variable cost per room of $20, total fixed costs of $15,000 and 300 rooms per night, the operating leverage would be calculated as shown in Example 14.

EXAMPLE 14:

$$\frac{\text{Percent change in EBT}}{\text{Percent change in sales}} = \frac{(\$100 - \$20) \times 400}{([\$100 - \$20] \times 400) - \$15,000} = 1.88$$

Thus, for every 1% increase in sales, its EBIT will increase by 1.88%.

Financial Leverage

Only fixed operating costs are taken into account when calculating operating leverage. In the calculation of financial leverage, the fixed financing costs are also taken into account. These fixed costs are interest and preferred stock dividends. Additionally, the number of common shares outstanding must be considered as an income-diluting factor. The formula for calculating the ratio of growth in earnings per share (EPS) and EBIT can be calculated in one of the following two ways:

Financial Leverage

Percent Change Calculation Method

$$\frac{\text{Percent change in EPS}}{\text{Percent change in EBIT}} = \frac{(\text{New EPS} - \text{Original EPS})/\text{Original EPS}}{(\text{New EBIT} - \text{Original EBIT})/\text{Original EBIT}}$$

Unit Values Calculation Method

$$\frac{\text{Percent change in EPS}}{\text{Percent change in EBIT}}$$

$$= \frac{\{([\text{Unit price} - \text{unit variable cost}] \times \text{units sold}) - \text{Fixed costs}\}}{\left\{\begin{array}{c}([\text{Unit price} - \text{unit variable cost}] \times \text{units sold}) - \text{Fixed costs} \\ - \text{Fixed Financial Charges}\end{array}\right\}}$$

Fixed financial charges (FFC) are interest (a pre-tax amount) and any preferred dividends divided by (1 – income tax rate) to adjust them to a pre-tax basis. Assuming that in addition to the information given for Example 14, Trendy Hotel also pays interest of $1,000 and has preferred stock dividends of $3,000 and an income tax rate of 40%, its financial leverage would be calculated as shown in Example 15.

EXAMPLE 15:

$$FFC = \$1,000 + \$3,000/1 - 0.40) = \$6,000$$

$$\frac{\text{Percent change in EPS}}{\text{Percent change in EBIT}} = \frac{([\$100 - \$20] \times 400) - 15,000}{([\$100 - \$20] \times 400) - \$15,000 - \$6,000} = 1.55$$

Thus, for every 1% increase in EBIT, its EPS would increase by 1.55%.

Total Leverage

Total leverage is the leverage that exists over the entire range of the income statement, including net income divided by outstanding common shares. It is the leverage between sales and EPS, the percentage change in EPS produced by a given percent change in sales, or:

$$\frac{\text{Percent Change in EPS}}{\text{Percent Change in sales}}$$

It is calculated by multiplying operating leverage by financial leverage as follows:

$$\frac{(\text{Unit price} - \text{unit variable cost}) \times \text{units sold}}{([\text{Unit price} - \text{unit variable cost}] \times \text{units sold}) - \text{Fixed costs}} \times$$

$$\frac{\{([\text{Unit price} - \text{unit variable cost}] \times \text{units sold}) - \text{Fixed costs}\}}{\left\{\begin{array}{c}([\text{Unit price} - \text{unit variable cost}] \times \text{units sold}) - \text{Fixed costs} \\ - \text{Fixed financial charges}\end{array}\right\}}$$

Thus, by multiplying the operating leverage obtained in Example 14 (1.88) by the financial leverage obtained in Example 15 (1.55) a total leverage of 2.91 is obtained, indicating that for every 1% increase in sales there will be a 2.91% increase in EPS. The hypothetical income statements in Example 16 explain the relationship between the percent and per unit leverage calculations.

EXAMPLE 16:

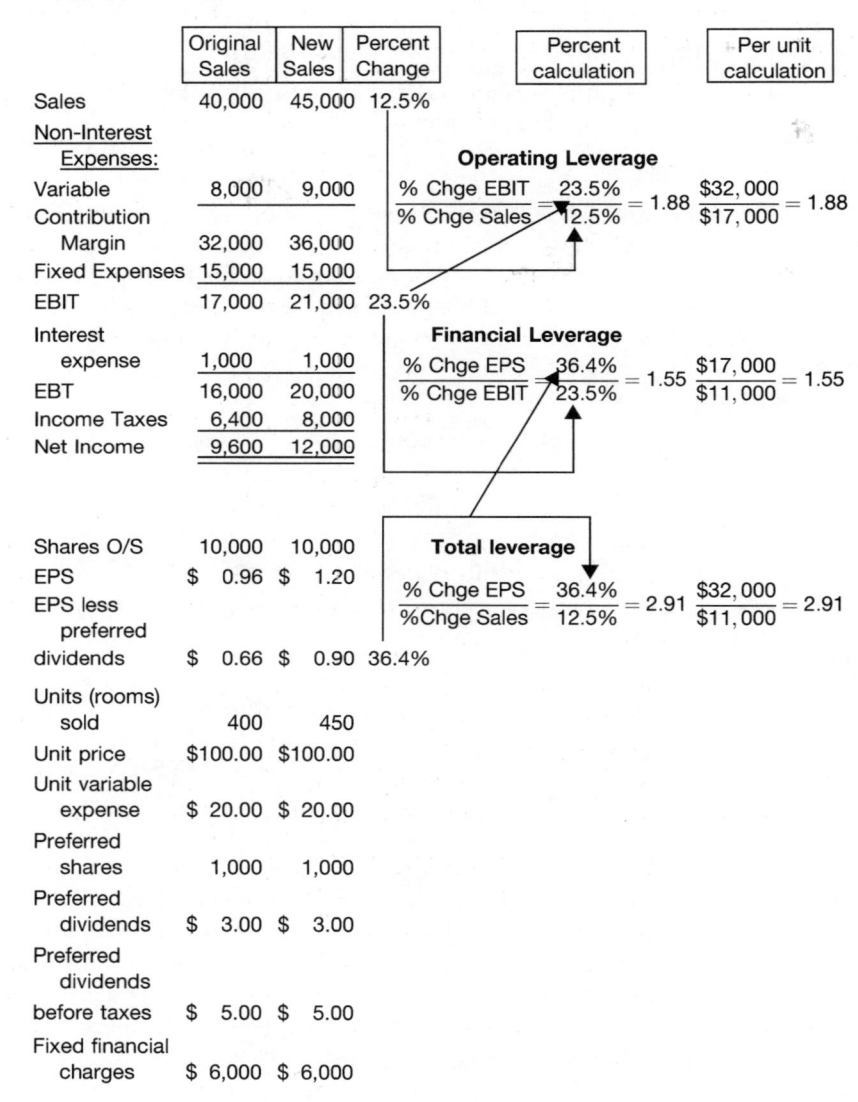

	Original Sales	New Sales	Percent Change
Sales	40,000	45,000	12.5%
Non-Interest Expenses:			
Variable	8,000	9,000	
Contribution Margin	32,000	36,000	
Fixed Expenses	15,000	15,000	
EBIT	17,000	21,000	23.5%
Interest expense	1,000	1,000	
EBT	16,000	20,000	
Income Taxes	6,400	8,000	
Net Income	9,600	12,000	
Shares O/S	10,000	10,000	
EPS	$ 0.96	$ 1.20	
EPS less preferred dividends	$ 0.66	$ 0.90	36.4%
Units (rooms) sold	400	450	
Unit price	$100.00	$100.00	
Unit variable expense	$ 20.00	$ 20.00	
Preferred shares	1,000	1,000	
Preferred dividends	$ 3.00	$ 3.00	
Preferred dividends before taxes	$ 5.00	$ 5.00	
Fixed financial charges	$ 6,000	$ 6,000	

Percent calculation — **Per unit calculation**

Operating Leverage

$$\frac{\% \text{ Chge EBIT}}{\% \text{ Chge Sales}} = \frac{23.5\%}{12.5\%} = 1.88 \quad \frac{\$32,000}{\$17,000} = 1.88$$

Financial Leverage

$$\frac{\% \text{ Chge EPS}}{\% \text{ Chge EBIT}} = \frac{36.4\%}{23.5\%} = 1.55 \quad \frac{\$17,000}{\$11,000} = 1.55$$

Total leverage

$$\frac{\% \text{ Chge EPS}}{\% \text{ Chge Sales}} = \frac{36.4\%}{12.5\%} = 2.91 \quad \frac{\$32,000}{\$11,000} = 2.91$$

Factors Affecting Leverage and Favorability of Leverage

Examination of the financial leverage ratio reveals that the three major factors contributing to an increase in financial leverage are:

1. Decrease in EBIT
2. Increase in interest rate paid and/or preferred stock dividends
3. Increase in the amount of debt incurred

Of these three factors, the first two are detrimental to a business, and the third factor, increased debt, can also be detrimental to the business if borrowed funds are not invested properly. Money must be borrowed under favorable leverage conditions, which means the rate of return on any investments made with borrowed funds must be higher than the interest rate paid for these funds. This may sound obvious, but businesses often originate investments under favorable leverage conditions but as return on investment deteriorates, do not verify the continuing favorability of leverage on the various investments made with borrowed funds. Favorability of leverage is calculated for a business as a whole by comparing its total return on assets with the after-tax interest rate paid on interest-bearing debt. Total return on assets should be greater than the business's average after-tax interest rate, as calculated below.

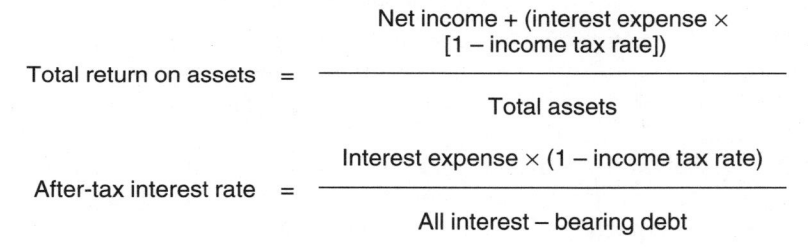

$$\text{Total return on assets} = \frac{\text{Net income} + (\text{interest expense} \times [1 - \text{income tax rate}])}{\text{Total assets}}$$

$$\text{After-tax interest rate} = \frac{\text{Interest expense} \times (1 - \text{income tax rate})}{\text{All interest} - \text{bearing debt}}$$

If this is not the case, then the financial leverage of the business is working against it by lowering return on equity, rather than increasing it. The above comparison can also be made for individual investments or responsibility centers to evaluate each one's favorability of leverage.

Because most of the factors causing financial leverage to increase are unfavorable to a business, the risks involved in using leverage become more apparent. If a recessionary economy is expected, then a business should try to reduce financial leverage by selling stock and using the money to reduce its fixed financial charges, such as interest and preferred stock dividends.

On the other hand, because interest is tax-deductible, if a company does not borrow as much as it can, it will be paying part of the unused EBIT to the government in the form of taxes, rather than using it to obtain additional borrowed funds for faster growth. Basically, if a company uses all of its EBIT to pay interest on borrowed funds used to fund a more rapid profitable growth under favorable leverage conditions, then it is foregoing current earnings, but it is also foregoing the dilution of earnings (reduced EPS) that would have occurred had it obtained this money by selling common stock. When a company reduces its borrowing because it has achieved market saturation, it will not only generate higher earnings as a result of its rapid debt-financed growth, but will also have fewer common shares outstanding if it had obtained its growth funds by selling stock. This, in addition to the company's rapid debt-financed growth, is a second contributing factor to its increase in EPS resulting from the use of debt (leverage) versus equity financing. Unfortunately, the business community has focused on net income as a measure of management performance. However, their focus should be on rapid growth in EBIT instead of net income.

INDIFFERENCE EARNINGS BEFORE INCOME TAXES AND MARGIN OF SAFETY

The *indifference* earnings before income taxes (EBT) is the amount of earnings before EBT that enables a hospitality company to conclude that it would generate the same earnings per share (EPS) (1) if it sold stock to raise a given amount of money or (2) if it raised the money by borrowing at a given interest rate. As is evident from the approximate EPS formula below, used to calculate an adequate approximation of EPS for this purpose, both of these approaches involve a trade-off.

$$\text{EPS} = \frac{\text{Net income}}{\text{Common shares outstanding}}$$

If the funds are raised by borrowing, then interest expense increases and net income decreases, resulting in a decrease in EPS. If the funds are raised by selling stock, then the number of common shares outstanding increases, also resulting in a decrease in EPS. When a hospitality company's EBT is exactly equal to its indifference EBT, then the impact on EPS is the same regardless of which method of raising the funds is used. In other words, it is "indifferent" to the stockholders, strictly from the perspective of EPS (excluding additional risk factors).

Indifference EBT

A company can determine the best method of obtaining additional needed funds by borrowing (which increases leverage and risk), or by selling common stock, by calculating a business's indifference EBT. If a business's current EBT plus any additional EBT (called *adjusted EBT*) expected to be generated by investing the additional new funds is equal to the indifference EBT, then strictly from the point of view of EPS it will not matter whether the funds are raised by borrowing or by selling common stock. If the adjusted EBT is greater than the indifference EBT, then EPS will be maximized by borrowing the needed funds. In the opposite case, EPS will be maximized by selling common stock to raise the needed funds.

EXAMPLE 17: The indifference EBT is calculated as follows:

$$\text{Financial Indifference EBT} = \text{Interest expense} \times \frac{\text{New Shares} + \text{Original Shares}}{\text{New Shares}}$$

Thus, if a business needs to raise $1,000,000 and its alternatives are to:

1. Borrow the money at 10% interest, or
2. Sell 10,000 shares of common stock at $100 per share,
3. It already has 200,000 common shares outstanding, and
4. Its EBT will increase by $100,000 as a result of investing these funds and
5. Its income tax rate is 40%, then its financial indifference EBT is:

$$\text{Financial Indifference EBT} = \$100,000 \times \frac{10,000 + 200,000}{10,000} = \$2,100,000$$

The following income statements are presented for clarification of the calculations presented in the above example.

	Adjusted EBT	Borrow Needed Funds	Sell Stock to Obtain Funds
EBT (current)	1,900,000	1,900,000	1,900,000
EBT (increase)	200,000	200,000	200,000
EBT (adjusted)	2,100,000	2,100,000	2,100,000
Additional interest		100,000	
New EBT	2,100,000	2,000,000	2,100,000
Income Taxes	840,000	800,000	840,000
Net Income	1,260,000	1,200,000	1,260,000
Common shares O/S	200,000	200,000	210,000
EPS	$6.30	$6.00	$6.00

It is evident not only that EPS are the same regardless of the financing option used, but also that this investment will reduce EPS, at least initially.

EXAMPLE 18: An example of a business with an adjusted EBT ($2,300,000) greater than the indifference EBT is as follows:

	Adjusted EBT	Borrow Needed Funds	Sell Stock to Obtain Funds
EBT (current)	2,100,000	2,100,000	2,100,000
EBT (increase)	200,000	200,000	200,000
EBT (adjusted)	2,300,000	2,300,000	2,300,000
Additional interest		100,000	
New EBT	2,300,000	2,200,000	2,300,000
Income taxes	920,000	880,000	920,000
Net income	1,380,000	1,320,000	1,380,000
Common shares O/S	200,000	200,000	210,000
EPS	$6.90	$6.60	$6.57

Based on the above example, it is better to borrow the funds rather than sell common stock. This calculation not only helps decide whether to borrow or issue common stock; it also facilitates evaluation of the risk involved in taking the recommended action. In Example 19, for instance, the adjusted EBT of $2,300,000 is very close to the indifference EBT of $2,100,000, indicating that it would not require much of a decrease in EBT to render the decision to borrow an incorrect one.

Margin of Safety

Another way to measure the risk involved in a new venture is to calculate the margin of safety as follows:

$$\text{Margin of safety} = \frac{\text{Expected sales} - \text{Break-even sales}}{\text{Expected sales}}$$

A hotel chain wishes to build a new hotel and projects its sales to be $3,500,000. Break-even sales are $3,000,000. The margin of safety would be:

$$\text{Margin of safety} = \frac{\$3,500 - \$3,000,000}{\$3,500,000} = 14.29\%$$

Another margin of safety calculation can also be made using indifference EBT instead of break-even sales and adjusted EBT instead of expected sales. This latter method would help to visualize the risk involved in choosing borrowing over the sale of stock, or vice versa, as a financing option. This modified ratio is shown below.

$$\text{Margin of safety} = \frac{\text{Adjusted EBT} - \text{Indifference EBT}}{\text{Adjusted EBT}}$$

CONCEPTS UNDERLYING CVP ANALYSIS

To apply CVP analysis successfully, it is important to take certain underlying concepts into account. Understanding these concepts will help to avoid misinterpreting the results of the analysis and arriving at erroneous conclusions. These concepts are listed as follows:

1. If unit price or unit variable costs change, this will cause the variable expense ratio and contribution margin ratio to change.

2. When using CVP to analyze multiple products or services, a change in the percentage sales of any of the products or services will change the weighted-average variable expense ratio and contribution margin ratio.

3. If sales are expected to increase, it is better to have a higher contribution margin ratio (lower variable expense ratio); and if sales are expected to decrease, a lower contribution margin ratio (higher variable expense ratio) is preferable.

4. A higher contribution margin ratio is usually associated with higher fixed expenses. Therefore, the company's break-even point sales will also be greater, thus implying greater risk.

5. The risk of sales decreasing to the break-even point is less when there is a large margin of safety.

6. In a multi-product or multi-service business, it is important not only to consider market share, but also to emphasize those products or services that generate a higher contribution margin. For instance, when planning a menu, a restaurant should try to maximize sales of high gross-profit items. Or, if two restaurant concepts generate different contribution margins, the one with the highest contribution margin should be expanded, not the one with the highest post-allocation income.

7. Higher leverage produces faster growth if leverage is favorable, but also increases a company's risk by increasing the break-even point sales.
8. Leverage should be reviewed for favorability throughout the life of an investment.
9. Every new financing decision should be tested for its effect on EPS.
10. Within the limits of item 9, if the growth potential exists, businesses should borrow as much as possible to use EBIT to buy the use of creditors' funds instead of paying it to the government in the form of income taxes.
11. When using the indifference EBT calculation, consideration should be given to the following factors: (a) closeness of the indifference EBT to the adjusted EBT (risk of wrong decision); (b) the expected economic and competitive environment (if a recession is expected, it might be safer to sell stock regardless of what the indifference EBT indicates); (c) the type of stockholders (risk-takers versus safety-oriented).

SEPARATION OF MIXED COSTS INTO VARIABLE AND FIXED ELEMENTS

CVP analysis cannot be applied if there are mixed costs in an income statement because mixed costs are not predictable. In the hospitality industry, few expenses are fully 100% variable. Cost of food or beverages sold is almost the only truly variable expense in a restaurant. In addition, there are few 100% fixed expenses. Fixed rent payments, property taxes, property insurance, interest, and depreciation are the most common fixed expenses in this industry. Because most hospitality industry expenses are mixed expenses, before performing CVP analysis, one of the following techniques must be implemented to separate mixed expenses into their variable and fixed elements:

1. Graph method
2. Min-Max (high-low) method
3. Regression method

Graph Method

The graph method is the least accurate method, but it serves two purposes: (1) it enables a practitioner to identify statistical outliers that should be ignored when using the other two methods; and (2) in some cases it helps identify inefficient managers. Example 19 demonstrates the use of the graph method.

EXAMPLE 19: Demonstration of the Graph Method of Separating Semi-Variable Expenses into Their Fixed and Variable Elements

	Jan	Feb	Mar	Apr	May	Jun
Sales	$10,000	$19,000	$24,000	$30,000	$26,000	$20,000
Electricity expense	$ 400	$ 375	$ 500	$ 550	$ 450	$ 425

A plot of these amounts would produce the following graph:

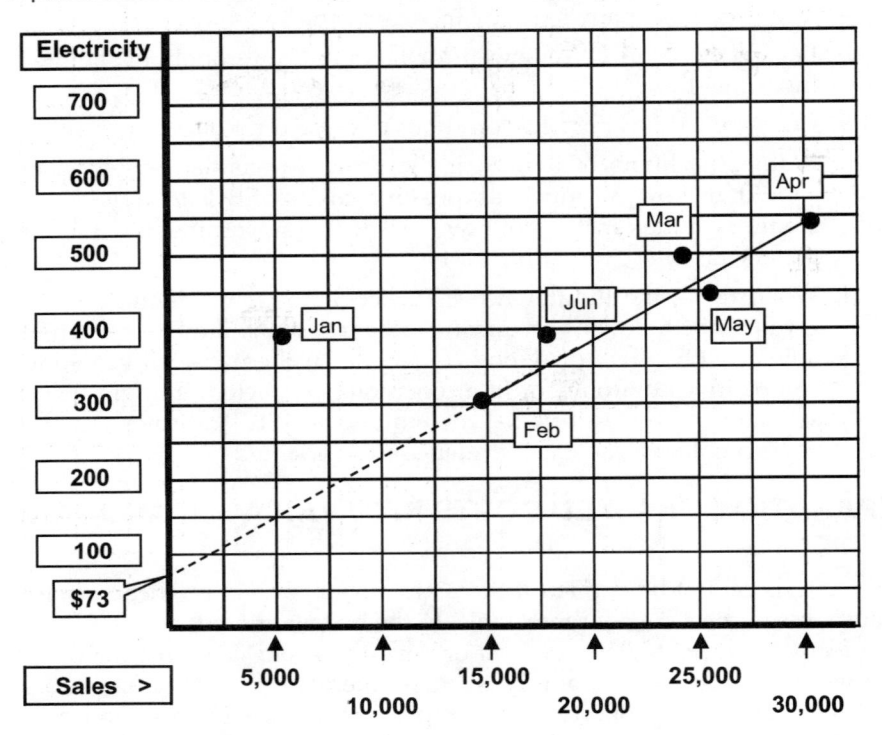

Electricity

```
700
600                                           Apr
                                        Mar
500
                              Jun
400         Jan                         May
300
                        Feb
200
100
$73
        5,000      15,000      25,000
Sales >      10,000    20,000      30,000
```

When using the graph method, one must guess the best-fitting line among all the plotted points. This line is then extended until it reaches the "Y" (vertical) axis. The point of intersection identifies the amount of the fixed element in the mixed expense. The min-max method involves a calculation that provides results equivalent to drawing a line between the plot for the maximum and minimum sales points. It is obvious that when guessing at the best-fitting line or when using the min-max method, the closer all the plotted points are to a single plane, the more accurate are the results.

Identify Outliers. This highlights the usefulness of the graph method. In the above graph, all the monthly plots lie fairly close to a plane except for the month of January. Perhaps a prolonged severe cold spell reduced traffic to the restaurant and required a higher than usual heating bill (assuming this restaurant uses electric heating). Although January generated the lowest sales, it should not be used in the min-max calculation because it is a statistical outlier, an aberration. The next lowest monthly sales plot (February) should be used for the min-max calculation. Drawing this graph identifies such outliers and enables them to be excluded from the min-max calculation, which is the easiest non-spreadsheet calculation to make.

Identify Inefficient Managers. A second benefit of graphing mixed expenses is that a plot of points that do not lie on a plane, but rather are scattered about haphazardly on the graph, may indicate a lackadaisical manager who is not responding rapidly to changes in sales. Below is an example of such a graph:

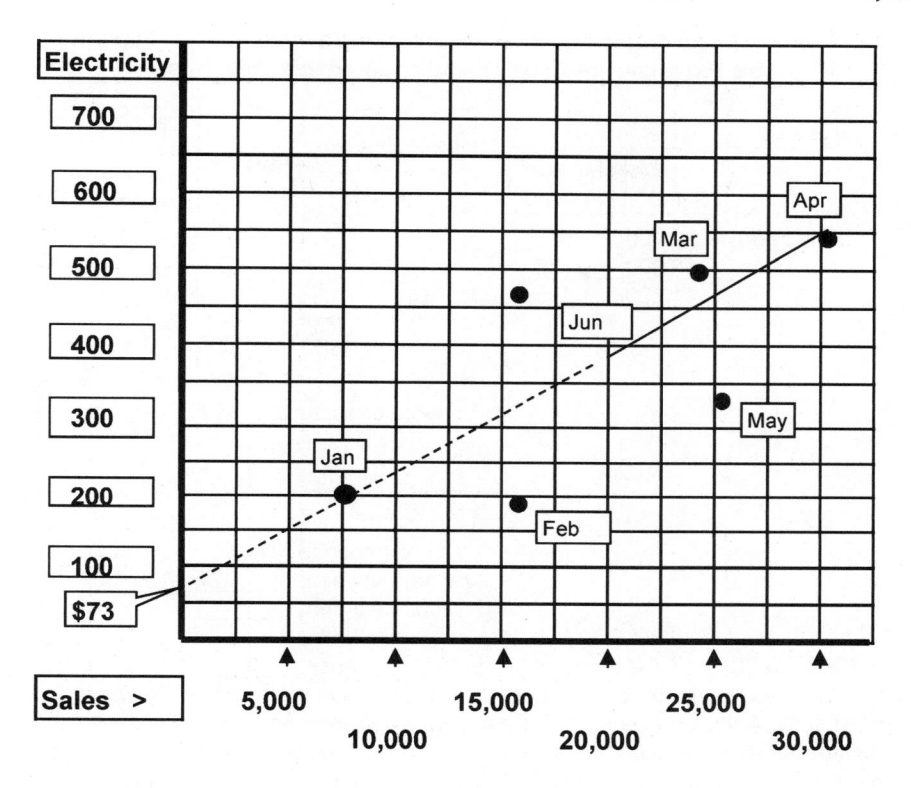

```
Electricity
  700
  600                                              Apr
                                         Mar
  500                              •
                                  Jun
  400
  300                                          •
                                              May
                         Jan
  200                    •        •
                                 Feb
  100
  $73

Sales >   5,000      15,000       25,000
              10,000      20,000       30,000
```

Min-Max Method

The min-max calculation for the above example would be performed as shown in Example 20:

EXAMPLE 20: Demonstration of the Min-Max Method of Separating Semi-Variable Expenses into Their Fixed and Variable Elements

Step 1

	Sales	Mixed Expense
Maximum	30,000	550
Minimum	19,000	375
	11,000	175

Step 2

$$\frac{175}{11,000} = 1.59\%$$ Variable element percent (VEP)

Step 3

Sales	30,000	19,000
VEP	× 1.59%	× 1.59%
Variable element	477	302

Step 4

Mixed expense	550	375
Variable element	477	302
Fixed element	73	73

In Example 20, the fixed element in electricity expense is $73, and it agrees with the "Y" axis intercept of the dotted line extension of the line between the maximum (April) and minimum (February) sales months. That is because the results of the Min-Max Method are based on a hypothetical line between the minimum and maximum sales points on the first graph shown above. It is obvious from the graph that, had the January plot been used in the min-max calculation, the "Y" axis intersect would have been approximately $350.

Regression Method

The most accurate method of separating mixed expenses into their variable and fixed elements is the regression method. This method calculates the "Y" intersect of the best-fitting line among all the plotted points. The equation is as follows:

$$\text{Fixed element} = \frac{(\sum Y)(\sum X^2) - (\sum X)(\sum XY)}{N(\sum X^2) - (\sum X)^2}$$

Y = mixed expense

X = sales

N = number of measurements (5 in the above example because we omit January as an outlier)

Σ = sum or total of a series of numbers

Regression calculations can be easily performed using Microsoft Excel. A short sample solution to the above equation is presented in Example 21.

EXAMPLE 21:

	Y	X²	X	XY
February	375	361,000,000	19,000	7,125,000
March	500	576,000,000	24,000	12,000,000
April	550	900,000,000	30,000	16,500,000
May	450	676,000,000	26,000	11,700,000
June	425	400,000,000	20,000	8,500,000
S =	2,300	2,913,000,000	119,000	55,825,000

$$SX^2 = (119,000 \times 119,000) = 14,161,000,000$$

When these values are placed in the regression equation it appears as follows:

$$\text{Fixed element} = \frac{(2,300 \times 2,913,000,000) - (119,000 \times 55,825,000)}{5(2,913,000,000) - 14,161,000,000} = 140$$

In Example 21, the fixed element per this equation is $140 (rounded). The large difference between the min-max and regression methods is due to the small sample size and the low dollar value of the fixed element. But mainly it is due to the fact that drawing a line through the minimum and maximum sales plots is really an arbitrary choice of two points that do not necessarily minimize the total distance of all the points from the plotted line, as does regression analysis, rendering the latter the more accurate calculation.

BOTTOM-UP PRICING

A method of pricing used in the hospitality industry that is based on identifying variable and fixed expenses, as required for CVP analysis, is the bottom-up approach or Hubbart Formula approach. This approach is used to determine if a particular investment will generate the targeted or desired net income at an average room rate (for hotels) or average cover price (for restaurants) that is competitive.

Conceptually, under this approach, net income is considered the first cost of running a business. A hypothetical income statement is constructed based on various expense assumptions, beginning at the bottom of the income statement with the desired net income assumption. The desired net income is then added to all the assumed expense amounts to arrive at a sales value sufficient to generate this net income after covering all the expenses. A calculation for a restaurant is shown in Example 22:

EXAMPLE 22: Hubbart Formula Applied to a Restaurant

Assumptions regarding the Tasty Spoon Restaurant:
Variable expense ratios

Cost of food sales %	35%
Variable labor cost	18%
Rent-contingent fee	2%
Other variable expenses	20%
Total variable expense ratio	75%

Part IV: Management Accounting

Fixed expense amounts

Management and other fixed salaries	$195,000
General and administrative expenses	37,000
Maintenance, repairs, and utilities	43,000
Insurance–property and liability	24,000
Rent-fixed	48,000
Depreciation expense	63,000
Total fixed expenses	$410,000
Desired net income	$ 42,000
Income tax rate	40%

Based on this information required sales are calculated in three steps:

Step 1—Calculate income tax expense.

Earnings before income taxes must be calculated by dividing net income by (1–tax rate), as follows:

$$\text{Earnings before income taxes} = \frac{\$42,000}{(1 - 0.40)} = \$70,000$$

Income tax expense is $70,000 (EBT) – $42,000 (NI) or $28,000.

Step 2—Calculate total nonvariable expenses plus net income.

The total variable expense ratio is 75% of sales. Therefore, the net income plus income taxes, plus all other fixed expenses must be 25% of sales.

The dollar total of these amounts is:

Net income desired	$ 42,000
Income tax expense	28,000
Total fixed expenses	410,000
Total nonvariable expenses	$ 480,000 = 25% × required sales

Step 3—Calculate sales amount required to cover all expenses and generate the desired net income of $42,000 by dividing total nonvariable expenses by their percentage in relation to the required sales, as follows:

$$\frac{\$480,000}{0.25} = \$1,920,000 = \text{Required sales}$$

The objective of bottom-up pricing is not to determine what dollar sales are required to obtain the desired net income—this is an intermediate objective only. The ultimate objective is to determine what average cover price would have to be charged to generate the required sales in order to determine if it is a competitive market price. Prior to this determination, the following further assumptions concerning the Tasty Spoon Restaurant in Example 22 must be made:

Number of seats	200
Expected seat turnover	3x
Number of days open	350 days

With this data, the required average cover to generate $1,920,000 in sales can be calculated as follows:

$$\text{Required average cover price} = \frac{\$1,920,000}{(200 \times 3 \times 350)} = \$9.14$$

$$= \text{average cover required to generate } \$1,920,000 \text{ in sales.}$$

If this $9.14 amount is considered competitive for comparable menus in the area, then the investment seems reasonable.

Suppose the Tasty Spoon serves both lunch and dinner and has found in other similar restaurants that 30% of its revenue comes from lunch sales and 70% from dinner sales. It has also found that seat turnover during lunch is 2x and at dinner only 1x because lunch prices are lower than those at night. Furthermore, it is only open 300 days per year for lunch. It could calculate the required average check for lunch and dinner as shown in the following example:

EXAMPLE 23:

$$\text{Required average lunch cover} = \frac{\$1,920,000 \times 30\%}{(200 \times 2 \times 300)} = \$4.80$$

$$\text{Required average dinner cover} = \frac{\$1,920,000 \times 70\%}{(200 \times 1 \times 350)} = \$19.20$$

Caution: For this calculation to be meaningful, the average food cost and other variable expense ratios for both lunch and dinner menus must be approximately the same.

Bottom-Up Pricing for Hotels (Hubbart Formula)

The same bottom-up approach used to price restaurant average covers can be applied to a hotel investment, with the additional variation that departmental income assumptions will have to be made for all the revenue-generating departments other than the targeted department for which one seeks to determine required sales. An example of bottom-up pricing applied to a hotel is provided below. In this example the income statement will be turned upside down, with net income at the top of the calculation.

EXAMPLE 24: Hubbart Formula Applied to a Hotel

General assumptions regarding the Fairly Priced Hotel:
- The targeted department for which required sales are to be determined is the rooms department.
- The hotel also has a restaurant that will help generate part of the required earnings, for which the following income assumptions are made:

19,028   Part IV: Management Accounting

- Expected investment $1,000,000
- Income tax rate 40%
- Desired net income (25% × $1,000,000 =) 250,000

Bottom–up calculation and specific expense assumptions:

Step 1—Calculate EBT based on desired net income:

Earnings before income taxes ($250,000/(1 − 0.40)) $416,667

Step 2—Add EBT to all expected expenses and subtract any income from contributing departments other than the target department (the rooms department in this case):

Earnings before income taxes	$416,667
Fixed Charges:	
Interest expense	40,000
Depreciation	
Building—400,000 × 4%	16,000
Furniture & equipment—150,000 × 20%	30,000
Insurance expenses	35,000
Property taxes	30,000
Fixed rent expense	10,000
Management fees (2.5%)	24,000
Total net income, income taxes, and fixed charges	$601,667
Undistributed Operating Expenses:	
Administrative and general	$125,000
Human resources	187,000
Information systems	134,000
Security	87,000
Marketing	94,000
Franchise fees	34,000
Transportation	37,000
Property operation and maintenance	98,000
Utility costs	77,000
Total undistributed operating expenses	$873,000
Rooms department direct expenses	234,000
Total net income and expenses required to be covered	$1,708,667
Less contributing departments' income:	
Expected restaurant departmental income (an estimated amount)	(183,000)
Revenue required to be generated by rooms department	$1,891,667

Step 3—Calculate required average room rate based on available rooms, occupancy percentage and number of days the hotel will be open:

  Available rooms: 100

Expected occupancy percentage: 65%
Number of days expected to be open: 365 days

$$\text{Required average room rate} = \frac{\text{Required sales}}{\text{Available rooms} \times \text{Occupancy percent} \times \text{Days open}}$$

$$= \frac{\$1{,}891{,}667}{(100 \times 65\% \times 365)}$$

Required average room rate = $80 (rounded)

If an average room rate of $80 is competitive in the intended market and if an occupancy percentage of 65% is reasonable, then there is a good probability that this investment will be successful.

Double and Single Occupancy Rates

Step 4—Double and single occupancy rates are calculated as follows:

In addition to the above assumptions, a $12 rate differential between a single and double occupied room will also be assumed.

Number of guests	23,725
Number of rooms occupied	18,000
Number of double occupied rooms	5,725

$$\frac{\text{Number of double occupied rooms}}{\text{Number of rooms occupied}} = \frac{5{,}725}{18{,}000} = 32\% \text{ double occupied rooms}$$

Daily occupied rooms = 65% × 100 rooms = 65 rooms

Daily double occupied rooms = 65 rooms × 32% = 21 double occupied rooms (rounded)

Daily single occupied rooms = 65 rooms × 68% = 44 single occupied rooms (rounded)

Daily room revenue required = 65 rooms × average room rate = 65 × $80 = $5,200

The $5,200 required daily revenue will be raised by selling 44 rooms at the single room rate of $Y plus selling 21 rooms at the double room rate of $Y + $12, where $12 is the predetermined room rate differential between single and double occupied rooms.

Thus: $5,200 = 44 Y + 21 (Y + $12)
        5,200 = 65 Y + $252
        4,948 = 65 Y
        76 (rounded) = Y (single room rate)
        76 + 12 = 88 (double occupied room rate)

The calculations in Example 24 indicate that, on average, the hotel must sell 21 double occupied rooms daily at $88 and 44 single occupied rooms at $76 in order to have the sales required to cover all expenses and generate the desired net income.

CHAPTER 20
TAXATION

CONTENTS

Depreciation—Hospitality Issues	20,002
Smallwares Accounting Method	20,002
Section 179 Deduction	20,003
Depreciable Life for Restaurant Building Improvements	20,003
Cost Segregation for Depreciation	20,004
Longer Depreciation Lives	20,004
Leasehold Improvements	20,004
Amortization of Leasehold Improvements	20,004
Who Should Pay for Leasehold Improvements?	20,005
Historic Building Credit	20,005
Recapture of the Credit	20,006
Rehabilitation Expenditures Made by a Lessee	20,007
Net Leases and Leases Shorter Than 80% of a Building's Recovery Period	20,008
Energy Tax Credit for Building Improvements	20,008
Allowed Deductions	20,008
How to Claim Deductions	20,009
Property Basis Reduction	20,009
Tax Laws Related to Tips	20,009
Tips Deemed Wages	20,010
Tip Reporting Procedures	20,010
When Tips Are Deemed to Be Paid	20,010
Penalties	20,011
Allocated Tips	20,011
FICA Tax-Related to Tips	20,011
FICA Tax Tip Credit	20,012
IRS Tip Rate Determination/Education Programs	20,012
Empowerment Zone and Renewal Community Benefits	20,014
Work Opportunity Tax Credit	20,014
Empowerment Zone and Renewal Community Employment Credit	20,015
Exclusion of Capital Gains	20,015
Upfront Payments Received from Suppliers	20,015
Bartering	20,015
Franchising Fees	20,016
Gift Card Sales Deferral Rules	20,016
Deductible Food and Beverage Contributions	20,016
Contributions of Used Items	20,017
Guest Loyalty Programs	20,017
Lobbying Deductions	20,018
Expansion Costs	20,019
Property and Sales Taxes	20,019

Exhibit 20-1. Lessee Claim of Rehabilitation Tax Credit

Tax laws provide a number of alternative methods for reporting income and expenses. Thus, an understanding of important choices available under the income tax laws should be taken into consideration by a controller or financial manager. This chapter provides an overview of several tax laws applicable to the hospitality industry, such as (1) tax implications of the tip credit, (2) certain special depreciation and amortization provisions of the tax law pertaining to specific hospitality industry segments, (3) historic building and energy tax credits, (4) empowerment zone and renewal community benefits, (5) upfront payments received from suppliers, (6) bartering income, (7) recording of franchise fees, (8) deferral of income from the sale of gift cards, (9) tax treatment of contributions of food, beverages, and used equipment, (10) proper deduction of costs related to guest loyalty programs, (11) lobbying expenses eligible for deduction, and (12) tax implications of expansion costs incurred by hospitality industry chains. This chapter is not intended to explain the full details of the tax laws that apply in these situations. Rather, its objective is to indicate some situations in which these laws may apply, and in which further investigation or consultation with a tax professional may be required. See Resources on the Web for references to some helpful Internet sites.

DEPRECIATION—HOSPITALITY ISSUES

Because it is such a highly capital-intensive industry, depreciation of property and equipment in the hospitality industry can be a significant expense. A judicious application of the different methods of accelerated depreciation and write-offs permitted by the Internal Revenue Code (IRC) can minimize current taxable income and enable a company to postpone the payment of income taxes, freeing up funds for use in one of the four beneficial expenditures: (1) buying more revenue-generating or cost-reducing assets, (2) reducing interest-bearing debt, (3) buying treasury stock, and (4) increasing the dividend payment. Note that a company's circumstances will determine which of these are beneficial at any particular time. Therefore, the hospitality controller or financial manager should be conversant with these methods and review the company's tax depreciation schedules frequently to ascertain that new acquisitions of depreciable assets are being depreciated in the most beneficial manner.

The IRC provides certain depreciation-related income tax benefits for restaurants and taverns based on the fact that restaurant businesses have a higher failure rate than other businesses (approximately 80% of restaurants fail within the first two to three years) and, therefore, shorter lives than other types of business. These tax benefits are discussed below.

Smallwares Accounting Method

The smallwares accounting method allows restaurants and taverns that prepare food and beverages to expense the cost of replacement dishware, glassware, and other items that previously had to be depreciated. The deduction must be taken in the year of purchase but is not available for new business start-up purchases. In addition, it cannot be used for items that are purchased and stored at any location other than the restaurant where they are used.

Smallwares consists of glassware, flatware, dinnerware, pots and pans, tabletop items, bar supplies, food preparation utensils and tools, storage supplies, service items and small appliances costing $500 or less.

When electing this method, a company must submit Form 3115, "Application for Change in Accounting Method." See Revenue Procedure 2002-12 for further details concerning the use of this method.

Section 179 Deduction

The Economic Stimulus Act of 2008 increased the limits for the total amount of property that can be expensed under IRC section 179 from the previous $128,000 to $250,000. Furthermore, the total amount of section 179 property that can be purchased by a company in a given year before the section 179 accelerated write-off begins to be phased out has been increased from $510,000 to $800,000. There are also new higher limits for the section 179 write-off of business vehicles.

For eligible section 179 property purchased prior to January 1, 2010, an additional $35,000 deduction may be taken in the year that personal property is purchased and put into service. This raises the maximum section 179 deduction, prior to 2010, from $250,000 to $285,000.

Depreciable Life for Restaurant Building Improvements

The IRC allows restaurants to depreciate "qualified leasehold improvement property" and "qualified restaurant property" over a 15-year period for improvements made in 2008 and 2009. Restaurant buildings acquired in 2009 may also be amortized over as short a period as 15 years.

Qualified restaurant property is any section 1250 property that is an improvement to a building and meets the following requirements.

1. The improvement is placed in service more than three years after the date the building was first placed in service, and

2. More than 50% of the building's square footage is devoted to preparation of meals and to on-premise consumption of prepared meals.

Qualified leasehold improvement property is any improvement to an interior part of a building that is nonresidential real property, provided certain requirements are met. An improvement made by the lessor does not qualify as qualified leasehold improvement property to any subsequent owner unless it is (1) acquired from the original lessor by reason of the lessor's death, (2) a Section 381(a) transaction, (3) a mere change in the form of conducting the business (business must retain a substantial interest), (4) a like-kind exchange, or (5) a certain transaction in which gain or loss is not recognized.

Cost Segregation for Depreciation

The IRS has issued a suggested nonofficial list (referred to as Exhibit A) indicating an acceptable segregation of restaurant assets for purposes of determining their classification as section 1245 or section 1250 assets, as well as for purposes of determining their depreciation lives. This list is reproduced in Appendix 2 of this manual. The IRS has stated that this large- and medium-size business directive is not an official pronouncement of the law or the position of the IRS and cannot be used, cited, or relied on as such. Nevertheless, the IRS has also stated that if the taxpayer's tax return position for these assets is consistent with the recommendations in Exhibit A, examiners should not make adjustments to categorization and lives. If the taxpayer reports assets differently, then adjustments should be considered. Exhibit A will be updated regularly.

A cost segregation list has also been issued for the gaming industry segment. No list has yet been prepared for hotels, but the IRS suggests that the lodging industry segment use both the gaming and the retail industry segment cost segregation lists, both of which are included in Appendix 3 and list assets similar to those a hotel might own.

Longer Depreciation Lives

If a business wishes to depreciate its assets over longer periods (deferring depreciation to later years in which it expects to have higher taxable income), it should use the Alternative Depreciation System (ADS) permitted in IRC section 168(g). For recovery periods under IRC section 168(g), see Revenue Procedure 87-56, 1987-2 CB 674 or publication 946, "How to Depreciate Property."

A hospitality business should be aware that any assets purchased prior to 1999 must be depreciated using the ADS if the business is subject to the alternative minimum tax (AMT). For real property purchased and utilized beginning in 1999, the Modified Accelerated Cost Recovery System (MACRS) method of depreciation may be used for the calculation of both the regular income tax and the AMT. Property that is not real property and that was purchased in 1999 or later must be depreciated using a modified form of MACRS for AMT purposes.

LEASEHOLD IMPROVEMENTS

Although there seems to be some controversy regarding the amortization period of leasehold improvements for income tax reporting purposes, the position of the IRS, stated below, is clear. The logic for determining who should pay for these improvements in order to maximize the tax deductions available from their amortization is also explained.

Amortization of Leasehold Improvements

The IRS position is that leasehold improvements must be amortized over their MACRS lives for income tax purposes. If the term of the lease is shorter than the MACRS life of the leasehold improvements and the asset is no longer used at the end of the lease term, then at the end of the lease term the lessee can write-off the unamortized portion of the leasehold improvements as a leasehold acquisition expense.

Who Should Pay for Leasehold Improvements?

When a chain owns a building that it rents to a lessee (e.g., to a franchisee) the decision as to whether the lessor or the lessee will bear the cost of leasehold improvements should take into account the current and expected future income tax brackets of both parties in order to minimize the combined income tax paid by both parties. Deductible expenses should be maximized for the entity that will benefit the most. For example, these deductions may bring the taxable income of a small hospitality company to a lower income tax bracket, or, in the case of large hospitality companies, if one has large loss carryovers, the one without the loss carryovers should take the deduction. The combined tax savings can be distributed among the parties by taking them into account when determining the conditions of the lease contract.

HISTORIC BUILDING CREDIT

The Historic Building Credit is a dollar-for-dollar tax reduction included in Section 47 of Title 26 of the IRC. This credit may be claimed for the cost of rehabilitating historic structures. To claim the credit, the following conditions must be met:

1. The costs were incurred for the rehabilitation (renovation, restoration, or reconstruction) of buildings that were put into service prior to 1936.

2. The costs were incurred for the rehabilitation (renovation, restoration, or reconstruction) of buildings that have been declared historic structures by the National Register of Historic Places and are listed there individually.

3. The costs were incurred for the rehabilitation (renovation, restoration, or reconstruction) of buildings that are determined to contribute to a registered historic district. To qualify, they must be located in a registered historic district (as defined in Section 47(c)(3)(B) of the federal tax code) and certified by the Secretary of the Interior as being of historic significance to the district.

4. The costs were not incurred to acquire, enlarge, or expand an eligible building or construct new buildings, nor were they incurred to acquire any asset that is classified as personal property by the IRC. The credit is only available for the rehabilitation of real property.

5. The rehabilitation expenditures incurred during a 24-month period must exceed the greater of $5,000 or the adjusted basis of the building at the commencement of the 24-month period. The adjusted basis should be used on the first day of the 24-month period or the first day of the holding period, whichever is later. (A building that is being rehabilitated in phases under a written architectural plan, with specifications that were completed before the rehabilitation began, has 60 months to be completed.)

6. The building must not be permanently retired from service. It must have been placed in service by any person at any time before the beginning of rehabilitation. If the building is damaged, it is not considered permanently retired from service when the taxpayer returns it to actual service within a reasonable period of time.
7. The expenditures must be capitalized and depreciated using the straight line method.
8. The rehabilitation must be certified by the Secretary of the Interior as being consistent with the historic character of the property or district in which the property is located. This requirement does not apply to a building in a registered historic district if (a) the building is not a certified historic structure, (b) the Secretary of the Interior certifies that the building is not of historic significance to the district, and (c) the certification in (b) occurs after the rehabilitation began, the taxpayer certifies in good faith that he or she was not aware of that certification requirement.

If eligible for the credit, the hospitality company must comply with the following:

1. The qualified expenditures should be taken into account for the tax year in which the qualified rehabilitated building is placed in service. However, with certain exceptions, expenditures may be taken into account for the tax year in which they were paid (or, for a self-rehabilitated building, when capitalized) if (a) the normal rehabilitation period for the building is at least two years and (b) it is reasonable to expect that the building will be a qualified rehabilitated building when placed in service. (See section 47(d) of the tax code.)
2. The basis in the building must be reduced by the amount of the credit.
3. Form 3468 (Investment Credit) should be included with the first income tax return filed after receipt of the final certification of the completed work. This form is available at http://www.irs.gov/pub/irs-pdf/f3468.pdf.

Generally, the percentage of costs that can be taken as a credit is:

- 10% for buildings placed in service before 1936
- 20% for certified historic structures

The rehabilitation credit was increased for qualified rehabilitation expenditures on buildings located in the Gulf Opportunity zone paid or incurred after August 27, 2005, and before January 1, 2009.

Recapture of the Credit

With certain exceptions, it may be necessary to recalculate or recapture the credit if:

- The investment credit property is disposed of before the end of five full years after the property was placed in service (recapture period).

- The business use of the property decreases before the end of the recapture period so that it no longer qualifies (in whole or in part) as investment credit property.
- Any building to which section 47(d) applies will no longer be a qualified rehabilitated building when placed in service.

Rehabilitation Expenditures Made by a Lessee

A lessee may claim the rehabilitation credit provided that (a) the lessor does not claim it, (b) the lessee incurs the rehabilitation costs, and (c) the lease term is greater than the recovery period determined under IRC section 168(c), currently 39 years for nonresidential real property and 27.5 years for residential rental property. The lessee must meet a substantial rehabilitation test that is different from that for an owner. The combined qualified rehabilitation expenditures incurred by the owner and any lessees must exceed the aggregate adjusted basis of all parties who have an interest in the building (i.e., the adjusted basis of the owner in the building plus the adjusted bases of the lessees in the leasehold and any leasehold improvements that are structural components of the building). As a result, the property owner and several lessees could all qualify for the rehabilitation tax credit as long as the combined rehabilitation expenditures of all parties are considered when determining if the project meets the substantial rehabilitation test. The amount of credit each party can claim is based on the amount each party expended during the rehabilitation. A lessee claim of a rehabilitation tax credit is shown in Exhibit 20-1.

Exhibit 20-1: Lessee Claim of Rehabilitation Tax Credit

Owner's adjusted basis before rehabilitation	$ 75,000
Prior improvements made by lessees	5,000
Combined adjusted basis of all parties	$ 80,000
Owner's additional rehabilitation expenditure	$ 10,000
Expenditures paid for by lessee "A"	25,000
Expenditures paid for by lessee "B"	20,000
Expenditures paid for by lessee "C"	45,000
	$100,000

Tests met:
1. Building is historic; therefore, credit is 20% of the rehabilitation expenditure.
2. Lease is in excess of 39 years.
3. Combined rehabilitation expenditures exceed the combined adjusted bases of all parties who have an interest in the building.

   The $90,000 rehabilitation cost is greater than the $80,000 adjusted basis.

The rehabilitation credit each lessee can take is:

Owner	20% × $10,000 = $2,000
Lessee "A"	20% × $25,000 = $5,000
Lessee "B"	20% × $20,000 = $4,000
Lessee "C"	20% × $45,000 = $9,000

In the above exhibit, the basis of the owner in the building must be reduced by the owner's $2,000 credit. In addition, the owner's credit is subject to the recapture rules. Instead of reducing their bases, the lessees must include in their annual gross income the amount of the credit divided by the years in the recovery period, which is the class life determined by the IRS.

Note: The income tax brackets of the lessor and lessee should be taken into account when negotiating who will be allowed the rehabilitation credit so that the minimum amount of combined total income tax is paid by the lessor and lessee together.

Net Leases and Leases Shorter Than 80% of a Building's Recovery Period

Different rules apply for net leases in which the lessor is guaranteed a specific return or protected partially or entirely against loss of income (see IRC sections 57(c)(1)(B) and 48(d)(4)(D)). Different rules also apply for leases shorter than 80% of the class life of a building (i.e., shorter than 31.2 years for nonresidential rental property and shorter than 22 years for residential rental property). The rules applicable under these circumstances are explained in IRC section 48(d)(5)(B).

ENERGY TAX CREDIT FOR BUILDING IMPROVEMENTS

On October 3, 2008, the Emergency Economic Stabilization Act of 2008 (HR-1424) extended the benefits of the Energy Policy Act of 2005 (Public Law No. 109-58, 119 Statute 594-2005) through December 31, 2013. Based on this law, IRC section 179(d) provides a tax deduction during the year in which the property is ready to be placed in use to owners of commercial buildings (including garages) that are higher than three stories and who install in them certain energy-efficient property. Exceptions to these, and to some of the following rules, can be made on a case-by-case basis, so a tax expert should be consulted.

Two Internet sites containing information pertinent to the energy credit are:
1. Procedure Enabling Commercial Property Owners to Qualify for Energy Efficiency Deduction
   http://www.irs.gov/newsroom/article/0,,id=158395,00.html
2. Deduction for Energy Efficient Commercial Buildings—Notice 2006-52
   http://www.irs.gov/pub/irs-drop/n-06-52.pdf

Allowed Deductions

The allowed deduction is up to $1.80 per square foot of building floor area for buildings that achieve a 50% energy savings target. The 50% target is measured against a reference building that meets the minimum requirements of the American Society of Heating, Refrigeration, and Air Conditioning Equipment Standard 90.1-2001. Deductions are allowed for the cost of any energy efficiency investments in (1) interior lighting systems; (2) heating, cooling, ventilation, and hot water systems; and (3) the building envelope. The cost includes any capitalizable cost, including labor. The installations must be made as part of a plan designed to reduce the annual energy costs in one or more of these three areas. A modification made by the IRS in March 2008 allows the 50% deduction to be taken on a piecemeal basis using the following percentages:

	Target
1. Interior lighting:	20%
2. Heating, cooling, ventilation, and hot water systems	20%
3. Building envelope	10%

For each of the above areas that meet its relevant targeted percent, $0.60 per square foot may be deducted up to the maximum deduction of $1.80 per square foot. The IRS allows a partial deduction, less than 20%, for interior lighting. IRS Notice 2006-52 explains this procedure.

How to Claim Deductions

Before claiming a deduction, the taxpayer must obtain certification from a qualified person stating that the required energy savings will be achieved. Inspections by qualified engineers or contractors are required. IRS Notice 2006-52 (http://www.irs.gov/pub/irs-drop/n-06-52.pdf) explains the certification requirements, and the Department of Energy will create and publish a list of software that must be used to calculate energy savings for purposes of providing this certification. No special form is required to claim the deduction; it should be deducted in the "Other deductions" line of the company's federal tax return. However, the company should retain all pertinent supporting documentation.

Property Basis Reduction

The basis of any property for which an energy efficiency deduction is made must be reduced by the amount of the deduction. The remaining value should be depreciated over its asset class life.

TAX LAWS RELATED TO TIPS

Employee tip income is an important type of remuneration in the hospitality industry. The Fair Labor Standards Act defines *tipped employees* as those who earn more than $30 in tips per month. Tips are considered by tax law to be remuneration for services rendered, not gifts. Because of the difficulty of verifying actual tips received, the IRS has made ongoing efforts to simplify the process of tip reporting. This section explains the tax ramifications of tips, as well as the latest tip-reporting programs developed by the IRS. Appendix 3 contains a list of helpful IRS publications and forms, Internet sites, and court cases related to the taxation of tips.

Tips Deemed Wages

Deemed wages are tips that are taken into account by the employer when calculating the minimum wage paid to employees. An employer may pay as little as $2.13 per hour to employees whose tips are sufficient to bring their total hourly remuneration up to the legal minimum wage. From July 24, 2008, to July 23, 2009, the federal minimum wage was $6.55 per hour, and from July 24, 2009, onward the federal minimum wage is $7.25 per hour. Thus, the maximum amount of tips deemed wages from July 24, 2008, to July 23, 2009, was $4.42 and $5.12 thereafter. If tips are not sufficient to bring a tipped employee's hourly remuneration up to the legal minimum wage, the employer is responsible for paying the difference. For employees younger than 21 years, the minimum wage is $4.25 for the first 90 days of employment. Employers may not deduct charges against employees for walkouts, breakages, and cash register shortages against tips deemed wages, because tips are the property of the employee. Such charges may only be made against real wages. Employees are allowed to share their tips; however, a charge added to a check by the establishment is not considered a tip, even if so named, as it is part of the establishment's earnings.

Various states have different minimum wage requirements with which a hospitality company needs to comply. These are listed in the Department of Labor site attainable through the link http://www.dol.gov/esa/whd/state/tipped.htm.

Tip Reporting Procedures

Employees who receive up to $20 of tips per month are not required to report them to their employers, although they are required to report them on their personal income tax return (IRS Form 1040) at year-end.

Employees who receive more than $20 per month in tips must report them to the employer at least once a month by the tenth day of the following month. These tips may be reported on IRS Form 4070, on a time card, or electronically, such as a point-of-sale tip program. Employees are encouraged to use IRS Form 4070A to keep a daily record of tips received. Large food and beverage establishments must report their calendar year sales on IRS Form 8027, which must be filed by February 28 of the following year. If the form is filed electronically, it may be filed by March 31. A large food and beverage establishment is one that has more than 10 employees, or their equivalent (see IRC section 6053(c)(4)), whose work relates to the preparation and serving of food (regardless of whether they are tip-earning), sells food and beverages for consumption in the establishment, and where tipping of some employees is customary (this excludes quick-service and carryout establishments). In addition to their annual calendar year sales, employers must include on IRS Form 8027 charge-card sales, charge-card tips, and employee-reported tips.

When Tips Are Deemed to Be Paid

Tips are considered paid at the earliest of the following times:
- When an employee reports the tips to the employer.

- If an employee does not report tips, then the employee is deemed paid when the tips are either received from a customer or, in the case of charge slips, when the employer remits them to an employee.
- In those cases when insufficient tips are reported and the IRS takes action against a company, they are deemed to be paid when notice and demand for the related Federal Insurance Contributions Act (FICA) tax is made to the employer by the IRS.

There have been cases in which a company with tip-earning employees has been assessed the FICA tax on tips that the IRS considered under-reported based on an aggregate estimate of tips, without investigating whether employees had in fact under-reported. These "employer only" audits are viewed by some as a way of motivating food and beverage establishments to join one of the tip-reporting methods developed under the IRS Tip Rate Determination/Education Program. These safe-harbor tip-reporting programs are explained later in this chapter.

Penalties

A penalty of 50% of the unreported FICA tax is imposed on violators.

Allocated Tips

If reported tips are less than 8% of total gross sales, an amount of tips sufficient to bring reported tips up to the 8% amount must be allocated and reported in box eight of the W-2 form of each employee who did not report tips equivalent to at least 8% of their individual gross sales. Tips may be allocated in one of three ways:

1. *Hours worked method.* Establishments with less than 25 full-time tipped plus nontipped employees may allocate tips based on the hours worked by an employee.
2. *Gross receipts method.* This method allocates tips based on the actual sales of an employee.
3. *Negotiation method.* The establishment negotiates with its employees in each category of tipped employees an allocation of tips needed to bring total tips up to the amount of 8% of gross sales. In this case, at least two-thirds of the employees in a category must accept the negotiated allocation.

When one of these methods is used correctly, the establishment is not liable to any employee for over-allocation of tips. See IRC Section 6053(c)(3)(B).

If an establishment can prove that average tips are less than 8% of gross sales, it, or a majority of its employees, may apply to the IRS to have the allocation reduced to an amount between 8% and 2%.

FICA Tax-Related to Tips

The establishment can deduct from an employee's wages the FICA taxes due on tips. If these taxes exceed an employee's current wages, they may be withheld from wages when they are paid in the future. The establishment should show any employee FICA taxes due that were not collected from an employee as an adjustment on IRS Form 941, "Employer's Quarterly Federal Tax Return." Uncollected FICA taxes should also be entered in box 12 of the employee's W-2 form. Social Security taxes should be coded as "A" and Medicare taxes should be coded as "B." Withheld amounts should be reported in box 4 for Social Security and box 6 for Medicare. Employers are responsible for the timely payment of the FICA tax on tips, regardless of whether the employee portion of the FICA tax was withheld.

FICA Tax Tip Credit

Because it was considered an excessive burden to impose the FICA taxes on employers for tips not deemed wages, IRC Section 45B allows employers an income tax credit for FICA taxes. For purposes of this section, the minimum wage is frozen at $5.15 indefinitely, regardless of the minimum wage increase to $7.25 in 2009. Therefore, even after this minimum wage increase goes into effect, employers will still be able to take this credit for FICA taxes paid by the employer on tips in excess of $5.15 per hour, instead of in excess of the new and higher $7.25 minimum wage. The FICA tax on service fees charged by an establishment is not eligible for this credit because it is a nonrefundable credit, meaning the credit may only be used to offset an income tax liability, including one created by the alternative minimum tax. It may not be used to offset liability for employment taxes. In addition, the deduction for FICA taxes must be reduced by the amount of this credit. Unused credits may be carried back 1 year and forward 20 years. IRS Form 8846 should be used to claim the credit, which is available at http://www.pro1040.com/Occupations/Restaurant/8846_cr_for_fica_on_tips.pdf.

The credit is available regardless of whether the tips were reported to the employer. Thus, it is available for the employer FICA tax paid under an IRS assessment. In this case, the credit is available to the employer in the year of notice and demand, not the year in which the unreported tips were received by the employee.

IRS Tip Rate Determination/Education Programs

IRS estimates have indicated that fewer than 50% of all tips received are reported, representing billions of dollars in unreported income. Collecting taxes on tip income is especially problematic because they are often received in cash with no easy way of verifying receipt. The IRS established the Tip Rate Determination/Education Program in 1993 for developing simplified tip reporting approaches that would encourage employees to report all their earned tips to employers and would provide some safe-harbor status for businesses employing tip-earning employees. Since the start of the program, declared tip income has approximately doubled.

The Tip Rate Determination/Education Program resulted in the creation of five separate programs for reporting tips. Included is the year in which they were introduced:

1. Tip Rate Determination Agreement (TRDA) (1993).
2. Tip Reporting Alternative Commitment (TRAC) (1995).

3. Employer-Designed Tip Reporting Alternative Commitment (EmTRAC) (2000).
4. Gaming Industry Tip Compliance Agreement (GITCA) (2003). (See Revenue Procedure 2003-35, 2003-1 C.B. 919, revised by Revenue Procedure 2007-32.)
5. Attributed Tip Income Program (ATIP) (2006). (See Revenue Procedure 2006-3.)

Employers who enter into these agreements and comply with their terms are not subject to challenge on audit with respect to the amount of tips they are reporting as wages. The TRDA offers a similar assurance to employees. The TRAC or EmTRAC programs do not include a predetermined tip rate; rather, they attempt to increase compliance through employer education of tipped employees. Although not specifically stated, there is an implied protection from an audit given to an employee who follows the educational guidelines provided by an employer under these latter two programs.

The TRDA attempts to ensure tip reporting by requiring at least 75% of employees to sign Tipped Employee Participation Agreements with their employer. Under this agreement, employees agree to report tips at a predetermined rate. This rate is established by negotiation between the IRS and the employer. If employees fail to do this, their employer will report them to the IRS.

The TRAC and EmTRAC programs attempt to ensure adequate tip reporting by requiring employers to continuously educate their employees regarding tip-reporting laws and procedures. They also require that the employer:

1. Provide to the employee, at least monthly, a written statement of attributed charged tips.
2. Allow employees to affirm or correct the statement of attributed tips.
3. Establish a procedure whereby each indirectly tipped employee reports tips at least monthly.
4. With regard to directly tipped employees, establish a procedure whereby a statement reflecting all cash tips attributable to sales of each employee is prepared at least monthly.

EmTRAC differs from TRAC in that it allows employers to design their own employee education program and reporting procedures.

Although it is a revenue procedure, GITCA is similar to the TRDA. Revenue procedures are more easily enforceable than programs, but they also provide more reliable safe-harbor protection for employer and employees.

The Attributed Tip Income Program (ATIP), which was established by the IRS in 2006, is a three-year pilot program that expires in 2009. ATIP differs from the other programs in that employers are not required to enter into an individual agreement with the IRS. The employer simply checks a box in Form 8027 and submits a copy of last year's Form 8027. At least 75% of employees must enroll in the program, where tips are attributed based on the charge tip rate from the prior year's Form 8027, less 2%.

Note: The employees' portion of FICA taxes and withheld income taxes are not a liability of the employer company. These taxes are a debt of the company's employees. Therefore, this debt is not extinguished upon the bankruptcy of the employer company. The employees of the employer company who have the authority to withhold and remit these funds to the IRS are considered to be personal trustees of the IRS charged with collecting and remitting to the IRS the employees' portion of payroll taxes. Therefore, these employees are held personally responsible to the full extent of their personal assets for any failure to collect and remit these taxes to the IRS. The bankruptcy or liquidation of the employer company does not relieve any of the company's payroll responsible employees of personal liability for nonpayment of these funds. Officers and even bookkeepers who have the authority to pay or withhold payment of the employees' portion of the payroll taxes have been held personally responsible by the courts.

EMPOWERMENT ZONE AND RENEWAL COMMUNITY BENEFITS

The Empowerment Zone/Enterprise Community program was established in 1993 under the Federal Omnibus Budget Reconciliation Act. Under the Act certain communities were selected for designation as renewal communities, empowerment zones, or enterprise communities. The purpose is to encourage the public and private sectors to cooperate in the development and rehabilitation of these distressed urban and rural areas. This program is primarily managed through partnerships between the local entity and either the Department of Housing and Urban Development for renewal communities and urban areas or the U.S. Department of Agriculture for rural empowerment zones and enterprise communities. The program ended on December 31, 2009, although some benefits extend beyond that date. As this edition goes to press, H.R. 4213, the Tax Extenders Bill, is in the process of being reconciled in the Senate. Businesses can obtain the location of the empowerment zones and renewal communities at www.hud.gov/crlocator. Detailed information concerning the tax incentives available under this program is included in IRS Publication 954, "Tax Incentives for Distressed Communities."

Work Opportunity Tax Credit

Businesses can take an income tax credit of up to $2,400 for each employee who is 18 to 39 years old and lives and works for them in an empowerment zone or a renewal community. This particular income tax credit is available even if the business is subject to the alternative minimum tax. To claim this credit, a company should file IRS Form 8850 with its State Workforce Agency, and IRS Form 5884 with the IRS. The credit is available only during the first year of employment for employees who begin work before September 1, 2011. The credit is based on the first $6,000 of earnings and is two-tiered as follows: Businesses can take a 25% credit for workers who worked at least 120 hours but less than 400 hours, and a 40% credit for workers who worked at least 400 hours, up to the $2,400 maximum credit.

Empowerment Zone and Renewal Community Employment Credit

Businesses can take an income tax credit of up to $3,000 annually for each employee who lives and works in an empowerment zone. This credit is calculated by multiplying an employee's annual wages by 20% up to a maximum of $15,000. They can also take an annual tax credit of up to $1,500 for each employee who lives and works in a renewal community. This credit is calculated by multiplying an employee's annual wages by 15%, up to a maximum of $10,000. IRS Form 8844 is used to claim these credits. The credits are available through December 31, 2009, although they may extend to December 31, 2010 (H.R. 4213, the Tax Extenders Bill).

Exclusion of Capital Gains

Capital gains income from the sale of eligible stock, partnership interest, or eligible tangible property held by a renewal community business for more than five years is nontaxable. The property must have been acquired after December 31, 2001, and before January 1, 2010. If the property is not sold in 2015, the gain up to that period may be substantiated and is exempt from the capital gains tax. IRS Tax Form 4562 provides further information on this exemption. Taxpayers other than corporations may exclude up to 60% of their capital gains on qualified business stock in a qualified empowerment zone business if held for more than five years. The stock must have been acquired after December 2000. Gains attributable to periods ending after 2014 do not qualify for this partial exclusion. IRS Publication 954, "Tax Incentives for Distressed Communities," offers details concerning these and other tax benefits available in empowerment zones and renewal communities.

UPFRONT PAYMENTS RECEIVED FROM SUPPLIERS

Hospitality companies that receive an advance from a supplier for purposes of inducing the hospitality company to purchase products of a particular kind exclusively from that supplier must record the payment received as income when it is received. IRS Technical Advice Memorandum 9719005 further discusses such upfront payments. The IRS does not accept that they be treated as loans or that they be reported as income over the life of the contract with the supplier.

BARTERING

Barter transactions are taxable transactions. If a hotel exchanges room nights for advertising services, the room rate for the rooms exchanged must be credited to an income account when the advertiser uses the rooms. When the hotel receives advertising services, they are considered an expense. The Uniform System of Accounts for Lodging (USAL) recommends that at the time the barter contract is signed, both a liability account and an asset account of the same value are created. When the advertising agency uses the hotel's rooms, it should debit the liability account while crediting revenue. When the hotel receives advertising services, it should debit advertising expense and credit the asset account created when the barter contract was signed. If the exchange takes place through a barter exchange or broker, the barter exchange or broker will send each party to the

FRANCHISING FEES

Franchising fees that are nonrefundable should be reported as taxable income in the year they are received. The IRS is aware of, and does not agree with, the fact that some businesses report these fees ratably over the franchise contract period.

GIFT CARD SALES DEFERRAL RULES

Businesses that sell gift cards must generally report the sale as current income for tax-reporting purposes and as deferred income for accounting purposes. Under Treasury Regulations Subchapter A, Part 1, sections 1.451-5, advance payments from the sale of a gift card can be deferred until the last day of the second tax year after the sale. To make this deferral, a business must have sufficient food and beverages or other gift-card-related salable product on hand during the redemption period. An information schedule must also be attached to the business's tax return specifying gift tax income from the current tax year that is being deferred, as well as previously deferred gift tax income that is reported as income in the current tax year. This is a complex topic in the IRC, and various other factors may need to be taken into consideration. IRS Form 3115, "Application for Change in Accounting Method," must be filed when changing to the deferral method.

DEDUCTIBLE FOOD AND BEVERAGE CONTRIBUTIONS

IRC Section 170(e)(3) allows C corporations an enhanced deduction for qualified contributions of food or beverage inventory to qualified organizations. The deductible amount equals the lesser of:

1. The donor's tax basis in the property, increased by one-half the difference between fair market value and basis: ((FMV − Basis) divided by 2) + Basis, or
2. Twice the donor's tax basis.

A sample calculation is provided in Example 1 below.

>**EXAMPLE 1:** A restaurant donates food with a fair market value (FMV) of $12,000, the price at which the food or beverage could be sold. Its basis is $15,000, the amount it paid for the food.
>
>| | |
>|---|---|
>| FMV on date of contribution: | $12,000 |
>| Donor's basis in the food and/or beverages | $15,000 |
>
>The allowable deduction would be the lesser of either:
>
>(A) Basis + 1/2 the difference between FMV and basis
>$15,000 + (1/2 × ($15,000 − $12,000)) = $16,500
>
>or
>
>(B) Twice the basis
>2 × $15,000 = $30,000
>
>**Note:** If the food and/or beverages were sold in the restaurant, the deductible amount would be only $15,000, its basis.

To qualify for this increased deduction, food or beverages must be made to a public charity described in IRC sections 509(a)(1), (2) or (3), or to a private operating foundation described in section 4942(j)(3). In addition, the recipient may not sell the food or beverages. Certain public charities, such as Gleaning for the World, will assist in making donations under this section of the tax code.

A donor C corporation must submit Form 8283, "Non-Cash Charitable Contributions," if the total for all noncash gifts is over $5,000; however, a written qualified appraisal is not required for donations of property by C corporations. If the donor corporation's noncash gifts exceed $5,000, the charity receiving the gift must also complete the appropriate section of Form 8283. Furthermore, the donor must obtain from the recipient a statement acknowledging receipt of the donation and a signed statement confirming that the recipient will use the gift for the care of the ill, the needy, or infants (minors).

CONTRIBUTIONS OF USED ITEMS

Hotels and restaurants may contribute used items, such as beds or kitchen utensils, but they may deduct only their fair market value. Care should be taken not to overstate this market value and to ascertain that the recipient is a qualifying organization. Publication 78, *Cumulative List of Organizations Described in Section 170(c) of the Internal Revenue Code of 1986*, is a list of organizations eligible to receive tax-deductible charitable contributions. This publication is available on the Internet.

GUEST LOYALTY PROGRAMS

Guest loyalty programs and reward point programs are the subject of current IRS scrutiny. Although the IRS has not developed a safe-harbor position regarding these programs, it has prepared a list of questions to answer in case of an audit.

1. What is the proper character of a reward point? Is a reward point a rebate or refund, as provided in Treasury Regulation 1.461-4(g)(3), or a trading stamp or premium coupon, as provided in Treasury Regulation 1.451-4(a)? A trading stamp or premium coupon may reduce gross income at the time of the corresponding sale, while a rebate or refund will not reduce gross income until payment is made to the person to which the liability is owed.

2. What is the cost of a reward point? How was the estimated average cost of redeeming each point computed? Did the taxpayer include only the costs to acquire the merchandise, cash, or other property required to redeem the points or did the taxpayer include other costs, such as advertising catalogs, transporting and storing merchandise, or operating redemption centers?

3. What methodology was used to estimate future redemptions? Does the methodology result in a reasonably accurate estimate of the points outstanding at the end of the taxable year that will ultimately be

presented for redemption? Although an expense may be deductible before it is due and payable, the liability must be firmly established.

4. When is the liability fixed—at the time a customer is issued the reward points or when the business redeems them? Is the liability fixed prior to the customer's accumulation of the minimum number of points needed to earn a reward certificate?

5. How is the expiration date of previously earned points taken into consideration?

6. Does the recurring item exception provided under Treasury Regulation 1.461-5 apply? (Treasury Regulation 1.461-5 is a complex regulation concerning which tax specialist should be consulted.)

LOBBYING DEDUCTIONS

The hospitality financial manager should be careful when deducting lobbying expenses in the process of calculating taxable income. IRC section 162(e) specifies which types of lobbying expenses are deductible and which are not. Non-deductible expenses include any expense incurred to (a) influence legislation, (b) support or oppose the candidacy of any public official, (c) influence the general public, or segments thereof, with respect to elections, legislative matters, or referendums, or (d) influence the actions or position, by direct communication, of a covered executive branch official.

There is an exception to (a) above with regard to the legislation of a local council or similar governing body. When attempting to influence legislation of these governing bodies, a deduction is allowed for all ordinary and necessary expenses, including, but not limited to, travel expenses and the cost of preparing testimony, that are related to:

1. Appearances before, submission of statements to, or sending communications to the committees or individual members of such council or body with respect to legislation or proposed legislation of direct interest to the taxpayer.

2. Communication of information between the taxpayer and an organization of which the taxpayer is a member with respect to any such legislation or proposed legislation which is of direct interest to the taxpayer and to such organization.

3. The portion of the dues so paid or incurred with respect to any organization of which the taxpayer is a member, which is attributable to the expenses of the activities described in paragraphs (1) and (2) carried on by the organization.

There is also a de minimis exception if in-house expenditures for any taxable year do not exceed $2,000. In determining whether a taxpayer exceeds the $2,000 limit under this clause, reference should be made to IRC section 162(e), as it contains an extensive definition of in-house expenses.

EXPANSION COSTS

The case of the *IRS v. Specialty Restaurant Corporation* demonstrates that it is best for a chain to expand under the existing corporate structure. If a separate corporation is formed when a new restaurant is developed, the IRS has ruled, expansion costs become pre-opening costs for the new corporation and are not currently deductible. The new corporation may deduct its pre-opening expenses over a 60-month period, but only if the new corporation makes this election on its initial return. Otherwise, the expenses must be capitalized and deducted as part of the basis of the restaurant when it is eventually sold. If the new restaurant is kept within the existing corporate structure, however, the opening expenses become part of the ongoing cost of doing business and are currently deductible.

PROPERTY AND SALES TAXES

Because property tax rates vary according to the location of a hospitality property, they are beyond the scope of this text. However, a hospitality manager should realize that this industry is very capital-intensive due to the large investments in property and equipment required to operate a hospitality company. Therefore, tangible property taxes and, in some locations, intangible property taxes will affect the hospitality company's operating results significantly. The same applies to sales taxes, most of which are levied by states rather than by the federal government.

PART V

INVESTING AND FINANCING DECISIONS

CHAPTER 21
LONG-TERM FINANCING

CONTENTS

Equity Financing	21,002
Common Stock	21,002
Advantages and Drawbacks of Common Stock Financing	21,002
Preferred Stock	21,003
Features of Preferred Stock	21,004
Warrants	21,005
Publicly Held Securities versus Privately Held Securities	21,006
Long-Term Debt Financing	21,006
Long-Term Bank Loans	21,007
Mortgage Financing	21,007
Bond Financing	21,007
Bonds and Their Features	21,008
Calling Bonds: When Should They Be Called?	21,009
Types of Bonds	21,009
Mortgage Bonds	21,009
Unsecured Bonds	21,009
Income Bonds	21,010
Zero-Coupon Bonds	21,010
Convertible Bonds	21,010
Use of Convertible Debentures as a Form of Financing	21,011
Subordinated Debentures	21,012
Factors Influencing Long-Term Financing Decisions	21,013
Alternative Sources of Financing	21,015

Exhibits

Exhibit 21-1.	Main Characteristics of External Debt and Equity Financing	21,004
Exhibit 21-2.	Characteristics of Selected Bonds	21,012

Long-term financing refers to financing with a term of at least ten years. Hospitality companies need cash to finance new projects and working capital requirements. For some companies, the main source of funds is the cash that is generated from operations, net of cash received to service existing debt. When internally generated cash is not adequate to finance expansion and maintain existing assets, the hospitality company must raise additional funds from external sources in the form of debt or equity capital. Choosing the proper financing instrument will provide the company with desired cash on attractive terms and the opportunity to maximize the company's value. An improper selection will result in unnecessary risk and excessive costs. Sources of borrowed funds used in the hospitality industry include mortgages, bank loans, bonds, and leases. External sources of equity capital include the issuance of preferred and common stock to existing and new shareholders.

EQUITY FINANCING

Equity capital comes from a variety of sources, depending to some extent on whether the hospitality company is privately held or publicly traded and in part on the company's growth and risk characteristics.

Privately held hospitality companies have fewer choices available than do publicly held companies, since they are not in a position to sell stock to raise equity capital. As a result, they depend on the owner or venture capitalist to raise capital needed to maintain the company's operations and expansion. Conversely, publicly traded hospitality companies are able to raise equity financing from two sources: (1) common stock and (2) preferred stock. For recently listed companies, the issuance price is estimated by an investment banker based on the price that the market is willing to pay. For an existing hospitality company, it is based on the current market price.

Common Stock

Common stock is the residual equity ownership in the hospitality company. Common shareholders have voting power and have a claim on any income remaining after the payment of all obligations, including interest on debt and dividends on preferred stock. Common shareholders control the hospitality company through their right to elect the board of directors of the corporation. The board of directors in turn appoints the members of top management who supervise the daily operations of the company.

Common stock has no maturity dates. Despite the lack of priority in earnings and liquidation, the investing public has great interest in common stock, and it is a key component of a hospitality company's long-term financing. Some hospitality companies have more than one class of common stock outstanding, one of which does not carry the voting privilege. For example, owners of class A common stock may have the right to vote, whereas owners of class B common stock may not. The nonvoting stock may or may not provide the same claim to dividends, income, and assets as the voting shares.

Since the common shareholders of a hospitality company are the owners, they have the right to elect the board of directors. In a small hospitality company, the owners usually have direct control over the operation of the business. However, in a large hotel or restaurant, the owners only indirectly control the operations of the business. This is accomplished by having the shareholders elect the board of directors, who in turn select the management team that will run the business.

Advantages and Drawbacks of Common Stock Financing

With common stock, there is no fixed obligation to pay dividends. However, with debt financing, the interest costs are fixed obligations that are legally binding on the hospitality company. As noted before, common stock has no maturity, which lessens the likelihood of the hospitality company having to retire the issue. Additionally, common stock helps to increase the creditworthiness of the hospitality company by enhancing the debt-to-equity ratio and acts as a hedge against inflation during periods of increasing prices.

However, long-term financing associated with common stock has a number of drawbacks. When common stock is issued, the potential dilution of control through the expansion of more voting rights can be a serious predicament for small- and medium-size hospitality companies. If the control factor is an issue, management may decide against the common stock alternative as a means of long-term financing.

Another factor to consider is the fact that the cost structure associated with common stock financing is much greater than that related to other forms of financing. Due to the risk associated with common stock in terms of claims on income and assets, the cost of capital is considerably higher for common stock than for debt or preferred stock financing. The dividends paid on common stock are not tax-deductible as with interest on debt financing. This in itself leads to a higher component of the cost-of-capital figure.

Preferred Stock

Preferred stock is usually considered a hybrid form of security that contains features of both debt and common stock. Similar to debt, preferred stock has a fixed dollar dividend, and preferred shareholders normally do not have voting rights. Similar to common stock investors, preferred stock investors hold claims with no maturities. Dividends paid to preferred shareholders are not tax-deductible and are available from after-tax cash flows. In terms of priority, preferred stock is subordinated to all debt with regard to earnings and assets. In fact, preferred stockholders have to wait until the debt holders' claims have been met before receiving their portion of the assets of the hospitality company.

Preferred stock is not a widely used form of long-term financing. From the hospitality company's perspective, preferred stock has three primary advantages:

1. Returns on preferred stock are generally limited and unusually high earnings will accrue to the common shareholders, who are the real owners of the hospitality company.
2. Nonpayment of preferred dividends does not place the hospitality company into default, as is the case if interest on debt is not paid.
3. Control of the company remains with the hospitality company's common shareholders.

Some hospitality managers regard preferred stock as cheap equity. They believe that preferred stock provides management with flexibility regarding dividend payments and maturity dates that common equity provides. Yet, because preferred shareholders have no right to participate in the future growth of the hospitality company, they consider preferred stock to be less expensive than equity. In addition, preferred stock can be considered as debt with a tax disadvantage, thus resulting in lower residual earnings to shareholders with preferred stock than with debt, even if the interest rate on the debt equals the dividend rate on the preferred stock.

Features of Preferred Stock

To make preferred stock a more viable financing instrument and to draw the interest of investors, a preferred issue may include several special features, including cumulative dividends, participation features, and convertibility features.

The cumulative dividend feature enforces the rule that common stock dividends cannot be paid until all preferred dividends in arrears have been paid. Thus the cumulative feature of having unpaid dividends on preferred stock carried forward is the main line of protection for the preferred shareholder.

In the case of participating preferred stock, the shareholders can participate in residual earnings of the hospitality company according to a specified formula. For example, a 6% preferred issue may have a participating feature whereby the preferred shareholders can equally participate in any common stock dividends in excess of $6. If the common stock dividend is $9, then the preferred shareholders can receive an additional $3 per share in dividends.

Convertible preferred stock gives holders the option to convert their shares of preferred into common stock at a stated price. This convertible feature can be added to enhance the success of the flotation and as a means for acquisitions. For example, the feature can be used as a sweetener for a preferred issue when the market perceives greater risk with the hospitality company and would demand a much higher dividend yield to have the issue successfully absorbed. In the acquisition of another company, convertible preferred stock is used because the exchange of shares is a nontaxable exchange and it avoids the dilution of earnings per share.

The main characteristics of external debt and equity financing are summarized in Exhibit 21-1.

Exhibit 21-1: Main Characteristics of External Debt and Equity Financing

Long-Term Debt	Preferred Stock	Common Stock
Debt holders are creditors with no voting rights.	Preferred shareholders have no control but may have some voting rights under certain circumstances.	Common stockholders have full control and voting rights.
There is a maturity date.	There is no maturity date.	There is no maturity date.
Debt holders have priority in the event of liquidations.	Preferred shareholders are paid after payment to debt holders but before payment to common shareholders.	Common stockholders are paid after payment to debt holders and preferred shareholders.
Interest payments represent fixed charges.	Dividends are return of capital.	Dividends are return of capital.
Interest payments are tax-deductible.	There is no tax deductibility for dividends.	There is no tax deductibility for dividends.

Long-Term Debt	Preferred Stock	Common Stock
Debt is lower cost than preferred stock and common stock.	Preferred stock has a higher cost than debt but lower cost than common stock.	Common stock has a higher cost than debt and preferred stock.
Debt is issued to raise capital for expansion.	Preferred stock is issued to raise quasi-equity without losing control.	Common stock is issued to raise permanent capital to finance a firm's growth.
Debt increases the firm's debt-to-equity.	Preferred stock decreases a firm's debt to equity.	Common stock decreases a firm's debt to equity.

WARRANTS

Warrants are options issued by the hospitality company that give the holder the right to purchase a specific amount of the company's common stock at a stated price (the exercise price). Warrants may be distributed along with debt and can be used to induce investors to buy a company's long-term debt at a lower interest rate than would otherwise be required.

Warrants are used by small, rapidly growing companies as "sweeteners" for public issues of debt or preferred stock. These companies may be regarded as high risk, and their bonds can be sold only if a company is willing to pay extremely high rates of interest and to accept very restrictive indenture provisions. To prevent this situation, companies often offer warrants along with their bonds. In addition, warrants are sometimes used in the founding of a company as compensation to underwriters and venture capitalists.

The warrant exercise price is generally set at 10% to 30% above the market price of the stock on the date the bond is issued. For example, if a stock sells for $10, the exercise price may be set in the $12 to $13 range. If the company grows and its stock price rises above the exercise price at which shares may be purchased, warrant holders may turn in their warrants, along with cash equal to the exercise price in exchange for the stock.

Warrants do not have an investment value, because there is no interest or dividends paid to holders or voting rights given. As a result, the market value of the warrant is only derived from the right given to purchase common stock. However, the market price of a warrant is usually more than its theoretical value, which is referred to as the premium on the warrant. The theoretical value of a warrant can be calculated as follows:

Value of a warrant = (market price per share − exercise price) × number of shares that may be bought

Due to the speculative nature of the warrant, the investor is able to obtain a good degree of leverage, and thus the value of the warrant is usually lower than the market price of the stock.

EXAMPLE 1: An investor has a warrant for FRT Hospitality giving him the right to buy a share of common stock for $20. The market price of the common stock is $45. Thus, the value of the warrant is $25 {($45 − 20) × 1}

PUBLICLY HELD SECURITIES VERSUS PRIVATELY HELD SECURITIES

Debt and equity securities may be issued either privately or publicly. In a public issuance of securities by a hospitality company, the debt or shares are purchased by the general public. The issuance of private securities has greater flexibility, is less costly, is less time-consuming, and does not require Securities and Exchange Commission (SEC) filings nor disclosure of information to the public. However, private placements require compliance to strict credit standards, and it is more difficult to obtain significant amounts of funds. Moreover, there is a higher interest rate for debt private placements and a shorter maturity than for public issuances. Most private placements in the hospitality industry involve small- and medium-size companies and debt securities.

Private placements of securities have the following benefits relative to public issuances:

- Lower flotation costs (flotation costs are costs incurred in registering and issuing the stock issue, such as brokerage commissions and underwriting fees).
- More flexibility.
- No need to disclose financial information to the public.
- No need to comply with SEC filing requirements.
- Less impact from the Sarbanes-Oxley Act requirements.
- Faster access to funds.
- Less costly to place debt securities privately.

Private placements of securities have the following drawbacks relative to public issues:

- Greater difficulty obtaining significant amounts of funds.
- Greater ability of large institutional investors to obtain voting control of the company.
- In the case of debt securities, a higher interest rate (e.g., lower liquidity).
- More stringent credit standards.
- More restrictive terms.
- In the case of debt securities, a lower maturity period.

LONG-TERM DEBT FINANCING

Long-term debt by definition has a maturity of more than ten years. The principal feature that distinguishes debt from other types of long-term financing is the contractual nature of the lender's claims against the income and assets of the borrowing hospitality company. In addition, long-term debt agreements usually include several provisions designed to reduce the likelihood of the hospitality company defaulting on the loan. Many of these provisions place restrictions on the hospitality company's financing and investing activities, including the payment of dividends and the acquisition of new businesses.

Long-term instruments may be classified based on (1) seniority, (2) security, (3) type of interest rate (fixed or floating), (4) convertibility/call ability, and (5) tradability.

Long-Term Bank Loans

Long-term loans are extended by banks and insurance companies to the hospitality industry. Similar to intermediate term loans, they are repaid in equal periodic installments that include the loan reimbursement as well as interest on the loan. If a hospitality company has no access to debt markets, then bank loans provide an important source of borrowed funds.

Mortgage Financing

Mortgages are notes payable collateralized by real estate that requires periodic payments of principal and interest. They are widely used in the hospitality industry to finance the construction of new hotels and restaurants as well as the renovation of facilities. Most mortgage loans are between 60% and 90% of the value of the collateral. They are obtained from banks, insurance companies, pension funds, and other financial institutions.

There are two types of mortgages: (1) a *senior mortgage*, also referred to as a *first mortgage* and (2) a *junior mortgage*, also referred to as a *second* or *third mortgage*. The first or senior mortgage has first claim on assets and earnings, whereas the second or third mortgage (e.g., a junior mortgage) has subordinated claims against the pledged assets.

Mortgages have distinct advantages in financing capital investments, including favorable interest rates, fewer financing restrictions, extended maturity dates for loan repayment, and relatively easy availability. Their main drawback is the collateral requirements. A mortgage may relate to specific land and buildings or may be a blanket mortgage covering all the real estate owned by the hospitality company.

Bond Financing

The alternative to borrowing long-term funds through bank loans or mortgage financing is to borrow by issuing corporate bonds that can be either sold to the public at large or placed privately. Corporate bonds are long-term contracts issued by hospitality companies to raise debt capital over periods ranging from 10 to 30 years.

The bondholder receives a specified annual interest payment and a specified amount of principal at maturity. The issuing hospitality company has a contractual obligation to pay bondholders a fixed annual coupon payment over the bond's life and to repay the borrowed funds at maturity. The difference between bonds and other forms of debt is that bonds are issued in denominations of $1,000 per bond. After issue, the bonds may be traded by investors in organized security exchanges.

Similar to other forms of debt, a bond is generally a fixed-income security. Because of large fluctuations in interest rates in recent years, some bonds have been issued with variable or floating interest rates. In the case of floating-rate bonds, also referred to as floaters, the interest rate is restated at specified intervals based on a particular market index such as LIBOR (the London Interbank Offer Rate) or the prime rate (the rate charged by the bank to its best customers).

A bond indenture is a written agreement that describes the main features of the bond issue, including payment dates, call and conversion provisions, if any, and other restrictive covenants. Some of these covenants may provide for specific limitations on the payment of dividends or minimum working capital requirements. The bond indenture represents a contractual agreement between the hospitality company, the bondholder, and the trustee. The trustee must ensure that the hospitality company is in compliance with all the terms of the agreement. If that is not the case, the bonds are in default.

Bond prices and market interest rates are inversely related. As market interest increases, the price of an existing bond declines because investors will be in a position to earn a higher interest rate by investing in new bonds.

Bonds and Their Features

Bonds issued by hospitality companies may include several provisions attached to them that provide specific rights to either the bondholder or the issuing hospitality company. The bondholder is protected by the bond's security, seniority, and sinking funds provisions. The issuing hospitality company is protected against a possible drop in interest rates by a call provision.

The issuer of a secured bond provides collateral to the lender. If the hospitality company is unsuccessful in servicing the bond, the lenders can take hold of property and resell it. Unsecured bonds, sometimes called debentures, are issued pursuant to the general credit rating of the issuing company. A senior bond has a claim on the hospitality company's assets that precedes the claim of junior or subordinated debt, which in turn takes precedence over the claims of the company's stockholders.

A sinking fund provision requires the bond issuer to set aside cash in a special trust account according to a regular schedule. This cash accumulates during the bond's life to allow the hospitality company to either redeem the bonds at maturity or to cash in part of the outstanding bonds before they reach their maturity date. If a sinking bond requirement is attached to the bond issue, the issuing hospitality company will be required to make periodic payments to the trustee.

Some bonds contain a clause giving the issuing company the option to retire the bonds before they reach maturity. As a result, the callable bond is less valuable to its holder than the same bond that is not callable. The company will most likely call the bond when it can issue new ones at a lower coupon rate, thus forcing the bondholder to replace the original bond with a lower coupon one. However, the more attractive the call provisions to the issuer, the higher the coupon rate on the bond.

Calling Bonds: When Should They Be Called?

Many bonds contain a call provision. In these cases, the hospitality company has the option to call the bond for redemption before it reaches maturity. To the issuing company, the inclusion of a call feature in the bond indenture can provide added financing flexibility. If, for instance, interest rates declined sharply, it would be beneficial to the hospitality company to call the existing bond issue and float another issue at a reduced rate of interest. This could save the hospitality company a substantial amount of money in interest payments. In addition, if the covenants in the bond agreement are too restrictive, the call option provides the opportunity for the hospitality company to seek a more favorable financing arrangement.

Although the call provision is valuable to the hospitality company, it is potentially detrimental to the bond investor, especially if the bond was issued in a period when interest rates were relatively high. As a result, the interest rate on a new issue of callable bonds will exceed that on a new issue of noncallable bonds.

> **EXAMPLE 2:** On June 1, 2007, Oh Hospitality issued bonds yielding 12.3%; these bonds were callable immediately. On the same day, UY Hospitality sold a bond issue of similar risk and maturity yielding 12%; its bonds were not callable for eight years. It is evident that bondholders were willing to accept a .3 percentage point's lower interest rate on UY's bonds for the assurance that a higher rate of interest would be earned for at least eight years. Conversely, Oh Hospitality had to incur a higher annual interest rate to have the opportunity of calling the bonds in the event of a future decline in interest rates.

TYPES OF BONDS

There are a wide variety of bonds that can be issued by a hospitality company, such as mortgage bonds, debentures, convertible debentures, serial bonds, income bonds, and zero-coupon bonds.

Mortgage Bonds

Under a mortgage bond, a hospitality company pledges certain property and equipment as collateral for the bond. Mortgage bonds are issued subject to an indenture, which is the legal document that describes the property in question that is being collateralized for the bondholders. In addition, the indenture provides a detailed explanation of the rights of the bondholders and the hospitality company. In most cases, the market value of the collateral will exceed the dollar amount of the bond issue.

Unsecured Bonds

The term "debenture" applies to unsecured bonds, and as such it provides no lien against specific assets as security for the obligation. Because these bonds are unsecured, the earning ability of the issuing corporation is of great concern to the bondholder. In addition, the bonds are considered to have greater risk than secured bonds and as result must provide investors with a higher yield than secured bonds.

Unsecured bonds, or debentures, are backed by the general credit of the hospitality company—that is, by all the company's assets that are not pledged as security for a loan. Therefore, these bonds are not secured by any specific property. Large companies with excellent credit ratings are most likely to issue straight debentures instead of secured bonds.

Income Bonds

Income bonds are a form of unsecured debt that requires payment of interest only to the extent that it is earned by the company. For instance, if the annual interest on the bonds is $100,000 and the hospitality company earns only $80,000 (before interest and taxes), the hospitality company has to pay only $80,000 interest on the income bonds. If the hospitality company had earned $200,000, then $100,000 of interest would be paid on the income bonds. Income bond indenture provisions vary. Interest payments are at times cumulative; that is, if they are not paid in a given period, they must be paid in a future period if earned by the hospitality company.

Income bonds are frequently used by hospitality companies whose capacity to meet interest payments is questionable—for example, after corporate restructuring. Yet income bonds may also be used by successful hospitality companies as an alternative to preferred stock. The advantage of income bonds is that interest is tax-deductible, whereas preferred stock dividends are not.

Zero-Coupon Bonds

Zero-coupon bonds do not require any periodic coupon payments; however, they are offered at a substantial discount below their par values and hence provide capital appreciation to the potential investor. Bondholders earn their return on investment entirely through capital gains, which is the difference between the price at which the bonds are issued and their redemption value (face or par value).

Convertible Bonds

A convertible bond (also referred as convertible debenture) can be exchanged at the option of the holder into the hospitality company's common stock. Specific terms are established at the time of issuance to regulate the conditions under which the conversion will take place. A specified number of shares are received by the bondholder at the time of the exchange. This is referred to as the conversion ratio, as follows:

$$\text{Conversion ratio} = \frac{\text{Par value of convertible bond}}{\text{Conversion price}}$$

The conversion ratio and the conversion price are set at the time the bond is issued. The conversion price applies to the effective price the bondholder pays for the common stock when the conversion takes place. Usually the conversion price is set from between 10% to 20% above the current market price of the common stock. The greater the expectation for growth, the greater will be the conversion price. Many convertible issues have a protection clause that protects the issue from dilution through stock splits, stock dividends, or the sale of common stock at a lower price.

EXAMPLE 3: X Hospitality Company issues 10-year, 8% bonds at $1,000 face value that are convertible into 10 shares of X stock

$$\text{The conversion price is: } \frac{\$1,000}{10} = 100 \text{ shares}$$

Shares of X Hospitality Company are currently trading at $80 per share, so the conversion premium is 25% ($100 − $80 ÷ $80) and the bonds' conversion value is $800 (10 × $80). If X Hospitality Company issued 10-year straight debentures, it would have to pay a coupon rate of 10%. Thus, the firm has reduced its interest cost by two full percentage points by providing investors the option to convert the bonds into common stock.

Use of Convertible Debentures as a Form of Financing

There are several reasons why convertible securities have become a widely used financing instrument in the hospitality industry. Many times, the convertible feature is used as a sweetener in selling debt. By giving the bondholder the opportunity of participating in the company's future growth, the hospitality company can issue debentures at a lower interest rate than would normally be expected with a debenture issue. Another feature of convertible debentures is that the protective covenants are usually less restrictive.

As a delayed equity issue, the convertible debenture gives management an opportunity to sell common stock at a higher price than the current value. If the stock is temporarily depressed, another flotation can only further depress the stock.

The fundamental principle in a convertible issue is that the market price of the stock will increase sufficiently to allow the issue to be converted. However, a crucial aspect of a convertible issue is that if the stock declines, the company will be caught with a bond issue with a fixed interest commitment. In addition, the lack of price movement can expose a future convertible issue when investors know that the previous one did not convert because of price stagnation. Thus, convertible features would lose their appeal for debenture holders.

The hospitality company's decision to sell a convertible debenture must be based, like other financing decisions, on the company's special circumstances and on market conditions. As previously noted, convertible bonds are generally issued at a yield lower than that required if the securities were nonconvertible. However, whether this presumed advantage results in a benefit to the hospitality company depends on the future movement in the company's stock price. If the hospitality company's stock price does not appreciate much in value, then the common stockholders are in a better position because conversion will never occur. In contrast, if the hospitality company's stock value rises, conversion will occur, and the bondholders will effectively have bought the company's stock at a bargain price. In this case, the company's common shareholders benefit less than they would have if the company had initially issued common stock.

Real benefits may be provided by convertible debentures if the hospitality company wishes to increase its leverage position in the short run but reduces these fixed-charge securities later by replacing them with common stock. In so doing, they would only incur flotation costs one time. That is, the company could issue convertible debt, which would be converted into common stock at a later time, with flotation costs incurred only in the current period.

Subordinated Debentures

Subordinated debentures are unsecured debentures that have a subordinated claim on assets below regular debentures. Accordingly, they have a lower priority claim to the company's assets in the event of bankruptcy because they are of inferior quality. The bond indenture clearly specifies whether the debentures are subordinated and which debt has the preferred position relative to the debentures. In the event of bankruptcy or reorganization, the subordinated debentures holders are not paid until the senior debt, as named on the indenture, has been paid.

The cost associated with subordinated debentures is obviously going to be considerably higher than the cost of interest yield that is associated with regular debentures. This is simply because the claim on assets is subordinated, and, due to the perceived increase in risk, the required return in terms of yield will be higher. One way to lessen the yield requirement is to allow the subordinated debentures to be converted into common stock. This added feature provides a sweetener to the issue.

Junk bonds are a very risky type of subordinated debenture that emerged in the 1980s as a source for financing leveraged buyouts and takeovers. Even though there was a collapse in the junk bond market in the late 1980s, they are still used by companies with below-investment-grade credit ratings when issuing publicly traded, high-yield debt.

A summary of the main characteristics and priority claims associated with different types of bonds is presented in Exhibit 21-2.

Exhibit 21-2: Characteristics of Selected Bonds

Type of Bond	Unique Features	Claim on Assets
Straight debentures	Available only to financially strong hospitality firms	General creditor
Mortgage bonds	Collateralized with land and buildings	Paid from the proceeds of the sale of the land and buildings
Income bonds	Interest is paid only if the hospitality firm generates earnings	General creditor
Zero-coupon bonds	Issued at zero coupon rate at prices significantly below face value	Unsecured or secured status

Type of Bond	Unique Features	Claim on Assets
Floating rate bonds	Interest rates are restated at specified intervals based on a particular market index such as LIBOR	Unsecured or secured status
Convertible debentures	Can be exchanged into shares of common stock at the option of the bondholder	General creditor
Subordinated debentures	Inferior quality High-interest costs	Subordinated claim on assets below senior debt

FACTORS INFLUENCING LONG-TERM FINANCING DECISIONS

Many factors influence a hospitality company's long-term financing strategy. For example, some companies obtain a high percentage of their financing from issuing stock and from earnings retained in the business. Other companies borrow as much as possible and raise equity capital only when they have no access to debt financing. However, most companies are somewhere in the middle.

The financial manager is concerned with selecting the best possible source of financing that will result in value creation for the company's shareholders. The factors that affect the long-term financing decision will vary among hospitality companies at any time and for any specified company in the long run. However, it is important to consider the following points in formulating a financing strategy and determining the mix of financing required:

- Adherence to the company's target capital structure.
- Cost and risk of various financing strategies.
- Current and future trends in interest rate levels. For example, if interest rates are expected to rise, the hospitality company may prefer to borrow rather than issue common or preferred stock.
- Future trends in market conditions and how they will impact future fund availability.
- Current debt-to-equity ratio. For example, a very high ratio indicates that the hospitality company is using high leverage and is subject to added financial risk. Hence, additional financing should come from equity sources.
- Maturity dates of present debt instruments. For example, the company should avoid having all debt come due simultaneously, because in the case of an economic slowdown, the company will not be able to meet its debt commitments.
- Restrictions in loan agreements. For instance, there might be a restriction on the amount of additional borrowings that the company can undertake.
- Type and amount of collateral required by long-term creditors.

- Ability to change financing strategy to adjust to varying economic conditions.
- Adequacy of present lines of credit for current and future needs.
- Inflation rate, since with debt the repayment is in cheaper dollars.
- Company's current and forecasted position. If the hospitality company's financial position is weak, management may be reluctant to issue new long-term debt because it would be more costly and restrictive for a company experiencing financial difficulties. At the same time, if the company has a frail financial position but is forecasting a major improvement in the future, management would be disposed to delay permanent financing until conditions improve. Conversely, a financially strong company with a poor forecast for the future would be motivated to finance long-term debt rather than wait.
- Availability of collateral. Hospitality companies with large amounts of property and equipment that have a ready resale value are likely to use relatively large amounts of debt financing, especially mortgages.

EXAMPLE 4: His Hospitality is considering the acquisition of a hotel business and various options to finance the acquisition. The current debt-equity position is within the industry average. In the past few years, the market price of the company's common stock has shown great volatility due to disappointing earnings reported by the firm. Currently, however, the market price of stock is strong.

The company's effective tax rate is relatively low.

The hotel acquisition should be financed through the issuance of equity securities for the following reasons:

- The market price of stock is currently at a high level.
- The issuance of long-term debt will cause greater instability in earnings because interest is a fixed cost. Moreover, it could result in volatility of stock prices.
- The issuance of debt will result in a higher debt-equity ratio relative to industry averages. This will have an adverse impact on the company's cost of capital and its ability to obtain financing in the future.

EXAMPLE 5: HYT Hospitality is in the process of undertaking a major expansion program. Therefore, it must secure $10 million in financing. The current market price of its common stock is $100. The interest rate on the long-term debt is 15% and the dividend yield on preferred stock is 12%. The company's effective tax rate is 40%, and it has a fairly good credit rating.

HYT ratios compared to the industry average follow:

	HYT	INDUSTRY
Return on assets	20%	10%
Long-term debt to total assets	25%	30%
Total liabilities to total assets	50%	67%
Current ratio	1.5	1
Interest coverage	10	5

The current earnings show evidence of stability, and the current owners would like to retain control of the firm. There are no sinking fund requirements on the debt. The after-tax cost of long-term debt is 9% (15%×60%). What would be the most appropriate way to finance the firm's capital expansion?

The issuance of long-term debt is more appropriate for the following reasons:

1. It has a fairly low after-tax cost of debt.
2. The firm appears to be in a very good position to borrow funds for expansion, because both the debt ratio and the long-term debt to total asset ratios are far below the industry average.
3. The liquidity position is strong based on the current ratio relative to the industry standard.
4. The interest coverage is double the industry standard, and the company's earnings are fairly stable. Hence, the company is showing a great ability to cover future interest charges resulting from the use of additional debt financing.
5. The firm's credit rating is satisfactory.
6. There are no required sinking fund provisions.
7. The firm is in a good position to use positive leverage and thus magnify the return to the owners without dilution of control.

If HYT Hospitality would prefer not to finance the capital expansion program by issuing debt, the next best alternative would be to issue preferred stock. The cost of preferred stock is lower than the cost of common stock, and there will be no dilutive effect on the current owner's control of the firm.

ALTERNATIVE SOURCES OF FINANCING

As a result of the depressed hotel and restaurant real estate market conditions in recent times, the hospitality industry had difficulty in accessing traditional hotel financing sources. This resulted in the emergence of creative and innovative sources of long-term financing to partially fill in the financing gap, such as:

- Evolution of a secondary mortgage market.
- Securitization of commercial real estate (including hotels) involving the design and development of innovative financial instruments. This resulted in the creation of new financing structures such as collateralized mortgage obligations (CMOs) and real estate mortgage investment conduits (REMICs). Each of these securities was designed to suit different investors and to improve tax efficiency. Thus, selling debt securities such as CMOs to the broader public market increased the flow of capital to the lodging industry.
- Emergence of the equity real estate investment trusts (REITs) in addressing the dilemma of shortage of capital for commercial hotel financing. A REIT may be a corporation, business trust, or association primarily developed to own or finance real estate. Since the traditional financing sources (such as banks and insurance companies) did not continue financing the lodging industry, a void was produced. This prompted hospitality managers as well as real estate developers and owners to view REITs as a conduit to raise capital and finance expansion plans.

CHAPTER 22
SHORT-TERM AND INTERMEDIATE FINANCING

CONTENTS

Short-Term Financing	22,002
Major Sources of Short-Term Financing	22,002
Short-Term Credit	22,002
Advantages and Drawbacks of Trade Credit	22,003
Analyzing Credit Terms	22,003
Taking the Cash Discount	22,003
Accruals	22,004
Short-Term Bank Loans	22,005
Compensating Balances	22,006
Lines of Credit	22,006
Revolving Lines of Credit	22,007
Commercial Paper as a Source of Short-Term Financing	22,007
Secured Loans	22,009
Accounts Receivable Loans	22,010
Loans Secured by Marketable Securities	22,010
Other Secured Loans	22,010
Intermediate Financing	22,012
Term Loans	22,012
Small Business Administration Term Loans	22,013
Conditional Sales Contracts	22,013
Leasing	22,014
Comparing Short-Term Financing to Long-Term and Intermediate Financing	22,015
Exhibit	
Exhibit 22-1. Summary of Short-Term Financing Sources Used in the Hospitality Industry	22,011

Among the various decisions the hospitality financial manager must make, the financing decision is one of the most important ones. Short, intermediate, and long-term financing sources are available for consideration. Associated with each alternative financing source are the considerations of risk-return tradeoffs and the effect of the decision on the leverage position of the company. This chapter focuses on financing instruments available to a hospitality company for use on both a short-term and intermediate financing basis, including their benefits and drawbacks.

SHORT-TERM FINANCING

Short-term financing refers to financing that will be repaid in one year or less. It is important to all hospitality companies, but it becomes essential to meet seasonal operations and temporary fluctuations in funds positions. Most hospitality companies use short-term financing to meet temporary shortfalls, while permanent financing is used to meet long-term capital requirements.

For the most part, hospitality companies have access to a wide variety of sources of short-term financing. One of the key distinctions between these alternatives is whether the financing is spontaneous or negotiated. When compared to long-term financing, short-term financing has several advantages, including being less expensive, more flexible, and easier to obtain.

Offsetting these advantages of short-term financing is the need for repeated renewals, which create an added element of risk. Other drawbacks of short-term financing include the fluctuations of interest rates and the additional risk of not being able to pay the debt when due, thereby resulting in a potential negative impact on the credit rating of the hospitality company.

MAJOR SOURCES OF SHORT-TERM FINANCING

Major sources of short-term financing used in the hospitality industry include:

- Trade credit
- Accruals
- Bank loans
- Commercial paper

Some forms of short-term financing are more desirable than others because of interest costs or collateral requirements. Yet the hospitality financial manager should consider the merits and demerits of the various sources of short-term financing available to the company and take into consideration the main factors affecting the short-term financing decision. These variables include interest costs, impact on the company's credit rating, risk factors, flexibility, tax considerations, restrictions and effect on the company's liquidity position, and expected market conditions.

SHORT-TERM CREDIT

Accounts payable or trade credit is one the most prevalent forms of short-term financing available to a hospitality company. Trade credit is mainly used for purchases of food and beverage inventories, furniture, equipment and supplies, as well as for electric, telephone, and other services. Trade credit is a primary source of spontaneous or on-demand financing. That is, it arises from normal business operations. To arrange for trade credit, the hospitality company needs to place an order. The supplier checks the company's credit and, if satisfactory, will extend the credit with usually no collateral and very little contractual support. With the high cost of holding cash balances, short-term credit has become an important source of liquidity for many hospitality companies. If the company has financial difficulties, it may be able to extend due dates for repayment; however, among the drawbacks of doing so are giving up any cash discount offered and the prospect of lowering the company's credit rating.

Advantages and Drawbacks of Trade Credit

As a source of short-term financing, trade credit has a number of benefits. The most significant advantage is that trade credit is readily available to most hospitality companies. Generally, there are no restrictions associated with trade credit that are common with other forms of short-term financing. The only specific limitation is the amount of trade credit that will be extended at a particular time.

Trade credit is crucial to small hospitality companies having difficulty obtaining loans from financial institutions due to their lack of creditworthiness. In a period of tight funds, where the ease of access of funds becomes constrained, trade credit is a pivotal form of short-term financing for the survival of the hospitality company. Moreover, the amount of credit extended expands and contracts with the needs of the hospitality company, which is why trade credit is classified as a spontaneous or on-demand source of financing.

A distinct drawback of trade credit is that it might become costly to the hospitality company due to the extension of the accounts payable by delaying payment beyond the agreed credit term, a very unstable situation based on the assumption that no harm will come because management considers trade credit a free source of financing. The extension of accounts payable deadlines may require accessing additional bank financing in order to meet the repayment of the accounts payable. In some instances, it might bring forth a liquidity crisis and cause the refusal of creditors to extend future credit to the hospitality company.

Analyzing Credit Terms

The credit terms offered by suppliers may enable the hospitality company to postpone payments for food and beverage inventory and other items purchased on account. Because the supplier's cost of having money tied up in credit sales is most likely included in the purchase price, the hospitality company is already ultimately paying for this rescheduling of payment. The hospitality company should therefore carefully examine credit terms to determine the utmost short-term financing approach. If a company is extended credit terms that include a cash discount, it needs to consider whether to take the discount.

Taking the Cash Discount

If a hospitality company plans to take a cash discount, it should make the payment on the last day of the discount period. There is no cost associated with taking a cash discount. Conversely, if the hospitality company decides to give up the cash discount, it should pay at the conclusion of the credit period. There is an implicit cost associated with giving up a cash discount. It is represented by the implied rate of interest paid to delay payment of an accounts payable for an additional number of days. The cost can be calculated as follows:

$$\text{Approximate \% cost} = \frac{\text{Discount \%}}{100 - \text{Discount \%}} \times \frac{365}{\text{Days credit outstanding} - \text{Discount period}}$$

EXAMPLE 1: XYZ Hospitality purchases $2,000 worth of food inventory per day from suppliers. The terms of purchase is 2/10, net 30 and the company pays on time. The accounts payable balance is:

$$\$2000 \text{ per day} \times 30 \text{ days} = \$60,000$$

The company should typically take advantage of a cash discount offered on the early payment of accounts payable because the failure to do so results in a high opportunity cost.

EXAMPLE 2: A hospitality company buys beverage inventory on the terms 2/10, net 30 and pays the full amount on day 100. By so doing, the company disregards the credit terms offered by the supplier, but obtains financing for the period from day 10 to day 100 by not taking the discount. For this company, the implied cost of trade credit is 8.27%, as follows:

$$\text{Opportunity cost of trade credit} = \frac{0.02}{1 - 0.02} \times \frac{365}{100 - 10} = 8.27\%$$

While financing at a cost of 8.27% may seem attractive, it might affect the company's relationship with the supplier if it is done on a consistent basis. In those cases, the supplier may decline to extend additional credit. This will result in cash on delivery (COD) purchase terms and thus will have an adverse impact on the company's credit terms.

EXAMPLE 3: A hospitality company purchases $2,000 of small kitchen equipment on terms of 2/10, net 30. The company fails to take the discount and pays the invoice on the 30th day. The opportunity cost of not taking the discount is:

$$\frac{\$40}{\$1960} \times \frac{365}{20} = 37.24\%$$

The company would benefit more by taking the discount, since the opportunity cost is 37.24%, even if it had to borrow the money from a financial institution. The interest rate on a bank loan would be much lower than 37.24%.

ACCRUALS

Accrued expenses provide another source of spontaneous short-term financing to a hospitality company. Arising from the normal course of the hospitality business, accruals are liabilities for expenses incurred for which payment has yet to be made. The most common items accrued by a hospitality company are wages, interest, and taxes.

Because hospitality companies pay employees on weekly, biweekly, or monthly bases, one of the principal accruals will certainly be accrued salaries and wages for payroll payments paid at the beginning of the month for work performed during the previous month. These accruals increase considerably as the hospitality company's operations expand. In large companies, accrued wages constitute an important source of financing. For instance, a hotel having 10,000 employees paid monthly, with an average salary of $3,000 per month, has the use of more than $30 million in accrued wages on average. If, for instance, the hospitality company invests this average amount over one year at an interest rate of 5%, it will be able to generate additional annual earnings.

SHORT-TERM BANK LOANS

Important negotiated sources of short-term financing include unsecured bank loans where the hospitality company does not have to pledge assets as collateral, or guarantee, in case of default. Most short-term unsecured loans made by banks to hospitality companies are self-liquidating. They are used to finance projects that have quick cash flows, for buildups in working capital requirements, and for seasonal cash shortfalls. They are highly recommended in cases where the hospitality company has a very good credit rating.

Short-term bank loans are used for access to immediate cash when the hospitality company can either repay the loan in the near future or rapidly obtain longer-term financing. A main objective of self-liquidating loans for 30 days, 90 days, and up to one year is to carry the hospitality company through seasonal peaks in financing requirements that are due primarily to buildups of accounts receivable and inventory. As receivables and inventories are converted into cash, the funds needed to repay these loans become available.

There are three forms of unsecured loans that are commonly used in the hospitality industry:

1. *Transaction loan*—a one-time loan used to finance a specific noncurrent need.
2. *Line of credit*—a nonbinding agreement in which the bank lends the hospitality company a specific amount of money over a set but renewable period of time, normally a year.
3. *Revolving line of credit*—a special line of credit in which the bank is legally committed to lend the money, a pledge for which the bank charges a commitment fee on the unused portion of the credit line.

Although savings and loan associations, credit unions, and other financial institutions provide banking services, commercial banks are the main source of unsecured bank loans in the hospitality industry. Commercial banks give hospitality companies the capability to keep a minimal amount of cash on hand and still expand operations. They are second in importance to trade credit as a source of short-term financing. A short-term commercial bank loan is generally made in the form of a note that the hospitality company agrees to pay interest on a regular basis and to repay the loan when it is due.

To receive an unsecured loan, a hospitality company must usually establish a good relationship with a bank by holding funds in the bank for checking accounts and other purposes. The interest rate on unsecured bank loans is typically based on the prime rate of interest and can be a fixed or a floating rate. The prime rate fluctuates over time with changes in the supply of, and demand for, loanable funds. Recently, a few large, highly profitable hospitality companies have been able to borrow at less than the prime rate. However, unsecured bank loans generally carry a higher interest rate than secured loans.

Interest on a loan may be paid either at maturity (ordinary interest) or in advance (discounting the loan). When interest is paid in advance, the loan proceeds are reduced and the effective (true) interest cost is increased.

EXAMPLE 4: The company borrows $100,000 at 12% interest per annum and repays the loan one year later.

The interest is $100,000 × .12 = $12,000

$$\text{Effective interest rate} = \frac{\text{Interest}}{\text{Proceeds}} = \frac{\$12,000}{\$100,000} = 12\%$$

EXAMPLE 5: Assume the same facts as in Example 4, except the note is discounted. The effective interest rate increases as follows:

Proceeds = principal − interest = $100,000 − $12,000 = $88,000

$$\text{Effective interest rate} = \frac{\text{Interest}}{\text{Proceeds}} = \frac{\$12,000}{\$88,000} = 13.6\%$$

Compensating Balances

Banks often require a hospitality company to maintain a portion of the loan amount on deposit in an account that does not earn interest. This deposit is a compensating balance, which is stated as a percentage of the loan and effectively raises the cost of financing. For example, if a bank issues a one-year loan for $10,000 and requires that 10% be left as a compensating balance, the hospitality company effectively receives $9,000; however, the company may still pay interest on this full $10,000. If the stated rate of interest on the loan is 10%, the hospitality company must pay $1,000 for the use of the borrowed funds. This represents an effective annual interest rate of $1,000/$9,000 = 11.11%.

Lines of Credit

A line of credit is generally an informal understanding between the bank and the hospitality company concerning the stated maximum amount the bank will provide the company at any one time. The bank does not have a legal commitment to supply the funds when the company requests them, but banks normally do so.

Lines of credit generally do not involve fixed rates of interest; instead, they state that credit will be extended at 1/2% over prime rate or some other spread over the bank's prime rate. They are normally established for a one-year period and may be renewed annually. The benefits of a line of credit are the easy and immediate access to funds during tight money market conditions and the ability to borrow only as much as desired and repay at once when cash is available.

When the company borrows under a line of credit, it may be required to maintain a compensating balance, thus effectively increasing the cost of the loan.

A compensating balance may also be placed on the unused portion of a line of credit, in which case the interest rate would be reduced.

Lines of credit are highly recommended for hospitality companies working on large capital investment projects that require a major investment of funds without receiving any cash inflows until the conclusion of the project. The drawbacks relate to the additional financial information that must be presented to the financial institution and the likely limitations that the bank may impose on the hospitality company, such as an upper limit on capital expenditures or the maintenance of a minimum level of working capital or financial ratios.

Revolving Lines of Credit

Revolving lines of credit are similar to regular lines of credit except that the bank is legally committed to extend the credit up to a maximum amount. Revolving credit arrangements usually involve both seasonal and longer-term financing and may extend over several years. For this legal commitment, the bank requires the hospitality company to pay a commitment fee based on the unused portion of the credit line.

> **EXAMPLE 6:** A Hospitality company has a revolving line of credit in the amount of $1 million. The company has borrowed $300,000 against the line of credit. A compensating fee of 1/2 of 1% annually is charged on the $700,000 unused balance in addition to the interest costs.
>
> In this case, the company will be paying $3,500 annually to maintain the commitment by the bank, as follows:
>
> $$\$700{,}000 \times 0.50\% = \$3{,}500$$
>
> **EXAMPLE 7:** The hospitality company borrows $100,000 and is required to keep a 10% compensating balance. It also has an unused line of credit of $90,000, for which a 5% compensating balance is required. The minimum balance that must be maintained is:
>
> $$(\$100{,}000 \times 0.10) + (\$90{,}000 \times .05) = \$10{,}000 + \$4{,}500 = \$14{,}500$$

COMMERCIAL PAPER AS A SOURCE OF SHORT-TERM FINANCING

Commercial paper is a form of short-term financing that consists of unsecured promissory notes issued by hospitality companies. Only the largest and most creditworthy hospitality company with a very strong credit rating is able to borrow funds through the sale of commercial paper. Therefore, the interest rate is less than that of a bank loan, typically 1/2% below the prime interest rate.

Commercial paper is sold at a discount (below face value). Maturities on commercial paper at the time of issue range from several days to a maximum of nine months. If the maturity date is more than nine months, registration with the SEC is required. Since the commercial paper is sold at a discount, the interest is immediately deducted from the face of the note by the creditor, but the company will pay the full face value. Commercial paper may be issued through a dealer or directly placed with an institutional investor.

Commercial paper represents an attractive financing source for large, financially sound hospitality companies because interest rates on commercial paper issues tend to be lower than for other short-term loans. Moreover, there are no minimum balance requirements that are associated with commercial paper, and because it is widely recognized that only the most creditworthy borrowers have access to the commercial paper market, its use denotes a company's strong and prestigious credit status. Using commercial paper as a source of short-term financing, however, involves a very special risk. The commercial paper market is highly impersonal and denies even the most creditworthy borrower any flexibility in terms of repayment. When bank credit is used, the borrower has someone with whom the financial manager can work out any temporary difficulties that might be encountered in meeting loan deadlines. This flexibility simply does not exist for commercial paper issuances. A hospitality company that is abruptly faced with temporary financial difficulties may find that investors are unwilling to purchase new issues of commercial paper to replace maturing issues. In addition, the amount of funds available in the commercial paper market is limited to the amount of excess liquidity of the various purchasers of commercial paper.

EXAMPLE 8: X Hospitality Company's balance sheet appears below:

Assets

Current assets	$ 500,000
Property and equipment	700,000
Total assets	$1,200,000

Liabilities and Stockholders' Equity

Current Liabilities:	
Notes payable	$ 100,000
Commercial paper	600,000
Total current liabilities	$ 700,000
Long-term debt	200,000
Total liabilities	$ 900,000
Stockholders' equity	300,000
Total liabilities and stockholders' equity	$1,200,000

The amount of commercial paper issued by X Hospitality is a very high percentage of both its current liabilities, 85.7% ($600,000/$700,000), and its total liabilities, 66.7% ($600,000/$900,000). It might be desirable for the company to borrow additional funds from banks because in the event of tight money market conditions, the company would find it beneficial to have a working relationship with a bank.

EXAMPLE 9: B Hospitality Company needs $100,000 for the month of September. It is considering the following alternatives:

1. A one-year revolving line of credit for $100,000 with Third National Bank. The commitment fee is 0.5%, and the interest charge on the used funds is 12%.

2. Issue two-month commercial paper at 10% interest. Because the funds are needed for only the month of September, the excess funds ($100,000) can be invested in 7% marketable securities for November. The total transaction fee for the marketable securities is 0.2%.

The line of credit costs:

Commitment fee for unused period:

$$0.50\% \times 100{,}000 \times 11/12 = \$458.33$$

Interest for one month:

$$12\% \times 100{,}000 \times 1/12 = \underline{100{,}000.00}$$

Total cost $\underline{\underline{\$1{,}458.33}}$

The commercial paper costs:

Interest charge:

$$10\% \times 100{,}000 \times 2/12 = \$1{,}666.66$$

Transaction fee:

$$0.20\% \times 100{,}000 = 200.00$$

Less interest earned on marketable securities:

$$7\% \times 100{,}000 \times 1/12 = \underline{(583.33)}$$

Total cost $\underline{\underline{\$1{,}283.33}}$

Note: It is apparent that the commercial paper option has a lower financing cost than the revolving line of credit.

SECURED LOANS

Secured sources of short-term financing represent the pledging of specific assets of the hospitality company as collateral to secure the loan. Upon default of the loan agreement, the lender has first claim to the pledged assets in addition to its claim as a general creditor of the company, an added margin of safety to the lender.

Other things being equal, the preferred method to borrow is on an unsecured basis. However, if a hospitality company's credit rating is deficient, the bank may lend money only on a secured basis. In some instances, although the hospitality company may be able to obtain an unsecured bank loan, it might be advisable to give collateral to get a lower interest rate.

Several kinds of collateral can be employed, including accounts receivables, inventory, marketable securities, or property and equipment. However, it is important to note that secured short-term financing is not as commonly used in the hospitality industry as in other industries in which inventories are pledged as collateral for secured loans. In special cases a company's hospitality receivables might be considered by some lenders to be prime collateral for a secured loan.

Accounts Receivable Loans

Accounts receivable financing involves either the pledging of or the factoring of receivables. From the lender's perspective, accounts receivable represent a desirable form of collateral, because they are fairly liquid and their value is relatively easy to recover if the company becomes insolvent.

There are a number of techniques for structuring a loan secured by accounts receivables. The simplest and least expensive to administer is to require the hospitality company to pledge accounts receivables. Therefore, the company simply provides a given amount of accounts receivables as collateral. Since the lender has no control over the quality of the accounts receivables pledged, usually the loan represents a low percentage of the receivables' face value. As customers pay the accounts receivables that have been assigned for the loan, the proceeds must be turned over to the bank separately from other funds. The bank will normally preserve the right to audit the books from time to time. Pledging receivables in this way leaves customers oblivious to the fact that their accounts have been given as collateral for a loan.

Factoring accounts receivable takes place when a company sells them to a financial institution called a *factor*, who receives direct payment from customers. The cost of the factoring arrangement is the factor's commission for credit inquiry, the interest on the unpaid balance of advanced funds, and a discount from the face value of the receivables where high-credit risk exists. The advantages of factoring are immediate availability of cash, financial advice, receipt of advances as required on a seasonal basis, and strengthening of the company's financial position. The drawbacks of factoring include both the high cost and the negative perception left with customers due to the change in ownership of the receivables. In addition, factoring may upset customers due to the restrictive ways of collecting delinquent accounts.

Loans Secured by Marketable Securities

Stocks and bonds may be used as collateral for short-term loans. These marketable securities are welcomed as collateral because of their high value and marketability. Securities listed in one of the national exchanges are preferred because price quotations are readily available. Banks will loan from 60% to 70% of the market value of listed stocks and from 70% to 80% of the market value of high-grade bonds. Only assignable stocks and bonds are eligible for this type of collateral financing. In those cases, a stock or bond power is executed that authorizes the bank to sell or otherwise dispose of the securities should it become necessary to do so to protect the loan.

Other Secured Loans

Assets other than receivables and marketable securities, such as the cash surrender of life insurance policies and equipment, may be used as collateral for short-term bank loans. In addition, loans may be made pursuant to the guarantee of a third party.

However, secured forms of short-term financing are not widely used in the hospitality industry.

Exhibit 22-1 provides a summary of the major features of short-term financing sources used in the hospitality industry.

Exhibit 22-1: Summary of Short-Term Financing Sources Used in the Hospitality Industry

Type	Source	Cost or Terms	Comments
Accounts Payable or Trade Credit	Suppliers or purveyors	No explicit cost 2/10 net 30 days. Opportunity cost for not taking discount	Hospitality companies should take advantage of discount offered
Accrued Expenses	Employees and tax agencies	None	Payroll and tax expenses incurred but not yet paid
Unsecured Bank Loans	Commercial banks	Prime interest rate plus risk premium. Interest rate may be fixed or variable 30, 60, 90 or up to one-year repayment periods	Working capital shortages. Seasonal needs
Regular Line of Credit	Commercial banks	Prime interest rate plus risk Premium	Informal agreement between banks and hospitality company
Revolving Line of Credit	Commercial banks	Prime rate plus risk Commitment fee 1/4 to 1/2 of 1% of the unused balance of the loan	Formal agreement between bank and hospitality company
Commercial Paper	Commercial banks, Insurance companies, and other financial institutions	Interest rate lower than prime	Unsecured short-term of financially strong hospitality companies
Accounts Receivable Loans (Pledging)	Commercial banks and finance companies	2% to 5% above prime rate plus fees	Accounts-receivable served as collateral (Customers are not notified of the arrangement)
Accounts Receivable Loans (Factoring)	Factors, commercial banks and finance companies	2% to 3% discount from face value of factored receivables	Accounts receivables are sold on discount basis without recourse

INTERMEDIATE FINANCING

Once the financial manager has decided that the debt with a maturity greater than one year is appropriate, the particular maturity must still be selected. Intermediate-term financing is debt originally rescheduled for repayment in more than one year but in less than ten years. It is appropriate when short-term unsecured loans are unavailable or when market conditions are not appropriate for the issuance of long-term debt or equity financing. The interest rate on intermediate loans is generally higher than on short-term loans because of the longer maturity period. The interest rates may be fixed or variable. However, the cost of an intermediate-term loan varies according to the amount of financing and the company's financial strength. Loan provisions are similar to short-term financing and are usually obtained from the same sources. The major types of intermediate-term financing include:

1. Term loans
2. Conditional sales contracts
3. Lease financing

Term Loans

A *term loan* is a contract under which the company agrees to make payments to a lender of interest and principal on specific dates. Term loans are normally negotiated directly with a financial institution, such as a bank, an insurance company, or a pension fund. Although the maturities of term loans may vary between two and 30 years, most are for periods ranging between two and 10 years. Thus, a term loan is described as having an intermediate maturity.

Term loans may or may not be secured by assets of the hospitality company. Payment schedules are variable but do not extend further than 10 years. Term loans are usually retired by systematic repayments over the life of the loan. Security in the form of equipment might be employed, but the larger, stronger hospitality companies are able to borrow on an unsecured basis. Some term loans will carry restrictive provisions or constraints on the hospitality company. For example, the loan agreement may require that the hospitality company maintain working capital equal to a fixed percentage of the amount of the debt.

There are many different sources of term loans, including commercial banks, insurance companies, pension funds, commercial finance companies, and government agencies. Several commercial banks and some savings and loan associations are actively involved in term lending. For instance, about one-third of commercial and industrial loans made by commercial banks are term loans. In spite of this level of activity, banks generally tend to favor loans having fairly short maturities of less than five years. Conversely, life insurance companies and pension funds are more interested in longer-term maturities, which might extend over 10 years.

From a hospitality company's perspective, term loan agreements with pension funds and insurance companies have one significant limitation. If a company decides to retire a term loan with a bank, it usually may do so without a penalty. However, insurance companies will normally charge a penalty, as they are interested in having funds invested for longer periods of time. Term loans from life insurance companies and pension funds tend to have slightly higher stated rates of interest than bank term loans because they generally are created with longer maturities, and there are no compensating balance requirements.

Term loans have three major advantages over publicly issued securities: (1) speed, (2) flexibility, and (3) low issuance costs. The flexibility enables the hospitality company to change the terms of the loan as financing requirements change. Because term loans are negotiated directly between the lender and the borrower, formal documentation is minimized. The key provisions of a term loan can be determined much more quickly than those for a public issue.

The drawback of intermediate-term loans is the high interest costs as compared to short-term debt. In addition, there might be collateral and restrictive covenants, which will not be the case for commercial paper and for unsecured short-term loans. Moreover, financial information, including budgets and financial statements, may have to be submitted on an annual or quarterly basis to the lender.

Small Business Administration Term Loans

The Small Business Administration (SBA), an agency of the federal government, has served as guarantor of term loans issued to small hospitality businesses. The SBA was established in 1953 to make credit available to small businesses that could not reasonably obtain financing from private sources. There are different types of SBA loans, as follows:

- *Direct loans*—Financed by the SBA and are made only when a small hospitality company cannot borrow from private sources at reasonable rates.

- *Participation loans*—Obtained from a local bank with SBA guaranteeing up to 90% of the loan amount. The SBA prefers participation loans over direct loans. Typical SBA loans have a maximum 10-year maturity. In addition, they usually carry an interest rate that is considerably lower than the rate charged for a similar non-SBA loan.

- *Economic opportunity loans*—Designed to assist economically and socially disadvantaged individuals who own hospitality companies.

Conditional Sales Contracts

Conditional sales contracts may be used to finance the acquisition of equipment, especially transportation equipment used by hospitality companies. Under the sales contract, the hospitality company agrees to buy transportation equipment and pay for it in installments over a one-to-five-year period. The interest cost on this type of intermediate financing is usually five to seven percentage points above prime rate and thus has a high cost and should only be used in cases where the hospitality company has no access to other forms of financing.

When a conditional sales contract is used to finance equipment, the seller retains the title until the company has made all payments required by the financing contract. At the time of purchase, the company normally makes a down payment to the seller and issues a promissory note for the balance of the purchase price. The company then agrees to make a series of periodic payments (usually monthly) of principal and interest to the seller until the note has been paid off. When the last payment has been made, the title to the equipment passes to the buyer. In the case of default, the seller may repossess the asset.

Leasing

Leasing is an alternative source of debt capital that allows the hospitality company to finance the use of assets such as transportation equipment, computers, or aircraft without actually owning them. Recently, many hospitality companies have supplemented debt with leasing as a way of acquiring property and equipment. For example, restaurants often lease their kitchen equipment. In these cases, the companies engage in long-term lease contracts that require periodic fixed rent payments.

Because leasing does not require immediate cash outlays, companies are able to use temporary equipment, meet other property requirements, and maintain flexibility in operations. The full amount of the rental payments is tax-deductible, whereas only the interest portion of the mortgage payment is tax-deductible. At the same time, with the use of leasing as an alternative source of debt capital, there are fewer financing restrictions placed by the lessor in comparison to those that are imposed by the lender when obtaining a loan to purchase an asset.

There are a few drawbacks when using leasing as a source of financing. There is a higher cost in the long run than if the asset is purchased, since the lessee is not building equity and will not benefit from the property's residual value. In addition, the hospitality company has no control of the property and thus is not in a position to make improvements to the leased property without the consent of the lessor. Moreover, the lessee cannot use the asset as collateral for future borrowings. Different types of leases are operating leases, financial leases (or capital leases), sale and leaseback leases, and leveraged leases.

An operating lease is normally of short-term duration and can be canceled by the lessee before it expires. Maintenance and service are normally provided by the lessor, and the lease payments under the contract are not sufficient to recover the full cost of the property. This alternative is particularly valuable to the lessee when the asset leased is a piece of equipment that can quickly become obsolete because of rapid technological advances. Conversely, a financial lease is a long-term lease that differs markedly from an operating lease in that it cannot be canceled, and the lessee is responsible for the maintenance and insurance costs. In these cases, the life of the lease contract approximates the life of the lease.

A sale and leaseback occurs when a hospitality company that owns land, buildings, or equipment sells the property to another company (usually a financial institution) and immediately executes an agreement to sell the property back for a specified period under specific terms. The lessee receives cash from the sale of the asset and makes periodic lease payments, thereby retaining use of the property as if it had borrowed and mortgaged the property to secure the loan. In a leveraged lease, the leasing company finances the purchase of the asset with a substantial level of debt, using as collateral the lease contract and the residual or salvage value of the asset. In essence, a financial lease is an alternative to borrowing and using the proceeds of the loan to purchase the (leased) assets.

In deciding whether to lease or borrow, the net present value (NPV) of the difference in cash flow between leasing and buying the asset should be calculated. This NPV is known as the net advantage to leasing (NAL). If the NAL is positive, the asset should be leased; if it is negative, the asset should be purchased. This approach is illustrated in Chapter 24, "Capital Investment Analysis."

COMPARING SHORT-TERM FINANCING TO LONG-TERM AND INTERMEDIATE FINANCING

Short-term financing is easier to arrange, has lower interest cost, and provides greater flexibility than long-term and intermediate financing. However, short-term financing makes the hospitality company subject to interest rate fluctuations, requires quicker refinancing, and is more difficult to repay. Short-term financing should be used as additional working capital to meet cash shortfalls for seasonal operations or as interim financing on long-term hotels or restaurant projects. Long-term financing is more appropriate to finance the purchase of property and equipment or the construction of new hotels or restaurants.

CHAPTER 23
DIVIDEND POLICY

CONTENTS

Dividends and Dividend Policy	23,001
Alternative Dividend Policies	23,002
Managed Dividend Policy	23,002
Residual Dividend Policy	23,004
Factors That Influence Dividend Policy	23,005
Shareholder Factors	23,005
Company Factors	23,005
Other Constraints on Dividend Policy	23,006
Cash Flow Constraints	23,006
Contractual Constraints	23,006
Tax Considerations	23,007
The Dividend Controversy	23,007
Dividend Policy and Corporate Strategy	23,008
Dividend Payment Procedures	23,008
Stock Dividends and Stock Splits	23,009
Rationale for a Stock Dividend or a Stock Split	23,009
Stock Repurchases	23,010

A hospitality company's dividend policy is an important decision, because dividends represent a major cash outlay for several hospitality companies and assist in determining a company's value. The dividend decision is directly related to the earnings a hospitality company pays out in dividends in contrast to the amount it retains and reinvests for future expansion. Thus, paying dividends reduces retained earnings, which otherwise may be used as a source of funds for capital investment projects.

Dividends are an important part of the difficult choice management makes in allocating the hospitality company's capital resources—reinvesting the money within the company or distributing it to shareholders. The dividends paid to shareholders partly compensate them for investing in the hospitality company. As an alternative to paying cash dividends, a hospitality company can also distribute cash to shareholders by repurchasing shares of its common stock.

DIVIDENDS AND DIVIDEND POLICY

The issue of how much in dividends a hospitality company should pay its shareholders is one that has concerned managers for some time. Hospitality companies operate with the objective of generating earnings. Shareholders supply equity capital, with the hope of sharing in those earnings either directly or indirectly. Hospitality management has two alternatives in deciding how to dispose of the company's earnings: (1) pay all or a portion of the earnings to the shareholders as dividends or (2) reinvest all or part of the earnings in the company. When a hospitality company pays out a share of its earnings as dividends, the shareholder benefits directly. If instead of paying dividends, the hospitality company retains those funds to take advantage of growth opportunities, the stockholders expect to benefit indirectly through potential enhancement of stock market prices.

Dividend policy refers to the payout policy that management follows in determining the size and pattern of distributions to shareholders over time. A financial manager's objectives for the company's dividend policy are to maximize shareholders' wealth while providing adequate financing for the company. When a company's earnings increase, management does not automatically pay a higher dividend. Generally, there is a time interval between rising earnings and increasing the dividend payment. Only when management is confident that the increased earnings will be sustained over time should an increase in dividends take place. Once dividends are raised, they should continue to be paid at the higher rate.

A hospitality company's dividend policy is important for the following reasons:

- It influences investor outlook about the future of the company. When dividends are cut, shareholders will look negatively on the hospitality company, because they tend to link the reduction in dividend payment with corporate financial difficulties. Stockholder dissatisfaction raises the likelihood that they might sell their stock holdings, which in turn may have a negative impact on stock prices.
- Stockholder discontent with a dividend payment policy also raises the possibility that control of the company may be seized by an outside group.
- It impacts the financing program and capital budget of the hospitality company.
- It affects the company's cash flow. A company with a poor liquidity position may be forced to restrict its dividend payments.
- It lowers stockholders' equity, since dividends reduce retained earnings and hence results in higher debt ratios.
- The size and timing of the company's expected dividend payments ultimately determine the value of the hospitality company.

ALTERNATIVE DIVIDEND POLICIES

The primary issue to be determined in establishing a sound dividend policy revolves around why corporations pay dividends. Most hospitality companies choose one of the following dividend payment patterns: (1) managed dividend policy or (2) residual dividend policy.

Managed Dividend Policy

When following the managed dividend policy, the hospitality company attempts to achieve a specific pattern of dividend payment. These payments can take three structures: (1) stable dollar dividend policy, (2) constant payout ratio dividend policy, and (3) compromised policy.

In a stable dividend policy the hospitality company maintains the same dividend per share each quarter. Earnings may change, but dividends remain stable. Accordingly, this policy preserves a relatively stable dollar dividend policy over time. Many investors have a positive perception of a stable dividend policy, as dividend stability suggests a low-risk company. Management will not reduce the dividend until there is evidence that a continuation of the current dividend cannot be sustained. Thus, in a year that the hospitality company experiences a net loss, the dividend may be maintained to avoid negative implications by current and prospective investors. By continuing to pay the dividend, shareholders will consider the loss as temporary. Some stockholders rely on the receipt of stable dividends for income. A stable dividend policy is also necessary for a company to be placed on a list of securities in which insurance companies, pensions, and other financial institutions invest. Being on such a list provides greater marketability for corporate shares.

Most dividend-paying hospitality companies tend to follow a stable dollar dividend policy for the following reasons:

- Stockholders who rely on dividends to provide a steady source of income will be less likely to invest in the company if they cannot depend on steady dividends.
- Managerial perception that a stable dollar dividend policy leads to higher stock prices.
- Legal listing in many states requires dividend stability.
- A stable dividend policy provides less opportunity of conveying misguided information content in cases of the pessimistic warning sign that a dividend cut might produce.

A constant payout ratio dividend policy is one where the hospitality company promises to pay a set portion of its earnings to shareholders each quarter. As a result, a constant percentage of earnings are paid out in dividends. Due to the fluctuation of earnings, dividends paid will fluctuate using this approach. A potential difficulty of this policy is that if the company's earnings fall significantly or there is a loss, the dividends paid will be markedly reduced or nonexistent. This policy will not maximize market price per share because most stockholders do not want volatility in their dividend payments.

A compromise between the policies of a stable dollar amount and a constant payout dividend ratio is when a hospitality company pays a small, regular dollar dividend per share plus a specially designated dividend, if warranted, based on the hospitality company's earnings performance. While this policy offers flexibility, it also leads to uncertainty in the minds of shareholders as to the amount in dividends they are likely to receive. Stockholders typically do not like such uncertainty; however, this policy may be appropriate when earnings significantly change over the years. The percentage or extra portion of the dividend should not be paid regularly; otherwise, its objective may not be attained, as the recurring extra dividends will come to be expected by investors.

Residual Dividend Policy

When a hospitality company's investment opportunities are not stable, management may wish to consider a wavering dividend policy. With this type of policy, a hospitality company pays dividends from earnings left over after meeting its investment needs while maintaining its target capital structure. Accordingly, the amount of earnings retained depends on the availability of investment opportunities in a given year. Dividends comprise the residual amount from earnings after the company's investment needs are met.

Implementing a residual dividend policy requires the following steps:

1. Determining the company's planned capital spending.
2. Determining the amount of equity needed to finance the company's planned spending given the company's target capital structure.
3. Using available cash flows to the greater extent possible.
4. Paying dividends only if more cash flows are available than the hospitality company needs to support the equity portion of the intended capital spending.

The main drawback of the residual dividend model is that it may result in a highly unstable dividend policy. That is, it can lead to huge dividends during periods in which earnings are high and investment opportunities are insufficient. Conversely, it might result in small or no dividends during periods when earnings are low and there are ample investment opportunities.

EXAMPLE 1: ER Hospitality and GT Hospitality are alike in every respect except for their dividend policies. ER Hospitality pays out a constant percentage of its earnings in dividends (25% dividend payout ratio), while GT Hospitality pays out a constant dollar dividend. GT Hospitality's market price per share is higher than that of ER Hospitality because the stock market looks favorably on stable dollar dividends. It reveals less uncertainty about the hospitality company.

EXAMPLE 2: Extra Hospitality Corporation reported net income of 1,000,000 in 20X9. Earnings have grown at a 10% annual rate. Dividends in 20X9 were $200,000.

In 2X10, the net income was $1,200,000, which was double the usual 10% annual growth rate. It is expected that earnings will return to the 10% rate in future years. The investment for 2X10 is expected to be $400,000.

Using a constant dividend payout ratio of 20%, the dividends to be paid in 2X10 will be $240,000 ($1,200,000 × 20%). If a stable dollar dividend policy is used, the 2X10 dividend payment will be $110,000 ($1,000,000 × 1.10).

If Extra Hospitality used the residual dividend policy, 40% of the 2X10 investment is financed with debt and the 2X10 dividend will be:

Equity needed = $400,000 × 60% = $240,000

Because net income exceeds the equity needed, all of the $240,000 of equity investment will be derived from net income:

Dividend = $1,200,00 − $240,000 = $960,000

If the investment for 2X10 is to be financed with 80% debt and 20% retained earnings and any net income not invested is paid out in dividends, then the dividends will be:

$$\text{Earnings retained} = \$400,000 \times 20\% = \$80,000$$

$$\text{Dividend} = \text{Net income} - \text{Earnings retained:}$$

$$\$1,120,000 = \$1,200,000 - \$80,000$$

FACTORS THAT INFLUENCE DIVIDEND POLICY

The dividend decision involves the determination of whether to pay dividends and, if so, how much. If earnings are reinvested in the company, they can be used to stimulate growth in future earnings and, as a result, might have a positive impact on future share values. On the other hand, dividends provide shareholders with tangible current returns.

Many factors may influence a hospitality company's decision about its dividends. Ample consideration should be given to these factors in determining a company's dividend policy. They are classified into three broad categories:

1. Shareholder factors
2. Company factors
3. Other constraints

Shareholder Factors

Shareholders' perspective about dividend policy is influenced by their dividend requirements, their view of the extent to which dividends reduce risk, and the tax status of dividends. The potential effect of a hospitality company's dividend policy on dilution of ownership may also concern some shareholders.

Some hospitality investors, such as retirees, depend on dividend income to help pay their living expenses. They want companies to provide large and stable dividends because an omission or cut in dividends can cause them hardship. Similarly, the attitudes of shareholders about risk may affect their preferences for dividend policies. For example, cautious investors may prefer to receive cash dividends now, rather than taking a chance on the future sale price of the stock.

Investors in high tax brackets often prefer stocks paying low or no dividends in order to avoid the tax liability resulting from the dividend payment. Conversely, if the retention of earnings leads to a hospitality company's increase in stock prices, the investor would be deferring the payment of taxes on capital gains, thereby reducing the present value of their future tax payments.

Company Factors

The financial manager should also consider several company-related factors that may influence the dividend decision in setting dividend policy. Dividends often follow the life cycle of the hospitality company. A rapidly growing hospitality company will generally pay no dividends or have a low dividend payout ratio in order to keep needed funds within the company for growth. Conversely, matured hospitality companies tend to have a growing to liberal dividend payout policy.

Likewise, profitable hospitality companies with stable earnings are more apt to have a higher percentage of their earnings paid in dividends than those hospitality companies with more volatile earnings. Management that is reluctant to issue additional common stock in order to maintain legal control will also retain a higher percentage of earnings inasmuch as internal financing enables control to be kept within.

The amount of a company's financial reserves can also affect the dividend payment policy. If a company has limited access to financing or a small amount of cash, this may restrict the size of the dividends because a cash dividend payment reduces a company's cash and retained earnings. Conversely, companies with excess cash reserves will be more likely to pay dividends to reduce those reserves. At the same time, a hospitality company with greater access to external financing has a more stable higher dividend payment because it is less dependent on internally generated funds to finance growth.

A highly leveraged hospitality company is more likely to retain profits so that it will have the required funds to pay interest and principal on debt. Likewise, a company that is capable of entering the capital markets easily can afford to have a higher dividend payout ratio.

OTHER CONSTRAINTS ON DIVIDEND POLICY

In addition to the factors discussed above, other considerations that affect the dividend policy of the hospitality company include cash flow constraints, contractual constraints, and tax considerations.

Cash Flow Constraints

Companies pay dividends in cash, but those that have no available cash cannot pay dividends regardless of their earnings. In most financial contexts, this emphasizes the superiority of cash flow over earnings. Even if hospitality companies do not have cash on hand, they must borrow funds to pay dividends. However, this requires incurring the costs of borrowing and may be considered financially unwise.

Contractual Constraints

Restricted covenants may be contained in bond indentures, term loans, short-term borrowing agreements, and lease contracts. For example, bond indentures include restrictions to help ensure that the hospitality company will have sufficient funds to meet obligations to bondholders or other creditors. These restrictions limit the amount in dividends a hospitality company can pay. The main reason for limiting dividend distributions is to protect creditors. Without such provisions, a company could distribute its assets to stockholders and reduce its ability to pay creditors.

Sometimes debt covenants state that dividends cannot be paid until a company's earnings have reached a specified level. Another type of constraint might prohibit dividend payments unless the hospitality company's current ratio is sufficiently large. In addition, sinking fund requirements, which state that a certain portion of a company's cash flow must be set apart for the retirement of the debt, may limit dividend payments.

Moreover, state or federal laws may govern the dividend practices followed by hospitality companies and may constrain the company's dividend policy. As a rule, laws regulate dividend payments, thus in essence prohibiting the impairment of capital. Capital is impaired when the company strips itself of assets through the dividend payment.

Tax Considerations

At various times, the top personal marginal tax rates on dividend income have been higher than the top marginal tax on long-term capital gains income. At other times, the two top marginal rates have been equal. In some instances, possible tax penalties for excess accumulation of retained earnings may result in high dividend payouts. The IRS prohibits the undue retention of earnings in excess of the present and future investment needs if they are retained solely as a means of avoiding taxes. The IRS may impose the accumulated earnings tax to prevent privately owned companies from retaining earnings beyond what is regarded as reasonable for business purposes.

THE DIVIDEND CONTROVERSY

The central issue about dividends is whether paying them or paying larger rather than smaller dividends has a positive, negative, or neutral effect on the hospitality company's stock price. Some financial experts argue that dividend policy does not affect the value of a company's common stock, while others believe that dividend policy has a strong impact on stock prices. The main theoretical arguments, regarding investors' preferences for or against dividends, are presented below in order to place the dividend controversy in proper perspective:

- Miller and Modigliani's Dividend Irrelevance theory contends that what a company pays in dividends is irrelevant and that shareholders are indifferent about receiving dividends. This notion comes from the pioneering work of Nobel laureates Miller and Modigliani, who argue that shareholders are generally indifferent as to dividends or capital gains, because the investment policy of the company is set ahead of time and is not altered by changes in dividend policy. Hence, according to this theory, there is no optimal dividend policy. Dividend policies are considered equally suitable.

- Weston and Brigham et al., believe that the best dividend policy varies with the particular characteristics of the company and its owners, depending on factors such as the tax bracket and income requirements of stockholders and corporate investment opportunities.

- Gordon and Lintner's bird-in-the-hand theory believes that cash flows of a company having a low dividend payout will be capitalized at a higher rate because investors will consider capital gains resulting from earnings retention to be more risky than dividends.

- According to Litzenberger and Ramaswamy's tax preference theory, investors who receive favorable tax treatment on capital gains may prefer stocks with low dividend payouts. Historically, tax laws in the United States have taxed dividend income more heavily than long-term capital gains. However, the Tax Act of 2003 reduced and equalized the maximum rate on dividends and capital gains. Yet investors may defer the capital gains tax until they sell the stock but cannot defer paying taxes on dividends. This theory suggests that companies should hold dividend payments to low levels if they want to maximize stock market prices.

DIVIDEND POLICY AND CORPORATE STRATEGY

Recent developments affecting the economy and the hospitality industry and, in particular, the recessions of the early 1990s and early in the millennium, coupled with the events of 9/11 and their impact on the industry, prompted several hospitality companies to revisit corporate strategies that directly affect shareholder's wealth. This reassessment of corporate strategies has resulted in rethinking many aspects of corporate policies, including dividend policy.

DIVIDEND PAYMENT PROCEDURES

A hospitality corporation's board of directors is responsible for a company's dividend policy. A corporation does not have the legal obligation to declare a dividend. Once the board declares a dividend, the declared dividend becomes a liability of the hospitality company, and the company has the legal obligation to make the dividend payment. Dividends are usually paid quarterly. The actual dividend procedures follow:

1. **Declaration Date.** On the declaration date the board of directors declares the regular dividend, and thus the hospitality company becomes liable for the payment of the dividend. As a result, if a balance sheet was prepared, the amount of dividends per share times the number of shares outstanding would appear as a current liability, and retained earnings would be reduced by the same amount.

2. **Ex-Dividend Date.** The ex-dividend date is the cut-off date for shareholders to receive the dividend. Companies and stock exchanges report the ex-dividend to remove any ambiguity about the recipients of the dividend payment. Hospitality investors who buy the stock before the ex-dividend date are entitled to the dividend, whereas those investors who buy shares on or after the ex-dividend date are not.

3. **Record Date.** At the close of business on the holder-of-record date, the company closes its stock transfer books and makes a list of the shareholders who own the stock as of that date. These are the shareholders who will receive the dividend check. The board of directors sets the record date, which is typically about a month after the declaration date.

4. **Payment Date.** The payment date is the date when the hospitality company mails the checks to the holders of record on this date. As a result, the dividend is payable, and the cash accounts are reduced. The payment date is usually several weeks after the record date.

STOCK DIVIDENDS AND STOCK SPLITS

An integral part of dividend policy is the use of stock dividends and stock splits. Both involve issuing new shares of stock on a pro rata basis to the current shareholders while the percentage of ownership in the hospitality company remains unchanged. The only explicit outcome of either a stock dividend or a stock split is the rise in the number of shares outstanding. A 20% stock dividend, for instance, entitles the holder of 100 shares of stock to 20 additional shares, to a total holding of 120 shares. Conversely, a stock split increases the number of shares outstanding by replacing old shares with new shares on a proportional basis. A two-for-one stock split would double the number of shares outstanding, as well as doubling each stockholder's individual holdings.

Although both stock dividends and stock splits increase the number of shares outstanding, they do not provide the company with new funds or its stockholders with any added claims to company assets. Theoretically, a company's economic value remains unchanged, because stock distributions simply divide the corporate pie into more pieces.

A difference between a stock dividend and a stock split relates to their respective accounting treatments. The accounting treatment for a stock dividend requires the issuing companies to capitalize the market value of the dividend by transferring this amount from retained earnings to the common stock account. Conversely, when accounting for a stock split, the dollar amounts for retained earnings or common stock do not change. Only the number of shares outstanding changes, and the par value of each share is decreased proportionately. Despite this dissimilarity in accounting treatment, there is no real economic difference between a stock dividend and stock split.

> **EXAMPLE 3:** X Hospitality has 1,000,000 shares outstanding, with a $2 par value. Its market price is $14 per share. It issues a 15% stock dividend. Hence, the number of shares outstanding increases by 150,000 shares (1,000,000 shares × 15%), and the market value of this increase is $2,100,000 (150,000 shares × $14 per share). To record this transaction, X Hospitality will transfer $2,100,000 from retained earnings to common stock, resulting in a $300,000 increase in total par value (150,000 shares × $2 par value).
>
> If X Hospitality declared a two-for-one split instead of the 15% dividend, the accounting treatment for the split would be recorded as an increase in the number of shares outstanding from 1,000,000 to 2,000,000 shares, and a decrease in the per-share par value from $2 to $1. Accordingly, the dollar amount of each account within shareholder's equity does not change.

Rationale for a Stock Dividend or a Stock Split

Although stock dividends and splits take place less often than cash dividends, a considerable number of hospitality companies opt to use these share distributions either with or in lieu of cash dividends. Proponents of stock dividends and splits frequently maintain that stockholders receive a key benefit, because the price of the stock will not fall precisely in proportion to the share increase. Moreover, the announcement of a stock dividend or split has been perceived as favorable news, as it has generally been associated with companies with increased earnings. However, most studies indicate that if a stock dividend or split is not accompanied by a positive trend in earnings and increase in cash dividends, price increases surrounding the stock dividend or split are insignificant.

Another reason for stock dividends or splits is to conserve corporate cash. If a hospitality company is experiencing cash difficulties, it may replace a stock dividend for a cash dividend. However, as stated earlier, investors will most likely look beyond the dividend to ascertain the underlying reason for preserving cash. If the stock dividend is an effort to conserve cash for attractive investment opportunities, the shareholders may bid up the stock price. If the move to conserve cash relates to financial difficulties within the company, the market price will most likely react adversely.

STOCK REPURCHASES

Stocks repurchases (or stock buybacks) are alternatives to paying dividends. In either case, excess cash is distributed to existing shareholders. Stock repurchases occur when a company buys its own stock, which results in a reduction in the number of shares outstanding. Since outstanding shares will be reduced after stock has been repurchased, earnings per share (EPS) will increase (assuming net income is held constant). The increase in EPS may result in a higher market price per share.

Share repurchases are accomplished by either open-market purchases or tender offers for shares. In an open-market purchase, the hospitality corporation buys its stock in the secondary market as a regular investor, except that companies must publicly announce their intention to repurchase shares. Conversely, a tender offer is a formal offer to buy all shares tendered up to a given number. The repurchase price (or bid price) is stated in the tender offer announcement and is above the current market price.

For several decades, corporate management of several hospitality companies has been active in repurchasing their own equity securities as a way to increase shareholder returns. A case in point is McDonald's Corporation. The amount shown on the balance sheet for treasury stock (e.g., the amount paid for repurchasing its own stock), is several-fold the amount originally invested by the stockholders. This situation is not unusual for many large publicly held companies. There are several contributing factors to the rise in stock repurchase activity:

- Favorable impact on EPS
- Elimination of minority ownership group of shareholders
- Reduction in the company's costs associated with servicing small stockholders
- Approach for modifying the company's capital structure
- Elimination of a minority ownership group of stockholders
- Use for future acquisitions or for stock options

From an investor's perspective, a stock repurchase, as opposed to a cash dividend, has a potential tax advantage. Before the enactment of the Tax Reduction Act of 2003, dividends have been traditionally taxed at regular income rates, but share repurchases have been taxed as capital gains. This created a tax advantage to the repurchase alternative. Moreover, repurchasing stock when the hospitality company has excess cash may be regarded as a sound investment decision. When equity prices are depressed, management may view the company's own stock as being materially undervalued and as representing a good investment opportunity. Nonetheless, the decision to repurchase a company's stock should not merely be viewed in the context of an investment decision. A hospitality company cannot prosper (or even survive) by investing only in its own stock.

EXAMPLE 4: A company earned $3 million in 2X10. Of this amount, it decided to use 30% to purchase treasury stock.

Currently, there are 400,000 shares outstanding. Market price per share is $30.

The company can use $900,000 (30% of $3 million) to buy back 40,000 shares through a tender offer of $22.50 per share.

Current earnings per share is $7.50 ($3 million ÷ 400,000 shares outstanding).

The current P/E multiple is: $3 (Market price per share ÷ earnings per share).

Earnings per share after treasury stock is acquired become:

$3 million ÷ 360,000 shares outstanding = $8.33

The expected market price, assuming the P/E ratio remains the same, is:

P/E multiple × New earnings per share = Expected market price

3 × $8.33 = $25

In undertaking stock repurchase transactions, there are several drawbacks for hospitality companies that must be considered:

- If investors believe that the company is engaging in a repurchase plan because its management does not have alternative good investment opportunities, a drop in the market price of stock may ensue.
- If the reacquisition of stock makes it appear that the company is manipulating its stock price, the company will have problems with the SEC. Further, if the IRS concludes that the repurchase is designed to avoid the payment of tax on dividends, tax penalties may be imposed because of the improper accumulation of earnings as specified in the tax code.

CHAPTER 24
CAPITAL INVESTMENT ANALYSIS

CONTENTS

Significance of Capital Investment Analysis	24,002
Types of Capital Budgeting Decisions	24,003
Independent Versus Mutually Exclusive Projects	24,003
The Capital Investment Process	24,003
Estimating Project Cash Flows	24,005
Cash Flow Categories	24,006
Initial Investment	24,006
Operating Income and Expense	24,006
Project Termination	24,006
Capital Budgeting Models	24,007
Accounting Rate of Return	24,007
Payback Method	24,008
The Discounted Payback Period	24,010
The Net Present Value Criterion	24,011
NPV and Shareholder Wealth	24,013
Profitability Index	24,013
Internal Rate of Return	24,014
Use of Computers	24,016
Capital Budgeting Process Illustration	24,016
Special Considerations in Capital Investment Analysis	24,018
Mutually Exclusive Project Decisions	24,018
Capital Budgeting and Inflation	24,019
Income Taxes and Capital Investment Decisions	24,019
Risk and Uncertainty	24,019
Impact of Discount Rate on Capital Investment Analysis	24,020
Post-Audit Project Review	24,020
The Lease or Purchase Decision	24,021

Exhibits

Exhibit 24-1.	The Capital Investment Process	24,004
Exhibit 24-2.	Major Types of Cash Flows from Capital Investments	24,006
Exhibit 24-3.	The ARR Acceptance Criterion	24,007
Exhibit 24-4.	The Payback Acceptance Criterion	24,009
Exhibit 24-5.	The Discounted Payback Acceptance Criterion	24,011
Exhibit 24-6.	The NPV Acceptance Criterion	24,012
Exhibit 24-7.	The IRR Criterion	24,015

Capital investment analysis, or capital budgeting, as it is often referred to, relates to planning for the best selection and financing of long-term investment proposals presented to the hospitality company. Sound investment decisions that apply well-founded strategies are vital for creating shareholder value. These key decisions require spending cash now in order to acquire long-lived assets that will be a source of cash flows in the future. Whether the investment decision involves committing resources to new hotel properties, a new marketing program, additional working capital, or investing in a bond security, an economic exchange must be made between the resources expended now and the prospect of future cash benefits to be obtained in the future. Analyzing this trade-off is essentially a valuation process that makes a financial evaluation of a combination of positive and negative cash flow patterns.

Hospitality managers will be highly commended for their skills in identifying potentially successful projects and carrying them to completion. However, if the capital investment program is not successful, the hospitality company's performance may be affected negatively for a considerable period of time. In addition, the company's creditors and shareholders could lose confidence and may become reluctant to provide additional funds in the future.

This chapter discusses the various capital budgeting models that are available to make a capital investment decision in the hospitality industry. They include accounting rate of return (ARR), payback, discounted payback, net present value (NPV), profitability index (PI), and internal rate of return (IRR). Consideration is also given to mutually exclusive projects and the impact of inflation and taxation on capital investment analysis. The incorporation of risk into the analysis is also addressed.

SIGNIFICANCE OF CAPITAL INVESTMENT ANALYSIS

The effective appraisal and management of capital investments is critically important in the hospitality industry for several reasons:

1. The hospitality industry is capital-intensive. Once a capital investment is implemented, it can affect the profitability and value of a hospitality company over a significant period of time.

2. Often, a capital investment represents a strategic investment that shapes the future of the hospitality company, such as major expansion into global markets or the development of a new brand.

3. Many capital investment decisions involve a large expenditure of funds and a significant commitment of managerial time.

As a result of the significance of capital investments to the successful performance of hospitality companies, there should be a capital budgeting process that is designed to assist financial managers in identifying, evaluating, selecting, and monitoring capital projects. A key aspect of this process is the selection of a proper decision criterion for the evaluation of an investment's potential success.

Capital budgeting decisions involve comparing the amount of cash spent today on an investment with the cash inflows expected from it in the future. An investment proposal should be evaluated in relation to whether it provides a return equal to, or greater than, that required by investors. Projects must be tied into the company's long-range planning and take into account corporate strengths and weaknesses.

Taxes have to be considered in making capital budgeting decisions because a project that looks good on a before-tax basis may not be acceptable on an after-tax basis. Taxes have an effect on the amount and timing of cash flows. What-if questions are often the most crucial and difficult with regard to the capital expenditure budget, and informed estimates of the major assumptions are needed. Once an investment proposal is accepted, there has to be an implementation of controls over expenditures and a reporting system regarding the project's status. Expenditures should be traced to the project and controls put in place to ensure that the expenditures are in compliance with the approved investment proposal. Continuous examination should be made of how well the project is doing relative to the original plan.

TYPES OF CAPITAL BUDGETING DECISIONS

The basic types of investment decisions are selecting between proposed projects and replacement decisions. Selection requires judgments concerning future events over which there may not be direct knowledge. Discounted cash flow methods are more realistic than methods not taking into account the time value of money in evaluating investments. Among the many capital budgeting decisions made by the hospitality financial manager are the following:

- Construction of a new hotel or restaurant
- Cost reduction program
- Undertaking a new marketing program
- Replacement of assets
- Merger analysis
- Compliance with government regulations (e.g., American Disabilities Act)
- Expansion of brands into domestic or global markets

INDEPENDENT VERSUS MUTUALLY EXCLUSIVE PROJECTS

Before hospitality managers can apply decision rules, they need to be able to distinguish between independent and mutually exclusive projects. Independent projects are those in which the acceptance or rejection of one project does not prevent the acceptance or rejection of another project under consideration. In other words, the implementation of independent projects is unrelated to each other. Analysis can evaluate the effects of an independent project on a hospitality company's value without having to consider the effect on other investment opportunities. Conversely, mutually exclusive projects are those in which the acceptance of one of the projects implies that the rest have to be rejected.

THE CAPITAL INVESTMENT PROCESS

The capital investment decision, also called the capital budgeting decision, involves several steps, as summarized in Exhibit 24-1. The process begins when the hospitality manager identifies business prospects that can be turned into potentially valuable investments. This first step is considered the most important step in the process. Certainly, it is easier to evaluate and monitor profitable projects than it is to identify them. It is extremely important that management promotes an environment within the hospitality company that facilitates the identification of new investment proposals that could lead to successful investments.

Exhibit 24-1: The Capital Investment Process

Identification	Evaluation	Selection	Implementation
Finding out investment opportunities and generating investment proposals	Estimating the project's relevant cash flows and discount rate	Choosing a decision-making rule (accept/reject decision)	Establishing an audit and a follow-up procedure

Type of Investment	Input	Decision-Rule	Performance Evaluation
• Acquisitions • Renovations • Replacements • Diversification • Required investment standard • Expansion of facilities • Mergers • Refinancing debt issues • Cost reduction programs • Conversion	Expected cash flow stream Discount rate Risk factors	Net present value Internal rate of return Profitability index Payback Accounting rate of return	Monitor the timing of cash flows Check if project still meets selection standard Continue or discard project Monitor failure rate

The first step in evaluating the investment decision is to devise long-term goals. Identified investment proposals must then be evaluated financially. The inputs required for financial evaluation of a project include the estimation of its useful life, the cash flows the project is expected to generate over that period, and the appropriate cash flow stream. This is a challenging step in making the capital investment decision.

Proposals are frequently classified by how difficult it is to estimate the key parameters needed for financial evaluation. Required investments are those the hospitality company must make to comply with safety, health, and environmental laws. Estimating cash inflows should not be difficult in this case because, in most instances, they are already specified in the corresponding regulations. Replacement of less efficient systems are cost-savings projects that do not generate extra cash inflows. Their future cash benefits consist of reductions in anticipated costs that hospitality managers can also identify with relative ease. Financial evaluations for expansion investments are more challenging because these projects require the hospitality company to estimate the additional sales revenues, margins, and working capital that the project is expected to generate. Finally, economic evaluation for diversification investments is usually the most complex. The cash inflows these proposals are expected to generate are probably the hardest to forecast because the company will enter an industry or market segment it does not know as well as its own.

After the proposal's financial parameters have been estimated, an investment criterion should be applied to decide whether the proposal will be accepted or rejected. Several models are available: net present value, internal rate of return, accounting rate of return, profitability index, and payback method.

Lastly, accepted proposals must be implemented. But the capital investment process does not end at this point. Projects should be audited regularly throughout their lives to ascertain that they are in line with budgeted figures and to determine if estimated cash flows are meeting expectations. If the audit indicates that the expected remaining benefits of an existing investment are lower than the costs of terminating the investment, the company must abandon the project. Continually monitoring the failure rate is also important in order to advance the company's capital investment process by preventing the hospitality company from making the same mistakes on future projects. Sample questions in the capital investment process include:

- Is the proposal consistent with the company's long-term objectives?
- Is cost-benefit analysis being performed?
- Is risk considered in the analysis?
- What is the quality of the project?
- Is a discounted cash flow technique being used in the evaluating process?
- Is risk versus return considered in selecting the best projects?
- Are all results of the capital investment analysis considered and integrated?
- Are both dollars and time considered in evaluating the proposal?
- What assumptions were made in estimating cash inflows?
- Is there a post-audit review process in place?
- Are qualitative factors being considered (e.g., economic, social, marketing, and political variables)?
- Is the company's financial status being considered in evaluating the proposal?
- Are the capital investments adequate in light of the current industry and company environment?

ESTIMATING PROJECT CASH FLOWS

One of the most important but challenging tasks in making a capital investment decision is estimating future cash flows for a project. In arriving at projected cash flows, the hospitality financial manager must rely on forecasts of sales revenues, as well as cost savings arising from the proposed project. The task given to the financial manager is to determine which cash flow categories apply to a given investment proposal and to forecast the incremental cash flows arising from each.

Cash Flow Categories

Project cash flows can be grouped by their timing—that is, when they occur. The initial investment occurs at the beginning of a project's life, whereas operating income and expenses are annual cash inflows occurring during a project's life. Similarly, termination cash flows occur at the end of a project's life. Exhibit 24-2 presents a list of major types of cash flows arising from capital investments.

Initial Investment

The initial project cost (e.g., cash outflow) may include planning and design costs in the construction of a restaurant or hotel as well as transportation, insurance, setup, and prepaid maintenance. For simple projects, cash outflows occur at the present time, whereas for large projects such as construction of new hotel properties, cash outflows occur in the future, as projects may take several years to complete. Sale of existing assets may also affect net cash inflows in the case of replacement projects.

Operating Income and Expense

Operating income and expense are annual revenues and expenses occurring during the operating life of the project. Cash revenues include sales of rooms, food, and other incidental income. These cash inflows will fluctuate, because unit sales will not be constant from year to year. Similarly, cash expenses include payroll, utility costs, maintenance, and other operating costs. As with sales, they normally vary from period to period. Replacement projects may lower expenses, thereby producing cash savings.

Project Termination

Cash inflows from the sale of assets apply to projects that have an economic value beyond the life of the venture. Accordingly, the resale or residual value may represent a significant addition to a project's value. In addition, the tax effect of a project's sale (cash inflow or cash outflow) is treated the same as that of the sale of an existing asset.

Moreover, recovery of net working capital (cash inflow or cash outflow) occurs at the termination of a project, when the initial change in net working capital is reversed in order to return to the original net working capital position.

Exhibit 24-2: Major Types of Cash Flows from Capital Investments

Chronological List of Major Types of Cash Flows Arising from a Capital Investment Decision

    A. Initial Period
        1. Initial investment cost
        2. Increase in net working capital

B. Project Life
  1. After cash operating inflows
  2. Cost savings
C. Project Termination
  1. Salvage or residual value
  2. Decrease in net working capital

CAPITAL BUDGETING MODELS

In deciding whether to accept or reject a proposed project, major emphasis is placed on cash flows, as they represent the benefits generated from accepting a capital budgeting proposal. Capital investment evaluation criteria can be divided into two broad categories: (1) nondiscounted cash flow methodologies and (2) discounted cash flow methodologies.

There are two nondiscounted cash flow capital budgeting models that are not very sophisticated: the accounting rate of return (ARR) method and the payback method. These techniques are not considered reliable because they do not take into consideration the time value of money and thus can be misleading. Unfortunately, they are still being used by some hospitality managers to evaluate investment proposals.

Conversely, there are three models that account for time value considerations, including risk: (1) net present value, (2) profitability index, and (3) internal rate of return.

ACCOUNTING RATE OF RETURN

ARR measures profitability from a conventional accounting standpoint by relating the required investment and future annual (average) earnings, as follows:

$$ARR = \frac{\text{Average net income}}{\text{Investment}}$$

Acceptance Criterion. The ARR decision rule is slightly different for independent investments than for mutually exclusive investments. When a hospitality financial manager is faced with a number of independent projects, the manager can select any number of investments because each serves a different purpose. Conversely, for investments that are mutually exclusive, the acceptance of one precludes the acceptance of others. The acceptance criteria of the ARR methodology are shown in Exhibit 24-3.

Exhibit 24-3: The ARR Acceptance Criterion

Independent Investments	Accept all investment projects whose ARR is equal to or higher than the minimum rate of return acceptable to the hospitality company.

Mutually Exclusive Investments — Select the proposal with the highest ARR as long as it is higher than the minimum rate of return acceptable to the hospitality company.

EXAMPLE 1: Consider two investments, Project A and Project B, which are mutually exclusive investments:

	Project A	Project B
Average net income	$ 6,000	$ 5,000
Project life	5 years	5 years
Investment cost	$25,000	$20,000

$$ARR = \frac{\text{Average Net Income}}{\text{Initial Investment}} \qquad 24\% \qquad 25\%$$

Accordingly, the company will select Project B, since it has a higher ARR.

Note: When average investment is used rather than the initial investment, ARR is doubled, since the average investment is calculated by taking the initial investment divided by 2. Accordingly, the ARR for Project A will be 48%, whereas the ARR for Project B will be 50%.

The principal advantages of the ARR method are its simplicity and ease of understanding and analysis. In addition, it follows generally accepted accounting principles and is mathematically consistent with the return on investment measures (e.g., ROE and ROA) used by external financial analysts to evaluate the hospitality company's financial performance. The main disadvantages of the ARR method is that it ignores the time value of money and thus the timing of the benefits received. Moreover, it does not consider investment cash flows while relying on income statement data. It also uses a subjectively derived rate as the minimum rate of return required by the hospitality company.

PAYBACK METHOD

The payback method centers around the payback period, which is an expression of the number of years required to recover the initial cash outlay based on a project's expected cash flows. It is a second investment evaluation method that does not rely on discounted cash flow analysis.

According to the payback period rule, a project is acceptable if its payback period is shorter than or equal to a specified number of periods. If the choice is between several mutually exclusive projects, the one with the shortest payback period should be selected.

Generally, the faster the project pays back, the superior the project. An advantage of the payback method is that it permits hospitality companies that have limited cash resources to evaluate the turnover of scarce funds in order to recover earlier those assets invested. In addition, there is the likelihood that there will be a lesser possibility of loss from changes in economic circumstances, as well as other recognizable risks when the commitment is short term.

Because the payback criterion measures how quickly the proposed project will return its original investment, it deals with projected cash flows, which serve as a measure of the true timing of the benefits, rather than accounting earnings. For example, if XYZ Hospitality firm's desired payback period is five years and an investment proposal requires an initial cash outflow of $28,000 and yields average annual cash inflows of $4,000, the payback period is seven years. In this case, the project should be rejected because the company will need seven years to recover its initial investment of $28,000, which is more than the desired payback period. Unfortunately, the payback method ignores the time value of money by not discounting these cash flows to their present value.

Payback period supporters point to its use where preliminary screening is more essential than exact figures, in situations where a poor credit position is a major factor, and when investment funds are remarkably scarce. A hospitality company may establish a limit on the payback period beyond which an investment will not be made; a majority of executives want payback in three years or less. Another business may use payback to choose one of several investments and select the one with the shortest payback period.

Acceptance Criterion. The decision rules for the payback period methodology requires the financial manager to determine a maximum acceptable payback period. If the payback period calculated is less than this maximum acceptable payback period, the project is accepted; if not, the project is rejected. If the projects under consideration are independent, all projects that recover their initial investment in less time than this "hurdle" payback period may be undertaken. Conversely, if the projects are mutually exclusive, the investment with the lowest payback period is chosen. Exhibit 24-4 shows a summary of the acceptance criterion under the payback method.

Exhibit 24-4: The Payback Acceptance Criterion

Independent Investments	Accept all investments whose payback period is equal to or higher than the maximum acceptable payback period.
Mutually Exclusive Investments	Accept the single investment with the shortest payback period, as long as its payback period is equal to or lower than the maximum acceptable payback period.

The advantages of the payback method are that it is easy to use and understand. It uses cash flow as the basis for investment decisions and effectively handles investment risk. Moreover, it is a good approach when a weak cash flow position influences the selection of a proposal.

However, a major limitation of the payback method is that it fails to consider cash flows received after the expiration of the payback period. Thus, it is not considered a measure of profitability. For example, two proposed investments costing $20,000 each would have the same payback if they both had $10,000 cash inflows in the first two years. However, one project might be expected to provide additional cash inflows after year 2, while the other project is expected to provide no cash flows after year 2. In this case the payback method can be deceptive as a gauge of profitability.

In addition to the above, the payback method ignores the time value of money. It also penalizes projects that result in small cash flows in their early years and heavy cash flows in their later years.

Note. Although the payback period has been widely used in the hospitality industry, it does have some obvious drawbacks and thus should not be used as a basis for making investment decisions. Reliable methods include discounting methods such as the net present value and the internal rate of return.

EXAMPLE 2: Y Hospitality is considering the purchase of kitchen equipment with an initial cost of $10,000. Expected cash inflows in the form of cost savings are $2,000 for the next five years. The company would like to recover its initial investment in three years.

Initial investment = $10,000

Annual cash inflow = $2,000

Payback period = 10,000 ÷ 2,000 = 5 years

Because the payback period (5 years) is more than the cutoff payback period (3 years), Y Hospitality should not accept the proposal.

However, the calculation is a bit more complex for a project with uneven cash inflows. If there are unequal cash inflows each year, to determine the payback period the annual cash inflows are added to obtain the amount of the cash outlay. The answer is found by calculating the time it takes to recover the initial investment.

EXAMPLE 3: Z Hospitality invests $50,000 and receives the following cash inflows:

Year 1 $20,000
Year 2 $15,000
Year 3 $28,000

In the first two years, the company recovers $35,000 of the initial investment. Accordingly, the payback period will be calculated by adding to the two years the point in which the company recovers the full investment of $50,000 in year 3 (50,000 − 35,000 = 15,000), as follows:

$$2 \text{ years} + \frac{15,000}{28,000} = 2.54 \text{ years}$$

The Discounted Payback Period

A project's discounted payback period is the number of periods required for the sum of the present values of the project's expected cash flows to equal its initial cash outlay. The payback period will be longer using the discounted method because money is worth less over time. This happens because the discounted payback periods are measured with discounted cash flows that are smaller than the undiscounted cash flows used to calculate the normal payback periods.

Acceptance Criterion. According to the discounted payback period rule, a project is acceptable if its discounted payback period is shorter than or equal to a specified number of periods, called the cutoff period. If the projects are mutually exclusive, the one with the shortest discounted payback period should be selected. Exhibit 24-5 provides a summary of the acceptance criterion under the discounted payback method.

Exhibit 24-5: The Discounted Payback Acceptance Criterion

Independent Investments	Accept all investments whose discounted payback period is equal to or higher than the maximum acceptable payback period.
Mutually Exclusive Investments	Accept the single investment with the shortest discounted payback period as long as its payback period is equal to or lower than the maximum acceptable payback period.

EXAMPLE 4: Using the same facts as in Example 3 and a cost of capital of 10%, the discounted payback is:

$$\text{Discounted payback} = \frac{\text{Initial cash outlay}}{\text{Discounted annual cash inflows}}$$

Initial cash outlay $50,000
Annual cash inflows:

Year 1	Year 2	Year 3
$20,000	$15,000	$28,000
0.9091	0.8264	0.7513
$18,182	$12,396	$21,036

In the first two years, the company recovers $30,578 (18,182 + 12,396) of the initial investment. Accordingly, the payback period will be calculated by adding to the two years the point in which the company recovers the full investment of $50,000 in year 3 (50,000 − 30,578 = 19,422), as follows:

$$2 \text{ years} + \frac{19{,}422}{21{,}036} = 2.92 \text{ years}$$

Note: Present value factors from Table A-3 are in Appendix 1.

The discounted payback period has two major benefits over the normal payback period method. It considers the time value of money and the risk of the investment's expected cash flows. However, it still ignores cash flows received beyond the payback period.

THE NET PRESENT VALUE CRITERION

The net present value (NPV) method is a discounted cash flow approach to capital budgeting in which a comparison is made of the present value of future cash flows expected from an investment project to the initial cash outlay for the investment. A project's NPV is the sum of the present values of the net cash flows discounted at the required rate of return, as follows:

1. The NPV of each cash inflow and cash outflow discounted at the required rate of return is found.
2. The sum of these discounted cash flows is referred to as NPV.

$$\text{NPV} = \text{Sum of present value of cash inflows}$$
$$- \text{Sum of present value of cash outflows}$$

The NPV approach is considered the most unambiguous application of cost-benefit analysis. It takes into account the timing of cash flows by placing a higher value on those received immediately than on those received in the future. If a project's benefits exceed its costs, the NPV is positive and the project is acceptable. However, if a project's benefits are less than the costs, the NPV is negative, and the project is not acceptable. If the capital investment decision involves mutually exclusive alternatives, the project with the highest NPV is accepted, and the other alternatives are rejected.

Net cash flows are the difference between forecasted cash inflows received from the investment to its expected cash outflows. The appropriate discount rate to be used is the minimum rate of return earned by the company on its investment. The best discount rate to be used is generally the company's cost of capital.

Acceptance Criterion. When the NPV of a cash flow stream equals zero, that stream of cash flows provides a rate of return exactly equal to the investor's required return. Likewise, when an investment project has a positive NPV, the proposed investment offers an expected return that exceeds the investors' requirements. A hospitality company that consistently finds positive NPV investments will generally exceed the shareholders' requirements and enjoy a rising stock price. The NPV, in effect, represents the amount of additional value created by the investment. Thus, the acceptance of positive NPV projects is consistent with the hospitality company's value-creation goal. Conversely, if the company makes an investment with a negative NPV, the investment will destroy value and disappoint shareholders. A company that regularly makes negative NPV investments will generally see its stock price decrease as it continues to achieve lower-than-required returns for stockholders. Exhibit 24-6 provides a summary of the acceptance criterion under the NPV technique.

Exhibit 24-6: The NPV Acceptance Criterion

Independent Investments	Accept all investment projects whose NPV is positive.
Mutually Exclusive Investments	Select the proposal with the highest NPV.

Accordingly, an independent project in which the present value of planned cash inflows exceeds the present value of cash outflows is desirable. Conversely, a project in which the outflows are larger is undesirable. These situations correspond to projects with positive and negative NPVs, respectively. This rationale leads to the following stand-alone decision rule:

- NPV > 0 Accept
- NPV < 0 Reject

EXAMPLE 5: X Hospitality Company is considering the purchase of kitchen equipment with a cost of $200,000 and a salvage value of $10,000. The new equipment has an estimated useful life of 10 years and will result in annual savings of $40,000. The company's cost of capital is 12%. The NPV criterion is used to determine if the new piece of kitchen equipment should be purchased.

NPV = Present value of cash inflows − Project cost

Present value of cash inflows = 40,000 (5.6502)* + 10,000 (0.322) = 226,330

Thus, NPV = 226,330 − 200,000 = 26,330

Kitchen equipment should be purchased, because the positive NPV of 26,330 is indicative that the acceptance of the project will create value to X Hospitality Company and its shareholders.

Note: Present value factors from Tables A-3 and A-4 in Appendix 1.

* In cases where the cash inflows are constant, in order to determine the present value of a future sum, the annuity Table A-4 (see Appendix 1) is used.

NPV and Shareholder Wealth

An insightful way to view capital spending projects involves their impact on shareholder value. A project's NPV is the net effect that the undertaking is expected to have on the value of the company. If a positive NPV project is taken on and successfully completed, the economic value of the company should be raised by exactly the amount of the project's NPV. Conversely, a negative NPV project will decrease the value of the company by the amount of the negative NPV.

Therefore, a capital spending program that maximizes the NPV of completed projects will contribute to maximizing shareholder wealth, the ideal goal of management. This direct link to shareholder wealth makes NPV the most theoretically correct capital investment technique.

PROFITABILITY INDEX

A project's profitability index (PI), also called cost benefit ratio, is the ratio of the present value of future net cash flows to the initial cash outflow, as follows:

$$\text{Profitability index} = \frac{\text{Present value of cash inflows}}{\text{Initial project cost}}$$

The profitability index is a cost benefit ratio because it relates the benefit derived from the investment (e.g., discounted value of projected cash inflows at the cost of capital) to its initial project cost. When there are budget constraints, the index can be used to rank proposals of different dollar magnitude in descending order of attractiveness.

Acceptance Criterion. As long as the profitability index is 1.00 or greater, the investment proposal is acceptable. For a given project, the net present value and the profitability index methods have the same accept-reject feature. If the project has a profitability index equal to one, the hospitality company should be indifferent as to accepting and rejecting the project.

It is important to recognize that when competing projects have unequal times as well as capital rationing conditions, the internal rate of return and the net present value approaches may provide conflicting signals. The profitability index provides the right decision, however, and is a preferable method under these circumstances. Capital rationing takes place when a business is not able to invest in projects having a net present value greater than or equal to zero. Usually, the company establishes an upper limit to its capital budget based on budgetary constraints.

EXAMPLE 6: Consider the following information concerning two proposed projects:

	Project A	Project B
Initial investment	$500,000	$20,000
Present value of cash inflows	$800,000	$100,000

The net present value of Project A is $300,000 and that of Project B is $80,000. According to the NPV criterion, Project A is better. However, this evaluation is not valid when a budget constraint exists. In this case, proposal B's profitability index of 5 exceeds project A's index of 1.6. Thus, the profitability index should be used in evaluating proposals when budget constraints are present. In those instances, Project B should be selected over Project A.

INTERNAL RATE OF RETURN

Like the NPV method, the internal rate of return (IRR) is a discounted cash flow approach to capital investment analysis. The IRR is the discount rate that causes the project's net present value to equal zero and assumes cash inflows are reinvested at the IRR. A project's IRR is then compared to its required rate of return, which is commonly referred to as the hurdle rate by hospitality managers.

If the IRR equals or exceeds the hurdle rate, the project is accepted. The hurdle rate is typically a company's cost of capital, sometimes adjusted for risk. Like the NPV model, the IRR model is more realistic and accurate compared to the ARR and payback approaches because it considers the time value of money. The IRR is also superior to the ARR model because it is based on cash flows, not on accounting earnings. A disadvantage of the IRR model is that it is difficult and time-consuming to calculate, particularly when there are uneven cash flows. However, the use of a computer or programmable calculator simplifies the IRR process. In addition, the IRR does not consider the varying size of investments in competing projects and their respective dollar profitability. Further, in limited cases, when there are multiple reversals in the cash flow stream, the project could yield more than one IRR.

To determine the IRR where uneven cash inflows are present, the trial-and-error process can be used while working through the present value tables, as follows:

1. Calculate the NPV at the cost of capital (k).
2. Determine if the NPV is positive or negative.
3. If the NPV is positive, a higher discount rate should be used.
4. If the NPV is negative, a lower discount rate should be used. The exact IRR at which the NPV equals zero is somewhere between the two rates.
5. Perform interpolation to find the precise IRR.

Exhibit 24-7 provides a summary of the acceptance criterion under the IRR technique.

Exhibit 24-7: The IRR Criterion

Independent Investments	Accept all investments whose IRR is equal to or higher than the hurdle rate.
Mutually Exclusive Investments	Accept the single investment with the highest IRR, as long as it is equal to or higher than the hurdle rate.

EXAMPLE 7: A project costing $100,000 is expected to produce the following cash inflows:

Year 1	$30,000	Year 2	40,000
Year 3	30,000	Year 4	50,000

Using trial and error, the internal rate is calculated as follows:

Year	10%	PV	16%	PV	18%	PV
1	0.909	$ 27,270	0.862	$ 25,860	0.847	$ 25,410
2	0.826	33,040	0.743	29,720	0.718	28,720
3	0.751	22,530	0.641	19,230	0.609	18,270
4	0.683	34,150	0.552	27,600	0.516	25,800
		+$116,990		+$102,410		+$ 98,200
Project Cost		−100,000		−100,000		−100,000
NPV		+$ 16,990		+$ 2,410		−$ 1,800

The internal rate of return on the project is between 16% and 18%, closer to 18% (see Appendix 1, Table A-3) because at that rate the NPV of the project is approximately zero.

EXAMPLE 8: U Hospitality Company is considering two mutually exclusive investment proposals. The cost of capital is 10%. Expected cash flows are as follows:

Project	Initial Cost	Year 2	Year 6
A	$20,000	$25,000	
B	$20,000		$30,000

The IRR is:

$$\text{Project A} \quad \frac{\$20{,}000}{\$25{,}000} = 0.80$$

The factor from the present value (see Table A-3 in Appendix 1) is 0.7972 (across two years). It corresponds to an internal rate of return of 12%.

$$\text{Project B} \quad \frac{\$20{,}000}{\$30{,}000} = 0.667$$

The factor from the present value (see Table A-3 in Appendix 1) is 0.667 (across six years). It corresponds to an internal rate of return of 7%.

Project A should be selected because it has a higher internal rate of return than Project B.

Note: When a project has constant cash inflows, the internal rate of return can be calculated by determining a factor from the annuity Table A-4 in Appendix 1 and then looking up the rate of return on the annuity table.

EXAMPLE 9: G Hospitality invests $100,000 in a proposal that will produce annual cash inflows of $18,000 a year for the next 20 years.

$$\text{Internal Rate of Return} = \frac{100{,}000}{\$18{,}500} = 5.4054$$

By referring to the present value of an annuity of $1 (Table A-4 in Appendix 1) across 20 years, the factor closest to 5.4054 is 5.3527, in the 18% column. Accordingly, the internal rate is approximately 18%.

USE OF COMPUTERS

Spreadsheet programs such as Microsoft's Excel can be used for simplifying IRR calculations. Once cash flows have been entered into the spreadsheet, the input of the IRR formula is included in the spreadsheet cell, and the calculations are completed by the Excel program. The IRR formula that serves as input into the spreadsheet cell is IRR (values). Excel considers negative numbers as cash outflows (such as the initial project cost) and positive numbers as cash inflows. Many financial calculators have similar features.

CAPITAL BUDGETING PROCESS ILLUSTRATION

To provide a comprehensive view of the capital budgeting process, an example is provided below.

EXAMPLE 10: Mr. X is considering the purchase of a hospitality company. The initial cash outlay is $2 million. He will receive annual net cash inflows of $300,000 per year for 10 years. The cost of capital is 18%. The income tax rate is 40%. The annual cash inflow follows:

Accounting Rate of Return (ARR):

	Years 1–10 Net Income	Cash Flow
Annual cash savings	$300,000	+$300,000
Depreciation ($2,000,000/10)	200,000	
Earnings before tax (EBT)	$100,000	
Income tax (40%)	40,000	−40,000
Net earnings	$ 60,000	
After tax cash inflows		+$260,000

ARR:

$$\frac{\text{Average net income}}{\text{Investment}} = \frac{60,000}{\$1,000,000} = 6\%$$

Payback Period:

$$\frac{\text{Initial investment}}{\text{Annual net cash inflow}} = \frac{\$1,000,000}{\$260,000} = 3.8 \text{ years}$$

NPV:

NPV = Present value of cash inflows − Project cost

NPV = 260,000 × 4.4941 (factor from Table A-4 in Appendix 1) − 1,000.000

NPV = 1,284,660 − 1,000,000 = 284,660

Profitability Index:

$$\frac{\text{Present Value of Cash Inflow}}{\text{Present Value of Cash Outflow}} = \frac{\$1,284,660}{\$1,000,000} = 1.28$$

Internal Rate of Return:

$$\text{Factor from Table A-4 (Appendix 1)} = \frac{\text{Project cost}}{\text{Annual cash inflow}} = \frac{\$1,000,000}{\$260,000} = 3.8$$

The intersection of 10 years and a factor of 3.8 result in an IRR of approximately 24%. (Refer to the present value of annuity, Table 4, Appendix 1.)

Conclusion:

X should purchase the company for the following reasons:

- The profitability index is higher than 1.
- The payback period is acceptable.
- The NPV is positive.
- The 24% IRR exceeds the 18% cost of capital.

SPECIAL CONSIDERATIONS IN CAPITAL INVESTMENT ANALYSIS

In making capital investment decisions, the financial manager must address various case scenarios such as projects having different sizes or different life spans. For instance, a hospitality company's investment budget may not be adequate to fund all of its investment proposals that have a positive NPV. In those cases, managers need to decide which proposals with a positive NPV to accept and which to reject. This process is referred to as capital investment analysis under capital rationing. In addition, managers should consider the impact of risk, taxes, and inflation in making capital investment decisions.

Mutually Exclusive Project Decisions

In general, the discounting cash flow methods (NPV, IRR, and profitability index) result in the same decision for competing proposals that are independent. However, when two or more investment proposals are mutually exclusive, there will be conflicting rankings under the various capital budgeting models. In those cases, the conflict in rankings will be because of one or more combinations of the following conditions:

- Scale or size of the initial investment.
- Differences in cash flow patterns.
- Differences in project lives.

A manager in a hospitality company with more projects than resources must rank projects from highest to lowest in value. The NPV model generally provides correct rankings of mutually exclusive investment projects, as it provides a ranking consistent with value creation. However, if projects have unequal life spans, the capital investment decisions will not result in reliable decisions unless the manager can evaluate sequences of projects of the same duration. Two procedures available for handling the ranking problem for mutually exclusive projects with unequal lives are (1) the replacement chain method and (2) the equivalent annual annuity method. Both approaches are considered an expansion of the basic NPV model, and both methods provide the same ranking when comparing mutually exclusive projects with unequal lives and lead to wealth maximization when the company can repeat the investment to a comparable time horizon.

The replacement chain method requires finding a common ending period. This date can be no earlier than the end of the project with the longer life. After the date is identified, the process requires calculating the NPV of the extended cash flows. After comparing both projects' adjusted equal lives, the decision rule is to accept the project with the higher NPV. This method may involve tedious and unrealistic calculations in cases where the lowest common denominator is at least 35 (e.g., five and seven years). In such cases, a faster and easier method is the equivalent annual annuity. The project with the lowest annuity-equivalent cost or the highest annuity-equivalent benefit should be selected. It indicates how much NPV per year the company expects the project to generate for as long as it maintains the project.

Capital Budgeting and Inflation

The effectiveness of capital investment decisions depends on the accuracy of the data regarding cash inflows and outflows. Inflation can have a positive or negative impact on the value of an investment. During inflationary periods, the level of capital expenditures made by the hospitality company tends to decrease. Accordingly, failure to incorporate price-level changes due to inflation in capital budgeting situations can result in errors in predicting cash flows and thus in flawed decisions. Yet the financial manager can estimate future cash flows that reflect the expected inflationary rate. For instance, if prices are expected to rise by 6% annually over the life of the project, the estimated cash inflows should reflect this rising price trend. By taking these appropriate steps the financial manager will make better capital investment decisions.

Income Taxes and Capital Investment Decisions

Income taxes make a difference in many capital budgeting decisions. The project that is attractive on a before-tax basis may have to be rejected on an after-tax basis. Income taxes typically affect both the amount and timing of cash flows. Because earnings, not cash inflows, are subject to tax, after-tax cash inflows are not usually the same as after-tax earnings.

The timing of tax payments will also affect the capital investment decision. For instance, accelerated depreciation methods result in larger, earlier cash flows; thus, using an accelerated depreciation method as opposed to a straight-line method for tax purposes will result in a higher NPV and create value to the hospitality company.

Risk and Uncertainty

Risk analysis is important in making capital investment decisions in the hospitality industry due to the capital-intensive nature of the industry and the long-term nature of the investments being considered. The higher the risk associated with a proposed project, the greater the return rate that must be earned on the project to compensate investors for that risk.

The interrelationship of risk among all investments should be considered. By properly diversifying, a hospitality company can obtain the best combination of expected NPV and risk. Risk can be included in capital budgeting by computing probable cash flows on the basis of probabilities and assigning a discount rate based on the riskiness of alternative proposals. The probabilities are multiplied by the monetary values to derive the expected monetary value of the investment. A probability distribution function can be generated by computer. The tighter the probability distribution of expected future returns, the lower the risk associated with a project.

Using this approach, an investment's value is determined by discounting the expected cash flow at a rate allowing for the time value of money and for the risk associated with the cash flow. The discount rate is adjusted for a project's risk. A profitable investment is indicated by a positive NPV.

Impact of Discount Rate on Capital Investment Analysis

The major cause for different rankings of alternative projects under NPV and IRR methods relates to the varying assumptions regarding the reinvestment rate employed for discounting cash flows. The NPV method assumes cash flows are reinvested at the cost of capital rate. Conversely, the IRR method is based on the assumption that cash flows are reinvested at the internal rate of return.

Suggestion. The NPV method typically provides an accurate ranking because the cost of capital is a more realistic reinvestment rate. It is generally easier to work out than the IRR, though the use of computers and present value calculators have abridged this drawback. But research studies have revealed that hospitality financial managers prefer the IRR model because the results are easier to interpret.

Recommendations. Which method is best for a hospitality company clearly depends on which reinvestment rate is nearest the rate the business can earn on future cash flows from a project. The board of directors of the hospitality company typically reviews the company's required rate of return annually and may increase or decrease that rate depending on the company's current rate of return and cost of capital. The minimum rate of return required for a proposal may be waived in a situation where the proposal has a noteworthy future advantage (e.g., development of a new brand), applies to an essential program (e.g., compliance with environmental laws), and has a qualitative advantage (e.g., enhanced service quality).

POST-AUDIT PROJECT REVIEW

A final central step in capital investment analysis is the review of investment projects once they have been implemented. This can provide very valuable information on the hospitality company's selection process. While hospitality managers proposing projects will be more careful before recommending a project, the post-audit review will identify those managers who are constantly positive or negative regarding cash flow estimates. As a result, top management will be in a better position to appraise the inclination that may be expected when a hospitality manager proposes a project. The post-audit review also provides the opportunity to support successful projects, to reinforce or recoup projects facing difficulties, to abandon projects that have not lived up to expectations before excessive losses arise, and to enhance the overall quality of the capital investment process.

The post-audit project review compares the actual cash flows from an accepted project with those that were estimated when the project was adopted. In conducting a post-audit review, the same technique should be employed as was used in the initial approval process to maintain consistency in evaluation. For instance, if a given project was accepted based on the IRR method, the same process should be employed in the post-audit review.

For internal control purposes, the project performance appraisal should not be conducted by those employees responsible for the original proposal. Instead,

THE LEASE OR PURCHASE DECISION

The decision of whether to lease or purchase is one commonly confronting hospitality companies considering the acquisition of new equipment. It is a capital budgeting decision that forces a company to compare leasing and financing (purchasing) alternatives. There are tax benefits of leasing equipment rather than financing it with a term loan. Depending on the needs and nature of the business, the entire lease payment may be fully deductible as a business expense, thereby reducing the company's taxable income. With a loan, only the interest and depreciation can be used for deductions. Another benefit a lease offers is 100% financing plus an additional 10% of the equipment's costs to cover soft costs, such as taxes, shipping, and installation. Some term loans offer 100% financing but, typically, only cover the cost of equipment.

A lease can help a hospitality company manage its cash flow. Payments are usually lower than for a term loan. Because a lease payment requires no down payment or deposit, the hotel or restaurant can acquire the equipment it needs without depleting reserve capital. Because the business's capital is not being used for equipment, the hospitality company can use it for business development and expansion into domestic or global markets. On the other hand, borrowing might be a better alternative if the company wants to keep the equipment and build equity quickly.

Note. If the hospitality company wants to retain the equipment beyond the lease term and prefers to know the full cost of the financing up front, it may choose a lease purchase option. As its name implies, this option requires no additional payment to own the equipment at the end of the lease.

One way to make a sound financial decision on whether to lease or purchase equipment is to calculate the NPV of the difference in cash flows between leasing and buying. This NPV is often referred to as net advantage to leasing (NAL). If the NAL is positive, the asset should be leased; if it is negative, the equipment should be purchased. The following information is needed in order to compute the NAL.

1. The annual lease payment.
2. The company's effective tax rate.
3. The after-tax residual value at the end of the lease period.
4. The loss on tax savings of depreciation.
5. The after-tax cost of borrowing, which is used as the discount rate.
6. Calculation of the present value of the differential cash flows, using Tables A-3 and A-4 in Appendix 1.

EXAMPLE 11: JL Hospitality needs to replace its kitchen equipment. The question is whether the company should lease the equipment or borrow money to buy it. If purchased, the cost is $100,000. This expenditure will be financed over the equipment's useful life of five years with a loan of the same maturity. The interest rate on the loan is 10%. The equipment will be depreciated over five years using the straight-line method. The residual value of the equipment is estimated at $10,000. The corporate tax rate is 40%.

If the firm leases the equipment, the terms of the lease call for annual payments of $20,000. The lease payments are payable at the beginning of each year, and the company is responsible for maintenance and insurance, regardless of whether it leases or buys the equipment.

	Now	Year 1	Year 2	Year 3	Year 4	Year 5
After tax lease payments $20,000 × (1 – 40%)	$–12,000	$–12,000	$–12,000	$–12,000	$–12,000	
Loss on tax savings on depreciation		–8,000	–8,000	–8,000	–8,000	–8,000
After-tax loss of the residual value 10,000 × (1 – 40%)						–6,000
Cash savings for not buying equipment	+100,000					
Total differential cash flows	$+88,000	$–20,000	$–20,000	$–20,000	$–20,000	$–14,000

Using the factors from Tables A-3 and A-4 (see Appendix 1), the NAL is calculated as follows:

NAL = 88,000 – 20,000 (3.461) – 14,000 (.7473) = 8,236

Using the discount rate of 6% (10%×(1– 0.40), it is evident that leasing is less expensive than borrowing to buy the kitchen equipment, as there is a positive NPV (or net advantage of leasing) of $8,236. Accordingly, JL Hospitality should lease the kitchen equipment instead of borrowing the funds to purchase it.

CHAPTER 25
COST OF CAPITAL

CONTENTS

Significance of the Cost of Capital	25,001
The Weighted-Average Cost of Capital	25,002
Determining Individual Costs of Capital	25,002
Cost of Debt, *Kd*	25,002
Cost of Preferred Stock, *Kp*	25,004
Cost of Equity Capital	25,004
Measuring the Overall Cost of Capital	25,007
Book Value versus Market Value Weights	25,008
Factors That Affect the Weighted-Average Cost of Capital	25,008
Factors That the Hospitality Company Can Control	25,009
Factors That the Hospitality Company Cannot Control	25,009
The Optimal Capital Structure	25,010
Managerial Implications of Capital Structure Theory	25,010
Important Considerations	25,011
The Capitalization Rate	25,011

Cost of capital is the rate of return that must be earned on an investment project in order for the project to increase the value of the common stockholders' investment. In the hospitality industry, it is essential to the long-term success of the company to earn a satisfactory rate of return on the company's investments to keep investors satisfied. Financial managers use the cost of capital in (1) making capital budgeting decisions, (2) establishing the optimal capital structure, and (3) making decisions such as whether to lease or buy equipment. The cost of capital is determined as a weighted average of the various components of capital employed by the hospitality company. Sources of borrowed funds include mortgages, bank loans, bonds, and leases; external sources of equity capital include the sale of preferred and common stock to existing and new shareholders.

SIGNIFICANCE OF THE COST OF CAPITAL

The cost of capital is extremely important to financial managers in the hospitality industry for several reasons. First, capital budgeting decisions have a major impact on the hospitality company, and proper capital investment decisions require the estimate of the cost of capital. Second, many other financial decisions, including those related to bond refunding, leasing, and working capital policy, require the estimate of the cost of capital. Last, in order to maximize the value of the hospitality company, the financial manager must be able to minimize the company's cost of capital and thus measure it.

THE WEIGHTED-AVERAGE COST OF CAPITAL

The cost of capital for each component of a hospitality company's capital structure is the rate of return that is required in order to induce investors to purchase and hold the securities issued by the hospitality company. The cost of capital is a weighted average of the required returns on each capital source. In order to estimate the weighted-average cost of capital, it is necessary to determine the costs of each of the sources of capital and the capital structure mix. The major sources are identified below:

- ki = cost of debt before tax
- kd = cost of debt after tax; $kd = ki\,(1 - t)$, where t is the effective tax rate of the hospitality company
- kp = cost of preferred stock
- kre = cost of internal equity (retained earnings)
- kc = cost of external equity, or cost of issuing new common stock
- WACC = company's weighted-average cost of capital

DETERMINING INDIVIDUAL COSTS OF CAPITAL

In calculating the individual costs of capital, it is necessary to estimate the investor's required rate of return after properly adjusting for any transaction or flotation costs. Furthermore, there is a need to adjust the cost of capital for the effect of corporate income taxes, as the process requires the discounting of after-tax cash flows. In essence, the cost of a particular source of capital is equal to the investor's required rate of return after adjusting for the effects of flotation costs and income taxes.

Cost of Debt, Kd

The pre-tax cost of debt is the yield the company would have to offer debt holders in order to obtain new debt financing. Because interest payments are tax-deductible, the cost of debt must be stated on an after-tax basis. Therefore, the interest cost of debt expressed as a percent rate is multiplied by one minus the company's effective tax rate to calculate the company's after-tax cost of debt, as follows:

$$kd = ki\,(1 - t)$$

where ki = the before-tax interest rate, and t = company's effective tax rate.

When a hospitality company borrows from a bank, its cost of debt before taxes is simply the interest rate the bank charges to the company. In the case of large hospitality companies, the company can borrow from investors by selling bonds to them. In this case, the before-tax cost of debt can be found by determining the internal rate of return (or yield to maturity) on the bond cash flows.

The following formula may be used for approximating the yield to maturity on a bond:

$$ki = \frac{I + (M - V)/n}{(M + V)/2}$$

where

I = annual interest payments in dollars

M = face value of bonds, usually $1,000 per bond

V = value or net proceeds from the sale of a bond

n = term of the bond in years

Example 1: YTU Hospitality issues a $1,000, 9%, 20-year bond whose net proceeds are $950. The company's effective tax rate is 40%. Accordingly, the before-tax cost of debt is:

$$ki = \frac{I + (M - V)/n}{(M + V)/2}$$

$$ki = \frac{\$90 + (\$1{,}000 - \$950)/20}{(\$1{,}000 + \$950)/2} = \frac{95.2}{975} = 9.49\%$$

Accordingly, the after-tax cost of debt is:

$$kd = ki\,(1 - t) = 9.49\%\,(1 - 0.4) = 5.69\%$$

Implied in the calculation of an after-tax cost of debt is the fact that the hospitality company has taxable income. Otherwise, it does not gain the tax benefit associated with interest payments. The explicit cost of debt for a hospitality company without taxable income is the before-tax cost of debt ki.

It is important to note that the primary concern with the cost of capital is using it in a decision-making process. Accordingly, the company's financial manager must determine the minimum acceptable return on new capital investment projects—that is, the manager must determine the appropriate cost of debt of new borrowing, not the historic interest rates on old, previously outstanding debt. There are two approaches for the manager to identify ki. The first approach is to contact the company's commercial or investment bankers and inquire about the interest rate the company would have to pay to raise new debt capital. The second approach would be to calculate the yield to maturity on the company's presently outstanding bonds if the bonds are publicly traded. The rationale is that the same yield would apply to new debt as well because it already takes into consideration market conditions and the investors' view of the company's credit standing.

In the case of issuing new bonds, the hospitality company will usually pay flotation costs (e.g., fees or commissions) to an investment bank, which will assist in issuing the bonds. As a result, the net proceeds from the bond issuance will be less than the bond price paid to the investor who buys it.

Cost of Preferred Stock, Kp

Although preferred stock is not as widely used as common stock, a number of hospitality companies use this method of raising capital. Preferred stock combines features of debt and equity. Determining the cost of preferred stock is very straightforward, due to the nature of the cash flows paid to the investors. That is, the cost of preferred stock is a function of its stated dividend. Preferred dividends are fixed, like interest on bonds or notes, but they also have a continuous life like common stock dividends. The cost of preferred stock (kp) equals its required rate of return, which is found by dividing the annual dividend by the net proceeds from the sale of preferred stock, as follows:

$$kp = \frac{\text{Dividends per share}}{\text{Market price per share (net of flotation costs)}}$$

No tax adjustment is required when calculating *kp* because, unlike interest on debt, dividends are not tax-deductible; hence, there is no tax savings associated with the use of preferred stock.

As in the case of new debt when new preferred shares are sold, the investor's required rate of return is less than the cost of preferred capital to the hospitality company due to the flotation costs that are paid to investment banks that assist in selling the new issue of preferred stock.

Example 2: XYZ Hospitality has preferred stock that pays a $12 dividend per share. Its current market price is $100 per share, and the flotation (or underwriting) cost is 3%, or $3 per share. The cost of preferred stock is:

$$kp = \frac{12}{100 - 3} = 12.37\%$$

Cost of Equity Capital

The cost of equity capital is the most difficult cost to measure. Equity capital can be raised either internally by retaining earnings or externally by issuing common stock. In theory, the cost of both forms of equity capital may be regarded as the minimum rate of return that the company must earn on the equity-financed portion of an investment project in order to leave the market price of the common stock unchanged.

The challenge in calculating the cost of equity capital is that the rate of return investors require is not a contractual rate, as it is for debt and preferred stock. There is no precise interest payment or fixed annual dividend that is paid to common shareholders. Instead, stockholders have a claim to the cash flow that is left after the company's obligations to debt and preferred stock have been met. Stockholders also have the right to participate in any future growth in the hospitality company's earnings and cash flows.

Cost of Common Stock, *Kc*. The cost of common stock is generally viewed as the rate of return investors must earn on a company's common stock. As previously noted, both preferred stock and debt generally make fixed, predictable cash payments over time. Thus, determining the rate of return that investors require on these securities is relatively easy. However, the calculation of the cost of common stock is not straightforward, as there are three major factors that affect this calculation: (1) alternative yields available, (2) expected growth in dividends or earnings, and (3) riskiness of the company.

Three approaches for measuring the cost of common stock equity capital include (1) the constant-growth valuation model (also known as the Gordon model), (2) the capital asset pricing model (CAPM), and (3) the risk premium on debt approach.

Using the Constant-Growth Valuation Model. The constant-growth valuation model, also referred to as the Gordon model, is based on the premise that the value of a share of stock is equal to the present value of all future dividends. The assumption made is that dividends will grow at a constant rate over an infinite time horizon and thus the cost of common stock equity can be found by dividing the dividend expected at the end of year 1 by the current price of stock and adding the expected growth rate. Using the Gordon model, the cost of common stock (kc) is then determined as follows:

$$kc = \frac{D_1}{P_0} + g$$

where

P_0 = value of common stock

D_1 = dividend per share expected at the end of one year

g = constant rate of growth in dividends

Example 3: FTR Hospitality stock market price is $30 per share. The company expects to pay a dividend of $2 per share at the end of the coming year, 2010. Using present value tables or a financial calculator, it is determined that the annual growth rate of dividends (g) is approximately 8%. The cost of common stock (Kc) is then calculated as follows:

$$kc = \frac{D_1}{P_0} + g = \frac{\$2}{\$30} + 8\% = 14.67\%$$

Note: Because common stock dividends are paid after-tax income, no tax adjustment is required.

Using the Capital-Asset Pricing Model. An alternative approach to measuring the cost of common equity is to use the CAPM. The CAPM describes the risk-required return trade-off for securities. This model expresses the relationship between the required return and the nondiversifiable risk of the hospitality company as measured by the beta coefficient.

Beta values are normally estimated by using historic values of the relationship between a security's returns and the market returns. The Value Line Investment Survey and brokerage firms regularly compute and provide beta values for publicly held hotels, restaurants, and other companies in the hospitality industry.

Part V: Investing and Financing Decisions

The cost of common stock (kc) is calculated using the CAPM equation, as follows:

$$kc = kr + (km - kr)\, beta$$

where

kr = risk-free rate of return
km = return of market portfolio of assets
km − kr = market premium
beta = beta coefficient

Using the CAPM requires the following steps:

1. Estimating the risk-free rate kr.
2. Estimating the stock's beta coefficient, which is an index of systematic (or nondiversifiable) market risk.
3. Estimating the current expected market risk premium, km − kr.
4. Estimating the required rate of return on the company's stock, using the CAPM equation.

The CAPM equation shows that the determination of the cost of common stock begins with the risk-free rate, kr, to which is added a risk premium set equal to a premium on an average stock, km − kr, scaled up or down to reflect the specific company's stock relative risk, as measured by its beta coefficient.

Based on the foregoing, the starting point for using the CAPM is to estimate the riskless rate of interest. Many analysts use the yield on a 10-year Treasury bond as the risk-free rate, although the yields on 20- or 30-year Treasury bonds are also sound choices. These rates can be found in the *Wall Street Journal* or the *Federal Reserve Bulletin*.

The market risk premium is the expected market return minus the risk-free rate where the Standard & Poor's 500 Stock Composite Index or Dow Jones Industrial Average might be used as the expected rate of return on the market portfolio. The average market risk premium measured relative to a 30-day Treasury bill has been 9.4% over the past few decades. Conversely, the average market risk premium measured relative to long-term government bond returns has been 8.0 over the same period. These market risk premiums might be used in the CAPM equation.

> **Example 4:** FTR Hospitality wishes to calculate its cost of common stock equity, kc, by using the CAPM. Research findings indicate that the risk-free rate (kr) equals 5%; the company's beta equals 1.3; and the market rate of return equals 12%. Accordingly, the calculation of the cost of common stock equity, kc, follows:
>
> $$kc = kr + (km - kr)\, beta = 5 + (12\% - 5\%)1.3 = 14.1\%$$

This 14.1% cost of common stock can be viewed as consisting of a 5% risk-free rate plus a 7% risk premium, which reflects that the company's stock price is 1.3 times more volatile than the market portfolio due to the factors affecting systematic risk.

The CAPM model is a fairly simple approach in calculating the cost of common stock that many hospitality companies use. The model variables are readily available from various sources, with the possible exception of the beta coefficients for small/nonpublicly held hospitality companies. Moreover, the CAPM model does not rely on dividends or any assumptions about the future growth in dividends. As a result, it can be applied to hospitality companies that are not paying dividends or are not likely to experience a constant rate of growth in dividends.

Using the Risk Premium on Debt Approach. Another simple but useful approach to determine the cost of common stock is to add a risk premium to the company's own cost of long-term debt, as follows:

$$kc = \text{long-term debt rate} + \text{risk premium} = ki\,(1 - t) + \text{risk premium}$$

According to several studies, the cost of equity capital for an average risk premium company (a company with a beta of 1.0) can be estimated by adding 6.5 percent points to the company's current cost of debt. For companies with a lower than average level of systematic risk, a risk premium of 3 to 5 percent points over the cost of debt should be used. Conversely, for companies with higher than average level of systematic risk, a risk premium in excess of 6.5 percent points is warranted.

Cost of Retained Earnings, Kre. The costs of debt and preferred stock are based on the return investors require on these securities. Similarly, the cost of retained earnings, kre, is the rate of return stockholders require on equity capital obtained by retaining earnings.

Some analysts and hospitality managers incorrectly assume that retained earnings are a costless source of funds. Indeed, if the hospitality financial manager decides to retain earnings, there is an opportunity cost involved. If the funds were paid out to shareholders, they could reinvest the funds elsewhere to earn an appropriate rate of return. Thus, the company should earn on its retained earnings at least as much as its shareholders could earn on alternative investments of comparable risk.

The cost to the company of retained earnings is less than the cost of new common stock because the issuance of new stock requires the payment of issuance costs.

MEASURING THE OVERALL COST OF CAPITAL

The hospitality company's cost of capital is the weighted average of the individual costs of financing, with the weights being the proportions of each source of capital used. The calculation of the weighted-average cost of capital (WACC) requires the completion of the following steps:

1. Calculate the cost of capital for each individual source of financing used by the hospitality company, which generally includes debt, preferred stock, and common stock.
2. Determine the percent makeup of debt, preferred stock, and common stock used in financing future investments.
3. Compute the weighted-average cost of capital.

Part V: Investing and Financing Decisions

As an equation, the WACC can be expressed as follows:

$$WACC = (wd \times kd) + (wp \times kp) + (wc \times kc) + (wre \times kre)$$

where

- wd = % of total debt in capital structure
- wp = % of total preferred stock in capital structure
- wc = % of total common stock in capital structure
- wre = % of total capital supplied by retained earnings (or internal equity)

Example 5: Consider the following capital structure for FRE Hospitality:

Mortgage bonds ($1,000 par)	$25,000,000
Preferred stock ($100 par)	5,000,000
Common stock ($10 par)	15,000,000
Retained earnings	5,000,000
Total	$50,000,000

The book value weights and the weighted-average cost of capital are computed as follows:

Source of Capital	Book Value	Weight (1)	Calculated Component Cost (2)	Weighted Cost (1 × 2)
Debt	$25,000,000	50%	5%	2.50%
Preferred stock	5,000,000	10	10	1.00
Common stock	15,000,000	30	16	4.80
Retained earnings	5,000,000	10	14	1.40
	$50,000,000	100%		9.7%

Weighted-average cost of capital = 9.7%

Book Value versus Market Value Weights

Book value weights use accounting values to measure the proportion of each source of capital in the hospitality company's capital structure. Market value weights measure the proportion of each type of capital at its market value. The use of market value weights for computing a company's weighted-average cost of capital is theoretically more appealing than the use of book value weights because the market values of the securities closely approximate the actual dollars to be received from their sale.

FACTORS THAT AFFECT THE WEIGHTED-AVERAGE COST OF CAPITAL

Various factors affect a hospitality company's weighted-average cost of capital. Some of these factors are determined by the external financial environment and thus are beyond the control of the hospitality company, but others might be influenced through the financing, investing, and dividend decisions made by hospitality managers.

Factors That the Hospitality Company Can Control

A hospitality financial manager can have a direct impact on the company's cost of capital through the company's investing, financing, and operating decisions.

Capital Structure Policy. Since the after-tax cost of debt is lower than the cost of equity, a change in the company's target capital structure can reduce the hospitality company's weighted-average cost of capital. The decision made by the hospitality company's financial manager must balance risks and rewards, as an increase in the use of debt will increase the riskiness of both the debt holders and the equity holders.

Dividend Policy. Hospitality companies can obtain new equity capital through retained earnings or by issuing new common stock, but because of flotation costs, new common stock is more expensive than retained earnings. Since retained earnings represent accumulated earnings that have not been paid out in dividends, it follows that the hospitality company's dividend policy can affect the overall cost of capital.

Investment Policy. A change in the hospitality company's investment policy will affect the riskiness of the company. For example, the purchase of the ABC television network by Disney in the 1990s changed the nature and risk of that company in a way that affected its cost of capital. Accordingly, there is a direct impact of a company's investment decisions on the weighted-average cost of capital.

Factors That the Hospitality Company Cannot Control

Two factors a hospitality company cannot control include the level of interest and tax rates and the market environment.

Interest Rates. As interest costs rise, the cost of debt increases because issuing debt will result in higher debt costs when the hospitality company issues debt capital. In addition, higher interest rates have a domino effect on the costs of common stock and preferred stock. Since interest rates have been reasonably low in the late 1990s and in the early part of the new millennium, the reduced cost of capital encouraged additional investment and enabled domestic hospitality companies to compete successfully in the global market.

Tax Rates. Tax rates have an important impact on the determination of the cost of capital because tax rates are used in the calculation of the component cost of debt. In addition, lowering the capital gain tax rate relative to the ordinary rate makes stocks more attractive and that reduces the cost of capital.

Market Environment. The cost of capital will respond to changes in the perceptions of hospitality investors as to the degree of risk associated with investments in common stock or due to investors' attitudes toward risk or expectations about future inflation rates. These changes in the weighted-average cost of capital might occur without any direct action by the company's management.

THE OPTIMAL CAPITAL STRUCTURE

An optimal or target capital structure is the combination of debt, preferred stock, and common equity capital that minimizes the weighted-average cost of capital. At the optimal capital structure, the total value of the hospitality company's market value is maximized. This most favorable capital structure is determined by finding the best debt-equity mix that minimizes the company's cost of capital.

The amount of debt contained in the hospitality company's capital structure is often referred to as debt capacity. Factors that should be considered in determining this debt capacity include the business risk of the company, the tax structure, the extent of potential financial distress (e.g., bankruptcy) and agency costs, and the role played by capital structure policy in providing signals to the capital markets regarding the company's performance.

In determining a hospitality company's optimal capital structure, the link between the cost of debt and the capital structure should be taken into consideration. All other things being equal, debt holders consider debt less risky if the company has a low, rather than high, leverage position. As the proportion of debt in the capital structure rises, debt holders as well as equity holders will require a higher return on the more risky debt. And because the company's cost of debt is the investor's required rate of return, the cost of debt increases as the proportion of debt increases.

The optimal capital structure is primarily a trade-off between the tax advantage of debt and the expected costs of financial distress that determine the optimum debt ratio. Evidence suggests that the cost of debt increases rather slowly for moderate amounts of debt. However, there is a point at which the capital markets begin to consider any higher leverage excessive and extremely risky. These concerns cause the value of the hospitality company and its common shares to stop rising and begin to descend. Under these conditions, as the debt ratio increases, the cost of debt begins to rise quickly but varies among companies depending on the hospitality company's degree of risk.

At the same time, when a hospitality company has a relatively low debt ratio (i.e., low leverage), the issuance of new common stock is viewed as less risky than using high equity when the hospitality company is financed with a relative high proportion of debt. The greater the leverage, the greater the risk of financial distress. Accordingly, equity holders will demand extremely high rates of return resulting in increases in the cost of equity capital.

Managerial Implications of Capital Structure Theory

Determining a company's target or optimal capital structure is one of the centrally important decisions facing hospitality financial managers. It is well documented that changes in capital structure result in changes in market value of the hospitality company. Moreover, the optimal capital structure is influenced heavily by the business risk associated with the company. Many factors influence a hospitality company's business risks, including:

- The variability of sales volume over the business cycle. Hospitality companies are greatly affected during periods of economic downturns and

thus sales tend to fluctuate greatly. As a result, hospitality companies have higher business risks than companies in other industries.
- The variability of selling prices. In the hospitality industry price stability is much less certain and therefore there is a greater business risk.
- The variability of costs. Airline and cruise lines, for instance, have been affected significantly by the volatility of the price of fuel.
- Existence of market power.
- The level and rate of growth.

IMPORTANT CONSIDERATIONS

Important considerations in making capital structure decisions are:
- *Revenue stability.* Companies having stable and predictable revenues are in a better position to undertake highly leveraged capital structures than can hospitality companies with volatile patterns of sales revenue. Companies with strong growth in revenue tend to benefit from the use of positive leverage, which will result in magnifying their return on investment.
- *Cash flow.* Any changes in capital structure must be supported with a strong cash-flow generation and a good ability to service debt and dividends in preferred stock, if applicable.
- *Timing.* When the general rate of interest is low, debt financing might be more appealing. Conversely, when interest costs are high, the issuance of common stock may be more attractive. General economic conditions can have a significant impact on a company's capital structure.
- *Ability to raise funds.* The ability of a company to raise funds at favorable rates is dependent on the external risk assessment of lenders. The company must therefore consider the impact of capital structure decisions both on share value and on financial statements used by analysts and raters to assess risk.
- *Control of the company.* In situations where the company is threatened by takeover issues or in the case of closely held corporations, control issues are of major concern. In those cases, management may prefer to issue debt rather than voting common stock. If market conditions are favorable, the company may sell nonvoting shares.
- *Contractual obligations.* Some contractual obligations might restrict the company from issuing additional debt or the ability to pay dividends.

THE CAPITALIZATION RATE

The capitalization rate (cap rate) is an important component of investment value. It can be used to establish the value of a lodging property when using a valuation method referred to as income approach. This approach capitalizes or values the property's income stream produced by the property, in a three-step process, as follows:

Part V: Investing and Financing Decisions

1. Project the property's income stream over a specified future period. This is done by projecting earnings before depreciation and interest expense, which is, in essence, the same as cash flow.

2. Derive the cap rate.

3. Calculate the market value by dividing the projected earnings by the cap rate.

The formula to estimate a hotel property value follows:

$$\text{Market value} = \frac{\text{Projected earnings before depreciation and interest}}{\text{Cap rate}}$$

As the cap rate increases, the market value decreases. Conversely, as the cap rate decreases, the market value increases.

In essence, the market cap rate is generally weighed by the two components used to acquire the hotel property: mortgage financing and equity capital. Since the lender normally requires amortization of the mortgage principal, a mortgage constant is used in calculating the component cost of debt. The component cost of equity represents the rate of return that is required to induce equity investors to invest in the property. The cap rate is then calculated as follows:

$$\% \text{ of debt financing} \times \text{mortgage constant} + \% \text{ of equity financing} \times \text{required rate of return on equity}$$

Example 6: X is considering the purchase of two hotel properties. He has gathered the following information on the properties:

Hotel A Cash flow = $20,000 Cap Rate = 12%

Hotel B Cash flow = $30,000 Cap Rate = 10%

Which of the two properties has a higher market value?

$$\text{Hotel A Market Value} = \frac{\$20,000}{12\%} = \$166,667$$

$$\text{Hotel B Market Value} = \frac{\$30,000}{10\%} = \$300,000$$

Hotel B has a much higher market value than Hotel A because of a lower cap rate coupled with a higher projected cash flow.

The mortgage constant is the component cost for debt including interest and principal repayments. It represents the amount of principal and interest required to amortize the mortgage. If a $1 million mortgage loan requires monthly payments of $10,000, resulting in total payments of $120,000 annually, the mortgage constant is 12% ($120,000 ÷ $1,000,000). Accordingly, the mortgage constant is affected by the interest rate, the term of the loan, and the rate in which the principal is repaid.

Chapter 25: Cost of Capital 25,013

Example 7: X Hotel wants to determine its cap rate based on the following:

Mortgage constant	12%
Required rate of return	18%
Percentage of debt financing	70%
Percentage of equity financing	30%

Mortgage constant	70% × .12 =	0.084
Equity	30% × .18 =	0.054
		0.138

Cap Rate 13.8%

Another way to determine the capitalization rate is by rearranging the market value formula and referring to the property's selling price, as follows:

$$\text{Market value} = \frac{\text{Projected earnings before depreciation and interest}}{\text{Cap rate}}$$

Thus,

$$\text{Cap rate} = \frac{\text{Projected earnings before depreciation and interest}}{\text{Market value (sales price)}}$$

If a lodging property with an average annual income stream of $200,000 is sold for $1,900,000, the cap rate would be determined as follows:

$$\text{Cap rate} = \frac{\$200,0000}{\$1,900,000} = 10.5\%$$

When appraising a lodging property, an appraiser will be in a position to derive an overall capitalization rate by referring to selling prices and income streams of comparable properties sold recently. Nonetheless, the use of this approach to determine the cap rate relies on an average annual income stream instead of relying on projected income for specific future periods and is based on the assumption that this average income stream will continue in the future. Accordingly, this is perceived as a shortcoming in using this method to derive capitalization rates.

PART VI

RECENT DEVELOPMENTS

CHAPTER 26
TURNAROUND STRATEGIES

CONTENTS

Financial Challenges Faced By Hospitality Companies	26,002
Causes of Financial Failure	26,002
External versus Internal Factors	26,003
Managing in an Uncertain Environment	26,004
Early Warning Signs	26,005
Use of Operational Analysis as a Management Tool	26,005
Turnaround Defined	26,006
Factors Affecting a Turnaround Situation	26,006
Stages of Turnaround Strategy	26,007
Situation Analysis	26,008
Retrenchment	26,008
Recovery	26,009
Return to Normalcy	26,010
Selected Turnaround Strategies	26,010
Increased Focus on Managing Liquidity	26,010
Enhancing Relationships with Debt Capital Providers	26,012
Debt Restructuring	26,013
Operational Improvements	26,014
Monitoring Marketing Activities	26,017
Rebuilding a Profitable Core Business	26,017
Asset Repositioning	26,018
Strategic Reorientation	26,018
Evaluating Accounting and Financial Reporting Systems	26,018
Other Turnaround Strategies	26,019
Implementation	26,019
Exit Strategy	26,020
Lessons To Be Learned	26,020

The hospitality industry entered the second decade of the new millennium with many challenges that threaten the survival of a considerable number of hotels and restaurants as well as other hospitality organizations. In this competitive and uncertain economic environment many companies experienced various degrees of financial distress such as declining earnings, cash flow problems, and mismanagement of resources. However, some of these companies were able to successfully implement a turnaround to prevent disbanding, while others were unable to respond and their situation became irreparable.

Turnaround, as a business strategy, is significant to hospitality companies that are challenged by sustaining profitability and surviving in turbulent economic times. As the hospitality industry continues to evolve, hotel and restaurant operators compete for a larger share of a slowly growing market. Some organizations are able to curtail failure by recognizing the early symptoms of declining performance, thereby making the changes necessary for recovery. Other organizations are unable to recognize the early warning signs and ultimately fail or enter a period of financial distress.

This chapter looks at the financial challenges experienced by hospitality companies in recent times. It examines some of the major contributing factors to the declining performance of these companies, outlines various turnaround stages, and examines selected strategies for survival. It also emphasizes reassessing priorities, improving operational processes, and consistently monitoring performance as strategies for emerging from distressed situations.

FINANCIAL CHALLENGES FACED BY HOSPITALITY COMPANIES

Traditionally, the hospitality industry has had a high rate of business failure. Even well-established companies, such as McDonalds, Marriott and Starbucks, had financial problems at various times, forcing them to employ turnaround strategies, such as closing operations and developing innovative solutions. At the same time, some companies filed for bankruptcy over the past few decades because they did not successfully implement an effective turnaround strategy.

Global competition, natural disasters, a deep financial crisis, and a global recession have contributed to the negative economic environment that the hospitality industry faced in the recent past. In effect, the cyclical nature of the U.S. and international economies has affected the lodging industry's ability to respond to changing circumstances. As a result, hotels have experienced an all-time low occupancy leading to low revenue and profit levels. Times of corporate distress present strategic management challenges and force changes in a company's organizational structure and leadership. Companies that succeed are flexible, innovative problem-solvers, with the ability to uphold their competitive advantage.

Hotel and restaurant operators experience challenges on an ongoing basis, as well as significant opportunities resulting from changes in the economic environment. Management continues to examine cost structures to expose savings opportunities and identify new revenue and marketing prospects in order to achieve budget goals. Finding new ways to better manage costs and maximize revenues can increase profitability levels and, in extreme cases, prevent a financial crisis.

CAUSES OF FINANCIAL FAILURE

There are many reasons hospitality businesses fail. Studies show that less than 10% of all failures are directly attributable to natural events (i.e., earthquakes, floods) and neglect or dishonesty on the part of management or owners. Failure may occur as a result of:

- Poor execution
- Undercapitalization
- Nondiversification

- Abandoned successful concepts
- Economic slowdowns
- Market shifts
- Inadequate management or employee training
- Poorly maintained property
- Too rapid expansion
- Inadequate internal controls
- Reliance on an old stale theme
- Poor site selection
- Derisory market analysis

Businesses fail for both internal and external reasons. Declining performance may be the result of internal issues within the hospitality organization, such as mismanagement, or by external causes, such as economic business cycles and increased competition. Many financial failures are caused by a combination of internal problems that eventually create the company's inability to adapt to changes in the external environment. This is evident when a business is underperforming or when the entire industry is not performing as well as other industries within the domestic or foreign economy.

External versus Internal Factors

External factors are influences from the external environment such as economic downturns, competitive problems, and technological or social change. They include increased competition, rapidly changing technology, and economic fluctuations. External environments can change rapidly and companies may not be able to adjust. Many restaurants fail each year from an inability to anticipate market trends, especially given that some market trends are very difficult to predict.

Internal factors are indicators that appear from within hospitality companies that may range from an inability to pay debt service to eroding gross margin, decreased capacity utilization, increased turnover of management and staff, and lack of management competence and expertise to guide the organization. Moreover, main internal factors of decline include management's inability to cope with growth, increasing inventory in the presence of revenue decreases, and cash flow deficiencies.

The importance of these factors varies over time, depending on the state of the economy and the hospitality industry. Most business failures occur because of factors that make the business unsustainable. Indicators of business distress are generally apparent in a ratio analysis before the hospitality company actually fails, and analysts use ratio analysis to predict that a given company will go bankrupt.

Economic Causes. Economic factors that contribute to the collapse of a hospitality company include industry weakness and poor location. Economic activity also can contribute to the collapse of a hospitality company, especially during economic slowdowns. The performance of most hotels and restaurants is tied to the business cycle. If the economy experiences a recession, sales may decrease suddenly leaving the hospitality company with high fixed costs and insufficient revenue to cover them. At the same time, swift rises in interest rates and scarce capital can contribute to cash flow deficiencies and make it more difficult to obtain required financing. If the recession lingers, the likelihood of survival decreases. Undeniably, many of the recent failures in the hospitality industry resulted from the recessionary economy. More than any other class of commercial real estate, the lodging industry has seen the worst impact of the real estate downturn nationwide.

Financial Causes. Financial factors that contribute to a company's collapse include excessive debt and insufficient capital. The latest financial crisis included the collapse of the sub-prime mortgage market, as well as the financial and global economic crisis brought about a pronounced shift in the credit markets. As a result, both investors and lenders became more risk-averse.

Heavy reliance on debt financing to fund a hospitality company's growth can result in a major decline in net income as a result of increased debt servicing. This makes it increasingly difficult for hotels and restaurants to service their debts, resulting in a decreased return to shareholders, which, in turn, affects earnings per share and, in extreme cases, the ability to continue as a going concern.

MANAGING IN AN UNCERTAIN ENVIRONMENT

Before a feasible turnaround strategy can be devised, it is necessary to identify the causes of the company's crisis. Frequently encountered causes may include revenue downturn resulting from a weak economy, overly optimistic sales projections, high operating costs, insufficient resources, excessive debt burden, and high fixed costs. The development of the industry position should be evaluated so that a comparison between the hospitality companies' external and internal environment can be made.

In recognizing financial distress, management must look beyond the numbers to properly identify the underlying cause-effect relationship. For example, a revenue decline could indicate a new competitor has taken market share from the hotel or the overall market has declined. A deterioration of receivable liquidity could reflect customer cash flow problems as a result of economic slowdowns. The longer the information is ignored and underlying conditions worsen, the lower the likelihood of achieving a successful turnaround.

A comprehensive strategy will include, at a bare minimum, implementing a cost reduction program, enhancing purchasing procedures, speeding up cash flow, and extending cash preservation. A volatile hospitality environment requires fine tuning the entire business and ensuring that all the components work effectively.

EARLY WARNING SIGNS

Early signs that a hospitality company is being threatened are rarely obvious. The signs, though, do frequently appear in the financial statements well before circumstances reach a crisis stage, and effective management should recognize those indicators.

A weakening liquidity position, for instance, is a symptom that requires immediate attention. Factors that cause a dismal financial crisis begin to appear early. Sales may be decreasing, fixed costs may be too high in relation to revenue, or working capital may not be managed properly.

Other symptoms of potentially serious problems include:
- Drop in sales and net income;
- Declining operating margins;
- Consistent shortages of cash;
- Increases in sales accompanied by decreases in net income;
- Steady rise in expenses; and
- Vendor payments falling behind.

Another important early warning sign is the turnover of senior management and the attrition of middle management. The defections of middle and senior managers to other more stable, secure firms or industries, compounded by the shortage in both skilled and unskilled workers can have far-reaching implications for the hospitality company.

Because of the fast-moving and complex nature of distress, as well as the increasingly competitive hospitality industry environment, the earlier a hotel or restaurant responds to distress, the lower the risk to operations and stakeholder value erosion. Being prepared helps hospitality companies avoid near-distress situations, while positioning the business for long-term success.

USE OF OPERATIONAL ANALYSIS AS A MANAGEMENT TOOL

Operational analysis is an important management tool for identifying potential problem areas and seeking solutions. It encompasses the line-by-line comparison of all figures on the statement of income to determine if they differ from past performance as well as competitors. Monitoring operating performance against competition is vital. In fact, obtaining trends of comparable lodging facilities enhances the process of identifying problem areas.

A troubled hospitality company experiences phases of underperformance, early decline, and late decline. Unless satisfactorily addressed, leadership troubles as well as financial, organizational, and operational concerns eventually lead to declining profitability. These phases can be tracked by means of adverse trends using financial ratios to identify symptoms of failure. If not timely addressed, this will lead to declining liquidity or solvency.

An operational analysis facilitates the identification and isolation of the causes of decline in company performance. These difficulties should be addressed before they turn into major problems. A business may be deficient in certain areas that are not always obvious, but may be dormant and threaten its survival. Thus, isolating the causes of declining performance could mean the difference between survival and the collapse of a company. Low, negative, or adverse trends in operating profitability figures normally represent a distressed situation that requires serious turnaround managerial action.

TURNAROUND DEFINED

A turnaround occurs when a company undergoes a survival-threatening performance decline over a period of time and is able to reverse the declining performance to attain sustainable profitability. This implies that a turnaround will result in recovery to profitability from a loss situation. A turnaround plan provides a process for focusing the organization on the turnaround objective and rebuilding support from all stakeholders.

A turnaround is an action taken to prevent the occurrence of a financial disaster. A hospitality company faces a potential turnaround situation when it does not meet the expectations of its stakeholders and the industry in terms of performance results over a period of time. This includes both present and future outcome prospects.

FACTORS AFFECTING A TURNAROUND SITUATION

A turnaround strategy should be accompanied by actions that either pursue profitability with renewed resource commitment or seek new growth opportunities. This usually includes long-term measures taken by hospitality companies designed at stimulating financial improvements based on strategy that is deemed suitable by the company's management.

Turnaround strategy enables hospitality management to focus on the causes of poor results, in order to curtail losses and restore growth and prosperity. It may involve eradicating costs, restructuring finances, and redefining strategic objectives. Turnarounds often call for building a stronger management team, making acquisitions, or devising an exit strategy.

Although the recent economic downturn exacerbated the need for turnaround strategies, this is not a new occurrence. Most hospitality businesses experienced difficulties and potential declines somewhere in their life cycle. In the early 1990s, Marriott had difficulty because of an exorbitant amount of leverage used to finance its aggressive growth. This resulted in dividing Marriott Corporation into two separate companies: Marriott International and Host Marriott. Similarly, McDonald's struggled with the most serious crisis in its history at the beginning of the new millennium, as did Starbucks in recent years (see Example 7).

A turnaround requires a completely different managerial focus, albeit in the short term. Instead of emphasis on customers and revenue enhancements, the hotel or restaurant must concentrate on cash flow and soothing creditors in order to keep the company afloat. In some cases, this change is so disconcerting to management that some distressed companies frequently decide to have two management teams: one focusing on operations and the other directing the turnaround.

Once the turnaround process begins, immediate steps must be taken to look after the business, such as fostering open communication, preserving cash, and safeguarding assets. Although company management may be able to start the turnaround process on its own, in many cases stabilization requires a new management team or an outside consulting firm with turnaround experience. A turnaround specialist might be in an excellent position to assess the strengths and weaknesses of the current management team.

Most hotels and other hospitality organizations in a distressed situation have some level of dysfunction in their management structure. As a result, changing management leadership normally occurs in turnaround efforts, which provides symbolic action to creditors, shareholders, customers, suppliers, and employees that the company is serious about turning around its situation. Although in many instances it has been a crucial difference between hospitality companies achieving recovery versus those that have not, changing senior or middle management can be risky. In a turnaround, it is important to preserve the industry skills and knowledge of the management team in place because existing leadership understands core aspects to the business crucial to business recovery.

Distressed private companies have unique management issues of their own. The owner of a small hotel or restaurant may be reluctant to acknowledge serious financial difficulties since the company is perceived as an extension of that person's identity. As a result, acknowledging that the hospitality organization is in distress is regarded as a personal failure. Moreover, the owner of the small restaurant or hotel may lack the skills necessary to turn around the business.

STAGES OF TURNAROUND STRATEGY

A hospitality company will go through various stages to overcome a crisis. A full range of turnaround strategies is available for consideration, such as cost-cutting, strategic repositioning, and asset reduction. Moving from distress to performing well is much easier than directly moving from a major crisis to performing well, which is very doubtful.

The length of time necessary to complete a successful turnaround varies depending on the circumstances. The turnaround may commence at various stages of company decline. If the symptoms have been detected early, the hospitality company can move quickly through the first few stages. If turnaround activity starts when the company has reached a critical phase, it must go through all stages of a turnaround as follows:

1. Situation analysis
2. Retrenchment
3. Recovery
4. Return to normalcy

Situation Analysis

Once the need for a turnaround has been recognized, the first step is to perform a situation analysis to determine the true position of the hospitality business and the likelihood of its survival. This review assesses the company's turnaround situation in terms of both short-term survivability and long-term turnaround feasibility. Turnaround viability not only depends on whether the underlying causes of the distress can be reversed, but also on whether the internal and external constraints and the adverse industry conditions can be overcome. It includes an analysis of the extent and severity of the company's problems.

The primary goal of this stage is to establish whether management is able to articulate a well-conceived strategy that works for the company. In addition, it is important for the company to assess its condition in terms of likelihood of survival, impending risk of failure, or temporary declining performance. Following the initial assessment, a more detailed analysis of its strengths and weaknesses, current conditions, and organizational structure is required before an appropriate turnaround strategy can be developed. An evaluation of the external environment including competitive forces, threats, opportunities, and market attractiveness is also performed. The higher the degree of urgency, the less time is available. Turnaround situation assessment can be as short as a couple of weeks for a small company in impending risk of failure to several months for a large hospitality company facing temporary declining performance.

The early phase of a turnaround process should involve fact-finding and detecting the extent of the company's distress situation. If it is determined that the hospitality company is worth turning around, depending on the root causes of the financial difficulties, a detailed corrective action plan is developed. The plan should be clear and aim to reverse declining performance and restore the company's long-term profitability. A turnaround team is formed to oversee its implementation. The plan must be presented to important parties in the company, including the board of directors, management, and employees. In addition, the plan must be accessible to parties outside the hospitality business such as creditors, investors, and major suppliers.

Cash management is considered integral to this stage of a turnaround. Without cash, the hotel or restaurant cannot continue to operate. Thus, cash is the company's first concern with when it finds itself in a crisis situation. The hotel or restaurant must obtain control of its cash to provide the short time needed to complete the situation analysis. Preparation of a short-term cash flow forecast for a two-month period reflecting realistic working capital requirements is essential. In addition, settlement with creditors and government bodies for payments due is critical during this stage in order to prevent legal proceedings. Negotiations should be made involving vendors, employees for cash relief, credit lines, and strengthening terms of debt repayment.

Retrenchment

The next stage of the turnaround involves actions that lead to the stabilization of declining performance. This stage entails short-term measures that hotels and restaurant companies can take in order to reduce the level of asset investment and costs such as divestment and reduction of employees. The plan typically includes financial, marketing, and operations actions to restructure debts, improve working capital, reduce costs, and improve budgeting practices. The more severe the distress situation, the more far-reaching is the retrenchment process.

Retrenchment activities involve a reduction of a company's assets and cost base. It is an important strategy employed by a financially distressed company. Accordingly, many hospitality companies activate a turnaround strategy by sharply reducing operational expenses through aggressive retrenchment. However, cost-cutting and downsizing may be detrimental for some declining hospitality companies seeking a turnaround because of the potential risk to customer service and the quality of the overall experience.

Turnarounds of hospitality companies may prove difficult to achieve because of the important role played by front-line service staff in serving customers. As a result, competent management of staff is critical. Nonetheless, faced with poor financial performance, hotel or restaurant managers often cut costs and staffing levels, which, in turn, negatively affects the product service, lowers staff morale, and possibly affects the customer experience. This can be particularly damaging in a turnaround attempt if not managed effectively. In addition, the human side of retrenchment can result in significant social and economic costs, and create consequences in the way hotel and restaurant staff deal and care for customers.

Recovery

Once a hospitality company achieves the objectives of the retrenchment phase and cash flows are brought under control, the next step is business recovery. At this stage, it the company should focus on its strategic direction. There is a shift toward restoring profitability and deciding on the type of strategy for long-term growth. This is often a difficult stage of the turnaround, as the hospitality business is restructured with a clear focus on its core business, systems, and controls. Consistent communication is critical throughout the turnaround. Management must make sure all decisions are designed to achieve the goal of restoring the company's profitability and long-term growth.

Turnarounds provide an opportunity to reassess a hospitality company's overall strategy. They involve an in-depth analysis of customers, products, services, and geographies. The recovery phase involves collecting relevant data on competition, trends and market share, and establishing priorities and assessments of necessary actions to be taken and by whom and when. It focuses on meeting the company's objectives of growth and development by altering their resource commitment or by pursuing new brands and markets. Investments made in this regard should be long-term oriented, aimed at improving the company's financial position. It is important to challenge the value contribution of each business unit. If it is determined that the value is not there, it will be necessary to divest and redeploy.

Turnaround recovery is characterized by increased emphasis on profitability, as well as cash flow. It also emphasizes operational improvements and building the hospitality organization. In some cases, this is when there is a change in senior management as the stabilized and restructured company returns to normalcy. This stage is completed when the company has returned to normal performance on a sustainable basis. The recovery phase thus becomes the starting point for future successful operations. Accordingly, management will develop a going-forward strategy that concentrates on the effectiveness of the hospitality business and on leveraging its competitive advantage.

Return to Normalcy

In this final stage of the turnaround, emphasis is placed on growing the hospitality business and maintaining a healthy and strong balance sheet. The company should generate confidence in all of its stakeholders, including management, employees, suppliers and customers, while establishing the stage for continued success.

If successful, the company becomes profitable and the changes are internalized. While previous steps concentrated on correcting problems, this final stage focuses on profitability and enhancing the company's value. It requires periodic monitoring, planning, and reviewing on a continuous basis.

The emphasis shifts from cash flow concerns to maintaining a strong financial position, long-term financing, and strategic accounting and control systems. From a marketing perspective, emphasis is placed on a number of tactical efforts, including planning new marketing programs to expand the hospitality business base and increase market penetration, and carefully adding new rooms or restaurants and improving customer service.

SELECTED TURNAROUND STRATEGIES

The range or combination of strategies employed in successful turnarounds is extensive and unique to every situation. The type of strategy chosen depends on the factors influencing the turnaround. The more that external factors play a major role on the distressed situation, the more the company pursues strategies such as strategic repositioning and new product development, or revenue enhancement measures. In situations where internal factors lead to a turnaround, the company pursues operating measures intended at reducing costs and maximizing asset utilization. A review of selected turnaround strategies follows.

Increased Focus on Managing Liquidity

An unstable economy may cause hospitality companies to have cash flow problems and risk going out of business. Cash flow is a serious concern for most companies, but with the added unpredictability of the economy, there is less room for error.

In periods of financial distress, companies should increase efforts at managing investments in working capital, while keeping receivables as close to realistic payment terms as possible, ensuring that inventories track sales. As a result of changes in the operating environment, reassessing capital projects and giving comparable treatment to the initial factors supporting projects, is vital. In so doing, it is important to reprioritize capital investments. Failing properties may need to spend money immediately on capital expenditures. Many areas of the facility may require immediate attention in order to keep the business in operation. Yet, only new proposals that result in permanent cash flow enhancements should be undertaken. Moreover, the company should test the adequacy of credit lines and liquidate unproductive assets.

Conserving Cash. A hospitality company attempting a turnaround must have firm control of its cash flows. Lower demand affects margins and reduces liquidity. Accordingly, it is imperative to assess priorities and pursue efficiencies in managing cash flow. As a starting point, it is important to tighten discretionary spending policies. Actions to ensure that no payments occur without a proper approval are required. All disbursements must be approved by proper management personnel. An understanding of cash payments allows for the recognition of potential areas for cost reductions, while sending a clear message to the rest of the hospitality organization that this is no business as usual and the old spending patterns are now subject to reevaluation. Although cash-related best practices are applicable at all times, they are crucial during times of economic slowdowns. The axiom of cash conservation should focus on accelerating receivable collections, minimizing inventories, and properly managing payables.

Accelerating Cash Receipts. Managing receivables is difficult during healthy economic times and these challenges are made even more pressing in periods of economic downturns. Communication with customers is of primary importance to a collection. Customers must be kept informed of their debt commitments from the start, and the company must address any potential collection problems at the outset. This may likely prevent receivables from becoming actual collection problems.

There are several steps that the hospitality company can take to expedite the collection process. First, an invoice should be submitted on a timely manner, as it is more likely to be paid when the value of service is still regarded as new to guests. The earlier an invoice is sent to a customer, the faster the company will receive payment. In the event the customer has specific guidelines for processing payment, it is important to have this information from the beginning (this is important for companies requiring electronic submission of invoices, which has become a widely used practice in recent times).

Companies should look for warning signs of impending payment problems. If a customer is in danger of declaring bankruptcy, timing issues should be considered. For example, payments made 90 days before filing for bankruptcy are typically considered privileged payments (or preferences) and subject to certain exceptions; the bankruptcy trustee may file suit against the company for repayment.

As part of the collections process, customers may ask for discounts. If a discount is based on displeasure with service, the company should consider obtaining a release of liability in connection with any reduction in the receivable. At the same time, a credit against future services is more likely to guarantee additional sources of revenue at a later time. Restructuring payment terms is also a frequent request by customers experiencing financial distress. During these troubled times, however, it is essential to focus on rapid collection of receivables.

If customers pay in 60 days rather than 30 days, the additional time may affect the cash situation of the hospitality company in need of immediate cash to pay debt.

Delaying Cash Outflows. An important strategy during a turnaround is to delay payments as long as possible. A payment should be made only when it is absolutely necessary. It is also imperative to postpone expenditures such as dressing up offices or refurbishing hotel lobbies. Clearly, money must be spent carefully during difficult times. Extending the life of equipment and tooling by performing effective and timely maintenance should be considered, as it is normally less expensive in the short-term to fix up old equipment and cars than to purchase them. In extreme cases, delaying the frequency of payroll payments should be considered (e.g., making monthly or biweekly payroll payments in lieu of weekly payments).

Inventory purchases and payables represent significant uses of cash. Inadequate control of inventory supply means that the hospitality company will have less cash available to pay debt if the food or beverage inventory is not converted into cash relatively soon. Monitoring inventory and supply purchases through better tracking and controls means additional cash available to the company. At the same time, slowing down the cash outflows by properly managing accounts payable can free up cash.

Approaching Suppliers for Better Terms. A good relationship with trade creditors is important during tough economic times. Thus, suppliers should be approached for better terms. If a vendor offers extended payment terms, for instance, they are actually providing unsecured interest-free financing. Renegotiating terms of payment from 30 to 90 days improves a hotel's or restaurant's cash flow position. Because suppliers have a stake in the company's survival, they will often arrange special payment terms if the hotel or restaurant can demonstrate that it is seriously addressing its problems. If the hotel or restaurant is salvageable, it is in the suppliers' best interest to help it avoid bankruptcy.

In some cases, taking trade discounts and making early payments can reduce payments owed to suppliers. If a vendor were to offer a discount on invoices paid within 10 days versus their standard 30-day no interest terms, and the company was in a position to borrow at a reasonable (low) rate, the company may make money even if it borrowed the needed funds to take advantage of the discount.

Enhancing Relationships with Debt Capital Providers

The usual dependence on credit capital by a hospitality company can present unique challenges during periods when access to debt capital tightens. With credit capital less readily available during periods of economic slowdowns, suppliers of debt become even more important to the business. Providing profitable noncredit business can be an effective way of building goodwill and deepening the relationship with credit suppliers during this critical period. With changes occurring constantly in the economic cycle, it is important to position the relationship so providers perceive they are being well rewarded for committing their capital. Bankers need to be aware of business activity at all times. If the company expects to have a slow month, it should inform its creditors and listen to their advice. A company's close and honest relationship with its creditors is important during difficult times. Generally, creditors are most interested in the integrity of the people behind the business.

Tight Financing and Scarce Capital. In recent troubled times there have been limited funds available for new construction under the best of circumstances. The nation's biggest banks cut back on lending to small businesses. Traditionally, debt came from local or regional banks with participation from the United States Small Business Administration in the case of small hotels and restaurants. Accordingly, banks have become much more restrictive, with lending reflecting stricter covenants, shorter maturities, and higher financing fees. Non-recourse financing is only available to strong borrowers with stabilized properties. Most lenders provide repositioning financing. Funding for more expensive transactions has been nonexistent or rare. For the most part, funding has been available from local and regional sources for deals requiring $5 million to $10 million or less in capital.

Using Creative Financing Sources. Despite a challenging lending environment, there have been funds available for acquisitions or renovations, especially for the acquisition of underperforming or turnaround properties. Credit unions, private investors, the sale of assets, and other innovative financing structures increasingly are filling the void left by the continuing scarcity of bank loans. Many hotels and restaurants in need of cash are filling gaps in their operating budgets by selling real estate assets. In extreme situations, personal guarantees by owners have emerged, especially in the case of small hotels or restaurants.

Debt Restructuring

A recent trend that has greatly affected the hospitality industry is that lenders are increasingly willing to redo loans often backed by struggling properties rather than risk realizing an immediate loss. As creditors begin to see some positive signs in the economic recovery, including a rise in consumer spending and a slight decline in the unemployment rate, they are more likely to take back an asset and negotiate with the current borrower until values return. Lenders are also making arrangements with delinquent debt holders, including those whose property is worth less than their loan, based on debt taken during the commercial real estate boom of recent years.

The risks and costs of foreclosure is a major concern among banks and other real estate lenders. Foreclosing can be more costly than restructuring a loan. In fact, if a hotel or restaurant property's value falls below the amount owed, the lender must increase the cash held in reserve. As a result, a foreclosure will increase the funds the bank must set aside. Moreover, banks do not want to sell properties they take over; they would prefer not having to unload hotel or restaurant assets in a down market. Banks are also not interested in retaining hotel or restaurant property because they lack the expertise to run these businesses.

Banks as well as other lenders have, therefore, become more proactive. They are willing to negotiate with hotel and restaurant owners faced with financial distress. In addition, regulations enacted at the end of 2009 enticed banks to restructure their loans. Accordingly, lenders restructured more than $10 billion of troubled debt during the first quarter of 2010, and hotels were a main beneficiary of lenders' willingness to redo loan terms. In many instances, repayments were extended from two to seven years, compared with 30 to 60 days in 2009. Bondholders have also refinanced major hotel debt. Hilton, which is currently owned by Blackstone, completed a deal to reduce debt by almost $4 billion and extend maturities by two years.

Modifying Debt Scheduled Payments. One cash-generating strategy for a hospitality company is to renegotiate debt or agreed-upon terms, giving the company the ability to keep up with debt service payments. This debt renegotiation process may involve extensions of maturity dates, interest rate changes, or reductions of principal. Modifications are defined by Treasury Regulation Section 1.1001-3(c)(1)(i) as "any alteration, including any deletion or addition, in whole or in part, of a legal right or obligation of the issuer or a holder of a debt instrument, whether the alteration is evidenced by an express agreement (oral or written), conduct of the parties, or otherwise." Hence, an extension of maturity date, change in interest rate, or reduction of principal is a modification to the debt instrument.

A "significant modification" of debt may cause a hotel or restaurant to realize taxable income from the "exchange of the original debt instrument for a modified instrument that differs materially either in kind or in extent" [Regulations Section 1.1001-3(b)]. If a significant modification has occurred, IRC Section 108 and its underlying regulations determine whether the income created is excludible from gross income. A modification that changes the timing of debt payments, for instance, is significant if it results in the material deferral of scheduled payments. Similarly, a modification that changes the priority or releases, substitutes, adds or otherwise alters the collateral for, or guarantee on, a debt instrument is considered significant. Accordingly, the simple act of renegotiating a loan with a bank may have unintentional tax consequences for a hospitality company that must be carefully scrutinized in order to minimize future taxes.

Operational Improvements

In a volatile economic environment, hospitality management must place greater emphasis on operating improvements than brand development. At the same time, the erosion of profits that the industry suffered during recent recessions accompanied by its inability to raise room rates significantly focused on making money on sales. Yet, it is important to note that in a high-fixed cost business (i.e., hotels) generating additional revenue might be more productive than focusing on cutting costs.

Cost-Cutting Measures. A property in distress is more likely to be cost-cutting, and full-service hotels may be the most vulnerable, as they have the highest level of staffing and services. Thus, the first impulse of many hospitality managers when commencing a turnaround is to cut costs. Some hotels reduce room-service hours, close or reduce the hours of restaurants, or close entire floors. Cost reduction should be a main focus, as it produces results more quickly than revenue-generating strategies. Costs should be examined on a continual basis to minimize ineffectiveness and waste. An examination of large expense items on the operating budget, for instance, may reveal that the restaurant is not ensuring that they are paying the lowest possible price for food supplies. However, blanket cost-cutting such as a 15% reduction on everything in the operation's budget will not produce desired results (e.g., cutting advertising expenses will reduce expenses, but will also result in a sales decline).

Labor is often the first cut in a hospitality organization, as it is the largest expense. However, it is important to avoid employee lay-offs, whenever possible. Terminations and dismissals, especially when implemented over a long period of time, create morale problems. Instead, natural attrition should allow reducing staff levels to a point where they become effective within a workable period of time. If terminations are necessary, they should be done quickly.

Reducing variable costs can return greater bottom line benefits than simply cutting fixed costs. Although it is often common practice during tough times to shift focus from employee training, this can compromise long-term individual and organizational growth. Evaluating existing human resources practices strengthens the connection between individual performance, profit drivers and organizational growth, which has a positive impact on achieving long-term profitability and growth. Moreover, taking positive steps to offer individual incentives for cost-savings ideas should be considered. Making management and staff part of the budgeting process while rewarding them for their cost-cutting ideas, for instance, may generate effective cost-cutting measures during the turnaround process.

EXAMPLE 1: A review of Hotel A energy costs indicated non-energy awareness procedures that caused high energy costs. Hotel A implemented the following reduced energy consumption procedures based on cost-saving ideas suggested by selected managers and staff members:

- Installing more energy efficient compressors;
- Developing rigorous maintenance programs for air conditioning systems;
- Closing off parts of the hotel during low occupancy periods;
- Installing energy controlling devices on doors and windows; and
- Training maids to adjust thermostats to acceptable levels.

EXAMPLE 2: Luxury Hotel was in financial distress. In 2009, its occupancy was 55% and its revenue per available room (REVPar) declined 30%. In spite of average room rates of $400 a night, the hotel was unable to generate enough cash to pay its interest and operating costs. A turnaround strategy included outsourcing laundry, closing the restaurant on two slow nights, and replacing fresh flowers in the lobbies with sculptures or ornate vases. It also eliminated staff bonuses and discontinued turn-down bed service each evening.

Enhancing Revenue Growth. During periods of economic slowdown, finding new ways to generate revenue is difficult. However, it is important to seek revenue-generating strategies to expand the company, drive the business forward, diversify from poor performing areas, and identify new sales opportunities. Examples include offering incentives to customers for repeat business, as well as developing referral relationships with related business such as travel agencies and event planners.

Discounting Room or Menu Prices. Many hoteliers contend that discounting room rates is unavoidable during difficult times as well as a strategy to increase market share in good times. Accordingly, many hotels and restaurants typically reduce room rates or menu prices during turbulent economic times as a means of stimulating consumer demand and capturing additional market share from competitors. At the same time, competitors' decisions for discounted rates strongly influence a hospitality company's pricing decisions.

However, discounting may weaken the integrity of a hotel's brand. In addition, studies have revealed that hotels that price higher than competitors may have lower occupancies but higher RevPAR, especially if they price significantly higher than competitors. Because RevPAR rather than occupancy percent is considered the true measure of performance in the rooms department, price discounting relative to competition may not result in enhancing performance for hotels.

Accordingly, a number of luxury and mid market hotels are holding firm on rates. Instead, they are developing value-added strategies so that high room prices deliver added value. Similarly, some mid market properties may use the pay-before-you-stay tactic to assure bookings during difficult economic conditions while improving cash flow.

Selecting strategies for Revenue Growth. Some hotels may offer savings of up to 30 or 40% to those customers who book ahead and pay in full. This strategy is perceived as a way to offer a discount without cheapening the brand, especially an upscale brand. Prepayments also guarantee revenue and cash flow ahead of time. These prepay discounts are widely accepted for resort bookings where booking time is often shorter. The earlier customers make a reservation, the more they save. To illustrate, reserving more than two months in advance can result in savings of 30%; one month to two months beforehand, 20%; and a week before, up to 5%. Similarly, a growing number of independent lodging companies are rewarding advance bookings by offering 10% to 20% off posted rates. However, if a guest cancels more than 10 days before arrival, a fee is charged. A larger amount may be charged if the cancellation occurs late and the room is not booked by another guest. Prepaying appeals to guests who have budget constraints and has emerged as a very successful marketing strategy.

Another valuable add-on strategy includes offering room credits for other products or services such as spa treatments, dining, and airport transfers. Creating a package deal at the same rate (or at a slightly higher price than the room-only rate) and adding additional services or features to the offering may be an effective revenue-enhancing strategy. To illustrate, rather than lowering rates, hotels may offer guests, who stay three or four nights, a free night that includes a buffet breakfast and a two-hour massage at the hotel spa. In addition, guests may receive free wine, kitchen tours, or free kid's program. In those cases, guests may pay $250 for each of three nights when the actual price is more than $400 per night, including the value-added extras.

EXAMPLE 3: Rather than discounting rates, ER Resort in Key Largo, Florida offers each guest a free deep-sea fishing trip, a dolphin cruise, and beach chair set-up, plus discounts on meals, entertainment, and other attractions.

EXAMPLE 4: A hotel has a special package of $2,000 per couple, which includes eight nights for the price of six in a suite with its own outdoor pool plus round-trip airport transfer, breakfast, champagne, and free laundry service.

EXAMPLE 5: Luxury Hotel includes daily breakfast, champagne, and strawberries upon arrival, and a one-time resort credit for use in the hotel's restaurants, bar, and spa for a normally priced package deal.

Monitoring Marketing Activities

Company management should take a professional approach to marketing, including profitability analysis and market research. The company should have a thorough understanding of its customer base. For example, when performing marketing research on customer needs, hotels should group guests in categories such as corporate and leisure travelers. Profitability analysis helps identify the areas in which a business has been competitive. It reveals where a hotel is achieving higher earnings and where it has unprofitable operations.

Moreover, the company should analyze each product by market segment by focusing on the most significant customer groups. For instance, market segments for hotel rooms might include conventions or weekend leisure travel, while market segments for banquets include holiday parties, cultural events, and business meetings. As a result, the business may develop sales campaigns to increase both corporate and leisure travel. Understanding key performance indicators that drive room revenue (e.g., average daily rate, occupancy percent, and RevPar), as well as other sources of revenue, are important to achieving a successful turnaround.

Rebuilding a Profitable Core Business

Most failing companies have a fundamental problem in their core business, which is where they have the greatest competitive strength. As a result, an important turnaround strategy must focus on the core. While cost-cutting may achieve a cash-positive position in the short term, it will not solve the deeper structural problems of the core business. Therefore, it is important that employees focus on positive customer service and customer relations before spending resources on marketing and advertising. Cash spent on attracting new business will be wasted if frontline employees are not providing acceptable customer service.

A riskier strategy is for hospitality managers to supplement their core business by developing new brands or entering new markets. The premise is that the revenue and cash flow from successful new businesses will help fund the turnaround of the core. This is not considered a formula for success. Growth added to a defective business produces a larger defective business and thus does not fix the underlying problem. Managers must therefore identify and capitalize on the company's distinct competitive advantage. This advantage should propel the business and strengthen core operations over time.

Asset Repositioning

Many troubled properties have outstanding intrinsic value. Unlocking this value requires vision, insight, and carefulness. Focusing on the balance sheet allows management to realize hidden value in the business, as well as identify and mitigate financial risks. During the first stages of a turnaround, decisions to sell assets in order to generate cash must be made by restaurants or hotels striving to survive. In those cases, the focus is on which assets to sell quickly rather than what makes sense from a long-term perspective.

Once the company achieves stability, it must create value through performance and service excellence, considering long-term strategy by liquidating underutilized assets, especially real estate. Contraction may be the natural by-product of rediscovering core competencies; however, market conditions must be considered in making those decisions.

> **EXAMPLE 6:** Success Hotels considered selling some real estate assets during its turnaround process but it parted with relatively few properties because the market was unfavorable and it wanted to protect the company's franchise value over the long-term.

Strategic Reorientation

When the cause of a downfall is rooted in weak strategic positioning, failure to alter the overall strategic approach may lead to a company's downfall. Strategic reorientation entails a dramatic transformation of strategy that serves as an essential step in the process of turnaround.

Rebranding might be used as a turnaround strategy. It can serve many purposes, including the reorientation of the business toward a different target market, anticipated enhancement to financial performance, or increased value of the property. Rebranding provides the prospect for a hotel property to reposition itself for better financial returns or to make necessary changes in adapting to a changing market.

Evaluating Accounting and Financial Reporting Systems

Hospitality companies must disseminate accounting and operational data to management in daily, weekly, monthly, and quarterly reports. Although the existing software may be satisfactory, the system may not be properly configured to provide the needed data on a timely basis. During the turnaround process, failure to produce or distribute management and financial reports to operate a business becomes a major internal control weakness and can negatively impact the turnaround effort.

A hospitality company's information systems should provide relevant information on a timely basis. Poor information systems and weak financial controls hide symptoms and causes. In troubled companies, a lack of information is not only a cause of the crisis, but a major impediment to the company's turnaround.

In healthy organizations, poor information systems allow a progressive weakening in the organization that can go undetected until it is too late.

OTHER TURNAROUND STRATEGIES

The following reflects additional strategies that can be considered in a turnaround situation:

- Building strong relationships with existing and prospective guests;
- Broadening the understanding of risk in the company's market and tightening the primary support practices to lessen that risk;
- Creating special offers for local clients;
- Using the company website as business generator;
- Renegotiating contracts with suppliers and service providers;
- Loading promotional materials on Internet portals; using social networks (e.g., Twitter, Facebook);
- Monitoring competition on a regular basis;
- Developing new packages and programs to generate demand from new guests; and
- Pursuing and achieving a greater pace in decision-making to take advantage of shifting market conditions.

EXAMPLE 7: Faced with a challenging financial and operating position in 2008, Starbucks initiated MyStarbucksIdea.com as a forum for consumers to make suggestions. Starbucks implemented turnaround strategies, including cost-cutting measures to increase margins and improve same-store sales. In 2009, Starbucks closed 600 locations in the United States, as well as additional units abroad as part of its turnaround strategy. In addition, it slowed development worldwide. The moves, coupled with the elimination of more than 1,000 corporate positions resulted in savings of close to $200 million in fiscal 2009. To drive sales, Starbucks introduced new products such as a line of smoothie and sorbetto drinks. The chain also refined the recipes of its breakfast sandwiches, so their smell did not overpower the aroma of fresh ground coffee that had always been a major factor in the company's successful concept. Introductions of an instant coffee successfully met corporate sales and volume targets and helped to achieve a successful turnaround. Starbucks realized its first same-store sales gain in two years while relying on digital and social-media promotions. After reducing more than half a billion dollars in corporate costs, it was expected to continue with a new growth model in future years, focusing aggressive growth on its Seattle's Best Coffee brand.

IMPLEMENTATION

Consistent communication is vital throughout the turnaround. Management must ensure all decisions are designed to leverage the company's competitive advantage and achieve the outcome of restoring its profitability and growth. Although staff members may not agree with management's decisions, they need to understand them. During turnarounds, lack of information is always worse than having negative information. As a result, management must always disclose important information during the turnaround process.

A turnaround is complete when a company is on its way to long-term growth. This is evident to the board and management through results of improved performance on the financial statements and reports. In addition, staff turnover has subsided and strategies have been internalized.

EXIT STRATEGY

Turnarounds are not all successful, and distressed companies are not all salvageable. It is essential to recognize those distressed situations for which a turnaround is possible and those that will ultimately fail. Where a turnaround is feasible, the swift and crucial action of appointing a turnaround manager or team is essential to preserving value and embarking on a recovery. In some cases, the turnaround may be so successful that the hotel or restaurant becomes a target of a takeover bid. In cases where the prospects of the company continuing as an ongoing operation are not realistic, the process of managing the closure or disposal to maximize returns and minimize losses is essential for all stakeholders.

A company may put a quick end to its devastating losses but by no means achieve an acceptable return position. When this occurs, an exit strategy may be appropriate. Exit strategies may include a sale or merger of all or part of the hospitality business to a company better able to produce an acceptable return on the funds invested. Different strategies may be pursued. One abandonment strategy is exiting the market by immediately liquidating or selling to another company. In other situations, voluntary liquidation or reorganization in bankruptcy might be considered.

Companies should avoid a bankruptcy filing unless it is the last resort. Filing for bankruptcy protection under Chapter 11 is time-consuming and expensive and should only be considered if all turnaround efforts fail. Legal fees for large cases may run into millions of dollars. Moreover, statistics on successful reorganizations of hospitality companies filing for bankruptcy protection under Chapter 11 have not been positive. It is distracting to management and it could be devastating if consumers disappear because they lack confidence in the hospitality company's ability to survive. Nevertheless, in some circumstances, bankruptcy is the only choice for the company to restructure for survival. Whenever a company's survival is in jeopardy, a turnaround professional should be called to assess whether bankruptcy may be an appropriate tool and what contingency plan should be put in place. Under Chapter 11, the owner of the hospitality company retains control of the business and its assets while it reorganizes, whereas under Chapter 7, a court-appointed trustee takes control of the assets while the trustee liquidates the business.

LESSONS TO BE LEARNED

As a result of recessionary trends, a depressed real estate market, a major financial crisis, as well as other economic factors, a number of hospitality firms have been unable to meet debt service and operating costs in the recent past. As a result, these hotels and restaurants have been reporting massive losses and face the prospect of failure. In order to survive in this difficult and increasingly competitive and challenging environment, it is essential that steps are taken to turn around the business.

A summary of important lessons that hotels and restaurants in financial distress can learn from the turnaround process follows:

- A turnaround takes place when a hotel, restaurant, or other hospitality business experiences a survival-threatening performance decline over a period of time and is able to reverse the declining performance to attain sustainable profitability.
- Early response to distress and a focus on preserving and enhancing the hotel or restaurant value are critical to successful turnarounds. At the same time, periodic monitoring, planning, and reviewing results and ensuring that the process of change does not distract from the need to continue to manage daily operations are integral components of ensuring a thriving future.
- Hospitality management must have the will and the ability to achieve a successful turnaround or access to external resources (e.g., turnaround specialists) that can provide these skills when required.
- Turnarounds take time, and if they are not started early enough, they will either fail or require protection through bankruptcy proceedings.
- Turnarounds of hospitality firms may prove difficult to achieve due to the key role played by front-line service staff in serving customers. As a result, the skillful management of the staff becomes critical in a turnaround.
- A turnaround requires a completely different managerial focus. In the early stages instead of emphasis on customers and revenue enhancements, the hotel or restaurant must place emphasis on cash flow and reassuring creditors as a means to ensure the business survival. A hospitality firm attempting a turnaround must get a firm hold on cash inflows and outflows. The motto of conservation of cash should be on acceleration of receivable collections, minimizing inventories, and proper management of payables.
- There are costs associated with the initial restructuring of a hospitality firm. These initial costs as well as the financing of future growth of the business must be obtained either from within the business or from outside sources.
- Renegotiation of the hotel or restaurant debt, or key terms, is an important turnaround strategy, giving the company the ability to keep with its debt service payments and improve its cash flow position. However, this simple act of renegotiating a loan with a bank may have unintentional tax consequences for the hospitality firm that need to be carefully examined in order to minimize future taxes.
- During the retrenchment stage, it is essential to avoid termination and dismissals of employees, whenever possible. They normally create morale problems, which are difficult to rectify. Instead, decreasing the workforce through natural attrition should allow reducing staff levels to a point at

which they become effective within a workable period of time. If terminations become necessary, it is important that they are completed in the shortest time possible and only in extreme situations.

- Turnaround recovery is characterized by increased emphasis on profitability besides the earlier focus on cash flow; management will develop a going forward strategy that will concentrate on the effectiveness of the hospitality business and on leveraging its competitive advantage.
- It is important to use the skills and approaches that have been adapted during the early stages of the turnaround process in order to return the hotel or restaurant to being a healthy and strong business. This will ensure that it continues to prosper, keeping the strategy and business development plan under continuous review and assessment.
- Management must acquire the support of suppliers, customers, employees, bankers, shareholders, and others in completing a successful turnaround. These stakeholders need to understand management's structured approach in dealing with the distressed situation. In so doing, it becomes essential to have open lines of communication with all stakeholders during the turnaround process by keeping them involved and informed as the turnaround process unfolds and develops. Most importantly, the hotel or restaurant cannot afford deterioration of its customer base. Thus, communicating with customers and taking steps to retain their business is key for the turnaround's success.

In a turnaround the primary objective of the hospitality business is to conduct a concerted effort to stop the declining performance and reestablish key business differentials that give the hotel or restaurant a competitive advantage. By following an effective turnaround process and appropriate strategic planning and decision making, many hospitality companies can look forward to recovery and a long, prosperous future.

CHAPTER 27
INTERNATIONAL FINANCIAL REPORTING STANDARDS

CONTENTS

Progress on Convergence of IFRS and U.S. GAAP	27,002
SEC Considerations	27,004
Timing of the Implementation Process	27,005
Avoiding Implementation Problems	27,005
Effectiveness of IFRS Compared to U.S. GAAP	27,005
Specific Differences between IFRS and U.S. GAAP	27,006
Projected Role of the SEC in the Standard-Setting Process	27,007
SEC-Proposed Roadmap Milestones	27,007
SEC February 2010 Release and Work Plan	27,008
General Conceptual Framework	27,013
Proposed Financial Statement Presentation	27,015
Disaggregation	27,015
Cohesiveness	27,016
Other Financial Statement Characteristics	27,017
Sample of Proposed IFRS Financial Statements	27,017
Conversion Preparation Checklist	27,026
Cost versus Benefits of Conversion	27,028
Additional Guidance	27,028
iGAAP Information Sources	27,028

Exhibits

Exhibit 27-1. Memorandum of Understanding: Short-Term Convergence Goals	27,002
Exhibit 27-2. Memorandum of Understanding: Additional Convergence Goals	27,003
Exhibit 27-3. ABC Restaurant's Financial Statements: Statement of Comprehensive Income	27,018
Exhibit 27-4. ABC Restaurant's Financial Statements: Statement of Financial Position	27,020
Exhibit 27-5. ABC Restaurant's Financial Statements: Statement of Cash Flows	27,022
Exhibit 27-6. ABC Restaurant's Financial Statements: Statement of Changes in Equity	27,024
Exhibit 27-7. ABC Restaurant's Financial Statements: Reconciliation of Cash Flows to Comprehensive Income	27,024

The generally accepted accounting principles (GAAP) currently used to record and present financial information differ in various regions of the world. Although, the United States, England, Canada, Australia, France, Germany, India, and Japan have their own standard-setting bodies, globalization renders it increasingly imperative to establish a single set of accounting and reporting standards acceptable in all geographical jurisdictions. Consequently, there is a worldwide surge toward the unification of accounting and reporting standards. In the United States, the Securities Exchange Commission (SEC) stated that in 2011 they will decide whether or not to replace U.S. GAAP with International GAAP (iGAAP). iGAAP is being developed by the International Accounting Standards Board (IASB) in conjunction with the standard-setting bodies of various countries and includes both International Accounting Standards (IAS) and International Financial Reporting Standards (IFRS). If the SEC decides to replace U.S. GAAP with iGAAP, U.S. publicly owned companies will not be required to apply iGAAP until 2015 or later, as expressed in the SEC's February 2010 Release, "Commission Statement in Support of Convergence and Global Accounting Standards." As a result of this potential change in reporting standards, it is important to understand the nature of iGAAP and the ways in which it differs from U.S. GAAP. Although this change would not apply to privately owned and not-for-profit companies, the AICPA, in May 2008, amended Rules 202 and 203 to allow for the use of IFRS by such companies on a trial basis of three to five years. In addition, in December 2007, the SEC adopted rules permitting foreign private issuers (FPIs) to file financial statements using IFRS, as issued by the IASB, without reconciliation to U.S. GAAP.

PROGRESS ON CONVERGENCE OF U.S. GAAP AND INTERNATIONAL ACCOUNTING AND FINANCIAL REPORTING STANDARDS

The tentative date on which the SEC will determine whether to require U.S. public companies to use IFRS for accounting and reporting purposes is June 2011. The chairman of the IASB, David Tweedie, stated that by 2015, there will be few discrepancies between U.S. GAAP and IFRS. However, in February 2010, the SEC initiated a work plan to study the benefits and problems involved in mandatory convergence. The magnitude of the hurdles listed in this Work Plan leaves open the possibility that U.S. GAAP might be made more compatible with IFRS without mandatory conversion to IFRS, or that the potential mandatory conversion date may be postponed.

In February 2006, the FASB and IASB issued a Memorandum of Understanding (MoU), which reaffirms their commitment to develop a set of high-quality worldwide accounting standards within a specified time frame. The 2006 MoU short-term convergence goals appear in Exhibit 27-1.

Exhibit 27-1: Memorandum of Understanding: Short-Term Convergence Goals

To Be Examined by the FASB	Outcome as of September 2008
Fair value option	FASB issued ASC 825 (FAS-159)
Investment properties	FASB considering adopting IAS 40*

Chapter 27: International Financial Reporting Standards 27,003

Research and development	FASB issued ASC 805 (FAS-141(R)) and possibly
Subsequent events	FASB will publish in late 2008

To Be Examined by the IASB	Outcome as of September 2008
Borrowing costs	IASB revised IAS 23
Government grants	Deferred to a later date
Joint ventures	IASB issued exposure draft
Segment reporting	IASB issued IFRS 8

To Be Examined Jointly	Outcome as of September 2008
Impairment	Deferred to a later date
Income tax	IASB plans to revise IAS 12

* The IASs were developed by the International Accounting Standards Committee (IASC) before the creation of the IASB. There are 41 IASs and they have all been adopted as IFRSs by the IASB unless revised by them.

In addition, the 2006 MoU listed 11 other goals to be attained jointly by the FASB and IASB. The status of these goals, as of April 2010, is shown in Exhibit 27-2.

Exhibit 27-2: Memorandum of Understanding: Additional Convergence Goals

1.	Business combinations	Completed in 2007—ASC 805 (FAS 141(R)) issued in 2007 and IFRS 3 revised in 2008.
2.	Financial instruments	(1) IFRS concerning classification and measurement of financial liabilities is scheduled to be issued in the fourth quarter of 2010. (2) IFRS concerning impairments is scheduled to be issued in the fourth quarter of 2010. (3) IFRS concerning hedging is scheduled to be issued in the first quarter of 2011.
3.	Financial statement presentation	(1) IFRS concerning discontinued operations is scheduled to be issued in the fourth quarter of 2010. (2) IFRS concerning the presentation of items of other comprehensive income is scheduled to be issued in the fourth quarter of 2010. (3) IFRS to replace IAS 1 and IAS 7 is scheduled to be issued in the second quarter of 2011.
4.	Tangible assets	Removed from active agenda.

Part VI: Recent Developments

5.	Leases	IFRS concerning leases is scheduled to be issued in the second quarter of 2011.
6.	Distinction between liabilities and equity	IFRS concerning financial instruments with characteristics of liabilities and equity is scheduled to be issued in the second quarter of 2011.
7.	Revenue recognition	IFRS concerning revenue recognition is scheduled to be issued in the second quarter of 2011.
8.	Consolidations	(1) IFRS to replace IAS 27 is scheduled to be issued in the fourth quarter of 2010. (2) IFRS concerning disclosures of unconsolidated SPEs/structured entities is scheduled to be issued June 2010.
9.	Derecognition	IFRS concerning the derecognition of assets is scheduled to be issued in the fourth quarter of 2010.
10.	Fair value measurement	IFRS concerning measurement uncertainty analysis disclosure for fair value is scheduled to be issued in 4th quarter of 2010.
11.	Post-employment benefits (including pensions)	(1) IFRS concerning defined benefit plans is scheduled to be issued in the fourth quarter of 2010. (2) IFRS concerning termination benefits is scheduled to be issued in May 2010.

SEC Considerations

In deciding to adopt IFRS, the SEC stated that it will consider the following:

1. The impact of the conversion on the way companies report to other parties. This is the case with the determination of capital requirements imposed by financial institutions, and with the interrelatedness between U.S. GAAP and federal or state income tax reporting (a change from LIFO (last in, first out) to FIFO (first in, first out) might be required). The eligibility of an IFRS filer for continued inclusion in certain market indices (e.g., S&P 500) might also be affected.

2. The requirement of simultaneous changes to a company's policies, procedures, and internal controls. These changes may affect users of financial information in general as well as regulators. Additional costs would also be incurred, for example, when the equity method of reporting an investment is used and investee information must be converted to IFRS, or when a private company using U.S. GAAP is obliged to convert to IFRS as the result of going public.

3. Auditing firms with a nonglobal client base may have difficulty training personnel or hiring personnel already familiar with IFRS. Public Company Accounting Oversight Board (PCAOB) requirements might be more stringent than IFRS requirements, as in the requirement to provide for a contingent obligation. Audit inquiry letters from clients' attorneys may be affected by conversion to IFRS when the attorney is not familiar

with IFRS. Existing references to U.S. GAAP in the many sources of financial literature would then need to be modified.
4. The degree to which the milestones specified in its Projected Roadmap (discussed later in this chapter) have been attained.

Timing of the Implementation Process

When the SEC mandates the use of IFRS by all U.S. public companies, they will be required to present three years of audited IFRS financial statements. The 2011 proposed announcement date provides companies with sufficient time to initiate their internal accounting to IFRS no later than 2012. This will enable them to present IFRS-audited public financial statements for the years 2012, 2013, and 2014. Large accelerated filers, as defined by the Securities and Exchange Act of 1934, would be required to file using IFRS by 2014. Accelerated filers would file using IFRS for years ending on or after December 31, 2015, and all other public companies for years ending on or after December 31, 2016. This staggered approach is designed to mitigate the costs of conversion to IFRS by introducing predictability into the process and by giving smaller companies that are less capable of engaging in the additional effort involved more time to convert to the new standards.

Avoiding Implementation Problems

The staggered conversion to IFRS may also introduce a lack of comparability among companies in a given industry; thus, the SEC may attempt to create transition procedures that would permit more companies to convert at the earlier date. The SEC would also revisit and evaluate the propriety of allowing foreign private issuers to use the three alternative presentation formats currently available to them (i.e., IFRS, U.S. GAAP, or other standard reconciled to U.S. GAAP). The SEC's stated goal throughout the conversion process is to protect investors and ease cross-border capital formation.

Effectiveness of IFRS Compared to U.S. GAAP

In general, IFRS is less developed than U.S. GAAP (e.g., treatment of insurance contracts, certain common control activities, recapitalizations, reorganizations, and ownership of noncontrolling minority shares) and allows more presentation options in certain areas that might reduce comparability. U.S. GAAP, on the other hand, does not have a comprehensive standard in other areas (e.g., revenue recognition, and property, plant and equipment). Therefore, less specific implementation guidance may increase auditor-client discrepancies concerning the accounting treatment of certain situations and may also diminish the predictability of litigation outcomes. The SEC is aware that this greater flexibility in implementation guidance may allow for a more accurate presentation of the economics behind a transaction and thus make it more transparent.

In its final report of August 2008 the SEC Committee on Improvements to Financial Reporting (CIFiR) wrote:

> Investors are likely to benefit from more emphasis on principles-based standards, since rules-based standards may provide a method, such as through

exceptions and bright-line tests, to avoid the accounting objectives underlying the standards. In other words, without the exercise of judgment, rules in the form of bright lines may result in a false consistency—that is, ostensibly uniform accounting for differing fact patterns. If properly implemented, "principles-based" standards should improve the information provided to investors while reducing investor concerns about "financial engineering" by companies using the rules to avoid accounting for the substance of a transaction.

Specific Differences between IFRS and U.S. GAAP

One of the main differences between U.S. GAAP and IFRS is that the latter is more principles-based than U.S. GAAP. U.S. GAAP tends to provide specific guidelines with many safe harbor provisions applicable to recording and reporting transactions, while IFRS emphasizes recording and reporting transactions according to their substance. Thus management will be required to use judgment to maximize the transparency of many transactions for which clear guidelines were provided by U.S. GAAP. To offset the additional risk this involves, more thorough disclosures will be advisable.

Examples of specific differences between IFRS and U.S. GAAP are IFRS acceptance of the revaluation of assets, its prohibition of the use of LIFO inventory valuation methods, and the elimination of the four clear-cut distinctions between operating leases and capital leases provided by U.S. GAAP. Differences also include the definition and recognition of revenue and expense, the resolution of which is ongoing. Further areas in which U.S. GAAP differs from IFRS are listed as follows:

- Accounting policies
- Contingencies
- Current and long-term liabilities
- Earnings per share
- Fair value
- Financial statement presentation
- Foreign currency translation
- Impairment
- Income taxes
- Interim statements
- Investments (long- and short-term)
- Leases
- Long-term or construction contracts
- Mergers and consolidations
- Pensions and other postretirement benefits
- Revenue recognition
- Segment reporting
- Stock-based compensation

- Stockholders' equity
- Tangible and intangible assets
- Valuation of inventories and other current assets

As a result of the changing nature of these items, web sites have been updated with additional current information (see "Resources on the Web" in this book). It is evident from this list that conversion to, or convergence with, IFRS will affect more than the accounting reporting process. It will affect tax reporting, internal controls, and the information technology systems used to report on, measure and monitor performance, as well as any stock-based remuneration.

Projected Role of the SEC in the Standard-Setting Process

Because the IASB would be responsive to input from interested parties (i.e., investors, issuers, regulators) worldwide, the influence of U.S. regulators (including the SEC) and market participants on the standard-setting process would diminish. The SEC may solely become a member of the IFRS Foundation "Monitoring Board," which monitors an independent, geographically diverse body of trustees that oversees the IASB. (See the IAFS Foundation, January 2009 Press Release.) The board must ensure the trustees properly discharge their duties, as the parties may have different national reporting requirements and goals and may attempt to unduly influence the IASB by partially adopting IFRS, or by interpreting the standards differently than other parties. The agility of the process to elaborate new standards may be diminished by the wide geographic dispersal and broad range of interests of the parties involved.

SEC-Proposed Roadmap Milestones

In its November 2008 Proposed Roadmap, the SEC listed a series of goals or "milestones" that must be achieved before it mandates the use of IFRS. Before this mandate, the SEC will consider:

1. Whether IFRS (a) are of high quality and sufficiently comprehensive, (b) are established under a robust independent process that includes consideration of alternative approaches, (c) will be promptly expanded as the need for additional standards arises, and (d) improve the accuracy and effectiveness of financial reporting relative to any standards they replace.

2. Whether the IASC (a) has a secure funding mechanism (b) that does not render it subject to the influence of the fund providers, and (c) that there is an effective monitoring group (e.g., board) to supervise the IASC and protect its independence.

3. Whether the IFRS Foundation, named the IASC Foundation up to March 1, 2010, develops an appropriate taxonomy that enables the SEC to develop adequate XBRL (eXtensible Business Reporting Language) tags to support its proposed requirement (May 2008) that all IFRS and U.S. GAAP financial reports be presented using XBRL for fiscal periods ending on or after December 31, 2010. In this regard, in April 2010, the IFRS Foundation released the following statement:

The International Accounting Standards Committee (IASC) Foundation today released the International Financial Reporting Standards (IFRS) Taxonomy 2010. The 2010 taxonomy is consistent with IFRSs and with the *IFRS for Small and Medium-Size Entities* (SMEs), and for the first time both have been integrated into a single taxonomy.

The IFRS Taxonomy 2010 is a translation of IFRSs as issued at 1 January 2010 into XBRL (eXtensible Business Reporting Language). XBRL is rapidly becoming the standard format for the electronic filing of financial information—particularly within jurisdictions reporting under IFRSs—because it facilitates simpler and faster filing and comparison of IFRS financial data by companies, regulators, investors, analysts, and other users of financial information.

4. Whether the SEC believes that the education and training of investors, preparers, auditors, regulators, and other parties affected by financial statements prepared using IFRS is sufficient to enable them to work with the new structure of these statements and other financial information.

5. Whether the experience of early IFRS adopters, allowed by the SEC to certain issuers that meet its criteria, reveals obstacles or advantages resulting from conversion. In addition, the SEC realizes that permitting early adoption by some companies will hinder comparability and is aware that this may create pressure to accelerate mandatory conversion.

SEC FEBRUARY 2010 RELEASE AND WORK PLAN

In 2010, the November 2008 Road Map was superseded by a February 2010 Release, which encourages continued convergence toward a single set of accounting standards and anticipates fewer differences as a result of the convergence project.

In addition, the SEC established a new, more comprehensive work plan that calls for sufficient transition time for users and preparers of financial statements and provides transparency of the required work to incorporate IFRS into the U.S. financial reporting system for U.S. issuers. This includes the scope, timeframe, and methodology for this transition.

1. Will the IFRS be of sufficiently high quality and be based on neutral principles that require consistent, comparable, relevant, and reliable information that is useful for investors, creditors, and others who make capital allocation decisions? Furthermore, are the standards supported by an infrastructure, ensuring a rigorous interpretation and application? This question leads to the following three concerns:

    a. *Comprehensiveness of IFRS*—IFRS does not have a long history that validates U.S. GAAP, which has been modified to respond to various scenarios with detailed guidance. A concern is that the benefits of this guidance will be lost. According to the Financial Accounting Foundation (FAF):

[W]hile it is perceived that IFRS provides financial statement preparers more discretion in application than U.S. GAAP, such additional discretion may not result in major differences in the application of IFRS by U.S. companies because the U.S. institutional framework plays a major role in shaping how companies would apply the discretion.

In response to this concern, the SEC has proposed the following:

    i. It will inventory areas where IFRS provides no guidance or less than U.S. GAAP.

    ii. It will analyze how specific situations in these areas are being handled by issuers, auditors, and investors.

    iii. It will then identify those areas in which additional IFRS guidance is required.

b. *Auditability and enforceability of IFRS*—There is concern regarding potential divergent applications of IFRS due to its principles-based nature, which would diminish the auditability and enforceability of these standards, thus possibly allowing for opportunistic accounting. In response to this concern, the SEC proposes the following:

    i. It will analyze the factors that may impair the general auditability and enforceability of IFRS.

    ii. It will analyze the factors that impair consistency in the audit of financial statements prepared using IFRS and in the enforcement of IFRS.

    iii. It will propose changes to improve the auditability, enforcement, and consistency of the application of IFRS.

c. *Comparability within and across jurisdictions*—There is concern that the lack of comprehensive standards that address multiple scenarios, as well as their potential impaired auditability may undermine the comparability of recording and financial reporting. Although more than 100 countries require or allow the use of IFRS, there are variations among them based on jurisdiction. Furthermore, the remedy of extensive footnotes places a burden on the users of financial statements to understand these footnotes.

The SEC proposes the following response to this concern:

    i. It will analyze the factors that impair comparability under IFRS on a global basis.

    ii. It will investigate situations where incomparability of IFRS financial statements exist and study how investors are currently dealing with these situations.

    iii. It will develop ways to improve global comparability of IFRS financial statements with the goal of providing maximum benefit to investors.

2. Will the standard-setting entity be adequately funded, and will its governance structure be such that it is accountable, independent, and

free of undue influences? The SEC's response to this concern is as follows:

a. *Oversight of the IASB by the IFRS Foundation*—The SEC believes that effective oversight of the IASB is essential to ensuring that the above factors safeguard and support the independence of the IASB. Therefore, the SEC will analyze and determine the extent to which the Monitoring Board is functioning to ensure such independence.

b. *Composition of the IFRS Foundation and the IASB*—The IFRS Foundation has approved amendments to its Constitution that:

   i. Emphasize its commitment to developing standards for investors.
   ii. Provide guidelines to ensure trustees' geographical diversity.
   iii. Provide guidelines to ensure IASB members' geographical diversity.
   iv. Increase the maximum number of IASB members to 16, with three part-time members, by July 2012.

   The SEC will study whether all IASB members should be full-time to minimize the potential for conflict of interest and whether it should have greater investor representation.

c. *Funding of the IFRS Foundation*—As of 2008, most funds are obtained from national standard-setting bodies and national capital market authorities, as opposed to small voluntary sources and major accounting firms. The SEC will evaluate whether the trustees' funding approach is appropriate, monitor whether voluntary funding from individual organizations continues to decline, and explore alternative funding procedures for funding from the United States.

d. *The IASB standard-setting process*—The SEC has stated that the IASB's process must emphasize an investor perspective and result in the timely development of new standards, which bear proof of the application of an objective approach in their development. The expected benefits of these standards are expected to outweigh their cost.

   The IASB promotes objectivity by opening its meetings to public observers and broadcasting over the Internet, making all materials, letters, and other discussion papers publicly available on the IASB web site, seeking the assistance of the IFRS Interpretations Committee, consulting with the IFRS Advisory Council concerning practical application and implementation issues on single projects, cooperating with national accounting standard-setters and other official bodies to promote the convergence of worldwide accounting standards, and making the IASB due process subject to the oversight of the Trustee Due Process Oversight Committee.

3. Although improved comparability is the most obvious advantage of adopting a single set of globally accepted high-quality standards, this benefit will not be realized unless investors are sufficiently informed and

educated regarding IFRS. In response, the SEC proposes to do the following:

   a. Analyze U.S. investors' current knowledge of IFRS.

   b. Understand how investors educate themselves regarding the historically frequent changes in reporting standards.

   c. Estimate the effort and time required to ensure that investors have adequate understanding of IFRS prior to mandatory conversion.

4. How will United States regulatory agencies, such as the SEC, as well as other parties who rely on U.S. GAAP financial statements, be affected by financial reports issued based on IFRS? This question encompasses the seven concerns listed below:

   a. The SEC will analyze the manner in which it currently fulfills its mission in relation to providing rules, interpretations and guidance, and determine how this will be affected by adopting IFRS. In addition, the SEC will analyze its approaches to the FASB, including the logistics and time involved.

   b. The SEC will study the impact of adopting IFRS on issuer compliance with industry regulatory requirements, and the impact on industry regulators.

   c. The SEC will study the impact of adopting IFRS on federal and state income tax reporting. If the current tax codes are not modified, this may create a significant increase in the number of book to tax differences. In addition, certain procedures, such as the use of LIFO inventory accounting, are not acceptable under IFRS. Because LIFO must be used for reporting to shareholders for tax purposes, companies would have to change to an inventory accounting method acceptable under IFRS.

   d. The SEC will address the problem of differences between certain legal standards and IFRS. For example, existing laws governing the payment of dividends and stock repurchases may be different than IFRS requirements.

   e. The SEC will address three concerns related to the PCAOB: (1) whether PCAOB standards should be converged with, or adopt, auditing standards issued by the International Accounting and Assurances Board (IAASB); (2) if IFRS provides less specific audit guidance than PCAOB; and (3) references in PCAOB audit standards to U.S. GAAP would need to be changed to refer to IFRS-related literature.

   f. The SEC will address the concern as to whether certain investment companies and other regulated entities, such as broker-dealers, should be exempt, as well as the concern that there is sufficient time for the IASB and the SEC to develop an appropriate financial reporting model.

   g. Because the SEC does not govern private companies, these companies will incur a sudden great cost if they go public. Furthermore, a dual-standard system might impair the effectiveness of U.S. capital markets. Even if both private and public companies are required to adopt IFRS, there is a different set of IFRS for small- and medium-sized entities that would still leave a dual-standard system in place.

5. Though mitigated by the ongoing convergence process between IASB and U.S. GAAP, there is concern over the impact of conversion on large and small companies in terms of cost, changes to contractual arrangements, corporate governance, litigation contingencies, and other logistical changes involved in converting the entire U.S. financial reporting system to IFRS. This question encompasses the four areas of concern listed below, which the SEC will address in its work plan:

   a. *Impact on issuers' accounting systems, controls, and procedures*—Companies will need to survey all accounting policies because IFRS requires that all similar transactions in a company and its affiliates be accounted for in a similar manner. In addition, companies will have to supplement the more lax IFRS requirements with more detailed company policies. During the transition period, companies may have to maintain dual sets of books, especially for reporting purposes under section 404 of the Sarbanes-Oxley Act of 2002 (SOX). However, there should be sufficient lead time to make all of these changes.

   b. *Impact on existing contracts*—Many existing contract stipulations require the use of U.S. GAAP for reporting contract-related data and making contract-related calculations.

   c. *Impact on corporate governance*—SOX requires that at least one member of the audit financial committee have sufficient financial expertise. At this early stage of the process, it may be difficult for a large number of companies to each find an audit financial committee member who is an expert on IFRS.

   d. *Impact on smaller issuers versus larger issuers*—There are varying views on the impact of IFRS on large as opposed to small companies. Some expect substantially higher transition costs for small companies, while others anticipate that affected transactions will be few and of the type that would be subject to greater study under U.S. GAAP.

6. How will the conversion to IFRS affect the education and training of professionals involved in the financial reporting process, including investors, preparers, auditors, regulators and educators? Two aspects of this concern follow:

   a. *Education and training*—Because the training and education of accountants, lawyers, and other specialists in the United States currently concentrate on U.S. GAAP, the following professionals will require accelerated training in IFRS:

      i. Investors.

      ii. Issuers' accounting, audit, and investor relations personnel, as well as boards of directors and audit committee members.

iii. Specialists, such as actuaries and valuation experts, who are often hired by issuers to assist in the evaluation of certain assets and liabilities for financial reporting purposes.
iv. Attorneys who often advise clients on disclosures under securities laws and provide legal representation to external auditors.
v. External auditors.
vi. Regulators, such as SEC and PCAOB staff members, as well the staff of other regulatory agencies.
vii. State licensing bodies, professional associations, and industry groups that would need to integrate IFRS into their training and certification programs (e.g., the Uniform CPA Examination).
viii. Colleges and universities that would integrate IFRS into their curriculums. It would be costly for educators to switch to IFRS both in terms of training and of the greater need for judgment in its less prescriptive, principles-based approach. This problem would be particularly exacerbated if private companies continue to use U.S. GAAP, while public companies use iGAAP.

b. *Impairment of audit firms' capacity to audit and audit costs*—The difficulty of obtaining personnel trained in IFRS may limit the audit capacity of small audit firms as compared to large firms, because large firms are more likely to have performed IFRS audits abroad and thus have access to IFRS-trained personnel in their overseas offices. In addition, the existence of fewer specific guidelines in IFRS may increase internal and external audit costs because of the need for additional exercise and evaluation in judgment.

GENERAL CONCEPTUAL FRAMEWORK

As of May 2010, the IASB and the FASB are working on the convergence of the IASB's 2001 conceptual framework, as described in the MoU of 2006. The overall objective is to create a sound foundation for future accounting standards that are principles-based, internally consistent, and internationally converged. The project is divided into eight phases titled below, with phases A to D currently being developed. The topics of each phase are:

A. Objectives and qualitative characteristics
B. Definitions of elements, recognition, and derecognition
C. Measurement
D. Reporting entity concept
E. Boundaries of financial reporting, and presentation and disclosure
F. Purpose and status of the framework
G. Application of the framework to not-for-profit entities
H. Remaining issues

This Framework also serves as a guide to assist in resolving questions not addressed in iGAAP. The specific goals of the Framework are to:

- Define the objective of financial statements;
- Identify the qualitative characteristics that make information in financial statements useful;
- Define the basic elements of financial statements and the concepts for recognizing and measuring them in financial statements; and
- Provides concepts of capital maintenance.

The Framework recognizes that users of financial statements are present and potential investors, employees, lenders, suppliers and other trade creditors, customers, governments and their agencies, and the general public. It concludes that because investors are providers of risk capital to the entity, financial statements that meet their needs will also meet most of the general financial information needs of other users. It recognizes that all of these user groups are interested in the ability of an entity to generate cash and cash equivalents and in the timing and certainty of those future cash flows. It also identifies two basic assumptions on which financial statements are based:

1. *Accrual basis*—Transactions are recognized when they occur rather than when cash is exchanged.
2. *Going concern basis*—Assumes an entity will last indefinitely, and requires disclosure when this assumption is inappropriate.

It further proposes that financial statements should be:
- Understandable by users who have a reasonable knowledge of business.
- Relevant as helps users evaluate past, ongoing, and future events and helps correct previous evaluations. Both materiality and timeliness are important. An item is material if its omission or misstatement might influence the opinion of the user of the financial statements.
- Reliable as it should be free of material error. Because making financial statements relevantly timely usually requires the use of estimates, there can be a conflict between reliability and relevance. This conflict should be resolved in a neutral manner, using prudence to present a financial statement profile that is neither unrealistically favorable nor unfavorable, as well as using appropriate disclosures. In the case of both relevance and reliability, there should be a reasonable balance between the cost of presenting information and its value to users.
- Comparable through the use of accounting policy disclosures.

The Framework states that the financial statement elements related to financial position (balance sheet) are assets, liabilities, and equity; that the elements related to performance (income statement) are income and expenses; and that the cash flow statement contains income statement elements and changes in balance sheet elements. It defines assets, liabilities, equity, income, and expenses; and states when they should be recognized.

The Framework recognizes that four measurement bases exist:

1. Historical cost
2. Current cost

3. Net realizable value (settlement value)
4. Discounted present value

It further states that individual IFRS and interpretations indicate which basis to use in specific circumstances.

Because development of the Framework is an ongoing process, the definitions and recognition triggers in the original document are being modified. For further developments on the Framework, go to http://www.iasplus.com/standard/framewk.htm.

PROPOSED FINANCIAL STATEMENT PRESENTATION

IAS 1, *Presentation of Financial Statements*, requires the presentation of four financial statements, in addition to notes to the financial statements explaining the accounting policies applied as well as other appropriate explanations. In addition, IAS 1 has mostly been aligned with ASC 220, *Comprehensive Income* (FAS-130, *Reporting Comprehensive Income*). The IASB has changed the names of three of the four required financial statements as follows:

U.S. GAAP	iGAAP
Income statement	Statement of comprehensive income
Balance sheet	Statement of financial position
Cash flow statement	Cash flow statement
Statement of stockholders' equity	Statement of changes in equity

Concerning their proposed financial statement presentation format, the FASB and IASB included the following in a November 5, 2009, joint statement reaffirming their commitment to the 2006 MoU:

> The boards completed their deliberations on Phase A in December 2005. In their Phase B discussions, the boards developed two core principles for financial statement presentation based on the objectives of financial reporting and the input the boards received from users of financial statements and from members of their advisory groups. Those proposed principles state that (a) information should be presented in the financial statements in a manner that portrays a cohesive financial picture of an entity's activities, and (b) disaggregates information so that it is useful in predicting an entity's future cash flows.

In a discussion paper issued October 2008, a third goal was added, namely, that financial statements should help users assess an entity's liquidity and financial flexibility.

Disaggregation

The disaggregation goal requires that the presentation of assets, liabilities, revenues, expenses, and cash flows be shown separately according to their function, such as business operations, investing, and financing. Furthermore, assets and liabilities would be subclassified according to whether they are short-term or long-term and should be further subdivided according to their measurement basis. Revenues and cash flows would be classified according to their function. Expenses may be classified according to their function, such as cost of sales or selling; or according to their nature, such as food and beverage expense, labor, or depreciation. Note that an exception is made for those cases in which a listing of current assets and noncurrent assets in the order of liquidity is more reliable and relevant. In this regard, IAS 1 states:

> Only if a presentation based on liquidity provides information that is reliable and more relevant may the current/noncurrent split be omitted. [IAS 1.60] In either case, if an asset (liability) category combines amounts that will be received (settled) after 12 months with assets (liabilities) that will be received (settled) within 12 months, note disclosure is required that separates the longer-term amounts from the 12-month amounts. [IAS 1.61]

Cohesiveness

The cohesiveness goal requires that accounts be grouped into the same categories on all statements. They would be grouped in the same manner they are grouped in the cash flow statement—operating, investing, financing, and equity. Nevertheless, as the dominant statement, it is their classification in the statement of financial position that dictates the cash flow group in which asset-related cash flows would be included. For example, if some items that are classified as investing assets in the cash flow statement under U.S. GAAP are classified as operating assets in the statement of financial position under IFRS, then their related cash flows would likewise be classified as operating cash flows, rather than investing cash flows, in the cash flow statement under IFRS.

The parallels among these three statements are demonstrated as follows:

Statement of Financial Position	Statement of Comprehensive Income	Statement of Cash Flows
Business—Operating assets and liabilities	Business—Operating income and expenses	Business—Operating cash flows
Business—Investing assets and liabilities	Investing—Income and expenses	Investing—Cash flows
Financing—Assets and liabilities	Financing—Income and expenses, not shown net	Financing—Cash flows, not shown net
Income taxes—Benefits, deferred and payable	Income taxes—Not related to discontinued operations	Income taxes—Cash paid
Discontinued operations—Assets and liabilities	Discontinued operations and related taxes	Discontinued operations—Cash flows
Equity—Invested capital, Retained earnings, and other comprehensive income	Other comprehensive income and related taxes	Equity—Cash flows

The Statement of Changes in Equity would not be affected by the new groupings and would be about the same as the Statement of Stockholders' Equity under U.S. GAAP.

Concerning this order of presentation, the IASB, in a snapshot of its October 2008 Disclosure Paper provided the following information:

- All entities applying IFRS or U.S. GAAP would present each of the sections and categories shown in the table above.
- Each entity would decide on the order of the sections and categories, but would use the same order in each individual statement.
- Each entity would decide how to classify its assets and liabilities into the sections and categories, on the basis of how an item is used (the 'management approach'). The entity would disclose why it chose those classifications.
- All entities would present a single statement of comprehensive income; the boards would eliminate the option to present the same information split between two statements. The single statement of comprehensive income would still include a subtotal for net income or profit or loss and a separate section for other comprehensive income. The proposed format would not change existing requirements that 'recycle' items in specified circumstances from other comprehensive income to net income or profit or loss.

Other Financial Statement Characteristics

Business activities are those that indicate how a business uses capital to create value; and financing activities indicate how it obtains that capital. The cash flow statement would have to be prepared using the direct method rather than the indirect method. The notes to the financial statements would include a schedule to reconcile cash flows to comprehensive income. The reconciliation would show cash transactions, accrual transactions, and changes in values due to remeasurements based on fair value. An entity would be required to disclose its accounting policies, including a description of how and why it chose to classify its assets and liabilities in particular sections of the financial statements. It should also provide a description of its business activities to assist readers in forming conclusions concerning management. A list of all long-term contractual asset and liability maturities, including any probable realization and settlement dates that are materially different from contractual dates, will also be required.

SAMPLE OF PROPOSED IFRS FINANCIAL STATEMENTS

In October 2008, the IASB published a discussion paper, "Preliminary Views on Financial Statement Presentation." This Discussion Paper does not apply to not-for-profit entities, entities to which the IASB's forthcoming IFRS for private entities applies, and nonpublic entities per U.S. GAAP. The nonbinding presentation format presented in this discussion framework was modified slightly to better conform to a restaurant format and is presented in Exhibits 27-3 through 27-7 to give a preliminary indication of how the goals mentioned above might be applied to financial statements prepared in accordance with IFRS.

Two noteworthy differences in these financial statements are that (1) the direct method must be used to calculate operating cash flow, and (2) a new statement, "Reconciliation of Cash Flows to Comprehensive Income," has been added.

Exhibit 27-3: ABC Restaurant's Financial Statements (Proposed format)

STATEMENT OF COMPREHENSIVE INCOME		
	For the year ended 31 December	
	2010	2009
BUSINESS		
Operating		
Sales - ABC Restaurants	2,790,080	2,591,400
Sales - DEF Restaurants	697,520	647,850
Total revenue	3,487,600	3,239,250
Cost of food sold		
Food consumed	(1,046,280)	(971,775)
Loss on unsellable inventory	(29,000)	(9,500)
Total cost of food sold	(1,075,280)	(981,275)
Gross profit	2,412,320	2,257,975
Other food-production-related expenses		
Wages, salaries, and benefits	(697,520)	(647,850)
Other	(196,625)	(199,478)
Total other food-production-related expenses	(894,145)	(847,328)
Income after food-production-related expenses	1,518,175	1,410,647
Selling expenses		
Advertising	(60,000)	(50,000)
Wages, salaries, and benefits	(56,700)	(52,500)
Bad debt	(23,068)	(15,034)
Other	(13,500)	(12,500)
Total selling expenses	(153,268)	(130,034)
General and administrative expenses		
Wages, salaries, and benefits	(321,300)	(297,500)
Depreciation	(59,820)	(58,500)
Pension	(51,975)	(47,250)
Share-based remuneration	(22,023)	(17,000)
Interest on lease liability	(23,303)	(24,350)
Other	(15,768)	(14,600)
Total general and administrative expenses	(494,189)	(459,200)
Income before other operating items	870,718	821,413
Miscellaneous operating income (expense)		
Share of profit of associate A	23,760	22,000
Gain on disposal of property, plant and equipment	22,650	-
Realized gain on cash flow hedge	3,996	3,700
Loss on sale of receivables	(4,987)	(2,025)
Impairment loss on goodwill		(35,033)
Total miscellaneous operating income (expense)	45,419	(11,358)
Total operating income	916,137	810,055

(Continued)

Source: Adapted from IASB, Preliminary Views on Financial Statement Presentation, October 2008.

Chapter 27: International Financial Reporting Standards

STATEMENT OF COMPREHENSIVE INCOME (Continuation)		
	\multicolumn{2}{c}{For the year ended 31 December}
	2010	2009
Investing		
Dividend income	54,000	50,000
Realized gain on available-for-sale securities	18,250	7,500
Share of profit of associate B	7,500	3,250
Total investing income	79,750	60,750
TOTAL BUSINESS INCOME	995,887	870,805
FINANCING		
Interest income on cash	8,619	5,500
Total financing asset income	8,619	5,500
Interest expense	(111,352)	(110,250)
Total financing liability expense	(111,352)	(110,250)
TOTAL NET FINANCING EXPENSE	(102,733)	(104,750)
Profit from continuing operations before taxes and other comprehensive income	893,154	766,055
INCOME TAXES		
Income tax expense	(333,625)	(295,266)
Net profit from continuing operations	559,529	470,789
DISCONTINUED OPERATIONS		
Loss on discontinued operations	(32,400)	(35,000)
Tax benefit	11,340	12,250
NET LOSS FROM DISCONTINUED OPERATIONS	(21,060)	(22,750)
NET PROFIT	538,469	448,039
OTHER COMPREHENSIVE INCOME (after tax)		
Unrealized gain on available-for-sale securities (investing)	17,193	15,275
Revaluation surplus (operating)	3,653	-
Foreign currency translation adjust-consolidated subsidiary	2,094	(1,492)
Unrealized gain on cash flow hedge (operating)	1,825	1,690
Foreign currency translation adjust-associate A (operating)	(1,404)	(1,300)
TOTAL OTHER COMPREHENSIVE INCOME	23,361	14,173
TOTAL COMPREHENSIVE INCOME	561,830	462,212
Basic earnings per share	7.07	6.14
Diluted earnings per share	6.85	5.96

Exhibit 27-4: ABC Restaurant's Financial Statements (Proposed format)

STATEMENT OF FINANCIAL POSITION		
	\multicolumn{2}{c}{As at December 31}	
	2010	2009
BUSINESS		
Operating		
Accounts receivable, trade	945,678	541,375
Less allowance for doubtful accounts	(23,642)	(13,534)
Accounts receivable, net	922,036	527,841
Inventory	679,474	767,102
Prepaid advertising•	80,000	75,000
Foreign exchange contracts—cash flow hedge	6,552	3,150
Total short-term assets	1,688,062	1,373,093
Property, plant and equipment•	5,112,700	5,088,500
Less accumulated depreciation	(2,267,620)	(2,023,500)
Property, plant and equipment, net	2,845,080	3,065,000
Investment in associate A	261,600	240,000
Goodwill	154,967	154,967
Other intangible assets	35,000	35,000
Total long-term assets	3,296,647	3,494,967
Accounts payable, trade	(612,556)	(505,000)
Advances from customers	(182,000)	(425,000)
Wages payable•	(173,000)	(200,000)
Share-based remuneration liability	(39,586)	(21,165)
Current portion of lease liability	(35,175)	(33,500)
Interest payable on lease liability	(14,825)	(16,500)
Total short-term liabilities	(1,057,142)	(1,201,165)
Accrued pension liability	(293,250)	(529,500)
Lease liability (excluding current portion)•	(261,325)	(296,500)
Other long-term liabilities	(33,488)	(16,100)
Total long-term liabilities	(588,063)	(842,100)
Net operating assets	3,339,504	2,824,795
Investing		
Available-for-sale financial assets (short term)	473,600	485,000
Investment in associate B (long-term)	46,750	39,250
Total investing assets	520,350	524,250
NET BUSINESS ASSETS	3,859,854	3,349,045

(Continued)

Source: Adapted from IASB, Preliminary Views on Financial Statement Presentation, October 2008.

STATEMENT OF FINANCIAL POSITION (Continuation)

	As at December 31	
	2010	2009
FINANCING		
Financing assets		
Cash	1,174,102	861,941
Total financing assets	1,174,102	861,941
Financing liabilities		
Short-term borrowings	(562,000)	(400,000)
Interest payable	(140,401)	(112,563)
Dividends payable	(20,000)	(20,000)
Total short-term financing liabilities	(722,401)	(532,563)
Long-term borrowings	(2,050,000)	(2,050,000)
Total financing liabilities	(2,772,401)	(2,582,563)
NET FINANCING LIABILITIES	(1,598,299)	(1,720,622)
DISCONTINUED OPERATIONS		
Assets held for sale	856,832	876,650
Liabilities related to assets held for sale	(400,000)	(400,000)
NET ASSETS HELD FOR SALE	456,832	476,650
INCOME TAXES		
Short-term		
Deferred tax asset	4,426	8,907
Income taxes payable	(72,514)	(63,679)
Long-term•		
Deferred tax asset	39,833	80,160
NET INCOME TAX ASSET (LIABILITY)	(28,255)	25,388
NET ASSETS	2,690,132	2,130,461
EQUITY		
Share capital	(1,427,240)	(1,343,000)
Retained earnings	(1,100,358)	(648,289)
Accumulated other comprehensive income, net	(162,534)	(139,173)
TOTAL EQUITY	(2,690,132)	(2,130,462)

Total short-term assets	4,197,021	3,605,591
Total long-term assets	3,383,231	3,614,377
Total assets	7,580,252	7,219,968
Total short-term liabilities	(2,252,057)	(2,197,406)
Total long-term liabilities	(2,638,063)	(2,892,100)
Total liabilities	(4,890,120)	(5,089,506)

Exhibit 27-5: ABC Restaurant's Financial Statements (Proposed format)

STATEMENT OF CASH FLOWS		
	For the year ended 31 December	
	2010	2009
BUSINESS		
Operating		
Cash received in ABC Restaurants	2,108,754	1,928,798
Cash received in CDF Restaurants	703,988	643,275
Total cash collected from customers	2,812,742	2,572,073
Cash paid for food		
Food purchases	(935,544)	(785,000)
Total cash paid for food	(935,544)	(785,000)
Cash paid for other food-production-related activities		
Wages, salaries, and benefits	(584,895)	(591,216)
Other	(164,971)	(176,597)
Total cash paid for other food-production-related expenses	(749,866)	(767,813)
Cash paid for selling activities		
Advertising	(65,000)	(75,000)
Wages, salaries, and benefits	(58,655)	(55,453)
Other	(13,500)	(12,500)
Total cash paid for selling activities	(137,155)	(142,953)
Cash paid for general and administrative activities		
Wages, salaries, and benefits	(332,379)	(314,234)
Contributions to pension plan	(170,100)	(157,500)
Capital expenditures	(54,000)	(50,000)
Lease payments	(50,000)	-
Settlement of share-based remuneration	(3,602)	(3,335)
Other	(21,438)	(19,850)
Total cash paid for general and administrative activities	(631,519)	(544,919)
Cash flow before other operating activities	358,658	331,388
Cash from other operating activities		
Disposal of property, plant and equipment	37,650	
Investment in associate A		(120,000)
Sale of receivable	8,000	10,000
Settlement of cash flow hedge	3,402	3,150
Total cash received (paid) for other operating activities	49,052	(106,850)
Net cash from operating activities	**407,710**	**224,538**

(continued)

Source: Adapted from IASB, Preliminary Views on Financial Statement Presentation, October 2008.

STATEMENT OF CASH FLOWS (Continuation)		
	For the year ended 31 December	
	2010	2009
Investing		
Purchase of available-for-sale financial assets		(130,000)
Sale of available-for-sale financial assets	56,100	51,000
Dividends received	54,000	50,000
Net cash from investing activities	110,100	(29,000)
NET CASH FROM BUSINESS ACTIVITIES	517,810	195,538
FINANCING		
Interest received on cash	8,619	5,500
Total cash from financing assets	8,619	5,500
Proceeds from issue of short-term debt	162,000	150,000
Proceeds from issue of long-term debt	-	250,000
Interest paid	(83,514)	(82,688)
Dividends paid	(86,400)	(80,000)
Total cash from financing liabilities	(7,914)	237,312
NET CASH FROM FINANCING ACTIVITIES	705	242,812
Change in cash from continuing operations before taxes and equity	518,515	438,350
INCOME TAXES		
Cash taxes paid	(281,221)	(193,786)
Change in cash before discontinued operations and equity	237,294	244,564
DISCONTINUED OPERATIONS		
Cash paid from discontinued operations	(12,582)	(11,650)
NET CASH FROM DISCONTINUED OPERATIONS	(12,582)	(11,650)
Change in cash before equity	224,712	232,914
EQUITY		
Proceeds from reissue of treasury stock	84,240	78,000
NET CASH FROM EQUITY	84,240	78,000
Effect of foreign exchange rates on cash	3,209	1,027
CHANGE IN CASH	312,161	311,941
Beginning cash	861,941	550,000
Ending cash	1,174,102	861,941

Exhibit 27-6: ABC Restaurant's Financial Statements (Proposed format)

			STATEMENT OF CHANGES IN EQUITY					
	Share capital	Retained earnings	Foreign currency translation adjustment-consolidated subsidiary	Foreign currency translation adjustment—associate A	Revaluation surplus	Unrealized gain on cash flow hedge	Unrealized gain on available-for-sale financial assets	Total equity
Balance at 31 Dec. 2008	1,265,000	280,250	50,200	37,000	800	31,000	6,000	1,670,250
Issue of share capital	78,000							78,000
Dividends		(80,000)						(80,000)
Total comprehensive income		448,039	(1,492)	(1,300)		1,690	15,275	462,212
Balance at 31 Dec. 2009	1,343,000	648,289	48,708	35,700	800	32,690	21,275	2,130,462
Issue of share capital	84,240							84,240
Dividends		(86,400)						(86,400)
Total comprehensive income		538,469	2,094	(1,404)	3,653	1,825	17,193	561,830
Balance at 31 Dec. 2010	1,427,240	1,100,358	50,802	34,296	4,453	34,515	38,468	2,690,132

Source: Adapted from IASB, Preliminary Views on Financial Statement Presentation, October 2008.

Exhibit 27-7: ABC Restaurant's Financial Statements (Proposed format)

		RECONCILIATION OF CASH FLOWS TO COMPREHENSIVE INCOME					
		For the year ended 31 December 2009					
A	B	C	D	E	F	G	
		Changes in Assets and Liabilities, Excluding Transactions with Owners					
		Not from Remeasurements	From Remeasurements		Statement of Comprehensive Income		
Caption in Statement of Cash Flows	Cash Flows	Accruals, Allocations, and Other	Recurring Valuation Adjustments	All Other	Comprehensive Income (B + C + D + E)	Caption in Statement of Comprehensive Income	
BUSINESS						**BUSINESS**	
Operating						**Operating**	
Cash received from ABC Restaurants	1,928,798	662,602			2,591,400	Sales - ABC Restaurants	
Cash received from DEF Restaurants customers	643,275	4,575			647,850	Sales - DEF Restaurants	
Total cash collected from customers	2,572,073	667,177			3,239,250	Total revenue	
Cash paid for food						Cost of food sold	
Food	(785,000)	(165,922)	6,000		(944,922)	Food	
other		(26,853)			(26,853)	Change in inventory	
				(9,500)	(9,500)	Loss on unsellable inventory	
Total cash paid for food	(785,000)	(192,775)	6,000	(9,500)	(981,275)	Total cost of food sold	
Cash paid for other food-production-related activities						Cost of food sold	
Wages, salaries, benefits	(591,216)	(56,634)			(647,850)	Wages, salaries, benefits	
other	(176,597)	(22,881)			(199,478)	Other	
Total cash paid for food	(767,813)	(79,515)	0	0	(847,328)	Total other food-production-related expenses	

(Continued)

Source: Adapted from IASB, Preliminary Views on Financial Statement Presentation, October 2008.

Chapter 27: International Financial Reporting Standards

RECONCILIATION OF CASH FLOWS TO COMPREHENSIVE INCOME (Continuation)
For the year ended 31 December 2009

A	B	C	D	E	F	G
		Changes in Assets and Liabilities, Excluding Transactions with Owners				
		Not from Remeasurements	From Remeasurements		Statement of Comprehensive Income	
Caption in Statement of Cash Flows	Cash Flows	Accruals, Allocations, and Other	Recurring Valuation Adjustments	All Other	Comprehensive Income (B + C + D + E)	Caption in Statement of Comprehensive Income
Cash paid for selling activities						**Selling expenses**
Advertising	(75,000)	25,000			(50,000)	Advertising
Wages, salaries, benefits	(55,453)	2,953			(52,500)	Wages, salaries, benefits
		(15,034)			(15,034)	Bad debt
Other	(12,500)				(12,500)	Other
Total cash paid for selling activities	(142,953)	12,919			(130,034)	Total selling expenses
Cash paid for general and administrative activities						**General and administrative expenses**
Wages, salaries, & benefits	(314,234)	16,734			(297,500)	Wages, salaries, and benefits
Contributions to pension plan	(157,500)	104,250	6,000		(47,250)	Pension
Capital expenditures	(50,000)	50,000				
		(58,500)			(58,500)	Depreciation
Settlement of share-based	(3,335)	(8,665)	(5,000)		(17,000)	Share-based remuneration
Lease payments		(16,500)			(16,500)	Interest on lease liability
Other	(19,850)	(2,600)			(22,450)	Other
Total cash paid for general and administrative activities	(544,919)	84,719	1,000		(459,200)	Total general and administrative expenses

(Continued)

RECONCILIATION OF CASH FLOWS TO COMPREHENSIVE INCOME (Continuation)
For the year ended 31 December 2009

A	B	C	D	E	F	G
		Changes in Assets and Liabilities, Excluding Transactions with Owners				
		Not from Remeasurements	From Remeasurements		Statement of Comprehensive Income	
Caption in Statement of Cash Flows	Cash Flows	Accruals, Allocations, and Other	Recurring Valuation Adjustments	All Other	Comprehensive Income (B + C + D + E)	Caption in Statement of Comprehensive Income
Cash flow before other operating activities	331,388	492,525	7,000	(9,500)	821,413	Income before other operating items
Cash from other operating activities						Other operating income (expense)
Investment in associate A	(120,000)	120,000		22,000	22,000	Share of profit of associate A
Sale of receivable	10,000	(10,000)		(2,025)	(2,025)	Loss on sale of receivable
Settlement of cash flow hedge	3,150	(550)	1,100		3,700	Realized gain on cash flow hedge
				(35,033)	(35,033)	Impairment loss on goodwill
Total cash paid for other operating activities	(106,850)	109,450	1,100	(15,058)	(11,358)	Total other operating income
Net cash from operating activities	224,538	601,975	8,100	(24,558)	810,055	**Total operating income**
Investing						**Investing**
Purchase of available-for-sale financial assets	(130,000)	130,000				
Sale of available-for-sale financial assets	51,000	(43,500)			7,500	Realized gain on available-for-sale financial assets
Dividends received	50,000				50,000	Dividend income
				3,250	3,250	Share of profit of associate B
Net cash from investing activities	(29,000)	86,500		3,250	60,750	**Total investing income**
NET CASH FROM BUSINESS ACTIVITIES	195,538	688,475	8,100	(21,308)	870,805	**TOTAL BUSINESS INCOME**

(Continued)

RECONCILIATION OF CASH FLOWS TO COMPREHENSIVE INCOME (Continuation)
For the year ended 31 December 2009

A	B	C	D	E	F	G
		Changes in Assets and Liabilities, Excluding Transactions with Owners			Statement of Comprehensive Income	
		Not from Remeasurements	From Remeasurements			
Caption in Statement of Cash Flows	Cash Flows	Accruals, Allocations, and Other	Recurring Valuation Adjustments	All Other	Comprehensive Income (B + C + D + E)	Caption in Statement of Comprehensive Income
FINANCING						**FINANCING**
Interest received on cash	5,500				5,500	Interest income on cash
Total cash from financing assets	5,500				5,500	Total financing asset income
Proceeds from issue of short-term debt	150,000	(150,000)				
Proceeds from issue of long-term debt	250,000	(250,000)				
Interest paid	(82,688)	(27,563)			(110,251)	Interest expense
Dividends paid	(80,000)	80,000				
Total cash from financing liabilities	237,312	(347,563)			(110,250)	Total financing liability expense
NET CASH FROM FINANCING ACTIVITIES	242,812	(347,563)			(104,751)	**TOTAL NET FINANCING EXPENSE**
Change in cash from continuing operations before taxes and equity	438,350	340,912	8,100	(21,308)	766,054	Profit from continuing operations before taxes and other comprehensive income

(Continued)

RECONCILIATION OF CASH FLOWS TO COMPREHENSIVE INCOME (Continuation)
For the year ended 31 December 2009

A	B	C	D	E	F	G
		Changes in Assets and Liabilities, Excluding Transactions with Owners			Statement of Comprehensive Income	
		Not from Remeasurements	From Remeasurements			
Caption in Statement of Cash Flows	Cash Flows	Accruals, Allocations, and Other	Recurring Valuation Adjustments	All Other	Comprehensive Income (B + C + D + E)	Caption in Statement of Comprehensive Income
INCOME TAXES						**INCOME TAXES**
Cash taxes paid	(193,786)	(101,480)			(295,266)	Income tax expense
Change in cash before discontinued operations and equity	244,564	239,432	8,100	(21,308)	470,788	Net profit from continuing operations
DISCONTINUED OPERATIONS						**DISCONTINUED OPERATIONS**
Cash paid from discontinued operations	(11,650)		(23,350)		(35,000)	Loss on discontinued operations
		12,250			12,250	Tax benefit
NET CASH FROM DISCONTINUED OPERATIONS	(11,650)	12,250	(23,350)		(22,750)	**NET LOSS FROM DISCONTINUED OPERATIONS**
Change in cash before equity	232,914	251,682	8,100	(44,658)	448,038	**NET PROFIT**
						OTHER COMPREHENSIVE INCOME (after tax)
			15,275		15,275	Unrealized gain on available-for-sale securities
			1,690		1,690	Unrealized gain on cash flow hedge
				(1,492)	(1,492)	Foreign currency translation adjust - consolidated subsidiary
				(1,300)	(1,300)	Foreign currency translation adjust—associate A
						TOTAL OTHER COMPREHENSIVE
			16,965	(2,792)	14,173	**INCOME**
Change in cash before equity	232,914	251,682	25,065	(47,450)	462,211	**TOTAL COMPREHENSIVE INCOME**

CONVERSION PREPARATION CHECKLIST

If the SEC mandates IFRS financial statements for 2015, companies would have to present IFRS financial statements for the two years prior, 2013 and 2014. This does not leave much time to prepare for this eventuality. The experience of companies in countries where IFRS has been mandated has revealed that beginning this process late raises costs considerably. Hospitality companies should, therefore, begin their preparations now. Below is a checklist of some of the factors involved, revealing the potential complexity of the transition from U.S. GAAP to iGAAP.

1. Plan for conversion to IFRS
   - Has an IFRS transition assessment been performed?
   - Has a timeline been created of steps to be taken?
   - Has an estimate of the required resources been made?
   - Has a budget been made for the acquisition of these resources as well as for personnel and other costs of conversion?
   - Is there a need for an initial temporary parallel reporting system?
   - Have all affected departments, such as information technology, been brought into the planning process?
   - Are both the immediate and longer-term impacts of conversion being taken into account—the impact on current and planned changes?
   - Is there a system in place to maintain currency with evolving IFRS standards?
2. Attitude towards conversion
   - Is this conversion regarded as an opportunity to review and improve strategic management and operational policies?
   - Are the board of directors, audit committee and compensation committee working together to provide information that will enable management to make better decisions?
   - Has management been made aware of the fact that some specific accounting guidelines under U.S. GAAP will no longer exist under IFRS?
   - Is management aware of the risks implicit in such a broad-based conversion of accounting processes and reporting, and are these risks being addressed?
3. Communication within the company
   - Have potential changes been communicated to all parties within the organization?
   - Are affected employees being educated concerning their new roles?
   - Have employees been informed of the potential impact on employee compensation?
4. Impact of conversion on external stakeholders
   - What is the impact on tax and regulatory reports?
   - What is the impact on loan, lease, and other financing covenants?
   - What is the impact on subsidiaries' reports?
   - What are the implications with regard to SOX?
   - Are external auditors being brought into the conversion process?

Cost versus Benefits of Conversion

For large multinational companies, conversion to IFRS is a cost benefit trade-off, the benefit being compatibility with international subsidiaries, hence lower reconciliation costs. This cost saving would not apply to nonpublic subsidiaries that would probably be reporting under some form of local accounting standards that would require reconciliation with IFRS. U.S. national companies will not enjoy the benefits of compatibility. A less important benefit from the financial perspective would be the increased comparability with international companies in the same industry. In addition, increased demand from international investors who understand IFRS better than U.S. GAAP might be a factor in raising the market value of companies' shares. Seven possible non-SEC-sanctioned outcomes of the contest between U.S. GAAP and IFRS in the United States and a more detailed examination of the costs and benefits of conversion are discussed in a paper titled "Global Accounting Convergence and the Potential Adoption of IFRS by the United States: An Analysis of Economic and Policy Factors," which can be found at http://papers.ssrn.com/sol3/papers.cfm?abstract_id=1357331.

Additional Guidance

Companies that find themselves bereft of guidance with regard to a specific reporting situation should refer to IAS 8, *Accounting Policies, Changes in Accounting Estimates and Errors*. This standard ranks the authorities that should be used in selecting a reporting procedure when there is no specific IFRS or Interpretation that applies. In these cases, management should:

- Refer to IFRS or Interpretations applicable to similar situations
- Refer to the IASB's Conceptual Framework
- Refer to statements by other authoritative standard-setting entities
- Refer to other accounting literature
- Refer to industry practices

iGAAP INFORMATION SOURCES

As of May 2010, iGAAP included the following:

- 41 IAS (issued by the IASC) that have been adopted by the IASB or have been superseded by IFRS
- 9 IFRS issued by the IASB
- 19 Interpretations issued by the IFRS Interpretations Committee (IFIC)
- 33 Interpretations issued by the Standing Interpretations Committee (SIC)

For additional information on iGAAP developments, see www.iasb.org/IFRSs/IFRS.htm.

APPENDIX 1

Appendix 1

Table A-1 Future Value of $1 = T1\ (i, n)$

Interest Rate

Number of Years	1%	2%	3%	4%	5%	6%	7%	8%	9%	10%	12%	14%	15%	16%	18%	20%	24%	28%	32%	36%
1	1.0100	1.0200	1.0300	1.0400	1.0500	1.0600	1.0700	1.0800	1.0900	1.1000	1.1200	1.1400	1.1500	1.1600	1.1800	1.2000	1.2400	1.2800	1.3200	1.3600
2	1.0201	1.0404	1.0609	1.0816	1.1025	1.1236	1.1449	1.1664	1.1881	1.2100	1.2544	1.2996	1.3225	1.3456	1.3924	1.4400	1.5376	1.6384	1.7424	1.8496
3	1.0303	1.0612	1.0927	1.1249	1.1576	1.1910	1.2250	1.2597	1.2950	1.3310	1.4049	1.4815	1.5209	1.5609	1.6430	1.7280	1.9066	2.0972	2.3000	2.5155
4	1.0406	1.0824	1.1255	1.1699	1.2155	1.2625	1.3108	1.3605	1.4116	1.4641	1.5735	1.6890	1.7490	1.8106	1.9388	2.0736	2.3642	2.6844	3.0360	3.4210
5	1.0510	1.1041	1.1593	1.2167	1.2763	1.3382	1.4026	1.4693	1.5386	1.6105	1.7623	1.9254	2.0114	2.1003	2.2878	2.4883	2.9316	3.4360	4.0075	4.6526
6	1.0615	1.1262	1.1941	1.2653	1.3401	1.4185	1.5007	1.5869	1.6771	1.7716	1.9738	2.1950	2.3131	2.4364	2.6996	2.9860	3.6352	4.3980	5.2899	6.3275
7	1.0721	1.1487	1.2299	1.3159	1.4071	1.5036	1.6058	1.7138	1.8280	1.9487	2.2107	2.5023	2.6600	2.8262	3.1855	3.5832	4.5077	5.6295	6.9826	8.6054
8	1.0829	1.1717	1.2668	1.3686	1.4775	1.5938	1.7182	1.8509	1.9926	2.1436	2.4760	2.8526	3.0590	3.2784	3.7589	4.2998	5.5895	7.2058	9.2170	11.703
9	1.0937	1.1951	1.3048	1.4233	1.5513	1.6895	1.8385	1.9990	2.1719	2.3579	2.7731	3.2519	3.5179	3.8030	4.4355	5.1598	6.9310	9.2234	12.166	15.916
10	1.1046	1.2190	1.3439	1.4802	1.6289	1.7908	1.9672	2.1589	2.3674	2.5937	3.1058	3.7072	4.0456	4.4114	5.2338	6.1917	8.5944	11.805	16.059	21.646
11	1.1157	1.2434	1.3842	1.5395	1.7103	1.8983	2.1049	2.3316	2.5804	2.8531	3.4785	4.2262	4.6524	5.1173	6.1759	7.4301	10.657	15.111	21.198	29.439
12	1.1268	1.2682	1.4258	1.6010	1.7959	2.0122	2.2522	2.5182	2.8127	3.1384	3.8960	4.8179	5.3502	5.9360	7.2876	8.9161	13.214	19.342	27.982	40.037
13	1.1381	1.2936	1.4685	1.6651	1.8856	2.1329	2.4098	2.7196	3.0658	3.4523	4.3635	5.4924	6.1528	6.8858	8.5994	10.699	16.386	24.748	36.937	54.451
14	1.1495	1.3195	1.5126	1.7317	1.9799	2.2609	2.5785	2.9372	3.3417	3.7975	4.8871	6.2613	7.0757	7.9875	10.147	12.839	20.319	31.691	48.756	74.053
15	1.1610	1.3459	1.5580	1.8009	2.0789	2.3966	2.7590	3.1722	3.6425	4.1772	5.4736	7.1379	8.1371	9.2655	11.973	15.407	25.195	40.564	53.358	100.71
16	1.1726	1.3728	1.6047	1.8730	2.1829	2.5404	2.9522	3.4259	3.9703	4.5950	6.1304	8.1372	9.3576	10.748	14.129	18.488	31.242	51.923	84.953	136.96
17	1.1834	1.4002	1.6528	1.9479	2.2920	2.6928	3.1588	3.7000	4.3276	5.0545	6.8660	9.2765	10.761	12.467	16.672	22.186	38.740	66.461	112.13	186.27
18	1.1961	1.4282	1.7024	2.0258	2.4066	2.8543	3.3799	3.9960	4.7171	5.5599	7.6900	10.575	12.375	14.462	19.673	26.623	48.038	85.070	148.02	253.33
19	1.2081	1.4568	1.7535	2.1068	2.5270	3.0256	3.6165	4.3157	5.1417	6.1159	8.6129	12.055	14.231	16.776	23.214	31.948	59.567	108.89	195.39	344.53
20	1.2202	1.4859	1.8061	2.1911	2.6533	3.2071	3.8697	4.6610	5.6044	6.7275	9.6463	13.743	16.366	19.460	27.393	38.337	73.864	139.37	257.91	468.57
21	1.2324	1.5157	1.8603	2.2788	2.7860	3.3996	4.1406	5.0338	6.1088	7.4002	10.803	15.667	18.821	22.574	32.323	46.005	91.591	178.40	340.44	637.26
22	1.2447	1.5460	1.9161	2.3699	2.9253	3.6035	4.4304	5.4365	6.6586	8.1403	12.100	17.861	21.644	26.186	38.142	55.206	113.57	228.35	449.39	866.67
23	1.2572	1.5769	1.9736	2.4627	3.0715	3.8197	4.7405	5.8715	7.2579	8.9543	13.552	20.361	24.891	30.376	45.007	66.247	140.83	292.30	593.19	1178.6
24	1.2697	1.6084	2.0328	2.5633	3.2251	4.0489	5.0724	6.3412	7.9111	9.8497	15.178	23.212	28.625	35.236	53.108	79.496	174.63	374.14	783.02	1602.9
25	1.2824	1.6406	2.0938	2.6658	3.3864	4.2919	5.4274	6.8485	8.6231	10.834	17.000	26.461	32.918	40.874	62.668	95.396	216.54	478.90	1033.5	2180.0
26	1.2953	1.6734	2.1566	2.7725	3.5557	4.5497	5.8074	7.3964	9.3992	11.918	19.040	30.166	37.856	47.414	73.948	114.47	268.51	612.99	1364.3	2964.9
27	1.3082	1.7069	2.2213	2.8834	3.7335	4.8223	6.2199	7.9881	10.245	13.110	21.324	34.389	43.535	55.000	87.259	137.37	332.95	784.63	1800.9	4032.2
28	1.3213	1.7410	2.2879	2.9987	3.9201	5.1117	6.6488	8.6271	11.167	14.421	23.883	39.204	50.065	63.800	102.96	164.84	412.86	1004.3	2377.2	5483.8
29	1.3345	1.7758	2.3566	3.1187	4.1161	5.4184	7.1143	9.3173	12.172	15.863	26.749	44.693	57.575	74.008	121.50	197.81	511.95	128.5	3137.9	7458.0
30	1.3478	1.8114	2.4273	3.2434	4.3219	5.7435	7.6123	10.062	13.267	17.449	29.959	50.950	66.211	85.849	143.37	237.37	634.81	1645.5	4142.0	10143.
40	1.4889	2.2080	3.2620	4.8010	7.0400	10.285	14.974	21.724	31.409	45.259	93.050	188.88	267.86	378.72	750.37	1469.7	5455.9	19426.	66520	*
50	1.6446	2.6916	4.3839	7.1067	11.467	18.420	29.457	46.901	74.357	117.39	289.00	700.23	1083.6	1670.7	3927.3	9100.4	46890.	*	*	*
60	1.8167	3.2810	5.8916	10.519	18.679	32.987	57.946	101.25	176.03	304.48	897.59	2595.9	4383.9	7370.1	20555	56347	*	*	*	*

Table A-2 Future Value of Annuity of $1 = T2 (i,n)

Interest Rate

Number of Years	1%	2%	3%	4%	5%	6%	7%	8%	9%	10%	12%	14%	15%	16%	18%	20%	24%	28%	32%	36%
1	1.0000	1.0000	1.0000	1.0000	1.0000	1.0000	1.0000	1.0000	1.0000	1.0000	1.0000	1.0000	1.0000	1.0000	1.0000	1.0000	1.0000	1.0000	1.0000	1.0000
2	2.0100	2.0200	2.0300	2.0400	2.0500	2.0600	2.0700	2.0800	2.0900	2.1000	2.1200	2.1400	2.1500	2.1600	2.1800	2.2000	2.2400	2.2800	2.3200	2.3600
3	3.0301	3.0604	3.0909	3.1216	3.1525	3.1836	3.2149	3.2464	3.2781	3.3100	3.3744	3.4396	3.4725	3.5056	3.5724	3.6400	3.7776	3.9184	4.0624	4.2096
4	4.0604	4.1216	4.1836	4.2465	4.3101	4.3746	4.4399	4.5061	4.5731	4.6410	4.7793	4.9211	4.9934	5.0665	5.2154	5.3680	5.6842	6.0156	6.3624	6.7251
5	5.1010	5.2040	5.3091	5.4163	5.5256	5.6371	5.7507	5.8666	5.9847	6.1051	6.3528	6.6101	6.7424	6.8771	7.1542	7.4416	8.0484	8.6999	9.3983	10.146
6	6.1520	6.3081	6.4684	6.6330	6.8019	6.9753	7.1533	7.3359	7.5233	7.7156	8.1152	8.5355	8.7537	8.9775	9.4420	9.9299	10.980	12.135	13.405	14.798
7	7.2135	7.4343	7.6625	7.8983	8.1420	8.3938	8.6540	8.9228	9.2004	9.4872	10.089	10.730	11.066	11.413	12.141	12.915	14.615	16.533	18.695	21.126
8	8.2857	8.5830	8.8923	9.2142	9.5491	9.8975	10.259	10.636	11.028	11.435	12.299	13.232	13.726	14.240	15.327	16.499	19.122	22.163	25.678	29.731
9	9.3685	9.7546	10.159	10.582	11.026	11.491	11.978	12.487	13.021	13.579	14.775	16.085	16.785	17.518	19.085	20.798	24.712	29.369	34.895	41.435
10	10.462	10.949	11.463	12.006	12.577	13.180	13.816	14.486	15.192	15.937	17.548	19.337	20.303	21.321	23.521	25.958	31.643	38.592	47.061	57.351
11	11.566	12.168	12.807	13.486	14.206	14.971	15.783	16.645	17.560	18.531	20.654	23.044	24.349	25.732	28.755	32.150	40.237	50.398	63.121	78.998
12	12.682	13.412	14.192	15.025	15.917	16.869	17.888	18.977	20.140	21.384	24.133	27.270	29.001	30.850	34.931	39.580	50.894	65.510	84.320	108.43
13	13.809	14.680	15.617	16.626	17.713	18.882	20.140	21.495	22.953	24.522	28.029	32.088	34.351	36.786	42.218	48.496	64.109	84.852	112.30	148.47
14	14.947	15.973	17.086	18.291	19.598	21.015	22.550	24.214	26.019	27.975	32.392	37.581	40.504	43.672	50.818	59.195	80.496	109.61	149.23	202.92
15	16.096	17.293	18.598	20.023	21.578	23.276	25.129	27.152	29.360	31.772	37.279	43.842	47.580	51.659	60.965	72.035	100.81	141.30	197.99	276.97
16	17.257	18.639	20.156	21.824	23.657	25.672	27.888	30.324	33.003	35.949	42.753	50.980	55.717	60.925	72.939	87.442	126.01	181.86	262.35	377.69
17	18.430	20.012	21.761	23.697	25.840	28.212	30.840	33.750	36.973	40.544	48.883	59.117	65.075	71.673	87.068	105.93	157.25	233.79	347.30	514.66
18	19.614	21.412	23.414	25.645	28.132	30.905	33.99	37.450	41.301	45.599	55.749	68.394	75.836	84.140	103.74	128.11	195.99	300.25	459.44	700.93
19	20.810	22.840	25.116	27.671	30.539	33.760	37.379	41.446	46.018	51.159	63.439	78.969	88.211	98.603	123.41	154.74	244.03	385.32	607.47	954.27
20	22.019	24.297	26.870	29.778	33.066	36.785	40.995	45.762	51.160	57.275	72.052	91.024	102.44	115.37	146.62	186.68	303.60	494.21	802.86	1298.8
21	23.239	25.783	28.676	31.969	35.719	39.992	44.865	50.442	56.764	64.002	81.698	104.76	118.81	134.84	174.02	225.02	377.46	633.59	1060.7	1767.3
22	24.471	27.299	30.536	34.248	38.505	43.392	49.005	55.456	62.873	71.402	92.502	120.43	137.63	157.41	206.34	271.03	469.05	811.99	1401.2	2404.6
23	25.716	28.845	32.452	36.617	41.430	46.995	53.436	60.893	69.531	79.543	104.60	138.29	159.27	183.60	244.48	326.23	582.62	1040.3	1850.6	3271.3
24	26.973	30.421	34.426	39.082	44.502	50.815	58.176	66.764	76.789	88.497	118.15	158.65	184.16	213.97	289.49	392.48	723.46	1332.6	2443.8	4449.9
25	28.243	32.030	36.459	41.645	47.727	54.864	63.249	73.105	84.700	98.347	133.33	181.87	212.79	249.21	342.60	471.98	898.09	1706.8	3226.8	6052.9
26	29.525	33.670	38.553	44.311	51.113	59.156	68.676	79.954	93.323	109.18	150.33	208.33	245.71	290.08	405.27	567.37	1114.6	2185.7	4260.4	8233.0
27	30.820	35.344	40.709	47.084	54.669	63.705	74.483	87.350	102.72	121.09	169.37	238.49	283.56	337.50	479.22	681.85	1383.1	2798.7	5624.7	11197.9
28	32.129	37.051	42.930	49.967	58.402	68.528	80.697	95.338	112.96	134.20	190.69	272.88	327.10	392.50	566.48	819.22	1716.0	3583.3	7425.6	15230.2
29	32.450	38.792	45.218	52.966	62.322	73.689	87.346	103.96	124.13	148.63	214.58	312.09	377.16	456.30	669.44	984.06	2128.9	4587.6	9802.9	20714.1
30	34.784	40.568	47.576	56.084	66.438	79.058	94.460	113.28	136.30	164.49	241.33	356.78	434.74	530.31	790.94	1181.8	2640.9	5873.2	12940	28172.2
40	48.886	60.402	75.401	95.025	120.79	154.76	199.63	259.05	337.88	442.59	767.09	1342.0	1779.0	2360.7	4163.2	7343.8	22728	69977	*	*
50	64.473	84.579	112.79	152.66	209.34	290.33	406.52	573.76	815.08	1163.9	2400.0	4994.5	7217.7	10435	21813	45497	*	*	*	*
60	81.669	114.05	163.05	237.90	353.58	533.12	813.52	1253.2	1944.7	3034.8	7471.6	18535	29219	46057	*	*	*	*	*	*

Appendix 1

Table A-3 Present Value of $1 = T3\ (i,n)$

Interest Rate

Number of Years	1%	2%	3%	4%	5%	6%	7%	8%	9%	10%	12%	14%	15%	16%	18%	20%	24%	28%	32%	36%
1	0.9901	0.9804	0.9709	0.9615	0.9524	0.9434	0.9346	0.9259	0.9174	0.9091	0.8929	0.8772	0.8696	0.8621	0.8475	0.8333	0.8065	0.7813	0.7576	0.7353
2	0.9803	0.9612	0.9426	0.9246	0.9070	0.8900	0.8734	0.8573	0.8417	0.8264	0.7972	0.7695	0.7561	0.7432	0.7182	0.6944	0.6504	0.6104	0.5739	0.5407
3	0.9706	0.9423	0.9151	0.8890	0.8638	0.8396	0.8163	0.7938	0.7722	0.7513	0.7118	0.6750	0.6575	0.6407	0.6086	0.5787	0.5245	0.4768	0.4348	0.3975
4	0.9610	0.9238	0.8885	0.8548	0.8227	0.7921	0.7629	0.7350	0.7084	0.6830	0.6355	0.5921	0.5718	0.5523	0.5158	0.4823	0.4230	0.3725	0.3294	0.2923
5	0.9515	0.9057	0.8626	0.8219	0.7835	0.7473	0.7130	0.6806	0.6499	0.6209	0.5674	0.5194	0.4972	0.4761	0.4371	0.4019	0.3411	0.2910	0.2495	0.2149
6	0.9420	0.8880	0.8375	0.7903	0.7462	0.7050	0.6663	0.6302	0.5963	0.5645	0.5066	0.4556	0.4323	0.4104	0.3704	0.3349	0.2751	0.2274	0.1890	0.1580
7	0.9327	0.8706	0.8131	0.7599	0.7101	0.6651	0.6227	0.5835	0.5470	0.5132	0.4523	0.3996	0.3759	0.3538	0.3139	0.2791	0.2218	0.1776	0.1432	0.1162
8	0.9235	0.8535	0.7894	0.7307	0.6768	0.6274	0.5820	0.5403	0.5019	0.4665	0.4039	0.3506	0.3269	0.3050	0.2660	0.2326	0.1789	0.1388	0.1085	0.0854
9	0.9143	0.8368	0.7664	0.7026	0.6446	0.5919	0.5439	0.5002	0.4604	0.4241	0.3606	0.3075	0.2843	0.2630	0.2255	0.1938	0.1443	0.1084	0.0822	0.0628
10	0.9053	0.8203	0.7441	0.6756	0.6139	0.5584	0.5083	0.4632	0.4224	0.3855	0.3220	0.2697	0.2472	0.2267	0.1911	0.1615	0.1164	0.0847	0.0623	0.0462
11	0.8963	0.8043	0.7224	0.6496	0.5847	0.5268	0.4751	0.4289	0.3875	0.3505	0.2875	0.2366	0.2149	0.1954	0.1619	0.1346	0.0938	0.0662	0.0472	0.0340
12	0.8874	0.7885	0.7014	0.6246	0.5568	0.4970	0.4440	0.3971	0.3555	0.3186	0.2567	0.2076	0.1869	0.1685	0.1372	0.1122	0.0757	0.0517	0.0357	0.0250
13	0.8787	0.7730	0.6810	0.6006	0.5303	0.4688	0.4150	0.3677	0.3262	0.2897	0.2292	0.1821	0.1625	0.1452	0.1163	0.0935	0.0610	0.0404	0.0271	0.0184
14	0.8700	0.7579	0.6611	0.5775	0.5051	0.4423	0.3878	0.3405	0.2992	0.2633	0.2046	0.1597	0.1413	0.1252	0.0985	0.0779	0.0492	0.0316	0.0205	0.0135
15	0.8613	0.7430	0.6419	0.5553	0.4810	0.4173	0.3624	0.3152	0.2745	0.2394	0.1827	0.1401	0.1229	0.1079	0.0835	0.0649	0.0397	0.0247	0.0155	0.0099
16	0.8528	0.7284	0.6232	0.5339	0.4581	0.3936	0.3387	0.2919	0.2519	0.2176	0.1631	0.1229	0.1069	0.0930	0.0708	0.0541	0.0320	0.0193	0.0118	0.0073
17	0.8444	0.7142	0.6050	0.5134	0.4363	0.3714	0.3166	0.2703	0.2311	0.1978	0.1456	0.1078	0.0929	0.0802	0.0600	0.0451	0.0258	0.0150	0.0089	0.0054
18	0.8360	0.7002	0.5874	0.4936	0.4155	0.3503	0.2959	0.2502	0.2120	0.1799	0.1300	0.0946	0.0808	0.0691	0.0508	0.0376	0.0208	0.0118	0.0068	0.0038
19	0.8277	0.6864	0.5703	0.4746	0.3957	0.3305	0.2765	0.2317	0.1945	0.1635	0.1161	0.0829	0.0703	0.0596	0.0431	0.0313	0.0168	0.0092	0.0051	0.0029
20	0.8195	0.6730	0.5537	0.4564	0.3769	0.3118	0.2584	0.2145	0.1784	0.1486	0.1037	0.0728	0.0611	0.0514	0.0365	0.0261	0.0135	0.0072	0.0039	0.0021
25	0.7798	0.6095	0.4776	0.3751	0.2953	0.2330	0.1842	0.1460	0.1160	0.0923	0.0588	0.0378	0.0304	0.0245	0.0160	0.0105	0.0046	0.0021	0.0010	0.0005
30	0.7419	0.5521	0.4120	0.3083	0.2314	0.1741	0.1314	0.0994	0.0754	0.0573	0.0334	0.0196	0.0151	0.0116	0.0070	0.0042	0.0016	0.0006	0.0002	0.0001
40	0.6717	0.4529	0.3066	0.2083	0.1420	0.0972	0.0668	0.0460	0.0318	0.0221	0.0107	0.0053	0.0037	0.0026	0.0013	0.0007	0.0002	0.0001	*	*
50	0.6080	0.3715	0.2281	0.1407	0.0872	0.0543	0.0339	0.0213	0.0132	0.0085	0.0035	0.0014	0.0009	0.0006	0.0003	0.0001	*	*	*	*
60	0.5504	0.3048	0.1697	0.0951	0.0535	0.0303	0.0173	0.0099	0.0057	0.0033	0.0011	0.0004	0.0002	0.0001	*	*	*	*	*	*

Appendix 1

Table A-4 Present Value of an Annuity of $1 = T4 (i,n)

Interest Rate

Number of Years	1%	2%	3%	4%	5%	6%	7%	8%	9%	10%	12%	14%	15%	16%	18%	20%	24%	28%	32%
1	0.9901	0.9804	0.9709	0.9615	0.9524	0.9434	0.9346	0.9259	0.9174	0.9091	0.8929	0.8772	0.8696	0.8621	0.8475	0.8333	0.8065	0.7813	0.7576
2	1.9704	1.9415	1.9135	1.8861	1.8594	1.8334	1.8080	1.7833	1.7591	1.7355	1.6901	1.6467	1.6257	1.6052	1.5656	1.5278	1.4568	1.3916	1.3315
3	2.9410	2.8839	2.8286	2.7751	2.7232	2.6730	2.6243	2.5771	2.5313	2.4869	2.4018	2.3216	2.2832	2.2459	2.1743	2.1065	1.9813	1.8684	1.7663
4	3.9020	3.8077	3.7171	3.6299	3.5460	3.4651	3.3872	3.3121	3.2397	3.1699	3.0373	2.9137	2.8550	2.7982	2.6901	2.5887	2.4043	2.2410	2.0957
5	4.8534	4.7135	4.5797	4.4518	4.3295	4.2124	4.1002	3.9927	3.8897	3.7908	3.6048	3.4331	3.3522	3.2743	3.1272	2.9906	2.7454	2.5320	2.3452
6	5.7955	5.6014	5.4172	5.1421	5.0757	4.9173	4.7665	4.6229	4.4859	4.3553	4.1114	3.8887	3.7845	3.6847	3.4976	3.3255	3.0205	2.7594	2.5342
7	6.7282	6.4720	6.2303	6.0021	5.7864	5.5824	5.3893	5.2064	5.0330	4.8684	4.5638	4.2883	4.1604	4.0386	3.8115	3.6046	3.2423	2.9370	2.6775
8	7.6517	7.3255	7.0197	6.7327	6.4632	6.2098	5.9713	5.7466	5.5348	5.3349	4.9676	4.6389	4.4873	4.3436	4.0776	3.8372	3.4212	3.0758	2.7860
9	8.5660	8.1622	7.7861	7.4353	7.1078	6.8017	6.5152	6.2469	5.9952	5.7590	5.3282	4.9464	4.7716	4.6065	4.3030	4.0310	3.5655	3.1842	2.8681
10	9.4713	8.9826	8.5302	8.1109	7.7217	7.3601	7.0236	6.7101	6.4177	6.1446	5.6502	5.2161	5.0188	4.8332	4.4941	4.1925	3.6819	3.2689	2.9304
11	10.3676	9.7868	9.2526	8.7605	8.3064	7.8869	7.4987	7.1390	6.8052	6.4951	5.9377	5.4527	5.2337	5.0286	4.6560	4.3271	3.7757	3.3351	2.9776
12	11.2551	10.5753	9.9540	9.3851	8.8633	8.3838	7.9427	7.5361	7.1607	6.8137	6.1944	5.6603	5.4206	5.1971	4.7932	4.4392	3.8514	3.3868	3.0133
13	12.1337	11.3484	10.6350	9.9856	9.3936	8.8527	8.3577	7.9038	7.1889	7.1034	6.4235	5.8424	5.5831	5.3423	4.9095	4.5327	3.9124	3.4272	3.0404
14	13.0037	12.1062	11.2961	10.5631	9.8986	9.2950	8.7455	8.2442	7.7862	7.3667	6.6282	6.0021	5.7245	5.4675	5.0081	4.6106	3.9616	3.4587	3.0609
15	13.8651	11.8493	11.9379	11.1184	10.3797	9.7122	9.1079	8.5595	8.0607	7.6061	6.8109	6.1422	5.8474	5.5755	5.0916	4.6755	4.0013	3.4834	3.0764
16	14.7179	13.5777	12.5611	11.6523	10.8378	10.1059	9.4466	8.8514	8.3126	7.8237	6.9740	6.2651	5.9542	5.6685	5.1724	4.7296	4.0333	3.5026	3.0882
17	15.5623	14.2919	13.1661	12.1657	11.2741	10.4773	9.7632	9.1216	8.5436	8.0216	7.1196	6.3729	6.0472	5.7487	5.2223	4.7746	4.0591	3.5177	3.0971
18	16.3983	14.9920	13.7535	12.6593	11.6896	10.8276	10.0591	9.3719	8.7556	8.2014	7.2497	6.4674	6.1280	5.8178	5.2732	4.8122	4.0799	3.5294	3.1039
19	17.2260	15.6785	14.3238	13.1339	12.0853	11.1581	10.3356	9.6036	8.9501	8.3649	7.3658	6.5504	6.1982	5.8775	5.3162	4.8435	4.0967	3.5386	3.1090
20	18.0456	16.3514	14.8775	13.5903	12.4622	11.4699	10.5940	9.8181	9.1285	8.5436	7.4694	6.6231	6.2593	5.9288	5.3527	4.8696	4.1103	3.5458	3.1129
25	22.0232	19.5235	17.4131	15.6221	14.0939	12.7834	11.6536	10.6748	9.8226	9.0770	7.8431	6.8729	6.4641	6.0971	5.4669	4.9476	4.1474	3.5640	3.1220
30	25.8077	22.3965	19.6004	17.2920	15.3725	13.7648	12.4090	11.2578	10.2737	9.4269	8.0552	7.0072	6.5660	6.1772	5.5168	4.9789	4.1601	3.5693	3.1242
40	32.8347	27.3555	23.1148	19.7928	17.1591	15.0463	13.3317	11.9246	10.7574	9.7791	8.2438	7.1050	6.6418	6.2335	5.5482	4.9966	4.1659	3.5712	3.1250
50	39.1961	31.4236	25.7298	21.4822	18.2559	15.7619	13.8007	12.2335	10.9617	9.9148	8.3045	7.1327	6.6605	6.2463	5.5541	4.9995	4.1666	3.5714	3.1250
60	44.9550	34.7609	27.8656	22.6235	18.9293	16.1614	14.0392	12.3766	11.0480	9.9672	8.3240	7.1401	6.6651	6.2492	5.5553	4.9999	4.1667	3.5714	3.1250

29,001

APPENDIX 2

Item 1—List of Tip-Related IRS Publications, Forms, Internet Sites, and Cases

IRS Publications and Forms

Publication 1875:	Tips on Tips—A Guide to Tip Income Reporting for Employers in the Food and Beverage Industry
Publication 1872:	Tips on Tips—A Guide to Tip Income Reporting for Employees in the Food and Beverage Industry
Publication 505:	Tax Withholding and Estimated Tax
Publication 531:	Reporting Tip Income
Publication 1244:	Employee's Daily Record of Tips and Report to Employer
Form 4137:	"Social Security and Medicare Tax on Unreported Tip Income"
Form 4070:	"Employee's Report of Tips to Employer"
Form 8027:	"Employer's Annual Information of Tip Income and Allocated Tips"

Site for downloading IRS forms and publications:

http://www.irs.gov/forms_pubs/index.html

Site for accessing a historical presentation of tip-related cases brought to court:

http://www.journalofaccountancy.com/

In the above site enter: "Got tips? Better Report Them" in the search window.

Then search through the articles until you find the above-named article.

Some cases related to FICA taxes and tips:

- A.J. McQuatters (1973)
- 330 West Hubbard Restaurant Corp.—Doing Business as: Coco Pazzo Restaurant—(2000), http://www.altlaw.org/v1/cases/1362196.

  In this site enter the name of the above case in the search window.
- Morrison Restaurants, Inc. (1997), http://caselaw.lp.findlaw.com/ In the above site enter: Morrison Restaurants, Inc. in the search window that is in the upper right hand corner.
- The Bubble Room, Inc. (1996),
  - http://www.ll.georgetown.edu/ In the above site enter: The Bubble Room" in the search window.
  - http://findarticles.com/p/articles/mi_m3190/is_/ai_18851065
- Fior D'Italia, Inc. (S. C. 2002), http://supreme.lp.findlaw.com/

  In the above site enter: Fior D'Italia, Inc.

Although the Internet sites above are related here to specific cases, some of the above cases appear on more than one of the above search sites.

29,002 Appendix 2

An interesting case regarding incorrectly assessed FICA tax on unreported tips in which the restaurant won is: *Quietwater Entertainment, Inc. d/b/a Jubilee/Captain Fun Restaurant* (99- 2 USTC 50,695; U.S. District Court, No. Dist. Fla., Pensacola Div.) In this case it was held that the IRS improperly used the formula in A.J. McQuatters.

Item 2—LMSB Directive on Cost Segregation in the Restaurant Industry

EXHIBIT A

Note: In the case of certain leasehold improvements and restaurant property, the classifications in this directive are superseded to the extent that the American Jobs Creation Act of 2004 modifies IRC Section 168. Thus, a 15-year straight line recovery period should replace the recovery period shown in the following matrix if the asset is "qualified leasehold improvement property" (as defined in IRC Section 168(e)(6)) or "qualified restaurant property" (as defined in IRC Section 168(e)(7)) placed in service by the taxpayer after October 22, 2004, and before January 1, 2008.

[1]IRC Section 1245 can apply to certain qualified recovery nonresidential real estate placed in service after 1980 and before 1987. See I.R.C. Section 1245(a)(5).

Asset	Description	Property Type	Recovery Period
Beverage Equipment	Equipment for storage and preparation of beverages and beverage delivery systems. Beverage equipment includes the refrigerators, coolers, dispensing systems, and the dedicated electrical, tubing, or piping for such equipment. The dispensing system may be gravity, pump, or gas driven.	1245	57.0 Distributive Trades and Services—5 Years
Canopies & Awnings	Readily removable overhang or covering, often of canvas or plastic, used to provide shade or cover over a storefront, window, or door; or used inside a structure to identify a particular area. Examples include applications over an exterior door or window or attached to interior walls or suspended from ceilings to identify a buffet line or bar area of the restaurant. Does not include canopies that are an integral part of a building's structural shell, such as in the casino industry, or over docks.	1245	57.0 Distributive Trades and Services—5 Years
Ceilings	Includes all interior ceilings regardless of finish or décor, e.g., drywall or plaster ceilings, acoustic ceilings, suspended ceilings (including all hangers, frames, grids, and tiles or panels), decorative metal or tin finishes, kitchen plastic panels, decorative panels, etc.	1250	Building or Building Component—39 Years

Appendix 2 **29,003**

Asset	Description	Property Type	Recovery Period
Computers	Processors (CPU), direct access storage device (DASD), tape drives, desktop and laptop computers, CRT, terminals, monitors, printers, and other peripheral equipment. Excludes Point of Sale (POS) systems and computers that are an integral part of other equipment (e.g., fire detection, heating, cooling, or energy management systems, etc.).	1245	00.12 Information Systems—5 Years
Concrete Foundations & Footings	Includes formwork, reinforcement, concrete block, and pre-cast or cast-in-place work related to foundations and footings necessary for the proper setting of the building.	1250	Building or Building Component—39 Years
	Foundations or footings for signs, light poles, canopies and other land improvements (except buildings).	1250	00.3 Land Improvements—15 Years
Data Handling Equipment	Includes adding and accounting machines, calculators, copiers and duplicating machines. Excludes computers and computer peripheral equipment, see **Computers**.	1245	00.13 Data Handling Equipment, except Computers—5 Years
Doors	Interior and exterior doors, regardless of decoration, including but not limited to, double opening doors, overhead doors, revolving doors, mall entrance security gates, roll-up or sliding wire mesh or steel grills and gates, and door hardware (such as doorknobs, closers, kick plates, hinges, locks, automatic openers, etc.).	1250	Building or Building Component—39 Years
	Special lightweight, double action doors installed to prevent accidents in a heavily trafficked area. For example, Eliason doors providing easy access between the kitchen and dining areas.	1245	57.0 Distributive Trades and Services—5 Years
Door—Air Curtains	Air doors or curtains are air systems located above doors and windows that circulate air to stabilize environments and save energy by minimizing the heated/air conditioned air loss through open doorways and windows. They also effectively repel flying insects, dust, and pollutants.	1250	Building or Building Component—39 Years
Drive-Through Equipment	Drive-through equipment includes order taking, food delivery and payment processing systems whether mechanical or electronic. Excludes building elements such as doors, bays, or windows. See also **Walls—Exterior**, and **Windows** for drive-through bays and windows.	1245	57.0 Distributive Trades and Services—5 Years

Appendix 2

Asset	Description	Property Type	Recovery Period
Electrical	Includes all components of the building electrical system used in the operation or maintenance of the building or necessary to provide general building services such as electrical outlets of general applicability and accessibility, lighting, heating, ventilation, air conditioning and electrical wiring. See also **Kitchen Equipment Hook-ups.**	1250	Building or Building Component—39 Years
	Special electrical connections which are necessary to and used directly with a specific item of machinery or equipment or connections between specific items of individual machinery or equipment; such as dedicated electrical outlets, wiring, conduit, and circuit breakers by which machinery and equipment is connected to the electrical distribution system. Does not include electrical outlets of general applicability and accessibility. See Chapter 5 of the Cost Segregation Audit Techniques Guide for allocation examples.	1245	57.0 Distributive Trades and Services—5 Years
Elevators & Escalators	Elevators and escalators, which include handrails and smoke baffles, are permanently affixed to the building and intended to remain in place. They relate to the operation or maintenance of the building and are structural components.	1250	Building or Building Component—39 Years
Equipment Installation	Expenses incurred in the installation of furnishings and restaurant equipment. Some examples include booths, tables, counters and interior theme décor.	1245	57.0 Distributive Trades and Services—5 Years
Exit Signs	Signs posted along exit routes that indicate the direction of travel to the nearest exit. These signs typically read "EXIT" and may have distinctive colors, illumination, or arrows indicating the direction to the exit.	1250	Building or Building Component—39 Years
Fire Protection & Alarm Systems	Includes sensing devices, computer controls, sprinkler heads, piping or plumbing, pumps, visual and audible alarms, alarm control panels, heat and smoke detection devices, fire escapes, fire doors, emergency exit lighting and signage, and wall mounted fire extinguishers necessary for the protection of the building.	1250	Building or Building Component—39 Years
Fire Protection Equipment	Includes special fire detection or suppression systems located in equipment hoods or directly associated with a piece of equipment. For example, a fire extinguisher designed and used for protection against a particular hazard created by the business activity.	1245	57.0 Distributive Trades and Services—5 Years

Appendix 2 **29,005**

Asset	Description	Property Type	Recovery Period
Fireplaces	Includes masonry and gas fireplaces, flues, chimneys and other components of built-in fireplaces.	1250	Building or Building Component—39 Years
Floor Coverings	Floor covering affixed with permanent adhesive, nailed, or screwed in place. Examples include ceramic or quarry tile, marble, paving brick, and other coverings cemented, mudded, or grouted to the floor; epoxy or sealers; and wood flooring.	1250	Building or Building Component—39 Years
	Floor covering that is installed by means of strippable adhesives. For the restaurant industry, all carpeting will be treated as not permanently attached and not intended to be permanent. Excludes rugs or tapestries that are considered artwork and do not suffer wear and tear (e.g., Persian rugs that may appreciate are considered artwork).	1245	57.0 Distributive Trades and Services—5 Years
Floors	Includes concrete slabs and other floor systems. Floors include special treatments applied to or otherwise a permanent part of the floor. For example, "superflat" finish, sloped drainage basins, raised perimeter, serving line curb; or cooler, freezer, and garbage room floors.	1250	Building or Building Component—39 Years
Food Storage & Preparation Equipment	Food storage, cleaning, preparation, and delivery systems including all machinery, equipment, furniture, and fixtures used to process food items from storage through delivery to the customer.	1245	57.0 Distributive Trades and Services—5 Years
Heating, Ventilating, & Air Conditioning (HVAC)	Includes all components of a central heating, ventilating, and air conditioning system not specifically identified elsewhere. HVAC systems that are installed not only to meet the temperature and humidity requirements of machinery, but are installed for additional significant purposes, such as customer comfort and ventilation, are building components.	1250	Building or Building Component—39 Years

Asset	Description	Property Type	Recovery Period
	Only separate kitchen HVAC units that meet the sole justification test are included (i.e., machinery the sole justification for the installation of which is the fact that such machinery is required to meet temperature or humidity requirements which are essential for the operation of other machinery or the processing of materials or foodstuffs). Kitchen HVAC may meet the sole justification test even though it incidentally provides for the comfort of employees, or serves, to an insubstantial degree, areas where such temperature or humidity requirements are not essential. Includes refrigeration units, condensers, compressors, accumulators, coolers, pumps, connecting pipes, and wiring for the mechanical equipment for climate controlled rooms such as walk-in freezers and coolers. Allocation of HVAC is not appropriate.	1245	57.0 Distributive Trades and Services—5 Years
Kitchen Equipment Hook-ups	Includes separate water lines from the incoming water main to equipment (such as steam trays, cooking vessels, or ice machines), gas lines from the building's main gas line to equipment (such as fryers or ovens), and special drain lines from equipment (such as refrigerator or dishwasher) to the drain. Also includes ventilation system or kitchen air makeup unit solely to maintain specific ventilation requirements essential for operation of kitchen equipment, equipment exhaust hoods, and electric outlets and conduit extending back to the circuit box to provide a localized power source for specialized equipment. For example, a dishwasher requires electric and plumbing hook-ups, electrical from the dishwasher to the source of electricity (such as an outlet or junction box), and plumbing to connect the dishwasher to the water line and the drain. Excludes outlets of general applicability and accessibility or kitchen hand sink plumbing; see also **Electrical, HVAC,** and **Plumbing**.	1245	57.0 Distributive Trades and Services—5 Years
Light Fixtures— Interior	Includes lighting such as recessed and lay-in lighting, night lighting, and exit lighting, as well as decorative lighting fixtures that provide substantially all the artificial illumination in the building or along building walkways. For emergency and exit lighting, see **Fire Protection & Alarm Systems**.	1250	Building or Building Component—39 Years

Appendix 2 **29,007**

Asset	Description	Property Type	Recovery Period
	Decorative light fixtures are light fixtures, such as neon lights or track lighting, which are decorative in nature and not necessary for the operation of the building. In other words, if the decorative lighting were turned off, the other sources of lighting would provide sufficient light for operation of the building. If the decorative lighting is the *primary* source of lighting, then it is section 1250 property.	1245	57.0 Distributive Trades and Services—5 Years
Light Fixtures— Exterior	Exterior lighting whether decorative or not is considered section 1250 property to the extent that the lighting relates to the maintenance or operation of the building. Includes building mounted lighting to illuminate walkways, entrances, parking, etc.	1250	Building or Building Component—39 Years
	Pole mounted or freestanding outdoor lighting system to illuminate sidewalks, parking or recreation areas. See also **Poles & Pylons**. Note* asset class 00.3 Land improvements includes both section 1245 and 1250 property per Rev. Proc. 87-56.	See Note*	00.3 Land Improvements— 15 Years
	Plant grow lights or lighting that highlights *only* the landscaping or building exterior (but not parking areas or walkways) does not relate to the maintenance or operation of the building.	1245	57.0 Distributive Trades and Services—5 Years
Millwork— Decorative	Decorative millwork is the decorative finish carpentry in the restaurant. Examples include detailed crown moldings, lattice work placed over finished walls or ceilings, cabinets and counters. The decorative millwork serves to enhance the overall theme of the restaurant and is not related to the operation of the building. Excludes cabinets and counters in a restroom; see **Restroom Accessories**.	1245	57.0 Distributive Trades and Services—5 Years
Millwork— General Building or Structural	General millwork is all building materials made of finished wood (e.g., doors and frames, window frames, sashes, porch work, mantels, panel work, stairways, and special woodwork). Includes pre-built wooden items brought to the site for installation and items constructed on site such as restroom cabinets, door jambs, moldings, trim, etc.	1250	Building or Building Component—39 Years

Asset	Description	Property Type	Recovery Period
Office Furnishings	Includes desk, chair, credenza, file cabinet, table, or other furniture such as workstations. Also includes telephone equipment, fax machines, and other communications equipment. Does not include communications equipment included in other asset classes in Rev. Proc. 87-56.	1245	00.11 Office Furniture, Fixtures, and Equipment—7 Years
Parking Lots	Grade level surface parking area usually constructed of asphalt, brick, concrete, stone or similar material. Category includes bumper blocks, curb cuts, curb work, striping, landscape islands, perimeter fences, and sidewalks.	1250	00.3 Land Improvements—15 Years
Plumbing	All piping, drains, sprinkler mains, valves, sprinkler heads, water flow switches, restroom plumbing fixtures (e.g., toilets) and piping, kitchen hand sinks, electric water coolers, and all other components of a building plumbing system (water or gas) not specifically identified elsewhere. Excludes water or gas connections directly to appliances or kitchen drainage and kitchen hot water heater; see **Kitchen Equipment Hook-ups**.	1250	Building or Building Component—39 Years
	Includes water, gas, or refrigerant hook-ups directly connected to appliances or equipment, eyewash stations, kitchen drainage, and kitchen hot water heater. For example, a dishwasher would require special water hook-up.	1245	57.0 Distributive Trades and Services—5 Years
Point-of-Sale (POS) Systems	A register or terminal based data collection system used to control and record all sales. Includes cash registers, computerized sales systems, and related peripheral equipment. See also **Electrical** for hook-ups.	1245	57.0 Distributive Trades and Services—5 Years
Poles & Pylons	Light poles for parking areas and other poles poured in concrete footings or bolt-mounted for signage, flags, etc. Note* asset class 00.3 Land Improvements includes both section 1245 and 1250 property per Rev. Proc. 87-56.	See Note*	00.3 Land Improvements—15 Years
Restaurant Décor Accessories	Decorative mobile props such as playground equipment, potted plants, hanging mirrors, ceiling fans, and theme related props (such as coat of arms, sporting equipment or memorabilia, artifacts, pictures, plaques, etc., excluding non-depreciable artwork, antiques, or collectibles).	1245	57.0 Distributive Trades and Services—5 Years

Appendix 2 **29,009**

Asset	Description	Property Type	Recovery Period
Restaurant Furniture	Includes furniture unique to restaurants and distinguishable from office furniture. For example, a high stool in a bar, dining room table and chairs, booths, lockers, or benches. See also **Office Furnishings**.	1245	57.0 Distributive Trades and Services—5 Years
Restaurant Nonstructural Theme Elements	Interior non-load bearing decorative structures. These are items that do not function as part of the building and are not integrated with building elements such as wiring, plumbing or ventilation. For example a model castle constructed of gypsum board or plaster and wood studs would be considered a non-structural theme element that functions merely as ornamentation. Excludes a half wall whose function is to provide traffic control or space subdivision, see **Walls—Interior Partitions**. Excludes decorative ceilings, see **Ceilings**.	1245	57.0 Distributive Trades and Services—5 Years
Restroom Accessories	Includes paper towel dispensers, electric hand dryers, towel racks or holders, cup dispensers, purse shelves, toilet paper holders, soap dispensers or holders, lotion dispensers, sanitary napkin dispensers and waste receptacles, coat hooks, grab bars, mirrors, shelves, vanity cabinets, counters, ashtrays, baby changing stations, and other items generally found in public restrooms that are built into or mounted on walls or partitions.	1250	Building or Building Component—39 Years
Restroom Partitions	Includes shop made and standard manufacture toilet partitions, typically metal, but may be plastic or other materials.	1250	Building or Building Component—39 Years
Roof	All elements of the roof including but not limited to joists, rafters, deck, shingles, vapor barrier, skylights, trusses, girders and gutters. Determination of whether decorative elements of a roof (e.g., false dormers, mansard) constitute structural building components depends on their integration with the overall roof, not their load bearing capacity. If removal of the decorative element results in the direct exposure of building components to water, snow, wind, or moisture damage, or if the decorative element houses lighting fixtures, wiring, or other structural components, then the decorative elements are part of the overall roof system and are structural components of the building.	1250	Building or Building Component—39 Years

Appendix 2

Asset	Description	Property Type	Recovery Period
Security Systems	Includes security equipment for the protection of the building (and its contents) from burglary or vandalism and protection of employees from assault. Examples include window and door locks; card key access systems; keyless entry systems; security cameras, recorders, monitors, and related equipment; perimeter and interior building motion detectors; security lighting; alarm systems; and security system wiring and conduit.	1250	Building or Building Component—39 Years
Signs	Exit signs, restroom identifiers, and other signs relating to the operation or maintenance of a building.	1250	Building or Building Component—39 Years
	Interior and Exterior Signs used for menu display or theme identity. For pylon signs, includes only sign face. See also **Poles & Pylons**.	1245	57.0 Distributive Trades and Services—5 Years
Site Preparation, Grading & Excavation	In general, land preparation costs include one time cost of clearing and grubbing, site stripping, fill or excavation, and grading to allow development of land. Clearing and grubbing is the removal of debris, brush, trees, etc., from the site. Stripping is the removal of the topsoil to provide a stable surface for site and building improvements. The grading of land involves moving soil to produce a more level surface to allow development of the land.		Land
	Clearing, grading, excavating, and removal costs directly associated with the construction of buildings and building components are part of the cost of construction of the building.	1250	Building or Building Component—39 Years
	Clearing, grading, excavating and removal costs directly associated with the construction of sidewalks, parking areas, roadways, and other depreciable land improvements are part of the cost of construction of the improvements.	1250	00.3 Land Improvements— 15 Years
Site Utilities	Site utilities are the systems that are used to distribute utility services from the property line to the restaurant building. Includes water, sanitary sewer, gas, and electrical services.	1250	Building or Building Component—39 Years
Site Work	Site work includes curbing, paving, general site improvements, fencing, landscaping, roads, sewers, sidewalks, site drainage, and all other site improvements not directly related to the building. For sanitary sewers, see **Site Utilities**.	1250	00.3 Land Improvements— 15 Years

Asset	Description	Property Type	Recovery Period
Sound Systems	Equipment and apparatus, including wiring, used to provide amplified music or sound. For example, public address by way of paging a customer or background music. Excludes applications linked to fire protection and alarm systems.	1245	57.0 Distributive Trades and Services—5 Years
Stonework	Exterior decorative stonework embedded in half walls, such as patio half walls, that are an integral part of a building's structural shell. Such half walls relate to the operation or maintenance of the building.	1250	Building or Building Component—39 Years
	Includes patio stonework imbedded in the ground or applied to exterior half walls that are not an integral part of the building's structural shell.	1250	00.3 Land Improvements— 15 Years
Trash Enclosures	Enclosures for waste receptacles that are attached to the building. Typically constructed of the same materials as the building shell with either interior or exterior access. These trash enclosures are an integral part of the building shell and cannot be moved without damage to the underlying building.	1250	Building or Building Component—39 Years
	Freestanding enclosures for waste receptacles, typically constructed on a concrete pad with its posts set in the concrete. Serves both safety and decorative functions.	1250	00.3 Land Improvements— 15 Years
Upholstery	Any material used in the coverage and protection of furnishings.	1245	57.0 Distributive Trades and Services—5 Years
Wall Coverings	Includes interior and exterior paint; ceramic or quarry tile, marble, stone, brick, and other finishes affixed with mortar, cement, or grout; paneling, wainscoting, and other wood finishes affixed with nails, screws, or permanent adhesives; and sanitary kitchen wall panels such as Fiberglass Reinforced Plastic (FRP), stainless steel, or plastic wall panels.	1250	Building or Building Component—39 Years
	Strippable wallpaper that causes no damage to the underlying wall or wall surface.	1245	57.0 Distributive Trades and Services—5 Years

Appendix 2

Asset	Description	Property Type	Recovery Period
Walls—Exterior	Includes all exterior walls and building support regardless of construction materials. Exterior walls may include columns, posts, beams, girders, curtain walls, tilt up panels, studs, framing, sheetrock, insulation, windows, doors, exterior façade, brick, masonry, etc. Also includes drive-through bay, windows, and doors.	1250	Building or Building Component—39 Years
Walls—Interior Partitions	Includes all load bearing interior partitions regardless of construction. Also includes non-load bearing partitions regardless of height (typically constructed of studs and sheetrock or other materials) that divide or create rooms or provide traffic control. Includes rough carpentry and plaster, dry wall, or gypsum board, and other finishes.	1250	Building or Building Component—39 Years
	Interior walls where the partition can be 1) readily removed and remain in substantially the same condition after removal as before; or 2) moved and reused, stored, or sold in its entirety.	1245	57.0 Distributive Trades and Services—5 Years
Windows	Exterior windows, including store front windows, drive-through service and carousel windows, and vestibule.	1250	Building or Building Component—39 Years
Window Treatments	Window treatments such as drapes, curtains, louvers, blinds, post construction tinting, or interior decorative theme décor that are readily removable.	1245	57.0 Distributive Trades and Services—5 Years

Item 3—Large and Medium-Size Business (LMSB) Directive on Cost Segregation in the Gaming Industry

This matrix, which is part of the *Cost Segregation Audit Techniques Guide*, is intended to provide direction to effectively utilize resources in the classification and examination of property used in the operation of a casino/hotel property. General fact patterns specific to this industry have been considered in the classification of these assets and may not be applicable to other industries. Similarly, asset classification guidance issued for other industries is based on the general fact pattern for that industry and may not be applicable to a casino/hotel business situation. For example, for asset classification of restaurants located within a casino refer to the industry directive for restaurants. For examination techniques and historical background related to this issue, refer to the *Cost Segregation Audit Techniques Guide*.

Note: In the case of certain leasehold improvement property, the classifications in this directive are superseded to the extent that the American Jobs Creation Act of 2004 modifies IRC Section 168. Thus, a 15-year straight line recovery period should replace the recovery period shown in the following matrix if the asset is

Appendix 2 **29,013**

"qualified leasehold improvement property" (as defined in IRC Section 168(e)(6)) placed in service by the taxpayer after 10/22/04 and before 1/1/08.

Asset	Description	Property Type	Recovery Period
Ceilings	Dropped or lowered ceilings with decorative finishes (such as ornamental polished gold and copper metal panels suspended from the finished ceiling or glued to soffits or lowered drywall ceiling systems). The suspension grids are hung by hanger wires from hooks or eyes set in the floor above or bottom of the roof and attached to walls with nails or screws. Components such as lighting fixtures and air conditioning registers are placed on the grid. The ceilings conceal plumbing, wiring, sprinkler systems and air conditioning ducts. Includes grid systems where the actual building ceiling above the suspended ceiling can be seen. The actual building ceiling is generally painted a dark color so as to hide the various conduit, wires, and mechanical systems hanging from it.	§ 1250	39 years (40 years for purposes of § 168(g))
Doors and Door Locks	Interior and exterior doors, regardless of decoration, including but not limited to, double opening doors, overhead doors, revolving doors, entrance security gates, roll-up or sliding wire mesh or steel grills and gates, and door hardware (such as doorknobs, closers, kick plates, hinges, locks, automatic openers, etc.). Includes hotel guest room computerized door locks. Includes encoders, computers, and other associated hardware of the computerized lock system.	§ 1250	39 years (40 years for purposes of § 168(g))
	Special lightweight, double action doors installed to prevent accidents in a heavily trafficked area ("Eliason"-type door). For example, flexible doors, clear curtains, or strip curtains used between stock areas and selling areas.	§ 1245	5 years (57.0 Distributive Trades and Services)

Appendix 2

Asset	Description	Property Type	Recovery Period
Electrical Hook-ups (includes duplex, fourplex, junction box, conduit/ wiring and allocation of panels)	Includes electrical outlets of general applicability and accessibility located in *Accounting and Administrative Offices, Ballrooms, "Back of House" areas, Pre-function areas, and Support areas* (such as shop areas, engineering and construction offices). Includes but is not limited to outlets connected to copy machines, fax machines, personal computers, break rooms, coffee rooms, lounges, etc.	§ 1250	39 years (40 years for purposes of § 168(g))
	Includes electrical outlets located in hotel guest rooms and guest bathrooms of general applicability and accessibility (includes bathroom GFI outlet).	§ 1250	39 years (40 years for purposes of § 168(g))
	Includes electrical outlets specifically associated with particular items of machinery and equipment located in the Casino area. Includes ATM machines, slot machines, and other gaming related equipment. Also includes all electrical hook-ups associated with the activities described in Asset Class 79.0 of Rev. Proc. 87-56, 1987-2 CB 674, such as Theater and Showroom.	§ 1245	7 years (79.0 Recreation)
	Includes electrical outlets specifically associated with a particular item of machinery or equipment located in *Conference Rooms, Guest Rooms, Public Facility areas, Meeting Rooms, and Support Areas*, but not in the Casino/ Theater area. Examples include equipment in Exercise rooms, ice machines, vending machines, audio visual equipment, televisions (and the riser conduit and wiring), garbage disposals, refrigerators, and workbenches.	§ 1245	5 years (57.0 Distributive Trades and Services)
Exit Signs	Signs posted along exit routes that indicate the direction of travel to the nearest exit. These signs typically read "EXIT" and may have distinctive colors, illumination, or arrows indicating the direction to the exit.	§ 1250	39 years (40 years for purposes of § 168(g))
Facade— Exterior	Decorative exterior wall covering of the hotel/casino complex to help create the theme for the hotel/casino complex. Generally consists of a synthetic plaster, or stucco, that is cemented, or in some cases, bolted on in the form of a panel, to the frames of the exterior walls of the buildings.	§ 1250	39 years (40 years for purposes of § 168(g))

Appendix 2

Asset		Description	Property Type	Recovery Period
Facade— Interior	Interior Columns	Includes finishes on interior columns that are affixed with permanent adhesive or nailed or screwed in place. Examples include marble tile, millwork, and other coverings cemented, mudded, or grouted to the column.	§ 1250	39 years (40 years for purposes of § 168(g))
		Includes finishes on interior columns that are not permanently attached and not intended to be permanent. Located in the Casino area. Also includes interior columns associated with the activities described in Asset Class 79.0 of Rev. Proc. 87-56, such as Theater and Showroom.	§ 1245	7 years (79.0 Recreation)
		Includes finishes on interior columns that are not permanently attached and not intended to be permanent. Not located in the Casino/ Theater area.	§ 1245	5 years (57.0 Distributive Trades and Services)
	False Balcony	Finishes generally made of millwork or wrought iron (forged balconies and gates) and located in the Casino area. Also includes false balconies associated with the activities described in Asset Class 79.0 of Rev. Proc. 87-56, such as Theater and Showroom.	§ 1245	7 years (79.0 Recreation)
		Finishes generally made of millwork or wrought iron (forged balconies and gates). Not located in the Casino/ Theater area.	§ 1245	5 years (57.0 Distributive Trades and Services)
	Storefronts	Includes the framework, sheetrock, or any other component that comprises the framing of the storefront walls.	§ 1250	39 years (40 years for purposes of § 168(g))
		Includes storefronts made primarily of synthetic materials (foam, fiberglass, cast stone, or glass reinforced concrete) that are affixed with permanent adhesive or nailed or screwed in place. Also includes costs relating to the exposed millwork, trim	§ 1250	39 years (40 years for purposes of § 168(g))

Asset		Description	Property Type	Recovery Period
Facade— Interior— Continued	Storefronts— Continued	molding and lining around doors, windows, and baseboards. See also **Wall Coverings and Millwork.**		
		Includes false storefronts made primarily of synthetic materials (foam, fiberglass, cast stone, or glass reinforced concrete) that are not permanently attached and not intended to be permanent. Located in the Casino area. Also includes storefronts associated with the activities described in Asset Class 79.0 of Rev. Proc. 87-56, such as Theater and Showroom.	§ 1245	7 years (79.0 Recreation)
		Includes false storefronts made primarily of synthetic materials (foam, fiberglass, cast stone, or glass reinforced concrete) that are not permanently attached and not intended to be permanent. Not located in the Casino/Theater area.	§ 1245	5 years (57.0 Distributive Trades and Services)
	Painted Ceilings	Includes painted ceilings applied with spray guns and brushes (regardless of theme or design).	§ 1250	39 years (40 years for purposes of § 168(g))
		Includes *custom* painted ceilings designed on computers, transferred to canvases, and hand-painted with acrylics (fire-retardant materials).	§ 1250	39 years (40 years for purposes of § 168(g))
		Includes painted ceilings designed on computers, transferred to canvases, and hand-painted with acrylics that are not permanently attached and not intended to be permanent and located in the Casino area. Also includes painted ceilings that are not permanently attached associated with the activities described in Asset Class 79.0 of Rev. Proc. 87-56, such as Theater and Showroom.	§ 1245	7 years (79.0 Recreation)
		Includes painted ceilings designed on computers, transferred to canvases, and	§ 1245	5 years

Asset	Description		Property Type	Recovery Period
Facade—Interior—Continued	Painted Ceilings—Continued	hand-painted with acrylics that are not permanently attached and not intended to be permanent. Not located in the Casino/Theater area.		(57.0 Distributive Trades and Services)
	Rockscape	Includes rock finishes made of synthetic materials (such as interior fountains containing waterproofed liners and molded rockscape features) and decorative stonework embedded in walls that are an integral part of a building's structural shell. Includes non-load bearing rockscape and decorative stonework embedded in walls (regardless of height) that divide or create rooms or provide traffic control where the rockscape and stonework cannot be 1) readily removed and remain in substantially the same condition after removal as before, or 2) moved and reused, stored, or sold in its entirety.	§ 1250	39 years (40 years for purposes of § 168(g))
		Includes rockscape and decorative stonework that do not function as part of the building and would be considered as non-structural theme elements that function merely as ornamentation.	§ 1245	5 years (57.0 Distributive Trades and Services)
Fire Protection & Alarm Systems	Includes sensing devices, computer controls, sprinkler heads, piping or plumbing, pumps, visual and audible alarms, alarm control panels, heat and smoke detection devices, fire escapes, fire doors, emergency exit lighting and signage, and wall mounted fire extinguishers necessary for the protection of the building.		§ 1250	39 years (40 years for purposes of § 168(g))
Fire Protection Equipment	Includes special fire detection or suppression systems directly associated with a piece of equipment. For example, a fire extinguisher designed and used for protection against a particular hazard created by the business activity.		§ 1245	5 years (57.0 Distributive Trades and Services)

Appendix 2

Asset	Description	Property Type	Recovery Period
Floor Covering	Includes floor covering that is affixed with permanent adhesive or nailed or screwed in place. Examples include ceramic or quarry tile, marble, paving brick, most vinyl coverings and other coverings cemented, mudded, or grouted to the floor; epoxy or sealers; and wood flooring.	§ 1250	39 years (40 years for purposes of § 168(g))
	Includes floor covering that is not permanently attached and not intended to be permanent, such as vinyl composition tile (VCT) installed with strippable adhesive, sheet vinyl, and carpeting, and located in the Casino area. Also includes floor covering that is not permanently attached associated with the activities described in Asset Class 79.0 of Rev. Proc. 87-56, such as Theater and Showroom.	§ 1245	7 years (79.0 Recreation)
	Includes floor covering that is not permanently attached and not intended to be permanent, such as vinyl composition tile (VCT) installed with strippable adhesive, sheet vinyl, and carpeting, but not located in the Casino/Theater area.	§ 1245	5 years (57.0 Distributive Trades and Services)
Floors	Includes concrete slabs and other floor systems. Floors include special treatments applied to or otherwise a permanent part of the floor. For example "super flat" finish, sloped drainage basins, raised perimeter, serving line curb, or cooler, freezer, and garbage room floors.	§ 1250	39 years (40 years for purposes of § 168(g))
Furniture—Guest Rooms	Includes furniture unique to guest rooms and distinguishable from office furniture. For example, beds, dressers, armoires, and night-tables. See also **Furniture—Office**.	§ 1245	5 years (57.0 Distributive Trades and Services)
Furniture—Office (includes Communication Equipment and Hook-ups)	Includes desk, chair, credenza, file cabinet, table (whether located in Administrative Areas or Guest Rooms) and other furniture such as workstations. Also includes communication equipment and related hook-ups.	§ 1245	7 years (00.11 Office Furniture and Fixtures)

Asset	Description	Property Type	Recovery Period
Generators	Emergency power generators for building related operations (emergency/safety systems).	§ 1250	39 years (40 years for purposes of § 168(g))
	Depreciable assets, whether such assets are section 1245 property or 1250 property, used in the production and/or distribution of electricity with rated total capacity in excess of 500 Kilowatts and/or assets used in the production and/or distribution of steam with rated total capacity in excess of 12,500 pounds per hour for use by the taxpayer in its industrial manufacturing process or plant activity and not ordinarily available for sale to others. Does not include buildings and structural components as defined in section 1.48-1(e) of the regulations. See **Asset Class 00.4 (Rev. Proc. 87-56)**. Note* asset class 00.4 includes both section 1245 and 1250 property per Rev. Proc. 87-56.	See Note*	15 years (00.4 Industrial Steam and Electric Generation and/ or Distribution Systems)
	Emergency power generators for casino operations. (See **Cost Segregation Audit Techniques Guide** for allocation examples.)	§ 1245	7 years (79.0 Recreation)
Kitchen Equipment Hook-ups	Encompasses the electrical distribution system of the kitchen. Refer to the industry directive for **Restaurants—Kitchen Equipment Hook-up**.	§ 1245	5 years (57.0 Distributive Trades and Services)

Asset	Description	Property Type	Recovery Period
Light Fixtures— Interior	Includes lighting such as recessed and lay-in lighting, night lighting, and exit lighting, as well as decorative lighting fixtures that provide substantially all the artificial illumination (*primary* source of lighting). Includes guest room lighting, wall sconces (bathroom, guest room, and hallway), hallway chandeliers, and all electrical connections associated with these fixtures, such as power junction boxes, riser conduit, and wiring.	§ 1250	39 years (40 years for purposes of § 168(g))
	Includes decorative light fixtures such as chandeliers, wall sconces, down lighting, neon lighting, column lights which are decorative in nature and not necessary for the operation of the building and located in the Casino area plus cost of all wiring and electrical connections associated with these fixtures. Also includes all decorative lighting fixtures associated with the activities described in Asset Class 79.0 of Rev. Proc. 87-56, such as Theater and Showroom.	§ 1245	7 years (79.0 Recreation)
	Includes decorative light fixtures, such as neon lights, table lamps, or track lighting, which are decorative in nature and not necessary for the operation of the building and not located in the Casino/Theater area. In other words, if the decorative lighting were turned off, the other sources of lighting would provide sufficient light for operation of the building. If the decorative lighting is the *primary* source of lighting, then it is section 1250 property.	§ 1245	5 years (57.0 Distributive Trades and Services)
Light Fixtures— Exterior	Exterior lighting (whether decorative or not) to the extent that the lighting relates to the maintenance or operation of the building. This category includes building mounted lighting to illuminate walkways, entrances, parking, etc.	§ 1250	39 years (40 years for purposes of § 168(g))
	Pole mounted or freestanding outdoor lighting system to illuminate sidewalks, parking or recreation areas. See also **Poles & Pylons**. Note* asset class 00.3 Land improvements includes both section 1245 and 1250 property per Rev. Proc. 87-56.	See Note*	15 years (00.3 Land Improvement)
	Removable plant grow lights or removable lighting that highlights *only* the landscaping or building exterior (but not parking areas or walkways) and does not relate to the maintenance or operation of the building.	§ 1245	5 years (57.0 Distributive Trades and Services)

Appendix 2 **29,021**

Asset	Description	Property Type	Recovery Period
Loading Dock	Includes bumpers, permanently installed dock levelers, plates, seals, lights, canopies, and overhead doors used in the receiving and shipping of merchandise.	§ 1250	39 years (40 years for purposes of § 168(g))
	Includes items such as compactors, conveyors, hoists and/or balers.	§ 1245	5 years (57.0 Distributive Trades and Services)
Millwork— General Building or Structural	Includes millwork that is made of finished wood, for example, doors and frames, window frames, sashes, porch work, mantels, panel work, stairways, and special woodwork. Includes pre-built wooden items brought to the site for installation and items constructed on site such as restroom cabinets, door jambs, moldings, trim, etc.	§ 1250	39 years (40 years for purposes of § 168(g))
	Corner Guards and Wall Guards (includes guards made of stainless steel, e.g., diamond plate)	§ 1250	39 years (40 years for purposes of § 168(g))
Millwork— Decorative	Includes decorative finish carpentry in a Casino area. Examples include detailed crown moldings, lattice work placed over finished walls or ceilings, and cabinets. The decorative millwork serves to enhance the overall décor of the Casino area and is not related to the operation of the building. Cabinets and counters in a restroom are excluded from this category; see **Restroom Accessories.** Also includes decorative millwork associated with the activities described in Asset Class 79.0 of Rev. Proc. 87-56, such as Theater and Showroom.	§ 1245	7 years (79.0 Recreation)
	Includes decorative finish carpentry in the *hotel and retail* areas. Examples include detailed crown moldings, lattice work placed over finished walls or ceilings, and cabinets. The decorative millwork serves to enhance the overall décor of the hotel and retail areas and is not related to the operation of the building. Cabinets and counters in a restroom are excluded from this category; see **Restroom Accessories**.	§ 1245	5 years (57.0 Distributive Trades and Services)
Poles & Pylons	Light poles for parking areas and other poles poured in concrete footings or bolt-mounted for signage, flags, etc. Note* asset class 00.3 Land improvements includes both section 1245 and 1250 property per Rev. Proc. 87-56. See also **Pylon Sign— Exterior** and **Light Fixtures—Exterior**.	See Note*	15 years (00.3 Land Improvement)

Asset	Description	Property Type	Recovery Period
Pools & Pool Equipment	Includes swimming pools and pool equipment (and spas attached to the swimming pools) that are contained within, on, or attached to a building.	§ 1250	39 years (40 years for purposes of § 168(g))
	Includes exterior swimming pools and pool equipment (and spas attached to the swimming pools) that are built on land. Note* asset class 00.3 Land improvements includes both section 1245 and 1250 property per Rev. Proc. 87-56.	See Note*	15 years (00.3 Land Improvement)
Pylon Sign— Exterior	Pylons made of concrete, brick, wood frame, stucco, or similar materials usually set in the ground or on a concrete foundation, and usually used for signage. Note* asset class 00.3 Land improvements includes both section 1245 and 1250 property per Rev. Proc. 87-56. See also **Poles & Pylons**	See Note*	15 years (00.3 Land Improvement)
	Includes only the sign face and/or message screen and related components.	§ 1245	5 years (57.0 Distributive Trades and Services)
Restroom Accessories	Includes paper towel dispensers, electric hand dryers, towel racks or holders, cup dispensers, purse shelves, toilet paper holders, soap dispensers or holders, lotion dispensers, sanitary napkin dispensers and waste receptacles, coat hooks, handrails, grab bars, mirrors, shelves, vanity cabinets, counters, and ashtrays and other items generally found in public restrooms that are built into or mounted on walls or partitions.	§ 1250	39 years (40 years for purposes of § 168(g))
Restroom Partitions	Includes shop made and standard manufacture toilet partitions, typically metal, but may be plastic or other materials.	§ 1250	39 years (40 years for purposes of § 168(g))

Appendix 2 **29,023**

Asset	Description	Property Type	Recovery Period
Security Equipment	Includes security equipment for the protection of the building and its contents, including the building exterior and grounds, from theft or vandalism and protection of employees and guests from assault. Examples include security cameras, recorders, monitors, and related equipment (including those located in the elevator and elevator lobbies); building exterior and interior motion detectors; security lighting; alarm systems; security systems and related junction boxes, wiring, and conduit).	§ 1250	39 years (40 years for purposes of § 168(g))
	Includes surveillance cameras, recorders, monitors and related equipment the primary purpose of which is to surveil gaming activities and to minimize theft in the Casino area. Also includes surveillance equipment associated with the activities described in Asset Class 79.0 of Rev. Proc. 87-56, such as Theater and Showroom.	§ 1245	7 years (79.0 Recreation)
	Includes electronic article surveillance systems, including surveillance cameras, recorders, monitors, and related equipment the primary purpose of which is to minimize theft in the *retail* areas. Does not include the Casino/Theater area.	§ 1245	5 years (57.0 Distributive Trades and Services)
Signs	Exit signs, restroom identifiers, room numbers, and other signs relating to the operation or maintenance of a building. See also **Exit Signs**.	§ 1250	39 years (40 years for purposes of § 168(g))
	Includes interior signs used to display gaming related activities such as keno, slots, video poker, etc. Also includes interior signs associated with the activities described in Asset Class 79.0 of Rev. Proc. 87-56, such as Theater and Showroom.	§ 1245	7 years (79.0 Recreation)
	Includes interior signs used to display directories of names or indicate the location of business functions and departments, (registration desk, buffet, retail shops, etc.), but not associated with the Casino/Theater activities. Not related to the operation or maintenance of a building. Also includes exterior signs used to display names, symbols, directions, etc. For pylon signs, includes only the sign face and related dedicated wiring. See also **Pylon Sign— Exterior**.	§ 1245	5 years (57.0 Distributive Trades and Services)

Appendix 2

Asset	Description	Property Type	Recovery Period
Site Grading & Excavation	Nondepreciable land preparation costs, in general, include the one time cost of demolition, clearing and grubbing, blasting, site stripping, fill or excavation, dewatering, and grading to allow development of land. Clearing and grubbing is the removal of debris, brush, trees, etc., from the site. Stripping is the removal of the topsoil to provide a stable surface for site and building improvements. The grading of land involves moving soil for the purpose of producing a more level surface to allow development of the land. These costs would not have to be incurred again if the building was repaired, rebuilt, or even torn down and replaced with some other type of building.		Land
	Clearing, grading, excavating, and removal costs directly associated with the construction of buildings and building components are part of the cost of construction of the building and depreciated over the life of the building.	§ 1250	39 years (40 years for purposes of § 168(g))
	Clearing, grading, excavating, and removal costs directly associated with the construction of sidewalks, parking areas, roadways, and other depreciable land improvements are part of the cost of construction of the improvements and depreciated over the life of the associated asset. Note* asset class 00.3 Land improvements includes both section 1245 and 1250 property per Rev. Proc. 87-56.	See Note*	15 years (00.3 Land Improvement)
Site Utilities	Systems that are used to distribute utility services from the property line to the casino complex. Includes water, sanitary sewers, gas, and electrical services.	§ 1250	39 years (40 years for purposes of § 168(g)
	Storm Piping (for draining the site of rainwater). Note* asset class 00.3 Land improvements includes both section 1245 and 1250 property per Rev. Proc. 87-56.	See Note*	15 years (00.3 Land Improvement)
Site Work	Site work includes curbing, paving, general site improvements, fencing, landscaping, roads, sewers, sidewalks, site drainage, and all other site improvements not directly related to the building. Note* asset class 00.3 Land improvements includes both section 1245 and 1250 property per Rev. Proc. 87-56. See **Site Utilities** for sanitary sewers.	See Note*	15 years (00.3 Land Improvement)

Appendix 2 **29,025**

Asset	Description	Property Type	Recovery Period
Spa Hook-ups	Includes Jacuzzi, Whirlpools, and bathtubs located in Guest Rooms and Suites.	§ 1250	39 years (40 years for purposes of § 168(g))
	Includes Jacuzzi and Whirlpools located in the *Hotel Spa/Fitness Center*. Does not include spa hook-ups that may be associated with swimming pools or pool equipment. See also **Pools & Pool Equipment**.	§ 1245	5 years (57.0 Distributive Trades and Services)
Wall Coverings	Includes interior and exterior paint; ceramic or quarry tile, marble, stone, brick, and other finishes affixed with mortar, cement, or grout; paneling, wainscoting, and other wood finishes affixed with nails, screws, or permanent adhesives; and sanitary kitchen wall panels such as fiberglass, stainless steel, and plastic wall panels.	§ 1250	39 years (40 years for purposes of § 168(g))
	Includes strippable wall paper and vinyl that causes no damage to the underlying wall or wall surface and located in the Casino area. For purposes of this directive, such wallpaper is considered not permanently attached or intended to be permanent. Also includes strippable wall coverings associated with the activities described in Asset Class 79.0 of Rev. Proc. 87-56, such as Theater and Showroom.	§ 1245	7 years (79.0 Recreation)
	Includes strippable wall paper and vinyl that causes no damage to the underlying wall or wall surface and located in the *hotel and retail* areas. For purposes of this directive, such wallpaper is considered not permanently attached or intended to be permanent.	§ 1245	5 years (57.0 Distributive Trades and Services)

Item 4—Cost Segregation Guide for Retail Business

This matrix, which is part of the *Cost Segregation Audit Techniques Guide*, is intended to provide direction to effectively utilize resources in the classification and examination of property used in the operation of a retail business such as a department or grocery store. General fact patterns specific to this industry have been considered in the classification of these assets and may not be applicable to other industries. Similarly, asset classification guidance issued for other industries is based on the general fact pattern for that industry and may not be applicable to a retail business situation. For example, for asset classification of restaurants located within a retail store, refer to the industry directive for restaurants. For examination techniques and historical background related to this issue, refer to the *Cost Segregation Audit Techniques Guide*.

Note: In the case of certain leasehold improvement property, the classifications in this directive are superseded to the extent that the American Jobs Creation Act of

2004 modifies IRC Section 168. Thus, a 15-year straight line recovery period should replace the recovery period shown in the following matrix if the asset is "qualified leasehold improvement property" (as defined in IRC Section 168(e)(6)) placed in service by the taxpayer after 10/22/04 and before 01/01/08.

[1]I.R.C. §1245 can apply to certain qualified recovery nonresidential real estate placed in service after 1980 and before 1987. See I.R.C. § 1245(a)(5).

Asset	Description	Property Type	Recovery Period
Awnings & Canopies	Readily removable overhang or covering, often of canvas or plastic, used to provide shade or cover over a storefront, window, or door; or used inside a structure to identify a particular department or selling area. Examples include applications over an exterior door or window, or attached to interior walls or suspended from ceilings for bakery, deli, floral, meat, or produce departments. Also includes canopies designed to protect customers and gasoline fueling equipment from weather conditions and to act as advertising displays that are anchored with bolts and are not attached to buildings or other structures. Does not include canopies that are an integral part of a building's structural shell, such as in the casino industry, or over docks. See also **Concrete Foundations & Footings** and **Loading Docks**.	1245	57.0 Distributive Trades and Services—5 Years
Beverage Equipment	Equipment for storage and preparation of beverages and beverage delivery systems. Beverage equipment includes the refrigerators, coolers, dispensing systems, and the dedicated electrical, tubing, or piping for such equipment. The dispensing system may be gravity, pump, or gas driven. See also **Refrigerated Structures**.	1245	57.0 Distributive Trades and Services—5 Years
Ceilings	Includes all interior ceilings regardless of finish or décor; e.g., drywall or plaster ceilings, acoustic ceilings, suspended ceilings (including hangers, frames, grids, and tiles or panels), decorative metal or tin finishes, plastic panels, decorative panels, etc. See also **Awnings & Canopies, Millwork—Decorative** and **Millwork—General Building or Structural**.	1250	Building or Building Component—39 Years

Appendix 2 **29,027**

Asset	Description	Property Type	Recovery Period
Computers	Processors (CPU), direct access storage device (DASD), tape drives, desktop and laptop computers, CRT, terminals, monitors, printers, and other peripheral equipment. Excludes Point of Sale (POS) systems and computers that are an integral part of other equipment (e.g., fire detection, heating, cooling, or energy management systems, etc.).	1245	00.12 Information Systems—5 Years
Concrete Foundations & Footings	Includes formwork, reinforcement, concrete block, and pre-cast or cast-in-place work related to foundations and footings necessary for the proper setting of the building.	1250	Building or Building Component—39 Years
	Foundations or footings for signs, light poles, and other land improvements (except buildings).	1250	00.3 Land Improvements—15 Years
	The supporting concrete footings used to anchor gasoline pump canopies are inherently permanent structures and are classified as land improvements.	1250	57.1 Distributive Trades and Services—15 Years
Data Handling Equipment	Includes adding and accounting machines, calculators, copiers, and duplicating machines. Excludes computers and computer peripheral equipment. See **Computers**.	1245	00.13 Data Handling Equipment, except Computers—5 Years
Doors	Interior and exterior doors, regardless of decoration, including but not limited to, double opening doors, overhead doors, revolving doors, mall entrance security gates, roll-up or sliding wire mesh or steel grills and gates, and door hardware (such as doorknobs, closers, kick plates, hinges, locks, automatic openers, etc.).	1250	Building or Building Component—39 Years
	Special lightweight, double action doors installed to prevent accidents in a heavily trafficked area. For example, flexible doors, or clear or strip curtains used between stock and selling areas.	1245	57.0 Distributive Trades and Services—5 Years
Doors—Air Curtains	Air doors or curtains are air systems located above doors and windows that circulate air to stabilize environments and save energy by minimizing the heated/air conditioned air loss through open doorways and windows. They also effectively repel flying insects, dust, and pollutants.	1250	Building or Building Component—39 Years

Asset	Description	Property Type	Recovery Period
Drive-Through Equipment	Drive-through equipment includes order taking, merchandise delivery, and payment processing systems whether mechanical or electronic. Excludes building elements such as doors, bays, or windows. See also **Walls—Exterior**, and **Windows** for drive-through bays and windows.	1245	57.0 Distributive Trades and Services—5 Years
Electrical	Includes all components of the building electrical system used in the operation or maintenance of the building or necessary to provide general building services such as electrical outlets of general applicability and accessibility, lighting, heating, ventilation, air conditioning, and electrical wiring.	1250	Building or Building Component—39 Years
	Special electrical connections which are necessary to and used directly with a specific item of machinery or equipment or connections between specific items of individual machinery or equipment; such as dedicated electrical outlets, wiring, conduit, and circuit breakers by which machinery and equipment is connected to the electrical distribution system. Does not include electrical outlets of general applicability and accessibility. See Chapter 5 of the Cost Segregation Audit Techniques Guide for allocation examples.	1245	57.0 Distributive Trades and Services—5 Years
Elevators and Escalators	Elevators and escalators, which include handrails and smoke baffles, are permanently affixed to the building and intended to remain in place. They relate to the operation or maintenance of the building and are structural components.	1250	Building or Building Component—39 Years
Energy Management Systems	Energy management systems control all energy-using systems in a building, automatically checking occupancy schedules, reading temperatures, and re-circuiting light levels, causing all heating, cooling and lighting equipment to operate so as to minimize energy costs. Includes, for example, detection devices such as smoke, motion, and infrared devices, photocells, foil and contact switches, pressure switches, proximity alarms, sensors, alarm transmitting controls, data gathering panels, demand controllers, thermostats, computer controls, outside air economizers, occupancy sensors, electronic ballasts, and all related wiring and conduit. May also provide for fire and burglary protection.	1250	Building or Building Component—39 Years

Appendix 2 **29,029**

Asset	Description	Property Type	Recovery Period
Exit Signs	Signs posted along exit routes that indicate the direction of travel to the nearest exit. These signs typically read "EXIT" and may have distinctive colors, illumination, or arrows indicating the direction to the exit.	1250	Building or Building Component—39 Years
Fire Protection & Alarm Systems	Includes sensing devices, computer controls, sprinkler heads, piping or plumbing, pumps, visual and audible alarms, alarm control panels, heat and smoke detection devices, fire escapes, fire doors, emergency exit lighting and signage, and wall mounted fire extinguishers necessary for the protection of the building.	1250	Building or Building Component—39 Years
Fire Protection Equipment	Includes special fire detection or suppression systems directly associated with a piece of equipment. For example, a fire extinguisher designed and used for protection against a particular hazard created by the business activity.	1245	57.0 Distributive Trades and Services—5 Years
Floor Coverings	Floor covering affixed with permanent adhesive, nailed, or screwed in place. Examples include ceramic or quarry tile, marble, paving brick, and other coverings cemented, mudded, or grouted to the floor; epoxy or sealers; and wood flooring.	1250	Building or Building Component—39 Years
	Floor covering that is installed by means of strippable adhesives. For the retail industry, all vinyl composition tile (VCT), sheet vinyl, and carpeting will be treated as not permanently attached and not intended to be permanent. Also includes flooring that is frequently moved and reused to create a department theme or seasonal display.	1245	57.0 Distributive Trades and Services—5 Years
Floors	Includes concrete slabs and other floor systems. Floors include special treatments applied to or otherwise a permanent part of the floor. For example "super flat" finish, sloped drainage basins, raised perimeter, serving line curb, or cooler, freezer and garbage room floors.	1250	Building or Building Component—39 Years
Heating, Ventilating & Air Conditioning (HVAC)	Includes all components of a central heating, ventilating and air conditioning system not specifically identified elsewhere. HVAC systems that are installed not only to meet the temperature and humidity requirements of machinery but are also installed for additional significant purposes, such as customer comfort and ventilation, are building components.	1250	Building or Building Component—39 Years

Asset	Description	Property Type	Recovery Period
	Only separate HVAC units that meet the sole justification test are included (i.e., machinery the sole justification for the installation of which is the fact that such machinery is required to meet temperature or humidity requirements which are essential for the operation of other machinery or the processing of materials or foodstuffs). HVAC may meet the sole justification test even though it incidentally provides for the comfort of employees, or serves, to an insubstantial degree, areas where such temperature or humidity requirements are not essential. Includes refrigeration units, condensers, compressors, accumulators, coolers, pumps, connecting pipes, and wiring for the mechanical equipment for climate controlled rooms, walk-in freezers, coolers, humidors, and ripening rooms. Allocation of HVAC is not appropriate. See also **Refrigerated Structures, Refrigeration Equipment**, and **Ripening Rooms**.	1245	57.0 Distributive Trades and Services—5 Years
Kiosks	A small retail outlet, often prefabricated, which acts like a fixed retail outlet yet is not permanent. Kiosks may be used to retail merchandise such as newspapers and magazines, film and digital images, and food and beverages. Kiosks are also present in shopping centers or malls where they function as temporary or portable retail outlets for a variety of merchandise.	1245	57.0 Distributive Trades and Services—5 Years
Light Fixtures— Interior	Includes lighting such as recessed and lay-in lighting, night lighting, and exit lighting, as well as decorative lighting fixtures that provide substantially all the artificial illumination in the building or along building walkways. For emergency and exit lighting, see **Fire Protection & Alarm Systems**.	1250	Building or Building Component—39 Years
	Decorative light fixtures are light fixtures, such as neon lights or track lighting, which are decorative in nature and not necessary for the operation of the building. In other words, if the decorative lighting were turned off, the other sources of lighting would provide sufficient light for operation of the building. If the decorative lighting is the *primary* source of lighting, then it is section 1250 property.	1245	57.0 Distributive Trades and Services—5 Years

Appendix 2 **29,031**

Asset	Description	Property Type	Recovery Period
Light Fixtures—Exterior	Exterior lighting whether decorative or not is considered section 1250 property to the extent that the lighting relates to the maintenance or operation of the building. This category includes building mounted lighting to illuminate walkways, entrances, parking, etc.	1250	Building or Building Component—39 Years
	Pole mounted or freestanding outdoor lighting system to illuminate sidewalks, parking or recreation areas. See also **Poles & Pylons**. Note* asset class 00.3 Land improvements includes both section 1245 and 1250 property per Rev. Proc. 87-56.	See Note*	00.3 Land Improvements—15 Years
	Plant grow lights or lighting that highlights *only* the landscaping or building exterior (but not parking areas or walkways) does not relate to the maintenance or operation of the building.	1245	57.0 Distributive Trades and Services—5 Years
Loading Docks	Includes bumpers, permanently installed dock levelers, plates, seals, lights, canopies, and overhead doors used in the receiving and shipping of merchandise.	1250	Building or Building Component—39 Years
	Includes items such as compactors, conveyors, hoists, and balers.	1245	57.0 Distributive Trades and Services—5 Years
Millwork—Decorative	Decorative millwork is the decorative finish carpentry in a retail selling area. Examples include detailed crown moldings, lattice work placed over finished walls or ceilings, cabinets, cashwraps, counters and toppers. The decorative millwork serves to enhance the overall décor of the retail store and is not related to the operation of the building. Cabinets and counters in a restroom are excluded from this category; see **Restroom Accessories**.	1245	57.0 Distributive Trades and Services—5 Years
Millwork—General Building or Structural	General millwork is all building materials made of finished wood (e.g., doors and frames, window frames, sashes, porch work, mantels, panel work, stairways, and special woodwork). Includes pre-built wooden items brought to the site for installation and items constructed on site such as restroom cabinets, door jambs, moldings, trim, etc.	1250	Building or Building Component—39 Years

Asset	Description	Property Type	Recovery Period
Office Furnishings	Includes desk, chair, credenza, file cabinet, table or other furniture such as workstations. Also includes telephone equipment, fax machines, and other communications equipment. Does not include communications equipment included in other asset classes in Rev. Proc. 87-56.	1245	00.11 Office Furniture, Fixtures, and Equipment—7 Years
Parking Lots	Grade level surface parking area usually constructed of asphalt, brick, concrete, stone or similar material. Category includes bumper blocks, curb cuts, curb work, striping, landscape islands, perimeter fences, and sidewalks.	1250	00.3 Land Improvements—15 Years
Parking Structures	Any structure or edifice the purpose of which is to provide parking space. Includes, for example, garages, parking ramps, or other parking structures.	1250	Building or Building Component—39 Years
Plumbing	All piping, drains, sprinkler mains, valves, sprinkler heads, water flow switches, restroom plumbing fixtures (e.g., toilets), and piping, kitchen hand sinks, electric water coolers, and all other components of a building plumbing system (water or gas) not specifically identified elsewhere.	1250	Building or Building Component—39 Years
	Includes water, gas, or refrigerant hook-ups directly connected to appliances or equipment, eyewash stations, kitchen drainage, and kitchen hot water heater. For example, a hair salon in a retail outlet would require special hair washing sinks and water hook-up for the sinks.	1245	57.0 Distributive Trades and Services—5 Years
Point of Sale (POS) Systems	A register or terminal based data collection system used to control and record all sales (cash, charge, COD, gift cards, layaway, etc.) at the point of sale. Includes cash registers, computerized sales systems and related peripheral equipment, satellite systems, scanners, and wands. See also **Electrical** for hook-ups.	1245	57.0 Distributive Trades and Services—5 Years
Poles & Pylons	Light poles for parking areas and other poles poured in concrete footings or bolt-mounted for signage, flags, etc. Note* asset class 00.3 Land improvements includes both section 1245 and 1250 property per Rev. Proc. 87-56. See also **Signs** and **Light Fixtures—Exterior**.	See Note*	00.3 Land Improvements—15 Years

Appendix 2 **29,033**

Asset	Description	Property Type	Recovery Period
Refrigeration Equipment	Includes refrigeration units, condensers, compressors, accumulators, coolers, pumps, connecting pipes, and associated wiring. Refrigeration equipment is commonly found in climate controlled rooms, walk-in freezers, coolers, humidors, and ripening rooms.	1245	57.0 Distributive Trades and Services—5 Years
Refrigerated Structures	Includes structural components such as walls, floors, ceilings, and insulation to construct a climate controlled structure, room, or facility such as a cold storage warehouse, walk-in freezer, cooler, garbage room, or humidor. See also **Refrigeration Equipment**.	1250	Building or Building Component—39 Years
	A portable structure installed inside the building, consisting of prefabricated panels mounted on a movable framework. Portable structures are designed to be able to be disassembled and moved. See also **Refrigeration Equipment**.	1245	57.0 Distributive Trades and Services—5 Years
Restaurant—In Store	See Restaurant Industry Directive. For retail situations that include a restaurant or other food preparation property within a store, such as a deli or snack bar, the facts are similar to those considered in the industry directive on restaurants, and that directive may be relied upon for asset classification.		
Restroom Accessories	Includes paper towel dispensers, electric hand dryers, towel racks or holders, cup dispensers, purse shelves, toilet paper holders, soap dispensers or holders, lotion dispensers, sanitary napkin dispensers and waste receptacles, coat hooks, handrails, grab bars, mirrors, shelves, vanity cabinets, counters, ashtrays, baby changing stations, and other items generally found in public restrooms that are built into or mounted on walls or partitions.	1250	Building or Building Component—39 Years
Restroom Partitions	Includes shop made and standard manufacture toilet partitions, typically metal, but may be plastic or other materials.	1250	Building or Building Component—39 Years
Retail Accessories	Accessories used to better display merchandise that are not held for sale. Includes assets such as audio/video display devices, artwork (if depreciable), holiday decorations, lamps, mirrors, pictures, plaques, potted plants, and decorative mobile props (such as coat of arms, sporting equipment or memorabilia, etc., excluding non-depreciable art, antiques or collectibles).	1245	57.0 Distributive Trades and Services—5 Years

Asset	Description	Property Type	Recovery Period
Retail Conveying Equipment	Includes assets such as belt or roller conveyors and pneumatic tube systems used to distribute retail merchandise.	1245	57.0 Distributive Trades and Services—5 Years
Retail Equipment	Includes assets such as sewing machines, tackers, ironing equipment, pressing tables, steam presses, pinning machines, price mark guns, marking machines, work benches, power tools, check writers, endorsing machines, paper cutters, perforators, postage meters, money sorters, coin counting and dispensing equipment, and shopping carts.	1245	57.0 Distributive Trades and Services—5 Years
Retail Fixtures	Includes assets such as back cases or islands, cabinets, cubes, deli cases, end caps, floor stands, garment racks, gondolas, grid systems, mannequins, refrigerator/freezer cases, shelving, sign holders or stands, show cases, wall display units and other retail fixtures (such as dressing or fitting room partitions) needed in the business operation that are not a building component.	1245	57.0 Distributive Trades and Services—5 Years
Retail Furniture	Includes furniture unique to retail stores and distinguishable from office furniture. For example, a high stool in a cosmetic department, a shoe department footstool, a hair salon barber chair, or a bench outside a dressing room. See also **Office Furnishings**.	1245	57.0 Distributive Trades and Services—5 Years
Ripening Rooms	Special enclosed equipment boxes used to ripen produce by circulating special gases. The rooms are large boxes with special doors and large airplane-type propellers, which circulate the gases used to ripen the produce. The boxes are housed within a distribution center warehouse. These specialized facilities are considered to be part of the retail distribution equipment because they have a special retail purpose and can not be used for any other purpose. The boxes are not a part of the building structure.	1245	57.0 Distributive Trades and Services—5 Years

Appendix 2 **29,035**

Asset	Description	Property Type	Recovery Period
Roof	All elements of the roof including but not limited to joists, rafters, deck, shingles, vapor barrier, skylights, trusses, girders, and gutters. Determination of whether decorative elements of a roof (e.g., false dormers, mansard) constitute structural building components depends on their integration with the overall roof, not their load bearing capacity. If removal of the decorative element results in the direct exposure of building components to water, snow, wind, or moisture damage, or if the decorative element houses lighting fixtures, wiring, or other structural components, then the decorative elements are part of the overall roof system and are structural components of the building.	1250	Building or Building Component—39 Years
Security Systems	Includes security equipment for the protection of the building (and its contents) from burglary or vandalism and protection of employees from assault. Examples include window and door locks; card key access systems; keyless entry systems; security cameras, recorders, monitors and related equipment; perimeter and interior building motion detectors; security lighting; alarm systems; and security system wiring and conduit.	1250	Building or Building Component—39 Years
	Electronic article surveillance systems including electronic gates, surveillance cameras, recorders, monitors and related equipment, the primary purpose of which is to minimize merchandise shrinkage due to theft. Also includes teller-style pass-through windows, security booths, and bulletproof enclosures generally located in the cash office and customer service areas.	1245	57.0 Distributive Trades and Services—5 Years
Signs	Exit signs, restroom identifiers, room numbers, and other signs relating to the operation or maintenance of a building.	1250	Building or Building Component—39 Years
	Interior and exterior signs used for display or theme identity. For example, interior signs to identify departments or exterior signs to display trade names or trade symbols. For pylon signs, includes only sign face. See also **Poles & Pylons**.	1245	57.0 Distributive Trades and Services—5 Years

Asset	Description	Property Type	Recovery Period
Site Preparation, Grading & Excavation	In general, land preparation costs include the one time cost of clearing and grubbing, site stripping, fill or excavation, and grading to allow development of land. Clearing and grubbing is the removal of debris, brush, trees, etc., from the site. Stripping is the removal of the topsoil to provide a stable surface for site and building improvements. The grading of land involves moving soil for the purpose of producing a more level surface to allow development of the land.		Land
	Clearing, grading, excavating, and removal costs directly associated with the construction of buildings and building components are part of the cost of construction of the building and depreciated over the life of the building.	1250	Building or Building Component—39 Years
	Clearing, grading, excavating and removal costs directly associated with the construction of sidewalks, parking areas, roadways and other depreciable land improvements are part of the cost of construction of the improvements and depreciated over the life of the associated asset.	1250	00.3 Land Improvements— 15 Years
Site Utilities	Site utilities are the systems that are used to distribute utility services from the property line to the retail building. Includes water, sanitary sewer, gas, and electrical services.	1250	Building or Building Component—39 Years
Site Work	Site work includes curbing, paving, general site improvements, fencing, landscaping, roads, sewers, sidewalks, site drainage, and all other site improvements not directly related to the building. For sanitary sewers, see **Site Utilities**.	1250	00.3 Land Improvements— 15 Years
Sound Systems	Equipment and apparatus, including wiring, used to provide amplified sound or music. For example, public address by way of paging a customer or background music. Excludes applications linked to fire protection and alarm systems.	1245	57.0 Distributive Trades and Services—5 Years

Appendix 2 **29,037**

Asset	Description	Property Type	Recovery Period
Trash Enclosures	Enclosures for waste receptacles that are attached to the building. Typically constructed of the same materials as the building shell with either interior or exterior access. These trash enclosures are an integral part of the building shell and cannot be moved without damage to the underlying building.	1250	Building or Building Component—39 Years
	Freestanding enclosures for waste receptacles, typically constructed on a concrete pad with its posts set in the concrete. Serves both safety and decorative functions.	1250	00.3 Land Improvements—15 Years
Wall Coverings	Includes interior and exterior paint; ceramic or quarry tile, marble, stone, brick and other finishes affixed with mortar, cement or grout; paneling, wainscoting, and other wood finishes affixed with nails, screws, or permanent adhesives; and sanitary kitchen wall panels such as fiberglass, stainless steel, and plastic wall panels.	1250	Building or Building Component—39 Years
	Strippable wallpaper that causes no damage to the underlying wall or wall surface.	1245	57.0 Distributive Trades and Services—5 Years
Walls—Exterior	Includes all exterior walls and building support regardless of construction materials. Exterior walls may include columns, posts, beams, girders, curtain walls, tilt up panels, studs, framing, sheetrock, insulation, windows, doors, exterior façade, brick, masonry, etc. Also includes drive-through bay, windows, and doors.	1250	Building or Building Component—39 Years
Walls—Interior Partitions	Includes all load bearing interior partitions regardless of construction. Also includes non-load bearing partitions regardless of height (typically constructed of studs and sheetrock or other materials) that divide or create rooms or provide traffic control. Includes rough carpentry and plaster, dry wall or gypsum board, and other finishes.	1250	Building or Building Component—39 Years
	Interior walls for merchandise display where the partition can be 1) readily removed and remain in substantially the same condition after removal as before, or 2) moved and reused, stored, or sold in their entirety.	1245	57.0 Distributive Trades and Services—5 Years

Asset	Description	Property Type	Recovery Period
Windows	Exterior windows, including store front windows, drive-through service and carousel windows, and vestibule.	1250	Building or Building Component—39 Years
Window Treatments	Window treatments such as drapes, curtains, louver, blinds, post construction tinting, and interior decorative theme décor which are readily removable.	1245	57.0 Distributive Trades and Services—5 Years

RESOURCES ON THE WEB

Item A—Sites with information on the major spreadsheets
- http://office.microsoft.com/en-us/FX010858001033.aspx
- http://www.lotus.com/products/product2.nsf/wdocs/123home
- http://www.corel.com/servlet/Satellite?pagename=Corel3/Products/Display

Item B—Sites where other Excel add-ins may be found
- Type: "Excel business tools" in a search engine such as Google
- http://www.ozgrid.com
- http://www.modeladvisor.com

Item C—Links that offer budgeting and forecasting software
- http://www.business.com/directory/accounting/budgeting_and_forecasting
- http://www.business.com/search/rslt_default.asp?vt=all&type=web&query=expert+systems+forecasting

Item D—Links to business management software
- http://www.2020software.com/default.asp
- http://www.business.com/directory/food_and_beverage
- http://www.analyticsmagazine.com

Item E—Links to hotel management programs
- http://www.micros.com
- http://www.springermiller.com
- http://www.agilysys.com/home.com
- http://solutions.epicor.com/se/hosp-landing/?PROD=HOSPGOO&SRC=g-hos-2005

30,002 Resources on the Web

Item F—Leading point-of-sale system vendors
- Profitek Ultimate P.O.S Solutions (http://www.developer.ibm.com/gsdod/solutiondetails.do?solutionId=4269&lc=en)
- Micros (http://www.micros.com/products)
- Food Service Solutions, Inc. (http://www.foodserve.com/pos.htm)

Item G—Links to other restaurant management software
- Micros by Micros Systems, Inc. (http://www.micros.com)
- Execu/Touch by Executech Systems, Inc. (http://executouch.com)
- Business Plus Accounting (http://www.businesssoftware.com/restpro.asp?trackcode=bizcom)
- Compeat Restaurant Accounting Systems Software (http://www.find accountingsoftware.com/software/product/3039)
- Silverware Pos (http://www.silverwarepos.com)
- Restaurant Manager (http://www.actionsystems.com/?trackcode=bizcom)
- Maitre'D (http://www.maitredpos.com/MenuProducts/default.aspx?pub=google)
- Adaco Services, Inc. (http://www.adacoservices.com)
- Avero, Inc. (http://www.averoinc.com)
- CBORD Group, Inc. (http://www.cbord.com/products)
- Eatec Corp. (http://www.eatec.com/products.htm)
- ReServe Interactive (http://www.efficient-frontiers.com)

Item H—Links to Microsoft-related sites containing useful hospitality management programs
- http://www.microsoft.com/industry/hospitality/default.mspx
- http://www.microsoft.com/smarthospitality

Item I—Links to revenue management providers
- Micros (www.micros.com)
- Integrated Decisions and Systems, Inc. (IdeaS) (www.ideas.com)
- Manugistics (www.manugistics.com)

Item J—Links to yield management systems
- Integrated Decisions and Systems, Inc. (www.ideas.com)
- Micros (www.micros.com)
- Resort Data Processing (www.resortdata.com/index.htm)
- Manugistics (www.manugistics.com)

Item K—Links to sites with information on data warehousing and data warehousing providers
- Dataflux at: www.dataflux.com

Resources on the Web **30,003**

- DataMirror at: www.datamirror.com
- CIO at: www.cio.com/km/data
- InfoSphere at: www.datawarehousing.com
- Toolbox for IT at: www.datawarehouse.ittoolbox.com
- LGI Systems at: www.dwinfocenter.org

Item L—Link to the Knowledgestorm site, a site with information on investment in IT, and a partial list of topics covered

- http://www.knowledgestorm.com/ActivityServlet?ksAction=optInReq&solId=72990&pos=2&spId=LONGVIEWENTRPFINCLMGMT&trkpg=scname

    Partial list of topics covered in this site:

    —*Aligning IT and Business Goals*—Help the IT team understand, implement, and determine key business strategies.

    —*Maximizing IT Investments*—Reduce IT costs, stretch budget dollars, and make the financial case for IT projects.

    —*Integrating the Enterprise*—Build systems that help employees, customers, and partners create profits for company.

    —*Optimizing Infrastructure*—Maximize the value of existing hardware and software while planning wisely for the future.

    —*Managing Compliance Standards*—Understand regulations and turn compliance efforts into business opportunities.

    —*Outsourcing for Strategic Advantage*—Outsource when, where, and how it makes sense for the business.

    —*Empowering a Mobile Workforce*—Free employees from their desktops to unlock productivity and profitability.

    —*Leveraging Open Source*—Go beyond Linux and find real business value in enterprise applications.

Item M—Links to some hospitality industry and financial manager associations

- American Hospitality Institute—http://www.americanhospitalityinstitute.org
- American Hotel and Lodging Educational Foundation—http://www.ahlef.org
- American Hotel and Lodging Industry Association—http://www.ahla.com
- Club Managers Association of America—www.cmaa.org
- Council on Hotel, Restaurant and Institutional Education—http://www.chrie.org/i4a/pages/index.cfm?pageid=1
- Financial Executives International—http://www.financialexecutives.org
- Hospitality Financial and Technology Professionals—http://www.hftp.org

- Hotel and Catering International Management Association—http://www.ameinfo.com/news/Company_News/H/HCIMA
- Institute of Management Accountants—http://www.imanet.org
- International Hotel and Restaurant Association—http://ih-ra.com
- National Restaurant Association—http://www.restaurant.org

Item N—Links to some IFRS-related sites

- International Accounting Standards Board
  www.iasb.org
- IASB—Conceptual Framework
  http://www.iasb.org/Current+Projects/IASB+Projects/Conceptual+Framework/Conceptual+Framework.htm
- IASB—Stages of Completion of Various Projects
  www.iasb.org/Current+Projects/IASB+Projects/IASB+Work+Plan.htm
- Memorandum of Understanding Between the FASB and IASB (2006)—Roadmap to Convergence
  www.iasb.org/NR/rdonlyres/874B63FB-56DB-4B78-B7AF-49BBA18C98D9/0/MoU.pdf
- IASB and FASB Commitment to Memorandum of Understanding (of 2006)—Quarterly Progress Report—March 31, 2010
  www.iasb.org/NR/rdonlyres/184E570C-808F-45B9-9710-8249A76A0677/0/April2010progressreport
- Commission Statement in Support of Convergence and Global Accounting Standards
  www.sec.gov/rules/other/2010/33-9109.pdf
- Framework for the Preparation and Presentation of Financial Statements
  www.sba.pdx.edu/faculty/kathyr/kraccess/Winter%202010%20381/IASB%20Conceptualframework.pdf
- IASB Discussion Paper—Preliminary Views on Financial Statement Presentation
  www.iasb.org/NR/rdonlyres/92028667-6118-496E-B0FE-97F829858B5D/0/DPPrelViewsFinStmtPresentation.pdf
- iGAAP
  www.iasb.org/IFRSs/IFRS.htm
- IASB Standards for Small- and Medium-Size Entities (SME)
  www.iasplus.com/standard/ifrsforsmes.htm
- Comparison of IFRS for SME and U.S. GAAP
  http://wiki.ifrs.com/
- Deloitte, Touche and Tohmatsu
  www.iasplus.com/index.htm
- American Institute of Certified Public Accountants (AICPA) IFRS Resources
  www.ifrs.com

- Various Comparisons of U.S. GAAP and iGAAP

    —Grant Thornton
    www.grantthornton.com/staticfiles/GTCom/
    Grant%20Thornton%20Thinking/Resource%20centers/
    IFRS%20Resource%20Center/
    Comparison%20Document-09%2016%2009%20-%20Final%20Version%20(2).pdf

    —Deloitte, Touche, Kohmatsu
    www.deloitte.com/view/en_US/us/Services/additional-services/
    IFRS/92299342e630e110VgnVCM100000ba42f00aRCRD.htm

    —PricewaterhouseCoopers
    www.pwc.com/us/en/issues/ifrs-reporting/publications/ifrs-and-us-gaap-similarities-and-differences-september-2009.jhtml

    —KPMG
    http://www.kpmginstitutes.com/ifrs-institute/insights/active/ifrs-now-engaging-the-audience.aspx

- Guidance for First-Time IFRS Reporting
    www.pwc.com/en_US/us/issues/ifrs-reporting/assets/adopting-ifrs.pdf

INDEX

A

AAA (American Accounting Association), GAAP standards, . . . 2017

Accounting
. accounting rate of return (ARR), . . . 24,007-24,008
. accrual, . . . 2004-2005, 5002
. accuracy of, . . . 3019-3020
. call accounting systems, . . . 4018
. change in accounting principle, cumulative effect of, . . . 6016
. computer programs, . . . 4013-4014
. cost accounting
. . historical, . . . 11,009-11,010
. . internal management reports, . . . 2012-2015
. . management accounting vs., . . . 17,001-17,002
. . purpose of, . . . 17,001-17,002
. financial statement disclosures
. . accounting changes, . . . 9003-9006
. . accounting estimates, changes in, . . . 9004-9005
. . accounting policies, . . . 9002-9003
. . accounting principles, changes in, . . . 9003-9004
. . reporting entity, changes in, . . . 9005-9006
. Form 3115, "Application for Change in Accounting Method", . . . 20,003, 20,016
. historical cost accounting, . . . 11,009-11,010
. IT functions, . . . 4003
. management accounting
. . cost accounting vs., . . . 17,001-17,002
. . internal management reports, . . . 2012-2015
. . purpose of, . . . 17,001-17,002

Accounting—continued
. principles-based accounting system, . . . 3022
. reporting system evaluation, . . . 26,018-26,019
. smallwares accounting method, . . . 20,002-20,003

Accounting and recording functions of controllers, . . . 2002-2008
. accounting aberrations risk, . . . 2009
. accrual entries, . . . 2004-2005
. conservatism concept, . . . 2004
. consistency concept, . . . 2004
. internal management reports, . . . 2012-2015
. management accounting, . . . 2012-2015
. matching concept, . . . 2004
. materiality concept, . . . 2003
. realization concept, . . . 2003-2004
. USAL and USAR, . . . 2005-2008

Accounting Principles Board (APB)
. APB-17, Intangible Assets, . . . 7009
. APB-20, Accounting Changes, . . . 9003, 9004
. GAAP, . . . 5003

Accounts payable
. balance sheet presentation, . . . 7011
. operating activities analysis, . . . 15,007
. short-term credit, . . . 22,002-22,004, 22,011

Accounts receivable
. balance sheet presentation, . . . 7004
. factoring, . . . 22,010, 22,011
. liquidity analysis, . . . 10,005-10,007
. . accounts receivable percentage, . . . 10,006-10,007
. . accounts receivable turnover, . . . 10,005-10,006
. . average collection period, . . . 10,006

ACC

Index

Accounts receivable—continued
. operating activities analysis, . . . 15,007
. pledging, . . . 22,010, 22,011
. for secured loans, . . . 22,010

Accrual accounting
. accrual entries, . . . 2004-2005
. financial reporting, . . . 5002
. IFRS Framework, . . . 27,014

Accruals for short-term financing, . . . 22,004-22,005, 22,011

Accrued expenses
. balance sheet presentation, . . . 7011
. short-term financing, . . . 22,004-22,005, 22,011

Acid-test ratio, . . . 10,004

Activity-based costing, . . . 18,012-18,015
. activity-based management, . . . 18,015
. allocated costs as motivators, . . . 18,012-18,013
. measuring productivity, . . . 18,013-18,015
. unnecessary use of services, . . . 18,015

Administrative expenses, summary operating statement presentation, . . . 6012-6013

ADS (Alternative Depreciation System), . . . 20,004

Agency problem
. corporate governance, . . . 3002-3003
. shareholders, . . . 1006

AH&LA (American Hotel and Lodging Association), hotel statistics, . . . 1001

AICPA (American Institute of Certified Public Accountants), GAAP standards, . . . 2017

Almanac of Business and Industrial Financial Ratios, . . . 10,010

Alternative Depreciation System (ADS), . . . 20,004

Alternative minimum tax (AMT), . . . 20,004

American Accounting Association (AAA), GAAP standards, . . . 2017

American Hotel and Lodging Association (AH&LA), hotel statistics, . . . 1001

American Institute of Certified Public Accountants (AICPA), GAAP standards, . . . 2017

American Society of Heating, Refrigeration, and Air Conditioning Equipment Standard 90.1-2001, . . . 20,009

AMT (alternative minimum tax), . . . 20,004

Analytical techniques of controllers, . . . 2015

Annuity, present and future value of, . . . 28,002-28,005

Apani Networks, . . . 3013

APB. *See* Accounting Principles Board (APB)

APB-17, Intangible Assets, . . . 7009

APB-20, Accounting Changes, . . . 9003, 9004

Application service providers (ASP), . . . 4026

Area chart, . . . 4010

ARR (accounting rate of return), . . . 24,007-24,008

ASP (application service providers), . . . 4026

Assets
. asset management systems, . . . 4034-4035
. asset to equity ratio, . . . 11,005
. asset turnover, . . . 12,005, 12,006-12,007
. balance sheet presentation, . . . 7003-7010
. . assets, defined, . . . 7003
. . capital leases, . . . 7007-7008
. . cash and cash equivalents, . . . 7003
. . china, glass, silver, linen, uniforms, . . . 7007
. . construction in progress, . . . 7007
. . current assets, . . . 7003-7005
. . deferred expenses, . . . 7010
. . intangible assets, . . . 7009-7010
. . inventories, . . . 7004
. . investments, . . . 7008
. . leasehold and leasehold improvements, . . . 7007
. . life insurance value, . . . 7009

Index

Assets—continued
. balance sheet presentation,—continued
. . prepaid expenses, . . . 7005
. . property and equipment, . . . 7005-7008
. . receivables, . . . 7004
. . short-term investments, . . . 7003-7004
. current assets.*See* Current assets, liquidity analysis
. defined, . . . 7003
. impairment, GAAP vs. IFRS, . . . 2018
. net assets, . . . 13,008
. net return on assets, . . . 12,004, 12,006-12,007
. repositioning, . . . 26,018
. return on assets, . . . 12,003-12,004

@Risk, . . . 4006

ATIP (Attributed Tip Income Program), . . . 20,013

Attorneys
. professional conduct standards, . . . 3012-3013
. reporting of unresolved Board issues, . . . 3005

Attributed Tip Income Program (ATIP), . . . 20,013

Auditing Standard No. 2, An Audit of Internal Control over Financial Reporting Performed in Conjunction with an Audit of Financial Statements, . . . 3013

Auditor
. auditor's report in financial statements, . . . 5007
. external auditor independence and liability, . . . 3010-3012

Audits, internal control function of controllers, . . . 2011

Audubon Green Leaf Eco-Rating Program for Hotels, . . . 3028-3029

Average check target pricing, . . . 16,007

B

Balance sheet
. asset presentation, . . . 7003-7010
. . assets, defined, . . . 7003
. . capital leases, . . . 7007-7008
. . cash and cash equivalents, . . . 7003
. . china, glass, silver, linen, uniforms, . . . 7007
. . construction in progress, . . . 7007
. . current assets, . . . 7003-7005
. . deferred expenses, . . . 7010
. . intangible assets, . . . 7009-7010
. . inventories, . . . 7004
. . investments, . . . 7008
. . leasehold and leasehold improvements, . . . 7007
. . life insurance value, . . . 7009
. . prepaid expenses, . . . 7005
. . property and equipment, . . . 7005-7008
. . receivables, . . . 7004
. . short-term investments, . . . 7003-7004
. classified balance sheet, . . . 7002-7003
. liabilities, . . . 7010-7014
. . accounts payable, . . . 7011
. . accrued expenses, . . . 7011
. . bonds payable, . . . 7011-7013
. . compensating absences, . . . 7013
. . contingencies, . . . 7014
. . current liabilities, . . . 7010-7011
. . deferred income taxes, . . . 7013
. . defined, . . . 7010
. . long-term debt, . . . 7011
. . long-term liabilities, . . . 7011-7013
. . notes payable, . . . 7011
. . unearned revenue, . . . 7011
. objectives, . . . 7001-7002
. overview, . . . 7001
. owner's equity, . . . 7014
. property and equipment, . . . 7005-7008
. scope, . . . 7001-7002
. shareholders' equity, . . . 7014-7022
. . additional paid-in capital, . . . 7016
. . common stock, . . . 7016
. . comprehensive income, . . . 7017-7018
. . consolidated statement, . . . 7020-7021

BAL

Balance sheet—continued
. shareholders' equity,—continued
.. employee stock purchase plans, . . . 7018
.. preferred stock, . . . 7015-7016
.. retained earnings, . . . 7016-7017
.. stock options, . . . 7019, 7022
.. stock splits, . . . 7022
.. treasury stock, . . . 7017
. solvency and leverage analysis, . . . 11,002-11,005

Bank loans
. long-term financing, . . . 21,007
. short-term financing, . . . 22,005-22,007
.. compensating balances, . . . 22,006
.. interest, . . . 22,006
.. lines of credit, . . . 22,005, 22,006-22,007, 22,011
.. revolving lines of credit, . . . 22,005, 22,007, 22,011
.. transaction loan, . . . 22,005
.. unsecured loans, . . . 22,011

Bar chart, . . . 4008

Bartering, . . . 20,015-20,016

Basic earnings per share, . . . 6017-6018, 13,002

Benchmarking, financial accounting, . . . 2012

Beta analysis, . . . 13,009

Beverages. *See* Food and beverages

Blackstone Group LP, . . . 3019

Board of Directors, SOX requirements for credibility and independence, . . . 3005

Bonds
. balance sheet presentation, . . . 7011-7013
. call provision, . . . 21,009
. convertible bonds, . . . 21,010-21,011, 21,013
. convertible debentures, . . . 21,011-21,012, 21,013
. debentures, . . . 21,011-21,013
. features, . . . 21,008
. financing arrangements, . . . 21,007-21,008
. floating rate bonds, . . . 21,013
. income bonds, . . . 21,010, 21,012

Bonds—continued
. indenture, . . . 21,008
. junk bonds, . . . 21,012
. mortgage bonds, . . . 21,009, 21,012
. for secured loans, . . . 22,010
. subordinated debentures, . . . 21,012-21,013
. unsecured bonds, . . . 21,009-21,010
. zero-coupon bonds, . . . 21,010, 21,012

Book value per share, . . . 13,008

Boston Chicken, . . . 1007

Bottom-up pricing
. CVP analysis, . . . 19,025-19,029
. Hubbart formula, . . . 19,027-19,029

Bottom-up questions
. break-even formula, . . . 19,005, 19,006-19,009
. break-even graphical analysis, . . . 19,012
. sample questions, . . . 19,004

Budgets
. capital budgeting, *See also* Capital investment analysis . . . 24,001.
. controller functions, . . . 2014-2015
. data warehousing information, . . . 2013-2014
. inflation and, . . . 24,019

Business intelligence programs, . . . 4029-4030

Business life cycle, cash flow statement, . . . 15,017-15,018

Business performance management systems, . . . 4030

Business process integration systems, . . . 4031

Business risk, . . . 2009

C

Call accounting systems, . . . 4018

Capital
. additional paid-in capital, balance sheet presentation, . . . 7016
. budgeting, *See also* Capital investment analysis . . . 24,001.

Capital—continued
. cost of
. . book value vs. market value weights, . . . 25,008
. . capital-asset pricing model, . . . 25,005-25,007
. . capitalization rate, . . . 25,011-25,013
. . common stock, . . . 25,004-25,007
. . constant-growth valuation model, . . . 25,005
. . cost of debt, . . . 25,002-25,003
. . defined, . . . 25,001
. . equity capital, . . . 25,004-25,007
. . measuring overall cost, . . . 25,007-25,008
. . optimal capital structure, . . . 25,010-25,011
. . preferred stock, . . . 25,004
. . retained earnings, . . . 25,007
. . significance of, . . . 25,001
. . uses for information, . . . 25,001
. . weighted-average. *See* Weighted-average cost of capital (WACC)
. providers, enhancing relationships as turnaround strategy
. . creative financing sources, . . . 26,013
. . tight financing and scarce capital, . . . 26,013
. structure, . . . 25,010-25,011
. . cash flow, . . . 25,011
. . company control, . . . 25,011
. . contractual obligations, . . . 25,011
. . fund-raising ability, . . . 25,011
. . managerial implications, . . . 25,010-25,011
. . revenue stability, . . . 25,011
. . timing, . . . 25,011
. tight financing and scarce capital, . . . 26,013
. working capital
. . cash flow statement, . . . 15,006-15,007
. . indicator of management efficiency, . . . 15,006-15,007
. . liquidity analysis, . . . 10,002
. . profitability factor, . . . 16,055

Capital investment analysis
. accounting rate of return, . . . 24,007-24,008

Capital investment analysis—continued
. budgeting and inflation, . . . 24,019
. capital budgeting models, . . . 24,007
. cash flow estimating, . . . 24,005-24,007
. . categories, . . . 24,006-24,007
. . initial investment, . . . 24,006
. . operating income and expense, . . . 24,006
. . project termination, . . . 24,006
. computer use, . . . 24,016
. discount rate, impact of, . . . 24,020
. income tax implications, . . . 24,019
. independent vs. mutually exclusive projects, . . . 24,003, 24,018
. internal rate of return, . . . 24,014-24,016
. lease or purchase decision, . . . 24,021-24,022
. mutually exclusive project decisions, . . . 24,003, 24,018
. net present value criterion, . . . 24,011-24,013
. overview, . . . 24,001-24,002, 24,018
. payback method, . . . 24,008-24,011
. post-audit project review, . . . 24,020-24,021
. process of, . . . 24,003-24,005
. . illustrated, . . . 24,016-24,017
. profitability index, . . . 24,013-24,014
. reasons for, . . . 24,002
. risk and uncertainty, . . . 24,019
. significance of, . . . 24,002-24,003
. types of decisions, . . . 24,003

Capital leases
. balance sheet presentation, . . . 7007-7008
. history of corporate governance, . . . 3017
. solvency and leverage analysis, . . . 11,007-11,008

Capital-asset pricing model (CAPM), . . . 25,005-25,007

Capitalization rate, . . . 25,011-25,013

CAPM (capital-asset pricing model), . . . 25,005-25,007

Carlson Hotels Worldwide, . . . 4028

Cash and cash equivalents
. balance sheet presentation, . . . 7003

Cash and cash equivalents—continued
. cash equivalents
. . defined, . . . 8008
. . examples, . . . 8008
. . foreign currency, . . . 8008-8009
. discounts on purchases, . . . 22,003-22,004
. liquidity analysis, . . . 10,007-10,008
. liquidity analysis ratio, . . . 10,007
. turnaround strategies
. . cash conservation, . . . 26,011
. . cash outflow, delaying, . . . 26,012
. . cash receipts, accelerating, . . . 26,011-26,012

Cash flow
. capital structure and, . . . 25,011
. estimating project cash flows, . . . 24,005-24,007
. . categories, . . . 24,006-24,007
. . initial investment, . . . 24,006
. . operating income and expense, . . . 24,006
. . project termination, . . . 24,006
. importance in financial management, . . . 1006
. statement. *See* Cash flow statement

Cash flow statement
. analysis of, . . . 15,002, 15,015-15,017
. business life cycle, . . . 15,017-15,018
. cash and cash equivalents, . . . 8008-8009
. change in cash, . . . 15,003-15,004
. components, . . . 8003-8005, 15,002-15,003
. . financing activities, . . . 8003, 8004
. . investing activities, . . . 8004
. . operating activities, . . . 8003, 8004-8005
. . supplementary cash flow information, . . . 15,002
. . supplementary disclosure of noncash investing and financing activities, . . . 15,003
. direct approach, . . . 8005-8006
. example, . . . 8009-8010
. financing activities analysis, . . . 15,009-15,014
. . complex restructurings, . . . 15,012
. . debt to debt, . . . 15,012
. . debt to equity or equity to debt, . . . 15,012-15,013

Cash flow statement—continued
. financing activities analysis,—continued
. . dividends, . . . 15,014
. . financial restructurings, . . . 15,010-15,014
. . financing investments, . . . 15,010
. . simple financial restructurings, . . . 15,011-15,012
. . treasury stock, . . . 15,013-15,014
. importance of, . . . 15,020-15,026
. . cash flow questions, . . . 15,024-15,026
. . cash flow ratios vs. accrual ratios, . . . 15,022-15,024
. . EBITDA, . . . 15,020-15,022
. . evaluation of financing sources, . . . 15,024
. . evaluation of uses of cash, . . . 15,024
. indirect approach, . . . 8005-8008
. investing activities, . . . 8008, 15,003
. investing activities analysis, . . . 15,007-15,009
. . indicator of company growth, . . . 15,008
. . internal finance growth, . . . 15,008-15,009
. . quality of growth, . . . 15,009
. management of cash flows, . . . 8009
. noncash financing, . . . 8008, 15,003
. objectives, . . . 8001-8002
. operating activities analysis, . . . 15,005-15,007
. . adjustments of the income statement, . . . 15,006
. . warning signs, . . . 15,007
. . working capital management efficiency, . . . 15,006-15,007
. overview, . . . 8001
. possible profiles, . . . 15,015-15,017
. preparation, . . . 8002-8003
. ratios, . . . 15,018-15,020
. . cash flow to debt, . . . 15,019-15,020
. . free cash flow, . . . 15,018-15,019
. restructurings, . . . 15,010-15,014, 15,015-15,017
. scope, . . . 8001-8002
. shortcomings of, . . . 15,026-15,029
. . misleading reporting, . . . 15,029
. . what is not revealed, . . . 15,026-15,029

Cendant, . . . 1007

CFO (chief financial officer), responsibilities of, ... 1002

Channel management, ... 4024

Chart of Accounts, USAL system, ... 2006-2008

Chief financial officer (CFO), responsibilities of, ... 1002

Chief information officer (CIO), IT department interaction, ... 4003

China, accounting for, ... 7007

CIO (chief information officer), IT department interaction, ... 4003

Classified balance sheet, ... 7002-7003

CMOs (collateralized mortgage obligations), ... 21,015

Cohesiveness of proposed financial statement presentation, ... 27,016-27,017

Collateral for loans
. collateralized mortgage obligations (CMOs), ... 21,015
. secured loans, ... 22,009-22,011
.. accounts receivable, ... 22,010
.. equipment, ... 22,010
.. life insurance cash surrender, ... 22,010
.. marketable securities, ... 22,010
.. summary of sources, ... 22,011
.. third party guarantee, ... 22,010

Collusion, ... 16,032-16,033

Colony Hotel, Audubon Green Leaf Eco-Rating Program for Hotels, ... 3029

Commercial paper for short-term financing, ... 22,007-22,009, 22,011

Commitments
. defined, ... 9007
. financial statement disclosures, ... 9007-9008
.. long-term debt, ... 9007
.. pension plans and postretirement benefit plans, ... 9007-9008

Committee of Sponsoring Organizations of the Treadway Commission (COSO)
. attorney professional conduct standards, ... 3013
. GAAP standards, ... 2017

Common size analysis
. cost minimization, ... 16,049-16,056
. defined, ... 12,008, 14,002, 14,025
. horizontal analysis, ... 12,009, 14,026-14,028
. trend analysis (percent change), ... 14,028-14,030
. vertical analysis, ... 12,009, 14,025-14,026, 16,050-16,053

Comparative analysis
. defined, ... 14,002
. management analysis of operations, ... 14,023-14,024

Compensating absences, balance sheet presentation, ... 7013

Compensating balances, ... 22,006

Competitive advantage systems, ... 4022-4035
. application service providers, ... 4026
. asset management, ... 4034-4035
. business intelligence programs, ... 4029-4030
. business performance management, ... 4030
. business process integration, ... 4031
. customer relationship management systems, ... 4026-4027
. data mining, ... 4028-4029
. data warehousing, ... 4028-4029
. decision support software, ... 4033
. enterprise application integration, ... 4032
. enterprise resource planning, ... 4032-4033
. executive information, ... 4033-4034
. global distribution systems, ... 4029
. revenue management, ... 4022-4035
. REVPAG, ... 4021, 4022, 4027
. supply chain management systems, ... 4027-4028

Complex restructurings, ... 15,012

Comprehensive income
. balance sheet presentation, . . . 7017-7018
. income statement reporting, . . . 6020

Computer networks
. extranet, . . . 4004
. intranet, . . . 4004, 4028
. local area networks, . . . 4003
. secure sockets layers, . . . 4004
. TCP/IP, . . . 4004
. virtual local area networks, . . . 4003-4004
. wide-area networks, . . . 4004

Computers.*See also* Internet
. application programs, . . . 4004-4014
. . accounting and tax, . . . 4013-4014
. . databases, . . . 4007
. . Excel add-in programs, . . . 4006-4007
. . financial software, . . . 4013
. . forecasting, . . . 4012
. . graphics, . . . 4008-4012
. . modelling, . . . 4013
. . risk analysis, . . . 4012-4013
. . spreadsheets, . . . 4004-4006
. . statistical programs, . . . 4012-4013
. data-processing tools, . . . 4003-4014
. . application programs, . . . 4004-4014
. . networks, . . . 4003-4004
. evaluation of, . . . 4002-4003
. history of, . . . 4001-4002
. hospitality industry programs, . . . 4016-4021
. . call accounting systems, . . . 4018
. . cost minimization, . . . 4020-4021
. . electronic room access keys, . . . 4018
. . guest-tracking software, . . . 4018
. . key codes, . . . 4018
. . minibar systems, . . . 4018
. . point-of-sale systems, . . . 4017
. . property management systems, . . . 4017, 4018
. . restaurant management systems, . . . 4018-4019
. . revenue maximization, . . . 4020
. . sales and catering system, . . . 4018
. information technology to maximize ROI, . . . 4014-4016

Computers.—continued
. for IRR calculations, . . . 24,016
. networks.*See* Computer networks
. operational efficiency programs, . . . 4021-4022
. overview, . . . 4002-4003
. reasons for use, . . . 4002
. strategic alignment programs, . . . 4021-4022
. systems to increase competitive advantage, . . . 4022-4035
. . application service providers, . . . 4026
. . asset management, . . . 4034-4035
. . business intelligence programs, . . . 4029-4030
. . business performance management, . . . 4030
. . business process integration, . . . 4031
. . customer relationship management systems, . . . 4026-4027
. . data mining, . . . 4028-4029
. . data warehousing, . . . 4028-4029
. . decision support software, . . . 4033
. . enterprise application integration, . . . 4032
. . enterprise resource planning, . . . 4032-4033
. . executive information, . . . 4033-4034
. . global distribution systems, . . . 4029
. . revenue management, . . . 4022-4035
. . REVPAG, . . . 4021, 4022, 4027
. . supply chain management systems, . . . 4027-4028

Conditional sales contracts, . . . 22,013-22,014

Conservatism concept, . . . 2004

Consistency concept
. controller responsibilities, . . . 2004
. financial statement reporting, . . . 5002

Constant-growth valuation model, . . . 25,005

Construction in progress, balance sheet presentation, . . . 7007

Consumer price index (CPI), . . . 14,031

Contingencies
. balance sheet presentation, . . . 7014
. financial statement disclosures, . . . 9008-9009
. solvency and leverage analysis, . . . 11,008-11,009

Contribution margin
. CVP analysis, . . . 19,003, 19,013
. defined, . . . 19,003
. pricing, . . . 16,007-16,008, 16,011

Contribution pricing, . . . 17,010-17,014

Contributions
. food and beverages, . . . 20,016-20,017
. IRS rules, . . . 20,016-20,017
. used items, . . . 20,017

Control approach, . . . 3028

Controllable costs, . . . 17,019-17,020

Controller
. accounting and recording functions, . . . 2002-2008
. . accounting aberrations risk, . . . 2009
. . accrual entries, . . . 2004-2005
. . conservatism concept, . . . 2004
. . consistency concept, . . . 2004
. . internal management reports, . . . 2012-2015
. . management accounting, . . . 2012-2015
. . matching concept, . . . 2004
. . materiality concept, . . . 2003
. . realization concept, . . . 2003-2004
. . USAL and USAR, . . . 2005-2008
. characteristics, . . . 2022-2024
. . business judgment, . . . 2022
. . communications skills, . . . 2023
. . interpersonal skills, . . . 2023
. . managing dual accountability, . . . 2024
. . personal qualities, . . . 2022
. . technical competence, . . . 2022
. corporate controller, . . . 2001-2002
. division controller, . . . 2001-2002
. industry knowledge, . . . 2018-2020
. integrity of, . . . 2022

Controller—continued
. internal control function, . . . 2002, 2009-2011
. . accuracy of records, . . . 2009-2010
. . enterprise risk management, . . . 2009, 2010
. . evaluation of procedures, . . . 2010
. . internal audit, . . . 2011
. . internal control, defined, . . . 2009
. . minimizing expenses, . . . 2010
. . minimizing risk, . . . 2009
. . outsourced records, . . . 2011
. . overview, . . . 2002
. . summary of steps, . . . 2010
. . system evaluation, . . . 2010-2011
. . value maximization, . . . 2010
. international accounting GAAP, . . . 2018
. knowledge of accounting fundamentals, . . . 2017-2018
. knowledge of legal statutes, . . . 2018
. personal qualities and skills, . . . 2020-2024
. qualifications, . . . 2016-2017
. reporting function, . . . 2002, 2011-2016
. . advisor to management, . . . 2015-2016
. . financial accounting and reporting, . . . 2011-2012
. . insurance matters, . . . 2015
. . internal management reports, . . . 2011-2015
. . management accounting, . . . 2012-2015
. . reports to outside stakeholders, . . . 2012
. . tax matters, . . . 2015
. responsibilities
. . accounting and recording, . . . 2002-2008
. . control, . . . 2002, 2009-2011
. . corporate controller, . . . 2001-2002
. . division controller, . . . 2001-2002
. . overview, . . . 1002
. . reporting, . . . 2002, 2011-2016

Convertible bonds, . . . 21,010-21,011, 21,013

Core business, rebuilding, . . . 26,017-26,018

Corel Corporation's Quattro Pro, . . . 4004

Corporate controller responsibilities, . . . 2001-2002

COR

Index

Corporate governance
. accounting accuracy, . . . 3019-3020
. agency problem, . . . 3002-3003
. control environment, . . . 3021-3022
. corporate culture, . . . 3021
. defined, . . . 3002, 3018-3019
. drawbacks of, . . . 3022-3024
. ethical decision making, . . . 3020-3021
. history of, . . . 3016-3018
. improving of, . . . 3029-3036
. inhibited management, . . . 3023-3024
. instruments, . . . 3003
. international, . . . 3028-3029
. out-of-pocket cost, . . . 3023
. overview, . . . 3001-3002
. perspectives and importance, . . . 3002
. principles-based accounting, . . . 3022
. rewards of, . . . 3024-3028
. . culture of change, . . . 3025
. . market value increase, . . . 3025-3028
. . operating efficiency, . . . 3024-3025
. Sarbanes-Oxley Act of 2002, . . . 3004-3013, 3032-3036
. transparency, . . . 3020
. transparency through Web site, . . . 3036-3037
. U.S. Stock Exchanges and, . . . 3013-3016

Corrections, prior-period adjustments, . . . 9006-9007

COSO. *See* Committee of Sponsoring Organizations of the Treadway Commission (COSO)

Cost accounting
. historical, . . . 11,009-11,010
. internal management reports, . . . 2012-2015
. management accounting vs., . . . 17,001-17,002
. purpose of, . . . 17,001-17,002

Cost allocation
. activity-based costing, . . . 18,012-18,015
. . activity-based management, . . . 18,015
. . allocated costs as motivators, . . . 18,012-18,013
. . measuring productivity, . . . 18,013-18,015
. . unnecessary use of services, . . . 18,015

Cost allocation—continued
. basis of, . . . 18,005-18,006
. cost drivers, . . . 18,002, 18,004
. for cost minimization, . . . 2015
. cost object, . . . 18,002
. cost pool, . . . 18,002-18,003, 18,004
. direct expenses, . . . 18,002-18,005
. factors in, . . . 18,002
. indirect expenses, . . . 18,002-18,005
. laundry department, . . . 18,004-18,005
. post-allocation income, misinterpreting of, . . . 18,016-18,017
. steps, . . . 18,002
. traditional cost allocation
. . direct method, . . . 18,006-18,009
. . formula method, . . . 18,011-18,012
. . step method, . . . 18,009-18,011
. undistributed operating expenses, . . . 18,002-18,005

Cost analysis reports, . . . 2015

Cost benefit ratio, *See also* Profitability index (PI) . . . 24,013.

Cost-cutting measures, . . . 26,014-26,015

Cost/margin analysis, menu, . . . 16,012-16,015

Costs. *See also* Expenses
. allocation. *See* Cost allocation
. analysis of operations, . . . 14,003-14,004, 14,012-14,013
. capital. *See* Capital, cost of
. controllable, . . . 17,019-17,020
. cost accounting
. . historical, . . . 11,009-11,010
. . internal management reports, . . . 2012-2015
. . management accounting vs., . . . 17,001-17,002
. . purpose of, . . . 17,001-17,002
. cost segregation
. . depreciation, . . . 20,004
. . gaming industry, . . . 29,012-29,025
. . restaurant, . . . 29,002-29,012
. . retail business, . . . 29,025-29,038
. direct costs, defined, . . . 17,014

Costs.—continued
- direct vs. indirect, . . . 17,014-17,016
- expansion costs, . . . 20,019
- fixed
  - changes in, . . . 17,003
  - coverage ratio, . . . 11,006-11,007
  - defined, . . . 19,002
  - expanded income statement, . . . 17,017
  - income statement reporting, . . . 6006
  - mixed, . . . 19,002
  - overview, . . . 17,002-17,003, 17,005-17,007
  - relevant range, . . . 17,008
  - risk vs. rapid growth, . . . 19,011-19,012
  - summary operating statement, . . . 6007-6008, 6014
- income statement, expanded, . . . 17,017
- incremental, . . . 17,019
- indirect costs, . . . 17,014-17,016
- joint costs, . . . 17,018
- management accounting, . . . 17,001-17,002
- minimization of, . . . 4020-4021
  - common size analysis, . . . 16,049-16,056
  - labor costs, . . . 16,046-16,049
  - operating ratios, . . . 16,049-16,056
  - standard per-unit ratios, . . . 16,049
  - variance analysis, . . . 16,049-16,056
- mixed
  - contribution margin, . . . 17,004-17,005
  - overview, . . . 17,002-17,003
  - separation into variable and fixed elements, . . . 17,007-17,008
- noncontrollable, . . . 17,019-17,020
- opportunity cost, . . . 17,020
- period costs, . . . 17,017-17,018
- prime cost, . . . 16,002
- relevant cost, . . . 17,018-17,019
- relevant range, . . . 17,008-17,010
- service/product, . . . 17,017-17,018
- standard, . . . 17,020
- sunk cost, . . . 17,019
- uncontrollable, . . . 17,019-17,020
- variable, . . . 17,002-17,004
  - defined, . . . 19,002
  - expanded income statement, . . . 17,017
  - overview, . . . 17,002-17,004
  - relevant range, . . . 17,008-17,010

Costs.—continued
- variable,—continued
  - risk vs. rapid growth, . . . 19,011-19,012

Cost-volume-profit (CVP) analysis
- bottom-up pricing, . . . 19,025-19,029
- bottom-up questions
  - break-even formula, . . . 19,005, 19,006-19,009
  - break-even graphical analysis, . . . 19,012
  - sample questions, . . . 19,004
- break-even formula, . . . 19,005
- break-even graphs, . . . 19,012-19,013
- cost minimization, . . . 2015
- fixed vs. variable expenses, . . . 19,011-19,012
- income statement components, . . . 19,002-19,003
- income statement equation, . . . 19,012-19,013
- indifference earnings, . . . 19,018-19,020
  - adjusted EBT, . . . 19,018
  - before income taxes, . . . 19,018-19,020
  - margin of safety, . . . 19,019-19,020
- leverage, . . . 19,013-19,017
  - defined, . . . 19,013
  - factors affecting leverage, . . . 19,016-19,017
  - favorability of, . . . 19,017
  - financial leverage, . . . 19,013, 19,014-19,015
  - operating leverage, . . . 19,013, 19,014
  - total leverage, . . . 19,015-19,016
- multiple products or services, example, . . . 19,009-19,011
- purpose of, . . . 19,001, 19,003-19,004
- risk vs. rapid growth, . . . 19,011-19,012
- separating mixed costs into variable and fixed elements, . . . 19,021-19,025
  - graph method, . . . 19,021-19,023
  - min-max method, . . . 19,023-19,024
  - regression method, . . . 19,024-19,025
- single product or service example, . . . 19,004-19,009
  - bottom-up questions, . . . 19,005, 19,006-19,009

Cost-volume-profit (CVP) analysis—continued
- single product or service example,—continued
  - pro forma contribution format income statement, . . . 19,005-19,006
  - top-down questions, . . . 19,004
- top-down questions, . . . 19,003, 19,004, 19,012
- underlying concepts, . . . 19,020-19,021

Courtyard Marriott, Audubon Green Leaf Eco-Rating Program for Hotels, . . . 3029

CPI (consumer price index), . . . 14,031

Creative financing, . . . 26,013

Credit. *See* Trade credit

Culture of change, compliance mechanisms, . . . 3025

Current assets, liquidity analysis, . . . 10,007-10,009
- cash, . . . 10,007-10,008
- inventories, . . . 10,008-10,009
- receivables, . . . 10,008
- short-term investments, . . . 10,008

Current liabilities
- balance sheet presentation, . . . 7010-7011
- liquidity analysis, . . . 10,007-10,009

Current ratio, liquidity analysis, . . . 10,002-10,004

Customer relationship management systems, . . . 4026-4027

CVP. *See* Cost-volume-profit (CVP) analysis

D

Data mining, . . . 4012, 4028-4029

Data warehousing
- accounting and record keeping, . . . 2002
- defined, . . . 4028
- Harrah's, . . . 4022
- purpose of, . . . 2013-2014
- servers, . . . 4028-4029
- transmission of data, . . . 4028

Databases
- described, . . . 4007
- higher capacity databases, . . . 4007
- Oracle's Database 10g, . . . 4007
- query, . . . 4007
- small databases, . . . 4007
- standard query language, . . . 4007
- storage area network, . . . 4007

Debenture
- characteristics, . . . 21,012, 21,013
- convertible debentures, . . . 21,011-21,012, 21,013
- defined, . . . 21,009
- subordinated debentures, . . . 21,012-21,013
- unsecured bonds, . . . 21,009-21,010

Debt
- cost of, . . . 25,002-25,003
- debt to debt restructurings, . . . 15,012
- debt to equity ratio, . . . 11,004
- debt to equity restructurings, . . . 15,012-15,013
- long-term debt. *See* Long-term debt
- restructuring, . . . 26,013-26,014
- scheduled payment modifications, . . . 26,014

Decision support software (DSS), . . . 4033

Deferred expenses, balance sheet presentation, . . . 7010

Department income or loss, summary operating statement, . . . 6012

Department of Housing and Urban Development, Empowerment Zone/Enterprise Community program, . . . 20,014, 20,015

Depreciation
- Alternative Depreciation System, . . . 20,004
- alternative minimum tax, . . . 20,004
- building improvements, depreciable life, . . . 20,003
- cost segregation, . . . 20,004
- hospitality issues, . . . 20,002
- longer depreciation lives, . . . 20,004

Index

Depreciation—continued
- Modified Accelerated Cost Recovery System, . . . 20,004
- recovery periods, . . . 20,004
- Section 179 deduction, . . . 20,003
- smallwares accounting method, . . . 20,002-20,003

Derivatives, financial statement disclosures, . . . 9009-9010

Diluted earnings per share, . . . 6018-6020

Direct costs
- defined, . . . 17,014
- direct costs vs., . . . 17,014-17,016

Direct loans, . . . 22,013

Disaggregation of proposed financial statement presentation, . . . 27,015-27,016

Disclosures
- accounting changes, . . . 9003-9006
- - accounting estimates, changes in, . . . 9004-9005
- - accounting policies, . . . 9002-9003
- - accounting principles, changes in, . . . 9003-9004
- - reporting entity, changes in, . . . 9005-9006
- accounting policies, . . . 9002-9003
- commitments, . . . 9007-9008
- - defined, . . . 9007
- - long-term debt, . . . 9007
- - pension plans and postretirement benefit plans, . . . 9007-9008
- contingencies, . . . 9008-9009
- derivatives, . . . 9009-9010
- environmental issues, . . . 9009
- income tax, . . . 9010-9011
- notes to financial statements, . . . 9002
- overview, . . . 9001
- prior-period adjustments, . . . 9006-9007
- segment reporting, . . . 9011-9012
- stock options, . . . 9010
- subsequent events, . . . 9012-9013

Discontinued operations, income statement reporting, . . . 6015-6016

Discount rate, impact on capital investment analysis, . . . 24,020

Discounts on purchases, . . . 22,003-22,004

Dividends
- amount determination, . . . 23,001-23,002
- bird-in-the-hand theory, . . . 23,007-23,008
- Dividend Irrelevance theory, . . . 23,007
- dividend payout ratio, . . . 13,006
- dividend yield, . . . 13,006-13,008
- payment procedures, . . . 23,008-23,009
- - declaration date, . . . 23,008
- - ex-dividend date, . . . 23,008
- - payment date, . . . 23,009
- - record date, . . . 23,008
- policy
- - cash flow constraints, . . . 23,006
- - company factors, . . . 23,005-23,006
- - compromised policy, . . . 23,003
- - constant payout ratio, . . . 23,003
- - contractual constraints, . . . 23,006-23,007
- - controversy, . . . 23,007-23,008
- - corporate strategy, . . . 23,008
- - cost of capital, impact on, . . . 25,009
- - defined, . . . 23,002
- - importance of, . . . 23,002
- - influencing factors, . . . 23,005-23,006
- - managed dividend policy, . . . 23,002-23,003
- - overview, . . . 23,001-23,002
- - payment procedures, . . . 23,008-23,009
- - residual-dividend policy, . . . 23,004-23,005
- - shareholder factors, . . . 23,005
- - stable dividend policy, . . . 23,003, 23,004
- - tax considerations, . . . 23,007
- as resource allocation, . . . 23,001
- restructurings, . . . 15,014
- stock repurchases, . . . 23,010-23,011
- stock split vs., . . . 23,009-23,010
- tax preference theory, . . . 23,008

Division controller, responsibilities of, . . . 2001-2002

Division general manager, responsibilities of, . . . 2001-2002

DIV

Donaldson, William, . . . 3022

Donations. *See* Contributions

DSS (decision support software), . . . 4033

Dun & Bradstreet, *Industry Norms and Key Business Ratios*, . . . 10,010

DuPont and Leverage analysis, . . . 12,006-12,008
. drivers of return on equity, . . . 12,007-12,008

E

Earnings before interest, income taxes, depreciation and amortization (EBITDA), cash flow statement, . . . 15,020-15,022

Earnings per share (EPS)
. and analysts' forecasts, . . . 13,003-13,004
. basic earnings per share, . . . 6017-6018, 13,002
. diluted earnings per share, . . . 6018-6020, 13,002-13,004
. profitability for investors, . . . 13,002-13,004

EBITDA (earnings before interest, income taxes, depreciation and amortization), cash flow statement, . . . 15,020-15,022

Economic causes of financial failure, . . . 26,003-26,004

Economic impact of hotel industry, . . . 1001

Economic opportunity loans, . . . 22,013

Economic order quantity (EOQ)
. beverage purchases, . . . 16,039
. Excel spreadsheet, . . . 4006
. food purchases, . . . 16,020, 16,023-16,025

Economic Stimulus Act of 2008, . . . 20,003

Economist Intelligence Unit
. corporate governance statistics, . . . 3002
. obstacles to good corporate governance, . . . 3021

EDP (electronic data processors), . . . 4001

EITF (Emerging Issues Task Force), GAAP standards, . . . 2017

Electronic data processors (EDP), . . . 4001

Emergency Economic Stabilization Act of 2008 (HR-1424), . . . 20,008

Emerging Issues Task Force (EITF), GAAP standards, . . . 2017

Employer-Designed Tip Reporting Alternative Commitment (EmTRAC), . . . 20,013

Empowerment Zone/Enterprise Community program, . . . 20,014, 20,015

EmTRAC (Employer-Designed Tip Reporting Alternative Commitment), . . . 20,013

Energy Policy Act of 2005, . . . 20,008

Energy tax credit
. allowed deductions, . . . 20,008-20,009
. claiming deductions, . . . 20,009
. Energy Policy Act of 2005, . . . 20,008
. property basis reduction, . . . 20,009

England, control approach, . . . 3028

Enron, . . . 1007, 3020

Enterprise application integration, . . . 4032

Enterprise resource planning, . . . 4032-4033

Enterprise risk management (ERM)
. control function, summarized, . . . 2010
. defined, . . . 2009
. minimizing risk, . . . 2009

Environmental issues
. EPA regulations, . . . 9009
. financial statement disclosures, . . . 9009

EOQ. *See* Economic order quantity (EOQ)

EPS. *See* Earnings per share (EPS)

Equipment. *See* Property and equipment

Equity capital, cost of, . . . 25,004-25,007

Equity financing, . . . 21,002-21,005
. common stock, . . . 21,002-21,003, 21,004-21,005

Equity financing,—continued
. preferred stock, . . . 21,003-21,005

Equity to debt restructurings, . . . 15,012-15,013

ERM. *See* Enterprise risk management (ERM)

Ethics
. decision making complexity, . . . 3020-3021
. in financial management, . . . 1007

European Union, IFRS standards, . . . 2018

Excel spreadsheet
. add-in programs, . . . 4006-4007
. @Risk, . . . 4006
. EOQ, . . . 4006
. for IRR calculations, . . . 24,016
. restaurant management systems, . . . 4019
. uses for, . . . 4004-4006

Executive information systems, . . . 4033-4034

Exit strategy, . . . 26,020

Expansion chart, . . . 4010

Expansion costs, . . . 20,019

Expenses. *See also* Costs
. accrued expenses
. . balance sheet presentation, . . . 7011
. . short-term financing, . . . 22,004-22,005, 22,011
. administrative expenses, summary operating statement, . . . 6012-6013
. deferred expenses, balance sheet presentation, . . . 7010
. defined, . . . 6004
. fixed expenses. *See* Fixed expenses
. income statement reporting, . . . 6004-6005
. indirect expense reporting, . . . 6006
. minimization of, . . . 2010
. operating ratio analysis, . . . 14,012-14,013
. prepaid, balance sheet presentation, . . . 7005
. undistributed operating expenses
. . administrative and general expenses, . . . 6012-6013
. . allocation of, . . . 18,002-18,005
. . gross operating profit, . . . 6013

Expenses.—continued
. undistributed operating expenses—continued
. . property operations and maintenance, . . . 6013
. . sales and marketing, . . . 6013
. . summary operating statement, . . . 6007-6008, 6012-6013
. . utilities, . . . 6013

eXtensible Business Reporting Language (XBRL), . . . 27,007-27,008

External environment and stock value, . . . 1006

Extranet, . . . 4004

Extraordinary items
. defined, . . . 6014
. income statement reporting, . . . 6014-6015

F

Factoring accounts receivable, . . . 22,010

Fair Labor Standards Act, tipped employees, defined, . . . 20,009

FAS-5, Accounting for Contingencies
. balance sheet presentation, . . . 7014
. financial statement disclosures, . . . 9008-9009
. solvency and leverage analysis, . . . 11,008-11,009

FAS-13, Accounting for Leases, . . . 11,007-11,008

FAS-43, Accounting for Compensated Absences, . . . 7013

FAS-45, Accounting for Franchise Fee Revenue, . . . 6004

FAS-87, Employers' Accounting for Pensions, . . . 9007-9008

FAS-95, Statement of Cash Flows
. balance sheet presentation, . . . 8001, 8003, 8005
. EBITDA, . . . 15,020
. operating activities analysis, . . . 15,005

FAS

FAS-95, Statement of Cash Flows—continued
. supplementary cash flow information, . . . 15,002

FAS-109, Accounting for Income Taxes
. balance sheet presentation, . . . 7013
. financial statement disclosures, . . . 9010
. solvency and leverage analysis, . . . 11,004

FAS-114, Accounting by Creditors for Impairment of a Loan, . . . 7004

FAS-115, Accounting for Certain Investments in Debt and Equity Securities, . . . 7004

FAS-123R, Share-Based Payment
. balance sheet presentation, . . . 7019, 7022
. financial statement disclosures, . . . 9010

FAS-128, Earnings per Share, . . . 6017, 6018

FAS-130, Reporting Comprehensive Income
. balance sheet presentation, . . . 7017-7018
. income statement reporting, . . . 6020
. proposed financial statement presentation, . . . 27,015

FAS-131, Disclosures about Segments of an Enterprise and Related Information, . . . 9011

FAS-132, Employers' Disclosure about Pensions and Other Postretirement Benefits, . . . 9008

FAS-133, Accounting for Derivative Instruments and Hedging Activities, . . . 9009-9010

FAS-141, Business Combinations, . . . 7009

FAS-142, Goodwill and Other Intangible Assets, . . . 7010

FAS-144, Accounting for the Impairment or Disposal of Long-Lived Assets, . . . 6015-6016

FAS-154, Accounting Changes and Error Corrections, . . . 9003, 9005

FAS-165, Subsequent Events, . . . 9012

FASB.*See* Financial Accounting Standards Board (FASB)

FAS

FASB No. 2, Qualitative Characteristics of Accounting Information, materiality, defined, . . . 3020

FCPA.*See* Foreign Corrupt Practices Act of 1977 (FCPA)

Federal Insurance Contributions Act (FICA)
. Form 941 reporting, . . . 20,011-20,012
. tax tip credit, . . . 20,012
. tip income
. . deemed to be paid, . . . 20,010-20,011
. . employer liability, . . . 20,014
. . penalties for violations, . . . 20,011
. . tax related to, . . . 20,011-20,012

Federal Omnibus Budget Reconciliation Act, . . . 20,014

FICA.*See* Federal Insurance Contributions Act (FICA)

Financial accounting and reporting, controller functions, . . . 2011-2012

Financial Accounting Standards Board (FASB).*See also specific FAS*
. authoritative statements, . . . 5003
. background, . . . 5002-5004
. GAAP standards, . . . 2017
. Memorandum of Understanding, . . . 27,002-27,004
. Norwalk Agreement, . . . 2018
. purpose of, . . . 5002
. regulations, . . . 3004
. sections, . . . 5003-5004
. SFAC 6.*See* SFAC 6, Elements of Financial Statements

Financial expert, defined, . . . 3006-3007

Financial failure
. causes of, . . . 26,002-26,004
. . common causes, . . . 26,002-26,003
. . economic causes, . . . 26,003-26,004
. . external factors, . . . 26,003-26,004
. . financial causes, . . . 26,004
. . internal factors, . . . 26,003-26,004
. hospitality company challenges, . . . 26,002
. turnaround strategies.*See* Turnaround

Index

Financial leases, . . . 22,014-22,015

Financial leverage, CVP analysis, . . . 19,013, 19,014-19,015

Financial manager
. cash flow, importance of, . . . 1006
. controller responsibilities, . . . 2001, 2021
. external environment, impact of, . . . 1006
. profitability and investor analysis, . . . 13,001-13,002
. profitability factor, . . . 16,055
. responsibilities, . . . 1001-1002
. separation of ownership and control, . . . 1005-1006
. shareholder value influence, . . . 1005
. value creation, . . . 1003-1004

Financial reporting system
. annual reports to shareholders, . . . 5005-5007
. . auditor's report, . . . 5007
. . financial statements, . . . 5006
. . management discussion of financial condition and results of operations, . . . 5007
. . notes to financial statements, . . . 5006
. evaluation, . . . 26,018-26,019
. FASB, . . . 5002-5004
. general principles, . . . 5002
. goal of financial reporting, . . . 5001
. guidelines, . . . 5002
. internal reports, . . . 5008
. measurement rules, . . . 5002
. overview, . . . 5001
. prospective financial statements, . . . 5008
. SEC, *See also* Securities Exchange Commission (SEC) . . . 5004.
. Securities Act of 1933, . . . 5004
. Securities Act of 1934, . . . 5004-5005
. uniform system of accounts, . . . 5007-5008

Financial software, . . . 4013

Financial statements
. disclosures
. . accounting changes, . . . 9003-9006
. . accounting estimates, changes in, . . . 9004-9005

Financial statements—continued
. disclosures—continued
. . accounting policies, . . . 9002-9003
. . accounting principles, changes in, . . . 9003-9004
. . commitments, . . . 9007-9008
. . contingencies, . . . 9008-9009
. . derivatives, . . . 9009-9010
. . environmental issues, . . . 9009
. . income tax, . . . 9010-9011
. . long-term debt, . . . 9007
. . notes to financial statements, . . . 9002
. . overview, . . . 9001
. . pension plans and postretirement benefit plans, . . . 9007-9008
. . prior-period adjustments, . . . 9006-9007
. . reporting entity, changes in, . . . 9005-9006
. . segment reporting, . . . 9011-9012
. . stock options, . . . 9010
. . subsequent events, . . . 9012-9013
. IFRS proposed presentation, . . . 27,015-27,017
. . background, . . . 27,015
. . cohesiveness, . . . 27,016-27,017
. . conversion preparation checklist, . . . 27,026-27,028
. . disaggregation, . . . 27,015-27,016
. . financial statement characteristics, . . . 27,017
. . sample, . . . 27,017-27,026
. notes, . . . 5006, 9002
. prospective financial statements, . . . 5008

Financing activities. *See also* Loans
. cash flow from, . . . 8003, 8004
. cash flow statement, . . . 15,009-15,014
. . complex restructurings, . . . 15,012
. . debt to debt, . . . 15,012
. . debt to equity or equity to debt, . . . 15,012-15,013
. . dividends, . . . 15,014
. . financial restructurings, . . . 15,010-15,014
. . financing investments, . . . 15,010
. . simple financial restructurings, . . . 15,011-15,012
. . treasury stock, . . . 15,013-15,014

FIN

Financing activities.—continued
- creative financing, . . . 26,013
- disclosure of noncash financing activities, . . . 8008
- intermediate. *See* Intermediate financing
- long-term. *See* Long-term financing
- noncash financing, . . . 8008, 15,003
- off-balance-sheet financing, . . . 11,006-11,007
- short-term. *See* Short-term financing
- tight financing and scarce capital, . . . 26,013

Fixed asset turnover, . . . 12,002

Fixed expenses (fixed charges)
- changes in, . . . 17,003
- coverage ratio, . . . 11,006-11,007
- defined, . . . 19,002
- expanded income statement, . . . 17,017
- income statement reporting, . . . 6006
- mixed, . . . 19,002
- overview, . . . 17,005-17,007
- relevant range, . . . 17,009-17,010
- risk vs. rapid growth, . . . 19,011-19,012
- summary operating statement, . . . 6007-6008, 6014

Floating rate bonds, . . . 21,013

Food and beverages
- beverage consumption, . . . 16,040-16,045
- - cost percentage, . . . 16,040-16,042
- - portion controls, . . . 16,044-16,045
- - standard ratios, . . . 16,043-16,044
- beverage cost minimization, . . . 16,039-16,046
- - consumption, . . . 16,040-16,045
- - purchasing, . . . 16,039
- - storage, . . . 16,039-16,040
- - theft at the bar, . . . 16,045-16,046
- beverage operations analysis, . . . 14,018-14,021
- - accounting for beverages consumed, . . . 14,019-14,020
- - food sales vs. beverage sales, . . . 14,020
- - operating ratios, . . . 14,020
- - standard ratios, . . . 14,020-14,021

Food and beverages—continued
- beverage revenue maximization, . . . 16,033-16,039
- - cost/margin analysis, . . . 16,035-16,039
- - pricing, . . . 16,034
- - waiters' suggestion, . . . 16,034-16,035
- controller knowledge of costs, . . . 2018-2020
- deductible contributions, . . . 20,016-20,017
- joint costs and the yield ratio, . . . 17,018
- operating ratio analysis, . . . 14,011-14,012
- restaurants. *See* Restaurant
- storage, . . . 16,027-16,029
- - beverages, . . . 16,039-16,040
- - periodic inventory control, . . . 16,027, 16,039-16,040
- - perpetual inventory control, . . . 16,027-16,029, 16,039-16,040
- summary operating statement reporting, . . . 6010-6011

Forecasting computer programs, . . . 4012

Foreign Corrupt Practices Act of 1977 (FCPA)
- business ethics and accounting, . . . 2018
- internal control function of controllers, . . . 2010

Form 10-K
- NYSE requirements, . . . 3014
- overview, . . . 5005

Form 10-Q, . . . 5005

Form 941, "Employer's Quarterly Federal Tax Return", . . . 20,011-20,012

Form 1040, reporting tips, . . . 20,010

Form 1099-B, "Proceeds from Broker and Barter Exchange Transactions", . . . 20,015-20,016

Form 3115, "Application for Change in Accounting Method", . . . 20,003, 20,016

Form 3468, Investment Credit, . . . 20,006

Form 4070, reporting tips, . . . 20,010

Form 4070A, reporting tips, . . . 20,010

Form 4562, capital gains, . . . 20,015

FIX

Form 5884, tax credit, . . . 20,014

Form 8027, reporting tips, . . . 20,010, 20,013

Form 8283, "Non-Cash Charitable Contributions", . . . 20,017

Form 8844, tax credit, . . . 20,015

Form 8846, tax tip credit, . . . 20,012

Form 8850, tax credit, . . . 20,014

Framework for IFRS, . . . 27,013-27,015

France, Hospitality Extraordinaire, . . . 3028

Franchise fee revenue reporting, . . . 6004

Franchising fees, . . . 20,016

Fraud
. collusion, . . . 16,032-16,033
. purchasing incentives, . . . 16,020-16,021
. theft at the bar, . . . 16,045-16,046

Free cash flow, . . . 15,018-15,019

Fundamental analysis, . . . 14,002

G

GAAP. *See* Generally accepted accounting principles (GAAP)

Gains
. defined, . . . 6005
. income statement reporting, . . . 6005

Gaming industry
. cost segregation, . . . 29,012-29,025
. Gaming Industry Tip Compliance Agreement (GITCA), . . . 20,013

Generally accepted accounting principles (GAAP)
. cash flow statement, . . . 15,021, 15,026-15,029
. contingencies, . . . 11,008-11,009
. controller knowledge of, . . . 2017-2018
. deferred tax recognition, . . . 11,004
. disclosure of noncash financing and investing activities, . . . 8008
. earnings per share, . . . 13,002
. FASB and APB influence, . . . 5002-5004

Generally accepted accounting principles (GAAP)—continued
. financial report disclosures, . . . 3006
. financial statement disclosures, . . . 9002-9003
. financial statement reporting, . . . 5002
. historical cost accounting, . . . 11,009-11,010
. IFRS vs., *See also* International Financial Reporting Standards (IFRS) . . . 2018.
. iGAAP, *See also* International Financial Reporting Standards (IFRS) . . . 27,002.
. leases, . . . 11,006-11,008
. prior-period adjustments, . . . 9006
. subsequent event disclosures, . . . 9012

Gift card sales deferral rules, . . . 20,016

GITCA (Gaming Industry Tip Compliance Agreement), . . . 20,013

Glass, accounting for, . . . 7007

Global distribution systems, . . . 4029

Goal of the company
. compliance mechanisms, . . . 3024-3025
. financial management, . . . 1002-1003

Going-concern assumption, financial statement reporting, . . . 5002

Going concern basis, IFRS Framework, . . . 27,014

Gordon and Lintner's bird-in-the-hand theory, . . . 23,007-23,008

Graphics, . . . 4008-4012
. area chart, . . . 4010
. bar chart, . . . 4008
. break-even graphs, . . . 19,012-19,013
. expansion chart, . . . 4010
. informational Web site, . . . 4012
. line chart, . . . 4009
. pie chart, . . . 4009
. program listing, . . . 4012
. scatter chart, . . . 4011
. separating mixed costs into variable and fixed elements, . . . 19,021-19,023
. statistical chart, . . . 4011

Green Globe 21, . . . 3028-3029

"Green" Hotels Association, . . . 3028-3029

Gross operating profit
. defined, . . . 6013
. summary operating statement reporting, . . . 6013

Gross profit margin, . . . 12,005

Guarantees by third parties, secured loans, . . . 22,010

Guest loyalty programs, . . . 20,017-20,018

Guest-tracking software, . . . 4018

H

Harrah's
. data warehousing system, . . . 4022
. PROFPAR system, . . . 4026

Highest price method, . . . 16,006

Historic building credit, . . . 20,005-20,008
. compliance requirements, . . . 20,006
. defined, . . . 20,005
. leases shorter than recovery period, . . . 20,008
. net leases, . . . 20,008
. recapture of the credit, . . . 20,006-20,007
. rehabilitation expenditures made by lessee, . . . 20,007-20,008
. requirements, . . . 20,005-20,006

HITIS (Hospitality Information Technology Integration Standards), . . . 4022

Holiday Inn, energy-conserving practices, . . . 3029

Horizontal common size analysis, . . . 12,009, 14,026-14,028

Hospitality Extraordinaire, . . . 3028

Hospitality Information Technology Integration Standards (HITIS), . . . 4022

Host Marriott, . . . 3017-3018

Hotel operating ratios, . . . 14,004-14,013

Hotel Operating Statistics (HOST) Study, . . . 10,010

Hotel Sofitel, Audubon Green Leaf Eco-Rating Program for Hotels, . . . 3029

House profit, *See also* Gross operating profit . . . 6013.

Hubbart formula, . . . 19,027-19,029

I

IAASB (International Auditing and Assurance Standards Board), . . . 2018

IAS (International Accounting Standards), . . . 2018, 27,002

IAS 1, *Presentation of Financial Statements*, . . . 27,015

IAS 8, *Accounting Policies, Changes in Accounting Estimates and Errors*, . . . 27,028

IASB. *See* International Accounting Standards Board (IASB)

IBM's Lotus 1-2-3, . . . 4004

IFAC (International Federation of Accountants), . . . 2018

IFRIC (International Financial Reporting Interpretations Committee), . . . 2018

IFRS. *See* International Financial Reporting Standards (IFRS)

iGAAP, *See also* International Financial Reporting Standards (IFRS) . . . 27,002.

IHG (Intercontinental Hotel Group), . . . 4021

IHRA. *See* International Hotel and Restaurant Association (IHRA)

Income
. comprehensive income, . . . 6020
. before fixed charges, *See also* Gross operating profit . . . 6014.
. summary operating statement, . . . 6012

Income bonds, . . . 21,010, 21,012

Income statement
. change in accounting principle, cumulative effect of, . . . 6016

Income statement—continued
. components, . . . 6003-6005, 19,002-19,003
. . expenses, . . . 6004-6005
. . franchise fee revenue, . . . 6004
. . gains and losses, . . . 6005
. . income taxes, . . . 6005
. . number of units sold, . . . 19,002-19,003
. . revenue, . . . 6003-6004
. . total fixed costs, . . . 19,002-19,003
. . unit price, . . . 19,002-19,003
. . unit variable expense, . . . 19,002-19,003
. comprehensive income, . . . 6020
. discontinued operations, . . . 6015-6016
. earnings per share, . . . 6017-6020
. . basic earnings per share, . . . 6017-6018
. . diluted earnings per share, . . . 6018-6020
. expanded, . . . 17,017
. extraordinary items, . . . 6014-6015
. formats, . . . 6002-6003
. . multistep, . . . 6002
. . single-step, . . . 6002-6003
. objectives, . . . 6002
. overview, . . . 6001-6002
. pro forma contribution format, . . . 19,005-19,006
. restructuring charges, . . . 6016-6017
. scope, . . . 6002
. solvency and leverage analysis, . . . 11,006-11,007
. structure of, . . . 6005-6006
. summary, . . . 6007-6014
. . fixed charges, . . . 6007-6008, 6014
. . operated departments, . . . 6007-6012
. . undistributed operating expenses, . . . 6007-6008, 6012-6013
. USAL
. . income statement, . . . 6002
. . income statement development, . . . 6006-6007
. . income statement sample, . . . 2006-2008

Income taxes
. capital investment decisions and, . . . 24,019
. deferred, balance sheet presentation, . . . 7013
. financial statement disclosures, . . . 9010-9011

Income taxes—continued
. income statement reporting, . . . 6005
. leverage, impact of, . . . 19,017

Incremental cost, . . . 17,019

Indentures, bond, . . . 21,008

Independence
. Board of Directors, . . . 3005
. defined, . . . 3005

Independent projects, . . . 24,003

Indexing
. consumer price index, . . . 14,031
. defined, . . . 14,002
. management analysis of operations, . . . 14,030-14,031
. producer price index, . . . 14,031
. Twin Restaurants example, . . . 14,032-14,033

Indifference earnings, . . . 19,018-19,020
. before income taxes, . . . 19,018-19,020
. . adjusted EBT, . . . 19,018
. margin of safety, . . . 19,019-19,020

Indirect costs
. defined, . . . 17,014
. indirect costs vs., . . . 17,014-17,016

Indirect expenses
. defined, . . . 6006
. traditional cost allocation
. . direct method, . . . 18,006-18,009
. . formula method, . . . 18,011-18,012
. . step method, . . . 18,009-18,011

Industry averages, sources of, . . . 10,010-10,011

Information technology (IT)
. accounting and recording functions, . . . 2002
. accounting functions, . . . 4003
. attorney professional conduct standards, . . . 3013
. controller responsibilities, . . . 1002
. history of, . . . 4002
. to maximize ROI, . . . 4014-4016
. purchasing process, . . . 4040-4041

INF

Information technology (IT)—continued
. ROI calculations, . . . 4035-4040

Insurance
. controller functions, . . . 2015
. FICA. *See* Federal Insurance Contributions Act (FICA)
. life insurance
. . cash surrender value, balance sheet presentation, . . . 7009
. . for secured loans, . . . 22,010

Intangible assets, balance sheet presentation, . . . 7009-7010

Intercontinental Hotel Group (IHG), . . . 4021

Interest
. interest rates, impact on cost of capital, . . . 25,009
. short-term financing, . . . 22,006
. times interest earned, . . . 11,006

Intermediate financing, . . . 22,012-22,015
. conditional sales contracts, . . . 22,013-22,014
. leasing, . . . 22,014-22,015
. overview, . . . 22,001, 22,012
. short-term financing vs., . . . 22,015
. Small Business Administration term loans, . . . 22,013
. . direct loans, . . . 22,013
. . economic opportunity loans, . . . 22,013
. . participation loans, . . . 22,013
. term loans, . . . 22,012-22,013

Internal audit, controller functions, . . . 2011

Internal control
. attorney professional conduct standards, . . . 3012-3013
. controller functions, . . . 2002, 2009-2011
. . accuracy of records, . . . 2009-2010
. . enterprise risk management, . . . 2009, 2010
. . evaluation of procedures, . . . 2010
. . internal audit, . . . 2011
. . internal control, defined, . . . 2009
. . minimizing expenses, . . . 2010
. . minimizing risk, . . . 2009

Internal control—continued
. controller functions,—continued
. . outsourced records, . . . 2011
. . overview, . . . 2002
. . summary of steps, . . . 2010
. . system evaluation, . . . 2010-2011
. . value maximization, . . . 2010
. corporate governance and, . . . 3021-3022
. defined, . . . 2009

Internal management reports, . . . 2012-2015

Internal rate of return (IRR), capital investment analysis, . . . 24,014-24,016

Internal reports, . . . 5008

Internal Revenue Code/Service
. bartering, . . . 20,015-20,016
. building improvements, depreciable life, . . . 20,003
. contributions
. . Publication 78, . . . 20,017
. . used items, . . . 20,017
. contributions, food and beverages, . . . 20,016-20,017
. . Form 8283, . . . 20,017
. . Section 170(e)(3), . . . 20,016
. . Section 509(a)(1), . . . 20,017
. . Section 509(a)(2), . . . 20,017
. . Section 509(a)(3), . . . 20,017
. . Section 4942(j)(3), . . . 20,017
. depreciation issues, . . . 20,002-20,004
. . Form 3115, "Application for Change in Accounting Method", . . . 20,003, 20,016
. . publication 946, "How to Depreciate Property", . . . 20,004
. . Revenue Procedure 87-56, 1987-2 CB 674, . . . 20,004
. . Revenue Procedure 2002-12, . . . 20,003
. . Section 168(g), . . . 20,004
. . Section 179 deduction, . . . 20,003
. . Section 381(a), leasehold improvements, . . . 20,003
. . Section 1245, . . . 20,004
. . Section 1250 property, . . . 20,003-20,004
. energy tax credit, . . . 20,008-20,009
. . IRS Notice 2006-52, . . . 20,009
. . Section 179(d), . . . 20,008

Index

Internal Revenue Code/Service—continued
- expansion costs, . . . 20,019
- Form 10-K, . . . 3014, 5005
- Form 10-Q, . . . 5005
- Form 941, . . . 20,011-20,012
- Form 1099-B, bartering, . . . 20,015-20,016
- Form 4562, . . . 20,015
- Form 5884, . . . 20,014
- Form 8844, . . . 20,015
- Form 8846, . . . 20,012
- Form 8850, . . . 20,014
- franchising fees, . . . 20,016
- gift card sales deferral rules, . . . 20,016
- . Form 3115, . . . 20,016
- . Treasury Regulation 1.451-5, . . . 20,016
- guest loyalty programs, . . . 20,017-20,018
- . Treasury Regulation 1.451-4(a), . . . 20,017
- . Treasury Regulation 1.461-4(g)(3), . . . 20,017
- . Treasury Regulation 1.461-5, . . . 20,018
- Historic Building Credit, . . . 20,005-20,008
- . Form 3468, Investment Credit, . . . 20,006
- . Section 47 of Title 26, . . . 20,005
- . Section 47(c)(3)(B), . . . 20,005
- . Section 47(d), . . . 20,006, 20,007
- . Section 48(d)(4)(D), . . . 20,008
- . Section 48(d)(5)(B), . . . 20,008
- . Section 57(c)(1)(B), . . . 20,008
- . Section 168(c), . . . 20,007
- leasehold improvements, . . . 20,004-20,005
- lobbying deductions, Section 162(e), . . . 20,018
- property taxes, . . . 20,019
- Publication 954, "Tax Incentives for Distressed Communities", . . . 20,014, 20,015
- rehabilitation expenditures made by lessee, . . . 20,007-20,008
- sales taxes, . . . 20,019
- Section 6053(c)(3)(B), . . . 20,011
- Technical Advice Memorandum 9719005, . . . 20,015
- tip income, . . . 20,009-20,014
- . Form 941, . . . 20,014-20,012
- . Form 1040, . . . 20,010

Internal Revenue Code/Service—continued
- tip income,—continued
- . . Form 4070 and 4070A, . . . 20,010
- . . Form 8027, . . . 20,010, 20,013
- . . Form 8846, . . . 20,012
- . . Revenue Procedure 2003-35, 2003-1 C.B. 919, . . . 20,013
- . . Revenue Procedure 2006-3, . . . 20,013
- . . Revenue Procedure 2007-32, . . . 20,013
- . . Section 6053(c)(3)(B), . . . 20,011
- . . Section 6053(c)(4), . . . 20,010
- . Tip Rate/Determination/Education Program, . . . 20,011
- tip-related resources, . . . 29,001-29,002
- upfront payments from suppliers, . . . 20,015

International Accounting Standards Board (IASB)
- controller knowledge of, . . . 2018
- financial reporting system, . . . 5003
- iGAAP development, . . . 27,002
- Memorandum of Understanding, . . . 27,002-27,004
- SEC oversight, . . . 27,007
- truth and fairness principle, . . . 3021

International Accounting Standards (IAS)
- accounting standards, . . . 2018, 27,002
- IAS 1, *Presentation of Financial Statements*, . . . 27,015
- IAS 8, *Accounting Policies, Changes in Accounting Estimates and Errors*, . . . 27,028

International Auditing and Assurance Standards Board (IAASB), . . . 2018

International concept of corporate governance, . . . 3028-3029

International Federation of Accountants (IFAC), IAASB, . . . 2018

International Financial Reporting Interpretations Committee (IFRIC), accounting standards, . . . 2018

International Financial Reporting Standards (IFRS)
- conceptual framework, . . . 27,013-27,015

INT

International Financial Reporting Standards (IFRS)—continued
. convergence of U.S. GAAP and IFRS, . . . 27,002-27,008
. . additional convergence goals, . . . 27,003-27,004
. . differences between IFRS and U.S. GAAP, . . . 27,006-27,007
. . effectiveness of IFRS compared to U.S. GAAP, . . . 27,005-27,006
. . implementation problems, avoiding, . . . 27,005
. . SEC considerations, . . . 27,004-27,005
. . SEC-proposed roadmap milestones, . . . 27,007-27,008
. . SEC role in standard-setting process, . . . 27,007
. . short-term convergence, . . . 27,002-27,003
. . timing of implementation, . . . 27,005
. conversion of financial statements, . . . 27,026-27,028
. . checklist, . . . 27,027-27,028
. . cost vs. benefits of conversion, . . . 27,028
. . guidance, . . . 27,028
. European Union adoption of, . . . 2018
. financial statement presentation, proposed, . . . 27,015-27,017
. . background, . . . 27,015
. . cohesiveness, . . . 27,016-27,017
. . conversion preparation checklist, . . . 27,026-27,028
. . disaggregation, . . . 27,015-27,016
. . financial statement characteristics, . . . 27,017
. . sample, . . . 27,017-27,026
. GAAP vs., . . . 2018
. information sources, . . . 27,028
. overview, . . . 27,001-27,002
. SEC February 2010 release and work plan, . . . 27,008-27,013

International Hotel and Restaurant Association (IHRA)
. entitlement generation of workers, . . . 2019
. management accounting, . . . 2013, 2014
. marketing function, . . . 2015

Internet. *See also* Computers
. extranet, . . . 4004
. intranet, . . . 4004, 4028
. TCP/IP, . . . 4004

Intranet
. data warehouse information transmission, . . . 4028
. defined, . . . 4004
. uses for, . . . 4004

Inventory
. analysis of operations, . . . 14,004
. balance sheet presentation, . . . 7004
. beverage storage
. . periodic inventory control, . . . 16,039-16,040
. . perpetual inventory control, . . . 16,039-16,040
. expiring, . . . 14,004
. financial statement disclosures, . . . 9003
. food storage, . . . 16,027-16,029
. . periodic inventory control, . . . 16,027
. . perpetual inventory control, . . . 16,027-16,029
. ideal inventory quantity, . . . 16,025
. liquidity analysis, . . . 10,008-10,009
. physical, . . . 14,004
. single-image inventory, . . . 4024
. supply chain information technology, . . . 16,025

Investments
. balance sheet presentation, . . . 7008
. cash flow from, . . . 8004
. cash flow statement disclosure, . . . 8008
. cost of capital, impact on, . . . 25,009
. costs, GAAP vs. IFRS, . . . 2018
. financing activities for cash flow, . . . 8003, 8004, 15,010
. investing activities analysis, . . . 15,007-15,009
. . indicator of company growth, . . . 15,008
. . internal finance growth, . . . 15,008-15,009
. . quality of growth, . . . 15,009
. liquidity analysis, . . . 10,008
. profitability factor, . . . 16,056

Index

Investments—continued
. short-term
. . balance sheet presentation, . . . 7003-7004
. . liquidity analysis, . . . 10,008

Investor analysis of profitability
. beta analysis, . . . 13,009
. financial manager responsibilities, . . . 13,001
. market to book value, . . . 13,008-13,009
. market value, . . . 13,008-13,009
. measures of profitability, . . . 13,002-13,008
. . basic earnings per share, . . . 13,002
. . book value per share, . . . 13,008
. . diluted earnings per share, . . . 13,002-13,003
. . dividend payout ratio, . . . 13,006
. . dividend yield, . . . 13,006-13,008
. . earnings per share, . . . 13,002-13,004
. . earnings per share and analysts' forecasts, . . . 13,003-13,004
. . price earnings ratio, . . . 13,004-13,005
. overview, . . . 13,001-13,002

IRR (internal rate of return), . . . 24,014-24,016

IRS v. Specialty Restaurant Corporation, . . . 20,019

IT. *See* Information technology (IT)

J

Joint costs, . . . 17,018

Joint ventures
. defined, . . . 11,009
. solvency and leverage analysis, . . . 11,009

Junk bonds, . . . 21,012

K

Key codes, . . . 4018

KPMG International
. corporate governance white paper, . . . 3021, 3023
. Economist Intelligence Unit, . . . 3002, 3021

L

Labor
. controller knowledge of costs, . . . 2019
. cost-cutting measures, . . . 26,015
. cost minimization, . . . 16,046-16,049
. . staffing guide, . . . 16,046-16,048
. . standard ratios and variance analysis, . . . 16,048-16,049
. entitlement generation of workers, . . . 2019
. income statement reporting, . . . 6006
. as period cost, . . . 17,018
. recruiting and training, . . . 2019
. restaurant cost control, . . . 16,002-16,004

LANs (local area networks), . . . 4003

Laundry, cost allocation, . . . 18,004-18,005

Laws, controller knowledge of, . . . 2018

Leases
. balance sheet presentation, . . . 7007
. capital leases
. . balance sheet presentation, . . . 7007-7008
. . history of corporate governance, . . . 3017
. . solvency and leverage analysis, . . . 11,007-11,008
. financial leases, . . . 22,014-22,015
. history of corporate governance, . . . 3017
. for intermediate financing, . . . 22,014-22,015
. lease or purchase decision, . . . 24,021-24,022
. leasehold improvements
. . amortization, . . . 20,004-20,005
. . lessee or lessor expense, . . . 20,005
. leases shorter than recovery period, . . . 20,008
. leveraged lease, . . . 22,014
. net advantage to leasing, . . . 22,015, 24,021
. net leases, . . . 20,008
. net present value calculation, . . . 22,015
. operating leases
. . capital leases, . . . 11,008
. . fixed charges coverage ratio, . . . 11,006-11,007
. . for intermediate financing, . . . 22,014

Leases—continued
. rehabilitation expenditures made by lessee, . . . 20,007-20,008
. sale and leaseback, . . . 22,014-22,015

Leverage
. analysis. *See* Solvency and leverage analysis
. cost-volume-profit (CVP) analysis, . . . 19,013-19,017
. . factors affecting leverage, . . . 19,016-19,017
. . favorability of, . . . 19,017
. . financial leverage, . . . 19,013, 19,014-19,015
. . operating leverage, . . . 19,013, 19,014
. . total leverage, . . . 19,015-19,016
. defined, . . . 19,013
. leveraged lease, . . . 22,014

Levinson method of order size determination, . . . 16,022-16,023

Liabilities
. balance sheet presentation, . . . 7010-7014
. . accounts payable, . . . 7011
. . accrued expenses, . . . 7011
. . bonds payable, . . . 7011-7013
. . compensating absences, . . . 7013
. . contingencies, . . . 7014
. . current liabilities, . . . 7010-7011
. . deferred income taxes, . . . 7013
. . defined, . . . 7010
. . long-term debt, . . . 7011
. . long-term liabilities, . . . 7011-7013
. . notes payable, . . . 7011
. . unearned revenue, . . . 7011
. current liabilities. *See* Current liabilities

Life insurance
. cash surrender value, balance sheet presentation, . . . 7009
. for secured loans, . . . 22,010

Lifetime value of guests (LVoG), . . . 4021, 4027

Line chart, . . . 4009

Line of credit, . . . 22,005, 22,006-22,007

Linen, accounting for, . . . 7007

Liquidity analysis
. accounts receivable analysis, . . . 10,005-10,007
. . accounts receivable percentage, . . . 10,006-10,007
. . accounts receivable turnover, . . . 10,005-10,006
. . average collection period, . . . 10,006
. cash ratio, . . . 10,007
. composition of current assets and liabilities, . . . 10,007-10,009
. . cash, . . . 10,007-10,008
. . current liabilities, . . . 10,009
. . inventories, . . . 10,008-10,009
. . receivables, . . . 10,008
. . short-term investments, . . . 10,008
. current ratio, . . . 10,002-10,004
. industry averages, . . . 10,010-10,011
. liquidity, defined, . . . 10,001
. overview, . . . 10,001-10,002
. owners vs. creditors, . . . 10,004
. quick ratio, . . . 10,004-10,005
. ratio analysis considerations
. . ability to issue debt or stock, . . . 10,009
. . discounted notes, . . . 10,009
. . lawsuits, . . . 10,009
. . loan guarantees, . . . 10,009
. . long-term assets that can be converted into cash, . . . 10,009
. . unused bank credit lines, . . . 10,009
. working capital, . . . 10,002

Liquidity management in turnaround strategy, . . . 26,010-26,012
. better terms from suppliers, . . . 26,012
. cash conservation, . . . 26,011
. cash outlay, delaying, . . . 26,012
. cash receipts, accelerating, . . . 26,011-26,012

Litzenberger and Ramaswamy's tax preference theory, . . . 23,008

Loans. *See also* Financing activities
. long-term bank loans, . . . 21,007
. secured loans, . . . 22,009-22,011
. . accounts receivable, . . . 22,010
. . equipment, . . . 22,010

Loans.—continued
. secured loans,—continued
. . life insurance cash surrender, . . . 22,010
. . marketable securities, . . . 22,010
. . summary of sources, . . . 22,011
. . third party guarantee, . . . 22,010
. Small Business Administration (SBA) term loans, . . . 22,013
. . direct loans, . . . 22,013
. . economic opportunity loans, . . . 22,013
. . participation loans, . . . 22,013
. term loans, . . . 22,012-22,013

Lobbying deductions, . . . 20,018

Local area networks (LANs), . . . 4003

Long-term debt
. balance sheet presentation, . . . 7011
. characteristics, . . . 21,004-21,005
. defined, . . . 21,006
. financial statement disclosures, . . . 9007
. long-term debt to capitalization ratio, . . . 11,005
. long-term financing vs., . . . 21,006

Long-term financing
. alternative sources of financing, . . . 21,015
. bonds
. . balance sheet presentation, . . . 7011-7013
. . call provision, . . . 21,009
. . convertible bonds, . . . 21,010-21,011, 21,013
. . convertible debentures, . . . 21,011-21,012, 21,013
. . debentures, . . . 21,011-21,013
. . features, . . . 21,008
. . financing arrangements, . . . 21,007-21,008
. . floating rate bonds, . . . 21,013
. . income bonds, . . . 21,010, 21,012
. . indenture, . . . 21,008
. . junk bonds, . . . 21,012
. . mortgage bonds, . . . 21,009, 21,012
. . for secured loans, . . . 22,010
. . subordinated debentures, . . . 21,012-21,013
. . unsecured bonds, . . . 21,009-21,010
. . zero-coupon bonds, . . . 21,010, 21,012

Long-term financing—continued
. collateralized mortgage obligations, . . . 21,015
. defined, . . . 21,001
. equity financing, . . . 21,002-21,005
. . common stock, . . . 21,002-21,003, 21,004-21,005
. . preferred stock, . . . 21,003-21,005
. equity real estate investment trusts, . . . 21,015
. factors influencing financing decisions, . . . 21,013-21,015
. long-term debt, *See also* Long-term debt . . . 21,006-21,009.
. . bank loans, . . . 21,007
. . bond financing, . . . 21,007-21,009
. . long-term financing vs., . . . 21,006
. . mortgage financing, . . . 21,007
. privately held securities, . . . 21,006
. publicly held securities, . . . 21,006
. real estate mortgage investment conduits, . . . 21,015
. secondary mortgage market, . . . 21,015
. securitization of commercial real estate, . . . 21,015
. warrants, . . . 21,005

Loss leader pricing, . . . 16,006

Losses, income statement reporting, . . . 6005

Lotus 1-2-3, . . . 4004

LVoG (lifetime value of guests), . . . 4021, 4027

M

MACRS (Modified Accelerated Cost Recovery System), . . . 20,004

Management, activity-based, . . . 18,015

Management accounting, . . . 2012-2015
. cost accounting vs., . . . 17,001-17,002
. internal management reports, . . . 2012-2015
. purpose of, . . . 17,001-17,002

Management analysis of operations
. common size analysis, . . . 14,025-14,030
. . defined, . . . 14,002, 14,025

Management analysis of operations—continued
- common size analysis,—continued
  - horizontal analysis, . . . 14,026-14,028
  - trend analysis (percent change), . . . 14,028-14,030
  - vertical analysis, . . . 14,025-14,026
- comparative analysis, . . . 14,002, 14,023-14,024
- fundamental analysis, . . . 14,002
- indexing, . . . 14,030-14,033
  - consumer price index, . . . 14,031
  - defined, . . . 14,002
  - management analysis of operations, . . . 14,030-14,031
  - producer price index, . . . 14,031
  - Twin Restaurants example, . . . 14,032-14,033
- operating ratio analysis, . . . 14,003-14,023
  - advantages of ratios, . . . 14,003
  - beverage operations, . . . 14,018-14,021
  - costs, . . . 14,003-14,004, 14,012-14,013
  - cyclical comparisons, . . . 14,023
  - defined, . . . 14,002, 14,003
  - evaluation of, . . . 14,022-14,023
  - food and banquet revenue, . . . 14,011-14,012
  - hotel operating ratios, . . . 14,004-14,013
  - inventory, . . . 14,004
  - less common ratios, . . . 14,021-14,022
  - restaurant operating ratios, . . . 14,013-14,018
  - rooms revenue, . . . 14,008-14,011
  - Twin Restaurants example, . . . 14,033
  - units of input, . . . 14,003
  - units of output, . . . 14,003-14,004

Management discussion and analysis, financial condition and results of operations, . . . 5007

Management information systems (MIS), . . . 4001

Management-by-exception reports, . . . 2015

Manager
- financial manager. *See* Financial manager
- profitability measures, . . . 12,008

Margin of safety, . . . 19,019-19,020

Market cap, . . . 13,008

Market capitalization, . . . 13,008

Market environment, impact on cost of capital, . . . 25,009

Market to book value, . . . 13,008-13,009

Market value, . . . 13,008-13,009

Marketable securities, balance sheet presentation, . . . 7003-7004

Marketing
- costs, . . . 6013
- monitoring activities, . . . 26,017

Marriott
- Audubon Green Leaf Eco-Rating Program for Hotels, . . . 3028-3029
- history of corporate governance, . . . 3017-3018
- Host Marriott, . . . 3017-3018, 26,006
- Marriott International, . . . 3017-3018, 26,006
- turnaround strategies, . . . 26,002, 26,006

Matching concept, . . . 2004

Materiality
- accounting accuracy, . . . 3020
- concept of, . . . 2003
- defined, . . . 3020
- financial statement reporting, . . . 5002
- SAB-99, . . . 3020

McDonald's, . . . 26,002, 26,006

Memorandum of Understanding, . . . 27,002-27,004

Menu
- design, . . . 16,005
- pricing, . . . 16,005-16,012
  - average check target pricing, . . . 16,007
  - base selling price, . . . 16,012
  - contribution margin pricing, . . . 16,007-16,008, 16,011
  - discounts, . . . 26,016
  - highest price method, . . . 16,006
  - loss leader pricing, . . . 16,006

MAN

Index

Menu—continued
. pricing,—continued
. . markup price calculation methods, . . . 16,006-16,007, 16,009-16,010
. . objective methods, . . . 16,007
. . price by the ounce, . . . 16,011-16,012
. . pricing per customer, . . . 16,011
. . reasonable price method, . . . 16,006
. . sales volume considerations, . . . 16,007
. . subjective methods, . . . 16,006-16,007
. . target pricing, . . . 16,006
. . targeting competitors' prices, . . . 16,006
. . Texas Restaurant Association method, . . . 16,007
. . trial and error method, . . . 16,006
. sales mix analysis, . . . 16,012-16,015
. . cost/margin analysis, . . . 16,012-16,015
. . menu engineering analysis, . . . 16,012-16,015
. . per-unit contribution margin, . . . 16,012

Miami Mandarin Oriental Hotel, . . . 4027

Microsoft Excel spreadsheet
. add-in programs, . . . 4006-4007
. @Risk, . . . 4006
. EOQ, . . . 4006
. for IRR calculations, . . . 24,016
. restaurant management systems, . . . 4019
. uses for, . . . 4004-4006

Miller and Modigliani's Dividend Irrelevance theory, . . . 23,007

Minibar systems, . . . 4018

Min-max method of separating mixed costs, . . . 19,023-19,024

MIS (management information systems), . . . 4001

Mixed costs
. contribution margin, . . . 17,004-17,005
. overview, . . . 17,002-17,003
. separation into variable and fixed elements, . . . 19,021-19,025
. . graph method, . . . 19,021-19,023
. . min-max method, . . . 19,023-19,024

Modified Accelerated Cost Recovery System (MACRS), . . . 20,004

Mortgages
. bonds, . . . 21,009, 21,012
. collateralized mortgage obligations, . . . 21,015
. defined, . . . 21,007
. junior mortgage (second or third mortgage), . . . 21,007
. overview, . . . 21,007
. secondary mortgage market, . . . 21,015
. senior mortgage (first mortgage), . . . 21,007

Mutually exclusive projects, . . . 24,003, 24,018

N

NAL (net advantage to leasing), . . . 22,015, 24,021

NASDAQ, corporate governance, . . . 3013

Net advantage to leasing (NAL), . . . 22,015, 24,021

Net present value (NPV)
. acceptance criterion, . . . 24,012
. capital investment analysis, . . . 24,011-24,013
. discount rate, impact on capital investment analysis, . . . 24,020
. income taxes and capital investment decisions, . . . 24,019
. lease or purchase decision, . . . 22,015, 24,021
. mutually exclusive project decisions, . . . 24,002, 24,018
. risk and uncertainty, . . . 24,019
. shareholder wealth and, . . . 24,013

Net profit margin, . . . 12,005

Net return on assets (netROA), . . . 12,004, 12,006-12,007

NetROA (net return on assets), . . . 12,004, 12,006-12,007

Networks. *See* Computer networks

New York Stock Exchange (NYSE), corporate governance, . . . 3013-3016

Norwalk Agreement, . . . 2018

Notes payable, balance sheet presentation, . . . 7011

Notes to financial statements, . . . 5006, 9002

Notice 2006-52, energy tax credit, . . . 20,009

NPV. *See* Net present value (NPV)

Nucleus Research, . . . 4023

O

Objectives of financial management, . . . 1002

OECD (Organization for Economic Cooperation and Development), . . . 3002

Off-balance-sheet financing, . . . 11,006-11,007

OLAP (online applications processing), . . . 4029-4030

Online applications processing (OLAP), . . . 4029-4030

Operated departments, operating statement reporting, . . . 6007-6012
. department income or loss, . . . 6012
. example, . . . 6008-6009
. food and beverages, . . . 6010-6011
. objective, . . . 6008
. other operating departments, . . . 6011-6012
. rentals and other income, . . . 6012
. rooms, . . . 6009
. structure, . . . 6007-6008
. telecommunications department, . . . 6011

Operating activities, analysis of, . . . 15,005-15,007
. adjustments of the income statement, . . . 15,006
. warning signs, . . . 15,007
. working capital management efficiency, . . . 15,006-15,007

Operating activities, cash flow from, . . . 8003, 8004-8005

Operating efficiency
. compliance mechanisms, . . . 3024-3025
. ratio, . . . 12,001, 12,006

Operating income and expense, project cash flow estimating, . . . 24,006

Operating income margin, . . . 12,006

Operating leases
. capital leases, . . . 11,008
. fixed charges coverage ratio, . . . 11,006-11,007
. for intermediate financing, . . . 22,014

Operating leverage, CVP analysis, . . . 19,013, 19,014

Operating ratio analysis, . . . 14,013-14,018
. cost minimization, . . . 14,049-16,056
. defined, . . . 14,002
. evaluating food and banquet revenue, . . . 14,011-14,012
. expense evaluation, . . . 14,012-14,013
. hotel operating ratios, . . . 14,004-14,013
. . evaluating rooms revenue, . . . 14,008-14,011
. . expense evaluation, . . . 14,012-14,013
. . food and banquet revenue, . . . 14,011-14,012
. . room occupancy statistics, . . . 14,007-14,008
. . rooms in hotel, . . . 14,005-14,006
. management analysis of operations, . . . 14,003-14,023
. . advantages of ratios, . . . 14,003
. . beverage operations, . . . 14,018-14,021
. . costs, . . . 14,003-14,004, 14,012-14,013
. . cyclical comparisons, . . . 14,023
. . defined, . . . 14,002, 14,003
. . evaluation of, . . . 14,022-14,023
. . food and banquet revenue, . . . 14,011-14,012
. . hotel operating ratios, . . . 14,004-14,013
. . inventory, . . . 14,004
. . less common ratios, . . . 14,021-14,022
. . restaurant operating ratios, . . . 14,013-14,018
. . rooms revenue, . . . 14,008-14,011

Operating ratio analysis,—continued
. management analysis of operations,— continued
.. Twin Restaurants example, . . . 14,033
.. units of input, . . . 14,003
.. units of output, . . . 14,003-14,004
. restaurant operating ratios, . . . 14,013-14,018
.. accounting for food consumed, . . . 14,014-14,015
.. food operating ratios, . . . 14,016-14,018
.. restaurant sales, . . . 14,014
. restaurants.*See* Restaurant

Operational analysis as a management tool, . . . 26,005-26,006

Operational improvements, turnaround strategy, . . . 26,014-26,017
. cost-cutting measures, . . . 26,014-26,015
. revenue growth enhancement, . . . 26,015-26,017
. room and menu price discounts, . . . 26,016

Operations manager, controller responsibilities, . . . 2001, 2020

Opportunity cost, . . . 17,020

Oracle's Database 10g, . . . 4007

Organization for Economic Cooperation and Development (OECD), corporate governance, defined, . . . 3002

Outsourcing
. internal control function of controllers, . . . 2011
. payroll, . . . 4014

Owner's equity, balance sheet presentation, . . . 7014

Ownership, separation of ownership and control, . . . 1005

P

Par stock method of order size determination, . . . 16,021-16,022

Participation loans, . . . 22,013

Payback method, capital investment analysis, . . . 24,008-24,011
. acceptance criterion, . . . 24,009-24,010, 24,011
. discounted payback period, . . . 24,010-24,011

Payroll
. expense reporting, . . . 6012-6013
. outsourcing, . . . 4014

PBX (private branch exchange), . . . 4018

PCAOB.*See* Public Company Accounting Oversight Board (PCAOB)

P/E (price earnings ratio), . . . 13,004-13,005

Pension plans, financial statement disclosures, . . . 9007-9008

Period costs, . . . 17,017-17,018

PI (profitability index), . . . 24,013-24,014

Pie chart, . . . 4009

Point-of-sale (POS)
. computer systems, . . . 4017
. handheld input devices, . . . 2013
. for operational efficiency, . . . 4021

Population sampling, . . . 4013

POS.*See* Point-of-sale (POS)

Postretirement benefits
. expensing of, . . . 3020
. financial statement disclosures, . . . 9007-9008

PPI (producer price index), . . . 14,031

Prepaid expenses, balance sheet presentation, . . . 7005

Price earnings ratio (P/E), . . . 13,004-13,005

Prices
. average check target pricing, . . . 16,007
. bottom-up pricing
.. CVP analysis, . . . 19,025-19,029
.. Hubbart formula, . . . 19,027-19,029
. contribution pricing, . . . 17,010-17,014
. discounts, . . . 26,016

Prices—continued
. food and beverages. *See* Menu, pricing

Prime cost, . . . 16,002

Prior-period adjustments, . . . 9006-9007

Private branch exchange (PBX), . . . 4018

Producer price index (PPI), . . . 14,031

Profit margin
. operating efficiency ratio and, . . . 12,001
. profitability analysis, . . . 12,005, 12,006-12,007

Profit maximization
. beverage cost minimization, . . . 16,039-16,046
. . consumption, . . . 16,040-16,045
. . purchasing, . . . 16,039
. . storage, . . . 16,039-16,040
. . theft at the bar, . . . 16,045-16,046
. beverage revenue maximization, . . . 16,033-16,039
. . cost/margin analysis, . . . 16,035-16,039
. . pricing, . . . 16,034
. . waiters' suggestion, . . . 16,034-16,035
. factors affecting profits, . . . 16,055-16,056
. restaurant contribution margin, . . . 16,002-16,033
. . base selling price, . . . 16,012
. . consumption, . . . 16,030-16,033
. . elasticity of demand, . . . 16,015-16,018
. . mediocre food and labor cost control, . . . 16,002-16,004
. . menu design, . . . 16,005
. . menu pricing, . . . 16,005-16,012
. . menu sales mix analysis, . . . 16,012-16,015
. . optimum order size, . . . 16,021-16,026
. . prime cost, . . . 16,002
. . procurement of products, . . . 16,019-16,021
. . ratio analysis, . . . 16,018-16,019
. . receiving, . . . 16,026-16,027
. . restaurant design, . . . 16,004-16,005
. . storage, . . . 16,027-16,029
. value creation vs., . . . 1004-1005

Profit per available room (PROFPAR), . . . 4026

Profitability analysis
. common size analysis, . . . 12,008-12,009
. . horizontal analysis, . . . 12,009
. . vertical analysis, . . . 12,009
. DuPont and Leverage analysis, . . . 12,006-12,008
. . drivers of return on equity, . . . 12,007-12,008
. for investors. *See* Investor analysis of profitability
. measures of, . . . 12,001-12,006
. . asset turnover, . . . 12,005, 12,006-12,007
. . fixed asset turnover, . . . 12,002
. . managerial area of responsibility, . . . 12,008
. . net return on assets, . . . 12,004, 12,006-12,007
. . operating efficiency ratio, . . . 12,001, 12,006
. . profit margin, . . . 12,005, 12,006-12,007
. . return on assets, . . . 12,003-12,004
. . return on equity, . . . 12,002-12,003
. overview, . . . 12,001
. profitability, defined, . . . 12,001
. sustainable sales growth, . . . 12,009-12,010

Profitability index (PI), . . . 24,013-24,014

Profitability ratio, . . . 12,001

PROFPAR (profit per available room), . . . 4026

Projects
. cash flow estimating, . . . 24,005-24,007
. . categories, . . . 24,006-24,007
. . initial investment, . . . 24,006
. . operating income and expense, . . . 24,006
. . project termination, . . . 24,006
. mutually exclusive projects, . . . 24,003, 24,018
. post-audit project review, . . . 24,020-24,021

Property and equipment
. balance sheet presentation, . . . 7005-7008
. . capital leases, . . . 7007-7008

Property and equipment—continued
. balance sheet presentation,—continued
. . china, glass, silver, linen, uniforms, . . . 7007
. . construction in progress, . . . 7007
. . leasehold and leasehold improvements, . . . 7007
. GAAP vs. IFRS, . . . 2018
. property basis reduction for energy tax credit, . . . 20,009
. property management computer systems, . . . 4017, 4018
. property taxes, . . . 20,019
. real estate. *See* Real estate
. for secured loans, . . . 22,010
. summary operating statement reporting, . . . 6013

Proposed Roadmap, . . . 27,007-27,008

Public Company Accounting Oversight Board (PCAOB)
. attorney professional conduct standards, . . . 3013
. enterprise risk management, defined, . . . 2009
. GAAP standards, . . . 2017
. IFRS requirements and, . . . 27,004
. purpose of, . . . 3011-3012
. SOX creation of, . . . 3011

Publication 946, "How to Depreciate Property", . . . 20,004

Publication 954, "Tax Incentives for Distressed Communities", . . . 20,014, 20,015

Purchasing
. approaches and applications, . . . 16,025-16,026
. beverages, . . . 16,039
. food procurement, . . . 16,019-16,021
. order size determination, . . . 16,021-16,026
. purchase requisition and purchase order, . . . 16,026

Q

Quattro Pro spreadsheet, . . . 4004

Query, . . . 4007

Quick ratio, . . . 10,004-10,005

R

Racketeer Influenced and Corrupt Organizations Act of 1970 (RICO), . . . 2018

Ratios
. acid-test ratio, . . . 10,004
. accounts receivable turnover ratio, . . . 10,005-10,006
. asset to equity ratio, . . . 11,005
. asset turnover, . . . 12,005, 12,006-12,007
. beverage consumption, . . . 16,043-16,045
. beverage operations, . . . 14,018-14,021
. . accounting for beverages consumed, . . . 14,019-14,020
. . food sales vs. beverage sales, . . . 14,020
. . operating ratios, . . . 14,020
. . standard ratios, . . . 14,020-14,021
. cash flow, . . . 15,018-15,020
. cash flow to debt, . . . 15,019-15,020
. cash flow vs. accrual, . . . 15,022-15,024
. cash ratio, . . . 10,007
. constant payout ratio for dividends, . . . 23,003
. cost benefit, . . . 24,013
. cost minimization, . . . 16,049-16,056
. current ratio
. . liquidity analysis, . . . 10,002-10,004
. . owners vs. creditors, . . . 10,004
. debt ratio, . . . 11,003
. debt to asset ratio, . . . 11,003
. debt to equity ratio, . . . 11,004
. dividend payout ratio, . . . 13,006
. fixed asset turnover, . . . 12,002
. fixed charges coverage, . . . 11,006-11,007
. food consumption, . . . 16,030-16,031
. food-related operating ratios, . . . 16,018-16,019
. free cash flow, . . . 15,018-15,019
. hotel operating ratios, . . . 14,004-14,013
. *Industry Norms and Key Business Ratios*, . . . 10,010
. labor costs, . . . 16,048-16,049

Ratios—continued
. long-term debt to capitalization, . . . 11,005
. minority interest, debt ratio calculations, . . . 11,003-11,004
. net return on assets, . . . 12,004, 12,006-12,007
. operating efficiency ratio, . . . 12,001, 12,006
. operating income margin, . . . 12,006
. operating ratio analysis.*See* Operating ratio analysis
. price earnings ratio, . . . 13,004-13,005
. profit margin, . . . 12,005, 12,006-12,007
. profit margin and operating efficiency ratio, . . . 12,001, 12,006-12,007
. profit maximization, . . . 16,018-16,019
. profitability ratios, . . . 12,001
. quick ratio, . . . 10,004-10,005
. restaurant operating ratios, . . . 14,013-14,018
. return on assets, . . . 12,003-12,004
. return on equity, . . . 12,002-12,003, 12,007-12,008
. room operating ratios, . . . 14,004-14,011
. sales to fixed assets ratio, . . . 12,002
. solvency and leverage, . . . 11,002
. solvency ratio, . . . 11,002-11,003
. times interest earned, . . . 11,006
. yield ratio, . . . 17,018

Real estate
. collateralized mortgage obligations (CMOs), . . . 21,015
. real estate investment trusts (REITs), . . . 21,015
. real estate mortgage investment conduits (REMICs), . . . 21,015
. securitization of commercial real estate,*See also* Property and equipment . . . 21,015.

Realization concept, . . . 2003-2004

Reasonable price method, . . . 16,006

Rebranding, . . . 26,018

Receivables
. accounts receivable.*See* Accounts receivable
. balance sheet presentation, . . . 7004

Receivables—continued
. liquidity analysis, . . . 10,008

Recording.*See* Accounting and recording functions of controllers

Recovery as stage of turnaround strategy, . . . 26,009-26,010

Regression method of separating mixed costs, . . . 19,024-19,025

REITs (real estate investment trusts), . . . 21,015

Relevant cost, . . . 17,018-17,019

REMICs (real estate mortgage investment conduits), . . . 21,015

Rentals, summary operating statement presentation, . . . 6012

Reporting
. controller functions, . . . 2002, 2011-2016
. . advisor to management, . . . 2015-2016
. . financial accounting and reporting, . . . 2011-2012
. . insurance matters, . . . 2015
. . internal management reports, . . . 2012-2015
. . management accounting, . . . 2012-2015
. . reports to outside stakeholders, . . . 2012
. . tax matters, . . . 2015
. financial.*See* Financial reporting system
. internal reports, . . . 5008
. reporting entity, financial statement disclosures of changes, . . . 9005-9006
. reporting systems
. . ethical standards, . . . 1007
. . evaluation, . . . 26,018-26,019

Reservation systems, . . . 4024

Reserves, solvency and leverage analysis, . . . 11,004

Restaurant.*See also* Food and beverages
. consumption, . . . 16,030-16,033
. . built-in margin of error, . . . 16,033
. . collusion, . . . 16,032-16,033
. . errors using total sales and total costs, . . . 16,033

REA

Restaurant.—continued
- consumption,—continued
  - overcharging and underportioning, . . . 16,032
  - portion control, . . . 16,030
  - standard ratios and variance analysis, . . . 16,030-16,031
  - undercollection and excessive costs, . . . 16,031-16,032
- cost segregation, . . . 29,002-29,012
- elasticity of demand, . . . 16,015-16,018
  - quick determination method, . . . 16,018
  - snob demand, . . . 16,018
- layout and design, . . . 16,004-16,005
- management systems, . . . 4018-4019
- menu. *See also* Menu
  - base selling price, . . . 16,012
  - design, . . . 16,005
  - menu sales mix analysis, . . . 16,012-16,015
  - pricing, . . . 16,005-16,012
- operating ratios, . . . 14,013-14,018
  - accounting for food consumed, . . . 14,014-14,015
  - food operating ratios, . . . 14,016-14,018
  - restaurant sales, . . . 14,014
- optimum order size, . . . 16,021-16,026
  - economic order quantity, . . . 16,023-16,025
  - ideal inventory quantity, . . . 16,025
  - Levinson method, . . . 16,022-16,023
  - par stock method, . . . 16,021-16,022
  - purchase requisition and purchase order, . . . 16,026
  - purchasing approaches, . . . 16,025-16,026
  - supply chain information technology, . . . 16,025
- procurement of products, . . . 16,019-16,021
- profit maximization, . . . 16,002-16,033
  - base selling price, . . . 16,012
  - consumption, . . . 16,030-16,033
  - elasticity of demand, . . . 16,015-16,018
  - mediocre food and labor cost control, . . . 16,002-16,004
  - menu design, . . . 16,005
  - menu pricing, . . . 16,005-16,012

Restaurant.—continued
- profit maximization,—continued
  - menu sales mix analysis, . . . 16,012-16,015
  - optimum order size, . . . 16,021-16,026
  - prime cost, . . . 16,002
  - procurement of products, . . . 16,019-16,021
  - ratio analysis, . . . 16,018-16,019
  - receiving, . . . 16,026-16,027
  - restaurant design, . . . 16,004-16,005
  - storage, . . . 16,027-16,029
- ratio analysis, . . . 16,018-16,019
- receiving, . . . 16,026-16,027
- storage, . . . 16,027-16,029

Restructurings
- cash flow statement, . . . 15,010-15,014
- charges, income statement reporting, . . . 6016-6017
- complex restructurings, . . . 15,012
- debt to debt, . . . 15,012
- debt to equity or equity to debt, . . . 15,012-15,013
- simple financial restructurings, . . . 15,011-15,012

Retail business, cost segregation, . . . 29,025-29,038

Retained earnings
- balance sheet presentation, . . . 7016-7017
- cost of capital, . . . 25,007

Retirement benefits, . . . 3020, 9007-9008

Retrenchment as stage of turnaround strategy, . . . 26,008-26,009

Return on assets (ROA), . . . 12,003-12,004

Return on equity (ROE), profitability analysis, . . . 12,002-12,003, 12,007

Return on investment (ROI)
- calculation of, . . . 2013
- computer calculations, . . . 4002
- IT asset purchasing process, . . . 4040-4041
- IT investments, calculating ROI, . . . 4035-4040

Return on investment (ROI)—continued
. maximizing with information technology, . . . 4014-4016

Return on sales, . . . 12,005

Return to normalcy as stage of turnaround strategy, . . . 26,010

Revenue
. franchise fee revenue reporting, . . . 6004
. growth strategies, . . . 26,015-26,017
. income statement reporting, . . . 6003-6004
. management. *See* Revenue management systems
. maximization of, . . . 4020
. recognition of
. . GAAP vs. IFRS, . . . 2018
. . income statement reporting, . . . 6003-6004
. REVPAG (revenue per available guest), . . . 4021, 4022, 4027
. REVPAR (revenue per available room), . . . 14,011
. REVPOR (revenue per occupied room), . . . 14,009-14,010
. unearned revenue, balance sheet presentation, . . . 7011

Revenue management systems, . . . 4022-4026
. central reservation systems, . . . 4024
. channel management, . . . 4024
. defined, . . . 4022-4023
. procedures in programs, . . . 4023
. products, . . . 4023-4024
. profit per available room, . . . 4026
. REVPAG, . . . 4021, 4022, 4027
. single-image inventory, . . . 4024
. yield management, . . . 4024-4025

Revenue per available guest (REVPAG), . . . 4021, 4022, 4027

Revenue per available room (REVPAR), . . . 14,011

Revenue per occupied room (REVPOR), . . . 14,009-14,010

Revenue Procedure 87-56, 1987-2 CB 674, . . . 20,004

Revenue Procedure 2002-12, . . . 20,003

Revenue Procedure 2003-35, 2003-1 C.B. 919, . . . 20,013

Revenue Procedure 2006-3, . . . 20,013

Revenue Procedure 2007-32, . . . 20,013

Revolving line of credit, . . . 22,005, 22,007, 22,011

RICO (Racketeer Influenced and Corrupt Organizations Act of 1970), . . . 2018

Risk management
. accounting aberrations risk, . . . 2009
. business risk, . . . 2009
. internal control. *See* Internal control
. management inhibition in risk taking, . . . 3023-3024
. risk analysis computer programs, . . . 4012-4013

ROA (return on assets), . . . 12,003-12,004

Robert Morris Associates Annual Statement Studies, . . . 10,010

ROE (return on equity), . . . 12,012-12,003, 12,007

ROI. *See* Return on investment (ROI)

Rooms
. access keys, . . . 4018
. discounting prices, . . . 26,016
. operating ratios, . . . 14,004-14,011
. PROFPAR, . . . 4026
. revenue, . . . 14,008-14,011
. REVPAR, . . . 14,011
. REVPOR, . . . 14,009-14,010
. summary operating statement reporting, . . . 6009

Royalties, . . . 6004

RTTs, . . . 4028

S

SAB-67, Income Statement Presentation of Restructuring Charges, . . . 6016

Index

SAB-99, Materiality, . . . 3020

Sales
. conditional sales contracts, . . . 22,013-22,014
. defined, . . . 6013
. sale and leaseback, . . . 22,014-22,015
. sales and catering system (SCS), . . . 4018
. sales maximizing computer programs, . . . 4020
. sales taxes, . . . 20,019
. sales to fixed assets ratio, . . . 12,002
. summary operating statement reporting, . . . 6013
. sustainable sales growth, . . . 12,009-12,010

SAN. *See* Storage area network (SAN)

Sarbanes-Oxley Act of 2002 (SOX)
. attorney professional conduct standards, . . . 3012-3013
. business ethics and accounting, . . . 2018
. corporate governance, impact on, . . . 3004-3013
. . questions directed to management, . . . 3032-3036
. . penalties for violations, . . . 3019
. . traditional mechanisms, . . . 3004-3013
. corporate governance, traditional mechanisms
. . attorney reporting of unresolved issues, . . . 3005
. . Board of Directors credibility and independence, . . . 3005
. . categories, . . . 3004
. . corporate disclosures, . . . 3005-3007
. . whistleblower protections, . . . 3005
. cost of compliance, . . . 3023
. culture of change, . . . 3025
. disclosure requirements, . . . 3005-3007, 9001
. ethical standards, . . . 1007
. executive responsibility and legal liability, . . . 3007-3010
. external auditor independence and liability, . . . 3010-3012
. internal control function of controllers, . . . 2010-2011

Sarbanes-Oxley Act of 2002 (SOX)—continued
. management inhibition in risk taking, . . . 3023-3024
. PCAOB. *See* Public Company Accounting Oversight Board (PCAOB)
. principles-based accounting, . . . 3022
. purpose of, . . . 3004
. requirements, . . . 3004
. restoring compensation and reputation, . . . 3010
. Section 108, IASB accounting rules, . . . 3004
. Section 201
. . corporate disclosures, . . . 3005-3006
. . external auditor independence and liability, . . . 3010-3011
. Section 203, external auditor independence and liability, . . . 3011
. Section 204, external auditor independence and liability, . . . 3011
. Section 206, external auditor independence and liability, . . . 3011
. Section 301
. . Board of Directors credibility and independence, . . . 3005
. . questions to management, . . . 3032
. Section 302
. . attorney professional conduct standards, . . . 3013
. . executive responsibility and legal liability, . . . 3007-3008, 3009
. . financial statements, . . . 5001
. . questions to management, . . . 3033
. Section 303
. . external auditor independence and liability, . . . 3011
. . questions to management, . . . 3033
. Section 304, restoring compensation and reputation, . . . 3010
. Section 305, restoring compensation and reputation, . . . 3010
. Section 306, questions to management, . . . 3034
. Section 307, attorney reporting of unresolved issues, . . . 3005

SAR

Index

Sarbanes-Oxley Act of 2002 (SOX)—continued
. Section 401, questions to management, . . . 3034
. Section 401(a), corporate disclosures, . . . 3006
. Section 401(b), corporate disclosures, . . . 3006
. Section 401(c), corporate disclosures, . . . 3006
. Section 402, questions to management, . . . 3034
. Section 402(a), Board of Directors credibility and independence, . . . 3005
. Section 403
. . corporate disclosures, . . . 3006
. . questions to management, . . . 3034
. Section 404
. . attorney professional conduct standards, . . . 3013
. . executive responsibility and legal liability, . . . 3009
. . questions to management, . . . 3034
. Section 406
. . executive responsibility and legal liability, . . . 3009
. . questions to management, . . . 3034
. Section 407
. . corporate disclosures, . . . 3006-3007
. . questions to management, . . . 3035
. Section 409
. . corporate disclosures, . . . 3007
. . questions to management, . . . 3035
. Section 501, security analyst conflict of interest, . . . 3012
. Section 601, questions to management, . . . 3035
. Section 801, questions to management, . . . 3035
. Section 802
. . executive responsibility and legal liability, . . . 3009
. . external auditor independence and liability, . . . 3011
. Section 806
. . questions to management, . . . 3035
. . whistleblower protections, . . . 3005

Sarbanes-Oxley Act of 2002 (SOX)—continued
. Section 906
. . attorney professional conduct standards, . . . 3013
. . questions to management, . . . 3036
. . reporting requirements, . . . 3008-3009
. Section 1001, questions to management, . . . 3036
. Section 1102
. . executive responsibility and legal liability, . . . 3010
. . questions to management, . . . 3035
. Section 1103, restoring compensation and reputation, . . . 3010
. Section 1105, restoring compensation and reputation, . . . 3010
. security analyst conflict of interest, . . . 3012
. Title IX, executive responsibility and legal liability, . . . 3009-3010
. Title IX, restoring compensation and reputation, . . . 3010
. Title VIII, restoring compensation and reputation, . . . 3010
. Title XI, restoring compensation and reputation, . . . 3010

SAS-70, Service Organizations, . . . 2011

SBA. *See* Small Business Administration (SBA) term loans

Scatter chart, . . . 4011

Schulze, Karl, . . . 3020-3021

Scope of financial management
. cash flow, importance of, . . . 1006
. ethics, . . . 1007
. external environment, . . . 1006
. goal of the company, . . . 1002-1003
. managerial action influence on shareholder value, . . . 1005
. objectives, . . . 1002
. overview, . . . 1001
. profit maximization vs. value creation, . . . 1004-1005
. separation of ownership and control, . . . 1005-1006
. stakeholders' interests, . . . 1006-1007

SAS

Index

Scope of financial management—continued
. value creation, . . . 1003-1005

SCS (sales and catering system), . . . 4018

SEC. *See* Securities Exchange Commission (SEC)

Section 13(a), executive responsibility and legal liability, . . . 3007-3008

Section 15(d), executive responsibility and legal liability, . . . 3007-3008

Section 47 of Title 26 Historic Building Credit, . . . 20,005

Section 47(c)(3)(B), Historic Building Credit, . . . 20,005

Section 47(d), Historic Building Credit, . . . 20,006, 20,007

Section 48(d)(4)(D), leases, . . . 20,008

Section 48(d)(5)(B), leases, . . . 20,008

Section 57(c)(1)(B), leases, . . . 20,008

Section 162(e), lobbying deductions, . . . 20,018

Section 168(c), recovery period, . . . 20,007

Section 168(g) depreciation, . . . 20,004

Section 170(e)(3), deductible contributions, . . . 20,016

Section 179 deduction, . . . 20,003

Section 179(d), energy tax credit, . . . 20,008

Section 381(a), leasehold improvements, . . . 20,003

Section 509(a)(1), deductible contributions, . . . 20,017

Section 509(a)(2), deductible contributions, . . . 20,017

Section 509(a)(3), deductible contributions, . . . 20,017

Section 1245 assets, . . . 20,004

Section 1250 property, . . . 20,003-20,004

Section 4942(j)(3), deductible contributions, . . . 20,017

Section 6053(c)(3)(B), allocated tips, . . . 20,011

Section 6053(c)(4), reporting tips, . . . 20,010

Secure sockets layers (SSLs), . . . 4004

Securities
. long-term financing
. . privately held securities, . . . 21,006
. . publicly held securities, . . . 21,006
. for secured loans, . . . 22,010
. securitization of commercial real estate, . . . 21,015

Securities Exchange Act of 1933
. business ethics and accounting, . . . 2018
. overview, . . . 5004

Securities Exchange Act of 1934
. business ethics and accounting, . . . 2018
. corporate governance, . . . 3019
. Form 10-K, . . . 5005
. Form 10-Q, . . . 5005
. purpose of, . . . 5004-5005
. Section 10(b), restoring compensation and reputation, . . . 3010
. Section 13(a)
. . certified reports, . . . 3009-3010
. . corporate disclosures, . . . 3006
. . executive responsibility and legal liability, . . . 3007-3008
. . external auditor independence and liability, . . . 3011
. . reports required, . . . 3008
. Section 15(d)
. . certified reports, . . . 3009-3010
. . executive responsibility and legal liability, . . . 3007-3008
. . reports required, . . . 3008
. Section 21C, restoring compensation and reputation, . . . 3010
. Section 32(a), penalties for securities fraud, . . . 3013

Securities Exchange Commission (SEC)
. CIFiR, . . . 27,005-27,006
. expensing of postretirement benefits, . . . 3020
. February 2010 release and work plan, . . . 27,008-27,013

SEC

31,040   Index

Securities Exchange Commission (SEC)—continued
- GAAP standards, . . . 2017, 5003, 27,002
- IFRS adoption considerations, . . . 27,004-27,005
- internal control function of controllers, . . . 2010-2011
- Proposed Roadmap, . . . 27,007-27,008
- purpose of, . . . 5004
- SAB-67, . . . 6016
- SAB-99, . . . 3020
- standard-setting role, . . . 27,007

Security analysis conflict of interest, . . . 3012

Segment of a business
- defined, . . . 6015
- financial statement disclosures, . . . 9011-9012

SFAC 6, Elements of Financial Statements
- assets, . . . 7003
- expense reporting, . . . 6004
- gains, defined, . . . 6005
- liabilities, defined, . . . 7010
- revenue reporting, . . . 6003

Shareholders
- agency problem, . . . 1006
- annual reports to shareholders, . . . 5005-5007
- - auditor's report, . . . 5007
- - financial statements, . . . 5006
- - management discussion of financial condition and results of operations, . . . 5007
- - notes to financial statements, . . . 5006
- company value creation, . . . 1003-1004
- corporate governance, . . . 3018-3019
- as dividend policy factor, . . . 23,005
- interests of other stakeholders, . . . 1006-1007
- managerial action influence on shareholder value, . . . 1005
- market value increase, . . . 3025-3028
- minority interest, debt ratio calculations, . . . 11,003-11,004
- net present value and shareholder wealth, . . . 24,013

Shareholders—continued
- separation of ownership and control, . . . 1005-1006
- stakeholders
- - controller reports, . . . 2011-2013
- - financial accounting and reporting to, . . . 2011-2012

Shareholders' equity, balance sheet presentation, . . . 7014-7022
- additional paid-in capital, . . . 7016
- common stock, . . . 7016
- comprehensive income, . . . 7017-7018
- consolidated statement, . . . 7020-7021
- employee stock purchase plans, . . . 7018
- preferred stock, . . . 7015-7016
- retained earnings, . . . 7016-7017
- stock options, . . . 7019, 7022
- treasury stock, . . . 7017

Shoney's, . . . 3018

Short-term financing
- accruals, . . . 22,004-22,005, 22,011
- advantages of use, . . . 22,002
- bank loans, . . . 22,005-22,007
- - compensating balances, . . . 22,006
- - interest, . . . 22,006
- - lines of credit, . . . 22,005, 22,006-22,007, 22,011
- - revolving lines of credit, . . . 22,005, 22,007, 22,011
- - transaction loan, . . . 22,005
- - unsecured loans, . . . 22,011
- commercial paper, . . . 22,007-22,009, 22,011
- defined, . . . 22,002
- disadvantages of use, . . . 22,002
- intermediate financing vs., . . . 22,015
- overview, . . . 22,001
- secured loans, . . . 22,009-22,011
- - accounts receivable, . . . 22,010
- - equipment, . . . 22,010
- - life insurance cash surrender, . . . 22,010
- - marketable securities, . . . 22,010
- - summary of sources, . . . 22,011
- - third party guarantee, . . . 22,010
- sources of, . . . 22,002
- - accruals, . . . 22,004-22,005, 22,011

SEC

Short-term financing—continued
. sources of,—continued
.. bank loans, . . . 22,005-22,007
.. commercial paper, . . . 22,007-22,009, 22,011
.. trade credit, . . . 22,002-22,004
. trade credit
.. advantages of use, . . . 22,003
.. cash discount, . . . 22,003-22,004
.. credit terms, . . . 22,003
.. drawbacks of use, . . . 22,003
.. overview, . . . 22,002-22,004, 22,011

Short-term investments
. balance sheet presentation, . . . 7003-7004
. liquidity analysis, . . . 10,008

Silver, accounting for, . . . 7007

Simple financial restructurings, . . . 15,011-15,012

Single-image inventory, . . . 4024

Situation analysis as stage of turnaround strategy, . . . 26,008

Small Business Administration (SBA) term loans, . . . 22,013
. direct loans, . . . 22,013
. economic opportunity loans, . . . 22,013
. participation loans, . . . 22,013

Smallwares accounting method, . . . 20,002-20,003

Snob demand, . . . 16,018

Software. *See* Computers

Solvency and leverage analysis
. balance sheet approach, . . . 11,002-11,005
.. asset to equity ratio, . . . 11,005
.. debt ratio, . . . 11,003
.. debt to equity ratio, . . . 11,004
.. deferred taxes, . . . 11,004
.. long-term debt to capitalization, . . . 11,005
.. minority interest, . . . 11,003-11,004
.. reserves, . . . 11,004
.. solvency ratio, . . . 11,002-11,003
. capital leases, . . . 11,007-11,008

Solvency and leverage analysis—continued
. contingencies, . . . 11,008-11,009
. historical cost accounting, . . . 11,009-11,010
. income statement approach, . . . 11,006-11,007
.. fixed charges coverage ratio, . . . 11,006-11,007
.. interest coverage, . . . 11,006
. joint ventures, . . . 11,009
. overview, . . . 11,001-11,002
. ratios, . . . 11,002
. solvency, defined, . . . 11,001

SOX. *See* Sarbanes-Oxley Act of 2002 (SOX)

Spreadsheets, . . . 4004-4006
. Excel
.. add-in programs, . . . 4006-4008
.. @Risk, . . . 4006
.. EOQ, . . . 4006
.. for IRR calculations, . . . 24,016
.. restaurant management systems, . . . 4019
.. uses for, . . . 4004-4006
. for IRR calculations, . . . 24,016
. Lotus 1-2-3, . . . 4004
. Quattro Pro, . . . 4004
. tips for using, . . . 4006

SQL (standard query language), . . . 4007

SSLs (secure sockets layers), . . . 4004

Staffing guide, . . . 16,046-16,048

Stakeholder. *See also* Shareholders
. controller reports, . . . 2011-2013
. financial accounting and reporting to, . . . 2011-2012

Standard and Poor's Industry Surveys, . . . 10,010

Standard costs, . . . 17,020

Standard query language (SQL), . . . 4007

Starbucks, . . . 26,002, 26,006

Starwood Hotels, . . . 4024

Statement of Auditing Standards No. 70, Service Organizations, . . . 2011

Statement of earnings. *See* Income statement

STA

Statement of financial condition. *See* Balance sheet

Statement of financial position. *See* Balance sheet

Statement of income. *See* Income statement

Statement of operations. *See* Income statement

Statistics
. economic impact of hotel industry, . . . 1001
. Hotel Operating Statistics (HOST) Study, . . . 10,010
. statistical analysis computer programs, . . . 4012-4013
. statistical chart, . . . 4011

Stock
. balance sheet presentation
. . common stock, . . . 7016
. . employee stock purchase plans, . . . 7018
. . preferred stock, . . . 7015-7016
. . stock options, . . . 7019, 7022
. . stock splits, . . . 7022
. . treasury stock, . . . 7017
. book value per share, . . . 13,008
. buybacks, . . . 23,010-23,011
. common stock
. . balance sheet presentation, . . . 7016
. . cost of capital, . . . 25,004-25,007
. . equity financing, . . . 21,002-21,003, 21,004-21,005
. dividends. *See* Dividends
. earnings per share, . . . 6017-6020
. . basic earnings per share, . . . 6017-6018, 13,002
. . diluted earnings per share, . . . 6018-6020
. market value, . . . 13,008-13,009
. preferred stock
. . balance sheet presentation, . . . 7015-7016
. . cost of capital, . . . 25,004
. . equity financing, . . . 21,003-21,005
. repurchases, . . . 23,010-23,011
. for secured loans, . . . 22,010
. stock options
. . balance sheet presentation, . . . 7019, 7022
. . financial statement disclosures, . . . 9010

Stock—continued
. stock options—continued
. . history of corporate governance, . . . 3017, 3018
. stock split
. . balance sheet presentation, . . . 7022
. . dividends vs., . . . 23,009-23,010
. treasury stock
. . balance sheet presentation, . . . 7017
. . restructurings, . . . 15,013-15,014

Stock exchanges
. corporate governance, . . . 3013-3016
. NASDAQ, . . . 3013
. New York Stock Exchange, . . . 3013-3016

Stockholders. *See* Shareholders

Storage, food
. beverages, . . . 16,039-16,040
. perpetual inventory control, . . . 16,027, 16,039-16,040
. periodic inventory control, . . . 16,027-16,029, 16,039-16,040

Storage area network (SAN)
. data warehouse information transmission, . . . 4028
. purpose of, . . . 4007

Strategic planning computer systems
. asset management systems, . . . 4034-4035
. business process integration, . . . 4031
. decision support software, . . . 4033
. enterprise application integration, . . . 4032
. enterprise resource planning, . . . 4032-4033
. executive information systems, . . . 4033-4034

Strategic reorientation, . . . 26,018

Subordinated debentures, . . . 21,012-21,013

Subsequent events, financial statement disclosures, . . . 9012-9013

Summary operating statement, . . . 6007-6014
. fixed charges, . . . 6007-6008, 6014
. operated departments, . . . 6007-6012
. undistributed operating expenses, . . . 6007-6008, 6012-6013

Index

Sunk cost, . . . 17,019

Suppliers
. incentives, . . . 16,020-16,021
. just-in-time delivery, . . . 16,025
. negotiating better terms, . . . 26,012
. procurement of food products, . . . 16,019-16,021
. supply chain information technology, . . . 16,025
. upfront payments from suppliers, . . . 20,015

Supply chain information technology, . . . 16,025

Supply chain management systems, . . . 4027-4028

SurfControl, . . . 3013

T

Tablet PC, . . . 4021

Target pricing, . . . 16,006

Targeting competitors' prices, . . . 16,006

Tax Reduction Act of 2003, dividends, . . . 23,008, 23,011

Taxes
. alternative minimum tax, . . . 20,004
. bartering, . . . 20,015-20,016
. capital gains exclusion, . . . 20,015
. capital investment considerations, . . . 24,003
. computer programs, . . . 4013-4014
. contributions of used items, . . . 20,017
. controller functions, . . . 2015
. cost of capital, impact on, . . . 25,009
. deductible food and beverage contributions, . . . 20,016-20,017
. deferred, . . . 11,004
. depreciation issues, . . . 20,002-20,004
. . Alternative Depreciation System, . . . 20,004
. . alternative minimum tax, . . . 20,004
. . building improvements, . . . 20,003
. . cost segregation, . . . 20,004

Taxes—continued
. depreciation issues,—continued
. . hospitality issues, . . . 20,002
. . longer depreciation lives, . . . 20,004
. . MACRS, . . . 20,004
. . recovery periods, . . . 20,004
. . Section 179 deduction, . . . 20,003
. . smallwares accounting method, . . . 20,002-20,003
. as dividend policy factor, . . . 23,007
. dividend tax preference theory, . . . 23,008
. empowerment zone, . . . 20,014-20,015
. energy tax credit, . . . 20,008-20,009
. expansion costs, . . . 20,019
. FICA. *See* Federal Insurance Contributions Act (FICA)
. franchising fees, . . . 20,016
. gift card sales deferral rules, . . . 20,016
. guest loyalty programs, . . . 20,017-20,018
. historic building credit, . . . 20,005-20,008
. . compliance requirements, . . . 20,006
. . defined, . . . 20,005
. . leases shorter than recovery period, . . . 20,008
. . net leases, . . . 20,008
. . recapture of the credit, . . . 20,006-20,007
. . rehabilitation expenditures made by lessee, . . . 20,007-20,008
. . requirements, . . . 20,005-20,006
. income tax. *See* Income taxes
. leasehold improvements, . . . 20,004-20,005
. lobbying deductions, . . . 20,018
. property taxes, . . . 20,019
. renewal community benefits, . . . 20,015
. sales taxes, . . . 20,019
. solvency and leverage analysis, . . . 11,004
. tip income, . . . 20,009-20,014
. . allocated tips, . . . 20,011
. . deemed wages, . . . 20,010-20,011
. . FICA tax, . . . 20,011-20,012, 20,014
. . penalties, . . . 20,011
. . reporting procedures, . . . 20,010
. . tip rate determination, . . . 20,012-20,014
. upfront payments from suppliers, . . . 20,015
. work opportunity tax credit, . . . 20,014

TAX

TCP/IP, . . . 4004

Technical Advice Memorandum 9719005, . . . 20,015

Telecommunications department, summary operating statement reporting, . . . 6011

Term loan, . . . 22,012-22,013

Texas Restaurant Association pricing method, . . . 16,007

Theft at the bar, . . . 16,045-16,046

Tim Hortons, . . . 3019

Times interest earned ratio, . . . 11,006

Tip income, . . . 20,009-20,014
. allocated tips, . . . 20,011
. deemed wages, . . . 20,010-20,011
. Fair Labor Standards Act, . . . 20,009
. FICA tax, . . . 20,011-20,012, 20,014
. penalties, . . . 20,011
. reporting procedures, . . . 20,010
. tip rate determination/education programs, . . . 20,012-20,014
. . Attributed Tip Income Program (ATIP), . . . 20,013
. . Employer-Designed Tip Reporting Alternative Commitment (EmTRAC), . . . 20,013
. . Gaming Industry Tip Compliance Agreement (GITCA), . . . 20,013
. . Tip Rate Determination Agreement (TRDA), . . . 20,012, 20,013
. . Tip Reporting Alternative Commitment (TRAC), . . . 20,013
. Tip Rate/Determination/Education Program, . . . 20,011
. tipped employees, defined, . . . 20,009

Tip Rate Determination Agreement (TRDA), . . . 20,012, 20,013

Tip Reporting Alternative Commitment (TRAC), . . . 20,012, 20,013

Top-down questions, . . . 19,003, 19,004, 19,012

Total free cash, . . . 15,019

Total leverage, CVP analysis, . . . 19,015-19,016

TRAC (Tip Reporting Alternative Commitment), . . . 20,012, 20,013

Trade credit
. advantages of use, . . . 22,003
. cash discount, . . . 22,003-22,004
. credit terms, . . . 22,003
. drawbacks of use, . . . 22,003
. overview, . . . 22,002-22,004, 22,011

Transaction loan, . . . 22,005

Transparency
. corporate governance, . . . 3020
. defined, . . . 3020

TRDA (Tip Rate Determination Agreement), . . . 20,012, 20,013

Treadway Commission. *See* Committee of Sponsoring Organizations of the Treadway Commission (COSO)

Treasurer's responsibilities, . . . 1002

Treasury Regulation 1.451-4(a), . . . 20,017

Treasury Regulation 1.461-4(g)(3), . . . 20,017

Treasury Regulation 1.461-5, . . . 20,018

Treasury stock restructurings, . . . 15,013-15,014

Trend analysis (percent change), . . . 14,028-14,030

Trends in the Hotel Industry, . . . 10,010

Trial and error pricing method, . . . 16,006

Turnaround
. debt capital provider relationships, . . . 26,012-26,013
. . creative financing sources, . . . 26,013
. . tight financing and scarce capital, . . . 26,013
. defined, . . . 26,006
. early warning signs, . . . 26,005
. exit strategy, . . . 26,020
. factors affecting, . . . 26,006-26,007
. financial challenges, . . . 26,002

Index

Turnaround—continued
. financial failure, causes of, . . .
   26,002-26,004
. . common causes, . . . 26,002-26,003
. . economic causes, . . . 26,003-26,004
. . external factors, . . . 26,003-26,004
. . financial causes, . . . 26,004
. . internal factors, . . . 26,003-26,004
. implementation, . . . 26,019-26,020
. lessons to be learned, . . . 26,020-26,022
. liquidity management, . . . 26,010-26,012
. . better terms from suppliers, . . . 26,012
. . cash conservation, . . . 26,011
. . cash outflow, delaying, . . . 26,012
. . cash receipts, accelerating, . . .
   26,011-26,012
. managing in uncertain environment, . . .
   26,004
. operational analysis as a management
   tool, . . . 26,005-26,006
. operational improvements, . . .
   26,014-26,017
. . cost-cutting measures, . . . 26,014-26,015
. . revenue growth enhancement, . . .
   26,015-26,017
. . room and menu price discounts, . . .
   26,016
. overview, . . . 26,001-26,002
. significance, . . . 26,001-26,002
. stages of turnaround strategy, . . .
   26,007-26,010
. . recovery, . . . 26,009-26,010
. . retrenchment, . . . 26,008-26,009
. . return to normalcy, . . . 26,010
. . situation analysis, . . . 26,008
. strategies
. . accounting and financial reporting
     system evaluation, . . . 26,018-26,019
. . additional strategies, . . . 26,019
. . asset repositioning, . . . 26,018
. . debt capital provider relationships, . . .
   26,012-26,013
. . debt restructuring, . . . 26,013-26,014
. . liquidity management, . . . 26,010-26,012
. . marketing activity monitoring, . . . 26,017

Turnaround—continued
. strategies—continued
. . operational improvements, . . .
   26,014-26,017
. . rebranding, . . . 26,018
. . rebuilding a profitable core business, . . .
   26,017-26,018
. . strategic reorientation, . . . 26,018

Tweedie, David, . . . 27,002

Tyco, . . . 1007

U

Uncontrollable costs, . . . 17,019-17,020

Undistributed operating expenses
. administrative and general expenses, . . .
   6012-6013
. allocation of, . . . 18,002-18,005
. gross operating profit, . . . 6013
. property operations and maintenance, . . .
   6013
. sales and marketing, . . . 6013
. summary operating statement, . . .
   6012-6013
. utilities, . . . 6013

Uniform system of accounts, . . . 5007-5008

Uniform System of Accounts for Hotels. *See*
Uniform System of Accounts for the
Lodging Industry (USAL)

Uniform System of Accounts for Restaurants
(USAR), . . . 2005

Uniform System of Accounts for the Lodging
Industry (USAL)
. accounting for china, glass, silver, linen,
   uniforms, . . . 7007
. background of use, . . . 5007
. bartering, . . . 20,015
. chart of accounts sample, . . . 2006-2008
. development of system of accounts, . . .
   6006
. direct vs. indirect costs, . . . 17,014
. fixed charges, . . . 6014
. house laundry schedule, . . . 18,004-18,005

Uniform System of Accounts for the Lodging Industry (USAL)—continued
. income statement, . . . 6002
. income statement development, . . . 6006-6007
. income statement sample, . . . 2006-2008
. objectives, . . . 6006-6007
. overview, . . . 2005
. summary operating statement, . . . 6007-6014
. . fixed charges, . . . 6007-6008, 6014
. . operated departments, . . . 6007-6012
. . undistributed operating expenses, . . . 6007-6008, 6012-6013
. traditional cost allocation
. . direct method, . . . 18,006-18,009
. . formula method, . . . 18,011-18,012
. . step method, . . . 18,009-18,011

Uniforms, accounting for, . . . 7007

United States, control approach, . . . 3028

U.S. Department of Agriculture, Empowerment Zone/Enterprise Community program, . . . 20,014, 20,015

U.S. Stock exchanges.*See* Stock exchanges

USAL.*See* Uniform System of Accounts for the Lodging Industry (USAL)

USAR (Uniform System of Accounts for Restaurants), . . . 2005

Utilities, summary operating statement reporting, . . . 6013

V

Values
. future value of $1, . . . 28,002
. future value of annuity, . . . 28,003
. maximization of, . . . 2010
. present value of $1, . . . 28,004
. present value of annuity, . . . 28,005
. value creation
. . business decisions for, . . . 1004
. . goal of the company, . . . 1002-1003
. . importance of, . . . 1003-1004

Values—continued
. value creation—continued
. . managing for, . . . 1003-1004
. . profit maximization vs., . . . 1004-1005

Variable expenses
. defined, . . . 19,002
. expanded income statement, . . . 17,017
. overview, . . . 17,002-17,004
. relevant range, . . . 17,008-17,010
. risk vs. rapid growth, . . . 19,011-19,012

Vendors.*See* Suppliers

VeriSign, . . . 4004

Vertical common size analysis, . . . 12,009, 14,025-14,026, 16,050, 16,052-16,053

Virtual local area networks (VLANs), . . . 4003-4004

VLANs (virtual local area networks), . . . 4003-4004

Voice-over Internet protocol (VoIP), . . . 4018

VoIP (voice-over Internet protocol), . . . 4018

W

WACC.*See* Weighted-average cost of capital (WACC)

Wages and salaries
. deemed wages, . . . 20,010-20,011
. minimum wage requirements, . . . 20,010
. tip income, . . . 20,009-20,014

WANs (wide-area networks), . . . 4004

Warrants, . . . 21,005

Web sites
. asset management systems, . . . 4035
. corporate governance, . . . 3036-3037
. database comparison, . . . 4007
. enterprise application integration, . . . 4032
. enterprise resource planning, . . . 4033
. EOQ program, . . . 4006
. financial software, . . . 4013
. Form 3468, . . . 20,006
. Form 8846, . . . 20,012

Web sites—continued
. global accounting convergence, . . . 27,028
. graphics programs, . . . 4012
. HUD, . . . 20,014
. IASB, . . . 27,028
. iGAAP developments, . . . 27,028
. IRS Notice 2006-52, . . . 20,009
. minimum wage requirements, . . . 20,010
. Nucleus Research, . . . 4023
. resources, . . . 30,001-30,005
. restaurant management systems, . . . 4019
. RTTs, . . . 4028
. statistical analysis computer programs, . . . 4013

Weighted-average cost of capital (WACC)
. book value vs. market value weights, . . . 25,008
. calculation of, . . . 25,007-25,008
. defined, . . . 25,002
. factors affecting WACC, . . . 25,008-25,009
. . capital structure policy, . . . 25,009
. . dividend polity, . . . 25,009
. . interest rates, . . . 25,009
. . investment policy, . . . 25,009
. . market environment, . . . 25,009
. . tax rates, . . . 25,009
. sources, . . . 25,002

Wendy's, . . . 3019

Weston and Brigham dividend policy theory, . . . 23,007

Whistleblowers
. company protection of, . . . 3021
. SOX protections, . . . 3005

Wide-area networks (WANs), . . . 4004

Window dressing, . . . 10,003

Work opportunity tax credit, . . . 20,014

Working capital
. cash flow statement, . . . 15,006-15,007
. indicator of management efficiency, . . . 15,006-15,007
. liquidity analysis, . . . 10,002
. profitability factor, . . . 16,055

WorldCom, . . . 1007

X

XBRL (eXtensible Business Reporting Language), . . . 27,007-27,008

Y

Yield management, . . . 4024-4025

Yield ratio, . . . 17,018

Z

Zero-coupon bonds, . . . 21,010, 21,012